Ellen, I thank you for the wonderful work you do in our field—

Koen Stan

The Call of Memory
A Teacher's Guide

The Call of Memory:
Learning About the Holocaust Through Narrative
A Teacher's Guide

Karen Shawn and Keren Goldfrad, Editors
William Younglove, Associate Editor

Ben Yehuda Press
Teaneck, NJ

In cooperation with
Beit Lohamei Haghetaot
The Ghetto Fighters' Museum, Israel

Published by Ben Yehuda Press
430 Kensington Road
Teaneck, NJ 07666

http://www.BenYehudaPress.com

Ben Yehuda Press books may be purchased for educational, business or sales promotional use. For information, please contact:
Special Markets, Ben Yehuda Press
430 Kensington Road, Teaneck, NJ 07666.
markets@BenYehudaPress.com.

ISBN13 978-0-9789980-1-1
ISBN 0-9789980-1-4

Cover illustration: "Transports" © 1985 Netty Vanderpol

08 09 / 10 9 8 7 6 5 4 3 2 1

Dedication

Karen Shawn dedicates this work in honor of her mother, Rosalie Heller Shawn, and in memory of her father, Bernard Shawn.

Keren Goldfrad dedicates this work to her grandparents, Sarah Werzberger (may she be healthy and well), Yishyahu Michalovitz (of blessed memory), Bella Shtrochlitz (of blessed memory), and Yechezkel Shtrochlitz (of blessed memory); and to her father-in-law, Chaim Goldfrad (may he be healthy and well). All are survivors of the Holocaust. May their stories live on in our memories and never be forgotten.

Acknowledgments

In 1994, when a group of my students from the Yad Vashem Summer Institute for Educators from Abroad discussed with me their need to meet together to process their shared experience of learning about the Holocaust, I considered hosting a small gathering of seminar graduates for a weekend reunion and hesitantly broached the idea to my school's principal, Rabbi Harvey Silberstein. In his wisdom he urged me to invite them and other interested graduates from across America, and so I began what would become the nationally-respected Consortium of Holocaust Educators, the seminal think tank for many of the contributors to this volume. He supported me in its earliest incarnation in every way possible, and the founding members of the Consortium and I are grateful to him for his help and his belief in us and our work.

My colleagues and friends in the Consortium, a trusted and trusting community of learners, are among the finest Holocaust educators in America. I thank them for the extraordinary work they have done in their role as "teacher-researchers," crafting highly professional essays describing their personal classroom experiences in teaching about the Holocaust through literature. I thank as well each and every other contributor, the Israeli, American, and Australian professors whose profoundly insightful literary analyses will, I believe, reshape the teaching of Holocaust narratives.

It took a community to produce this book. The Covenant Foundation opened countless doors for me by granting me its most generous and prestigious award. Beit Lohamei Haghetaot, the Ghetto Fighters' Museum, contributed its good name to our pages. The American Friends of the Ghetto Fighters' Museum co-sponsored the Consortium yearly gatherings. As staff of the American Friends, Linda Ripps helped to bring the Consortium members together efficiently and safely, while Lana Bernhardt's quiet and constant help behind the scenes allowed us to work without distractions. Mark and Anita Sarna have offered me, from the moment we met, an unusual level of commitment and appreciation for the work that the group and I do; their great generosity, support, affection, trust, and friendship have always been a source of strength and inspiration, and I am exceedingly grateful to them. Dr. Charles and Rella Feldman have never wavered in their gracious support of my work; their outreach, warmth, and enduring friendship have touched my soul. Debbie and Nadav Nahshon were never too busy to listen, advise, and help. Pamela Vissing, teacher extraordinaire, helped edit and reflected wisely on every contribution; she also broke (for the most part) my extra-comma habit. I also thank our other peer review board members: Beryl Bresgi, Denise A. Coleman, Shannon Kederis, and Brooks Parmelee.

"Much wisdom I learned from my teachers, more from my colleagues, from my pupils most of all" (Maimonides, *Code*, "Laws Concerning the Study of the Torah," chapter 5, section 13). Lolle Boettcher, first a student and now a colleague and dear friend, has always offered just the right support at just the right time. My spring and summer 2007 classes at the Azrieli Graduate School of

Jewish Education and Administration contributed greatly to this volume, as my students' keen eyes and thoughtful perceptions helped me to proofread and to improve many essays.

"From all my teachers I grew wise" (Psalms 119:99). Ben (of blessed memory) and Vladka Meed were my first teachers of the Holocaust, and their guiding principles are evident in all of my subsequent work. Netty Vanderpol, Bernard Gotfryd, Evelyn Ripp and Dr. Norbert Ripp, Bella Bryks-Klein, and Susan Prinz Shear, survivors and children of survivors, contributed their trust and friendship along with their memorable and personal narratives and, from Netty, her exquisite and evocative needlepoint that graces our cover and tells a story all by itself. Dr. Yaacov Lozowick, former Director of the Archives at Yad Vashem, and Dr. Efraim Zuroff, Director of the Simon Wiesenthal Center in Jerusalem, have had an invaluable and incalculable influence on my thinking and on my work. I treasure their teaching, their always sage advice, and their abiding friendship.

Dr. Keith Breiman, my husband, supported, appreciated, and respected my work despite the endless time I spent doing it. Always a patient and thoughtful reader, he also graced this volume with his own perceptive essay. Dr. Jill Heller Rathus, my daughter, is an ongoing source of pride and inspiration to me in her work ethic, productivity, accomplishments, and brilliance in teaching: she is the perfect combination of scholar/practitioner and helped provide the model for this book. Eve Yudelson and Larry Yudelson, our publishers at Ben Yehuda Press, worked long and hard to ensure we would all be proud of this volume. Dr. Keren Goldfrad and Dr. William (Bill) Younglove, my esteemed co-editors, are patient and productive colleagues; I am proud and privileged to work with them. Despite our great geographical distance from one another (or perhaps because of it?), we worked more closely, harmoniously, and rigorously than we could have had we been in the same room. I am grateful for their never-ending commitment and devotion to this project, for sharing my vision and realizing it. Finally, Rachel Witty, our gifted and tireless copyeditor, kept me sane; without her skills, her virtually daily communication, her endless willingness to discuss every aspect of every word and punctuation mark, and her good humor, I could not have imagined completing this work.

Karen Shawn

Expressing thanks is universally recognized as appropriate conduct. Among the Jewish people, it is not just proper conduct but an integral part of our identity.

The descendants of the 12 tribes of Israel are referred to as the Jews, in Hebrew *Yehudim*, derived from the name of the tribe Yehudah (Judah). Like many names in Hebrew, the name Yehudah has an inherent meaning that signifies an integral attribute of the *Yehudim* throughout the generations. When Leah gave birth to Yehudah, she said: "'This time will I thank the Lord.' Therefore she called his name Judah." (Genesis 29:35). When he was named, this trait of thanksgiving (*hodaya*) became internalized in Yehudah's being and was passed on to all the Jewish people.

In keeping with the age-old tradition of giving thanks, a fundamental part of Jewish identity, I express my gratitude to all who assisted me in this work. First and foremost, I thank Karen Shawn for being a remarkable partner in this joint venture. Her resourcefulness, astuteness, and knowledge have been the guiding powers of this project. It was a pleasure, as well, to work with William Young-love, who has proven to be an indispensable collaborator every step of the way.

I thank all the participants for their significant contributions and active involvement in this project. In particular, Sharon Deykin-Baris read willingly and commented perceptively on a number of the essays. Chani Levene-Nachshon has provided invaluable counsel. Victoria Aarons, Phyllis Lassner, Miriam Sivan, Emily Budick, and Sarah Fraiman-Morris invested time and effort in their suggestions and comments.

My deepest thanks belong to my dear husband, Joseph Goldfrad, for his unwavering emotional support, encouragement, and wise counsel; and to my beloved children, Shani, Oriah, Eitan, and Yaniv. I express my gratitude to my grandmother Sarah Werzberger and to my devoted parents, Dov and Rachel Shachar, for their ongoing assistance. Other family members and relatives have also helped with this enterprise in various ways: Lior Porat, Tanya Goldfrad, and Batia Goldfrad.

Keren Goldfrad

I thank Stacey Myers, who valiantly strove to stifle every writing impulse I had to allow "Dr. Pedantic" to surface during the work on this book. Karen, Keren, and I, like so many of us, stand upon the shoulders of giants; without their groundwork we would never have been able to make this contribution.

William Younglove

The past is never dead. It's not even past.

—William Faulkner

The painful truth is that apprehending the Holocaust requires years of patient study, a long journey through history, literature, art, memoirs, human psychology, and countless other disciplines that illuminate its tangled origins and dreadful results.

—Lawrence L. Langer

For with much wisdom comes much grief, and he who increases knowledge increases pain.

—Ecclesiastes
(1:18)

CONTENTS

In the Beginning

The Gathering Storm

Under Occupation

Daily Life in the Ghetto

Choiceless Choices

The Gray Zone

The Abyss

Sparks of Humanity

Trying to Start Anew

The Second Generation and Beyond

Foreword

Josey G. Fisher

> *One can't say how life is, how chance or fate deals with people,*
> *except by telling a tale.*
> —Hannah Arendt

Ida Fink describes a pivotal moment in her short story "The End" (Shawn & Goldfrad, *Anthology*, 2008, pp. 57–60), and, in so doing, provides a window into that crucial time in 1939. A young couple has collapsed into sleep, waiting in dread for the black night to end.

> A low thrumming of windowpanes jarred her from her sleep. She bolted up in bed, wide awake, fully aware of what was happening. … She waited. After a few minutes she heard a heavy, dull rumbling, as if the earth were sighing. … Carefully, so as not to wake the boy, she moved over. … She watched him lying there. … Gently she stroked his hair. "Keep sleeping," she whispered. She bent over him and stayed this way, keeping watch, guarding his last peaceful moments of sleep. The dawn advanced, followed by the sun. The war was fifteen minutes old. (p. 60)

Alongside the historical documentation of the invasion of Poland, we have the gift of another prism—this young couple, still treasuring the first flush of intimacy, still protecting each other's innocence, but now vulnerable, isolated, and terrified. The details of the invasion, we may forget. This young couple, holding each other through this ominous night, awakening to glaring reality, we remember. Why do such stories stay with us? What is it about narratives that provide a unique entry into the experience of the *Shoah*? How do they illuminate moments in time that capture the complexity of historical events?

Readers of all ages respond to stories. Narratives provide a frame that our minds seek in our need to make sense of our world. Stories that engage us, that are powerfully and vividly told and provide narrators and characters with whom we connect—these are the ones we remember, because they resonate with a psychological reality that may flesh out and even transcend the historical experience.

Individual stories have become integral to Holocaust documentation, personalizing and humanizing the experience so that the historical context breathes with reality. We see beyond facts and statistics to the impact on human lives, the pain, the conflicts, the challenges that were not envisioned as anyone's life experience. Each of these stories is unique—in time and place and circumstance—but also in voice.

What is the power of narrative? It both magnifies the moment and condenses it. It focuses on details that become metaphorical in their power. It is the way people remember and the way they retell. It is the art of our great writers to telescope and focus their lens on a moment that may represent a greater whole.

In her psychoanalytic study of literature, Dalsimer (1986) states:

> The force of ... great drama lies not only in the power of language, but in the power of its insight into particular situations, which language delivers and which the reader, with a shock of personal recognition, acknowledges to be just. ... The experiences of characters bear a relation to the reader's own observations and experiences, real or imagined. This resonance, I believe, is essential if the text is to have the power to engage, to move—to haunt the reader. (pp. 2-3)

We suddenly grasp the meaning of social death in Nazi Germany when a young Jewish girl, vividly portrayed in Aichinger's "Fear of Fear," cannot buy a birthday cake. Seeing the girl's yellow star, the saleswoman screams,

> "Get out! Go! Now! Or I'll have you arrested!"
> None of the customers budged. Ellen turned toward them, looking for help. It was then they all saw the star on her coat. Some began to laugh jeeringly. Others produced pitying smiles. No one helped her. (Shawn & Goldfrad, *Anthology*, 2008, p. 80)

We shudder when a young girl is abruptly separated from her mother during a deportation graphically depicted in Gotfryd's "On Guilt":

> I raised my arm with a handkerchief as high as I could, hoping that Mother would notice me. I even called her name, but I don't imagine she could have heard me. I tried to shout good-bye to her, just to let her know that I was there. I wasn't sure any longer where she was. (p. 141)

We understand Fink's presentation in "The Threshold" of a young woman's need to deny the cruel realities of war so apparent to her family: "Elzbieta refused to cross the threshold of their room, which seemed haunted by the spirit of that terrible time," and we stand by her through the crisis that propels her transition into adulthood: "Elzbieta crossed silently into the room and took her place at the table" (p. 66).

The Value of Stories in Adolescent Development

The history of the Holocaust and of the people it transformed is overwhelming. A narrative frame has the ability to contain the uncontainable. We can enter a world we fear and leave it. Reading permits a journey not otherwise taken, and we accompany our narrator in safety. We have a secure perspective because it is not happening to us.

Is there something crucial in this process for the adolescent or young adult reader who is struggling to understand not only how this could possibly have happened but also how people lived through it? Adolescents are able to appreciate history from the standpoint of cause and effect and to assess shades of gray, to question ramifications and moral implications. Cognitive development intertwines with their biological coming of age. History makes sense to them now that both they and the world have gone through transitions, triggering curiosity, concern, and the need to know. It is no longer enough to know that Hitler was bad. They need to discover who Hitler was and what motivated him, and this exploration leads them to even broader philosophical and religious questions of evil.

Stories of the Holocaust offer students a template not only to examine this complex history but also to delve into the challenges and crises for those who experienced it. Through stories, students can examine the players on the historical stage: those who implemented this genocide, those who were targets of it, those who collaborated, those who stood by, and those who protested and asserted their humanity by saving lives.

Rationale

However, what our students—and we—might be looking for is much more personal. Where would I fit into this picture? What dilemmas would I have faced? How did people at that time react? Can the answers to these questions help me learn more about my own life?

When I first started teaching, I was asked to lead a discussion in a senior seminar on the Holocaust in a private, secular high school. Searching for an opening, I showed them a copy of *Life* magazine from the spring of 1945. Several graphic photographs of liberation were followed by one of German townspeople exiting a barrack, some covering their nose and mouth with a handkerchief, bearing witness to the atrocities at Eisenhower's order. I had no idea where the students would focus. What happened both surprised and informed me: They stared at the photograph of the townspeople. One of the students said simply, "That's who I would have been." Would they be the wounded woman in Nalkowska's "By the Railway Track" or the villagers who would "cast their eyes about nervously and quickly depart" (p. 183)? Would they be the numbed prisoners on the open, ice-covered flatcars "who had been stripped ... of the capacity to make a human gesture" (p. 207) in Nomberg-Przytyk's "The Camp Blanket" or the unknown woman "who wants to help" (p. 209)?

We are all taught by our students. I have been continually struck by the ways students of the Holocaust connect with the history. Sometimes it is based on their group of identity. More subtly, it may be based on developmental issues and personal struggles. Literature permits exploration into other worlds both external and internal. It provides not only a window into an otherwise unknown and confusing place but also a mirror for readers, reflecting their image against another backdrop. As adolescents make the transition into adulthood, eager yet conflicted in their separation from parent figures, the immersion in literature may provide a safe testing ground. Not only can literary characters serve as guides through the journey, they may also serve as surrogates for the experience. From a point of safety, adolescent readers can permit themselves not only to enter the world but also to examine conflicts and feelings more deeply through an identification they know is temporary.

In the safety of the story, readers can try out experiences. They can think about themselves as they observe and discuss the characters. Not only can the stories become a prototype for complex history, but also the characters and their dilemmas can provide language for examining and discussing the unthinkable. Adolescent development both permits and fuels the search; literature encourages and provides opportunities for discovery. These narratives are reflections of what many both seek and fear. The necessary separation from dependency on parents leaves adolescents in a temporary vacuum. Natural strides toward individuation may still be felt as a profound sense of loss, isolation, and vulnerability in the search to restabilize as an independent adult. These narratives may also echo real experiences—divorce, death, exclusion, or victimization—that the reader seeks to master. How can students find meaning in these tragic stories? Do they provide clues to independent survival, to ethical and spiritual connection, to dealing with challenges without giving up hope? Can these answers help them in their path toward independence, the defining task of adolescence?

The adolescent passage may be a short journey for some, a larger challenge for others. Individuation may occur, but the struggle for mastery may be revisited as we face crises throughout our lives. We heed the fact that Nelson Mandela read Anne Frank's diary while imprisoned in South Africa and "derived much encouragement from it."

The Challenge of Understanding Holocaust History

Students can use their evolving self-awareness to enter the stories empathetically, and the process can enhance both their historical understanding and emotional growth. Nevertheless, stories of the Holocaust may not be understood within a previous frame of reference. Empathy may not be sufficient to comprehend the situations victims confronted or choices required. Lack of resolution, one of the hallmarks of narrative, may distinguish stories about the Holocaust and leave readers themselves in an incomplete—and, for some, terrifying—state. Although students should be able to deal with ambiguity cognitively, the emotional demand to deal with moral contradiction, "choiceless choice," and crisis of faith may be too much for them to handle and even freeze their cognition.

The readers of these narratives find themselves outside "normal" reality, as Laub (1992) describes, "outside the range of associatively linked experiences, outside the range of comprehension, of recounting and of mastery" (p. 69). How can students connect with Nalkowska's dying victim, begging to be shot to end her misery? How can they connect with the villagers who must decide whether to do it? What demand, then, does this put on the teacher?

For some students, the narratives are too painful either in content or in lack of resolution. Their hunger for answers may not be gratified; their search for answers may lead to ongoing examination of morality, ethics, or the unanswerable. Some may be ready for these conflicts; others may not. Yet our obligation as teachers is not only to transmit passive knowledge but also to engage students in an active process of examination. In a study of traumatic narratives co-authored with Laub, Felman (1992) writes:

> As far as the great literary subjects are concerned, teaching must itself be viewed not merely as transmitting, but as accessing. ... Each great subject has a turning point within it, and that turning point has to be met. The question for the teacher is, then, on the one hand, how to access, how not to foreclose the crisis, and, on the other hand, how to contain it, how much crisis can the class sustain. It is the teacher's task to recontextualize the crisis and to put it back into perspective, to relate the present to the past and to the future and to thus reintegrate the crisis in a transformed frame of meaning. (p. 54)

Laub later comments, "The listener, therefore, has to be at the same time a witness to the trauma witness and a witness to himself" (p. 58). Alternatively, in the confrontation with traumatic stories, the reader not only witnesses the literary trauma but also may benefit from encouragement and opportunity to witness his own personal reaction.

The Importance of the Classroom Teacher

For these reasons, we offer the safe space of the classroom, which itself may support the individual processing of the narrative. An empathic teacher, aware of painful historical content yet unaware of how individual students might respond to it, stays alert to students' responses and provides alternative means for them to explore and express their reactions. Open-ended questions, facilitating both guided discussion and written reflection, permit students to not only enter the richness of the story but also to extrapolate beyond it.

The veteran educators who share their classroom experiences in this *Guide* illustrate this empathetic facilitation. Christopher Gwin (2008), for instance, in "Discarded Objects, Remnants of War: Zofia Nalkowska's 'By the Railway

Track'" (pp. 320–331) encourages group discussion of essential questions and moral issues:

> The conversation darted back and forth across the room. It was, as often happens, electrifying for a teacher: a room full of ticking brains, engaged, listening, pondering. ... Even though [the students] will never be able to understand the actions of the perpetrators and the bystanders in the Holocaust, they realized they can approach the particular actions they encounter on a personal level and make them make sense through these kinds of conversations. ... The diversity of thought and experience in the room enriched our interactions. Students heard ideas they had never considered in their isolated reading. (p. 326–328)

Carrie A. Olson, in "Ordinary People, Untold Stories: Ida Fink's 'The End' and 'The Threshold'" (pp. 102–116), asks her students to give advice to future readers of Fink's stories. Mariana responds, "Remember that Ida Fink writes this way on purpose. She wants you to think, maybe even be confused at times. Don't give up if you get confused. Talk to your group and it will make sense" (p. 113). Olson is committed to reading aloud; she comments, "They enjoy it, and I do not have to worry about those less fluent" (p. 105), and describes reading Fink's "The End":

> I read the story with passion. When she is angry, I am angry. When Piotr whines, I whine. When she whispers, I whisper. I don't stop during the whole reading. I also walk among the students, who become more engaged when I get within arm's length. At the conclusion, students look up, surprised that the story has ended. (p. 106)

My college class, surprised initially when I begin to read a difficult passage to them, becomes similarly immersed. "I heard it differently," one student said. "I think I couldn't hear it all by myself before. But we were all together."

Short stories that can be examined together in class permit students not only to finish the task of reading but also to offer time for the necessary processing of both the content and their personal connections. The teacher can ensure that students who have entered this "other" world have also returned from it. For some students, the mastery of one story might trigger their curiosity about others, including novels and memoirs, which might broaden their understanding. If the story has had meaning to them, they want to know more.

Robert Coles (1989) describes:

> Stories are renderings of life; they can not only keep us company, but admonish us, point us in new directions or give us the courage to stay a given course. They can offer us kinsmen, kinswomen, comrades, advisors—offer us other eyes through which we might

see, other ears with which we might make soundings ... [they] can be spiritual companions, can be persons, however "imaginary" in nature, who give us pause and help us in the private moments when we try to find our bearings. (pp. 159–160)

What the narrative intends may expand as the narrative is received. How the story resonates determines how it is eventually transmitted. If our students grow in their understanding of the history, the individual experience, and their personal response, this fulfills part of our goal in teaching. And just perhaps they will become part of the chain, as expressed by the prophet Joel (1:3):

Tell your children about it,
And let your children tell theirs,
And their children the next generation.

REFERENCES

Aichinger, I. (1963). Fear of fear. In K. Shawn & K. Goldfrad (Eds.). (2008). *The call of memory: Learning about the Holocaust through narrative: An anthology*, pp. 77–95. Teaneck, NJ: Ben Yehuda Press.

Coles, R. (1989). *The call of stories: Teaching and the moral imagination.* Boston: Houghton Mifflin Company.

Dalsimer, K. (1986). *Female adolescence: Psychoanalytic reflections on literature.* New Haven, CT and London: Yale University Press.

Felman, S. & Laub, D. (1992). *Testimony: Crises of witnessing in literature, psychoanalysis and history.* New York and London: Routledge.

Fink, I. (1997). The end. In K. Shawn & K. Goldfrad (Eds.). (2008). *The call of memory: Learning about the Holocaust through narrative: An anthology*, p. 57–60. Teaneck, NJ: Ben Yehuda Press.

Fink, I. (1997). The threshold. In K. Shawn & K. Goldfrad (Eds.). (2008). *The call of memory: Learning about the Holocaust through narrative: An anthology*, pp. 61–66. Teaneck, NJ: Ben Yehuda Press.

Gotfryd, B. (2000). On guilt. In K. Shawn & K. Goldfrad (Eds.). (2008). *The call of memory: Learning about the Holocaust through narrative: An anthology*, p. 139–148. Teaneck, NJ: Ben Yehuda Press.

Gwin, C. (2008). Discarded objects, remnants of war: Zofia Nalkowska's "By the railway track." In K. Shawn & K. Goldfrad (Eds.). *The call of memory: Learning about the Holocaust through narrative: A teacher's guide*, p. 320–331. Teaneck, NJ: Ben Yehuda Press.

Nalkowska, Z. (2000). By the railroad track. In K. Shawn & K. Goldfrad (Eds.). (2008). *The call of memory: Learning about the Holocaust through narrative: An anthology*, p. 181–186. Teaneck, NJ: Ben Yehuda Press.

Nomberg-Przytyk, S. (1985). The camp blanket. In K. Shawn & K. Goldfrad (Eds.). (2008). *The call of memory: Learning about the Holocaust through narrative: An anthology*, p. 205–209. Teaneck, NJ: Ben Yehuda Press.

Olson, C. (2008). Ordinary people, untold stories: Ida Fink's "The end" and "The threshold." In K. Shawn & K. Goldfrad (Eds.). *The call of memory: Learning about the Holocaust through narrative: A teacher's guide*, pp. 102–116. Teaneck, NJ: Ben Yehuda Press.

Introduction

Karen Shawn

Genesis

When I began to study the Holocaust in earnest, I traveled its tragic terrain with a group of like-minded colleagues. We were led by knowledgeable and sure-footed mentors and teachers, guides who had survived the real journey into that dark time and place and were, so many years later, forging a path for American educators who wanted to learn.

Without the watchful care and kindness of Ben Meed (of blessed memory) and his indefatigable wife, Vladka Meed, who coordinated the formative and intensive seminars in Poland and in Israel, without their willingness and unerring ability to walk us carefully through the fearsome thicket of death and destruction we encountered each day, albeit at a far remove, we would have been too bruised, anguished, and lost to continue our quest for knowledge and our search for understanding. They saw where we might stumble and fall; they held us back from tumbling, unprepared and alone, into the abyss. They took us into darkness, but they always offered a contrastive glimmer to help us to find our way through the bleak and enigmatic landscape of sorrow and despair and then to find a way out. They set us on a course we would all follow; we came home determined to share our journey with others. This volume grew out of that life-changing summer of learning, when I came to believe that travel into the nether region of such a past should not be undertaken alone.

Keren Goldfrad, William (Bill) Younglove, and I taught the Holocaust on different coasts, in different countries, and from different perspectives. Keren teaches English at Bar-Ilan University and Holocaust Literature at Orot College in Israel; Bill taught high school English for 30 years and now teaches pre-service teachers at California State University, Long Beach; I taught middle school English in New York, methods and materials in Holocaust education at Yad Vashem and at Beit Lohamei Haghetaot (The Ghetto Fighters' Museum) in Israel, and currently teach Holocaust education at Yeshiva University's Azrieli Graduate School in New York. We discovered that we had differing needs but similar frustrations with existing materials and methodologies; nothing appropriate was available to guide us. I sought specific literary criticism and current history resources to contextualize the narratives I taught. Keren, highly skilled in literary criticism and in teaching the literature of the Holocaust, searched for specific pedagogic strategies that extended the traditional lecture and discussion format but that were at the same time suitable for this subject and for her university students. Bill, a master at lesson design, was stymied by the dearth of pedagogic materials available to help teachers present historically contextualized Holocaust literature within the framework of state standards.

When Keren, Bill, and I began to talk about filling the needs we had identified, we envisioned a book of short Holocaust narratives enhanced by a complementary teacher's guide offering suggestions for teaching and analyzing text. We realized the potential for this two-volume project, but we recognized our limitations in attempting this without other points of view. First, our wide and disparate intended audience—high school through university students, teachers and professors, history and literature classes around the world—precluded generalized pedagogic suggestions; only particulars from which individuals could choose would be immediately useful in such diverse contexts. Similarly, broad guidelines for analyzing literature would not help readers searching for a focused understanding of specific narratives. Finally, our teaching experiences were too narrow, limited as they were to our own audiences. Fortunately, we were blessed with a wealth of learned and congenial colleagues, and we soon came to appreciate that only a compilation of their and our vision and voices could produce the variety, wisdom, and breadth necessary for an internationally useful classroom guide.

Why These Contributors?

All of our contributors are reflective practitioners, and each offers a unique voice, making this *Guide* a collection of learning and teaching opportunities rich in individual style and substance. Our writers are divided into two groups: College and university professors and museum educators who used their literary expertise and historical knowledge to analyze the narratives we selected; and teachers who wrote reflective pedagogic essays discussing their classroom teaching experiences with the same narratives. Within this *Guide,* the analysis precedes the pedagogy of each story under discussion; read together, they offer the educator a complete unit of study, providing literary insights and clearly organized suggestions for class activities and discussion prompts crucial to successful teaching of Holocaust literature.

The college and university professors who contributed their expertise are from the five leading academic institutions in Israel: Hebrew University of Jerusalem, Tel Aviv University, University of Haifa, Ben-Gurion University of the Negev, and Bar-Ilan University; from American universities, including Yeshiva University, Northwestern University, Boston University, and Trinity University; from New York's Museum of Jewish Heritage; and from the University of Melbourne in Australia. Several are Dr. Goldfrad's colleagues; all are experts in the field of literary criticism, the Holocaust narrative, or both. Some of these contributors chose to analyze one or two stories that directly relate to their teaching or their field of study, while others preferred to examine narratives they found particularly intriguing.

Most of those who contributed pedagogic essays are members of the Consortium of Holocaust Educators, a group of senior American educators whose early experiences with Holocaust study were also shaped by Ben and Vladka

Meed and other survivors, as well as by professors at Yad Vashem, Beit Lohamei Haghetaot, and the United States Holocaust Memorial Museum. They have long taught the subject in public and parochial schools, colleges, and resource centers across the United States. The Consortium meets yearly to learn together, discuss best practices, and share and critique participants' research and writings. Susan Prinz Shear's "Saving History: Letters from the Holocaust: Teaching 'No Way Out,'" for example, grew out of her field-tests with our group as well as her years of research. From an annual session in which we examined and reviewed new Holocaust literature came the formulation for criteria we ultimately used in choosing the 27 Holocaust narratives we anthologized in themed, chronological order as the companion volume to this *Guide*. During our 14 years together, the Consortium has become a haven of trust, support, and professional respect; we are one another's guides.

Why This Text?

This text provides specifics for teaching, thoroughly and wisely, the classroom treasures the *Anthology* offers. Make no mistake about content; while the collected stories are typically short in length, they are not short on substance. Thus the analyses included here are detailed and rich in scholarship, and the flexible lessons suggest methods and material for three or more class periods, presenting a unique blend of sound and scholarly literary exegesis, a commitment to historical and literary accuracy, and classroom-tested pedagogy. Each academic analysis offers deep insight through multiple and diverse literary approaches to the narrative at hand; each pedagogic essay meets state standards and presents a ruminative, first-person account of the author's day-to-day projected plan or actual teaching experience with one or two stories in the *Anthology*. These complementary essays reflect the belief expressed by Richard Libowitz (1988): "The student must confront history and its contemporary questions or the course is a fraud; the student must wrestle with his/her own soul or the course is a failure" (p. 71).

For decades, educators have feared that unsuitable presentation of the history of the Holocaust may cause learners to dismiss learning about the Holocaust altogether. Alan Rosenberg (1988) observed that

> it is often portrayed, understandably enough, as a horror story. … Limited to recounting atrocities and brutalities, attempting to extract no wider implications from the event, [such presentations] assault and overwhelm our emotions—and in the end either suffocate us or cause us to turn away. (p. 385)

Simone Schweber (2006) agrees, positing that teaching this subject "without generating deep understandings" and through "overexpos[ing]" students "to its horrors but not … to its explanations" leads students "not to take it seriously, not to care about it, and to become 'sick of the Holocaust' before graduating from high school" (p. 53). Each essay herein addresses this seminal concern. Mindful of the time and curricular constraints most teachers face, the contributors present options to introduce and personalize Holocaust history, accounting for students' sensibilities and going beyond the "atrocities and brutalities" inherent in the subject to probe the "wider implications," the essential questions, and the power of the narrative to engage, inform, and perhaps transform the young adult reader.

Learning From the Holocaust

Unless the event has meaning and significance for educators and students alike, the Holocaust will remain simply a singular event in history, and its facts and statistics, once learned, will soon be forgotten. Thus we often speak of teaching not only the history and literature of the Holocaust but its specific "lessons" as well. In searching for these lessons and their significance for our time, however, academicians confront the same difficulties met by theologians and philosophers and may conclude that there are no lessons that are easily and universally identifiable, none that can be pulled from the past, fully formulated and resonant to all learners. Ze'ev Mankowitz (in Shawn, 1991) explains,

> There is no voice that speaks out of the past dispensing binding lessons for the present. History, even where spelled with a capital "H," has no authority of its own. The power it possesses comes to it from the interpretation and social response of [those] in the present ... who attempt to understand the past in order to better see their way to the future. (p. 28)

Novick (1999), cited by Schweber, adds that "how you make sense of which analogies to draw ... or what lessons you believe the Holocaust bears are purely reflections of personal choice." Schweber continues, "It's clear ... that the lessons we draw from the Holocaust have everything to do with what we know about it, what we want from it, and what we're willing to do with it" (p. 53). Thus our contributors refrain from offering facile lessons, wisely recognizing that interpretations depend upon and may differ with the attitudes, needs, context, and goals of those who teach and study it. Instead, they allow readers room to acknowledge both the uniqueness of the Holocaust and the truth of the observation by James Joyce that "in the particular is contained the universal." In the exploration of "what's worth knowing" raised in each essay, readers will find possibilities for expansion as they guide and challenge their students to identify their own lessons from this event and apply them to their lives today.

Designed for a Wide Audience

The professors' highly readable and informative analyses and the teachers' detailed personal commentaries help even the novice teacher feel comfortable exploring this era. For those new to teaching Holocaust literature, here are clear and concise literary explications; myriad text and Internet resources; easy-to-implement goals, practical suggestions for evocative discussions; journal and essay prompts; highly engaging activities, including Readers' Theater; rubrics for assessment and evaluation; and a glossary. This volume includes a necessary overview on state standards and learning objectives, and the Afterword, on the web at *http://www.CallOfMemory.com*, adds teaching options designed as the book was piloted, providing still more materials, methodologies, and Internet sites.

For those teaching only classic Holocaust novels and diaries, a wealth of short literature is interpreted here, affording teachers the opportunity to present an overview of the Holocaust or an in-depth study of its various aspects. For an appropriate point of entry, for example, consider historian Brana Gurewitsch's "Trapped in Germany: 'No Way Out: Letters from the Holocaust,'" which details the history behind a poignant collection of family letters written with increasing desperation during the late 1930s and early 1940s. The letters enable us, Gurewitsch writes, to "learn about the large, traumatic events that affected an entire world through the narrower prism of the story of one family as they keep in touch by mail." Then turn to Susan Prinz Shear's "Saving History: Letters From the Holocaust: Teaching 'No Way Out'" to read her account of and step-by-step suggestions for teaching these letters, sent to and from her grandparents, aunts, uncles, and mother.

Our *Anthology* boasts multiple stories by several different authors, including Bernard Gotfryd, Ida Fink, and Elie Wiesel; this *Guide,* therefore, provides the background for in-depth author study. Chana Levene-Nachshon's "From the Gotfryd Family Album: 'A Chicken for the Holidays,'" for instance, helps readers understand Gotfryd's vision, explaining that "it is through the lens of a photographer and the eye of a benign human being that Gotfryd views the world and recounts his experiences." Abigail Gillman's "Traces of Goodness: Bernard Gotfryd's 'Kurt' and 'Helmut Reiner'" analyzes "the dark landscape of his boyhood" to help readers understand still more about the man behind the stories. Daniel Mayer's "Compliant Defiance: Rejecting a Chicken for the Holidays" teaches Gotfryd's personal account of his youth in the Radom Ghetto through the prism of aspects of Jewish law that help students understand the dilemmas faced by Jews in the ghetto, while Lolle Boettcher's "Two Tales of Protection: 'Kurt' and 'Helmut Reiner': Altruism or Opportunism?" provides an easy-to-follow blueprint for engaging students in an in-depth examination of the actions and motivations of those who risked their lives to help others.

Professors and teachers alike examine specific aspects of the Holocaust in units such as "The Gathering Storm," "Under Occupation," "Daily Life in the Ghetto," "Choiceless Choices," "The Gray Zone," and "Sparks of Humanity." Even the most painful experiences are presented with the goal of providing access to thoughtful methods of reading and teaching them. In a brief unit called "The Abyss," for example, co-editor Keren Goldfrad offers, in her essay "The Ethics of Aesthetics," a brilliant analysis of Cynthia Ozick's classic "The Shawl"; and Sarah Fraiman-Morris writes cogently in "Elie Wiesel's 'Yom Kippur: The Day Without Forgiveness': Manifestation of the Transcendental Paradox After the Holocaust." Lauren Kempton, in "Crisis of Faith," and associate editor William Younglove, in "An Examination of Loss in the Holocaust in Cynthia Ozick's 'The Shawl,'" suggest detailed, classroom-tested strategies for teaching these particularly intricate and difficult narratives.

The educators also explore with great sensitivity little-taught truths confronting survivors and their descendants. Thus in a unit on the aftermath entitled "Trying to Start Anew," Victoria Aarons affords readers entry into the history and the current state of a narrator "ambushed by memory and held captive by past trauma" in her compelling analysis "Memory as Accomplice to History: Trauma and Narrative in Elie Wiesel's 'An Old Acquaintance.'" In "Confronting the Memory of Evil in Elie Wiesel's 'An Old Acquaintance,'" William Younglove walks students carefully through the exquisitely complex and anguished world of the survivor in his personal account of teaching the same Wiesel narrative.

In the final unit, entitled "The Second Generation and Beyond," Dvir Abramovich offers a vivid analysis of a "compendium of the cardinal threads and fissures that permeated the canvas of the post-*Shoah* generation in Israel regarding memory and memorialization" in his essay "The Problem of Holocaust Remembrance in Israel of the 1950s: Aharon Megged's 'The Name.'" Evelyn Ripp and Norbert Ripp, themselves survivors and educators, offer personal insight into the same generation with their instructive pedagogic essay "Generational Divide: Tradition in Transition in Aharon Megged's 'The Name.'"

We believe these essays to be welcome additions to literature, history, religion, psychology, education, or humanities courses; the entire *Guide* and its companion *Anthology* might serve as the basis for a semester-long study of the Holocaust for pre-service and in-service teachers, offering a unique synthesis of superb short literature, sophisticated text study, and practical classroom applications.

Lawrence L. Langer (1998) notes that "the bleak landscape of Holocaust atrocity requires a guide" (p. 188). We offer this one with the hope that its wise and reassuring voices assist you as you find your own way to teach the intimate and profound narratives examined here.

REFERENCES

Langer, L. L. (1998). Opening locked doors: Reflections on teaching the Holocaust. *Preempting the Holocaust*, pp. 187–198. New Haven, CT: Yale University Press.

Libowitz, R. (1988). "Asking the questions: Background and recommendations for Holocaust study." In Z. Garber (Ed.). *Methodology in the academic teaching of the Holocaust*, pp. 57–73. New York: University Press of America.

Mankowitz, Z. (1991). Lessons from the Holocaust: Implications for morality and policy. Unpublished paper. In K. Shawn (1991). *The end of innocence: A literature-based approach to teaching young adolescents about the Holocaust*. New York: New York University: Unpublished dissertation.

Rosenberg, A. (1988). The crisis in knowing and understanding the Holocaust. In A. Rosenberg and G. E. Meyers (Eds.). *Echoes from the Holocaust: Philosophical reflections on a dark time*, pp. 379–395. Philadelphia: Temple University Press.

Schweber, S. (2006). "Holocaust fatigue": Teaching it today. *Social education: Research and practice*, January–February, 48–55.

In the Beginning

Born From Myth Into History:
Reading "The Hunt" by Aharon Appelfeld

Avidov Lipsker

The short story "The Hunt" (Shawn & Goldfrad, 2008, *Anthology*, pp. 3–13) is one of a large collection of Aharon Appelfeld's stories and short compositions depicting lives and events on the margins of the Holocaust in Europe, the first of which were anthologized during the 1960s and 70s.

Janek, the protagonist of "The Hunt," is the son of assimilated Jewish parents, a young man whose Judaism was hidden from him by his father and secretly revealed to him by his mother during his childhood. Now, during the war, as a young man he is a refugee fleeing through the Carpathians in Eastern Europe. His horse has died and to cross the vast distances beyond the river and lakes before him, he seeks the help of a Ruthenian fisherman who takes his boat out in the evening. Along the way, they come upon a group of Jews who are being pursued and have stopped on the riverbank in their flight. The fisherman convinces one of them to sell him salt, and when the Jew approaches, he pretends to take money out of his pocket, but he takes out a knife instead and uses it to kill him. The boat, the Ruthenian fisherman, and Janek then continue down the river into the darkness of night.

The breadth of the story is determined by its extraordinary musical opening. It is rhythmical and metrical, and puts the reader in mind of the almost-forgotten beginning of Appelfeld the poet. The vocal elements mark out the space in which the events take place: the lilt of the oars, the voices singing to themselves as echoes, and the measured song accompanying the fishermen as they take their boats onto the river. That musical element is not only thematic, that is, is not only recounted at the beginning of the story, it is vocal material made audible to the reader through the rhythm flowing and periodically cut off through iambs and anapests. They divide the opening sentences into a poem, into rows that do not coincide with the syntax of prose.

The metric flow presents an expositional, lyric block that can be arranged typographically as poetry; that is, it can be heard and seen (on the page) as a song sung by the fishermen:

> ∪ – / ∪ ∪ – / ∪ – / ∪ – / ∪ – /
> *Rinat ha-mshotim halcha ve-nish/tabra*
> ∪ – / ∪ – / ∪ – /
> *Halcha ve-nada/ma*

∪ – /∪∪–/∪∪ –/∪ ∪ –/∪∪ – /∪∪ –/
Kolot bodedim od himshichu lashir le-atzmam ke-hedim
∪ –/∪∪ –/∪∪ –/∪ –/∪
Ha-esh hecheli/ka al pney ha-ma/yim.
∪∪ –/∪∪ – /∪ – /∪–/∪∪ – / ∪∪ – /
Hasirot nimshechu el toch he-arutz she-halach ve-hutzar
∪ ∪∪–/∪ ∪ – / ∪ ∪ –/∪ ∪ – /
Ve-hashira ha-ktzuva ha-zkhura mi-dorot
∪– /∪∪–/∪∪ – /
Shira achreha demama.[1]

The song of the oars was gradually broken up
and silenced.
Stray voices still continued to sing to themselves like echoes;
fire glided on the surface of the water.
The boats were drawn into the ever-narrowing channel:
and the rhythmic singing, remembered through the generations,
left silence behind it. (Shawn & Goldfrad, *Anthology*, p. 3)

The internal metrical tensions are a perfect example of the ancient *melos* (melody), which cannot be halted during the transition from one rhythmic foot to the next. The addition *"od himshichu lashir"* ("continued singing") is cut off within the meter but is forced to continue the flow within the thematic rhythm of the necessity to sail and sing the fishermen's song. That necessity stems from a rituality preserved for generations, marked by the notes repeating the melody as it fades into the darkness and from which it will arise again during the following fishing season. Its force is like a force of nature itself: sun, wind, and water, and the solitary cow on the river bank. It is the mythic rituality that the fisherman tries to express in his simple, immediate language: "Like it or not … there's no point in lingering. … At this season you have to go a long way off" (p. 3).

The power of that statement, coming as it does at the beginning of the story, has ironic implications for the fate of Janek, who must, "at this season," wander afar.[2] The irony is in the blindness of the fisherman, who does not see the neces-

---

1   The reader can find similar metrically stressed openings in other Appelfeld stories, especially "Barunda" in *Pillars of the River*, p. 63, in which the meter of the opening sentence is anapestic: *"ha-mitzad ha-gadol, ha-mitzad ha-mfuar, hofia ve-shataf et ha-rhov,"* and in the short novel, *The Skin and the Gown*, Am Oved, Tel Aviv, 1971, p. 1: *"sof choref, leili zaram barchovot, ko iti ke-betokh pa'amon shaquf."* The poetic theme of all three always turns on the meter: in "The Chase," "the measured song," in "Barunda," "all mourned as if led by the rhythm," and in *The Skin and the Gown*, "nothing, nothing if not for the rhythm." For Appelfeld's poetry, see the first chapter of Yigal Schwartz, *Aharon Appelfeld: From Individual Lament to Tribal Eternity*, University Press of New England, 2001.

2   The significance of temporal notation in Appelfeld fluctuates between mythical space and concrete space, both trapped within the same semiotic expression. See the titles of

sary, factual truth the verse has for his passenger, but is like Charon, who carries the souls of the dead over the River Styx into Hades. He "sees" the universality of the mythic law and the necessity of nature which has yielded to it, the seasonality of life and death that is not linked to the knowledge of the details of the concrete reality involving his passenger with his hidden Judaism.

Within the mythic textual space Appelfeld created for the opening of "The Hunt," the statement is perceived in all its primal innocence as indicating the "wild" tribal culture in which the hunt is regarded not only as a response to the fight for survival but also as an act taking place within a system of intimate relationships between hunter and prey. That significance is revealed when Janek and the fisherman exchange rudimentary food and in the series of farming motifs that indicate the simple, earthy connection between the fisherman and both domesticated animals and animals hunted in the wild, whom he looks upon "like peasants who keep livestock and feel an affection for the beasts, so long as they are alive" (p. 6). At first the hunt is regarded as an act without hostility or aggression, but rather as part of innocent, wild, mythic rural space, a place where fisherman and hunter (which are inter-translational in Hebrew and Aramaic, the Hebrew *dayag*, fisherman, equaling the Aramaic *tzayda*, hunter), steeped in a relationship of mutual curiosity and attentiveness, intimate with no shred of hatred or fear. That relationship of wonder and investigation is revealed by the fisherman for the Jews he meets. He does not hate them, he rather examines them "as though he was about to buy them" (p. 6). He peers at them "calmly, with a faint affection" (p. 7) and he places them within his mythic-rural space as a category of his other prey: fish, fowl, fox, and bear.

Appelfeld's definition of the gentile's hatred of the Jew is metahistorical. It is not connected, at least not at this stage of his writing, to Christian theology and the hostile relationship developed during the ages by Christianity toward the Jews.[3] It is an explanation completely rooted in the space of nature in the Carpathians and its pre-Christological culture. Within that space Janek, the persecuted Jew, can live alongside the Ruthenian fisherman as prey live alongside their predators, grazing side by side until the moment of attack. Appelfeld describes the attack as presaged by a movement of the fisherman's face, when "an involuntary muscle under his jaw stirred of its own accord, a hint of gathering force" (p. 5). He is as tense as a leopard when he regards the pale, almost transparent fragil-

---

his books: *Years and Hours* (Hakibbutz Hameuchad, Tel Aviv, 1975), *The Age of Wonders* (Hakibbutz Hameuchad, Tel Aviv, 1978), *At One and the Same Time* (Keter, Jerusalem, 1985). His protagonists deal with identifying the quality of those temporal notations and what they reveal; that is, do they expose a mythic, symbolic significance or do they denote time which passes blindly, like the mechanical ticks of a second hand?

3   At a later stage Appelfeld's writing is characterized by a concentrated focus on the Christological element, especially in its Russian Orthodox form, for example, in *Katerina*, London, Quartet, 1995, and in many other later works. See Lipsker, A. (1993) "A mystical, ecstatic apprentice to the saint, on the legendary novel *Katerina*," *Efes Shtaim* 2, Jerusalem, pp. 87–98.

ity of the Jews, looking like plucked birds on the riverbank. The hunt and attack are fashioned as the outbreak of an instinctive response of force when faced with weak, exposed, unprotected fragility.

The Jew and gentile sail together in the same boat as if they were floating unconsciously in flowing mythic primordial material, a flow whose tranquility neither ceases nor is threatened by the future outbreak of the murderer against his victim. Appelfeld fashions the preconscious flow in a supremely Impression-istic section. Its aquatic nature is the material out of which the boat ride and nonreflexive dimness of the lives of the souls of the unconscious agonists are fashioned:

> For a while the fisherman sat lifeless in the cramped silence. Now Janek felt the damp in his shirt and the faint freezing of his limbs. The late summer sun gilded the shorn meadows, and the trees, their branches stained with gold, seemed stark and insubstantial, as though they had risen disjointed from the ground. He was un-certain where he was, or who was this fisherman who had agreed to take him to the lakes in his boat. (p. 4)[4]

To the extent that curiosity, wonder, or regard develop, they are the elements of the laws of the primal space of hunters and hunted in a society whose life is led in pre-Christian, flowing, instinctive nature: "The fisherman did not take his eyes off them; no doubt this was the way he tracked a shoal of fish, curiosity mingled with the thrill of the hunt" (p. 10). It is the curiosity of one race for another, one sex for another, and one form of life for another, but not of one culture for an-other: "It would be interesting to know how they mate" (p. 7), the fisherman says. The Jews are for him "a strange breed" (p. 8).

Janek's participation in the flow as a separate consciousness is more complex than the fisherman's. As an individual fleeing for his life from his Ruthenian pursuers, and as a Jew carrying the secret of his Judaism, whispered into his ear by his mother, he is not a full participant in the primal "wild innocence." He carries within him family consciousness dependent on cultural ties that distin-guish him from his environment. That discrimination, that barrier, is what does not allow him to float fully and innocently within mythic space. Nevertheless, he is not totally apart from it. He "belongs" to the space because of his father's denial, who ordered that no mention of Jews be made in his house. However, because it was denial, it is repressed material that breaks through the surface of the primal wholeness. That borderline existence of consciousness that lives in one space but looks at what is beyond it is described by Appelfeld as a kind of special optical memory: "He recalled now as though through thick but still transparent

---

4 I have found great similarity to my position regarding Impressionism in Appelfeld's works in Michael Gluzman, "Memory and blindness: Appelfeld and the politics of Im-pressionism" (Hebrew) (January 2005), in Domb, R., Rozen, I., & Ben-Mordechai Y., (Eds.), *Mi-Kan 5*, pp. 89–99.

glass that his mother used to whisper to him that they [the Jews] were wonderful people" (p. 7). That sense of memory experiences a special reality in an optic-vocal synaesthesis: the view through thick but transparent glass is like a whisper, quiet but audible. It is the "transparent whisper," that is, it is both as hard as glass and a strangled sound, generating the miracle of life in a silent, sealed—and perhaps fetal—envelope of lack of knowledge. Now, however, in the confrontation between the fisherman and the Jews, and especially when he kills one of them, the fear of the hunted takes on a clear, immediate external form from which he cannot escape. The Jew was murdered close by after the fisherman convinced him to approach the boat, and the sound of his howls of pain continue into the night, accompanying the boat for a long time. It is a new, direct optic-vocal presence, a kind of final tearing of the thick glass amnion and the whisper of his children. Nature, which created the illusion of the protected mythical womb, in fact, adds its presence to the murder: "Nocturnal birds of prey roused themselves from their sleep and came down as though after a kill, to be witnesses and accomplices" (p. 12). Exchanging primal for ethical terminology ("murder" instead of "hunt") means exchanging a mythic code for a social-historical code. They are not the relations between predator and prey (the picture Nazi ideology tried to paint as it uprooted Germany's moral-religious base), but rather between murderer and victim, relations occurring within a social–historical context and not within primal-feral space. The violent act is like cutting the thick glass, like raising a weak voice to a loud scream, and, for Janek, like the passage of birth from a rustic-primal-mythic existence to one that is historical, social, and moral.

From that point on, for Janek the boat ride in the dark becomes a journey of human social knowledge into his Jewishness, which is tragic and dark at the historical moment in which he finds himself:

> Janek knew now that this faint darkness which was spreading its nets was the gateway to another darkness, and even when they were inside, in the channel, in the current that would carry them to the lakes, he could still see their roaming eyes on top of the feelers and they themselves, too thin to be substantial, and then only the stares, as though their whole being was in those radiant stares. (p. 13)

Based on matters discussed in a research seminar devoted to the works of Aharon Appelfeld and held at the Hartman Institute in Jerusalem in 2006.

REFERENCES

Appelfeld, A. (1971). The hunt. In *Pillars of the river* (Hebrew), pp. 65–73, Hakibbutz Hameuchad, Tel Aviv.

Appelfeld, A. (1989). The hunt. (N. de Lange, Trans.). In K. Shawn & K. Goldfrad (2008) (Eds.), *The call of memory: Learning about the Holocaust through narrative: An anthology*, pp. 3–13. Teaneck, NJ: Ben Yehuda Press.

"The Hunt" by Aharon Appelfeld: A Portrait of the Antisemite at His Most Natural

Tova Weiss

*"As though in an endless nightmare they were once more on the run
and heaven alone knew when and where the chase would end."*
—Benjamin Ellis,
translated from the Yiddish
by Moshe Spiegel

"The Hunt" by Aharon Appelfeld, anthologized in Shawn & Goldfrad (2008, pp. 3–13), is not an easy story, nor was it easy for me to write this chapter. I had to read and reread the story a dozen times before I could even begin to clearly sort out my thoughts about how to use it in the classroom. Because this was my first encounter with an Appelfeld narrative, I expected to be able to appreciate the way my students would feel when they were first exposed to this story. I felt confident that I would empathize with what I imagined their initial feelings would be. I had found the story powerful, disturbing, and difficult to absorb; yet, it intrigued and haunted me, and I believed my students would have the same response.

I was invited to create an advanced placement senior seminar, called "The Experience of the Individual in Holocaust Literature and Film," for approximately 12 young women in a Jewish day high school in Scranton, Pennsylvania. All the students are from religiously observant homes. All are American-born, and a third of them are grandchildren of Holocaust survivors. They are well-versed in Jewish history and world history, thanks to a strong and solid curriculum. They will come to me knowing the broad outlines of Holocaust history as well as the specific experiences of several survivors, which they have read in their English literature classes and heard from survivors they know personally.

What drew me most to this story and to its potential as the introductory selection in the seminar was the notion of the fisherman as archetypical antisemite. As expressed by the author, the readers will confront precisely what the Jews faced—not from the trials they endured as the Nazis invaded and occupied their countries—but from ordinary people living among them throughout Eastern Europe.

"Portrait of an Antisemite"

In this story, Appelfeld has drawn—to paraphrase James Joyce (1916)—"a portrait of the antisemite at his most natural." That portrait, so taut and intimate, provides a window into the thoughts and feelings of the type of person—one of many like him—who simply assumes as the natural order of things the role of the Jew as quarry. In so doing, the portrait, with the detail of a photograph, offers insight into a kind of "natural" antisemitism that has plagued Jews for centuries.

Appelfeld, with deft strokes, illustrates the widespread perception of the Jew as outsider, the other, a creature different from "ordinary folk" such as the fisherman, one of two major figures in this narrative. Here, the fisherman gazes at a group of Jews on shore. "It was not a look of hatred" (Shawn & Goldfrad, *Anthology*, p. 6) he projected; he considered them "like peasants who keep livestock and feel an affection for the beasts, so long as they are alive" (p. 6). He watches them and muses, "It would be interesting to know … how they mate" (p. 7). Later, he recalls how, in his childhood, "We used to run after them and throw stones at them." He sums up: "A strange breed of human beings" (p. 8).

At the same time, I was not sure this would be a good choice for the seminar because, interestingly, the more I reread the story, the more strongly I felt that this highly literary, symbolic, poetic piece could be set in any place or time in which antisemitism flourished in Europe. Almost disturbingly, there is nothing in the setting that clearly identifies it as the time of the Holocaust. In fact, the *only* key to its historical placement is not in the words of the text but in the reader's knowledge of the author's life.

However, the power of Appelfeld's writing held sway, and I set out to design my senior seminar with this as its first assignment. My class will meet daily for 45 minutes; I anticipate spending no more than three days on this short narrative, depending upon the depth of the resultant discussion. What follows, then, is my plan for teaching "The Hunt."

The Author's Background: When Should It Be Examined?

Initially, I planned to begin the class with a brief description of Appelfeld's background, which I had compiled from information I had gathered by reading several interviews with him. I wanted my students to know that Appelfeld was a child survivor whose mother was killed early on; who initially lived in a ghetto with his father; who was sent to a concentration camp and escaped; and who survived both by hiding and by "passing" as a non-Jew because of his Aryan looks. I wanted them to know that he had wandered about the countryside, working as a farmhand where possible, moving on when he felt threatened. Appelfeld's parents were, in his own words, highly assimilated intellectuals who distanced themselves from their roots. I thought they could more easily understand the story if they learned that his father was adamant about disconnecting from his traditional Jewish past, although his mother had warm connections to her Jewish upbringing and her family and managed to convey to her son her admiration of, and longing for, that past and the people in it.

Ultimately, though, my intuition led me to reject this traditional approach and to plan instead to *not* provide such biographical information before the first reading. Knowing the author's background, I suspected, would make it too easy to superimpose it on Janek, the protagonist of "The Hunt," and thus remove from the readers the task of struggling with the text and the questions it raises.

Just who is Janek? Is he running because he has committed a crime? It soon becomes obvious that he is, in some way, Jewish. Now, more questions crop up: Is he from a mixed marriage? Is he from an assimilated family? Why does he have such conflicted feelings for the Jewish men onshore? "I can't abide them" (p. 6), he says. Does he truly "hate" (p. 10) them? What is he discovering about them and about himself?

The question of ancestry, of belonging, of peoplehood, in a sense, is actually raised by the fisherman outright and figures prominently in Janek's thoughts, although for different reasons. With Janek, we see Jews through a distorted lens no less than through the fisherman's eyes. His view of them changes from minute to minute; he sees their "pathetic transparency" (p. 5) as that of soon-to-be butchered fowl, then sees them with "a coat of gleaming armor" (p. 6). He feels "exposed to their stares" (p. 10), begins to see himself as if through their eyes, feels drawn to them—"He would have liked to approach them" (p. 10)—and connects with them by understanding their "sadness" and "hopelessness" (p. 10).

He remembers "that his mother used to whisper to him that they were wonderful people, that she missed them, that they were not like the peasants" (p. 7). He knows that his father "gave orders that they were not to be mentioned in his house" (p. 7) and that his mother, therefore, stopped talking about them. He feels distant from the Jews on shore, watches them as one watches an oddity, clearly seeing himself as separate and apart from them; yet, "the thought that his father and mother belonged to their ranks had still not abandoned him" (p. 9). Janek is working on solving the mystery of his own family history, ancestry, and peoplehood within the puzzle of the larger "Jewish question" that floats through the entire story.

It seemed to me, therefore, that *not* knowing Appelfeld's background would stimulate more thoughtful discussion and text-based analysis. My students would be forced to draw on their previous knowledge of history and literature and integrate it into their reactions to this text. They would be compelled to search for clues, think critically, make educated guesses, and defend their conclusions. Finally, I wanted to offer my students the opportunity to compare their interpretations of the story and its characters, especially Janek, before and after knowing Appelfeld's own story, and to pursue a discussion of the differences they would surely find; I suspected that using this technique would also help to imprint the story in their memories. I decided then that only after an initial discussion would I provide the biography and assign a second reading in light of it.

I realized the imperative of teaching Appelfeld's biography at the end of the first reading as well as historical background on, or at least a brief review of, the assimilation of Jews into Western European culture and life since the Enlightenment/Emancipation of the 1800s. I also planned to include content on the existence and attitudes of those Jews who wanted to escape their heritage/religion/ culture for a variety of reasons, including the lure of modernity. (For introductory sources, see the *Encyclopedia Judaica* (2007): "Antisemitism" (pp. 206-245) and "Emancipation" (pp. 374-386).

Making Connections: Literature

As I read and continued to plan, I could not help but think of the testimony of Cecilia K. excerpted in *Witness: Voices from the Holocaust* (Greene & Kumar, 2000) in which Cecilia, hidden by a Christian farmer directly underneath a floor in the barn, overhears conversations between peasant workers who brag about the number of Jews each caught that day to be exchanged for a sack of salt. Their talk was an echo of the fisherman's musings: "'Damn 'em, they're out of range,' the fisherman said" (p. 5); "When I was young, I used to practice Jewhunting. For every Jew you bagged you got a modest bounty" (p. 6); "If only they were closer, I'd have a go at them" (p. 6). The Cecilia K. reading would complement this story and reinforce the fisherman's attitude and actions.

I reflected on the stark differences between Janek's dilemma with his identity and the reaction of Moshe Flinker to his Holocaust experiences as reflected in his diary, excerpted in *Salvaged Pages* (Zapruder, 2002, pp. 90–121). Janek is a person who doesn't belong, not among the peasant fishermen ("I knew you weren't one of us" [p. 10]), not among the non-Jews who hunt Jews ("You're a strange chap, haven't you ever seen Jews before [p. 11]"), and not among those whose blood flows in his veins ("They," he believes, "would not admit him to their throngs" [p. 10]).

My understanding of Janek, whom I imagine as a young man, is of a person lost for lack of clear knowledge of who he is and to whom and where he belongs. His is a confusion of identity so profound that he can "hate" his own people without knowing them. "I can't abide them," he says several times, but when the fisherman asks why, Janek says, "No reason" (p. 6). His is an "inherited hatred" that "lacked force" and "contained a certain sadness" (p. 10). "Didn't your ancestors tell you about them," the fisherman asks. "Yes, they did" Janek replies, "but not much" (p. 11).

Moshe Flinker, by contrast, was raised in an Orthodox Jewish family in The Hague. He wrote his diary while his family was in hiding in Brussels. Moshe struggled with the events around him and even questioned why God was allowing these horrors to happen to His people; but his questioning was always from a perspective firmly rooted in belief in God and love and knowledge of his people and his place among them. Excerpts from this diary must, I decided, be read as a concurrent homework assignment with the understanding that the class would return to examine it in greater depth at a later time. "The Hunt" is a work of fiction that I see as semi-autobiographical, and the diary is nonfiction; a comparison of the two young men and their reactions based on their upbringing would be most instructive.

Making Connections: Film

Film images flooded my mind. I remembered vividly one of the two survivors of the 400,000 Jews sent to the Chelmno death camp, Simon Srebnik, whom I came to know from Claude Lanzmann's epic film, *Shoah* (1985). In Chelmno, Srebnik was a 13-year-old boy assigned by the Nazis to labor, shackled in leg chains, in a so-called Jewish work detail. Several times a week, Simon, under heavy guard, sang for the Nazis' entertainment. In the film, viewers are introduced to the now-grown Simon as he sits in a flat-bottomed boat being rowed up the Narew River in Poland, singing the songs he sang then. His narrative is chilling as it unfolds.

"The Hunt" stirred in me the evoked memory of Simon as a young boy, and I couldn't shake it. Certainly, the similar setting suggested the comparison: a young man, a victim, in a boat on a river. Perhaps, there was also a subconscious awareness of what Lipsker (2008) describes in this *Guide* as "the vocal elements" in Appelfeld's writing that "mark out the space in which the events take place: the lilt of the oars, the voices singing to themselves as echoes, and the measured song accompanying the fishermen as they take their boats onto the river" (p. 17).

The stronger connection, though, was the visual memory of Simon in the scene in which he stands near the church in the town square as a church service lets out. Lanzmann begins to ask townspeople if they remember a shackled young boy on the river who used to sing as he rowed. At first, people in the crowd speak excitedly and discuss their memories of him; they seem happy to learn that Simon survived. However, the tone, the faces, and the gestures of the very people who profess joy at seeing the now-grown Simon soon change; antisemitism is still evident in them as they speak freely to the interviewer.

As I read "The Hunt," I developed a specific mental image of the fisherman's facial gestures; the looks, the movements of the eyes and the mouth would be subtle and small, but seen up close, they would be filled with meaning, the same meaning, I thought, that students would appreciate in this segment of *Shoah*. Despite the fact that the historical chronology is not sequential, I felt I had to screen the relevant excerpts from *Shoah* at the end of our work on "The Hunt" and hear the reactions of the students. I set about taping from the DVD version, Chapters 1, 25, and 26, already anticipating their responses and eager comparisons.

A Broad Audience

I had initially worried that this story might be too specific to the Jewish experience to be comfortably taught to a non-Jewish audience; but as I gathered material, I began to understand the value of "The Hunt" in any advanced placement senior literature class or Holocaust seminar or college- or graduate-level Holocaust literature course because its themes are many, varied, and connected to so much that would be covered in such courses: antisemitism, identity, search for self and for meaning, exploration of hatred/prejudice and what has been called "the dislike of the unlike," including "inherited" hatred, victimization, group response, and the victim/bystander/perpetrator/rescuer paradigm of the Holocaust.

"The Hunt," I saw, would serve as a touchstone throughout the course. It is complex and works on many levels: emotional, psychological, philosophical, historical, and, of course, as a brilliant piece of literature. It can bring the reader to a visceral understanding of the fear, helplessness, weariness, the knowing-but-not-knowing, the sense of danger and much more, that Janek as the Jewish youth in his late teens? 20s?—we can only conjecture—feels. It can connect us emotionally, viscerally, to the dangers encountered by the innocent victims represented by the group of Jewish men. Literarily, it is rich in figurative language and imagery; psychologically, it makes us tremble with its deceptively calm structure of suspense and drama. Philosophically and historically, it raises the essential questions of the roots of, and responses to, the perception of the Jews as outsiders and the ongoing examination of to whom and to what Jews themselves belong. Finally, and perhaps most importantly, the image of the fisherman, for whom Jew hunting is as natural as fishing, would help my students understand and fully appreciate the attitudes and actions of other people they will encounter in our readings, when the image of the peasant Jew-hater will be countered by those of non-Jews who helped Jews even at the risk of their own lives. My students cannot come away from my course with the distorted view that every non-Jew in Europe was an antisemite. My hope is that they will be able to appreciate the different responses of people, and, perhaps, what made them different, as the course progresses. A perfect example is the personality and image of Magda Trocme and the villagers of Le Chambon in *The Courage to Care* (ADL, 1985), a film we will screen.

The Unit of Study

My planned unit on "The Experience of the Individual in Holocaust Literature and Film" includes excerpts from diaries, memoirs and testimonies, short stories, and several films chosen to enhance understanding about, and empathy towards, the young people encountered in them. The course further explores the role of the family in providing emotional and spiritual support in times of crises; hiding and seeking; questions of morality and beliefs; the role of faith in young people's responses to the Holocaust; and the nature of survival. The literature covers aspects of the larger Holocaust experience including life in Germany, the *Kindertransports,* life in the ghetto, in hiding, and in labor and concentration camps; the Righteous among the Nations, liberation, and life in the DP camps. Selections in addition to those already mentioned are from *Anthology of Holocaust Literature* (Glatstein et al, 1973), *Out of the Whirlwind* (Friedlander, 1977), *Hasidic Tales of the Holocaust* (Eliach, 1982), *To Live With Honor and Die With Honor* (Kermish, 1986), *We Are Children Just the Same* (Krizkova & Kotouc,1995), *Flares of Memory* (Brostoff, 1998), *The Unconquerable Spirit* (Hirschler, 1980), *Witness to the Holocaust* (Lewin, 1990), *A Brush With Death* (Wyszogrod, 1999), and Primo Levi's *Survival in Auschwitz* (1996). Film excerpts include *Children Remember the Holocaust* (1995); *Return to Life* (1995), local videotaped testimony of survivors from my community, and *There Once Was a Town* (Bieber, 1999), the documentary based on Eliach's book of the same name. I will also invite survivors to visit the class at different points in the seminar.

Beginning the Seminar

When I meet the class, I will ask each student to share her background in Holocaust history and literature, her reasons for choosing this elective, and what she hopes to get from it. I will distribute a timeline of the Holocaust and conduct a brief, open-ended discussion in which any questions the young women have are raised and noted; hopefully, the course will help to answer them. I will assign "The Hunt" as our first story, to be read at home. I will ask students to use a literature journal to jot down their thoughts about the title, about those passages that disturb or perplex them, questions they may have, and their general reactions. I will review common terms they have already learned to ensure that we have a common language:

1. Simile: a figure of speech that draws a comparison between two different things, containing the word "like" or "as"
2. Metaphor:
    a. the application of a word or phrase to somebody or something that is not meant literally but to make a comparison
    b. one thing used or considered to represent another
3. Allusion: a reference that is made indirectly, subtly suggested, or implied
4. Archetype:
    a. a typical, ideal, or classic example of something
    b. an image or symbol used repeatedly in art or literature
5. Foreshadowing: the act of providing vague advance indications
6. Prejudice:
    a. preformed opinion, usually an unfavorable one, based on insufficient knowledge, irrational feelings, or inaccurate stereotypes
    b. an unfounded hatred, fear, or mistrust of a person or group, especially one of a particular religion, ethnicity, nationality, or social status
7. Discrimination: treatment of one person or group, usually because of prejudice about race, ethnic group, age group, religion, or gender
8. Bigotry: intolerance toward people who hold different views, especially on matters of politics, religion, or ethnicity.

I have identified and will share with my students my desired outcomes for teaching this story; they include students' understanding of:
- the effective use of simile, metaphor, and other literary terms;
- the nature of prejudice as explored in this story;
- the language of antisemitism in this story;
- the nature of the hunter and his view of the hunted;
- Janek's situation and his resultant identity crisis;
- the role of such "fishermen" in the success of the Holocaust; and
- the importance of connecting to, and reflecting on, related readings.

Questions for Discussion

In our second meeting, I'll ask students to skim the story and their journal notes, and we'll begin by sharing their reactions. I've prepared my own notes so I can raise additional questions, both to check for understanding and to promote critical thinking and literary analysis. I formulated these questions, which range from simple comprehension to analytical:

1. What is the setting of the story? In what period of time might you place it? Why? Are there any literary or historical clues that mark this story as set during the Holocaust? Cite direct indications or references that you find.
2. Discuss the main character: Who is Janek? Where is he physically? How did he get there? Where is he emotionally? How did he get there?
3. What do we learn about the fisherman: his abilities? background? prejudices? How did he get to be this way? Where would you place him on a scale of good vs. evil? Why?
4. Who did you understand the people on the riverbank to be at the beginning of the story? When and why did your understanding change?
5. What memories does Janek have of his parents? Why are these memories important for us to know?
6. Who is hunting? Who is hunted?
7. In what way does the fisherman's livelihood echo the title?
8. Find direct references and allusions to religion/beliefs.
9. How does Appelfeld use color and light to enhance the mood and the theme of the story? Give specific examples. What does each signify?
10. Near the story's conclusion, both the fisherman and Janek feel a sense of bad luck. What are the different implications of each man's feeling?

For homework, after what I hope will be a provocative and engaging exchange, I will ask students to complete in their journals any questions left unexplored during our class. I will ask them, as well, to read the brief biography of Appelfeld, to reread the story, and to note changes in their interpretation.

Making Sense of a Complex Narrative

In our second class, they'll share observations, insights, and reinterpretations, particularly about who is hunted and who is/are the victim(s). It should be clear that the Jews are the prey and that the fisherman, who is not Jewish, is the hunter. I'll listen carefully for new understandings about Janek and his upbringing and probe to discover if these new realizations changed their response to the fisherman and his actions.

I will ask for a definition of "antisemitism" and focus the discussion on specific phrases that can be seen as prejudicial, as language of separation and "otherness." I've prepared discussion prompts:

1. Is there a body language as one confronts "the other?"
2. Is hatred learned, inherited, both?

3. Is there a difference between the fisherman's feelings about the people on the shore and Janek's feelings?
4. What do you think the lakes signify?
5. Can the fisherman be seen as a rescuer?
6. In what ways is the "hunt" literal? metaphoric?

I would hope that my students will recognize that the "hunt" itself takes place on many levels; the hunting imagery is almost overwhelming. There is the literal hunt for fish, which "for a modest catch a man must row to the home of the Devil himself" (Shawn & Goldfrad, *Anthology*, p. 3). There is the hunt as spoken of by the fisherman who shares his reminisces of hunting Jews in exchange for money, an echo of the peasants in Cecilia K.'s testimony that I would then read aloud in class. There is the hunt that unexpectedly takes place in front of Janek's eyes: "'I have an urge to hunt them,' the fisherman sat up. ... [He] ... tensed himself, drew a knife and threw it. The knife did not miss (p. 12)." There is the hunt from which Janek is attempting to escape by taking this boat trip, and the hunt—more a search—that the reader surmises Janek is undergoing to discover who he is, to whom he belongs. In addition, there is the physical description of the fisherman's anticipation of the hunt that my students will surely note and examine. As soon as he sees the group of Jewish men,

> The fisherman's eyes sharpened and his eyebrows stiffened. A network of red blood vessels stood out in the whites of his eyes. He measured the distance. ... For a long time the fisherman sat without moving. His whole being was concentrated. The skin around his eyes turned blue. Attention and watchfulness gnawed at his face, and an involuntary muscle under his jaw stirred of its own accord, a hint of the gathering force. ... It did not occur to Janek that these were hunting thoughts being woven in secret. (pp. 5, 6)

I will distribute brief excerpts from Moshe Flinker's diary (Zapruder, 2002) to be read at home and ask students to note comparisons between Moshe's experiences growing up as an observant Jew and Janek's experiences with religion and the resultant reactions to their fellow Jews. To continue the work with imagery, I'll also assign the task of examining the text to find at least three examples each of simile, metaphor, and allusion. Before class on the third day, I'll draw a grid (see below) on the board, and when students arrive, I'll ask them to take turns as three at a time fill in the grid. Samples include:

Simile	Metaphor	Allusion
The bristles ringed his jowl like peeling birchbark.	Their bodies took on a coat of gleaming armor.	For a modest catch a man must row to the home of the Devil himself.
Their bodies … like hens whose neck-feathers had been plucked out	They're human foxes/they [the Jews] used to descend in flocks.	He could see now the horse's dead eyes looking at him with a final comprehension.
They slip between your fingers like fish.	Fire glided on the surface of the water.	He prepared his nets for the night.

To extend the learning, I'll probe: Which descriptive phrases stand out for you? Why? What feelings do those phrases arouse in you?

Many choices are possible; to be prepared to deepen and expand our conversation, I selected the following that describe the hunted Jews in terms of insects and wildlife: "The feelers that were above them (p. 5)," "like grasshoppers" (p. 7), "they shook themselves like beetles," "a flock of black men" (p. 5); likened, through the fisherman's eyes, to livestock, studied by him "like a peasant feeling a beast" (p. 7), and branded "human foxes" (p. 9).

1. Which phrase best defines for you each of the main characters? Explain.
2. What affected you most in the story?
3. What lasting image or memory might you carry away from it?

When the homework is reviewed, I plan to screen the excerpt from *Shoah* and encourage the students to discover the commonalities with our story. My final question will close and summarize. I'll ask, "In what ways do these two selections work to begin this seminar?" My hope is that students will recognize that each illustrates both those who were antisemites by instinct and upbringing, and the deep-rooted, long-standing prejudice against the Jews that made the Holocaust possible. As educators, we know that Europe was replete with people like these peasants and this fisherman, and that, ultimately, understanding them, their society, and their attitudes towards Jews ("Around here they can't camouflage themselves. We know them. Sometimes they try but we know them, from way back" [p. 9]) goes a long way toward answering the most essential question: *How could the Holocaust have happened?*

My students will write essays throughout the course, as I find them a useful evaluative tool. For their final summative response to "The Hunt," which will be written at home, I will offer them the following four quotes and ask them to choose one, explain its meaning, and elaborate on its value as an epigraph, on how, in other words, it illustrates the story's theme.

1. "Hamlet said: 'To be or not to be, that is the question.' But that is no problem. We all want to be. The real problem, biblically speaking, is how to be and how not to be; that is our challenge, and it is what makes the difference between the human and the animal." (Heschel, 1996, p. 252)

2. "People see somebody different/Fear is the reaction shown/Then they think they've got him licked/The barbaric hunt begins/And they move in slow/A human spirit is devoured/The remains to carrion crow/I was told that life is change/And yet history remains." (Stills, 1992)

3. "As though in an endless nightmare they were once more on the run and heaven alone knew when and where the chase would end." (Ellis, 1973, p. 387)

4. "Confusion will be my epitaph/As I crawl a cracked and broken path/If we make it we can all sit back and laugh./But I fear tomorrow I'll be crying./Yes, I fear tomorrow I'll be crying." (King Crimson, 1969–1974)

The Author Speaks

To conclude this introductory lesson, I will share excerpts from a talk given by Appelfeld that I believe will ground our later discussions of differences between testimonial literature written by adults and by children. As the featured speaker for a Jewish Book Week program held at Cambridge University in March 2004, "Expressing the Inexpressible," Appelfeld compared the experience, memory, testimony, and writing of adult survivors and child survivors. His full text can be downloaded from *www.jewishbookweek.com/archive/020304d/transcripts2.php*. In the case of children who grew up in the Holocaust, he explained,

> Life during the Holocaust was something they could understand for they had absorbed it in their blood. They knew no other. They knew man as a beast of prey, not metaphorically but as a physical reality with its full stature and clothing.

He continues:

> For the child survivors, the war was their full life. They could not speak about the Holocaust in historical, theological, or moral terms. They could speak only about the fears, hunger, callousness, cellars, people who were good to them or people who treated them badly. The power of their testimonies lies in their limited horizon.

He concludes, "But through their limited horizon, we learn a lot about cruelty, generosity, hatred and love."

It is the power of Appelfeld's "testimony," then—the story of a child couched in the exquisite literary narrative of the adult—that I will offer my students as I begin my seminar with "The Hunt."

REFERENCES

Appelfeld, A. (1971). The hunt. Nicholas de Lange, Trans. In K. Shawn and K. Goldfrad (Eds.) (2008). *The call of memory: Learning about the Holocaust through narrative*: *An anthology*, pp. 3–13. Teaneck, NJ: Ben Yehuda Press.

Appelfeld, A. (2004). Retrieved 11/14/2007 from *www.jewishbookweek.com/archive/020304d/transcripts2.php*.

Bieber, J. (Dir. & Prod.). (1999). *There once was a town: A remarkable journey of hope and survival.* Arlington, VA: WETA.

Brostoff, A. (Ed.). (1998). *Flares of memory: Childhood stories written by Holocaust survivors.* Pittsburgh: Holocaust Center of the United Jewish Federation of Greater Pittsburgh.

Eliach, Y. (1982). *Hasidic tales of the Holocaust.* New York: Oxford University Press.

Ellis, B. (1973). The fugitives. (M. Spiegel, Trans.). In J. Glatstein, I. Knox, & S. Margoshes (Eds.), *Anthology of Holocaust literature*, pp. 385–391. New York: Atheneum.

Encyclopedia Judaica. (2007). Antisemitism, Vol. 2, A Hertzberg et al. Emancipation, Vol. 6, B. Dinur (Dinaburg). Jerusalem: Keter Publishing House Ltd.

Friedlander, A. H. (Ed.). (1977). *Out of the whirlwind.* New York: Schocken Books.

Gardner, R. (Producer & Director). (1985). *The courage to care.* Alexandria, VA: United Way Productions, ADL.

Glatstein, J., Knox, I., & Margoshes, S. (Eds.). (1973). *Anthology of Holocaust literature.* New York: Atheneum.

Greene, J. M. & Kumar, S. (2000) *Witness: Voices from the Holocaust.* New York: The Free Press/Simon & Schuster Inc.

Heschel, A. J. (1996). Choose life! In S. Heschel (Ed.), *Moral grandeur and spiritual audacity*, pp. 251–256. New York: Farrar, Straus and Giroux.

Hirschler, G. (Ed.). (1980). *The unconquerable spirit: Vignettes of the religious spirit the Nazis could not destroy.* New York: Zachor Institute.

Kermish, J. (1986) *To live with honor and die with honor: Selected documents from the Warsaw Ghetto underground archives.* Jerusalem: Yad Vashem.

King Crimson. 21st century schizoid man. *The 21st century guide to King Crimson: Volume one, 1969–1974* .(CD).

Kirkpatrick, D. S. (December 19, 1995). *Children remember the Holocaust.* New York: CBS Schoolbreak Special, Season 13, Episode 2.

Krizkova,M. R. & Kotouc, K. J. (1995) *We are children just the same: Vedem, the secret magazine by the boys of Terezin.* Philadelphia: Jewish Publication Society.

Lanzmann, C..(1995). *Shoah: The complete text of the acclaimed Holocaust film Shoah.* New York: Da Capo Press.

Lanzmann, C. (1985). *Shoah.* France. Les Films Aleph-Historia Films.

Levi, P. (1996). *Survival in Auschwitz.* New York: Touchstone/Simon & Schuster Inc.

Lewin, R. G. (Ed.). (1990). *Witness to the Holocaust: An Oral History.* New York: Twayne Publishers.

Lipsker, A. (2008). Born from myth into history: Reading "The hunt" by Aharon Appelfeld. In K. Shawn and K. Goldfrad (Eds.), *The call of memory: Learning about the Holocaust through narrative*: *A teacher's guide*, pp. 17–22. Teaneck, NJ: Ben Yehuda Press.

Return to life: The Holocaust survivors: From liberation to rehabilitation. (1995). Israel: Beit Hatefutsot, Beit Lohamei Hageta'ot, & Yad Vashem.

Stills, S. (1992). Word game. *Stephen Stills 2.* (CD).

Wyszogrod, M. (1999). *A brush with death: An artist in the death camps.* Albany, NY: State University of New York Press.

Zapruder, A. (2002). Moshe Flinker: Brussels, Belgium. *Salvaged pages: Young writers' diaries of the Holocaust*, pp. 90–121. New Haven, CT: Yale University Press.

Trapped in Germany:
"No Way Out: Letters From the Holocaust"

Brana Gurewitsch

No one writes letters any more. Today, we are in constant communication via Instant Messages, e-mail, voicemail, telephones, and cell phones. Communication is so inexpensive that even great geographic distances do not separate us; we remain in touch electronically, in quick bursts of information or reaction: sound bites, bits, and bytes.

Try to imagine a world where geographic distance had to be bridged by what we now deride as "snail mail," where communication depended on trains and trucks and ships to carry physical messages written or typed on paper and sent from one address to the other, where there was a delay of days or even weeks between the time one put a letter in the mailbox or post office and the delivery of that letter to its destination; remember, too, that there was a similar delay before a response was received. Under wartime conditions, civilian mail service almost completely stopped, and families living apart became quite isolated with no means of communicating except for telegrams, very expensive, brief text messages that were transmitted over electric telegraph wires and then typed out by an operator and hand-delivered to the designated recipient at a distant destination.

In the 1940s, people communicated via long-distance telephone lines (even more expensive than telegrams), telegraph wires, or by sending handwritten letters through the postal system. Letters were the way to share news, express feelings, and obtain or provide information. Although this was hardly as easy or as efficient as our current, electronic communication, it was much more durable. Today, our text messages are quickly deleted, and writing letters is almost a lost art. At one time, letters were often saved, treasured as mementos of relationships, special events, and important thoughts. Some people saved certain, special letters; others saved entire correspondences, and those saved letters constitute shared family history, reflecting the events, responses, and actions taken or not taken. These letters are the building blocks not only of individual family histories, but also of the larger historical context of the time, and they give us insight into what was happening to people and how they responded to the world around them.

The letters of the Deutsch family, collected in Susan Prinz Shear's "No Way Out: Letters From the Holocaust" (Shawn & Goldfrad, *Anthology*, 2008, pp. 14–43), reflect a world that had been turned upside down. Political events destroyed their secure world as prominent German Jews and forced the family to seek refuge outside Germany. From their letters we learn what obstacles they faced, how they coped, and how their troubles affected them individually and as a family. We learn about the large, traumatic events that affected an entire world through the narrower prism of the story of one family as they keep in touch by mail.

The Jews in Germany

In 1933, there were more than a half million Jews living in Germany, comprising approximately 1% of the population. There is a record of uninterrupted Jewish life in Germany beginning with the 10th century. Since the 18th century, German Jews, including the ancestors of the Deutsch family, were integrated into German society, participating fully in its economic, political, and cultural life. Some Jews lived in small towns, but most were urban. Most German Jews were not religiously observant, but the orthodox religious minority created institutions with world-wide influence and prominence. German Jews were loyal citizens, serving in the German Army in World War I, and participating in Germany's political institutions.

When the Nazis came to power in 1933, they began to implement their anti-semitic political platform. This encouraged prejudices that were already present. Parliament passed laws that gave the government dictatorial powers, dissolved political parties, expelled Jews from government jobs, and started the process of denying civil rights to Jews. These laws not only legalized prejudice but also created an atmosphere of persecution and fear.

German Jews were shocked and dismayed by these disturbing and dangerous developments. However, most felt that the Nazi regime was a temporary aberration that would pass. After all, there had been periods of prejudice in the past. Jews had learned to live with restrictions before, and they felt sure that they would be able to cope with the new challenge. German Jews such as the Deutsch family had a large investment in Germany—professional status and practices, thriving businesses, personal property, and substantial community institutions. They saw no reason to abandon them.

In 1935, a series of laws was legislated, called the Nuremberg Laws, after the city in which the German parliament convened in a special meeting held during the annual Nazi Party rally in Nuremberg (*Encyclopedia of the Holocaust*, 1990, p. 1076). At this special meeting, Jews were denied the rights to economic freedom, deprived of their German citizenship, rights to education, and freedom of movement, and isolated physically and psychologically from the rest of German society. A Flight Tax was instituted, taxing the property of German Jews who applied to emigrate at 25% of its value, creating a hardship for many who did not have a lot of cash to pay the tax.

For those Jews who tried to leave Germany the process was complicated. In addition to the Flight Tax, all other taxes had to be paid up. Businesses or other assets had to be sold, and sale prices were usually at a fraction of true value.

> Bureaucratic procedures obliged everyone seeking emigration to
> satisfy many exit requirements according to a preset sequence and

within the time limit set by a stamped expiration date. If paper or permit number two was not acquired before number one had expired, it was necessary to begin anew. Documents, signatures, transactions sealed with the proper stamps: the formalities seemed endless. After one acquired clearances affirming that one owed no past taxes—local, government, utility, sales, or even dog taxes—one needed a form testifying to one's "nonobjectionable" character and lack of a criminal record. (Spitzer, 1998, p. 33)

Once all the required German exit documents were assembled, would-be emigrants still needed permission to enter another country. Obtaining these permissions, or visas, was the crucial step for those seeking to leave. The most desirable destinations, such as the United States, England, or Palestine, where German Jews had family connections and felt they would adjust most easily, had very restrictive immigration policies. Limited numbers of visas were issued to immigrants each year. If the number of applicants exceeded the number of visas that could be issued, the applicants had to wait, sometimes several years, until a visa became available.

After the collapse of the New York Stock Exchange in 1929, the United States experienced a major economic depression and a worldwide economic crisis soon followed. The United States restricted the number of visas it would issue and instructed its consuls in Germany to interpret the immigration regulations very strictly. As a result, even the limited number of American visas that might have been issued—26,000 a year to German immigrants—were not all issued. The elderly, the sick, children, those who might not be able to work, and people who did not have close relatives in the United States were denied entry because they might not be able to support themselves. In spite of these difficulties, however, about 129,000 German Jews emigrated between 1933 and 1937; 38,000 of them came to the United States (Bauer, 1982, p. 109).

Kristallnacht

In March 1938, Germany annexed Austria, unleashing a wave of antisemitic attacks on Jews, including confiscation of Jewish property and freezing of Jewish assets. These circumstances precipitated a frenzied rush by Austrian Jews to emigrate. In response to public pressure in the United States for liberalization of American immigration policy, President Franklin Delano Roosevelt convened an international conference in Evian, France, in July, 1938, on the problem of Jewish refugees. The American delegate promised that the U.S. government would fully use its existing quotas but would not increase them. With the exception of the Dominican Republic, none of the 32 countries at the conference agreed to accept more refugees, for various reasons. The message was clear: Germany was now free to solve what they called the "Jewish Problem" their way (Abella, 1982, p. 32).

To prevent Polish Jews who were living in Germany and Austria from fleeing to Poland, the Polish parliament passed laws in March and October 1938, prohibiting them from entering Poland. On October 27–28, Germany deported some

18,000 Jews to the Polish border, where some were forced across by the Nazis, and others were interned in a camp at Zbaszyn, Poland, in miserable conditions. When 17-year-old Hershel Grynszpan, a student living in Paris, received a letter from his family describing their experiences in Zbaszyn, he went to the German embassy in Paris in a fury and shot and killed a secretary of the embassy, Ernst vom Rath. This act became a convenient justification for mass action—which had been planned long before—against the Jews in Germany and Austria. Barracks were already prepared in the concentration camps to accommodate thousands of new prisoners (Bauer, 1982, p. 108).

On November 9–10, 1938, organized attacks on Jews were conducted by Nazis and their sympathizers throughout Germany and Austria. These attacks were called *Kristallnacht* (Crystal Night, or Night of Broken Glass) and refer to the broken windows of Jewish stores and synagogues destroyed in that two-day pogrom. During those attacks more than 30,000 Jews were arrested and sent to concentration camps, more than 1200 synagogues were destroyed, 91 Jews were killed, and a similar number were wounded.

Kristallnacht was not the beginning of the Holocaust, although its violence marked a new phase in the Nazi persecution of the Jews. The Nazi rise to power created a climate that began with social ostracism of Jews by their Christian neighbors, continued with economic measures that gradually impoverished them, and climaxed with the legalization of denial of basic civil rights for Jews, first in Germany and then in Austria.

The Deutsch Family

We first meet the Deutsch family in a royal document dated November 20, 1790, which gave Gerson Guttman, their ancestor, the status of "Protected Jew" (Shawn & Goldfrad, *Anthology*, p. 15). At that time, Germany was still divided into regional governments and city-states. Jews were not allowed to live in many German cities. They could visit for a few days to conduct business, but could not establish businesses or professional practices or maintain a permanent residence in German cities. This restricted Jews from conducting anything more than small business transactions, forcing them to do business in German cities from afar.

Because German cities were major centers of commerce in the 18th century, this was a significant restriction on Jewish enterprise. A Jew who defied German law and set up a residence in a German city without permission could be jailed, have his assets confiscated, and permanently be barred from the city. When German rulers realized that Jews, who sometimes had business connections with other countries, could be useful to the expansion of business in their own city, they created a special status, "Protected Jew," which permitted individual Jews to live in certain German cities and conduct business there.

As long as the Protected Jew complied with the law, the prince or ruler guaranteed to "powerfully" protect his rights. Gerson Guttman, according to the royal document, was the first such Protected Jew in the medium-sized city of Breslau, Germany. The Protected Jews and their descendants were the wealthiest and most influential Jews of Breslau. By 1938, Guttman's descendants, the Deutsch family, had been living in Breslau for 148 years and owned a successful business. Their name means "German," an indication of their pride in their identity. The Royal Majesty of Prussia had conferred German status on Gerson Guttman, and his descendants considered themselves totally German. In an ironic twist of history, the Nazi regime was to deny them this identity.

By the time their letters began on November 18, 1938, Stefan Deutsch and his son Erwin had been arrested (on *Kristallnacht*) and were imprisoned in Buchenwald, a concentration camp built in 1937, one of the prewar camps built by the Nazis. Unlike most prisons, which are built to protect society from convicted criminals, concentration camps were set up by the Nazi regime for the purpose of "re-educating" political dissidents. The tactics used there included hard labor, beatings, and other forms of mistreatment. During the attacks of *Kristallnacht*, the thousands of Jewish men of all ages who were arrested were not charged with any crimes. They were sent to concentration camps simply to terrorize them and their families. This was intended to send a clear message to the Jews: You are not wanted in Germany. The prisoners were told that they would be released if they could produce evidence that they would be leaving Germany within a short time.

Prisoners in Buchenwald, like Stefan and Erwin Deutsch, were allowed to write to their families on specially supplied postcards or mail forms that allowed for very brief messages. The authorities permitted contact but did not allow for long descriptions of conditions, because the terror regime of the concentration camp was maintained better in secret. Prisoners had to restrict their notes to very essential requests and information. Father and son were comforted by the fact that they were together in Buchenwald, and on November 18, 1938, they asked their wives to send clothing for cold weather. They cautioned them not to send money, which was forbidden, and not to contact the camp commander, who did not respond to inquiries. The most urgent request was to continue to work on the emigration process, which had apparently been started prior to *Kristallnacht*.

In the letter of November 23, 1938, addressed to the Jewish Committee in Amsterdam, we learn that the Deutsch family owned a business "until a short while ago," indicating that the business had been "Aryanized" (*Anthology*, p. 16).

The Nazis took over Jewish enterprises in two stages (Hilberg, 1961, p. 60). In the first, "voluntary" stage, from January 1933 to November 1938, Jewish business people were put under great pressure to transfer ownership of their business to German buyers "voluntarily." Stefan Deutsch's business was probably transferred to a German non-Jew, more than likely a member of the Nazi Party, who took it over as "manager," purchasing it for a fraction of its value. If the new "manager" and the Jewish owner were acquainted and on good terms, the "manager" might keep the Jewish owner on as a salaried employee. Most often, however, the Jewish owner simply lost his business to the new "manager." Jews who refused to sign the "Aryanization" agreement were imprisoned.

It should be noted that after November 1938, the later stage of Aryanization was compulsory. Jews were forced to sell their property. On January 30, 1939, Stefan Deutsch received an official letter from the District Court in Breslau, "extinguishing" his business firm (*Anthology*, p. 20). Although he may have transferred his business to a non-Jew before that, at this point his Jewish business no longer existed as a corporate entity. Germany used its courts to legalize the expropriation and confiscation of Jewish assets, thus corrupting the legal system to serve the political goals of the government.

Mrs. Deutsch had appealed to the Jewish Committee in Amsterdam to permit her and her husband to enter Holland "for a short stay" (p. 16), indicating that they hoped to obtain entry visas to immigrate to the United States, where their son Martin already lived. Their daughter and son-in-law, Margot and Kurt Prinz, were already in Amsterdam, waiting for their visas to the United States. Presumably, the elder Deutsches would live with the Prinzes if they were permitted to enter Holland while they waited for their own American visas.

Holland, which shared a border with Germany, had a similar language and culture and a substantial Jewish community in Amsterdam, and, therefore, was the Deutsch family's haven of first choice. Between 1933 and 1940, when Holland was occupied by Germany, 34,000 Jewish refugees entered Holland, all but 15,000 temporarily, until they immigrated to other countries. (Yahil, 1990, p. 93). We learn from a letter dated November 30, 1938 that Holland closed its borders to further immigration, and Stefan and Frieda Deutsch did not receive entry visas to Holland. Meanwhile, their son-in-law Heinz Schottlaender had paid the taxes for his wife's parents, to eliminate impediments to their leaving if they should get visas.

We learn from that same letter that Erwin had been released from Buchenwald—probably because he had been able to secure an entry visa to Bolivia. A month later, his father was released and wrote to Erwin, who was already in Bolivia, not to complain about Bolivia but to be happy that he is out of Germany.

Where Can They Go?

Martin Deutsch, the only unmarried son, was by now living in Chattanooga, Tennessee, and had sent his parents an Affidavit of Support, a document required by the American government that asserted that the prospective immigrants would be supported by someone in the United States who was financially able to do so until the immigrants could support themselves. This fulfilled the American legal requirement that immigrants not become a burden on public resources.

Young, unmarried Jewish men often left Germany before their families, for several reasons. Dismissed from German schools, forbidden to work in German enterprises except in menial positions, there seemed to be no future for them in Germany. Young men, unencumbered by family responsibility, without financial or professional obligations, emigrated, many intending to return to their homes and families after the troubles in Germany subsided. Eighty-three percent of German Jewish youth between the ages of 15 and 24 left Germany by 1939 (Kaplan, 1998, p. 118).

The Deutsches, although they would have preferred to immigrate to the United States, where their son Martin lived, were willing to consider other options. Cuba seemed like a possibility because the Cuban government was still issuing visas, and Cuba is very close to the United States. Another option was Shanghai, China, according to Heinz's letter of December 6, 1938. Shanghai became a haven for German and Austrian refugees because it was the only place in the world that did not require entry visas. It was, however, very far from Germany, an Asian location with a foreign culture and climate, and ship tickets to Shanghai were very expensive, as Heinz notes—150 English pounds, a fortune for impoverished German Jews. It did not seem feasible for Stefan and Frieda Deutsch.

Still another possibility was Latin America. Heinz was not thrilled with the possibility of going to Bolivia, like Erwin and Steffi, but he was scolded by Martin, his brother-in-law, in a letter of December 9, 1938: "When it is a matter of life or death, one cannot be choosy" (p. 18). For German Jews, Bolivia seemed like the end of the civilized world. Leo Spitzer (1998), whose family emigrated from Vienna to Bolivia, wrote that European Jews

> knew virtually nothing about [Bolivia's] physical geography or climate and even less about its history, government, and economy. In their eagerness to find a country that would accept them, they had been ready to go anywhere that would permit them to live in safety. ... "We would have gone to the moon," [one refugee recalled]. "Bolivia was a closer possibility, but the moon we saw every night. It was more real to us." (pp. 81-82)

Heinz, coping with the stresses and restrictions of everyday life in Germany, still had a sense of normalcy. In late 1938 he was still living in his own home with his wife, speaking his native language, comfortable, if not secure. Restrictions on where Jews can live, curfews, and restricted shopping hours had not yet been imposed. We do not know enough about Heinz's economic situation and how he was coping with the Nazi restrictions to explain the seeming lack of urgency in his letters relating to his and his wife's own emigration. Did his wealth and social status give him a feeling of false security? Did he feel that as a young man he would manage in Germany and outlast the Nazis? Perhaps he had hidden funds that he felt would tide him over the crisis; perhaps he had non-Jewish friends or associates whom he felt he could rely upon. We do not know. Martin, with the perspective of distance, sees more clearly that the situation in Germany is precarious. For him, the priority is for his family to leave, regardless of destination.

By December 29, 1938, Steffi and Erwin Deutsch had arrived in Bolivia, and Erwin began to make further attempts to secure visas for his parents, sister, and brother-in-law. Visas for family members left behind in Germany could, apparently, be *purchased* from certain Bolivian government officials (Spitzer, 1998, p. 42). Another avenue for Jewish immigration to Bolivia was to bring them to settle in agricultural colonies where they would cultivate and develop the "vast, potentially rich but largely undeveloped semitropical and tropical areas of the country" (pp. 110-111). "Agricultural visas" were granted (or sold illegally above the prescribed fee) by Bolivian consulates in Germany and Austria and became the means by which several thousand Jews entered Bolivia.

Jews with engineering and mining skills were permitted to enter Bolivia to work in the mining and metal-producing industries. A Bolivian Jew, German-born Moritz Hochschild was a dominant figure in Bolivian industry. He had lived in Bolivia since after World War I, and by the late 1930s he controlled at least one-third of Bolivian mineral production. His prominence and influence, and his generosity in support of Jewish refugees in Bolivia, were instrumental in the Bolivian government's acceptance of Jewish refugees.

When Erwin and Steffi Deutsch arrived in Bolivia, it is likely that he discovered the possibility of bringing his brother-in-law Heinz Schottlaender to Bolivia as a chemical/mining engineer, for whom visas were available. In Heinz's letter of March 4, 1939, to Erwin, however, Heinz voiced skepticism about this ruse. After all, he was not a *chemical/mining* engineer, and although he said he would try, it was obvious that he had no confidence that he would be able to procure a document certifying that he had those skills. Although the German legal system had been corrupted by the Nazis, Heinz still wanted to obey the law. He simply did not know how to fabricate proof of a skill that he did not have. Heinz was so handicapped by his honesty that he did not mention the fact that he was an *electrical* engineer with specialties in telephone, telegraph, and television until his letter of March 17, 1939. Perhaps mentioning those skills earlier would have been helpful, but he interpreted Erwin's request too narrowly, and we will probably never know if this was a crucial error.

Erwin continued his efforts to bring Heinz and Gerda to Bolivia. Several thousand Jewish refugees arrived in Bolivia in 1938–1939, and many were in the cities, unemployed and in need of social services (Spitzer, p. 116). Antisemitic and anti-immigrant sentiments were published in Bolivian newspapers, along with concern about the corruption of immigration officials who were taking bribes. Throughout 1939, Moritz Hochschild tried to convince Bolivian government officials that supporting Jewish immigration to agricultural colonies would benefit the Bolivian economy and benefit Bolivian transactions with the U.S. banking industry. Hochschild also secured a commitment from the American Joint Distribution Committee (AJDC) for some financial support of the agricultural colonies. Finally, in March 1940, financial support was in place, and the Bolivian Colonizing Corporation was set up to manage the process of settling and training refugees in the agricultural colonies. By then, however, World War II was in progress, and immigration had slowed to a trickle.

The elder Deutsches arrived in Bolivia in the summer of 1939, and Mr. Deutsch immediately tried to secure entry visas for Gerda and Heinz. He went from one official to another, each holding out a vague promise of help. During this time, Hochschild was negotiating with the Bolivian government and with the AJDC to formalize an official policy of accepting a large number of Jewish refugees. Hochschild hoped that "we would make a real big colonization in Bolivia … [and] set an example to the surrounding countries that would induce each of them also to take tens of thousands of Jews … [But] the lack of money has made this impossible" (Spitzer, 1998, p. 121).

Also, the long start-up period, a difficult climate, lack of training, and insufficient development funds made large- scale development seem doubtful. In addition, Bolivia's president, whose personal power and word had promised that thousands of Jewish refugees could enter Bolivia and had pledged the land for their colonies, died in August 1939. As Gerda noted on August 24, "I hope this does not mean bad news for us" (*Anthology*, p. 24). With his death, the plans and promises faltered. Jews who were trying to secure entry to Bolivia for their families were stymied by unclear procedures and policies. Some private individuals promised to help Mr. Deutsch, but nothing worked out. In the interim, the Bolivian government had demanded a payment of $350 for visas (noted in Heinz's letter of July 25, 1939). Perhaps this was intended to be a guarantee against the possibility of refugees becoming a public burden. Perhaps it was simple bribery. The purpose of the funds was not clear, but Gerda and Heinz, impoverished by German taxes and a reduction in their monthly allotment of money for living expenses, could not produce this amount quickly.

After their businesses were "Aryanized," Jews had to deposit their remaining funds into accounts that were controlled by the German government. For access to this money beyond their monthly allotment, they had to "apply to the government and bring proof of why they needed it" (Kaplan, 1998, p. 146). Heinz still did not have an exit visa, and World War II began, which meant that civilian travel was severely restricted and dangerous. German passenger ships stopped leaving Germany because of the danger that they would be attacked on the seas, and the few foreign ships that did required payment in foreign currency. Gerda and Heinz were stymied yet again.

On September 5, 1939, Gerda wrote: "It's impossible now to think of leaving Germany. We believe that Heinz, and I too, will be drafted in the Work Corps" (Shawn & Goldfrad, *Anthology*, p. 25). In March 1940, "the Reich formally drafted all Jews between fifteen and sixty-five into forced labor" (Kaplan, p. 174). Until then, only unemployed Jews had been taken for forced labor, but the decree of March 1940 applied to all Jews. As young people, Gerda and Heinz were certainly subject to this decree. On August 29, 1939, Gerda wrote that the Work Corps was "something we would gladly want to do." In spite of the discrimination and persecution she had endured, she still felt loyal to her homeland; she was still "Deutsch," a loyal German. She would rather work than "be a bystander. For that we are still too German" (*Anthology*, p. 25).

With the outbreak of World War II and the reduced likelihood of emigration for Gerda and Heinz, we see a warmer style emerge in her father's letters to Gerda, despite the conditioning of men of that generation to restrain their expressions of emotion. In his letter of October 26, 1939, he calls her Gerdele, a diminutive form of her name. In response to the loneliness that he detects in her letter to her mother, he responds affectionately, "Stay well, best greetings and kisses, Your Father" (p. 26).

"Modern bourgeois culture prescribed distinct gender roles. … Men and women were considered temperamentally suited for their different roles, with men endowed by nature with rationality and physical and mental strength and women with tenderness and spirituality" (Hyman, 1998, p. 27). Women were expected to be more demonstrative. We see these gender distinctions in the Deutsch family letters. Those between sisters Margot and Gerda are more affectionate and emotional than those from their parents or between the men. While the men often end their letters tersely, Gerda's closing words are warmer and more affectionate: "Warmest greetings and lots of kisses, Gerda," or "All my love, Gerda."

The Last Chapter

By the end of October 1939, Heinz and Gerda's letters reflected Germany in wartime: ration coupons, a curfew, blacked-out windows. Still, they wrote, "We are feeling good" (Shawn & Goldfrad, *Anthology*, p. 26). It is hard to know what Heinz meant, because the last letter they received had been opened by a censor, so Heinz's vagueness might have been deliberate. Germany was making the requirements for leaving even more difficult to fulfill. Heinz's emigration tax was computed on the basis of the original value of the estate he inherited, rather than its value at the time it was seized. His assets could no longer pay the tax. The letters of December 4, 9, and 13, 1939 (pp. 26-27), indicate that Heinz has turned over his entire estate to the German government in return for an exit visa, and the government sent $350 to Bolivia for entry visas, which they needed by April, in order to board a ship that was scheduled to leave Genoa on April 6, 1940.

As his efforts to obtain Bolivian visas for Gerda and Heinz are stymied, Mr. Deutch's expressions of love for his daughter continued; he refers to himself as "Your loving Father who is longing for you" (p. 29). For a German man, expected to be stoic in the face of distress, this was a rare expression of emotion.

Margot and Gerda apparently confided in each other more than they expressed their feelings to their parents. Mr. Deutsch wrote to Gerda on April 25, 1940, saying he heard from Margot that Gerda thinks the family in Bolivia was not doing everything possible to obtain visas for them. He is anguished not only because of the objective situation, but also because he is afraid that he is losing his daughter's trust. "I don't blame you for not trusting us anymore. … We are desperate. Stay well, a thousand regards and kisses from your very unhappy Father" (p. 30). As the situation deteriorated, Mr. Deutsch articulated his love more openly, uncharacteristic for a German father. "A thousand kisses" is a typically affectionate conventional closing for a German letter between family members, but we see it from Mr. Deutsch only when his emotions overcome him (Polt, 1999, *A Thousand Kisses*, title).

In Bolivia, Carnival intervened; in an ironic counterpoint to the Deutsches' feelings of desperation, Bolivians were celebrating. Government offices were closed, officials made "phony promises" (*Anthology*, p. 28), and Mr. Deutsch and Erwin spent days going from one government office to another to obtain immigration numbers and visas for Gerda and Heinz. Their hopes were raised countless times by officials who assured them that the numbers would be issued very soon. On April 26, 1940, Mr. Deutsch reported that he had arranged with a man who was building a chemical plant to bring Heinz to work for him, but in his letter of May 18, 1940, he reported with great disappointment and sadness that this man, too, was a "crook" (p. 31). Yet he tried another deal with a rancher who said he could bring 15 Jewish families to Bolivia. Mr. Deutsch no longer worried about whether Heinz had the qualifications for this work. If there was a possibility that visas were available for agricultural workers, he wanted Heinz to take the opportunity; but this effort also failed. On June 12, 1940, Heinz, out of concern for the health of his in-laws, asked them to desist from further efforts. Of course, Mr. Deutsch refused to give up. "I will continue the efforts and hope you won't blame me" (p. 33).

Margot's own immigrant experience gives her insight into that of her father, who, as Gerda writes, "can't be understood well by strangers" and is "nervous and excitable" (p. 32). Mr. Deutsch is overwhelmed by his expected traditional role as all-powerful father, the contradictory messages that are coming from various corrupt government officials in Bolivia, and the objective, wartime situation that separates the family. He writes, "I cannot get over the fact that I am unable to help you, of all people, who did so much for us and the rest of the family" (p. 33).

Mr. Deutsch is experiencing the powerlessness of the refugee. Separated from the social structure and culture in which he was competent, after the severe trauma of his incarceration in Buchenwald, he is cast adrift in a strange country, with a language, laws, and customs that he does not understand. His previous competencies and strengths seem useless. He feels useless. For the first time in these letters, on June 13, 1940, there is a mention of God and faith. When all else has failed, Mr. Deutsch feels blessed by God for loyal children but abandoned by God in the matter of their immigration. This is our first hint of Mr. Deutsch's feelings of Jewish identity. Secular German Jews, kept aware of their Jewish identity by the persistence of antisemitism, did not generally refer to it, considering themselves German first and Jewish second. We do not know the extent of Mr. Deutsch's identification with the Jewish community or with Jewish observance. However, as he realizes his powerlessness to protect Gerda, his child, he falls back on his religious identity, which has perhaps been dormant until now.

Mr. Deutsch's tenacity was admirable and quite in character, both for him as a German head-of-family with a strong sense of duty, and as the father who knew that his child was in grave danger. He would not give up responsibility for his family. He even tried to make Gerda and Heinz feel guilty for giving up by suggesting that perhaps they do not want to come to Bolivia. Then, startling news from Germany put a new face on the situation. Gerda was pregnant, expecting a baby in June 1941.

> [In Germany] Jewish couples who chose to have a baby faced an unpredictable future, in which they, as outcasts, would be able to offer their children far less than they themselves had received or achieved. At best, they could hope for a change of regime or emigration. (Kaplan, 1998, p. 82)

Very few Jewish children were being born in Germany by the late 1930s, mostly because a large percentage of young Jews had emigrated. In 1939, the number of Jewish children born in all of Germany was either 325 or 284, depending on how Jews were defined (Kaplan, p. 249). The number of Jewish babies born in Germany after 1939 would have been smaller still.

In Bolivia, the Deutsches heard dreadful news from Europe: Jews were being murdered in Romania, others were sent to camps and were starving, and "no one can leave Germany now even if they have visas" (*Anthology*, p. 34).

Gerda's February 1941 letter to her sister, Margot, focused on her pregnancy, her hopes for the baby, and baby names. According to a German law passed on August 17, 1938, Jews were allowed to have only certain recognizably Jewish, mostly biblical names (*Jewish Black Book*, p. 491). Jews whose first names were not on the approved list had to add "Sara" for females or "Israel" for males as a middle name. This rule, like the law requiring Jews to wear a yellow Star of David (September 1, 1941) was designed to separate Jews from other Germans and isolate them socially.

Gerda's baby boy was born on June 24, 1941, in a hospital in Breslau, in perfect health. His parents were overjoyed. They were still living in their home, they seem to have had a car, and they drove to the hospital where Gerda was cared for by a midwife and a doctor. In an environment that was increasingly restrictive, Jews were not denied medical care for childbirth. Breslau, one of Germany's larger Jewish communities, must have had a Jewish hospital, and it was probably there that Gerda delivered her son. The Jewish community umbrella organization that supported social welfare and religious functions was still functioning and supporting Jewish hospitals in 1941 and paying the salaries of Jewish doctors and medical personnel who were still working. By 1941, they were not permitted to care for Aryan patients but were certainly allowed to care for Jews.

The birth of a grandson inspired a certain level of sadness in Mr. and Mrs. Deutsch in that they could not help the new parents. They sent their good wishes and extended the hope that the new baby would "grow up to be as good a Jew as your father and grandfather and also Grandfather Deutsch." The letter ended with "a thousand kisses from your loving Grandfather and father who longs for you" (*Anthology*, p. 36). This is the first mention of Jewish identity by any of the Deutsch family. Inspired by the fact of family continuity, Mr. Deutsch expressed a feeling of Jewish identity that must have been present but not articulated all along. Even assimilated German Jews knew who they were, and Nazi persecution reinforced their Jewish identities. Mr. Deutsch, a descendant of the Protected Jews, probably did not regularly practice Jewish religious customs and rituals such as praying daily or observing the Sabbath or Jewish dietary laws (Meyer, 1997, v. 2, p. 103). Like other prominent Breslau Jews, he was probably affiliated with the Reform Jewish movement, which adopted many "modern" changes in synagogue ritual and religious observance. Despite his minimal his Jewish lifestyle, he remained identified as a Jew, and saw the new baby as a link in the chain of Jewish generations.

Gerda and Heinz focused on their pleasure in their child, even taking movies of him. It is interesting to note that they still had their movie camera—they even had film for it (the law ordering confiscation of electric appliances, typewriters, bicycles, and other mechanical devices was not passed until June 1942). Although individual Nazis might have confiscated such commodities from individual Jews at any time, Gerda and Heinz did not give any indication that this has happened to them. Perhaps their prominent social status was still affording them a certain measure of protection. They continued their efforts to find a country that would take them, perhaps Ecuador, Brazil, Santo Domingo.

> Anyone who still had some savings was prepared to pay whatever price was necessary for a South American entry visa. Brazil and Argentina had tightened their entry regulations, but it remained possible to arrange immigration there on the basis of fictitious land purchases or even serious settlement projects. (Meyer, v. 4, p. 329)

In September 1941, Breslau Jews were forced to move into specially designated *Judenhauser* (Jewish houses), leaving behind their homes, most of their possessions, and the relative security of the lives they had known (EH, pp. 244–245).

Mr. Deutsch and Erwin continued their efforts to obtain visas for Heinz and Gerda to enter Bolivia. In his letter of December 19, 1941, when the United States had already entered the war, Mr. Deutsch described a heart-stopping visit to the government ministry, shared the exciting news that they had obtained immigration numbers for Heinz and Gerda (the baby was probably listed on Gerda's visa), and urged them to leave as quickly as possible. A month later there still had been no response from Heinz and Gerda. In his excitement over his apparent success in obtaining immigration numbers for them, Mr. Deutsch did not anticipate the difficulties they would encounter in trying to travel in a wartime situation.

Where Are the Children?

Mr. Deutsch wrote to Heinz's cousin in Chile saying that he hadn't heard from Heinz and Gerda since December 7, 1941. On that date, the Japanese attacked American forces in Pearl Harbor, Hawaii, an event that propelled the United States into World War II. Travel now became almost impossible; very few passenger ships sailed on oceans that were patrolled by German torpedo boats, and those that did had to travel in convoy, escorted by warships for protection against attack. Meanwhile, the situation in Breslau had deteriorated badly for Jews.

Mr. Deutsch's letters to Heinz's cousin reflected his grief at losing contact with his children and his fears that they might be in a ghetto. He was grasping at the slim possibility that life in a ghetto might be safer than in Germany, but he was not really consoled by it. This was an illusion of safety that had its roots in medieval Jewish history, when Jews were forced to live in ghettos that were locked at night. Although this was a restriction on Jewish freedom, it also protected Jews from attack. German Jews had no way of knowing the implications of deportation from Germany and certainly no way of judging whether this development would be good or bad for them, since the Nazis were developing a diabolical plan to kill all the Jews, a plan that had never before been devised and implemented by any enemy of the Jews. Mr. Deutsch simply hoped that God would end the war and bring the criminals to justice.

At the end of August, a final telegram arrived from Heinz and Gerda in Breslau, dated February 16, 1942. The middle names "Israel" and "Sara" had been added to Heinz and Gerda. Although they had been required to add these names to their official documents prior to this date, their private correspondence would not have revealed this. A telegram, however, sent from a telegraph office in a public transmission, would have had to include these names. The telegram stated that they were all well, had received their Bolivian visas, but could not get passage on a ship. This pro forma statement probably concealed untold stress and fear. A telegram was an expensive means of communication for which one paid by the word, so each word had to count. Knowing that they might be deported at any time, Gerda and Heinz probably wanted to send a hopeful, pleasant, last message to their loved ones. Why distress their family when they were helpless to alleviate their pain?

In January 1941, a Nazi ruling stated that Jewish property and money "should not be regarded as Jewish but rather as property serving the purposes of the Reich." This was further explained on April 2, 1942: "The main function of the [Jewish] property … is now to aid in implementing the final solution of the Jewish Question in Europe." In other words, Jewish money and assets would be confiscated and used to pay for the process of destroying European Jewry.

On June 10, 1942, the Nazi administrator in Berlin informed Heinz's attorney that Heinz's fortune had become the property of the Reich on April 21, 1942. This was the last "legal" step taken by the German government and stripped Heinz and Gerda of their property and money. By then, German Jewish communities had had to provide the government with a list of Jewish apartments, their possessions, bank accounts, and other property (Meyer, v. 4, pp. 350–351). Without access to their money Gerda and Heinz could no longer bribe officials to delay their deportation. They could no longer buy food or other necessities to supplement their allotted rations.

Between November 20, 1942, and April 1944 all the Jews of Breslau—with the exception of 150 who were married to Aryans—were transported east, most to the Terezin ghetto/camp in Czechoslovakia, and from there to death camps in Poland. According to a Red Cross letter received by Mr. Deutsch in 1943, Gerda, Heinz, and their son were deported to the East on May 4, 1942, shortly after their property had been expropriated by the German state.

In July 1945, Mr. and Mrs. Deutsch received their entry permit to the United States through the efforts of Margot and her husband. Finally, in December 1947, in St. Louis, they received a letter from Mrs. Leuschner, Heinz's former employee, describing Heinz and Gerda's last days in Breslau.

Three of the four children of the Deutsch family were reunited with their parents in the United States after the war. Only Heinz, Gerda, and their baby were killed. That does not diminish their tragedy or their sorrow. The letters of the Deutsch family are documentary evidence of their strong family ties and loyalties, their fierce determination to protect and save each other. They also provide a window into the conditions German Jews faced and underscore the intensity of their repeated attempts to navigate the impossibly complicated and difficult regulations and requirements for emigration. We learn about the obstacles they faced in Germany, in Bolivia, and in the United States. We learn, by reading between the lines, about the experience of being a refugee and its devastating effects on people made homeless and helpless. Their letters humanize and personalize an experience that affected millions of people. The documents, telegrams, and even the single letter from Mrs. Leuschner provide additional historical context by giving us the chronological and historical outline of events; we can see the profound impact these circumstances had on specific people, and how and why they reacted to them.

Yet, the letters conceal as much as they reveal. We see that family members were protecting each other as they communicated. We do not learn much about how Gerda and Heinz coped with the gradually worsening restrictions. We do not learn about the journeys of their parents and siblings to Bolivia and the United States. We do not learn about the difficult process of adjustment and acclimatization—learning new languages, becoming familiar with cultural norms, and earning a living under new conditions. The family does not share troubles, except as they relate to the redemptive and hopeful process of reunification. Within that process, they share their hopes and love and wishes for a brighter future without expressing their individual pain, horrors, and nightmares.

Historians can use this kind of epistolary literature to confirm and provide a human dimension to a story that is too huge to imagine. Personal letters complement the documentary evidence and make it approachable. We learn from the Deutsch family that German Jews were not passive; that they tried every possible means of saving their lives, even when they did not know the ultimate outcome of Nazism. During the Holocaust, unfortunately, circumstances were such that even the strongest will could not entirely prevail.

REFERENCES

Abella, I., and Troper, H. (1982). *None is too many: Canada and the Jews of Europe 1933–1948*. Toronto: Lester & Orpen Dennys.

Bauer, Y. (1982). *A history of the Holocaust*. NY: Franklin Watts.

Encylopedia of the Holocaust. (1990). NY: Macmillan.

Encyclopedia Judaica. (1971). Jerusalem: Keter.

Hilberg, R. (1961). *The destruction of the European Jews*. Chicago: Quadrangle.

Hyman, P. E. (1998). "Gender and the Jewish family in modern Europe," in *Women in the Holocaust*, D. Ofer & L. J. Weitzman, (Eds.). New Haven: Yale University Press.

Jewish Black Book Committee. (1946). *The black book: The Nazi crime against the Jewish people*.

Kaplan, M. (1998). *Between dignity and despair: Jewish life in Nazi Germany*. NY: Oxford University Press.

Meyer, M. A. (Ed.). (1997). *German-Jewish history in modern times*. Vols. 2, 4. NY: Columbia University Press.

Polt, R. (1999). *A thousand kisses: A grandmother's Holocaust letters*. Tuscaloosa, AL: University of Alabama Press.

Seltzer, R. (1980). *Jewish people, Jewish thought: The Jewish experience in history*. NY: Macmillan.

Shear, S. P. (2008). Saving history: Letters from the Holocaust: Teaching "No way out." In K. Shawn & K. Goldfrad (Eds.)., *The call of memory: Learning about the Holocaust through narrative: An anthology*, pp. 14–43. Teaneck, NJ: Ben Yehuda Press.

Spitzer, L. (1998). *Hotel Bolivia: The culture of memory in a refuge from Nazism*. NY: Hill & Wang.

Yahil, L. (1990). *The Holocaust: The fate of European Jewry*. NY: Oxford University Press.

Saving History:
Letters from the Holocaust:
Teaching "No Way Out"

Susan Prinz Shear

What a wonderful thing is the mail, capable of conveying across continents a
warm, human hand clasp.
—Anonymous

Several years ago, I discovered hundreds of letters written by my family as they tried to escape the Nazis and find a haven. I soon came to appreciate their didactic power. I was drawn in with the first letter my mother showed me, wrinkled and yellowed with age, yet filled with information and insights I could never have learned from a history book. I found the immediacy compelling: a conversation between two people, oceans and cultures away from one another, yet as connected as if they were sitting at a kitchen table having coffee.

Now I, too, had a seat at the table, and it was then that "No Way Out" (Shawn & Goldfrad, *Anthology*, 2008, pp. 14–43) was born. At once personal and historical, these letters tell a story of what my family thought, felt, and experienced as the Nazi bureaucracy took hold of their lives and changed them forever.

The Jews of Breslau

My maternal grandfather, Stefan Deutsch, was a third-generation German Jew. He and my grandmother Frieda lived in Breslau, Germany, with their four grown children and their extended family nearby. Their life centered around family parties and holiday celebrations, as it had for generations of Deutsches in Breslau.

The earliest known Jews arrived in Breslau in 1203 and lived the restricted life commonly imposed on the Jews in Europe. As restrictions eased, many Jews became valued citizens, contributing their knowledge, skills, and talents to enrich every sphere of German life. By the beginning of the 20th century, many Breslau Jews, including the Deutsch family, had risen to prominence in the economic, political, and cultural life of the city. By 1933, Breslau, then a highly cultured, modern city of 700,000 in the state of Silesia in eastern Germany, was home to 20,000 Jews.

Implications of Hitler's Rise to Power

In 1933, Hitler came to power, and by 1938, the lives of all German Jews, including my family, had changed dramatically. As their businesses were taken from them, professions and schools closed to them, and family and friends forced to scatter to all parts of the world, what had been a beautiful life became, inexorably, grim, frightening, and lonely. By the end of 1938, everyone in my family had emigrated from Germany except my grandparents and their daughter Gerda and her husband, Heinz Schottlaender. It was then that the letter writing, their only means of communication with their relatives, began.

"No Way Out" offers students a chance to "peer over the shoulder" of the letter writers and enter the personal lives of the Deutsches, an ordinary German Jewish family. Through these intimate letters, we step back into their world. We hear the parents, sons, and daughters struggle to make sense of the Nazi policies of identification, separation, isolation, and humiliation of the Jews, even as they attempt valiantly to maintain a sense of normalcy in a world that, for them, is anything but normal. We listen as they share the everyday details of their lives as well as their desperate attempts to deal with the ever-changing events and policies that swirl out of control around them. We learn about Nazi measures that slowly, insidiously segregate them and destroy their once-vibrant lives, and we recognize the indifference of nations that chose to look the other way.

As students "eavesdrop" on these discussions, they gain a sense of the effects of the regulations and laws of Nazi Germany on every Jewish family. They hear the Deutsch family retaining their optimism in a life filling slowly with fear, frustration, worry, uncertainty, and despair. They gather inferences, as well as direct information, about what and when the Deutsch family knew about circumstances in and out of Germany and how they communicated via a censored mail system.

Teaching "No Way Out"

"No Way Out" is epistolary literature and, as such, combines the advantages of a short story with the authenticity of primary sources. Like many stories, it has characters for the reader to embrace, including Stefan, Frieda, Margot, Gerda, Heinz, Martin, and Erwin. Yet, unlike fictitious characters, these people are real.

I have not taught "No Way Out" in a classroom of my own, but, as its author, I have shared the story in various formats with thousands of students across the country. Before each four- or five-hour workshop I conduct, in advance of or following the presentation of this story as a theater piece, I contact the classroom teacher to ensure that his/her students have an appropriate appreciation of the historical background. In these initial conversations, I also share my favorite resources and extended learning activities (see Appendix D) that can enhance student understanding of the broader context of Germany and the Jews. Each time I exchange ideas with teachers, I increase my understanding of how I would teach this story to my own students. I hope we have, together, found a way to make "No Way Out" a successful, meaningful, and compelling learning experience.

Goals, Audience, and Learning Context

"No Way Out" addresses the overarching questions asked so often as students seek to understand the rise of Nazi Germany and the situation of the Jews caught in its web: Why didn't the Jews leave Germany earlier? Where could they go to escape? How could they get there? Who could have helped them? How and when did they become outsiders in their own country? My first goal is to guide students through the text to discover the answers; my second is to contextualize the story by familiarizing students with terms and concepts used explicitly or implicitly in the letters.

My third goal is to help students recognize and appreciate the challenges Jews faced as they tried to escape Germany and enter another country. The letters detail the complicated emigration and immigration issues and processes that made leaving and resettling problematic, frustrating, and exhausting at best and impossible at worst. They document "Aryanization," the Nazi expropriation of Jewish property and money, and they reflect laws the Nazis put into effect to delay emigration and immigration possibilities and to make the daily lives of Jews difficult and demeaning (see Appendix B).

My fourth goal is to put a human face on the term "German Jews" and to provide students with a crucial perspective of Jews as people, rather than merely as victims.

Finally, I want students to appreciate the importance, uniqueness, advantages, and limitations of primary sources, in this case, letters, in the study of history and literature.

"No Way Out" is most appropriate for high school and college students; teachers of advanced eighth graders who have some background in Holocaust history may find the story a useful tool as well. Ideally, "No Way Out" would be taught as a one-week interdisciplinary unit combining literature, history, and drama.

While this chronicle stands on its own for any reader who has studied the Holocaust, I suggest that for students to benefit fully from its implications, they should have at least a general knowledge of German antisemitism and Germany between the Wars, including pre-Nazi Jewish/non-Jewish relations, the Weimar Republic and its fall, socio-economic conditions, the rise of the Nazi regime, and Hitler's ascent to power. Two teaching curricula that offer excellent background information are Lacey & Shephard's (1997) *Germany 1918-1945* and Bakker's (1994) *Crisis, Conscience and Choices*. An excellent film is Yad Vashem's *Outcast* (1997).

To begin my workshops, I ask students the following questions about "letters" per se:

1. When was the last time you sent or received a letter by "snail-mail"?
2. How common is letter writing today among your peers?
3. Does snail-mail seem more special than e-mail? Why?
4. Does handwritten mail seem more special than e-mail? Do you usually save more mailed letters or e-mails? Why?

5. What are the benefits and limitations of letters as primary sources of historical information?

6. When you write a letter or send an e-mail, are you aware of the fact that it might, one day, be made public? How would you modify your writing if you expected strangers to read what you send?

7. If you know what you write will be censored, how might you try to share important information without alerting the censors? How might your knowledge of this censorship change what you write? How might your changes affect your readers' understanding of the information you were trying to convey?

I explain that my grandfather Stefan made carbon copies of the letters he wrote, so that family members could read the same information no matter where they were. I ask: Under what circumstances might people today make copies of their letters? Under what circumstances would you copy the e-mails you send?

Meet the Deutsch Family

I provide background information on the Deutsch family (and a pronunciation key to their names) and on Breslau, Germany, by using a family tree and a map of pre-World War Two Germany (see Appendix A). You might draw the tree on the board or show it, along with the map, on an overhead projector. Because I want students to have a sense of the family before they read their letters, I offer an overview that you might read aloud or have one of your best readers present to the class:

> My grandfather Stefan Deutsch was a decorated veteran of the Great War. Clearly the head of the household, he was warm-hearted, emotional, and devoted to his children. Frieda, my grandmother, was reserved, quiet, and practical: a quintessential housewife and caring mother. Margot, their daughter who was to become my mother, was sociable, family-minded, and fun-loving; she hoped to work in a musical field. Gerda, her sister, was fashionable, creative, adventurous, and optimistic; she wanted to become a designer of hats. She married Heinz Schottlaender, a wealthy, influential German Jew whose family had contributed a great deal to the city of Breslau. Margot and Gerda's brother Martin was an introvert. He was fastidious, serious, and realistic. He was preparing to work in his father's grain brokerage business. Their brother Erwin was active, athletic, and creative, and planned on becoming an architect. My family was upper-middle class, economically comfortable, and socially and religiously assimilated fully into the culture. In 1933, had someone asked them to describe themselves, they would have said they were proud Germans.

Glossary

Following this introduction, I distribute a glossary (see below), which we discuss. I ask students to keep the glossary in their notebooks for easy reference, and I suggest that they highlight each word as they encounter it in the story so they can read and understand it in context.

1. **Affidavit:** A legal document required for immigration into the United States, bearing the signature of a citizen who took financial responsibility for the immigrant; also called "sponsorship."
2. **Aryan:** A term used by the Nazis to describe non-Jewish Caucasian Germans, although the term originally referred to Indo-European-speaking peoples. Hitler used it to refer to what he believed was the "superior" race of Nordic-looking Germans. In fact, there is no such race as "Aryan."
3. **Aryanization:** The transfer of ownership of a Jewish enterprise into Aryan hands. The Aryan population and the German Reich absorbed most of the Jewish businesses and property in so-called voluntary (using harassment, pressure, and boycotts) and later, compulsory (forced), transfers. Aryanization most often involved businesses that had goods and equipment. Jews received very little, if any, compensation for the actual value of their properties and businesses. Often, the meager proceeds were not enough to pay the high taxes mounted against the Jews. By 1939, assets, including compensation received from forced sales, were placed in frozen accounts, and Jews could not transfer money abroad or exchange currency needed for their emigration and immigration. All expenditures required Nazi approval.
4. **Emigrate:** The act of legally leaving one place of residence to live elsewhere.
5. **Exit Permit:** A certificate issued in Germany that showed you didn't owe or own anything and therefore were permitted to leave the country.
6. **Expropriation:** To take away and/or dispose of someone's property. According to the Nazis, Jews were no longer Germans and therefore were required to return acquired assets to the State.
7. **Immigrate:** To legally enter and set up residence in a country.
8. **Immigration Numbers:** Numbers assigned to immigrants prior to an official visa.
9. **Liquidation:** The process of simply dissolving a business or enterprise so that it ceased to exist.
10. **Quota:** A set number of people allowed to immigrate into a country.
11. **Reichsmark:** German currency (Hitler changed the name from Deutschmark to Reichsmark). During the Nazi era, the exchange rate was approximately 4 RM to the dollar.
12. **Visa:** Endorsement made on a passport by proper authorities giving permission to enter a country, most often for a fee.

I then tell the class that we are going to "meet" the Deutsch family through reading their letters, first at home and then in a Readers' Theater presentation with all students involved in oral reading, directing, set design, stage management, or props and costumes. If we decide to present a theatrical performance to other classes and/or to parents, there will be invitations and programs to prepare as well. You might choose to wait to tell them about the theater piece as a culmination of the unit; I prefer to tell them from the beginning because I think the idea of a performance appeals to them and provides a concrete rationale for their focused attention to the text.

I distribute the story and, to ensure understanding of the basic plot line and characters, I ask students to read it through at home and come to class the next day with at least one written question about the history that surrounds the story, the actions of one of the characters, the actions of the Nazis, or the letters themselves.

I also ask that students think about which person they would like to portray; if they prefer to work "off-stage," which position do they wish to hold? I ask them to write a brief explanation for their first two preferences. (This is my way of directing students away from their usual rationale for choosing a part based solely on its length—either the longest or the shortest!) If time permits, you may prefer to have the students read the story aloud in class; each student's reading of a letter serves as a nonthreatening tryout for Readers' Theater.

Reading the Letters in Context

Our second meeting always begins with questions and comments. Students want to know more about the historical context. Anna, for example, asked, "Why did the Nazis allow Jews to write letters?" I tell her that this was a way of monitoring what the Jews were writing and also a way of giving the impression of normality.

They try to understand the thinking of the people within that context.

"Why would Heinz and Gerda have a baby in those dangerous times?" wondered Anya.

They want to know how people functioned within the ever-tightening Nazi net of restrictions.

"How was it possible for Gerda to have a baby in a hospital?" Manuel asked. Martin noted, "Gerda and Heinz were still sending photographs even though Jews were not allowed to have cameras. How was that possible?" I point out that cameras were not confiscated until October 1941; Gerda's last letter referencing pictures was September 25th of that year. Another likely possibility is that a non-Jewish friend took the pictures.

They want to know more about the characters and the setting, especially from me, the author. Jeri asked, "What happened to Gerda and Heinz's house after they were deported?" I tell her that their house is gone, but barns, stables, and a servant house remain. Denise observed that the letters don't mention Heinz's family, and she asked what happened to them. I tell her that his father died in 1938; his sister survived in hiding with the help of gentiles; his brother survived in Kenya; his mother married a Swiss man and therefore had immunity and survived. Christopher wondered, "Do you think it's possible that Denny survived?"

"Tragically," I say, "no."

They show empathy by asking about the feelings of the characters. Kindra wondered if my family "hates Germans for what they put them through." Trevor was interested to hear what it was like for someone in such a close family "to leave Germany all alone." Tommy, having heard other survivor testimony, asked if my grandparents suffered from nightmares after losing their daughter and grandson.

They are interested in the American response as well. Nick wondered, "What was it like for them when they arrived in America?" while Cody asked, "What were American attitudes toward Jews when refugees came to this country?" [For a lesson on what life was like for American Jews in the 1930s, see Witty in this *Guide*, pp. 78–94.]

They ask the essential question that plagues us all: "I am a Catholic," says John, "and I was taught to be a 'good Christian.' How is it possible for 'good Christians' to have done these terrible things to others?"

Classroom Activities

An effective whole-class learning experience is the "Decision-Making Activity" (Marcus, 1999). I use it to help answer the question most often asked: "Why didn't more Jews leave earlier?"

First, I pose the question, "How do we make decisions?" and assign a typical decision based on the class. I might ask juniors and seniors to analyze the factors that go into their decisions regarding post-high school and college plans. What must one consider, for example, in choosing a college?

As students offer various factors, I write them on a chalk board or transparency, and the intricacies of the decision-making process become clear. I ask, "What did the Jews of Germany have to consider as they struggled with the decision to leave Germany?" Student responses include when to leave, where to go, how to get a visa and secure travel, how to make a living in a new country, how to get money for travel expenses and relocation, how to master a new language, and how to find support in the new country. Many students also consider the loyalty and love Jews had for their homeland, the affection they had for their community and home, and the worry and guilt they felt over leaving friends and family, especially the sick and elderly. I conclude this activity with a quote:

> How could anyone wonder why so many stayed so long? ... There was one reason. Germany was home. They should leave everything that was, if flawed, familiar? Jewish Germans rationalized, adjusted, hoped each new insult was the last and waited for the return of their normal, orderly German way of life. (Owings, 1999, p. 27)

Historically, Jews had endured discrimination and prejudice. They were hoping this earthquake, too, would pass.

Included here might be an examination of the anti-Jewish laws and restrictions (see Appendix C) to clarify the insidiously gradual nature of the restrictions. The following quote offers insight:

> If the last and worst act of the whole regime had come immediately after the first and smallest, thousands, yes, millions, would have been sufficiently shocked … but of course, this isn't the way it happens. In between come all the hundreds of little steps, some of them imperceptible, each of them preparing you not to be shocked by the next. (Mayer, 1955, pp. 177–181)

A collaborative learning activity might involve using groups of five or six students, depending upon your enrollment, to represent Stefan, Frieda, Heinz, and Gerda; or additional but smaller groups to represent all the characters, including Gertrud Leuschner, Margot, Erwin, Martin, and the Royal Majesty of Prussia.

I assign each group questions specific to their letters, such as "What do the tone and the mood tell us about Stefan's letters from Bolivia? What do you think Gerda and Heinz understood their future to be? Do you think they felt safe because of Heinz's wealth and his standing in the community? Where is the evidence of optimism? Of rationalization?" I require that they find evidence in the letters to support all responses.

Because "No Way Out" presents complex historical information, it's important to check in periodically with students to see if they need clarification on the characters, setting, or background. I also monitor each group's close examination of individual letters so I can assess the progress students are making towards achieving my teaching goals. As groups share and compare their findings, noting in particular the alternating hope and despair, I see, for instance, that they have understood that changes in the characters' emotions document the changing times.

As another option, you might assign students to groups representing the years from 1939 through 1942 and ask them to identify in each character's letters the changes that reflect the escalating impediments they confront. When such groups come together to read aloud, in chronological order, the sentences they have highlighted, the increasing difficulties facing the Jews are starkly outlined.

For extended learning, enrichment, individualized research, and writing opportunities, you might use excerpts of specific letters to encourage students to think about both the individuals and the time in which they lived. For example, using the narrative excerpt that illustrates the relationship between the Jews and the Germans 150 years before the Holocaust, you might ask:

1. What phrases or words are significant? (The "Jewish situation," "The Protected Jews," "to the extent he complies … and fulfills his obligations" *Anthology*, p. 15.)

2. Note the use of the phrase "Jewish situation," a phrase used by the Nazis. To what does it refer in this letter? To what did it refer during the Holocaust?

Questions about the letter of May 25, 1939, require research on immigration laws.

1. How many refugees were allowed into America each year between 1938 and 1942?
2. Based on those numbers, how many years would it be before Heinz and Gerda's numbers would qualify them for a visa?
3. What does this letter tell us about American immigration policy at that time?
4. Why was the American government unwilling to let more Jews in?
5. How did American immigration policy compare to policies of other countries?

Another research question is: "Where could the Jews go if they were able to leave Germany?" In the "Immigration Exercise," students identify all the countries that Gerda and Heinz contacted about immigration possibilities. Students, individually or in pairs, research and compare policies of these countries, which include Philippines, Ecuador, Chile, Australia, Bolivia, United States, Cuba, Switzerland, England, Santa Domingo, Brazil, Kenya, Holland, British Colonies, Uruguay, and China.

Students might research mail censorship in Germany, or they might analyze the similarities and differences between letters and a history text and explain the benefits of both in studying this subject. You may also encourage students to write to surviving members of the Deutsch family, Margot, Martin, and Erwin. Send all correspondence to Janice@patentseminars.com. Finally, you might assign readings and videos suggested in Appendix D to expand and enrich this study.

Readers' Theater

After spending one or two 50-minute periods in discussion and group work, I prepare for our one-period Readers' Theater presentation, the culmination of the unit.

What is the rationale for this methodology? When used to dramatize literature, Readers' Theater links oral reading, literature, and drama and sparks interest in students who may not be engaged by silent or traditional oral "round-robin" classroom reading. Seeing stories come alive in a classroom that has been magically transformed into a theater gives unique meaning to literature and helps students interpret a text actively through sights and sounds as well as words. Readers learn the subtleties of meaning by experimenting with the pitch, stress, tone, projection, and rhythm of their voices. This provides readers and listeners with varied opportunities to relate to, interpret, and find personal meaning in the text and the characters.

It offers the teacher the chance to individualize instruction, capitalizing on students' strengths and minimizing weaknesses as students volunteer for the work in which they will have the greatest success; therefore, in addition to having tryouts for readers, you might hold them for set designers, stagehands, directors, prop managers, and program designers as well.

I assign the nine character roles from the text to the students who requested them, trying to ensure that they get their first or second choice. (If more than nine apply, we draw straws.) I ask the stagehands to move the desks to the back of the room so we can have a "stage." If you have a more appropriate space in your school, so much the better!

We divide the stage into three locales: Germany, America, and Bolivia. I've identified my set designers (those who are adept at sign writing, in marker or on the computer), and I ask them to make signs, one for each country, and hang them on an easel or the blackboard to identify the spaces. Explain to your "actors" that they will move from one locale to another as indicated in the story. As the family separates, and Gerda and Heinz are left alone in Germany, the physical scene on stage dramatizes the disintegration of the family unit and Gerda and Heinz's isolation.

For stage seating, I use chairs, stools, benches, or old suitcases. I like using suitcases, which characters take with them when they move, creating a metaphor for their uprooted lives. Finding old suitcases in the community is an engaging task for the props people and the set designers, who feel proud when they succeed!

Before taking on character roles, students must be familiar with the pronunciation and meaning of all words; with the point at which they move from Germany to another country; with the emotional tone and vocal expression each character expresses thorough his/her letters; and with the historical context that informs each letter, each move, each change of plans. Because this is not meant to be a polished performance, and because everyone has read the story at least once, I hold only one rehearsal with my cast before they present it to the whole class. You may have more rehearsals, depending upon your readers' abilities and your time to meet with them.

There are other ways as well to create a Readers' Theater using this story. If you have 27 students, for example, you can form three casts of nine readers each. These casts then present a performance for other classes or for parents. Of course, Readers' Theater can also be a program for the entire school with tryouts, many rehearsals, and elaborate sets, props, and period costumes, a perfect commemoration, for example, for Kristallnacht.

Assessment Opportunities

There are many effective techniques to evaluate your students' learning and overall performance. To help students understand evaluation criteria, you might want to design a rubric to assess their understanding of segments of the unit such as knowledge of anti-Jewish laws, expropriation and emigration policies, and historical events, or to assess their applied skills in drama and oral reading. Measurable drama/oral reading skills include projection, rate, enunciation, tempo, expression, characterization, reading ability, body language, and group interaction.

I have found success with the following assessment techniques:

1. **Pros and Cons:** Assess students' critical thinking skills as they examine the pros and cons of an issue. For instance, students might argue the pros and cons that the family might have raised about remaining in Germany after the Nuremberg Laws.

2. **Content, Form, and Purpose:** Ask each student to analyze the content, form, and purpose of one letter. What specific historical and/or personal information is available? What is the tone and mood? Was the writer's intent implicit or explicit?

3. **Compare:** Ask students to compare issues, concepts, and/or words. What is the difference, for example, between *visa* and *affidavit*?

4. **Retell:** Ask each student to retell one line of the Deutsch family story in his/her own words, in chronological order, to help assess understanding of plot, characters, and setting.

5. **Rewrite the Ending:** Assess students' critical thinking skills by asking them to imagine what might have happened if history had not unfolded as it did. For example, what if Gerda and Heinz had left Germany before Stefan and Frieda? What if Gerda and Heinz had gotten a visa for Kenya? What if they had fled east to Poland? To Russia? What if Heinz had not come from a wealthy and famous family? What if the Deutsch family had not been Jewish?

6. **Keep a Journal:** Journals are excellent tools for assessing students' affective and cognitive growth. To confirm students' connection to and empathy for the characters, ask students to write their impressions, feelings, and questions in a journal to which you respond periodically. Word journals are also effective assessment tools. Ask students to summarize a letter in one word, i.e., "despair" or "guilt" and write the explanation of that word choice.

The Deutsch Family Legacy

It is my hope that your students, having learned about Nazi Germany and the Jews in a novel and compelling way, will continue their studies of the Holocaust with a particular interest in reading about other Jewish families who faced monumental challenges trying to live among, and then escape from, the Nazis. I hope, as well, that you and your students will come away with the certainty that the Deutsches and countless other Jewish families maintained their love and devotion to one another, their humanity, and their dignity despite the Nazis' attempts to destroy them. The legacy of this story lies in its ability to inspire and educate and in its power to represent and memorialize all those who found no way out.

> "Letters are among the most significant memorials a person can leave behind."
>
> —Johann Wolfgang Von Goethe

Appendix A

Deutsch Family Tree

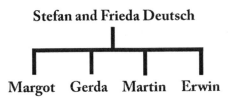

Stefan and Frieda Deutsch

Margot   Gerda   Martin   Erwin

Pronunciation of Names

Deutsch (Doitsch); Gerda (Gairda); Gerdele (Gair-de-la)."W" sounds are pronounced as v," i.e., Erwin (Ervin), Wallstrasse (Vallstrasse), and Wessig (Vessig). Margot (silent "t"), Gertrud Leuschner (Loishner), Schottlaender (Shotlander).

Maps

http://www.ushmm.org/museum/exhibit/focus/maps/
Gilbert, M. (1988) *Atlas of the Holocaust.* New York: William Morrow and Company, Inc. p. 17, map 6.

Appendix B

Expanded Information on Emigration and Immigration

Jews needed an exit permit issued by the Gestapo requiring Jews to:

1. submit character references. As so-called enemies of the State, Jews were frequently denied permits due to minor infractions, political association, or bogus charges.
2. possess a valid passport.
3. obtain a certificate demonstrating formal dissolution of their residence in Germany.
4. prove that they no longer owned properties or businesses. In Heinz Schottlaender's case, the process of dissolving his large and encumbered land and business holdings, which involved Jews, non-Jews, local and national authorities, banks, government departments, and even foreign countries, was complex and time-consuming.

Jews needed verification that they did not owe anything. The Nazis imposed high taxes on Jews, including an emigration tax, the Kristallnacht tax, capital transfer tax, and a charity tax for wealthy Jews, which often amounted to more than their assets. The Nazis also required Jews to pay fees to trustees, attorneys, advisors, banks, and local officials. These exorbitant fees and taxes left many Jews in debt.

Jews had to prove that they had obtained a visa to another country and secured travel.

Expanded Information on Immigration: Getting into Another Country

Assuming one could pay the exorbitant taxes, Jews still could not transfer their after-tax money abroad but had to deposit it in "frozen accounts" that could be accessed only with Nazi approval. If Jews tried to transfer funds, a hefty deduction was made. By June 1938, a 90% deduction was made.

Visas and ship passage had to be paid in foreign currency. Jews could buy foreign currency at unfavorable exchange rates; by September 1939, Jews received only 4% of the sum; shortly thereafter, the Nazis forbade all money transfers abroad or the exchange of foreign currency.

Immigration quotas, changing requirements and laws, time limits, antisemitism, bureaucratic red tape, securing ship passage, visa regulations, and fees made the process increasingly difficult as time went on. Foreign officials, lawyers, consuls, travel agencies, and intermediaries demanded high fees and often bribes.

Appendix C

Anti-Jewish Laws

There were nearly 2,000 Nazi anti-Jewish laws enacted against the Jews between 1933–1945. Below are those most relevant to the story.

Nazi Anti-Jewish Laws/Events

April/May 1933
- One-day boycott of Jewish stores staged.
- Jewish civil servants dismissed.
- Attendance in German schools limited for Jewish students.
- Nazis burn books.

September 1935
- German citizenship taken from Jews with enactment of Nuremberg Laws
- Jewish/non-Jewish marriages forbidden

March 1936
- Jews denied the right to participate in elections

November 1937
- Travel abroad restricted for German Jews

March 1938
- The *Anschluss*: Germany invades Austria, the country becomes incorporated into the German *Reich*, now called Greater Germany, and all Austrian Jews are subject to German restrictions.

April 1938
- German Jewish property must be registered

June/July 1938
- Jewish doctors, now called "caretakers," are allowed to treat only Jewish patients.
- Jews cannot work as brokers, guides, musicians, actors, journalists, or authors.
- Jews must carry identification cards at all times.
- "Jewish" street names are replaced with German names.

July/August 1938
- Jews over the age of six must add "Jewish" names to their passports: "Israel" for men and "Sara" for women.

September/October 1938
- German Jews cannot practice law.
- All German Jewish passports must display letter "J" on front.

November 9/10, 1938: *Kristallnacht*
- Nazis destroy Jewish synagogues and stores throughout Germany and Austria.
- 30,000 Jewish men are sent to concentration camps.
- Jews are fined 1 billion Reichsmark to pay for damages done to their homes and businesses during *Kristallnacht*.

November 1938 after *Kristallnacht*
- German Jewish children are removed from pubic schools.
- German Jewish businesses are closed.
- Jews are not permitted at movies, concerts, or swimming pools.
- Jews may no longer bear arms.

December 1938
- Jews must turn in drivers' licenses and registration.
- Jews must turn in jewelry and securities.
- Jews cannot attend universities.

September 1939
- Jews must turn in radios and other electrical items.

October/November 1939
- Jewish bank accounts are frozen.
- Permission is required to purchase goods; Jews are given fixed allowances.
- Fines, due November 15th, are increased to 1.25 billion Reichsmark.

February 1940
- Unlike other Germans, Jews no longer get clothing coupons.
- More Jews are deported to concentration and labor camps.

July 1940
- Telephones are confiscated from German Jews.

June/July 1941
- Beginning of "Final Solution."

September 1941
- German Jews must wear yellow Star of David on clothing.
- Jews need permission to leave their homes.
- Jews are banned from libraries.

October 1941
- Jewish emigration from Greater Germany is banned.
- Large scale deportations of Jews to concentration camps begin.
- Jews can no longer sell belongings.
- Nazis confiscate typewriters, bicycles, adding machines, and cameras from Jews.

December 1941
- Jews may no longer use public phones.

January 1942
- Jews must hand in wool and fur clothing.
- Jews can no longer subscribe to magazines and newspapers.

March/April/May 1942
- Jews cannot use public transportation.
- Jews cannot use barber shops or salons.
- Deportations intensify.
- Jews cannot visit non-Jewish homes.

Appendix D

Additional Individualized Assignments and Research Opportunities

"No Way Out" invites individualized assignments and research that will help your students confirm and/or question information in the letters. Below are optional study questions followed by a list of effective resources:

1. How do greed and career opportunism explain the reactions of Germans to Nazi policies?

2. It has been said that most German Jews considered themselves Germans first and Jews second. What impact did this have on their thinking about leaving Germany? Are there direct or inferential references to this in any of the letters?

3. To whom could Jews turn for help?

4. Anti-Jewish laws and restrictions happened slowly. What might have happened if Nazi anti-Jewish laws had been enacted more quickly? In a different order?

5. What did the average German Christian and German Jew know about anti-Jewish laws? Were laws made public?

6. How could the Holocaust have happened in a cultured, advanced, educated society such as Germany?

7. What made Nazi propaganda such a powerful force in the Nazi war against the Jews?

8. How much did Americans know about Nazi atrocities against the Jews?

9. How prevalent was antisemitism in America in the 1930s and 1940s?

Suggestions for Resources

The resources listed below are my favorites because they are, for the most part, stories that deepen an understanding of the Jews in Germany during the Nazi regime. Much of the literature is autobiographical; some might also be turned into Readers' Theater, offering additional performance opportunities.

Resources for Students in Grades 8–9

Author	Title	Genre
Baer, Edith	*A Frost in the Night*	Fictionalized Autobiography
Baer, Edith	*Walk the Dark Streets*	Fictionalized Autobiography
Hanf Noren, Catherine	*Camera of my Family*	Book and Video
Richter, Hans Peter	*Friedrich*	Fictionalized Autobiography
Richter, Hans Peter	*I Was There*	Fictionalized Autobiography
Wolff, Marion Freyer	*The Shrinking Circle: Memories of Nazi Berlin*	Memoir
Yad Vashem	*Outcast*	Video

Resources for Students in Grades 10–University

Author	Title	Genre
Auden, W. H.	"Refugee Blues"	Poem
Durlacher, Gerhard	*Drowning: Growing Up in the Third Reich*	Memoir
Elon, Amos	*The Pity of It All: A Portrait of the German-Jewish Epoch 1743–1933*	Nonfiction
Fisher, Josey G.	*The Persistence of Youth: Oral Testimonies of the Holocaust*	Nonfiction
Friedlander, Saul	*Nazi Germany & the Jews*	Nonfiction
Fromm, Bella	*Blood & Banquets: A Berlin Diary 1930–1938*	Nonfiction
Heck, Alfons & Sauvage, Pierre	*Heil Hitler: Confessions of a Hitler Youth*	Video
Hegi, Ursula	*Stones from the River*	Fiction
Kaplan, Marion A.	*Between Dignity and Despair*	Nonfiction
Klemperer, Victor	*I Will Bear Witness 1933-1941: A Diary of the Nazi Years*	Nonfiction
Kressman Taylor, Katherine	*Address Unknown*	Fiction
Wollenberg, Jorg	*The German Public and the Persecution of the Jews*	Essay

REFERENCES

Auden, W. H. (1939). Refugee blues. In *Collected poems*. New York: Random House Inc.

Baer, E. (1998). *A frost in the night*. New York: Farrar, Strauss and Giroux.

Baer, E. (1998). *Walk the dark streets*. New York: Farrar, Strauss and Giroux.

Bakker, D. (1994). *Crisis, conscience and choices: Weimar Germany and the rise of Hitler*. Choices for the 21st-Century Education Project, Thomas J. Watson Jr. Institute for International Studies. Providence, RI: Brown University.

Durlacher, G. (1993). *Drowning: Growing up in the Third Reich*. (Susan Massotty, Trans.). London and New York: Serpent's Tail.

Elon, A. (2003). *The pity of it all: A portrait of the German-Jewish epoch 1743–1933*. New York: Henry Holt and Company.

Feuchtwanger, L. (1934; 2001). *The Oppermanns*. Carroll & Graf Publishers. Video, 1982, Director, Egon Munk. Available from Jewish Media Fund.

Fisher, J. G. (Ed.). (1991). *The persistence of youth: Oral testimonies of the Holocaust*. New York: Greenwood Press.

Friedlander, S. (1997). *Nazi Germany & the Jews. Vol.1, The years of persecution 1933–1939*. New York: HarperCollins Publisher.

Fromm, B. (1990). *Blood & banquets: A Berlin diary 1930-1938*. New York: Simon & Schuster.

Heck, A. & Sauvage, P. (1991). *Heil Hitler: Confessions of a Hitler youth*. Video. 30 minutes, *HBO Project Knowledge*. New York: *Ambrose Video Publishing, Home Box Office*. Arthur Holch, producer.

Hegi, U. (1994). *Stones from the river*. New York: Simon and Schuster.

Kaplan, M. A. (1998). *Between dignity and despair: Jewish life in Nazi Germany*. Oxford and New York: Oxford University Press.

Klemperer, V. (1998). *I will bear witness 1933–1941: A diary of the Nazi years*. Translated by Martin Chalmers. New York: The Modern Library.

Lacey, G., & Shephard, K. (1997). *Germany 1918–1945: A study in depth*. London: John Murray, LTD.

Marcus, W. (1999). Decision-Making Activity. Washington, DC: Division of Education, United States Holocaust Memorial Museum.

Mayer, M. (1955) *They thought they were free*. Chicago: University of Chicago Press.

Noren, C. H. (1976). *Camera of my family*. New York: Knopf. Video published in New York: The Anti-Defamation League, 1986.

Owings, A. (1999). *Frauen: German women recall the Third Reich*. New Brunswick, NJ: Rutgers University Press.

Richter, H. P. (1970). *Friedrich*. (Edite Kroll, Trans.). New York: Puffin Books.

Richter, H. P. (1972). *I was there*. (Edite Kroll, Trans.). New York: Holt, Rinehart and Winston.

Shear, S. P. (1999). No way out. In K. Shawn & K. Goldfrad (Eds.). (2008) as Saving history: Letters from the Holocaust: Teaching "No way out." *The call of memory: Learning about the Holocaust through narrative: An anthology*, pp. 14–43. Teaneck, NJ: Ben Yehuda Press.

Taylor, K. K. (1939). *Address unknown*. New York: Simon and Schuster.

Witty, E. A. (2008). A look at the American Jewish experience in 1938: Was "Prelude" only the beginning? In K. Shawn & K. Goldfrad (Eds.). *The call of memory: Learning about the Holocaust through narrative: A teacher's guide*, pp. 78–94. Teaneck, NJ: Ben Yehuda Press.

Wolff, M. F. (1989). *The shrinking circle: Memories of Nazi Berlin 1933-1939*. New York: UAHC Press.

Wollenberg, J. (Ed.). (1996). *The German public and the persecution of the Jews: No one participated, no one knew.* New Jersey: Humanities Press.

Yad Vashem (1997). *Outcast: Jewish Persecution in Nazi Germany 1933-1938.* (1997). DVD, VHS. Israel. 40 min.

When There Are No Orders to Follow: Albert Halper's "Prelude" and Antisemitism in America

Aden Bar-Tura

> *Anywhere else is someone else's land.*
> —Melanie Kaye-Kantrowitz

Albert Halper's short story "Prelude" (Shawn & Goldfrad, 2008, *Anthology*, pp. 44–54) poses questions about the nature of antisemitism in the United States. Halper's story takes place in America, in Chicago, Illinois. Even though Chicago serves as site of many of Halper's works, the placement of "Prelude" in Chicago has a particular resonance. Both the references to the "EL" (short for elevated train lines) and the employees of the various factories that support the newsstand draw readers' attention to the fact that this occurs in the United States, in Chicago in particular.

Father Charles Edward Coughlin's antisemitic radio broadcasts were carried on Chicago radio stations in the 1930s. Chicago was a popular destination for a large German-American population that actively participated in German cultural activities. For the most part, the German population in the 1930s was not vocal in its support of Hitler. Even though some individuals, such as Otto Schmidt, warned against Germany's increasing power, many German-Americans preferred to remain quiet after experiencing the anti-German sentiment of World War I.[5] Given Chicago's position as a center for German-American culture, that city would appear to be an area where tensions with the Jewish population would arise.

Despite the story's conspicuous placement in America, the events that were occurring in Europe were never far away. The newspapers sold by the Silversteins report the news of people fleeing Austria; upon reading the news, Mr. Silverstein responds there is no other place other than "this country" (p. 48) to go. While firmly situated in America, the story considers the events in Europe and, at the same time, questions whether these events could happen in the United States,

---

5 Dr. Otto L. Schmidt (1863–1935) was a physician and historian. He was the president of the German American Historical Society of Illinois and president of the Chicago Historical Society. A letter to *Time* magazine on Monday, May 6, 1929, referred to him as "the leading German-American of the Middle West."

a place that historically prided itself on openness to and acceptance of foreign newcomers. A reader can view this story in several ways: as a prelude to the destruction of Jewish life in Europe during World War II, as a prelude to rising antisemitism in the United States, and as an example of American literature that presents recognizable aspects of an American immigrant story.

In this pedagogical guide to using narrative to teach the Holocaust, "Prelude" is one of four stories under discussion by American authors (the others are by Cynthia Ozick, Susan Prinz Shear, and Kurt Vonnegut). Certain aspects of Halper's story set it apart from other stories discussed in this book. Most obviously, it is not a Holocaust story in that it does not depict a scenario of World War II Europe. Instead, this story presents an immigrant family living in the United States before the outbreak of the war. It conjectures about the nature of scapegoats, how gangs get out of control, and how bystanders allow violence to happen to the innocent.

Reading "Prelude" in the 21st century is undeniably a different experience than it was in 1938, when it was first published. His story may have been more of a prelude than Halper imagined it would be. The 21st-century reader can immediately identify events and themes that were unavailable to the 1938 reader. In August 1938, the elevated railcars rumbling by the Silversteins' newsstand were not particularly sinister; disclosures about mass transports to concentration camps were not reported until 1941. By contrast, in the 21st century, the roar of the EL can be read as a salient prefigurement of the eventual transport of Jews in Poland and Germany. However, this is not to say that Europe was a quiet place at the time. In August 1938, the newsworthy events behind the headlines of "Austria and how the people were fleeing toward the borders and trying to get out of the country before it was too late" (p. 50) were the *Anschluss* (annexation of Austria) and the ongoing restrictions and elimination of Jewish rights and privileges in Europe.

Germany's annexation of Austria occurred in March 1938, and "Prelude" was published just five months later. The headlines of the events in Austria, as Mr. Silverstein reads about "mobs … robbing people they hated and spitting on them and making them go down on their hands and knees" (p. 51), could also be the prelude of what was to happen to Harry, forced down on the sidewalk while a group of eight or nine boys wrecked the newsstand.

In its depiction of the harassment of the Silversteins, "Prelude" considers the nature of antisemitism. In contrast to Europe, the United States did not have a state-sanctioned policy of antisemitism. When Mr. Silverstein first approaches the authorities to complain about the harassment by the gang of boys, he is told, "Don't worry any more about it, Mr. Silverstein, we'll take care of it. You're a respectable citizen and taxpayer and you're entitled to protection. We'll take care of it" (pp. 45–46). The "official" response acknowledges the Silversteins as citizens entitled to full privileges and protection under the law. This statement clearly reflects the American ideal that all Americans, regardless of background and immigrant status, were to be treated equally before the law and to be protected against harm. The city police department goes as far as to send a policeman to

Silverstein's newsstand and, at first, the policeman's presence seems to warn the gang away.

However, the authority of the policeman is eventually undermined. The boys recognize the cop Butch as cousin to one of their own members, Fred Gooley, which suggests that the policeman's own sympathy might be closer to the gang's than to that of the respectable Silversteins. When a gang member taunts the policeman with, "Listen who's talkin'!" Halper suggests that "who's talkin'" may once have engaged in the same kind of behavior (p. 46). Eventually, the policeman shrugs off both the gang and the Silversteins. He advises Mr. Silverstein that "It'll blow over" (p. 46), as he turns into a local bar. The official intervention, while seeming to take the complaint seriously, proves itself to be ineffective at best and possibly part of the problem at worst.

In discussions of the Nazi era, reference is often made to the frequent refrains of the Nazi soldiers, namely, that they were just following orders. The orders to Butch, the policeman, were to protect the Silversteins. The question of Nazi officers just following orders becomes less important in the face of ingrained cultural beliefs. The source of the gang's antisemitic behavior was not state-sponsored indoctrination; no Hitler-*Jugend* was in place in the United States. Instead, this behavior could be seen as a reaction to their perception of the powerlessness of the Jewish community, a minority group unsure of its status in a new country.

"Prelude" expands the discussion of possible sources of antisemitic attacks to include not only a system that authorizes them but also the cultural milieu that shrugs off antisemitism as something that will simply pass. Even without a state apparatus in place, this group of boys saw a "little fat old man" (p. 46) and two children as suitable targets. Moreover, as Harry was held down to the ground, both Mrs. Oliver and Syl begged bystanders for assistance. No one intervened on the Silversteins' behalf. When the police began to investigate, no one except Mrs. Oliver offered to be a witness.

The question of following orders is entirely absent here. This story questions fundamental relationships between people and the prejudices held by some. I am reminded of the 1947 film by Elia Kazan, *Gentleman's Agreement,* in which overt antisemitism was never expressed. The film examined the unspoken ways antisemitism was apparent in various venues, such as the workplace and in social situations. "Prelude" is not quite as subtle; the Silversteins had clearly been menaced by the gang for years. However, the same reticence to address the issue is apparent in both the film and this short story, at least among the bystanders. "Prelude" further suggests that latent antisemitism may pose a no-less-potent threat than do state-sponsored laws denying rights to Jews.

As a text written by an American author, placed in an American context, how does the narrative function as a piece of American literature? "Prelude" presents two well-established elements of American culture: the story of immigrants adjusting to a new country and the conflict of the individual struggling against a constrictive society. Traditionally, America has been populated by those who left one country behind and settled in a new place. Certainly the immigrant is part of the story of America, and on some level "Prelude" is an immigrant story.

Although it is unclear whether Harry and his sister Sylvia were born in the United States, Mr. Silverstein's reaction to the news in Europe shows that he understands the implications of the news from Europe as well as the long-standing tradition of Jews being unwelcome in another country. There is no mention of his country of origin; nevertheless, Mr. Silverstein gives the impression that immigration is part of his family's history.

Syl's questioning of Harry's grades in algebra and his need to lie to her, claiming an A instead of the C he really received, reflect a familiar emphasis on the immigrant's drive to succeed. Harry thinks about his father's timid reaction to the gang:

> My Pa said we got to watch our step extra careful now because there's no other place besides this country where we can go. We've always been picked on, he said, but we're up against the last wall now, he told me, and we got to be calm because if they start going after us here, there's no other place where we can go. (p. 48)

"We've always been picked on" could possibly refer to the pogroms of Russia and Eastern Europe of the 19th and 20th centuries. In contrast to stories of immigration, such as Israel Zangwill's 1908 play *The Melting Pot*, which celebrates the process of becoming an American through the cultural procedure of the melting pot, the need to blend in for Harry and his father is the result of fear, of feeling that there is no place else to go. Interestingly, when Harry's father expresses his future hopes for Harry to Mrs. Oliver, his explanation is also a reminder of an immigrant drive: "He should only grow up to be a nice young man and a good citizen and a credit to his country. That's all I want" (p. 49).

For the immigrant Silversteins, America is less a new beginning and more of a continuation of the old worry that plagued them in their previous homeland. In this story, the American dream of the immigrant enthusiastically becoming an American citizen is not realized.

Part of the American mythos is respect for individuals who follow the dictates of conscience instead of bowing to societal pressure. "Prelude" is a story of named individuals and identifiable groups. The Silversteins are not fighting a nameless, faceless Nazi machine. The gang that has menaced the Silversteins for more than a year calls Harry by a first name, even if it is not his correct name. The leader of the gang is Fred Gooley, and the policeman is Fred's cousin Butch. Mrs. Oliver is a longstanding customer. All of the witnesses who stood by and watched Harry being beaten knew the Silversteins.

Throughout the story, the work at the newsstand is punctuated by the quitting times of various factories, with conspicuously Jewish-sounding names: Hartman's furniture factory, Hillman's cocoa factory. Several customers knew them well enough to call Mr. Silverstein by name: "Hi, there, Silverstein … what's the latest news, you king of the press?" (p. 51). Presumably these are the individuals who stood by as the newsstand was being wrecked. Even Nick, who owns the bar where Harry's father sits next to the radiator, is well known to the family. Nick does not physically step in to defend the Silversteins, but at least he calls the police. These named individuals could easily have stood up for the Silversteins.

The American hero of this story is Mrs. Oliver. She is characterized as vaguely problematic; the story hints that her past and her "nice red hair … hanging loose down her back" have made her fodder for gossip; she has "started to get talked about" (p. 44). She visits the newsstand almost daily, buys movie magazines as well as the newspaper, and flirts mildly with both Harry and his father, behaviors that may also be somewhat unacceptable. In a June 2006 conversation I had with Karen Shawn (co-editor of this book), she suggested that the non-Jewish Mrs. Oliver, who comes to the defense of the Silversteins, might be seen as similar to those European non-Jewish helpers and rescuers of Jews who, by their own actions, engaged in behavior that also went against norms of their communities.

Sylvia, Harry's sister, with her refusal to be intimidated (she will not even cross the street to get away from the pool hall where the gang spends most of its time) clearly follows her conscience when stating uncomfortable truths: "When men hide behind Elevated posts and throw rotten apples at women, you know they're not men but just things that wear pants" (p. 49). During the attack on Harry, Syl shouts at the passive bystanders, "Why don't you help us? What are you standing there for?" (p. 53). She screams that Jews are victimized because "we're weak and haven't any country" (p. 54). In 1938, the modern-day state of Israel was not yet in existence. Israel came into being in 1948 in response to the destruction of 6 million Jews during World War II.

In considering the various ways in which Halper's story functions as a prelude, finally we should consider that it works as yet another call for the creation of a Jewish state. Perhaps, in its time, Halper's "Prelude" furthered the discussion about the need for a Jewish homeland as a possible response to American anti-semitism; current history confirms the Jewish state as a haven for Jews threatened by antisemitism worldwide. Today, the story raises salient issues in a discussion of antisemitism then and now. In contrast to Nazi-occupied Europe, where antisemitism was government-mandated through the reduction of rights and privileges, the antisemitism of government officials in the United States that led to strict and severe limitations on Jewish immigration was covert. Furthermore, even when immigrants are allowed entrance and their rights are protected by law, no government can legislate good will; making newcomers feel at home and welcome cannot be mandated. "Prelude" presents one Jewish family's experience in America; the story considers the possibility that antisemitism is a cultural rather than a legal construct and thus cannot be simply legislated away.

As I sit in Jerusalem, reading of Mr. Silverstein's fear and Sylvia's anguished scream, I wonder if the existence of Israel would have changed Halper's story. Despite the current and ongoing threats to the existence of the Jewish state, the "country of our own" that has existed since 1948, Syl's belief in its necessity as a haven for Jews remains valid.

REFERENCES

Halper, A. (1938). Prelude. In K. Shawn & K. Goldfrad (Eds.). (2008). *The call of memory: Learning about the Holocaust through narrative: An anthology*, pp. 44–54. Teaneck, NJ: Ben Yehuda Press.

Kazan, E. (Dir.). (1947). *Gentleman's agreement*. DVD release 2003, Twentieth Century Fox.

Zangwill, I. (1908, 1994). *The melting pot drama in four acts*. Manchester, NH: Ayer Company Publishers.

A Look at the American Jewish Experience in 1938: Was "Prelude" Only the Beginning?

Emily Amie Witty

> *In times of evil, indifference to evil is evil.*
> *Neutrality always helps the killer, not the victim.*
> —Elie Wiesel

I recall an e-mail we received in the office when I worked at the International School for Holocaust Studies at Yad Vashem in Jerusalem. It was from an eighth-grade student in a Jewish day school in the New York area. She wrote: "I am doing research for a project on the Holocaust. Please send me information about how the Mossad [Israeli Secret Service, formed on April 1, 1951] helped save the Jews during the Holocaust."

While my Israeli colleagues laughed, I cried. It was at that moment that I understood that we were not simply responsible for teaching about the Holocaust; we would need to recreate the world that existed during the Holocaust years. This realization hit me yet again when, during the piloting of my curriculum, "It *Is* My Business: Selected History from 1933–1945" (BJENY, 2005), in a Jewish school in Manhattan, my sixth-grade students asked me, "But where was the United Nations?" [The United Nations officially came into existence on October 24, 1945.] and, "Why didn't America just go in and stop the Nazis?"

As I internalized this reality, I understood that it wasn't enough for students to be able to recall the facts, figures, and chronology of the Holocaust. It was not enough for my students to *know* what happened without *understanding* what had happened. As an educator, I realized that in order for my students to understand, I needed to be able to anticipate their misunderstandings and address the constructs and assumptions that they were applying as they wrestled with understanding the Holocaust.

Because the Holocaust occurred in the 20th century, the modern period, I found that teaching the Holocaust was qualitatively different from teaching biblical or medieval Jewish history. Students somehow thought that the world in which they were living now was more or less the same as the world during the years of WWII and the Holocaust. It was this very assumption that was contributing to, if not causing, much of their frustration.

To make sense of what happened more than 70 years ago, students were applying their 20th- and 21st-century realities and understandings. This caused them great frustration and reminded me to take a step back in my own teaching. Before teaching the events of the Holocaust, my responsibility was to find a way to recreate a world and a reality that no longer existed.

How do we do this in a motivating and meaningful way? Enter literature, an excellent educational vehicle for depicting realities, attitudes, and feelings of a world that no longer exists. A history book, while rich with information, has no "eyes," whereas through a piece of literature, a reader can "see" into a period in history.

As one colleague noted in his personal reflection on the story,

> The short story is my genre of choice for this subject. Rather than having multiple characters with a range of experiences and emotions, there are few main characters, and readers learn more about each. The story expresses the feelings and mood of the characters and the setting. When I read stories, I feel a connection to the characters.

One story that offers insight into the American reality during the Holocaust is "Prelude" by Albert Halper. First published in 1938 and now in Shawn & Goldfrad (2008, *Anthology*, pp. 44–54), it offers students an opportunity to see what American life and American Jewish life was like during the 1930s. The plot and the characters give the student concrete representations of historical facts, concepts, perceptions, and attitudes, which are difficult to recreate for the student of pre-Holocaust history.

Through metaphor and symbolism, "Prelude," set in Chicago, Illinois, subtly offers the reader insight into what was happening to the Jewish community in Greater Germany. While one Jewish family in America was being persecuted by a local gang, Jews an ocean away were being brutalized under Hitler's Nazi regime.

Through the dialogue and actions—or failure to act—of the characters, the reader enters the mindset of the perpetrator, victim, bystander, and rescuer. (In addition to the term "rescuer," Facing History, a national Holocaust education organization (*www.facinghistory.org*), has used the term "upstander." This refers to those, who, unlike the bystander, do something proactive to help the victim. The actions of the "upstander" may or not result in saving the victim, highlighting the difference between the "upstander" and the "rescuer.")

The story, while complex in theme, is relatively easy for middle-school students to understand because of its clear writing and simple vocabulary. Because it is a story, with language accessible to a middle-school student, it allows the teacher to devote class time to discussions and literature extensions, rather than to reading the text.

"Prelude" is rich in dialogue and nuanced action and lends itself to two or three 45-minute class sessions ideally team-taught by history and literature teachers.

Extensions and research assignments may take an additional class or two, provided students have done some work independently. Two films also offer excellent background information. *Outcast* (Yad Vashem, 1997) emphasizes the early 1930s in Nazi Germany and its anti-Jewish legislation. Ostrow's *America and the Holocaust: Deceit and Indifference* (Shanachie Entertainment Corporation, 1994) depicts the antisemitism prevalent in the United States during this period and the difficulties facing Jews who, fleeing Hitler, sought refuge in the United States. The first 40 minutes of this video are appropriate for middle-school students and relevant to "Prelude." The following points are explored in one or both of the above-mentioned videos:

- Germany's role during WWI and the Versailles Treaty
- Hitler's rise to power; rise of the Nazi/National Socialist German Workers Party *(Nationalsozialistische Deutsche Arbeiterpartei)*
- Nazi anti-Jewish legislation, including the Nuremberg Laws
- The free world's policy of appeasement toward Hitler
- *Kristallnacht,* the "Night of Shattered Glass"
- The immigration policy of the United States during the 1920s–1930s
- The Evian Conference

Terms helpful to define before beginning the story include:

- prejudice, discrimination, antisemitism, scapegoating
- Nazism
- quotas
- perpetrator, victim, bystander, rescuer
- Universe of Obligation: the circle of individuals and groups toward whom obligations are owed, to whom rules apply, and whose injuries call for amends (Fein, 1979, p. 4).

Main Characters

Mr. Silverstein (father and owner of a newsstand)	Mrs. Oliver (a good customer)
Harry Silverstein (his son)	Fred Gooley and his gang
Sylvia Silverstein (his daughter)	Butch, the policeman (Fred Gooley's cousin)
Nick (the restaurant owner)	The factory workers and crowd

Plot Summary

After taunting the Jewish Silverstein family with antisemitic comments and name calling, neighborhood bullies (or possibly antisemites) wreak havoc on their newsstand and attack the owner's son, Harry. They attempt to force him to do exercises, and when he refuses, they trip him, causing him to fall to his knees.

While her brother is being beaten up, Sylvia screams at the passersby for help, but to no avail. Mrs. Oliver, a good customer and a kind neighbor, admonishes the gang for their actions. The police arrive, but by then it is too late. The newsstand has been destroyed, and Harry is badly hurt.

Using a Journal

Using a journal is an effective way for students to reflect on ideas they encounter. Fulwiler & Gardner (1999) write, "When people write about something, they learn it better" (p. 9). In addition, asking students to keep a journal allows you, the teacher, to know how the class is reacting to the material presented. I recommend the double-entry dialectical journal because it requires the student to go back into the text and identify a passage upon which to reflect in writing. These steps demand critical reading, which leads to critical thinking. Students may choose a passage with which they disagree or agree, or one they find interesting.

On one side of the page, they copy their selection; on the other, they record their response, allowing textual support for questions or reflections. The dialectical journal lets you see if multiple students are responding to similar passages. If so, you might address these during discussions. As a variation, you may open a dialogue with students by writing your comments in their journal. If you do, students should understand that you are not grading them. I initial my comments to personalize the interaction.

Sample Student Reflections
Using the Dialectical Journal Format with Teacher's Response

Selected Text	Student's Reflection	Teacher's Response
"Don't worry any more about it, Mr. Silverstein, we'll take care of it. You're a respectable citizen and taxpayer and you're entitled to protection" (pp. 45–46).	I think it's interesting that the sergeant says that because Mr. Silverstein is a respectable citizen and a taxpayer that he is entitled to protection. I wonder, was it surprising for a Jew to be both of those in the United States at that time? Would the officer have said that to a non-Jewish person? What if the person being harassed was a homeless vagrant; would he then not be entitled to police protection?	Thoughtful questions, Marc. I, too, wonder whether the officer would have said that to a non-Jewish person or to a homeless person. Where might you be able to find out more information about whether it was surprising for a Jew to be both a respectable citizen and a taxpayer in the United States at that time? Let me know what you find out! "Vagrant": good word choice! You remembered last week's bonus vocabulary word! —EAW

Discussion Points and Literature Extensions
- Define the word "prelude."
- Discuss the significance of the title. To what might this incident be a "prelude"?
- Discuss the significance of the fact that Mr. Silverstein is referred to as "the Yid" (p. 46) by one of the gang members.
- Ask your students if the nursery rhyme "Sticks and stones may break my bones but names will never hurt me" is true. Have them explain.
- Use a Venn diagram to compare and contrast Harry's reaction to the gang and Sylvia's reaction to the gang. Compare that with their father's reaction to the gang's taunting.
  1) What are the similarities and difference in their reactions?
  2) To what might they be attributed?
  3) How does each reflect different attitudes toward combating antisemitism?

Harry's Reaction

Sylvia's Reaction

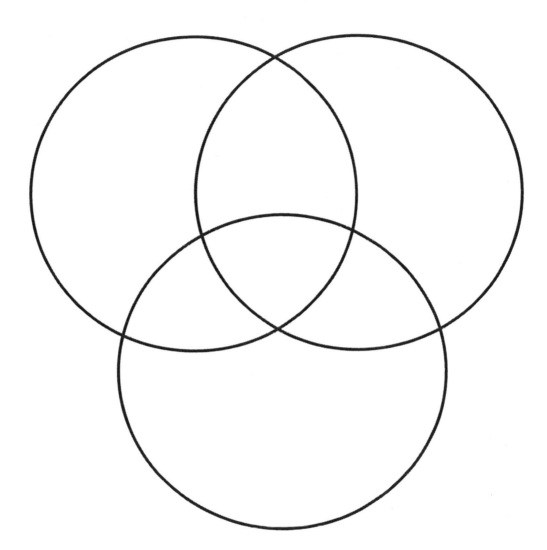

Mr. Silverstein's Reaction

Mini-Research Assignment

As an extension, the mini-research assignment below will give your students an idea of what was happening in other countries at the same time as this story takes place. The following chart is a sample of a research assignment. I often incorporate the jigsaw method in my teaching; it promotes interdependence and provides individual accountability. First introduced by Aronson, et al. (1978), the basic premise of jigsaw is to divide a problem into parts, one for each group member. The students responsible for the same part join each other and form a temporary learning community where each is responsible to learn and master the concepts in his/her part. Group members are also responsible for developing a plan to teach what they have learned to the other students.

Questions	Evian Conference July 6–15, 1938	Kristallnacht The Night of Shattered Glass November 9–10, 1938
Where did these events take place? (Group #1)		
What was the purpose of these events? (Group #2)		
Who was involved in these events? (individuals, countries, groups) (Group #3)		
What was the result or outcome of these events? (Group #4)		

Discussion Suggestions

The beauty of literature, unlike historical data, is the quality of discussion that can be elicited by focusing on selected sections or passages. Below are passages that I feel lend themselves to rich class discussion; I have also included suggestions for open-ended questions. The passages appear in order of the text of the short story. Other passages may speak to you and your students; you might include them instead of, or in addition to, the ones mentioned here.

TEXT: In the beginning of the story, Harry tells us,

My Pa said we got to watch our step extra careful now because there's no other place besides this country we can go ... we got to be calm because if they start going after us here, there's no other place where we can go (p. 48).

1. Why did Mr. Silverstein feel that there was no other place to go?
2. Based on the research you did earlier, do you agree or disagree with Harry's Pa? Explain.
3. List the names of the different companies and factories mentioned in the story.
4. What do they have in common? What might that tell us about Jews during the 1930s in the United States?
5. Notice and record the language used to describe Mr. Silverstein after he reads the headlines of the newspapers that are delivered.
6. What language is used to describe his reaction?
7. What emotion or feeling does this language evoke?

As the men are filing out of the factories at the end of the day, they call out,

"'Hi, there, Silverstein, ... what's the latest news, you king of the press?' They took the papers, kidding him, and hurried up the stairs to the Elevated, reading all about Austria and going home to eat" (p. 51).

1. Why do the workers call him "the king of the press"?[1]
2. What might "king of the press" mean?
   - Do you think it is a harmless, friendly greeting?
   - Do you think it is an insult about his job?
   - Do you think it is an antisemitic slur referring to the stereotype that "the Jews control the media"?
3. What is a stereotype?
4. Why is a stereotype dangerous even if it is phrased in a positive manner?

---

[1] The assertion that Jews "control" Hollywood, the media, *banking, and finance*, among other things, is an antisemitic canard that dates back more than 70 years to an anti-Jewish campaign waged in the 1920s by the *Dearborn Independent*, a long-defunct publication.

5. What is racial and ethnic humor? Why do you think people tell such "jokes" and make such comments?

6. Look back at the passage. What message might the author be conveying about responsibility to others and our "Universe of Obligation"?

TEXT: As Harry describes his beating, he tells us,

> "And while I was down, my face was squeezed against some papers on the sidewalk telling about Austria and I guess I went nuts while they kept hitting me, and I kept seeing the headlines against my nose." (p. 53)

1. Why does the author stress that Harry's face is in the headlines as he is being beaten?

2. What might the newspapers symbolize in this story?

TEXT: Toward the end of the story, Sylvia screams,

> In another few years, you wait! Some of you are working people and they'll be marching through the streets and going after you too! They pick on us Jews because we're weak and haven't any country; but after they get us down they'll go after you! And it'll be your fault; you're all cowards, you're afraid to fight back! (pp. 53–54)

1. Compare Sylvia's words with the following:

- The speech attributed to Protestant clergyman Reverend Martin Niemoller (1945):

   > First they arrested the Communists but I was not a Communist, so I did nothing. Then they came for the Social Democrats—but I was not a Social Democrat, so I did nothing. Then they arrested the trade unionists—and I did nothing because I was not one. And then they came for the Jews and then the Catholics, but I was neither a Jew nor a Catholic and I did nothing. At last they came and arrested me—and there was no one left to do anything about it. (available online at *http://www.ccla.org/schools/fund.shtml*

- "Hangman" by Maurice Ogden (available online at *http://edhelper.com/poetry/The_Hangman_by_Maurice_Ogden.htm*).

2. Why does Sylvia think that after the gang gets the Jews, they will go after "them"?

3. What is Sylvia saying about hatred and perpetrators?

4. What is she attempting to teach the bystanders?

In Their Own Words: Students Respond to "Prelude"

Students wrestle with the multiple layers in the story. Some students emphasize the roles of perpetrator, victim, bystander, and upstander/rescuer, while others connect to modern-day tragedies and our respective responsibilities to those in need. These journal responses illustrate that students are engaged in critical thinking, reflecting, and making meaning.

> **D:** This episode illustrates the silence of Americans in response to the plight of the Jews seeking refuge during World War II.

> **J:** Albert Halper has confirmed my grandparents' stories and helped me realize how strenuous [sic] the situation was in America. … [Halper] opened my world to what was happening and confirmed what my grandparents told me and more.

> **R:** The characters of "Prelude" were effective in humanizing the history of America during the early years of the Holocaust. Each character represented the larger groups of people in America at that time. The father represented recent immigrants still scared that America would not be the haven it promised to be. Syl represented the young idealistic American who wished to change the world. Harry represented youth forced to grow up fast due to the world situation, [or] the young Jews who fought in the Warsaw Ghetto, who, after realizing they had no better option, decided to stand up for themselves. The bullies represented the Nazis who, despite their numbers and strength, were not above hiding behind posts after throwing things at unsuspecting people. The people who just watched as Syl cried for help represented the Allies until 1939, who closed their eyes, acted as if they saw nothing, and refused to get involved. Mrs. Oliver represented the few righteous gentiles who were willing to risk their health and lives to stop injustice.

> **Y:** These stories have humanized the history of this period for me.

> **J:** I still fail to understand the passivity of American Jews during that time.

> **Y:** My understanding of life in America in the early years of the Holocaust was drastically changed after reading "Prelude." I had always thought that Jews in America did not suffer blatant anti-semitism. There was religious prejudice, such as getting fired for not working on [the Jewish Sabbath], but I never envisioned an

America with Jews getting beaten up in public with citizens just staring and offering no help.

Literature Extensions

"Prelude" is not only about a moment in time and a Jewish newsstand owner; it has haunting echoes to the events occurring in Europe. As educators, we can help our students discover those extensions and make the connections through structured re-reading.

With an eerie parallel to events in Europe, particularly *Kristallnacht*, the Night of Shattered Glass (the eve of November 9–10, 1938, in Germany and Austria), Halper depicts four categories of individuals: (1) the victim, (2) the perpetrator, (3) the bystander, and (4) the upstander/rescuer.

One strategy to emphasize this with the class is to divide the students into pairs or groups and have students assign each character in "Prelude" to one of these categories. Remind them to use textual evidence to support their decision; discuss disagreements that may arise. Once the textual analysis is complete, students can do a Readers' Theater presentation of the story.

I found that an interesting conversation developed about the fact that Nick called the police from the safety of his restaurant, whereas Mrs. Oliver directly confronted the perpetrators. We discussed differences in the level of their help and whether it mattered.

Character Map

Character	Victim	Perpetrator	Bystander	Upstander/ Rescuer
Harry Silverstein				
Sylvia Silverstein				
Mr. Silverstein				
Mrs. Oliver				
Fred Gooley and His Gang				
The Police				
Nick				
The Factory Workers/Crowd				

PYRAMID OF HATE

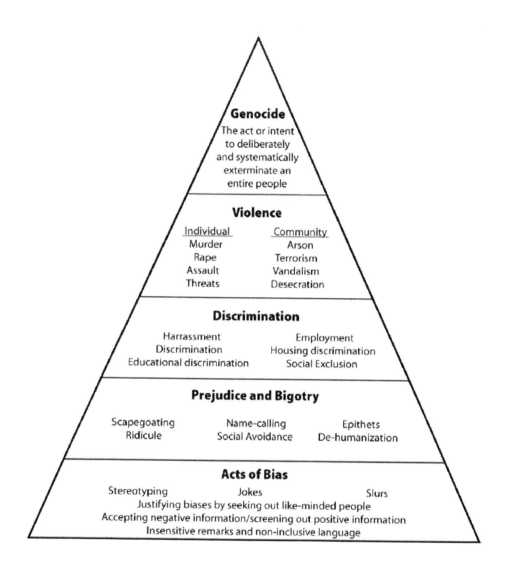

Genocide
The act or intent
to deliberately
and systematically
exterminate an
entire people

Violence

Individual
Murder
Rape
Assault
Threats

Community
Arson
Terrorism
Vandalism
Desecration

Discrimination

Harrassment
Discrimination
Educational discrimination

Employment
Housing discrimination
Social Exclusion

Prejudice and Bigotry

Scapegoating
Ridicule

Name-calling
Social Avoidance

Epithets
De-humanization

Acts of Bias

Stereotyping   Jokes   Slurs
Justifying biases by seeking out like-minded people
Accepting negative information/screening out positive information
Insensitive remarks and non-inclusive language

The *Pyramid of Hate* depicts the progression of hate in its various and increasingly violent forms. Using the following template, have your students complete their own *Pyramid* using "Prelude" as supporting evidence. Encourage them to identify specific dialogue or incidents that trace the increasing violence in the story and write it in the correct part of the blank pyramid.

Please Note: The template is meant to help the students map the story and see how verbal violence eventually escalated into a physical assault. As you guide the students, help them realize that this story depicts one incident of hate in one town, and caution them not to draw extreme conclusions about the potential for genocide in the United States of America based on this story.

Name: _____

When Does the Violence Against the Silversteins Begin?

Directions: Identify the increasing stages of violence in the story "Prelude." In each section of the pyramid, write specific dialogue or incidents from the story to support your answer. The top section is reserved for the most violent episode in the story.

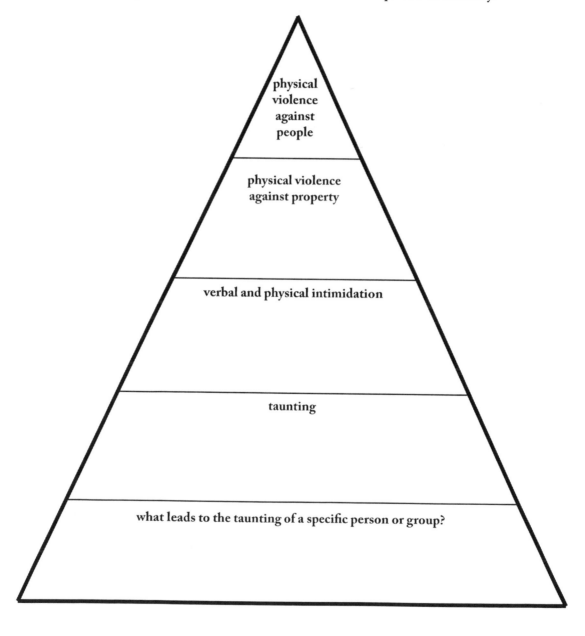

physical
violence
against
people

physical violence
against property

verbal and physical intimidation

taunting

what leads to the taunting of a specific person or group?

A Note on Assessment

Two sayings capture my view on assessment: (1) "Learning is what you remember after the test is over," and (2) "Don't let school interfere with your education." As educators, our goal is to encourage our students to want to learn more. Because "Prelude" poignantly addresses Elie Wiesel's (1979) comment that "neutrality always helps the killer, not the victim," one idea for assessment is to have your students rewrite the ending to this story. What if the workers had gotten involved? What might have happened? How might things have ended differently? Another idea is to have your students debate Wiesel's comment. Do they agree with his conclusion about neutrality?

Another one-period alternative assessment is to have students create an artistic expression that summarizes their learning, understanding, and internalization. I would encourage the cooperation of the art teacher to ensure that this will be more than a picture with a caption. Students should use a variety of materials, including clay, paints, mosaic tiles, and fabrics. Each expression should be accompanied by an oral explanation of the relationship between the art and the student's understanding of or response to the story. If the art is to be on display, it should include a brief written explanation. I suggest developing a rubric with your students so that they can be active partners in the evaluation process.

As your students complete their journal writing activities and the class discussions come to a close, it is key to remind the students that their study of the Holocaust ought not to end. As you leave the Silversteins and move to other areas of study, remind your students that what they have explored with you is but a prelude to future learning about the Holocaust.

REFERENCES

Aronson, E., Blaney, N., Stephin, C., Sikes, J., & Snapp, M. (1978). *The jigsaw classroom*. Beverly Hills, CA: Sage Publishing Company.

Fein, H. (1979). *Accounting for genocide*. City: Free Press.

Fulwiler, T. & Gardner, S. (1999). *The journal book: For teachers of at-risk college writers*. Portsmouth, NH: Boynton/Cook.

Halper, A. (1938). Prelude. In K. Shawn & K. Goldfrad (Eds.), (2008). *The call of memory: Learning about the Holocaust through narrative: An anthology*, pp. 44–54. Teaneck, NJ: Ben Yehuda Press.

Niemoller, M. Retrieved July 2, 2007, from *http://www.ccla.org/schools/fund.shtml*.

Ogden, M. (1964). (Writer). L. Goldman & P. Julian (Dirs.). *The Hangman*. Animated film. 12 min.

Melrose Productions. The hangman. Poem. Retrieved July 2, 2007, from *http://edhelper.com/poetry/The_Hangman_by_Maurice_Ogden.htm*).

Ostrow. M. (1994). (Prod., Dir.). *America and the Holocaust: Deceit and Indifference*. Shanachie Entertainment Corporation.

Wiesel, E. (Chairman) (September 27, 1979). Presentation of the Report of the President's Commission on the Holocaust to the President of the United States. The Rose Garden, Washington, DC: The White House. Retrieved April 25, 2007, from *http://xroads.virginia.edu*.

Witty, E. (2005). *It is my business: Selected history from 1933–1945*. New York: Board of Jewish Education.

Yad Vashem. (1997). *Outcast: Jewish Persecution in Nazi Germany 1933-1938*. DVD, VHS. Israel. 40 minutes.

The Gathering Storm

Portraits in Time:
Ida Fink's "The End" and "The Threshold"

Miriam Sivan

> *Spare us what we can learn to endure.*
> —Yiddish Proverb

Ida Fink is a unique voice in the *oeuvre* of writings about the *Shoah*. Though she has lived in Israel since 1957, and though she began writing about her war-time experiences only decades after her immigration, she did not develop her literary voice in Hebrew. Fink continues to write and publish in Polish, the language of her birth, the language of the culture that both nurtured and rejected her, first as a teenager and then later as a woman in her thirties. For Fink, Polish is the language of exile; and though many of her readers will come to her work in their English or Hebrew translations, knowing that the language of composition is Polish underscores the movement of looking back that is prevalent in her fiction. The Polish language itself becomes a sign of what remains; it is a trace of how much has been lost.

Her stories "The End" and "The Threshold" (Shawn & Goldfrad, *Anthology*, 2008, pp. 57–60 & 61–66) characterize a young woman's introduction to a world at war. These are elegiac narratives about a crossing over in time and more importantly in the protagonists' consciousness. Maybe it is because these are stories that take place before the violence and horror of the ghettos, the transports, and the concentration camps; maybe it is because Fink is more concerned with the slow movements of psychological discernment. However, in these two stories, her characters "identify and recognize themselves as primarily consisting of their dreams, hopes, and possibilities, rather than their physical bodies" (Best, 2002). These are not stories of deprivation: hunger, thirst, exhaustion. Fink does not use the body, as the French writer Charlotte Delbo does, for example, to convey the extent of the atrocities committed against humanity by those who served and carried out the policies of the Third Reich. For Delbo, deep memory—one that is known through the senses, one that conveys physical imprints—is most able to accurately convey the trauma of internment in German concentration camps (Delbo, 2001).

Ida Fink, however, was fortunate enough not to have shared these horrific experiences with Delbo and with the millions of others who perished and the relatively few who survived the death camps. Born in Zbaraz, Poland, she spent

1941–1942 in the Lvov ghetto and was able to escape. She spent the remaining war years on the Aryan side with false identity papers. Her stories, then, are about psychological and emotional reckonings. They are about the collapse of characters' worlds, emotionally and ontologically. It is not the body being ravaged she is 'de-scribing,'[1] but the psyche's forced adjustment to a new world order.

"The End" and "The Threshold," like the other stories collected in *Traces* (1997) and in *A Scrap of Time* (1995), Fink's compilations of short fiction, deal with the "small" moments. These are not stories of the grand sweep of history, but the minute-by-minute scraps, the small pieces that not only make up a life, but, like traces, are also the small pieces of memory that remain. They are often all that remain.

"The End" is a short story that manages simultaneously to capture the poignancy of young love, the eclipse of all that is familiar, and the terror and shadow that enveloped the citizens, particularly the Jews, of Europe. It is the end not only of the world as this young couple knows it, but it is the end of Modernism, of any notion that human construction—scientific, artistic, theological, ideological—can lead to advancement on a humane or ethical level. The end of the beginning of a relationship of young love, wherein all the promise, beauty, hope, and fertility abound in potential, is used to highlight the pain of rupture and of war.

The story begins on the night of the day when the Germans have entered the city. The opening line of the story describes the pair of young lovers: "They were still standing on the balcony, although it was the middle of the night and only a few hours kept them from dawn" (*Anthology*, p. 57). The *still* that describes their standing connotes a literal stillness or physical immobility, though this young couple is anything but. They are afraid and nervous; he felt "her body shaking" (p. 58). The *still* also implies continuity, a lingering motion, which in this case is a non-motion. Their *stillness* embodies their yearning to hold on to the world as they know it, to hold back the encroaching dread that plows forward relentlessly.

The stillness might also be read as a kind of foreshadowing of the still-like—both in terms of non-movement and endurance—phenomena that await the Jews: hours of standing in cattle cars, hours of standing in camp yards for roll call, hours, days, and weeks waiting in a kind of extended psychic and physical immobility in the ghettos and then in the camps to see what and when something more radical would befall them.

The boundary between times—the now, the then, the future unraveling—is not always clear in these characters' minds. It is no coincidence, then, that Fink interweaves the German entrance into the city with a description of a classical music concert. Standing on the balcony at night the young man thinks how he can remember perfectly

---

1 Maurice Blanchot has insightfully claimed that the Shoah exposes the limitations of language to express the complex anguish of the victims. He writes that the "disaster describes." Written language collapses in the confrontation with atrocity. Both writer and reader are affected with the loss of this foundational human characteristic: to name and give meaning to our world (Blanchot, 1995).

a faint buzz coming from the direction of the city. As if swarms of locusts were flying from far away. Maybe not locusts, but simply the dense tremolo of the strings, rising to a forte, closer and closer, fleeing before the storm." (p. 58)

As in some stories where Fink "exploits linguistic polyphony to orchestrate delusions, ironies, and unpredictable twists of fate" (Wilczynsji, 1994, p. 31), in this narrative Fink employs a kind of musical polyphony between the tanks and the orchestra to obfuscate the boundary between linear time, to highlight the floundering definitions of normalcy, and most egregiously to expose the sinister undermining of aesthetics as a product of the Platonic definition of the Good. Indeed, the Nazis very deliberately exploited music and other arts as part of their propaganda apparatus. The confluence of tanks and a musical performance at the center of Fink's story functions as a kind of "proof" that unto themselves aesthetics do not lead to the Good, but only to themselves.

This has added meaning because each one in this pair of young lovers is an artist. She is a musician. Piotr, the young man, is a painter. The tension in the story lies in their respective reactions to the "loud and brutal thunder" of the German tanks that blend in with the music the pianist is generating. His "fingers attack his silent keyboard" (*Anthology*, p. 58) just as the German tanks are about to attack the silent civilian population. The young woman is pessimistic. Her lover remains optimistic. He keeps repeating to her, and one is inclined to think mostly to himself, that what they are hearing is of little significance. He chastises her for mourning the finale of their relationship and of their world. He shouts at her to stop and comfortingly says he will make them coffee.

By comparison she is gloomy; but one wonders at what point does a pessimist become a realist? For it is only if one were able to boldly and clearly read the signs that one could even begin to think ahead and possibly figure out some way to escape the horrors about to destroy their lives. As the hours pass, his Pollyannaish insistence that nothing has or is happening becomes hollow, for despite himself he is listening hard to the changes in atmosphere and against all his wishes "the darkness resounded with dull thuds. ... It was the same ominous music that had overpowered Chopin in the park. Tanks were once again riding down the city streets" (p. 59).

At the story's end, Piotr is sleeping and his lover is awake, taking it all in: the end of their love affair, the end of their art, the end of their world. She tells him to keep sleeping: why not remain in contented denial for as long as possible? For her this is not feasible. She remains awake, and when the sun rises, the narrative voice acknowledges that the "war was fifteen minutes old" (p. 60). The war is actually fifteen minutes *young* at this moment, and she who is indeed young has quickly become old with the incisive entrance of enemy forces into her city.

"The Threshold" has a similar narrative movement. This story is about the entrance of the Germans into a small Polish town in July 1941, and the termination of a young woman's worldview. Though one week has passed since the Russian army fled Eastern Poland and the Germans arrived, and though the "first pogrom had already taken place" (p. 61), like Piotr in "The End," Elzbieta resists accepting the new order that has trapped her.

Hers is a gradual awakening to the new reality of the German occupation. There are layers of penetration, of various kinds of crossings over, before she can fully acknowledge the radical and lethal transformations. When her parents cannot return home for "the war had caught [them] by surprise in L." (p. 61), she is forced to begin to consider the new reality of her life—but only a little. Like her parents who did not acknowledge that danger was rife and the enemy close by, who left their home and young daughter to visit a neighboring city, their, and in turn, her innocence is destined to be shattered.

Once her own town is occupied, Elzbieta continues to resist facing the menace that surrounds her. She insists on going into the woods and down to the river, as is her habit. She takes her dog for walks, she lies in the sun, and she justifies her actions by claiming, "The Germans never go down there—after all, these days there aren't too many Jews interested in swimming" (p. 62). Her blatant refusal to see herself in the category of the threatened would be admirable if it were an expression of cynicism or even heroism, but it is, in actuality, rather tragic, for it stems from a combination of youthful inexperience and indifference.

Even when her house is ransacked by German soldiers, Elzbieta is not shaken out of her stubborn naiveté. It is only when she is made to witness the killing of a young Russian soldier by an equally young German soldier that her emotional threshold is violated. Until this moment, she has been able to pretend that little has changed. Then, the "something cold jabbing into her cheek" (p. 66) and the Russian "boy's final, bewildered gaze" (p. 66) force her out of the interior space she has deliberately constructed for herself. Until this moment, this inner sanctuary successfully "kept the others out" (p. 62).

The others are not only the enemy from without—the Germans. They are also the enemy from within—her relatives who have sought refuge in Elzbieta's family's country home. Elzbieta is engaged in an open struggle with these aunts and uncles. They criticize her for carrying on as if nothing has changed in their world, and she abhors them for they and even their room seem to her to be "haunted by the spirit of that terrible time" (p. 63).

However, once she is forced to witness the murder, she is able to see honestly, without cover or delusion. Only then is she able to cross the final threshold, which leads to the room of her relatives. Until this moment she has refused to enter for she scorned their endless whispering and worries. Finally, when Elzbieta recognizes that this is the room where a wartime atmosphere already exists, she enters and joins them at the table.

In her book, *One, by One, by One: Facing the Holocaust* (1990), Judith Miller claims that abstract remembering veils the reality of individual lives, of individual suffering. To continue to refer only to 6 million Jews, to not consciously consider that people suffered and died as one, plus one, plus one is to obscure the fact of their pain and of the perpetrators' culpability.

Similarly, Fink recreates one moment at a time. One moment followed by another moment that makes up a minute, an hour, a day, a week. Her moments are traces, a remnant of what remains. "There's always a remnant. A piece of a piece of a piece" (Cohen, 1972, p. 248). This remnant, or *shearith* as it is called in Hebrew, are the people who are still alive and still remember; it is their stories of those who are not and cannot.

The French philosopher Emanuel Levinas (1998) has also written about the idea of the trace, but from a metaphysical point of view. He claims that the trace is what remains of the face of the God who has retreated from our world. "But the trace is not just one more word," he says. "[I]t is the proximity of God in the countenance of my fellowman" (p. 57). The small frames of time and portraiture that Fink's stories create lead her readers to confront the faces of those lost, to see in their gestures and in their slowly spun awareness the traces that, according to Levinas, enigmatically remain for us to hold on to from the Infinite and immemorial past.

REFERENCES

Best, J. (2002). Life against death: The writings of Ida Fink and Tadeusz Borowski. *The Samaritan Review*. Retrieved April 25, 2007, from *http://www.ruf.rice.edu/~sarmatia/902/223best.html*.

Blanchot, M. (1980, 1995). *The writing of the disaster*. Lincoln, NE and London: University of Nebraska Press.

Cohen, A. A. (1972). *In the days of Simon Stern*. New York: Random House.

Delbo, C. (2001). *Days and memory*. (R. Lamont, Trans.). Chicago: Northwestern University Press.

Fink, I. (1997). The end. (M. Levine & F. Prose, Trans.). In K. Shawn & K. Goldfrad (2008). (Eds.), *The call of memory: Learning about the Holocaust through narrative: An anthology*, pp. 57–60. Teaneck, NJ: Ben Yehuda Press.

Fink, I. (1997). The threshold. (M. Levine & F. Prose, Trans.). In K. Shawn & K. Goldfrad (2008). (Eds.), *The call of memory: Learning about the Holocaust through narrative: An anthology*, pp. 61–66. Teaneck, NJ: Ben Yehuda Press.

Fink, I. (1997). *Traces*. (P. Boehm & F. Prose, Trans.). New York: Metropolitan Books.

Fink, I. (1995). *A scrap of time*. (M. Levine & F. Prose, Trans.). Chicago: Northwestern University Press.

Howe, I., & Greenberg, E. (Eds.). (1953). *A treasury of Yiddish stories*. Cleveland and New York: Meridien Books.

Levinas, E. (1998). *Entre nous: Thinking of the other*. (M. Smith & B. Harshav, Trans.). New York: Columbia University Press.

Miller, J. (1990). *One, by one, by one: Facing the Holocaust*. London: Weidenfeld & Nicolson.

Wilczynsji, M. (1994). Trusting the words: Paradoxes of Ida Fink. *Modern language studies*, 24(4), 25–37.

Ordinary People, Untold Stories:
Ida Fink's "The End" and "The Threshold"

Carrie A. Olson

People just don't realize that the Holocaust is not about
Anne Frank and Oscar Schindler;
it is about the millions of people whose stories were never told.
—Isabel, a 10th-grade student

As I choose Holocaust literature, I reflect on what I want students to understand when they read it. Isabel's quote reflects one objective: for students to gain the sense of how ordinary young people, close to the age of my students, reacted as the Holocaust was beginning to touch and tear apart their lives. I want them to "see" snapshots in time by reading vivid accounts of the daily lives of young people who lived as the Nazis swept into Poland; I want readers to translate the figure of 6 million into the experiences of a few young men and women caught in a specific place and time.

Thus, I chose Ida Fink's "The End" and "The Threshold" (Shawn & Goldfrad, *Anthology*, 2008, pp. 57–60 & 61–66), two stories in which young adults are confronted with the changing world of 1939 and 1942 in Poland. The themes of endings, beginnings, and irrevocable change wrought by circumstances beyond one's control are reflected in my students' lives and thus understandable to them. Too, my students can relate to the characters' longings, desires, fears, and confusion, age-appropriate points of entry to this study.

Fink's writing is sparse, sometimes frustratingly so, but this compression of emotion creates room for meaning-making, a task crucial for learning about the Holocaust. As students begin to construct meaning, their vague ideas of genocidal actions against millions become specific and detailed knowledge of the experience of a few youngsters who could have been their friends—friends who were murdered simply and solely because they were Jewish. As Sivan (2008) notes, these "are not stories of the grand sweep of history, but the minute-by-minute scraps, the small pieces that ... make up a life" (Shawn & Goldfrad, *Guide*, p. 98).

Fink's stories are moving vignettes that seem designed to help those who were not there to begin to comprehend not the magnitude of the Holocaust, but the moments that made it up. While historical context is important for a fuller understanding, I believe a thoughtful educator can teach these stories effectively regardless of the depth of his/her or the students' background knowledge of Holocaust history.

A Snapshot of My Classes

I taught this two-story mini-unit to 8th and 10th graders in the inner city of Denver, Colorado. Ninety-four percent of the students live in poverty; many are from immigrant families, mainly Hispanic, but also some of Asian descent. In the middle-school classes, the majority speak English as a second language and struggle to catch up to their native English-speaking peers. Classes have between 25 and 32 students. Most learners have little knowledge of the Holocaust other than "a lot of Jews died" and "Hitler was a bad man." One of the 8th-grade classes was my own; in one 8th-grade and one 10th-grade class, I was a "guest teacher." The students were in language arts classes or in my elective class for preparation on the state standardized test. I piloted these chapters with the idea of incorporating them into other classes where I also taught the Holocaust.

The 8th graders have studied European history, where teachers touched on the Holocaust to varying degrees, and many have been introduced to the concept from movies or novels. In the 10th-grade class, only two girls have studied it; several have never heard of it.

Teaching Goals

I want students to be informed and reflective, examining essential questions raised by any story of genocide. I teach for "understanding and transformation," (Ritchhard & Boix-Mansilla, 2004, p. 2) I want my students to understand basic Holocaust history, but I also want them to be transformed by what they learn. When I was a student at Yad Vashem, my professor and co-editor of this volume, Karen Shawn, told us, "You can't be the same person in the world after learning about this watershed. The Holocaust has within it the seeds of every question humans must confront if they are to live an examined life." For the middle- and high school students, I provide not only a historical framework but also a personal connection to the events: enter literary narrative. I want students to think about their thinking, to begin the work necessary to live "an examined life." As they analyze their thoughts and reactions, they begin to ask questions that enlarge the scope of the stories:

- How can the Holocaust be both the end and the beginning for the characters?
- What did people gain from trying to ignore what was happening? What did they gain from recognizing the dangers when they could not avoid them?
- How were other teenagers affected by the Holocaust?
- How did kids survive when their parents were taken away?
- Why did Fink choose to tell her stories in such a compact way? Is it because she wants us to feel as confused as the Jews must have felt?

These initial questions set the stage for raising the essential questions this learning provokes. I remind my students that their study with me is only a beginning; they will leave with more questions than they had when they entered.

Laying the Groundwork

Before beginning, I reread the *Guidelines for Teaching the Holocaust* (USHMM, 2001, pp. 11–18) to review concepts I need to remember as I teach. This helps me to be conscious of the captive, trusting audience I have. I strive for historical accuracy while not unduly traumatizing them, as then they will not study further. I recommend the USHMM Web site (*www.ushmm.org/education*) because it clarifies crucial pedagogic issues in short video guidelines.

To begin, I ask my students what they know about the Holocaust, an effective way to gauge their collective starting point. I list the facts on chart paper; for the *misinformation* they share, I find the grain of truth and turn it into a fact, never posting incorrect offerings. I tell students that we will focus on how these young Jewish people in Poland *lived* during this time, not how they died, and on how they understood and reacted to the tragedy that was engulfing them.

Students gain more understanding from group discussions than from lectures. I use group work structures suggested by Kagan (1994, 2004) and the Reciprocal Teaching Model (Oczkus, 2003) to prepare students for discussion and collaboration. Any framework that encourages children to work cooperatively to build meaning will be helpful as one teaches.

Methodology: Day One

I allot five 50-minute periods for an introduction, historical overview, reading, discussion, and follow-up activity; you can condense or expand as necessary. Our time together begins as I seat students in groups of three to four and explain that we'll be reading about and discussing the Holocaust. I acknowledge that learning about this period of history is difficult, but I reassure them that they are capable of doing so.

To provide the necessary historical framework, I give them a brief overview, including a basic timeline, particularly of the events leading up to Hitler's invasion of Poland, and a clear definition; the USHMM site offers both. When I am confident they have the fundamentals, I move on.

I introduce these stories with a brief overview of the life and work of Fink, reading a review of her work, "Images of an Extinguished World" (Eberstadt, 1997), from *The New York Times*. I want my students to understand the sparse prose Fink uses, her understated description of the impact of the war on everyday citizens. Although parts of the review are difficult, I appreciate its specificity in preparing students for what they will read.

I begin by reading it aloud, stopping often to model how I think about what I read. I focus on the following points:

1. Eberstadt writes that the "theme of the teen-ager frantic to know love before she dies is a constant in Fink's fiction." I explain that Fink writes about ado-

lescents facing the fact that their world is coming to an end. She writes about their longings, especially their budding interest in the opposite sex.

2. She discusses Fink's "intermingling of normalcy and terror, acknowledging the avid need of her characters to live fully even in the shadow of death." I explain that she writes about people going about their daily lives in the midst of a drastically changing world of death and destruction.

3. "Her work," Eberstadt notes, " ... is marked by a spare and urgent lucidity." Fink purposely writes sparsely, I explain. As we read, we need to keep in mind that she will not give us all the details we may want, but the ones she does offer help us see the characters and the events with remarkable clarity. (It's not easy to explain the phrase "spare and urgent lucidity," but, with enough synonyms, most students seem to get the point.)

4. Eberstadt tells us, "Born in Poland in 1921, Fink ... survived the Holocaust first in the ghetto and then in hiding" where she remained until the end of the war. She writes about what she knows best, not the concentration camps, but "the fates of families who survive by hiding," although she does not write specifically about her own personal experiences. (At this point, many students wonder why. I ask them to keep thinking about this as we read.)

5. Fink sets her stories, as Eberstadt describes, in "the borderlands claimed by both Poland and the Ukraine ... a countryside whose rich fields and lush forests are ... at odds with the ... atrocities committed in them by the occupying Russian and German armies." We define "atrocity"; I explain that while the stories are set in Poland, the Russians occupied part of the country until the Nazi invasion. Knowing these basic facts assists the children in making sense of what they read.

Explorations

Welcoming students back the next day, I ask them to sit and recall with their respective groups three facts about the Holocaust and three about Fink's work. By talking with each other, they learn to express and solidify their thinking. I circulate, listening, suggesting, clarifying. I give points to all the students in the group when any student volunteers information; this motivates participation.

We begin with "The End." I model a running internal monologue of what I think as I read by highlighting the title on my overhead, saying, "I wonder why Fink called her story 'The End' when it is about the beginning of the war?" I tell them I really do wonder about this, and this wondering is an example of what they are to do. I prepare overheads of each page; then it's easy to note specific places in the text.

I choose to read aloud to my students; they enjoy it, and I do not have to worry about less-fluent readers. As they follow, I instruct: "Think about what is going through your mind as you hear the story. Highlight or put a Post-It note next to at least four passages that

- connect to your life in some way, or remind you of something you've seen, heard, or read before;

- make you wonder;
- seem to be important for understanding the story;
- confuse you; or
- you want to remember to talk about later" (Tovani, 2004, p. 72).

I write these instructions on a chart and leave them as a reminder. I also use the sage advice of two of my 8th graders. Sabdy said, "Find a passage you can go along with and write about that." Her friend Edgar added, "Find passages you don't go along with and tell why."

Because I want them to focus without distraction on the story's meaning, I define, in advance, terms that may confuse, giving definitions instead of strategies for defining words in context. In "The End," I know my students will struggle with these words: *tousled, larghetto, locusts,* and *tremolo,* and the names *Chopin* and *Bach.*

As I write the definitions, I read aloud the sentence from which they came. Each teacher will decide which words, if any, will interfere with meaning. Some students may be confused by figures of speech, such as the comparison of Nazi tanks to a storm, but I want them to wrestle with that a bit.

I read the story with passion. When she is angry, I am angry. When Piotr whines, I whine. When she whispers, I whisper. I don't stop during the whole reading. I also walk among the students, who become more engaged when I get within arm's length.

At the conclusion, students look up, surprised that the story has ended! I tell them to note that for later comment. I allow students time to go back and high-light more, resisting the temptation to talk with them, as I want them to capture their own thinking. I circulate, though, to ensure everyone has at least something marked, and I highlight at least one passage on my overhead about which I would like to comment, again providing a model. For homework, I ask students to re-read the story and confirm the passages they want most to discuss.

Active Reading

I introduce the "comprehension constructor," adapted from Tovani (2004), on an overhead, explaining that we will discuss the text by writing the passages we highlighted along with our thoughts and/or reasons for picking that particular segment. The "New or Deeper Thinking" column should be ignored for now; it will be filled out after discussion. I pass out a sample comprehension constructor:

Comprehension Constructor Sample

Page Number	Quote Highlighted	My Thinking (reason for highlighting)	New or Deeper Thinking
Write the page number here.	Write your passage here. Copy it word for word from the book. If it is too long (more than 15 words), write the first three words, put three dots, and write the last three words. If you want to comment on the whole story, write "The Whole Story."	Now you need to think about why you highlighted the words you did. Write the page number and the words. Under "My Thinking," share your thinking as to why you marked that passage. You can use these sentence beginnings if they help (Tovani 2004): • This connects to my life in this way... • I wonder... • This part is important because... • I don't understand ... (write the passage here or record it on the sheet)... because... (tell why you didn't understand it)... • I want to remember this... (write the passage here or record it on the sheet)...because... (tell why you want to remember it)... You also could do the following: • Comment on a character's action. • Give an opinion about a sentence or the whole story. • Think of questions that don't have easy answers. Summarize what you've read.	AFTER YOU DISCUSS WITH YOUR GROUP This is where you show me how your thinking has changed about your particular passage or thinking through the discussion you had with your group and the class. How do you understand the text better now that you have discussed it with your group?
Example: p. 57	"The End"	I wonder why the story is called "The End." To what is the end referring: The end of their lives? their youth? Could she have called it "The Beginning"?	

When I am confident they understand, I pass out the blank comprehension constructor and ask a student to model by sharing a passage and his/her thinking on the constructor on the overhead. The students fill out their own as I circulate, checking work, encouraging, and reminding them of the grading rubric: four passages earn an A; three, a B; two, a C; one, a D; and none, an F.

Several students have difficulty finding something to write. I coach them to point to a part they had highlighted and ask them to explain their choice. When they do, I tell them to write exactly what they said!

In the 10th-grade "guest" class, a struggling reader, Justin, says he understands "nothing about this stupid story." When I ask him why it was stupid, he says, "They're young and it's the middle of the night. Why are they on the balcony? Why aren't they in bed? I know where I'd be if I was that boy." To this, his friends laugh, and I reply, "Excellent thinking! Find the part that says they are on the balcony and write that down as your passage. Then, write why you're confused and think it's stupid. Justin, that's an excellent place to start."

He may have been looking for an argument, but I accept all thinking if it is based on the text. His regular teacher was ready to jump in; she had warned me that he'd give me problems, but I wanted Justin to give it a shot. Much to everyone's surprise, he ended up writing and leading his group in a lively and insightful discussion. Earlier, we had defined the word "mood," and now I ask, "What is the mood created by the narrator? How does it help to shape your feelings about the story?" Students give specific examples and discuss how the mood differs from their first assessment.

When everyone has at least two passages, I ask volunteers to model for the class and then in their groups. I circulate and eavesdrop. When it's time to wrap up, I bring the whole class together and ask for volunteers to select passages and thinking that impressed them, modeling how discussion produces new and deeper thinking. I also comment on the conversations I heard.

For example, at a table of 14-year-old girls, Mariah couldn't interpret Piotr's failure to understand that war has broken out in Poland. Here is her comprehension constructor:

Page Number	Quote Highlighted	My Thinking (reason for highlighting)	New or Deeper Thinking
p. 57	"You see," he said, "it was nothing."	Why does the boy not understand what is happening and the girl does? He is always trying to show her that there is nothing happening.	

Her friends point out that Piotr did know what was going on but acted as if he didn't. They cite, "I love her, I don't want her to be afraid" (p. 58); his talking about the earlier concert in the park instead of what is happening now; and the passage describing that he wants to make coffee and sleep, but his face is white with pain. They recognize that the boy again and again tries to reassure the girl that "It was nothing" (p. 57), and yet he fails in his attempts. Mariah's group concludes that Piotr *did* know what was happening but wanted to protect the girl and himself as long as he could. Their conversation reflected Eberstadt's comment that "Fink is brilliant when it comes to conveying the 'false hopes and inaccurate calculations' by which ordinary men and women" dealt with their fears in those rapidly changing times. Mariah then wrote in her "New or Deeper Thinking" column, "What I now think is that he *does* know what is happening but wants to protect himself and the girl. He is scared, too."

The group has acknowledged that, ultimately, it is the girl who protects the boy, "keeping watch, guarding his last peaceful moments of sleep" (p. 60). I ask them if they believe that when the boy wakes up, he, too, will confront the realities of the war, and I leave them to debate and defend their thinking.

Olga wrote, "Why aren't boys like that anymore, wanting to protect you from stuff?" Her friend countered, asking "Do you really want to be protected from reality? Why can't we be strong?" and conducted a productive discussion connecting their own lives to those of the characters.

They complete their constructors, and the session ends by identifying the theme of the endings and beginnings; as the war began, they concluded, happiness and normal life ended. As they heard in Eberstadt's review, "Whatever joys these young [people] have thus far sampled are likely to be their last."

I remind them of the participation points each group earned and encourage them to find and cite at least two descriptors that support our supposition that these were "ordinary people." I ask: "Could 'The End' have just as easily been called '"The Beginning'?"

"The Threshold"

I begin by thanking the students for their hard work and asking them to review their learning. I give them five minutes in groups to compare their reactions and to discuss the following question: Will these characters be forever changed? They summarize insights they gained as they finished their homework; many prefer the title as it stands, noting that the idea of beginnings is a hopeful one, and what these young people face is not hopeful. I ask for questions; I ask how the story has deepened their understanding of this aspect of the Holocaust. I remind them that this is just one story of two people out of 6 million.

We discuss the apparent lack of details; one 8th grader complained that he didn't know the characters were Jewish. How was he supposed to know, he asked, if the author didn't tell him? Before I could respond, another student, Alejandra, told him, "The details are there if you know how to look! You have to sort of be a detective to figure it out. I think Ida Fink wants us to feel confused a bit." I tell the students they should focus on what and how the author tells them, and the conversation continues.

We begin the second story, "The Threshold." I challenge them to think of the reason I paired these stories. I ask them to keep in mind the theme of ordinary people; I reread a line from the Eberstadt essay: "As Fink insistently reminds us, her characters … merely went about the business of living—until a neighboring nation decided they had no right to do so." I ask them to think as well about the theme of beginnings and endings. The word *threshold*, I point out, can mean verge, brink, edge, dawn, beginning, onset, inception; any place or point of entering or beginning. Could "The Threshold" have just as easily been called "The Beginning"? Could it have been called "The End"? I will ask them to explain and support their responses.

I give them definitions of difficult words and cultural contexts: *nasturtiums, lopsided, pogrom, L.* (instead of mentioning the town), *Czing* (the dog's name), *Kuba* (a young man's name), *pierogi, incessant, incomprehensible*; when Kuba rolls a cigarette, he is smoking tobacco, not marijuana; *SS men, ransacking, kilims*; and German and Russian words.

Using the strategies and plan from the day before, we read, fill out our charts, and discuss. They are more comfortable, so the second day of reading and taking notes needs less intervention. Their passages are more insightful and complex. Many students comment on Elzbieta's not wanting to go into her relatives' room. For instance, Tashiba writes:

Page Number	Quote Highlighted	My Thinking (reason for highlighting)	New or Deeper Thinking
p. 62–63	Elzbieta kept her distance from them … She locked herself in her own world … Elzbieta refused to cross the threshold of their room, which seemed haunted by the spirit of that terrible time.	Why is she so distant from the only family she has left?	I now think that she saw the death and pain in their eyes and chose to ignore it. But at the end she can't ignore it anymore because she saw the boy get shot. Now she wants to be with her family because of this.

Tabitha didn't understand how Elzbieta could be so distant from her only family. In discussion with her group, she begins to see the reasons and fills in the third column. The students also focus on Kuba and Elzbieta walking together in the midst of so much danger. Teens themselves, many are quick to note that the two are likely boyfriend and girlfriend who have visited the field of chamomile before. Students are deeply pained when the German solider made Elzbieta watch him shoot the unarmed Russian boy. I point out that the description of the young German SS men is quite detailed, particularly in the specifics of their ransacking of the house. The killer is even described as having "sky blue eyes." I ask why they think Fink gives us such details. They understand immediately that details make characters more real to us. They draw parallels between this and the war in Iraq, wondering about the soldiers there. Some talk about how the Nazis in this story remind them of the terror that gang members create.

We meet as a class to present passages and clarify confusions. I ask how their understanding of the Holocaust has deepened. What are they learning? How are they feeling about the characters, the subject? What has ended and what has begun in the story? Several students observe that the teenagers were without their parents and acknowledge how hard that must have been. They comment on the universal longing to have a boyfriend or girlfriend, unchanged even in the Holocaust. Clearly, these stories have similar themes. I ask, "Is the end of something always the beginning of something else? The 'end of innocence' may describe a young person's experience of the events of the Holocaust. Are 'The End' and 'The Threshold' stories of the end of innocence?" The discussion continues unabated until the bell ends class. Their homework is to reread the story to resolve lingering questions and to complete the comprehension constructors.

Checking for Understanding

As I check students' passages and comments, I see that they focus on the idea of ordinary people, recognizing that the victims were very much like them. Today they will evaluate the literature, helping me to see what they have learned.

This check for understanding will be in the form of a letter. Because I will be teaching these stories to others, I say, I would like them to help me by writing to a future student to express what they have learned and understood, explain a favorite scene, defend the themes of catastrophic change on ordinary people and/ or beginnings and endings, and/or delineate reading strategies that help readers gain meaning.

We list the contents of a good letter, and I offer a rubric and point value for grading this letter, to be worth 45 points:

Guidelines for Our Letters about "The End" and "The Threshold"

1. Date (3 pts.)
2. Greeting: Dear Reader, (2 pts.)
3. A short introductory paragraph explaining why we are writing (5 pts.)
4. A paragraph stating what we have learned and understood about young people's responses to the beginning of the Holocaust in Poland (5 pts.)
5. A paragraph explaining a favorite scene (5 pts.), or
6. A paragraph on the theme of beginnings and endings or ordinary people forever changed (5 pts.)
7. A paragraph of advice for readers (5 pts.)
8. A closing: Yours truly, (3 pts.)
9. Our name and class (2 pts.)
10. Correct spelling, grammar, and punctuation. (10 pts.)

They write their first drafts eagerly; final copies will be done at home. Samples of students' writing, below, reflect their understanding and help me evaluate their learning:

A paragraph on a favorite scene

The part I like is when Elzbieta crosses the threshold in "The Threshold." She crosses it because she finally realizes the danger in her life and that people are dying and her parents are gone and she may die too. I like it because it tells about how she changed. —Peter

I like the part in "The End" where the girl is talking about how it is the end of everything, of youth, or music, of love, of his painting. I liked it because I think the author was having her explain to us the meaning of the theme and the title. That's a tight way of explaining the title. —Mario ("tight" means "cool.")

What do you understand about young people's responses to the early years of the Holocaust now that you have read these stories?

The most important thing for me is to learn how the Jewish people actually felt and lived right before the end of their regular lives and the beginning of the war. It was interesting to see that they were like me with a girlfriend but not like me because it was their last days. —Pablo

I think Fink writes this way, especially in "The End," to show how sometimes people look back on their life when they think it is ending. The girl in the story is looking back and remembering the good things. She knows the boy doesn't get it so she lets him sleep in the end. This must have been what it was like for some people. —Antonia

Advice for future readers

To make these stories less confusing, highlight the parts you didn't get, the ones you go along with, and the parts you have a connection with. Then, when you talk about it, you'll have something to say and you'll understand the story better. —Miguel

Write your connections and thoughts. Visualize and put yourself in the teenagers' place. They are a lot like us. You will understand the story better if you do. —Tabitha

Remember that Fink writes this way on purpose. She wants you to think, maybe even be confused at times. Don't give up if you get confused. Talk to your group and it will make sense. —Mariana

As they write, I circulate and talk with them; candid interactions help me understand what they want to say. They follow classroom-established protocol for writing, revising, and publishing, and they submit thoughtful, heartfelt letters, which I will use spring semester. The assignment is a wonderful way for students to reflect on their learning and to communicate with peers about the stories.

Assessment and Evaluation

I struggle with assessment. Sometimes it appears that the most effective learning is not easily measured, but it is important to find a way to give feedback that honors the work we do together. So, I continue to work to find ways to represent and measure what students have learned.

All students receive a grade based on the passages they note per story. Full credit requires completion of all four columns; extra credit is offered to those who synthesize ideas. I also track participation. Combining the comprehension constructors with the letters and discussions, I can analyze the level of my students' understanding to assess their success—and mine.

My Own Questions and Struggles

During this unit I realized I needed more time than I had allotted to provide a thorough framework of history, crucial for students to understand the stories. However, I am reminded of my own advice: If the starting point is accessible and intriguing, students' questions and interest will lead them to continue learning. I was rewarded by students from other classes who asked me when I would return to teach. It is important for me to remember that I don't always have to have the perfect lesson, but I need the perfect beginning, which I think these stories provide.

I am intrigued by students' comments that the characters reminded them of themselves: having boyfriends/girlfriends, not understanding adults in their lives, being fearful of and upset by violence. Next time, I will allow more time for students to draw parallels between the characters' lives and their own to assist them in understanding, as much as they can, both similarities and differences.

Most students took away an understanding of ordinary lives that became extraordinary because of circumstances forced on them and saw how the characters tried to cling to routines and habits to establish some sense of order in a changing world. While I found many eighth graders to be mature enough to comprehend the themes of beginnings and endings and of ordinary people in terrible times, tenth graders and older students, on the brink of young adulthood, can more appropriately reflect on these themes and draw personal parallels unavailable to middle schoolers.

I will also incorporate more varied assessment opportunities. An assignment of a poem, song, painting, PowerPoint presentation, illustration, or collage would address all learning styles and abilities.

Several closure activities are appropriate; following students' leads helps individualize instruction. Several 10th graders, for example, wanted to read more of Fink's work; I suggested two stories from her collection *Traces* (1997) that they would be able to understand independently: "An Address" (p. 121), and "Cheerful Zofia" (p. 143). Several asked for more book recommendations, which I gave, including Fink's other anthology, *A Scrap of Time* (1995). I made sure all students knew I was available for further conversation. I would also recommend guided investigation into the historical context of the Holocaust as found on the USHMM Web site.

Asking a survivor to speak is a profoundly meaningful way to have students witness history. I have a Hidden Child survivor speak to my students because he can explain so clearly what it was like to be a child experiencing the changes brought about by the Holocaust in 1939. Although he had some horrific experiences, he never scares my students, and this, too, is one of my goals: to use such encounters as a catalyst for further study rather than a catharsis, which often marks the end of learning.

Extended Learning/Enrichment Opportunities

The following questions require students to analyze, characterize, compare, conclude, explain, interpret, synthesize, take a position, and cite text to support stated opinions, allowing evaluation within specific parameters of achievement. Time constraints prevented my use of them, but I plan to incorporate them when I teach these stories again as assignments, discussion starters, journal prompts, and short essay topics to elicit specific nuances that may otherwise be missed.

1. The young women in both stories are referred to as children: "But you are a child" (p. 57), the boy says to the girl in "The End"; and the narrator in "The Threshold" says of Elzbieta, she "was still very young" (p. 61). Do you agree that they are "children"? Explain by referring to the text.
2. At the end of "The Threshold," "Elzbieta crossed silently into the room and took her place at the table" (p. 66). Has she become, by this action, more like the girl in "The End"? Defend your thinking. Might "taking your place at the table" be a metaphor for growing up? Explain.
3. In "The End," the boy wants desperately to protect the girl; in "The Threshold," the girl's aunts and uncle try "to reason with her, to explain things, to open her eyes" (p. 63). What accounts for the difference in the treatment of each girl?
4. With which girl's attitude do you more closely identify? Do you tend to want to know the truth, no matter how bad it is, or do you prefer to deny ("I just can't accept" (p. 63), Elzbieta says of the situation confronting her) or try to ignore terrible things that happen and live in your own world as long as you can? Explain.
5. In "The End," Fink describes tanks rolling through the streets during an outdoor concert, writing "The storm crested and subsided" (p. 58). What was "the storm" in this story, and how did it "crest" and then "subside"?

6. In "The End," he is a painter and she is a musician, and there are numerous references to music throughout. What is the significance of these references?

7. "Compression" is an attribute of short stories, when things that might take a page in a novel are said in a word or two, or simply implied. In "The Threshold," an example of compression is the description of bits of conversation Elzbieta overhears coming from her aunts' room: "Mostly cries and sighs" (p. 63). Another example is the time lapse, without words, from the murder of the young Russian soldier to his burial that evening. Find at least two examples of compression in "The End" and discuss what *isn't* written.

8. In "The End," the girl is a static character; she begins and remains strong. Elzbieta, in "The Threshold," is a dynamic character. Explain, giving examples of her growth from the text.

Conclusion

Adolescents and young adults confront beginnings and endings. They try to make sense of a world where they find themselves caught between growing up and remaining a child, shaped by events beyond their control. As they articulate their feelings of leaving the protection of childhood and being thrust into a world not of their making, as they grapple with ideas of innocence ending, they begin to recognize who they are becoming. They are eager to learn about other young people, those who came of age in the world of the Holocaust. Fink's "The End" and "The Threshold" introduce them to young people much like themselves, providing relevant and immediate connections to the otherwise unfathomable events of the past century.

References

Eberstadt, F. (1997). Images of an extinguished world. 24 August 1997. *The New York Times*. Retrieved October 1, 2006, from *http://www.nytimes.com/books/97/08/24/reviews/970824.24eberstt.html*.

Fink, I. (1995). A scrap of time and other stories. (Madeline Levine & Francine Prose, Trans.). Evanston: Northwestern University Press.

Fink, I. (1995). The end. In K. Shawn & K. Goldfrad (Eds.). (2008). *The call of memory: Learning about the Holocaust through narrative: An anthology*, pp. 57–60. Teaneck, NJ: Ben Yehuda Press.

Fink, I. (1995). The threshold. In K. Shawn & K. Goldfrad (Eds.). (2008). *The call of memory: Learning about the Holocaust through narrative: An anthology*, pp. 61–66. Teaneck, NJ: Ben Yehuda Press.

Fink, I. (1997). *Traces*. (Philip Boehm & Francine Prose, Trans.). New York: Henry Holt and Company.

Kagan, S. (1994). *Cooperative learning*. San Clemente, CA: Kagan Publishing.

Oczkus, L. D. (2003). *Reciprocal teaching at work: Strategies for improving reading comprehension*. Newark, DE: International Reading Association.

Ritchhard, R. & Boix-Mansilla, V. (2004). *Arthur and Rochelle Belfer: Exemplary lessons initiative*. Washington, DC: United States Holocaust Memorial Museum.

Sivan, M. (2008). Portraits in time: Ida Fink's "The end" and "The threshold." In K. Shawn & K. Goldfrad (Eds.). (2008). *The call of memory: Learning about the Holocaust through narrative: A teacher's guide*, pp. 97–101. Teaneck, NJ: Ben Yehuda Press.

Tovani, C. (2004). *Do I really have to teach reading? Content comprehension, grades 6–12*. Portland, ME: Stenhouse Publishers.

United States Holocaust Memorial Museum. *Teaching about the Holocaust: A resource guide for teachers*. (2001). Washington, DC: United States Holocaust Memorial Museum.

Young, A. (2004). Lesson one: Pre-World War II European Jewish life photo project. *Arthur and Rochelle Belfer: Exemplary lessons initiative*. Washington, DC: United States Holocaust Memorial Museum. See also *www.ushmm.org/education*.

Elijah the Prophet Questions Jewish Tradition: Elie Wiesel's "An Evening Guest"

Mark Gelber

In a very short prose text entitled "An Evening Guest" (Shawn & Goldfrad, *Anthology*, 2008, pp. 67–73), Elie Wiesel draws on the extensive Jewish literary and religious legacy surrounding the biblical prophet Elijah in order to enact a dialogue between tradition and modern experience. More precisely, within the framework of a depiction of traditional Jewish life, focusing on the Passover *seder* rituals, the radically "other" experience of modern brutality and industrialized genocide impinges on and calls into question the time-tested Jewish strategies for mediating and understanding Jewish life, the same ones that provided for the possibility of its continuation. The text, in effect, suggests that the *Shoah* represents a historic cultural rupture with the past, and in face of the attempted genocide, Jewish tradition is basically helpless. Thus, it is rendered meaningless. However, according to possible readings of Wiesel's text, it may be that alternatives to the tradition or simple answers regarding the future of Jewish life are not easily proffered in a post-*Shoah* world.

There is a vast amount of literature concerning Elijah the Prophet beyond the biblical material, which forms part of the background to Wiesel's narrative. This literature belongs to the Jewish canon, and it constitutes a literary corpus that was especially resonant in Jewish folk life for centuries. Also, the memory of Elijah, which was incorporated into Jewish religious and national life in numerous ways, appears in the text as part of the legacy of the Passover holiday celebrations.

It is probably fair to say that a good part of the literature concerning Elijah the Prophet has slipped into oblivion, and thus no longer strikes a chord of recognition within the literary and cultural memory of many Jewish readers today, or with other readers who encounter Wiesel's text. Yet Elijah, as a cultural icon, continues to be a presence in Jewish life because of those ritualistic aspects that have preserved his legacy, to the extent that these rituals are practiced or recalled by living Jewry and are known to others beyond it. Early descriptions of the biblical Elijah included the one based on his chief role as the righteous and implacable defender of the faith against the evil pagan prophets of Ba'al. His stentorian voice also warned of the immorality and sinfulness typical of the Northern Kingdom of Israel ruled by King Ahab and Queen Jezebel, as well as the fantastic account of his dramatic ascent to heaven in a fiery chariot at the end of his life. These images were extended eventually in order to accommodate many additional qualities that were integrated into his composite image over the centuries.

The post-biblical Jewish literature on Elijah depicts him variously, that is, often in different guises and in diverse contexts, as a savior of Jewish communities in distress or as a savior of individual Jews from agents and agencies of death. Often, Elijah appears unexpectedly and out of nowhere, in order to heal the sick, to feed the hungry, to right a wrong, to restore possessions to the dispossessed, to enrich the impoverished, to warn those in potential distress, to reveal mysteries to the unknowing, to demonstrate solidarity with the disenfranchised, and to dispense acts of loving-kindness in general. Sometimes, he appears as a poor, disheveled, and homeless beggar, who tests the commitment of Jewish hosts to the religious commandment of providing hospitality to strangers. Additionally, for vulnerable Jewish communities regularly threatened by antisemitic excesses and brutality over centuries throughout the Diaspora, the figure of Elijah, who, as harbinger of the Messiah and the messianic age promised an end to Jewish suffering, assumed central importance in Jewish national consciousness.

The memory of Elijah has been kept alive largely by means of the incorporation of numerous facets of his various images into Jewish religious life. For example, the spirit of the prophet presides over the circumcision rites of every Jewish boy. The *sandek* (godfather), the man who holds the infant in his arms, traditionally sits in the "chair of Elijah," while the *mohel* performs the circumcision. Another example is the figurative presence of Elijah at the weekly *Havdalah* service, which marks the separation of the sacred and the profane at the conclusion of the holy Sabbath day of rest. The Sabbath is bid a sorrowful farewell, as the mundane work week is inaugurated once again; Jews normally sing hymns that refer to Elijah during or at the conclusion of this service, which serve as a reminder of the prophet's invisible presence. A third example is the "cup of Elijah," which adorns the table at the annual Passover *seder*. Late in the evening ritual, at the conclusion of the meal, during which the miraculous tale of the exodus of the Jewish nation from Egyptian slavery is solemnly recounted, the door is opened to allow symbolically for the spirit of Elijah to enter as a guest and to partake of the wine, which has been poured in his honor and awaits his arrival. His anticipated presence confirms the authenticity of the *seder* ritual. It is this very same sequence that appears in Wiesel's text. As these examples and others illustrate, Elijah is a mediating figure, who in general presides over critical transitional stages of Jewish life and existence, in addition to the more specifically defined roles enumerated above.

In Wiesel's text, the narrative unfolds precisely on the evening of the Passover holiday, which is associated with Elijah the Prophet. Thus, when the evening guest arrives and is identified by the narrator as an incarnation of the prophet, the literary landscape of associations is easily established. However, Elijah's diverse literary incarnations and traditional roles as a prophet of warning and as a harbinger of rescue ("herald of deliverance" [*Anthology*, p. 67]) are neutralized or rendered feckless in this narrative, because the guest is perceived to be mentally unbalanced or mad, and his words of warning cannot therefore be taken seriously by the family members. The irony is heavy, because the reader and the narrator (partially, as will be explained) are completely aware of the gruesome reality facing European Jewry in the spring of 1944, the one date mentioned in the story.

In addition to this specific timeframe, the writer provides the reader with two temporal perspectives. The text incorporates narrative perspectives from the time before the family members are subjected to the destructive forces unleashed by the *Shoah*, that is, before it impinged on their insular traditional Jewish family life and terminated it. The story also offers retrospective perspectives that are dreadfully cognizant of the terrible toll and forbidding fate suffered in the end by the family.

The narrator accomplishes this dual or split temporal perspective by identifying himself, on one hand, with the child who is present at the *seder*, but also, on the other hand, with the "older," retrospective narrative voice that reports that this will be the last Passover that the family will spend together. The combination of these two vantages lends the text an uneven or ruptured quality, as well as an even more ironic ("I did not know that this was to be the last *Seder*" [p. 69]) but fateful solemnity, given the anticipation of death and destruction, which the "evening guest" has witnessed and implicitly predicts for his hosts and their community. In a sense, the image of Elijah is conflated here with another mythic image, namely the image of Cassandra, whose prophetic words of truth are destined to be disbelieved; they are condemned never to appear credible to their listeners.

Wiesel's partial but dominating identification of the narrative voice and point of view with that of a child is a well-known literary technique that tends to engender sympathy for the world and outlook of the innocent and vulnerable child in an uncaring, harmful environment. In this case, moreover, the child is identified as a Jewish child who also manifests solidarity with other Jewish children ("all the persecuted Jewish children" [p. 67]). Thus, the particularly exposed condition of Jewish children throughout history is emphasized. The childhood fascination for Elijah is linked directly to fire imagery ("chariot of fire" [p. 67], "fiery chariot" [pp. 72, 73]), which is implicitly linked to the fires of the crematoria that incinerated Jewish bodies in the concentration camps. This fire imagery permeates the text in order to guarantee that this linkage, while implicit, remains constantly in the mind of the reader: "setting mountains and hearts on fire" (p. 70); "my cheeks on fire" (p. 72); "eyes … aflame" (p. 68); "a burning glance" (p. 70).

The focus on the biblical narrative of the Passover exodus underscores the traditional Jewish tendency to understand the present with the interpretive tools of the Jewish past. However, because there is no deliverance this time around, the validity of this tendency and the tradition itself are called into question. The irony of the setting—Passover is the Jewish "festival of freedom" (p. 68)—is intensified by the fact that the child's perspective, while sympathetic with the visitor, does not fully comprehend the dire and impending tragic situation that faces the Jews in his immediate vicinity or Jewry at large. There was to be no miraculous deliverance or redemption in face of the Nazi threat to Jewish existence, and Jewry in a post-*Shoah* world would remain bereft of its traditional interpretive tools, which have informed its very mode of consciousness.

The poetical language of Wiesel's prose also contributes to the tension generated by the disjunction between traditional ways of the past, which worked successfully in favor of Jewish survival, and the brutal, modern threat, which cannot be eliminated or rendered void or useless by the tradition or by any other means. The poetic prose is replete with antiquated diction, sometimes recalling biblical lexical items or ancient linguistic patterns. This is the case especially when the syntax is awry and the text manifests inverted word order, for example, when adjectives follow nouns ("a prince ageless" [p. 67]), or when it uses anaphora: "Let him ... Let him. ..." (p. 67) Also, sentence fragments and awkward or repetitious rhetorical questions contribute in the same way to create the sense or aura of outdated, worn usage: "Is it not written ...? Is it not written?" (p. 65). Antiquated expressions such as "in the hour of punishment" (p. 69) or "at the gates of this city" (p. 70) complement the several quotations from the *seder* ritual, as established in the Passover *Haggadah*, but also the Aramaic quotation, *"Kol dichfin yetei veyochal"* (p. 68), which appears transliterated in the body of the story, but is glossed as: "Let him who is hungry come eat with us."

While Wiesel wrote this story in French, its linguistic object is the biblical language and Jewish ritualistic prose, which complement the focus on Elijah the Prophet. The topographical object, however, is the landscape of Eastern Europe; thus, mention of the place names that are the new sites of the modern Jewish tragedy grate against the familiar and comprehensible sounds of recognizable place names ("Jerusalem," "Rome," "Kiev" [p. 66]), by presenting strange sounds characteristic of the foreign: "Körösmezö," "Kolomei," "Kamenetz-Podolsk" (p. 69). That the "o" sound dominates in these place names seems to suggest that by their very names they are loci of woe. Also, that the three "o's" of Körösmezö are each written with an "Umlaut" (or double acute accent) in the original yields an additional, visual alienation effect.

Both the evening guest and the narrative voice of the "man/child" formulate critiques of Jewish tradition, which strain against aspects of the plot, and in the end, the "narrator-man/child" becomes the disciple of the evening guest. While the guest claims to have no time and certainly demonstrates no patience for the cumbersome, outdated Passover rituals, given the pressing need he feels to respond to the precariously dangerous situation before the catastrophe strikes, he nevertheless remains at the *seder* meal for most of the ritual, an inordinate amount of time. His role is to question the holiday's assumption of divine salvation and to doubt that divine intervention would play a role in the present, grave situation. By posing questions, he becomes an active participant in the *seder* and the tradition, since asking questions is a formal and integral part of the holiday ritual ("My little sister asked the traditional four questions" [p. 69]). At the same time he departs from the ritual, in a sense rewriting the *Haggadah*, by reformulating the standard questions and supplying new answers, which present a serious challenge to the Jewish tradition ("Discontent with both the question and answer, our guest repeated them in his own way" [pp. 69–70]). In effect, he urges his hosts to abandon the tradition and make some decisive move in order to elude the very real dangers lurking just outside the home. The idea is that perhaps the family can save itself, if it takes immediate action, rather than relying on divine intervention, which will never come, even though the message of the tradition is one of hope and deliverance.

However, the impact of the evening guest on the family, but especially on the narrator, is registered in a different way. Close to the conclusion of the *seder*, when the door is opened ritually for the arrival of Elijah the Prophet, the evening guest disappears, leaving his hosts dumbstruck and uncomprehending. It is at this point that the narrator assumes the role of the guest's disciple: "Had our guest stayed with us, he is the one who would have asked these questions. In his absence, I took them up on my own" (p. 73). Thus, the narrator, combining the perspectives of child participant and knowing adult well after the fact, questions the logic of the traditional and much-loved song about the little goat ("Chad Gadya") sung at the very end of the *seder*, which he now labels as "terrifying" (p. 72): "But that evening the song upset me. I rebelled against the resignation it implied. Why does God always act too late?" (p. 73). The dual or split perspective achieves both identification with the tradition while simultaneously undermining it from the vantage of the narrator, who survived the *Shoah* (and became a man) ostensibly without divine aid and without utilizing the successful strategies and narratives of the Jewish past in order to do so. This time, or in this day and age given the *Shoah,* they no longer have any efficacy.

Still, the numerous ironies of the text are framed by a large paradox, which seems to encompass all of the textual irregularities. Some of the ironies are patently obvious, as when the Hungarians who shout "Death to the Jews!" are called "our dear Hungarian neighbors" (p. 69). Another example might be the characterization of Elijah the Prophet as a "saint" (p. 67), which is really an idealized Christian designation, whereas he appears in the story as "pitiful" and "stoop-shouldered" (p. 68), a poor, bewildered Polish Jewish refugee. The paradox is that in retrospect, despite having lost belief in the tradition, the narrator "still believes" that it was Elijah whom he had encountered at that fateful moment long in the past; the visitor was, he continues to believe, an incarnation of the biblical prophet. Thus, the story that is told is just one more in the Jewish corpus, which is based on the Elijah tradition, despite the fact that the tradition has no more validity for the narrator in the post-*Shoah* world. "Elijah" is in this sense a Jewish way of understanding reality, a trope or model for ordering Jewish existence. The narrator, by constructing his tale within the literary tradition of Passover and Elijah, has, in effect, not abandoned that way, even though he has doubted it and denied its validity. Perhaps he cannot escape it. In accordance with the example of the evening guest, who by his questioning at the *seder* rewrites the *Haggadah,* it might be said that a new "Chad Gadya" is being written here, as the narrator wishes, when he asks: "Why didn't he [God] get rid of the Angel of Death before he even committed the first murder?" (p. 73). For while the narrator has reported that this *seder* would be the last one that the family celebrated together, he does not report that it is the last one in which he would ever participate. The difference is crucial.

REFERENCES

Klapholtz, Y. Y. (1974). *Stories of Elijah the prophet.* (4 vols.). (Abigail Nadav, Trans.) Bnei Brak, Israel: Pe'er Hasefer Publishers.

Wiesel, E. (1968). An evening guest. In K. Shawn & K. Goldfrad (Eds.). (2008). *The call of memory: Learning about the Holocaust through narrative: An anthology*, pp. 67–73. Teaneck, NJ: Ben Yehuda Press.

Let Us Tell Tales:
Teaching Elie Wiesel's "An Evening Guest"

Lauren Kempton

> *Let us tell tales—all the rest must wait.*
> *Let us tell tales—that is our primary obligation.*
> *Commentaries will have to come later,*
> *Lest they replace or becloud what they mean to reveal.*
> —Elie Wiesel

In our lives as teachers, especially teachers of the Holocaust, we gather stories to tell to our students. Some of these stories become lessons; some become etched in our *neshama* (soul) and being; the best become both. I first learned the story of the Holocaust from an extraordinary teacher, a survivor named Vladka Meed. As a teenager, Vladka was a courier for the Jewish Fighting Organization in the Warsaw Ghetto. Hiding her Jewish identity and posing as a Pole, she smuggled weapons into the ghetto and rescued Jewish children by finding Christians who would hide them. For 21 years Vladka and her husband, Ben Meed, of blessed memory, devoted themselves to Holocaust education, running three-week seminars in Israel underwritten by the American Gathering of Jewish Holocaust Survivors. I was among the first of the hundreds of teachers in this yearly seminar. In 1986, as our weeks of learning came to a close, Vladka, her eyes fixed on us, summed up: "Remember, when you teach, teach stories of Jewish life in Eastern Europe; teach stories about Jewish resistance." Today, Vladka's words have become the touchstone of my teaching and the background for this unit of study.

My course, a literature and history overview of the Holocaust, is offered to 24 sophomores in MAKOM, a supplementary Hebrew high school in Woodbridge, Connecticut. It runs one hour a week for one semester; this unit takes four of our 20 sessions. I struggle with time constraints, asking myself:

- Have I structured each class so students have time to process their learning?
- Is the history context a strong-enough foundation to support the literature?

Ideally, this course would be taught concurrently by teachers of history and English; my 30 years of teaching reinforce my commitment to interdisciplinary instruction, which doubles the time the students have for this subject and ensures the most effective teaching of history and literature. However, I teach alone, dependent on history texts and documents to contextualize the literature. While I am not required to meet the state or national standards for English/language arts or social studies, their sound principles (pp. 490–492 in this *Guide*) inform my teaching and reflect my goals.

Setting the Stage for Learning

While I weave literature throughout the semester, this story is introduced midway, following an introduction to Jewish life and culture in pre-war Eastern Europe and an overview of Holocaust history that I take from Michael Berenbaum's *The World Must Know* (1993) and *A Promise to Remember: The Holocaust in the Words and Voices of Its Survivors* (2003). I tell my students that all that we learn must be contextualized. All Jews were targeted for annihilation by the Nazis, but all Jews did not have the same experiences: Those on the run, in hiding, in ghettos, in concentration camps, and in death camps tell very different stories. I give examples of each. Secular and religious Jews may focus on different aspects of their experiences; I give examples of each of those as well.

This narrative by Elie Wiesel will introduce my students to the complicated relationship between the author and God during the Holocaust. For background, I download and discuss the PBS Web site "Elie Wiesel: First Person Singular" (*http://www.pbs.org/eliewiesel/life/index.html*) including "The Life and Work of Wiesel: A Biographical Overview," and, by Gary Henry, "Story and Silence: Transcendence in the Work of Elie Wiesel" (*http://www.pbs.org/eliewiesel/life/henry.html*).

"An Evening Guest"

In "An Evening Guest" (Shawn & Goldfrad, *Anthology*, 2008, pp. 67–73), we meet the Wiesel family as they celebrate the first night of Passover, unaware this *seder* will be their last as a family. We also learn, by inference, the fate of Hungarian Jews, among the last of Hitler's victims. Reviewing the religious symbols and rituals in the story is an additional goal I set as we discuss the continuity of the traditions that accompany the festival of Passover, traditions that remain timeless, rooted in the Torah, precisely the same now as they were before the Holocaust. Finally, we consider an essential question evoked by this and all tales told by survivors: Is there such a thing as "the triumph of memory"?

To begin, I review countries conquered and occupied by Hitler's armies as of 1944, and I show them, on a posted map from Gilbert's *Atlas of the Holocaust* (1982), Sighet, Romania, the hometown of Elie Wiesel and story's setting. I distribute the story and review vocabulary, providing definitions. Many will be familiar to my students, but not all:

- Passover/*Pesach:* The Jewish holiday celebrating the Exodus from Egypt.
- Elijah/*Eliyahu* in Hebrew: Ancient prophet who ascended to heaven alive, believed to be the herald of the Messiah
- Saul: First king of Israel, anointed by Samuel the Prophet

- Samson: Judge of ancient Israel, famous for his superhuman strength and for leading the struggle against Israel's archenemy, the Philistines.
- *Seder:* Passover ritual and meal; *seder* means "order" in Hebrew.
- *Haggadah:* Hebrew textual guide to the Passover *seder* that recounts the story of the Israelites' Exodus from Egypt
- Four Questions: Traditional *seder* questions asked by the youngest child
- Rebbe: the title of respect accorded a teacher of religious studies
- "*Chad Gadya*": song sung at the conclusion of the *seder*
- "Next Year in Jerusalem": Proclaimed at the *seder* to signify the wish for the return of the Jewish people to Jerusalem
- Beadle: a synagogue official

From the beginning of the semester, my students have used journals for note taking and reflective writing. I value journals as a place where students can record their feelings and reflect on the meaning they make of the text and its relation to their lives and to the broader community. I don't grade, but do assess, this writing, and I do respond to what they write. Now, I ask them to note, as they read, words or sentences that evoke for them their own *seder* experiences and to write a paragraph on one symbol or ritual that holds for them personal meaning.

"Who asks the Four Questions in your house, for example?" I ask. We talk about Elijah and his cup which, as Mark Gelber (Shawn & Goldfrad, *Guide*, 2008) explains,

> adorns the table at the annual Passover *seder*. Late in the evening ritual, at the conclusion of the meal, during which the miraculous tale of the Exodus of the Jewish nation from Egyptian slavery is solemnly recounted, the door is opened to allow symbolically for the spirit of Elijah to enter as a guest and to partake of the wine, which has been poured in his honor and awaits his arrival. (p. 118)

"Who opens the door for Elijah?" I ask. "What are your thoughts as these rituals are enacted in your home? What significance do they hold for you personally?"

We begin to read aloud, stopping frequently to clarify ideas and note the rhythms of Wiesel's writing. Some students have already begun to identify words they wish to discuss—"Elijah," "festival of freedom,"—and they share and compare family anecdotes. We read and talk until class ends.

In our second meeting, we exchange vignettes of *Pesach* in our homes, sharing personal connections to objects and rituals in Wiesel's story. I don't think my students will celebrate another Passover without thinking of the Wiesels' *seder* and the life the family lived before the catastrophe.

Questions for Discussion

I move from personal connections to an explication of the text by requiring discussion of questions I have written on the board:

1. Refer to this passage about Elijah: "In his eyes he holds a promise he would like to set free, but he has neither the right nor the power to do so, not yet" (*Anthology*, p. 67). What is the promise? For what or whom is he waiting to set it free?
2. Why does Elie, in his fantasy, endow Elijah "with the majestic beauty of Saul and the strength of Samson"? (p. 67)
3. What is the role of Elijah in the world, according to Jewish tradition?
4. Why does Elie come to believe that Elijah is a "pitiful, stoop-shouldered" Polish Jew?
5. What tradition does the elder Wiesel follow when he invites the stranger home to participate in the *seder*?
6. The guest implores the Wiesels, "Close your books!... Listen to me instead" (p. 69). If they had, would anything have changed for them?
7. How might you answer Elie's question to himself concerning Elijah?: "How then had I deserved what is refused so many others?" (p. 71).
8. When the guest fails to return to the *seder*, where does Elie believe he has gone? How is he transported? What message does he bring to God?
9. Elie asks the questions he says his guest would have asked had he stayed: "Why does God always act too late? Why didn't he get rid of the Angel of Death before he even committed the first murder?" (p. 73).
10. Why did the guest "seem more at ease" than the other Jews on the transport? Why is he the only empty-handed one on the transport, without "bundles on their backs, blankets, valises"? (p. 73)

I ask students to read the questions carefully, go to the board, and initial at least two they can answer using specific text citations to support their conclusions. All questions must be chosen, and no more than five students can initial the same one, a technique that permits both focused work with flexible grouping options and a broad whole-class discussion. All questions are quickly chosen. I ask those who initialed the same one or two questions to form groups; they will have 10 minutes to discuss their responses and pick a representative to summarize conclusions.

As they work, I check for understanding of plot, characters, and allusions; as they report to the whole class, I note varied inferences and interpretations and plan individualized extended research options.

In formulating a response to question 4, Ariella points out that "Eliyahu's disguise allowed him to be invited for the *seder*." Michelle adds, "Elijah was envisioned as the 'poor Jewish refugee from Poland.' So, he knew the horrors before anyone else and had to process that information alone."

Shai explains his group's thinking about question 6: "Elijah's charge, 'Open your eyes to the present' raises Dr. Kempton's questions: What could the Jews of Europe have done had their eyes been open? What could have come of being hopelessly aware of an inevitable death? On the other hand, was the father, in his refusal to hear their guest, wiser than Elijah himself, giving his children a last Passover filled with hope of salvation rather than despair?" These questions, all agree, lead only to more questions.

This discussion engages and focuses them on the essential question articulated by Wiesel himself: "Why does God always act too late?"

"This is ridiculous!" Ariella announces, as her group struggles with question 9. "Why *does* God always come too late? He is our savior if He let 6 million die? Couldn't God be a savior earlier and not make God's people feel lost? Ahhhhh, I'm so frustrated!"

It's clear that students need more time to articulate and clarify their thinking on this profoundly important question. I ask them to review the story, find five passages that have particular significance for them, that move, touch, impress, puzzle, or, yes, frustrate them, and to write the passages with page numbers in their journals for discussion next week. I have come to believe that passages are touchstones for memory; as readers choose and record them on paper, they record them as well in their hearts and minds. The students remain after class, talking heatedly about God's role in the Holocaust. I promise them the next class will be devoted entirely to conversation.

A Silent Conversation

Students arrive for our third class to discover that I have covered the walls with sheets of chart paper, each with a student's name and one with my own. They want to know the purpose, but they are also curious about their classmates' choices of passages.

"We will exchange passages and responses, as promised," I tell them, "but the exchange will be silent. On the chart paper, you'll write your passages with markers—there are 25 of them on my desk—and you'll respond to your classmates' passages the same way. Oral discussion will take place next week."

This technique, an adaptation of "A Conversation without Words" by the Facing History and Ourselves National Foundation (Brookline, Massachusetts), actively engages every student for the entire period, both in citing passages and in responding to others'. It affords the teacher the opportunity to check all students' thinking; as she circulates and reads, she can note what is of particular interest to students.

The students scatter in silence, first writing one passage on their own paper, then circling to assess and write reactions to others, and finally, revisiting each to read the comments and respond to those. I post my own passage: "The first convoy was leaving the ghetto; he was in it. He seemed more at ease than his companions, as if he had already taken this route a thousand times" (*Anthology*, p. 73); and I respond to others'. The only sound is that of markers on paper. The bell rings, students reluctantly finish writing, cap their markers, and leave with a nod, still silent.

We all have those moments in teaching when we know our labors have borne fruit. This was one of mine as I walked around the empty classroom reading, moved by the depth of thought and passion evidenced in the writing. I took the pages home to analyze, savor, and type up to distribute to the class so all students could reflect on their classmates' thinking and ponder the essential questions implicitly raised by the responses.

Below is a small selection of our "Silent Conversation." Each passage is followed by representative responses, edited for length:

Passage 1

"For the child I then was, Yemen was not to be found on any map but somewhere else, in the kingdom of dreams where all sad children, from every city and every century, join hands to defy coercion, the passing years, death." (p. 67)

Responses

"To European Jews, Yemen was a magical place, one that they'd never seen. It was a haven for children. For Eli, he needed a dream place to imagine, where nothing bad could reach him." (Anna)

"This quote reminds me of Israel. On the world map, it's so tiny you could almost not even notice it. And yet its size does not affect it, because Israel is the most amazing place ... magical for people who love it, the same with the Yemenite Jews." (Maya)

"To Wiesel, Yemen is more like heaven or Eden; the belief in which gives hope to despairing children, hope of a better place, much like children in Terezin painted pictures of the moon, away in a different world where Nazis don't exist. Yemenite Jews represent a diversion from the broken Jews of Europe, downtrodden and sad, so removed from the days of Jewish glory. Ironically, this image of the vital Jew was reborn after the Holocaust as the *sabra*, the next Elijah." (Harry)

Passage 2

"It was simply a question of holding out for a few days, a few weeks. Then ... once again the God of Abraham would save his people, as always, at the last moment, when all seems lost." (p. 69)

Responses

"Liberation does not justify extermination or prove the existence of God. What about the 6 million? Does the end of internment show divine intervention or our utterly alone humanity whose will can destroy and save?" (Harry)

"How can hope spring eternal in a place of utter despair, where there is no way out? Because we can draw on our history as Jews, a history filled with tragedy and death. Yet, we are still here. Despite Hitler and Pharaoh, we are still God's beloved people and there will always be hope that God can, and will, save us." (Shai)

"God has always saved his people, through good and bad times. It gave people hope to know that one day they'd be saved. For some, it would help them hang on for one more day." (Anna)

Passage 3:
"Pharaoh is not dead, open your eyes and see, he is destroying our people. Moses is dead … but not Pharaoh; he is alive, he's on his way, soon he'll be at the gates of this city, at the doors of this house: are you sure you'll be spared?" (p. 70)

Responses
"Perhaps this is pure, unadulterated truth, spoken by a true prophet who reflects his time. Elijah gives them not words of hope and encouragement but words of despair in the face of the worst tragedy to have ever affected the human race. Pharaoh will always live, but Moses will not. Therefore, hatred can never be truly eradicated." (Harry)

"So true; hate comes in many forms: Pharaoh, the Church, Hitler, Ahmadinejad. We (as Jews) will never stop being hated. It's like as one pharaoh is gone, a new one comes. Elie was enthralled with this "Elijah" who brought the news about the new pharaoh. But no one listened." (Ariella)

"This is the message of Wiesel's Elijah to us today—to bring value to the tradition of retelling our Jewish stories—it is not merely for the story's sake. Telling the Passover story (in fact, reliving it as tradition commands us) should remind us of the frailty of human nature, the presence of evil in our society." (Shai)

Passage 4
"Each generation begets a prophet in its own image. Wrathful preacher … student … messenger … beadle. … Today, he had the appearance and fate of a poor Jewish refugee from Poland who had seen, too close and too many times, the triumph of death over man and his prayer." (pp. 70–71)

Responses
"A sad commentary on the generation of the Holocaust. Elijah the Prophet, the last bastion of hope, the last stand against evil, even he had been extinguished." (Shai)

"This reminds me of a line from Noah that says, 'He was a good man in his time'; in other words, man is considered good for/in his generation. The mystique of Elijah is his identity. He is one of 'us'—whoever 'us' may be—indiscernible from the rest unless we look hard for him, open our hearts to him. This quotation may say that there really is no Elijah or prophets, but only good men within their times." (Harry)

"I really like that it [the passage] doesn't specify who the prophet is. The prophet could be rich, poor, black, white, or man or woman, young or old." (Ariella)

Passage 5
"His fiery chariot was waiting to carry him up to the heavens: is that not proof enough that he was the prophet Elijah?" (p. 73)

Responses
"I believe the boy realize[d] that the strange guest was a symbolic sending from God, warning the Jews." (Michelle)

Fiery chariot, or train to certain death, both can be the same given different frames of reference. Each generation molds the prophet. For the generation of the Holocaust, Elijah's mode of transportation could be none other than the trains, the trains that led millions to near certain death." (Shai)

Finding Essential Questions in Classroom Conversation

Our fourth session begins as I distribute copies of students' written responses and we share reflections. All students say that they appreciated the activity because their writing to one another was authentic, public, purposeful, and uninterrupted; responses from peers were immediate and honest; and because standing and writing was a liberating change from writing at their desks, "a serious assignment that was really cool and different," comments Julia.

I tell them that it was even more than that. I explain that I have seen in their work the seeds of inquiry crucial to the study of the Holocaust, inquiry that forms the heart of their attempt to make this subject personally meaningful. I have "grown" these seeds into essential questions and typed them on the cover sheet of their packet of responses, and we discuss these as well. This is, perhaps, the most important part of the silent conversation, and one which will provide thoughtful discussion prompts for the entire semester. I explain how I arrived at these questions.

For passage one, Anna, Maya, and Harry identified the need for "a haven for children," "a dream place," a "magical" place, "hope to despairing children," and "the next Elijah." In essence, I felt, they were investigating the question, "What role does the mechanism of hope play in the survival of children?"

The second and third passages provoked Harry, Shai, Anna, and Ariella to debate the existence of God, raising the essential theological issue, "How do we balance belief in God with the reality of the Holocaust?" In responses that balanced hope and despair, Elijah and his warnings, they evoked several more foundational queries: "How can optimism and pessimism each serve both as an ally and an enemy in the face of a threat to one's existence? Can one choose one's outlook? Do the values of tradition and learning help to maintain the Jewish people?"

When the comment "We as Jews will always be hated" is underscored by the names of Pharaoh and today's enemies, the students' underlying concern may be seen as "In what ways is Israel an answer to the questions posed by Holocaust?"

Harry's and Shai's notes about the generation of the Holocaust, that "there are only good men within their times" and "each generation molds the prophet," raised for me profoundly relevant questions of leadership: Are leaders judged only in comparison to others in their time and culture? If so, what are the ramifications of these limits?

The students are surprised, pleased, and proud that their comments bear such rich fruit. They agree that these questions demand ongoing examination and recognize that their silent conversation was, in fact, a search for meaning.

Assessment and Evaluation

Assessment consists of gathering evidence of learning for the process of evaluation. My evidence includes students' reflections on essential questions, those that raise issues larger than the story content, that have no specific answers, that are applicable to our lives. Raising and exploring such questions help me meet another of my goals: encouraging students to want to keep learning.

My assessment is also based on journal responses, discussion, reactions to text-based questions, outside learning, and attitude toward and interest in aspects of the Holocaust. If a student researches Jewish life in Sighet before the war, or Wiesel's childhood, or the prophet Elijah as seen throughout history, changing roles to reflect the times, I would consider my objective met. If a student finishes a lengthy journal entry on the traditions of Passover, as Shai did, by writing, "It is our mandate as Jews to live for justice and peace. Because we were slaves in Egypt, we must protect not only our fellow Jews but also all who are downtrodden," I consider my goal fulfilled. When students remain after class to ask questions and share opinions, I evaluate their ongoing interest as evidence of success.

If students remember Elie Wiesel and his father at their *seder* table and their mysterious, stoop-shouldered *seder* guest; if they remember and retell these stories to their parents and, someday, their children, does this signify a triumph of memory over murder? Is there such a thing? Perhaps not. However, as teachers, we are creating the storytellers of the future. By sharing survivors' stories, we give our students voice; they, in turn, give voice to memory.

As the survivors of the *Shoah* pass into history, leaving no witnesses but their words, succeeding generations must assume responsibility for keeping the knowledge of the *Shoah* alive, for telling its tales: for "that is our primary obligation."

REFERENCES

Berenbaum, M. (1993). *The world must know.* Boston: Little, Brown and Company.

Berenbaum, M. (2003). *A promise to remember: The Holocaust in the words and voices of survivors.* Boston: Bulfinch Press.

Gelber, M. (2008). Elijah the prophet questions Jewish tradition: Elie Wiesel's "An evening guest." In K. Shawn & K. Goldfrad (Eds.), *The call of memory: Learning about the Holocaust through narrative: A teacher's guide*, pp. 117–122. Teaneck, NJ: Ben Yehuda Press.

Gilbert, M. (1982). *Atlas of the Holocaust.* Great Britain: Michael Joseph Limited.

PBS Web sites: "Elie Wiesel: First person singular" (Retrieved April 17, 2007, from *http://www.pbs.org/eliewiesel/life/index.html*) including "The life and work of Wiesel: A biographical overview," and, by Gary Henry, "Story and silence: Transcendence in the work of Elie Wiesel" at *http://www.pbs.org/eliewiesel/life/henry.html*.

Wiesel, E. (1968). An evening guest. In K. Shawn & K. Goldfrad (Eds.), (2008). *The call of memory: Learning about the Holocaust through narrative: An anthology*, pp. 67–73. Teaneck, NJ: Ben Yehuda Press.

Under Occupation

Children with a Star:
Ilse Aichinger's Unique Perspective

Jakob Hessing

Ilse Aichinger shares the fate of writers like James Joyce: she is famous, but she is hardly ever read. Her first and only novel[1]—*Die größere Hoffnung* (1948), translated as *Herod's Children* (1964)—is considered a masterpiece, but its unique narrative structure makes for difficult reading. "Fear of Fear" (Shawn & Gold-frad, *Anthology*, 2008, pp. 77–95), the story under discussion here, is the fifth chapter of the novel, but Aichinger has given it no number. Her narrative has no plot in the traditional sense, and to a large extent, the chapters can be read as independent stories with very little information needed to fill in the gaps, provided readers have prior knowledge of the particular aspects of the Holocaust that Aichinger explores.

The protagonist of the novel and of the story "Fear of Fear" is Ellen, a young girl living in Vienna during the years of the Holocaust with only her Jewish grandmother to support her. Her mother, who is Jewish, has apparently immigrated to America; her father, a non-Jew, has abandoned her; and in this story her grandmother has left their apartment to learn what she can about rumored deportations, leaving Ellen alone. This circumstance thus creates the narrative perspective of a child who is orphaned in more than one sense. Throughout the novel, no grownup person looks back upon his childhood under Hitler, as so many characters do in Germany's postwar literature.[2] Instead, Aichinger presents a world of children *without* the wisdom of hindsight and with almost no adult logic superimposed upon its meaning.

Aichinger was born to a Jewish mother and a non-Jewish father in Vienna in 1921. Her parents were divorced in 1926, and at first glance, her novel seems to be an autobiographical memory. However, Ellen, in fact, is very different from the author. She is much younger than Aichinger was in the early 1940s, and neither mother nor daughter emigrated before the war. While her twin sister, Helga, went to England when it was still possible, Ilse deliberately stayed in Austria to protect her mother. Under Nazi rule Ilse was considered "half Jewish," and the

---

[1] Aichinger has later concentrated on writing poetry and short prose like her famous "Story in a Mirror," where the limitations of an artificial plot could be evaded more easily.

[2] The best known example is Oskar Matzerath in Günter Grass's *The Tin Drum*, but the phenomenon is ubiquitous in the literature of the period.

fact that she was partly "Aryan" saved her mother from deportation,[3] although many other members of the family were murdered.

Rather than being autobiographical, the novel inverts Aichinger's actual experience. While in real life mother and daughter survived the war together, Ellen's mother has, oddly, left her child behind. The reader does not know, however, whether this "emigration" is merely a euphemism employed by, say, her grandmother who does not want Ellen to know that her mother was deported. So far, no critic has considered this possibility,[4] but our reading of the story will try to take account of such implications.

"Fear of Fear" begins with Ellen laughing "happily" as she looks at herself wearing the star, "that wonderful star" (p. 77). It is the star that the Nazis have forced upon the Jews in order to separate them from the general population. Children do not live by the calendar, and, accordingly, there are no dates in the novel; but the star, nevertheless, gives us a clue. It was introduced by law on September 1, 1941 (Rosenkranz , 1978, p. 280), and by that time, Jews in Vienna were already being sent to the East. The first deportations—still obscured as a program of "resettlement"—took place in February and March 1941 (p. 255). In the opening chapter of the novel, sometime between spring and autumn, Ellen goes to the consulate in order to obtain a visa. She dreams of her mother who has, apparently, left for America, and now she wants to join her. Judging by the historical background of Ellen's experience, it is quite possible that the adults are hiding the truth from her, and that her mother did not immigrate but had been deported earlier in the spring.

Ellen, looking at herself in the mirror, is shown to be laughing happily at the image of the star, and we as readers are, from this moment, drawn to wonder why. Her view of the star will be central to our understanding of the compelling narrative that unfolds. In the eyes of the Nazis, she is a *Mischling*, a half-breed who, because of her "Aryan" father, does not have to wear the yellow badge. The privilege, however, leaves her in a void. Being left without her parents, she is now about to lose her friends as well. Gentiles do not accept her, and she has become a stranger to them; without the yellow badge she does not belong to the outcast, either.

In her loneliness, Ellen chooses to join the children with the star. It was her Jewish grandmother who, after having lost her daughter already, tried to prevent her from doing so—"'Never in the world!' her grandmother had said. 'Be happy

---

[3] In Austria, Jewish mothers of half-Jewish children under the age of 21 were not deported.

[4] Even Rosenberger, who has published the most comprehensive and illuminating study of the text, accepts the emigration of Ellen's mother at face value. Cf. Nicole Rosenberger, *Poetik des Ungefügten. Zur Darstellung von Krieg und Verfolgung in Ilse Aichinger's Roman 'Die größere Hoffnung.'* Wien: Braumüller, 1998, p. 50. As a rule, critics tend to concentrate on textual and structural analysis of the novel; neglecting the historical background to which it refers, they have little to say about the real world in which this novel of Jewish children under Hitler is situated.

you're spared that'" (*Anthology*, p. 77)—but Ellen, whose central perspective we continue to follow, needs friends. Staying alone in the apartment, she seizes the opportunity to put on the coveted star. As she watches her grandmother leave the house, we get a glimpse at the way in which a child transforms the elements of an incomprehensible situation into pieces of the imagination:

> Her grandmother had gone away. She had turned the corner, like a rolling ship. As long as she could still be seen, her umbrella drove like a black sail against the wet wind. Indecisive rumors blew frostily down the alleys of the island. Her grandmother had gone away to discover more information. (p. 77)

A "wet wind" is blowing in the streets; it is almost winter now. The season offers another clue to the reader: After a break during the summer of 1941, the deportations began again in October and continued without intermission until the end of 1944 (Rosenkranz, p. 282). When her grandmother goes out to gather information about "indecisive rumors," we get a clear hint about developments unintelligible to the child, which she must internalize in her own way. Such hints, as we shall see, are interspersed throughout the text as a means of emphasizing young Ellen's feelings as they develop.

In this scene, for example, the child does not know what is going on, but the images in her mind are closely linked to her desire to escape. She wishes to join her mother in America and often dreams of a ship that will take her across the ocean.[5] Now, watching her grandmother in the street, she sees her "like a rolling ship" with her umbrella "like a black sail," as the author allows these images to suggest ambivalent possibilities in the young girl's mind. They may conjure up the hopes of rescue, but they also speak of Ellen's fear of being abandoned once again, this time by her grandmother going across the sea.

Near the end of this same scene, the word "island" marks another transformation in the mind of the child and can be traced to historical facts. Connected with the imagery of the ship and the sail, this passage also suggests that Ellen sees herself as is living on an island. As early as 1938, Jews were being forced to leave their apartments in Vienna, and by May 1941, they had to move into designated areas, sites of segregated living, that can be defined as a semi-ghetto (Rosenkranz, p. 230).[6] As a half-breed, Ellen could perhaps have lived somewhere else, but by staying with her grandmother, she is confined to a circumscribed living space and thus imagines herself to be the inhabitant of an island.

The ghetto existence becomes palpable as we read about George, who is celebrating his birthday. He belongs to the group of Jewish children who must wear the star, and whom Ellen wishes to join. This, actually, is the reason she happily wears the star on this day—she wants to go to George's birthday party.

---

5 This is the central imagery in the first chapter of the novel, where Ellen visits the consulate.

6 Areas reserved for Jews were the II., IX. and XX. quarter of Vienna.

When we first see George in his home, no one has yet arrived. He wears a special suit for the occasion, but the star on the jacket has "spoiled all George's joy. ... Despairingly George laid his hand over it, then let it fall" (*Anthology*, pp. 81, 82).

While Ellen is happy to wear the star, George wants to get rid of it. It blacks out the sun for him, the source of life and the symbol of his happy childhood. When his guests arrive, Ellen is not among them, and as they take their seats at the table, George stands up to give a speech; but crying from "the young man next door" "drowned George's words" (p. 83).

The "young man next door" does not live in a different apartment. He shares the same flat with several tenants, just like the lady who has given George the tablecloth for his party. George, too, is one of these tenants, and he gives his party in the narrow space he shares with his father, their beds "pushed to the wall in order to make room" (p. 81). They are all strangers here, perched together in the area allocated to them by the Nazi authorities.

The young man next door is crying because he has been uprooted like every-body else in this house, and the birthday party, like all other events of the story, is merely a game of children in a world of disaster. In their own way they are aware of it, of course, but they can only react as children do, sharing and revealing, wanting and not wanting to know secrets that reflect their understanding of the realities they all face.

"I don't want to know!" screamed George. "Today's my birthday and I don't want to know!" Even so, Herbert tells him: "Bibi said: the star means death" (p. 85).

In the beginning, Ellen's grandmother leaves the house to find out about the "indecisive rumors" in the ghetto. Now we see how these rumors find their way into the world of the children: Bibi has heard something—"the star means death"—and she passes it on in her childish way. Aichinger represents Jewish life under Hitler through the games children play, and historical chronology bears out their performance: in the autumn of 1941 the deportations were taken up again.

As soon as the secret is given away, however, the children cannot go on with their party. It has become hot in the room; they let in some air and imagine one final game of ultimate escape:

> "If we were to jump now?" Kurt said hoarsely. "One right after the other. It would take just a moment, and then we wouldn't be afraid any more. Not afraid. Just think of it!"
> The children closed their eyes and saw themselves clearly, jump-ing one after the other. Black, quick and straight, as though there were water below. ... "Today's my birthday," George reminds the children. "You're all very impolite." (p. 86)

"Birthday" versus suicide—life and death is in the balance. In their fear of fear, the children reveal the despair underneath their games, and it is worth noting

Aichinger's use of water imagery here to convey her central focus upon the child's interpretive point of view. When Ellen dreams of her escape, she conjures up ships and oceans; and the children in the ghetto think of water, too: leaning out of the window and imagining their death as a final escape, the invisible courtyard seems to them "as dark and deep as the sea" (p. 86).

Ellen, on her way to the party, has stopped to buy a birthday cake. She enters the bakery, but she is wearing her star for the first time and does not know what it means. Putting her money on the counter, she asks for the cake, but the saleswoman refuses to sell it to her, a child with a star. The cake is her present for George, and he is waiting for it, but her attempt to buy it turns out to be a catastrophe for Ellen. Empty-handed, she is thrown out of the bakery. She is deeply shocked, and the star takes on a new meaning for her. She has lost her way, and the star, her source of pride, now leads her where she does not really want to go: to Julia, a Jewish girl a few years older than Ellen and quite different from her. Julia is required to wear a star, but she refuses to do so; she no longer leaves her house. She has obtained a visa for America and has cut herself off from the other Jewish children. George and his friends despise her and consider her a traitor, but Ellen, against her own will, suddenly finds herself at the door to Julia's apartment.

Ellen is, in effect, paying a visit to a possible alter ego. Having been deeply wounded at the bakery because of the star to which she is by now committed, Ellen is far more ambivalent and confused. She begins to take a look at the other side, the dark underside of her position including the meanings of the central star. For a moment, it seems as though she wishes to fulfill her dreams of escape through the figure of Julia; in talking to lucky Julia, Ellen projects her hopes, her fears, and her envy. There is a tacit irony to their conversation. Julia may have been granted a visa for America, but it is highly improbable that she will ever escape. In October 1941, while the deportations were being taken up again, Himmler issued another restriction, according to which all emigration of Jews was to be prohibited immediately (Rosenkranz, p. 284).

Now another friend, Anna, enters the room wearing a "gleaming" star. "I washed it yesterday," Anna says. "If I've got to wear it, it might as well gleam." Here is yet another glimpse of childhood reactions to that central image.

Ellen responds bitterly. "I'm not allowed to wear one! I've got two wrong grandparents too few. And so they say I don't belong."

Anna answers with a laugh. "Maybe it's all the same whether you wear it on your coat or in your face" (*Anthology*, p. 90).

By now it is obvious that the star is the central issue in the story. Ellen decides to wear it, although she does not have to, and she is punished for it; George feels tortured by it; the children whisper about it; Julia tries to avoid wearing it by all possible means; and Anna relates to it in terms far beyond its material dimension: if you can wear it "in your face," it is surely more than a yellow badge.

What, then, can we understand the meaning of the star to be, especially as this story presents it from the children's point of view? Although it is not easy to answer, the question is of crucial importance to any profound reading of the text. The perspective of children leaves little room for abstract language, and theoretical concepts about symbols and their meaning won't help us to understand Ellen's experience.[7] In meeting Julia and Anna, Ellen is faced with two distinct alternatives that become clearer as the dialogues unfold. Julia asks Anna, "Do you always have a reason for being so cheerful?"

"Yes," replied Anna. "Don't you?"

"No," said Julia hesitatingly. "Even though I'm going to America next week" (p. 90). Although Julia seems to be the lucky one, she is not cheerful. However, Anna is, and Ellen wants to know why. She identifies Anna with the star, just as Anna had done when she noticed that Ellen wore the star in her face. It has become a part of their nature, and they recognize each other by its gleam. When Anna says that she is going away, too, Ellen "saw for a moment a break in the shine. In Anna's face she saw fear, deathly fear, and a tortured mouth" (p. 92). Anna is calm and cheerful; her sudden "deathly fear" seems incoherent, but we think so merely because the dialogue has not yet reached its final point.

"Can we travel together?"

"No," said Anna. "Our directions are different…. I've been—I've been ordered to Poland" (p. 92).

Things fall into place. Anna is being deported, but the fear in her face does not concern herself. She is afraid for Ellen; both of them adhere to the star, and the young girl will try to follow her wherever she goes. Anna knows, however, that she is going to her death. She has come to say good-bye, and when she is asked, "Can we travel together?" we do not know who is asking. Julia wants her company on the journey across the ocean, Ellen will go wherever Anna is going, and she answers both of them: "Our directions are different." She is not going to America, and she does not want Ellen to come along.

Anna hesitates for a moment before she reveals her destination. The sentence hits Ellen, raising the hidden fear lurking under her dream of joining her mother: "For the first time, Ellen heard it aloud. All the fear in the world was locked in it" (p. 92). Whether Ellen, at this moment, is aware of the possibility that her mother, too, was "ordered to Poland," we cannot say. However, Anna's enormous hope wipes away the fear in her face, and Ellen recognizes the gleam again. Now she thinks that she has understood the meaning of the star, and happy with her new knowledge, she runs off to call the children who are at George's birthday party.

As she rushes into the room, they are still at the window pondering their suicide. In vain George has tried to lure them away, and it is only Ellen's entrance and request to follow her and find the meaning of the star that breaks the spell. Afraid of their suicidal moment, they are happy to follow Ellen's call. As they run through the streets, Aichinger explicitly describes a scene of deportation, but the children are filled with new hope and "no longer saw the small heavily laden vans

---

7 Rosenberger convincingly reads the novel in the context of Albert Camus's myth of Sisyphus, but this only makes sense in Aichinger's, not Ellen's, perspective; cf. Rosenberger, pp. 160 ff.

at the edge of the railroad in the dark, nor the tearful faces nor the smiles of the uncaring guards. Like Ellen, they saw only the star" (p. 93).

They enter Julia's house and they, too, are captivated by Anna's personality. They gather around her, and once again the images of mother and child, of a ship and a journey are evoked. "They sat down in a circle on the floor. Steerage passengers. It suddenly seemed as if they'd been traveling a long time."

"We want to know what the star means" (p. 93), they say to Anna.

It is the beginning of the final scene, and one cannot easily decide whether or not it is a successful ending to the story. Anna is expected to explain the meaning of the star, but the star means everything, and "everything" cannot be cut to proportions handed down in a lesson. It represents the *größere Hoffnung* of the original title, the *greater hope* that will always be greater than reality. While Anna tries her best, she has to rely on the logics of adult thinking. She asks the children why they want to learn about the star, and they admit their fear of the secret police:

"They hate us."

"Have you done something to them?"

"Nothing," said Herbert (p. 94).

The dialogue is weak because it tries to find a reason for evil. Of course, the kind of evil associated with the Gestapo has no reason, and the "explanation" Anna and the children finally come up with is not really convincing: "The secret police is afraid!"

"Of course," said Anna. "The secret police *is* fear. Living fear, nothing else."

…"The secret police is afraid!"

"And we're afraid of them!"

"Fear of fear—they cancel out" (p. 94).

In the darkness of its fear—thus Anna teaches the children—the secret police is searching for the light of the star. Her "lesson" may have helped them to get out of their depression, but is it really more than a sophisticated game she has played with the youngsters? Is the equation it has produced—"The secret police *is* fear"—an honest attempt to come to grips with the situation? Can it actually be understood by the children? Or isn't it rather a kind of theodicy, invented by adults—by Anna or, for that matter, by Aichinger—who replace evil with something else so that they can deal with it more easily?

These are questions that every reader will have to decide for himself, and Aichinger is rather ambivalent about it. One should, therefore, be careful not to mistake Ellen's adherence to the star for any "Jewish" solidarity on Ellen's or on Aichinger's part. "The secret police *is* fear. Living fear, nothing else" sounds more Christian than Jewish. This is reflected in the English title of the novel, *Herod's Children*; Ellen's last remark and Anna's reply contain an overt reference to the star of Bethlehem and the birth of Jesus: "'The star!' said Ellen, with glowing cheeks. 'The Wise Men's star—I knew it all the time!'—'Be sorry for the secret police,' said Anna. 'They're afraid of the King of the Jews again'" (p. 95).

Towards the end of the story, there is a certain irony in the words that Anna says to the children: "Don't let yourselves be led astray. … That's all I can tell you.

Follow the star. Don't ask grownups; they won't tell you the truth, not the deep truth" (p. 95).

Aichinger wants to make sense of the incomprehensible, but by introducing an adult perspective into the world of the children, she breaks the rules of her imagination. The grownups do not keep their promises, and even Anna does not have the answer. Not in this story, but by the end of the novel, Ellen and all the other children will have died. It is no accident that in trying to cope with the Holocaust and its implications, her narrative has reached the breaking point: Aichinger will never again try to write a novel.

REFERENCES

Aichinger, I. (1964). Fear of fear. In K. Shawn & K. Goldfrad (Eds.). (2008), *The Call of memory: Learning about the Holocaust through narrative: An anthology*, pp. 77–95. Teaneck, NJ: Ben Yehuda Press.

Aichinger, I. (1964). *Herod's children*. New York: Atheneum.

Rosenberger, N. (1998). *Poetik des Ungefügten. Zur Darstellung von Krieg und Verfolgung in Ilse Aichinger's Roman 'Die größere Hoffnung.'* Wien: Braumüller.

Rosenkranz, H. (1978). Verfolgung und Selbstbehauptung. *Die Juden in Österreich 1938–1945.* Wien: Herold.

Dignity Amidst Despair
in Ilse Aichinger's "Fear of Fear"

Barbara Appelbaum

> *We lived permanently between fear and hope.*
> *Our situation really could not have been more absurd.*
> —Helmut Kruger

As the former director of the Jewish Community Federation's Center for Holocaust Awareness and Information in Rochester, New York, I often worked with students and teachers from public and Catholic schools. When I brought Holocaust survivors into these classrooms, students frequently asked them, "Were you ever sorry to be Jewish?" or "Did you or your parents consider converting?"

I was frankly surprised by how often such questions were asked, however hesitantly, until I realized what lay behind them: the naïve assumption that being Jewish then, as now, was a choice. These young learners did not realize that, in Nazi ideology, being Jewish was not a religious or a cultural identity that one could exchange, if one wished, for another, but was instead an imposed "racial" identity determined by bloodline.

As Freund and Safrian (1997) note in "Reflections on Project 'Registration by Name: Austrian Victims of the Holocaust'":

> Religious, cultural, and political affiliation did not play a definitive role in Nazi persecution of Jews; classification as a Jew by the Nazi regime was the only decisive factor. ... In 1933, the Nazis declared a Jew to be anyone of "non-Aryan descent," [that is,] people with at least one Jewish parent or grandparent—regardless of his [or her] religious affiliation. (*http://www.doew.at/thema/themalt/holocaust/namerfass/engl2.html* p. 1)

"Aryans" were those people who had no Jewish grandparents and no connection to the Jewish community.

Mischlinge

The Nuremberg Laws, enacted in September 1935, forbade marriage between "Aryans" and "Jews" and classified children and grandchildren of those already intermarried as *Mischlinge* (*Mischling*, singular). The denotation of the word *Mis-*

chlinge is "of mixed blood" or "hybrid," but it has negative connotations, as in "mixed breed" or "mongrel." Kaplan (1998) writes that "there may have been as many as 300,000 '*Mischlinge*' and another 100,000 persons who, 'in one degree or another counted Jews among their immediate ancestry' and were thus affected by racial laws" of Nazi Germany (p. 75).

People who were thus labeled were differentiated according to degree. Those who did not belong to the Jewish community and did not have a Jewish spouse but who had two Jewish grandparents were "first-degree *Mischlinge*." Those who had one Jewish grandparent were "second-degree *Mischlinge*." Grandparents were considered Jewish if they belonged to the Jewish religious community. (Note the irony. In spite of their attempts to label Jews as a race, in the final analysis, the Nazis had to rely on the religious affiliation of the grandparent as the basis for Jewish identity.)

One might assume, Freund and Safrian write, "that all those *defined* as Jews by the Nuremberg racial laws ... *identified* themselves as Jews [italics mine], [but] this assumption does not apply ... to 'Jews' of Christian persuasion or certain assimilated Jews" (p. 1). Many Jewish Germans and Austrians were so assimilated into the modern, secular, Western European culture that they did not even have an idea of what being Jewish meant. Some had converted to Christianity before the Holocaust and did not consider themselves to be Jewish at all. *Mischlinge* who were raised as Christians or with no religious affiliation also did not consider themselves Jewish. To find themselves classified as Jews and subject to humiliation, segregation, and deprivation raised unique issues not typically presented in Holocaust literature.

"Fear of Fear"

Ilse Aichinger, herself a *Mischling*, explores this experience in "Fear of Fear" (Shawn & Goldfrad, *Anthology*, 2008, pp. 77–95), a story about young secular Jews and *Mischlinge* living in Greater Germany in the early 1940s, isolated by the Nazis from their friends and families as the net of death tightened around all the Jews of Europe. This narrative, from Aichinger's *Herod's Children*, a postwar classic published in German in 1948 and in English in 1964, offers rare insight into the lives of these fully secularized and part-Jewish children as they face isolation and discrimination, as they see family and friends emigrating or deported, and as they struggle to make sense of the inexplicable disintegration of their lives.

Memoirs such as Victor Klemperer's *I Will Bear Witness 1933–1941: A Diary of the Nazi Years* (1998); Cynthia Crane's *Divided Lives: The Untold Stories of Jewish-Christian Women in Nazi Germany* (2000); and Bella Fromm's *Blood & Banquets: A Berlin Diary 1930–1938* (1990); as well as those analyzed in Josey G. Fisher's *The Persistence of Youth: Oral Testimonies of the Holocaust* (1991), detail the lives of adults in Germany; but little beyond Ilse Koehn's *Mischlinge, Second Degree: My Childhood in Nazi Germany* (1977) is written from the perspective of a *Mischling* child. Teaching students of the circumstances of these children, all cruelly victimized by Nazi ideology, may help readers understand the deadly racial antisemitism that infected the German State and led to the murder of 6 million Jews and the torment of hundreds of thousands of others, simply and solely because they were descended from Jewish grandparents.

Audience and Goals

"Fear of Fear" is best suited for a senior advanced-placement English, Holocaust studies, or theology class, or a literature of the Holocaust or theology course in college or graduate school. This cryptic story, with its sophisticated philosophical concepts and Christian allusions, needs close reading and analysis. At least four class periods of 50 minutes are necessary to do justice to this story.

I had ideal 80-minute periods and the privilege of teaching it to seniors at Aquinas Institute, a co-ed Catholic school in Rochester, New York, in a theology class that focuses on the Holocaust and was taught by my colleague and friend Patrick Connelly. Patrick, author of an essay in this *Guide* (pp. 384–397), sat in daily as an active participant. With its Christian themes, this story is particularly appropriate for this audience, and I was eager to see how these students would react to the issues and essential questions it raises. Through oral reading, guided small- and large-group discussions, outside reading assignments, journal writing, and careful attention to setting, characters, theme, figurative language, and plot conflicts, we hoped that our students would

- understand the concepts of racial antisemitism and Nazi racial ideology and their effects on the Jewish and nominally Jewish population of Greater Germany through 1941;
- identify, understand, and appreciate the challenges particular to secular Jews and *Mischlinge*;
- articulate, analyze, and empathize with the choices these youngsters made as they tried to make sense of their ruptured world, maintain their sense of self and a semblance of their former lives, and prepare for the future; and
- examine and respond to the author's skillful use of dialogue and figurative language to convey both the dignity and the desperation of the characters.

Setting the Scene

At Aquinas, each class begins with the traditional Lord's Prayer and prayers for people students wish to mention. Now settled and attentive, they turn to the work at hand. I tell them we will read a story about young people during the Holocaust, but first I will present material to contextualize the literature, necessary even with the broad background in Holocaust history they have gained in this class. I refer them to the abridged list of anti-Jewish laws decreed between April 1933 and May 1942 that they have read in Susan Prinz Shear's "Saving History: Letters from the Holocaust: Teaching 'No Way Out'" (Shawn & Goldfrad, *Guide*, 2008, pp. 52–71), since these laws will help us later to clarify the setting.

I highlight March 13, 1938, the *Anschluss*, when Austria, our setting, was annexed to Germany, its Jews to suffer the same fate as those in Germany; and October 23, 1941, when all emigration from Greater Germany was stopped, effectively trapping its Jews. I review the Nuremberg Laws and the Law for the

Protection of German Blood and Honor, reminding students that the edicts, among other restrictions, deprived Jews of their German citizenship (they are now "State subjects") and forbade marriages between Jews and non-Jews.

In a brief lecture, I establish that when the Nazis took over Austria, Austrian Jews became subject to the Nuremberg Laws. Non-Jews already married to Jewish spouses were encouraged to divorce them and abandon their Jewish children, even if those children had been formally converted to Christianity. Children of such mixed marriages were classified as *Mischlinge,* a term I write on the board and define. By 1939, I note, there were close to 110,000 such children of mixed marriages in German and Austria (Noakes, 1989; Abrams, 1985).

Although in most cases these children were not persecuted as severely as *Volljuden,* "full Jews," a term I explain as well, and were not subject to all the restrictive laws, they nonetheless suffered their own kind of hell, completely isolated from both Jewish and Christian communities. Coming from secular or Christian families, many such children knew little or nothing about Judaism. Even if a youngster wanted to identify as a Jew, the Jewish community would naturally focus their attention first on alleviating the increasingly dire circumstances of their own members, the "full Jews" who were most at risk. Not considered Aryan either, *Mischlinge* had to face persecution and exclusion from the very society into which they had assimilated.

The Nazis created "Jewish houses" *(Judenhauser),* another term I define, apartments set aside, usually in the Jewish sections of cities where, from the end of April, 1939, Jewish families were consolidated; students need this information to understand the story. Although not ghettos in the strict sense of the word, they had the effect of concentrating Jews into one place where the Nazis could more easily supervise them. As more and more Jewish families were forced to live in a limited number of houses, whole families wound up in one room. Adults, themselves struggling with the increasing difficulties that their mixed marriage now caused them and their extended families, whose loyalties were more often than not strained to the breaking point, tried to maintain a degree of normalcy despite increasing deprivations and the threat of deportation to the "East." They protected their children by telling them little about their actual situation. In truth, adults *knew* very little about what awaited them but feared the worst. Although they desperately sought avenues of escape, their options were constantly diminishing.

"To help you understand the situation of Ellen, our protagonist, a child of a mixed marriage," I begin, "I'm giving you a chapter from Marion Kaplan's book *Between Dignity and Despair: Everyday Life in Nazi Germany* (1998, pp. 74–93) and an excellent article from Gutman's (Ed.) *Encyclopedia of the Holocaust* (Volume 3, New York: Macmillan, pp. 981–983). Read them before or after you read the short story; you'll get a much clearer sense of the conditions under which Ellen and others like her lived under Nazi rule."

In the powerful and complex narrative we're about to read, I explain, we see these young adolescents struggling to break through their ignorance, to understand what is happening around them as they live in their island of isolation. Surrounded by peers in similar circumstances, they maintain friendships, celebrate a birthday, and try to hold onto a sense of freedom, normalcy, and control over their lives. Like the adults, the children do not know what is happening or what the future holds, but they accept, as their parents cannot, that uncertainty may be the only certainty. The children try to put on a brave face, their struggles to do so emphasized by the story's title, "Fear of Fear."

Scaffolding

I write the title on the board and request random associations. I'm hoping a student will recall President Franklin D. Roosevelt's words, "The only thing we have to fear is fear itself," but no one does, so I give them the relevant paragraph of the speech that I had readied, noting that the line comes from the Roosevelt's first Inaugural Address, given on March 4, 1933:

> This great nation will endure as it has endured, will revive, and will prosper. So, first of all, let me assert my firm belief that the only thing we have to fear is fear itself—nameless, unreasoning, unjustified terror, which paralyzes needed efforts to convert retreat into advance. In every dark hour of our national life, a leadership of frankness and vigor has met with that understanding and support of the people themselves, which is essential to victory.

I suggest that as students read they reflect on the author's choice of those famous words as her title, given the reality of the Holocaust. If time and interests allow, there are current applications as well; you might suggest, for instance, that students consider President Roosevelt's words in the aftermath of 9/11 and other acts of terror worldwide. Do his thoughts resonate today? Where, today, have our collective fears led our country and us as individuals?

We turn to "Fear of Fear," and I distribute stapled packets of lined paper for students to use as their writing journal and a stack of Post-It notes for students to mark passages worthy of special comment. Author Ilse Aichinger, I tell them, was born in Vienna, Austria, in 1921. Like Ellen, the protagonist, Ilse's father was Christian and her mother Jewish, making Ilse a *Mischling* under Nazi law. Ilse's parents divorced when she was five years old. Her maternal great-grandmother, aunts, and uncles were all deported and murdered during the Holocaust.

I had considered assigning the story to be read as homework, but Patrick and I agreed that it was too challenging for students to tackle alone. Reading it in class would help me monitor understanding and afford me the opportunity to explain references.

Methodology

Since there are many characters and much dialogue, I chose the methodology of Readers' Theater (see Shear's essay in this *Guide*, pp. 52–71), and with Patrick's help assigned readers for the narrator, Ellen, Grandmother, deaf old man, saleswoman, customers, George, Kurt, Leon, Ruth, Bibi, Herbert, Hannah, Julia, and

Anna. We divided the narration among five strong readers because the part is quite long; expand or limit your readers as necessary to involve all students.

Cold readings are difficult, and this story is complex, but I assure students that after they rehearse the story and attend to its tone and nuances at home, complete it in tomorrow's class, and analyze it with their peers, they will master it. Now, beginning the reading in class will ground them for tonight's reading.

The vocabulary is simple, but they will not know the word *escutcheon* in the first sentence, so before we begin to read, I give two definitions of the word and ask the class to write them in their journals.

1. A shield or shield-shaped emblem used to display a coat of arms
2. An ornamental or protective plate fixed around something, such as a light switch or a keyhole.

The first short page is narration; at its end, we stop reading aloud.

"What do you make of these enigmatic paragraphs, of the star, darkness, happiness, and secrets?" I ask. "Why was Ellen so happy wearing the star?" Students are silent; there is more puzzlement than understanding.

The Central Metaphor

To help them relate to the story's central metaphor, the yellow star, I say, "Many of you are wearing today an item that serves to define you: jewelry, an item of clothing, a school uniform, or something you are carrying. It might be something that you chose to wear, or, like the uniform, is chosen for you. Take five minutes and, in your journal, briefly describe the item and the impression of you it may create to someone who sees you for the first time. Would this impression be accurate or misleading? What would you choose to wear that would best reveal who you really are?"

In the sharing that follows their writing, students agree that people frequently draw inaccurate or incomplete conclusions about us from what we wear. For example, Bethany says that because she often wears a necklace with a cross, people think she is very religious, but, in fact, she is not. She likes to wear it because her favorite grandmother gave it to her. The class notes that how people view us varies with what we wear; much is interpreted. What we intend and what people see can be two different things, as in a school uniform, which may stereotype its wearers as "rich and snobby," but which students themselves believe represents the school and its values of "respect, honesty, and kindness."

Again, connections to today's headlines are limited only by your time restraints. Muslim women wearing head scarves, Jewish men wearing *yarmulkes*, black men wearing bandanas, and white men wearing baseball caps backwards all project an image that may be at odds with what the wearer intends, desires, or assumes.

Our discussion, though, has been about choices. I remind students of the German edict requiring every Jew six years old and over to wear a yellow Star of David with the German word for Jew, *Jude*, printed on it in black. Wearing the star to indicate one's Jewish identity was not a choice during the Holocaust; failure to wear it could be a death sentence. Jews had to use their limited resources to purchase these stars, which had to be sewn on the left side of the chest and displayed on each item of clothing. Once a symbol of pride, the six-pointed star was then used by the Nazis as a badge of shame that marked its wearer for torment, cruelty, isolation, and separation from the rest of the community. (Curiously absent from "Fear of Fear" is any sense of the star's origin as the *Magen David,* the Star of David, a Jewish symbol. For more information about the star and its antecedents, see *http://history1900s.about.com/od/holocaust/a/yellowstar.htm;* the chapter on "The Star of David" in Kaplan, pp. 157–160; and Rotenberg's essay in this *Guide,* pp. 224–239).

I have brought an artifact from our Holocaust Center, a worn star with its hand-stitched hem, poignant in its readiness to be sewn onto an item of clothing. I give it to the students, who feel the coarse cloth and see the yellow star outlined with a crude black line. They are silent as they examine it, pass it along, and turn to their journals to analyze Ellen's response.

In place of such an artifact, you may choose to show a photograph from *ushmm. org/education/for students/;* click on "Photographs of Artifacts." Point out that the word *Jude* is written in a script that looks like Hebrew lettering; show an example of such lettering if necessary. (For contrast, show the modern pride in the blue and white Star of David used today on the Israeli flag at *www.stateofisrael.com.*)

Students return to the reading with growing interest, eager to make sense of the plot and the characters. I ask them to practice their parts aloud for homework to improve their speed, fluency, and comprehension, and, as an exercise in empathy, to identify their character's primary emotions, using dialogue to support their opinions. I remind them to read the articles and to refer to the list of restrictions as they read to enrich their understanding of the context.

Insights

In class the second day, students share their insights. "Ellen" speaks of her character's determination, describing her as willful, assertive, adventurous, rebellious, and impulsive. "Julia" feels that her character was in some ways the opposite of Ellen, refusing to leave her house wearing the star and yet highly independent and self-directed. "Anna" sees her character as brave and proud, with the ability to turn a negative into a positive; she "shines" the star she is forced to wear.

Today the reading is stronger and more confident as students pick up their lines on cue. As we finish, though, some students murmur, "I still don't get it," and others nod in agreement. They enjoyed participating in the oral reading, but they need time now to dissect the text.

I ask what inferences they were able to draw from the timeline and readings.

"We know from the first paragraph that the story takes place in September 1941, when all Jews were required to wear a yellow Star of David," Emily offers. "The experience is still new, and children don't know what to make of it. Ellen must be a *Mischling* because she doesn't have to wear the star."

"But her grandmother has one," Marisa says. "Presumably she is the Jewish member of the family, the mother of Ellen's mother."

"In October and November 1939, bank accounts are frozen, and permission is required to buy things. This affects the gifts George receives at his birthday party; it's why he doesn't have a real cake," says Chris.

"There's very little they can buy," adds Mike. "They have to rely on what they have: a silk handkerchief, a leather tobacco pouch, and especially that red ball that becomes communal property."

Alison raises a tentative hand. "By February 1940, Jews can't get clothing, fabric, or even coupons to repair their shoes. That's how I understood the passage that describes Ellen: 'Her hair was long and wet on the collar of her old coat. The coat was much too short, and her plaid skirt showed two hands' breadths beneath it'" (*Anthology*, p. 79).

I nod, and she continues.

"The shortage affects George, too. In the description of him at his own birthday party," she refers to p. 81 in the text, "'his father had lent him a dark-gray suit. A narrow leather strap held his trousers up.'"

She looks up. "It's so sad," she concludes with a shake of her head.

"By October 23, 1941, emigration ends for the Jews and deportations begin. What did you infer from that?" I ask.

Kristen says, "It seems that Julie got out just in time. Anna, though, is part of the large-scale deportation."

Now more hands wave.

"Ellen refers to herself as having 'two wrong grandparents too few'" (p. 90), says Glenn. "I have to say that that description confused me."

"I think it's ironic; it's meant as a reversal," Alison responds. "Most people at that time, including her Jewish grandmother, would consider her as having two 'right' grandparents—Christian ones! Because of them, she was exempt from many of the restrictive laws. But she thinks they are 'wrong' because she doesn't want to be different from her Jewish friends."

"There is other irony as well," I add. I ask students to recall our two definitions of *escutcheon* and to identify the irony in each as applied to Ellen as she regards herself in a mirror wearing her grandmother's star.

"In the first definition, a shield with a coat of arms," hazards Elizabeth after a silence, "I think the irony lies in the fact that, under Nazi rule, Aryans had to trace their ancestry and prove there were no Jews in their family. Here, Ellen reacts to her reflection as if her star is a badge of honor. Just as the Nazis have reversed the Jewish star into a badge of shame, Ellen again makes it a mark of distinction, her coat of arms."

"Elizabeth has it just right!" I say with pleasure. "And in the second definition, 'a protective plate'?"

John raises his hand. "Rather than protect its wearers, the star subjects them to ridicule and worse."

"Exactly!" I say. "I think you may have understood more than you realized."

"Why has her mother gone to the United States and left Ellen?" Nick asks. Several students suggest that her mother, as a "full Jew," is more at risk and is there perhaps trying to get a sponsor for Ellen. They recall what they have learned from "No Way Out: Letters from the Holocaust": the almost insurmountable stumbling blocks put in the way of the Jews: the myriad and contradictory forms, the visa, and the affidavits of support necessary from an American sponsor.

Seth reasons, "No one knew that all Jews would be trapped inside Greater Germany; perhaps the plan had been for Ellen to emigrate later with her grandmother." I support his point by reminding the class that of the 185,000 Jews living in Austria, 120,000 of them were able to leave before the borders were sealed. (Intriguingly, Jakob Hessing, in this volume, notes that the reader "cannot tell whether her mother has really gone to America or whether her 'emigration' is merely a euphemism by, say, her grandmother who does not want Ellen to know that her mother was deported" [p. 136]. He adds, "So far no critic has considered this possibility," but his reading raises it.)

"Why is there no mention of her father?" I ask. Stephany answers, "I guess he's Christian and has abandoned Ellen, just as the Nazis wanted."

We conclude that Ellen's situation as a *Mischling* is particularly poignant because she has been, in effect, abandoned by her parents to live in a Jewish neighborhood with her Jewish grandmother. As we can infer from her longing to wear the yellow star, she wants desperately to be like her Jewish friends, but she is not "allowed." Since the Nuremberg Laws, non-Jews were not supposed to associate with Jews.

When someone wonders why Ellen did not realize the implications of wearing the star to the bakery, or, as the text says, "had forgotten" (*Anthology*, p. 80) them, I note the many laws that preceded the 1941 mandate requiring it. For German and Austrian Jews, it comes relatively late in the long list of restrictions meant to isolate and impoverish them. While adults understand that this additional law signals a new stage in persecution, children do not. Ellen sews on the star so she can fit in with her friends, her immediate and overwhelming need.

"What did she learn from her experience in the bakery?" I ask.

"That everyone in the place is a Nazi," Larry says, and the class laughs.

"That's really true," says Amy. "But she also realizes that 'One had to choose between one's star and all other things' [p. 80]. At least *she* has to; her Jewish friends don't have that choice."

"So why does she continue to wear it?" Kevin asks. "She's a *Mischling*; she can remove the star and its stigma."

Jim summarizes, "Her desire to be like her friends is stronger than her fear."

As they share their conclusions, they sympathize with Ellen's desperate attempt to buy the cake and her realization of what she has done. In giving in to the temptation of wearing the star, she has made herself one of Germany's unwanted and will be treated accordingly. She goes from ignorance to knowledge as she experiences the rejection that wearing the star brings. Up until that point "she hadn't understood their fear" (p. 80); now she shares it. She is terrified, as are the children at George's birthday party, who are so overcome by the fear that the star means death that they are tempted to jump out of the window.

I refer to Jean Paul Sartre and other existentialists who emphasize the importance of choices for human dignity, that even in the most extreme situation, when death is imminent, human beings still have a choice; they can choose when and how they die. Powerless to control the world around them, they can, nevertheless, choose how they respond. Because I am using their writing as an evaluation tool, I ask them again to turn to their journals to express their thoughts on this choice that was not a choice.

"Fortunately," writes George, "the children reject suicide as an option. Even though the characters are powerless, they, like Anna, have a choice. They can give in to their fears and commit suicide, or they can choose to respond in a positive way, following the star, finding comfort and strength in a higher power."

Richard writes, "The characters try to gain power; by contemplating suicide, they make a bold statement: *they* will decide if and when and how they die. They are so desperate that they find some freedom in believing they can control the circumstances of their own death. Their fear is of the unknown, of what will happen, of how they will die, so they want to choose. However, it shows even more strength that they find comfort in God and not in having power."

When I ask students to identify passages that conveyed life in the *Judenhauser*, their responses are immediate:

1. "On the floor above, Aunt Sonya was giving piano lessons. Secretly."
2. "In the room to the left, two boys were fighting. Their clear, angry voices were very audible."
3. "In the room to the right, the deaf old man was shouting to his bulldog."
4. "Ellen got two saucepans lids out of the cupboard and clanged them angrily" (p. 78).

To change the pacing of the class, I ask them to sit with a partner and take a few minutes to identify strategies the children used to cope with this stressful and oppressive setting and help themselves maintain a sense of normalcy and a sense of self. As I circulate and visit the dyads, I hear many references to George's party with its incessant background voices. They identify the varied responses of the children—ignorance, denial, wanting/not wanting to know—as coping strategies. Several pairs focus on Hannah's insistence on knowing the cause of the crying next door and George's refusal to let her investigate, as he asserts, "It's bad enough that we have to live door to door with strangers. Why they laugh or cry is none of our business" (p. 84).

"I guess 'ignorance is bliss' is a coping mechanism," Jordan says, wryly.

"How is that coping?" Amy protests. "This highlights the abnormal conditions of the Jewish houses. Hannah insists that another's pain 'always has been our business' [p. 84]. The normal response would be to see what's wrong and to help."

"But normally," Jordan responds, "people don't live so close to one another. In this case, perhaps they should be given their privacy. It's like we don't look at other people when we're in a crowded elevator. People need their space. Denial is a form of coping and maintaining dignity."

Andrew spoke. "The noise was constant, and the children couldn't escape it. They had all they could do keep up a brave appearance, and I don't know how they could stand it. Hearing such noises would drive me insane!"

"I hate to say this," Tom began, "and I would never do it, but I could see how suicide could be seen as a choice, a sure way to end the uncertainty and the fear they feel all the time. I think it's admirable that they chose life. It shows their strength and their dignity."

Amy turned to me. "You know, I had *no idea* what this story was about when I first read it, but I really do get it now, and I think it's so deep!"

"It gets even deeper!" I laugh.

The time has gone quickly. For homework I ask them to identify and analyze five images using the guidelines offered in this volume by Younglove: "The key to teaching about figurative language is not simply to define the terms nor merely locate the figures of speech." Rather, students should consider "what image is the author trying to evoke in the reader's mind at the moment and why" (*Guide*, p. 364).

Imagery and Understanding

The third class begins with students charting their images on the board, identifying their parts of speech and their evocation. Examining just the images of the star is revealing, and much work can be done with "fog," "mist," and "darkness" as well. Students spoke of the star "darker than the sun and paler than the moon"; of "its radius undefined, like the palm of a stranger's hand"; of its resplendence "on the thin, dark blue cloth, as though convinced it was in the heavens"; of it burning "like flaming metal through her coat and dress to her skin." Leah noted that for George, the star "had unmasked the sun" (*Anthology*, p. 81).

"He feels regret and a sense of loss," she said, "for the sun was 'that beloved, beaming constellation of childhood'" (p. 81). Jerry identified the extended imagery that even the dusk is guilty as it hides the star.

The work on figurative language leads to the most challenging part of the story, the way in which Ellen transforms the meaning of the star from a source of depression and fear to one of hope and the fact that the children connect the story of a child born in Bethlehem to their own lives. To tackle it, I suggest that the pairs from yesterday now form groups of four and continue their analysis. Again I circulate, sometimes listening and commenting, sometimes speaking to the whole class, assessing their understanding to help me evaluate the effectiveness of my lesson as I visit each group. I call their attention to Ellen's struggles with two conflicting voices, her grandmother's warnings and her own sense of the star's magical powers as she runs from the bakery and from George's house. It is here that she begins to search for meanings for the star other than the obvious one.

I write on the board, "'Wasn't it within the star's power,' Ellen wonders, 'to … break through fear?'" (p. 87).

"This is where she begins to control her own life," Susan says. "Even though she experiences the stigma of the star, she refuses to let it, an object, control her. She will not give in to the force of hate and allow the star to define her; instead, she will define the star. So she changes it from an object of oppression and fear and shame into one of strength and hope and beauty."

I point out that Ellen urges the others "weakened by fear": "If you want to know what the star means" (p. 93), and they, without questions, run outside with her to meet Anna. "They no longer saw the … vans at the edge of the railroad … nor the tearful faces nor the smiles of the uncaring guards. Like Ellen, they saw only the star" (p. 93).

"Is it realistic," I ask, "that these young people can ignore the reality of vans loaded with Jews and instead fill themselves with a sense of courage and hope by focusing on the star?"

"Isn't it natural for us to ignore what we don't want to think about?" Alison responds with her own question. "Isn't that how we all cope with stress sometimes?"

"I don't think that they were ignoring reality. They were just looking for hope. Filling yourself with a sense of hope and courage pushes you to keep going and look and wait for something good to come out of something evil. That's their coping, and that's their strength," Leone answers.

Stacy also is not sure they ignored the vans. "I think they tried to avoid the reality, but deep inside they know what is happening and fear that they, too, might one day suffer the same fate. In a way, the kids have to have a sense of hope to keep on going."

Amy agrees. "Courage allows us to face evil head on. But it is amazing that the children can even think of hope and courage in this situation."

John also agrees. "Hope pushes us to keep on going, to look for something good to come."

Supporting Amy's and John's insight, I tell them, "Many survivors claim what kept them going was a feeling deep inside that they would pull through," and I ask, "How does Anna's response to her situation affect Ellen?"

"Anna shows that hope can conquer fear even when the worst happens," says Matt.

"Do you agree with Anna's explanation that fear motivates the secret police?"

Sara does. "It's amazing that the children came to this conclusion! They realize that the secret police fear them, and that is why they persecute them. Aren't they right? At the root of it all, isn't that the reason?"

Adam, recalling earlier learning in his Scriptures class, concurs. "The Secret Police harass the Jews because, as Anna says on p. 95, 'they're afraid of the King of the Jews again' just as King Herod was. The secret police do not want morality or Christ to be brought into this world."

"Do you all understand Anna's comment here?" There are more silences than nods.

A Discussion of Antisemitism

I had earlier discussed with Patrick a brief but sophisticated analysis of antisemitism by Maurice Samuel (1940), who wrote, as others also have, that the Jews are hated not as "Christ-killers," but as "Christ-givers," the people who gave the world a strict moral code and a conscience.[1] To Samuel, the Nazis' hatred of Jews was actually a rejection of the most important Judeo-Christian message: that no person is too humble to be precious to God, and that all of us are called to the brotherly love of even strangers. Patrick nodded; this was the time to share it with the class. Samuel explains,

> We shall never understand the maniacal, world-wide seizure of antisemitism unless we transpose the terms. It is of Christ that the Nazi-Fascists are afraid; it is in his omnipotence that they believe; it is he that they are determined madly to obliterate. But the names of Christ and Christianity are too overwhelming, and the habit of submission to them is too deeply ingrained after centuries and centuries of teaching. Therefore, they must, I repeat, make their assault on those who were responsible for the birth and spread of Christianity. They must spit on the Jews as the "Christ-killers" because they long to spit on the Jews as the Christ-givers. (*www. religion-online.org/showarticle.asp?title=383*, paragraph 6)

We distribute the paragraph and read it aloud together, validating students' concerns that it is very difficult to understand. We assign it for rereading and parsing at home.

The "Wise Men's Star"

In our fourth and final session, Patrick joins me to respond to students' journal questions, expand on Samuel's thesis, and reiterate the basis for Adam's comment.

"Let's begin with a question," Patrick addresses the class. "When Anna says, 'They're afraid of the King of the Jews *again*,' why did Adam think she was referring to Herod?"

No one is sure, so he continues. "Do you guys remember our conversation about Herod the Great? He ruled over Judea in from 37 B.C.E. until his death in 4 B.C.E He was a tyrant and, like the Pharaoh, he ordered the murder of all male Jewish children from birth to the age of two in an attempt to prevent the "Christ Child prophesy" from coming true. The story is found in the New Testament's Gospel according to Matthew, 2:1–12." [For further reading about Mat-

---

1 It may be that Aichinger was acquainted with Samuel's view of antisemitism through the writings of French philosopher and theologian Jacques Maritain, a Roman Catholic convert. In the October 6, 1941, issue of *Christianity and Crisis* Maritain quotes Samuel in his article "On Anti-Semitism." In it, Maritain agrees with Samuel's analysis of the underlying causes of antisemitism and takes it one step further. He considers what is happening to the Jews as a crucifixion. "Jesus Christ suffers in the passion of Israel. In striking Israel, the antisemites strike him, insult him, and spit on him." (Retrieved June 7, 2007, from *www.religion-online.org/showarticle.asp?title=383*.) Using the entire Maritain article in college classes studying "Fear of Fear" could be most fascinating.

thew 2:1–12, see "The Visit of the Wise Men" (Ross) found at *http://www.bible.org/page.asp?page_id=3822.*]

"The star that leads the Gentile visitors from the East brings the Magi[2] to Jerusalem," Patrick continues. "They ask where they can find the newborn King of the Jews, and, according to Matthew, the chief priests and scribes tell them of the Micah prophecy, which Matthew interprets as predicting that the messiah is to be born in Bethlehem. The religious authorities are indifferent to the news of the birth of the king; it is only the Magi who travel to Bethlehem to pay homage. They leave to return home by another way, warned in a dream not to return to Herod. Without a report of the newborn's exact location, Herod orders the Slaughter of the Innocents, the massacre of males two years and younger in and around Bethlehem."

Tom, listening intently, responds slowly, "So Anna and the children make the parallel between Herod's determination to destroy Jesus and the Nazi desire to destroy the Jews, both for the same reasons, because they bring morality into the world."

That's the analogy that we want the students to make, drawing on Samuel's theory. Just as Herod desired the slaughter of the innocents, so too, according to Anna, have the Nazis marked these Jewish children for death. I think it is key to be explicit about that parallel, which illustrates why the novel from which this narrative is taken is called *Herod's Children*.

Patrick was pleased with the discussion relating their critical study of the story in Scripture class to the issues of "Christ-killers and Christ-givers" alluded to in Samuel's article. However, most students were overwhelmed with this aspect; I would not refer to it again. The material is too sophisticated for this age level, difficult even for adults to grasp, despite its allusions to the story.

We move to conclude our discussion of the story, which ends abruptly with the final transformation of the star. I ask questions, including,

- To Anna, and now Ellen, what does the star symbolize?
- What do the police lack and the children have? Is it a sense of moral values, a spiritual direction, a faith? What gives the star its power?

---

2 So who were these Magi? We should say at the outset that the tradition that these men were three kings, and that their names have been preserved for us, has no foundation in biblical history at all. Here again you could check out the facts in a good Bible dictionary, looking under "Magi" as they were called. You will probably find that these were a priestly caste of very wise men from Mesopotamia, somewhere in the east, perhaps Persia or Babylonia—we are not told. They were famous for their learning, and for their wisdom. They were very interested in astronomy/astrology; when they observed the movements of stars and planets, they carefully recorded everything they saw. Anything out of the ordinary was taken by them to be some kind of an omen. Now they had seen a star that could not be identified (Ross, *http://www.bible.org/page.asp?page_id=3822*).

- What is the significance of Anna and then Ellen transforming the star into a Christian symbol, "the Wise Men's star" (*Anthology*, p. 95)?

The students have a hard time making sense of the Jewish star and its relation to the Wise Men's star. They feel the author has left them hanging. To help them surmount this hurdle and enter the minds of Ellen and Anna, I ask them to put aside their usual images of Jews as victims wearing the yellow star, to forget for a moment their associations of the star with the *Magen David*, often a symbol of the Jewish religion; even to forget, as Ellen has, that wearing the star makes one an object of scorn.

I remind them that we are dealing with Ellen, a *Mischling*, who, for all we know, was brought up as a Catholic, and Anna, who does not seem to have any Jewish identity, even though she is being deported to Poland. Both girls have been exposed to the dominant Christian culture, to Christmas and the story of the Magi.

"So consider: What do they gain by seeing their star as the Wise Men's star?"

"Maybe they are wishing for a miracle," suggests George.

Alison agrees. "The children, like the Magi, are looking for a savior. Just as Herod did not succeed in killing the baby Jesus, they hope the star will protect and save them."

However, Leone disagrees. "By transforming the star into a guide to salvation and joy, the children were creating a false sense of hope and courage. They must eventually face the fact that the star means pain and death; it is no guiding light to salvation."

"And the secret police?" I ask.

Kristen suggests, "When Anna says, 'It's very dark around the secret police' (p. 94), she may be claiming that the police have lost their faith."

"Uh, huh," John agrees. "Deep down they may know they are wrong in persecuting the children and fear being punished."

The students are still tentative, not quite sure if this works, but, at the end of our time together, they have gotten beyond looking at all Jews in the Holocaust in the same way. They have met children who were victimized although they did not even know they were Jewish, which deepened students' understanding of the ferocity of the Nazi intention to murder every Jew they could find.

Concluding Activities and Discussion

As a final writing assignment, I ask students to choose two of the following questions and respond to them in their journals.

1. What insights and understandings about the Holocaust did you gain from reading "Fear of Fear?"
2. What further questions does this story raise for you?
3. What do you think is the message of the story?
4. How satisfying is the conclusion of the story for you?

To conclude the class, we discuss the ultimate question: Were the characters able to conquer their fear of fear? If so, what were their strategies?

Rachel begins. "Yes, the children were able to conquer their fear of fear because they found hope. The strategies they used were listening to Anna and believing what she was saying. They conquered their fears when they surrendered themselves to faith. They found security even though uncertainty surrounded them."

Ken adds, "Fear immobilizes people; it prevents them from acting. Failure to act can further degrade a situation, creating more problems. So they acted. They found meaning in the insanity around them, and they used this meaning to survive."

Kristen has the last word in what has been a lively and remarkably insightful discussion. "Allowing themselves to continue despite uncertainty takes more strength than giving up. I think this is how they conquered their fear of fear."

What Comes Next?

After the story, you might provide survivor testimony, available from Rochester's Center for Holocaust Awareness and Information (*www.jewishrochester. org*) or from your local resource center or Holocaust museum. I particularly recommend one of the profiles in *Perilous Journeys: Personal Stories of German and Austrian Jews Who Escaped the Nazis* (Lovenheim & Appelbaum, 1990). Many of these profiles are about young children. The story of Evie Jacobson, entitled "Who Am I?" would be particularly appropriate. (Evie had a Jewish father and Christian mother and was persecuted as a *Mischling*. Also available from the Rochester Center is a companion DVD in which Evie speaks of how her parents tried to protect her. She struggles to this day with bouts of depression and problems of personal identity.) For enrichment, individualized learning, or research, you might assign Aichinger's *Herod's Children* in its totality, but only for college or graduate students. In addition, Clara Asscher-Pinkhof's very short and simple stories "White Lie" (Shawn & Goldfrad, *Anthology*, 2008, pp. 107–109) and "Shopping" (Asscher-Pinkhof, 1986, pp. 58–61) offer similar scenes of children with the star shopping in stores, but they are set in Amsterdam and make for a fascinating comparison.

Art, even for young adults, may be a satisfying activity that allows readers to respond to this nontraditional narrative with a nontraditional medium. Supply collage materials, such as scraps of fabric, irregular pieces of shiny and matte paper, feathers, tissue, and small silver and gold stars, along with oak tag, glue sticks, and oil crayons, and ask students to illustrate a theme or represent the meaning the story had for them, and, most importantly, to explain their artistic response to the class. Such tactile products often serve as a catharsis for students and are an excellent evaluative tool for the teacher; furthermore, they offer less-verbal students alternate assessment opportunities. Finally, such an exercise also provides a counterpoint to what has been an intellectually challenging story that requires complex thinking and that raises more questions than it answers.

Students at Aquinas felt the unit was well worth the effort in spite of the difficulties it poses. They found that the story "personalized the events of the

Holocaust and helped us relate as never before to the victims' inner lives as they searched for the strength to conquer fear."

REFERENCES

Abrams, A. (1985). *Special treatment—The untold story of Hitler's third race*. Secaucus, NJ: Lyle Stuart, Inc.

Aichinger, I. (1964). Fear of fear. In K. Shawn & K. Goldfrad, (Eds.). (2008). *The call of memory: Learning about the Holocaust through narrative: An anthology*, pp. 77–93. Teaneck, NJ: Ben Yehuda Press.

Aichinger, I. (1964). *Herod's children*. New York: Atheneum.

Asscher-Pinkhof, C. (1986). *Star children*. Detroit: Wayne State University Press.

Crane, C. (2000). *Divided lives: The untold stories of Jewish-Christian women in Nazi Germany*. New York: St. Martin's Press.

Fisher, J. G., (Ed.). (1991). *The persistence of youth: Oral testimonies of the Holocaust*. New York: Greenwood Press.

Freund, F. & Safrian, H. (1997). Reflections on project "Registration by name: Austrian victims of the Holocaust." *Expulsion and extermination. The fate of the Austrian Jews 1938–1945*. Vienna: Austrian Resistance Archive. Retrieved June 12, 2007, from *http://www.doew.at/*.

Fromm, B. (1990). *Blood & banquets: A Berlin diary 1930–1938*. New York: Simon & Schuster.

Gutman, I. (Ed.). (1990). *Encyclopedia of the Holocaust* (Volume 3). Mischlinge, pp. 981–983. D. Bankier, (Ed.). New York: Macmillan.

Hessing, J. (2008). Children with a star: Ilse Aichinger's unique perspective. In K. Shawn & K. Goldfrad (Eds.). *The call of memory: Learning about the Holocaust through narrative: A teacher's guide*, pp. 135–142. Teaneck, NJ: Ben Yehuda Press.

Hilberg, R. (1987). *The destruction of the European Jews*. Chicago: Quadrangle Books.

Jacobson, E. (2007). *Who am I?* DVD Testimony. Rochester, NY: Jewish Community Federation of Greater Rochester.

Kaplan, M. (1998). *Between dignity and despair: Everyday life in Nazi Germany*. Oxford: Oxford Press.

Klemperer, V. (1998). *I will bear witness 1933–1941: A diary of the Nazi years*. New York: Random House.

Koehn, I. (1977) *Mischlinge, second degree: My childhood in Nazi Germany*. New York: William Morrow.

Lovenheim, B. & Appelbaum, B. (1990). *Perilous journeys: Personal stories of German and Austrian Jews who escaped the Nazis*. Rochester, NY: Jewish Community Federation of Greater Rochester.

Noakes, J. (1989). Development of Nazi policy towards German-Jewish *Mischlinge* 1933–1945. In *Leo Baeck Institute yearbook of 1989*. New York: Center for Jewish History.

Ross, A. The visit of the Wise Men (Mathew 2:1–12). Retrieved June 14, 2007, from *http://www.bible.org/page.asp?page_id=3822*.

Samuel, M. (1940). *The great hatred*. New York: Alfred A. Knopf. Quoted in the online article "On Anti-Semitism" by Jacques Maritain. Retrieved April 25, 2007, from *www.religion-online.org/showarticle.asp?title=383*.

Younglove, W. (2008). An examination of loss in the Holocaust in Cynthia Ozick's "The shawl." In K. Shawn & K. Goldfrad (Eds.). *The call of memory: Learning about the Holocaust through narrative: A teacher's guide*, pp. 358–371. Teaneck, NJ: Ben Yehuda Press.

Retrieved June 7, 2007, from http://history1900s.about.com/od/holocaust/a/yellowstar.htm.
Retrieved June 7, 2007, from www.ushmm.org/education/forstudents/.
Retrieved June 7, 2007, from www.stateofisrael.com.

From the Gotfryd Family Album:
"A Chicken for the Holidays"

Chana Levene-Nachshon

In his foreword to his father's book, *Anton the Dove Fancier and Other Tales of the Holocaust* (2000), Howard Gotfryd writes,

> One of the most difficult problems I can imagine ... is for a survivor of Nazi atrocities in the 1940s to describe his experience to someone who was not in Europe during that time, in a manner that will ensure the listener's full understanding and empathy. (p. xi)

Gotfryd senior did indeed recount his tales at the dinner table for many years to a variety of guests. However, their comprehension of the horrific implications of the tales was very limited, as the tales were "contained in a code that was uncrackable to most of the people. ... Only other survivors knew the code ... and their children probably intuited the same things I did" (p. xi).

It was not until the mid-1980s, upon his return from a work assignment in his native Poland, that Bernard Gotfryd was no longer content with just telling his stories over dinner. "I have always been concerned that if I didn't set these moments down on paper, I would forget them," he wrote (p. xiii).

Gotfryd puts pen to paper in a manner that is sometimes deceptively simple and devoid of the horrors we have come to expect in tales of the Holocaust, whether they are fact or fiction. According to his son, Gotfryd is more concerned with conveying the sensation of what it meant to be a human being and a Jew during the Holocaust than with the terrible, bloody events themselves.

> In these simple and sensitive narratives, spread before the reader like an album of family photographs, lies the irony that makes them so effective, because one does not need to know the gritty details of forced labor, torture, beating, and execution in order to understand these details to be horrible. (p. xii)

To comprehend the essence of Gotfryd and to do justice to any discussion of his tales, one must keep in mind Gotfryd's concerns, as described above by his son, as well as his photographer's eye and sensibilities, which afford his writing the clarity and focus of an album of cherished family photographs. These concerns and perceptions frame all of Gotfryd's tales, for it is through the emotional response and vision of a benign human being and the eye, lens, and focus of a photographer that Gotfryd views the world and captures and recounts his experiences. No matter what the surroundings, he inevitably and invariably zooms in on the goodness, the moment of humanity of the people he recalls in startling detail.

As we open the Gotfryd family album, *Anton the Dove Fancier and Other Tales of the Holocaust*, we see a variety of photographs, each telling its own individual tale. At the same time, these photographs comprise part of a collective tale interconnected by virtue of time, location, and relation to a young Bernard Gotfryd. Yet, had Gotfryd intended to ensure that we view this album in its entirety, page by page, surely he would have named it accordingly. The very title includes the words "and other tales," implying that each narrative can be read independently and conclusions can be drawn from one that are not necessarily supported by another. It is in this context that the equation of tales with photographs is so relevant, for, in photography, the use of specific techniques (framing, angle, perspective, distance, depth, camera movement) make a significant difference in the images photographs project, the tales they tell, and the perceptions they elicit. Such techniques allow us to see things in one tale that may or may not be borne out by the larger context of the entire collection; it enables us to reconcile inconsistencies and disparities between and among stories, for all impressions are valid.

One such disparity between tales is the omission of certain details in "A Chicken for the Holidays" (Shawn & Goldfrad, *Anthology*, 2008, pp. 96–103) and the inclusion of similar details in others. For example, in the former, not one Jewish character is referred to by name. Yet in "Helmut Reiner" (pp. 170–180), the Jewish characters, Mr. and Mrs. Orenstein, are both named and described in detail.

In contrast, the non-Jews, relatively minor characters, are all referred to by name in "A Chicken for the Holidays": The Polish couple are the Dombroskis; the narrator's friend is George; the German SS officer is Schultz; and the "enterprising" Polish prostitute is Stasia, while in "The Last Morning" (pp. 131–138) neither the non-Jewish caretaker nor the SS men are named.

The author's decision not to ascribe names to Jewish characters in this story may be, on the one hand, intentional because this is Gotfryd's own story, and it is apparent that he is the boy and the parents are his parents. On the other hand, perhaps the Jewish characters remain nameless because they represent any and every mother, father, and child who experienced the horrors of the Holocaust. Beyond these possibilities, yet another explanation offers itself. The namelessness may be a reflection of the Nazis' dehumanization of their victims, herding them into cattle cars like animals, stealing their names and their very identity by branding them only with numbers.

The second omission is that of the specific venue of this story. We are told merely that it takes place in a city occupied by the Nazis in September 1939. A Polish farmer enters the furniture store of the narrator's father in October 1940, "some months before the ghetto was established" (p. 96). The actual action of the story begins after "some months went by" and "shortly before the Jewish High Holidays" (p. 96), which means a year had passed and it was now the fall of 1941.

We have not been told the name of the city or whether the family has been moved to the ghetto. It is from Gotfryd's biographical profile that we learn the city in "A Chicken for the Holidays" is Radom, and, by 1941, the Jews all live behind ghetto walls.

Is this second omission unintentional? Did the narrator see this detail as unimportant in this particular story or did he see its omission as serving the cause of universality? After all, was one ghetto really so different from another? Was the fate of the inhabitants of one so different from that of the inhabitants of another?

When viewed on its own, "A Chicken for the Holidays" is a childhood adventure, typical of those depicted in children's literature or on film, of a young boy eager to go to great lengths to please someone he loves.

> The anticipation of adventure and the risk involved must have appealed to me, but above all I could visualize my family at the holiday dinner eyeing a cooked chicken at the center of the table. My mouth started watering at the mere thought of being able to savor a chicken giblet, as in the old days. (p. 97)

No Jewish family album is complete without photographs of a festive family meal. The role of food in the Jewish family repertoire is legendary; and of all the foods associated with Jews, none is more quintessentially Jewish than chicken soup, the ultimate remedy for all ailments; physical, spiritual, and emotional. Yet, when viewed in its larger context, that of the Holocaust, the entire narrative, including this absurdly normal image of a family sitting down to a holiday meal, takes on an entirely different aspect, one of imminent danger. Seemingly minor particulars suddenly assume major importance; seemingly innocent and harmless details suddenly take on sinister proportions. One cannot help but recall Howard Gotfryd's sentiment that one does not need to know the details in order to understand that they were indeed horrible. The evil is always present, lurking, if not in the foreground, then in the shadows.

In this unnamed ghetto, the backdrop of "A Chicken for the Holidays," rigid restrictions are in force against Jews, with even minor offenses punishable by death. The narrator, a teenaged Bernard Gotfryd, (yet clearly gifted with a foresight that can only come from hindsight), sets his mind on collecting a debt owed to his father by a Polish farmer. He does not even consider that the Pole might not honor his promise, let alone turn him over to the Nazis. When he asks his Polish friend the safest way to the Polish farm, his friend refuses, adding, "It's an insane idea" (p. 97). Yet, young Gotfryd is not deterred. "Although I knew how risky it was to cross the city line without a pass. ... I wasn't going to let ... anyone discourage me" (p. 97).

En route to the Polish farm, "the rain intensified; the sky began to darken. ... Flocks of crows [omens of death] pecked away ... taking off noisily at the slightest motion" (p. 97). The setting grows darker as nature suddenly turns threatening, reflecting the danger to the boy. "When I stopped for a moment to orient myself I realized how insane I was to be there" (p. 97).

Passing the cemetery, young Bernard sees a military truck surrounded by people in uniform. Neither he nor we are given any indication of who, if anyone, is in the truck. He is already out of range when he hears a salvo of rifle shots ring out from the direction of the cemetery. He no longer sees—he only hears—and what he hears clearly disturbs him; he is horrified. We, the readers, however, do see: a blurry, fog-enveloped photograph, in which we are able to discern the images through sound, context, and hindsight. The implication is more than horrifying, for it is obvious that the truck contained Jews who were herded out by SS soldiers and shot, perhaps even after having dug their own mass grave.

In the next paragraph, when he writes, "There was not a living soul in sight" (p. 98), one cannot help but recall the shots he has just heard. When he feels the fog all around him "like a procession of floating ghosts" (p. 98), one cannot help but think of the victims of those shots; and when he hears children's voices but sees no one, one cannot help but wonder how many children had been among those victims. "I didn't think I was hallucinating," he says, "for I could still hear the voices, a whole chorus" (p. 98).

Once again, nature reveals the unseen truth: "I looked up and saw the wind-whipped treetops move in a wild dance, twirling and rotating; they were creating all sorts of squeaking sounds. It was eerie" (p. 98). For us, it is far more than eerie, for we know for certain what he only sensed at the time; he was indeed witnessing the dance of the dead and hearing their voices cry out. What had begun as an adventure for the teenager was fast becoming a nightmare.

Then, suddenly, "through a thick haze" he sees "the farmhouse in a clearing between the woods and a small lake surrounded by weeping willows. As I came closer to the fence a dog started barking; moments later a woman opened the door of the house" (p. 98). The picture-perfect Polish farmhouse, somehow seen in vivid detail on an evening when fog had enveloped the countryside (as the fog of the Third Reich had already enveloped Europe) and the sky had already turned a dark grey (like the uniforms of the SS), is too idyllic. The thick haze of danger clears long enough to enable young Gotfryd to reach his destination. For the narrator, the weeping willows and the dog that barks as he approaches the fence may be part of an idyllic scene, but for us they portend what is yet to come.

The owners of the farmhouse, the Dombroskis, could have sent the lad away; they could have turned him in. Yet they do not, for they have retained their humanity in an increasingly inhumane world by honoring their word. They give him fresh milk, freshly baked bread, potatoes, and the live chicken he so coveted. "[D]on't forget to tell your father that we're even," Mr. Dombroski cautions, sending a clear message that this repayment of debt is to be seen as final (p. 100).

One cannot help but draw an analogy between the chicken that Mr. Dombroski gives the boy and the Jewish victims of the Nazis. It is "a gray-yellow bird, not very big, with scared eyes. It kept turning its head nervously without making a sound" (p. 99), its color reminiscent of the yellow Star of David that Jews were forced to wear and the gray-white striped clothing of labor/concentration camp inmates. The chicken's fear is palpable; it seems to be far more aware of the danger than the boy. Its feet and wings have been tied with straps by Mrs. Dombroski "to prevent its escape" (p. 99). Like the Jews, its freedom has been curtailed, and its fate is fairly obvious and unavoidable. Sooner or later, under one set of circumstances or another, it will be killed.

Having secured his prize, young Gotfryd sets out on his journey home. Mr. Dombroski walks him to the road and, as he leaves him, says, "If they catch you, you don't know me, and I don't know you" (p. 100). He is fully aware of the potentially dire consequences of his actions. The idyll has been shattered.

As in a thriller, the narrator steps up his pace in the final part of this story, recording the action as successive rather than individual frames. The journey home is a roller coaster of emotions; heart-stopping tension alternates with merciful relief. Once the boy leaves the safety of the farmhouse, nature again turns dark and ominous. "The whole landscape seemed to be drowning in the rain" (p. 100). Gotfryd expresses fear in two consecutive paragraphs: "I feared that I might not be able to make it back in time" and "I realized I was just as scared wearing the arm band as I was without it" (p. 100). [See Mayer's "Compliant Defiance: Rejecting a Chicken for the Holidays," pp. 168–183 in this volume, for a discussion on the further implications of this passage.]

After he crosses the city line, he encounters a German soldier. In most stories this would surely have signaled the end for the Jewish teenager. However, fortuitously, the soldier turns out to be Schultz of the *Waffen SS*, whom Gotfryd had photographed at the studio where he worked. Instead of shooting, as German soldiers usually did without slightest provocation, Schultz waves him off, yelling, "Now hurry home" (p. 100).

The chicken, silent until now, begins to squawk. For the first time in the entire tale, the narrator expresses extreme anxiety: "I was desperate; the walk back was the most risky of all, and I knew there was no turning back" (p. 101). Also for the first time, he invokes God's help in keeping the chicken silent and delivering him home safely. God is not perceived as one who has placed him in this situation, but rather as one who can extricate him from it. "Please, God, help me … I must get this chicken home alive so we can celebrate the holidays" (p. 101). Ironically, he must get the chicken home alive so that it can be killed according to Jewish ritual. It is almost as if his family's celebrating the holidays is contingent upon this scrawny chicken.

Interestingly, he does not think of God directly but through a story told to him by his grandmother. This is a prelude to the mother's religious sentiments expressed at the end of the tale. It is apparent that in his family, as in many Jewish families of the time, the women were more knowledgeable than men in the practical observances of the laws pertaining to the Jewish home, and as such, were the arbiters and guardians of Jewish tradition in the home.

Bernard's prayers for the chicken's silence are not immediately answered, and panicky that its squawking will bring him to the attention of the SS, he strangles the chicken. In the space of a short time, he has gone from successfully achieving his goal to experiencing panic and desperation. As he espies a German police patrol on the opposite side of the street, his emotions manifest themselves physically as he breaks out in a sweat. "I was trapped" (p. 101), he writes. Nonetheless, garnering his last vestiges of strength, he climbs fences lined with barbed wire and finally reaches his street.

Though weary and frightened, young Gotfryd is still able to add a few photographs to his family album. One is of a friendly stray dog, unlike the barking dog of the Dombroskis. Another is of Stasia's pleasure house and the Germans who frequent it. Gotfryd's description of Stasia as an "enterprising Polish woman who—with the help of the German authorities—had taken over three adjoining sheds, evicting the tenants" (p. 102) is somewhat cynical or, at best, understated, making it difficult to discern whether the narrator is a young or adult Bernard Gotfryd. A third is of another nonstereotypical German soldier who addresses the young lad "in a sort of friendly tone of voice" (p. 102) and lets him run safely home.

Finally, when Gotfryd reaches home, he is greeted by a very worried mother with tears in her eyes. "Did you know how many arrests and executions for curfew violation there are every night?" (p. 102) she berates him. In reply, he illustrates the adage "One picture is worth a thousand words" by throwing the dead chicken on the doormat.

After hearing her son recount his adventure with boyish bravado (a tale within a tale that bears little resemblance to reality), the mother immediately and instinctively thanks the Almighty for returning her son. While she appreciates what her son has done for the family, her celebration of the holidays is unconditional: "We would survive even if it meant having a meatless holiday" (p. 102), she says. Her statement implies that their situation is not life-threatening, thus validating her pronouncement that they cannot eat a nonkosher chicken. When her son protests that it is wartime and there is a food shortage, she stands firm. Even when he pleads, "Does it matter that the chicken isn't kosher? Who'll know? Won't God forgive us?" she is unrelenting. Unlike her son, she does not make deals with God. Bernard has no choice but to accept his mother's decision as final.

Rather than throw out food that was nonkosher, Jews often gave such food to their non-Jewish neighbors. Here, Gotfryd's mother gives the chicken to the janitor's family. The janitor's wife is still talking about the chicken weeks later, "reminding my mother what a tasty and fat bird it had been" (p. 103). How did the nervous, gray-yellow chicken, not very big during its lifetime, become tasty and fat after death? Short of a miracle, the answer must lie in the eyes of the viewer or in a change of perspective, distance, and/or angle.

While the Germans are busy indulging their appetites for pleasures of the flesh and the Polish janitor's wife is relishing the memory of pleasures to the palate, Gotfryd's mother is committed to survival of the spirit. "In wartime or peacetime, we're a people who must abide by the laws, or else we'll cease to be a people" (p. 103). She clearly knows what it means to be a Jew; she understands that the survival of the Jews as a people depends on unwavering commitment. Religion/tradition is seen here not as a coercive or oppressive force, but rather as the lifeblood of the Jew, both individually and collectively.

As we put down these pages of the Gotfryd family album, we are aware that more remain for us to pick up any time we wish. From what we have already seen in "A Chicken for the Holidays," we know the benign eye of Gotfryd will inevitably focus on the moments, however few, of goodness in a world turned evil. If we are looking for grotesque, horrific images of the Holocaust, we shall not find them here. However, if we are looking for people who retained a semblance of humanity and kindness amidst and despite the horrors of the Holocaust, whether they are German soldiers, Polish farmers, or Jews in the most desperate of conditions, (and even God's four-legged creatures), their photographs will surely appear in this album as a testimony to Gotfryd's ability to find such goodness and capture it for posterity.

REFERENCES

Gotfryd, B. (2000). *Anton the dove fancier and other tales of the Holocaust*. Baltimore: Johns Hopkins University Press.

Gotfryd, B. (2000). A chicken for the holidays. In K. Shawn & K. Goldfrad (Eds.). (2008). *The call of memory: Learning about the Holocaust through narrative: An anthology*, pp. 96–103. Teaneck, NJ: Ben Yehuda Press.

Mayer, D. (2008). Compliant defiance: Rejecting a chicken for the holidays. In K. Shawn & K. Goldfrad (Eds.). (2008). *The call of memory: Learning about the Holocaust through narrative: A teacher's guide*, pp. 168–183. Teaneck, NJ: Ben Yehuda Press.

Compliant Defiance:
Rejecting a Chicken for the Holidays

Daniel Mayer

> *One resists with a gun; another, with his soul.*
> —Rabbi Ephraim Oshry (1975)

In the years that I have been teaching about the Holocaust, I have come to believe that students must come away from such study with a sense that the Holocaust was not merely a horrible display of man's inhumanity, a litany of atrocities to be examined with morbid fascination and used to inform future generations of the need to be vigilant against evil's insidious and relentless search for willing recruits. It was also the canvas upon which ordinary people painted the story of their tenacious wish to live, love, and celebrate their family and their faith, to preserve all that they held dear. In simple and subtle ways, Jews who experienced the Holocaust showed that they were very much alive spiritually even as they endured hunger and abuse and awaited almost certain death. One story of such spiritual resistance is "A Chicken for the Holidays" by Bernard Gotfryd (Shawn & Goldfrad, *Anthology*, 2008, pp. 96–103). It is a tale simple in its easy prose but rich in its imagery and genuine to the protagonist/narrator, who tells this story of rebellion, danger, love, and resistance about himself as a young man living in the Radom Ghetto in Poland.

I turn to narrative to accomplish my goals because I am convinced that this genre, with its brief but powerful presentation of moments of daily Jewish life during the Holocaust, engages students in the history of this subject as it rekindles their childhood fascination with stories. I teach "A Chicken for the Holidays" to bright, eager, inquisitive eighth graders in the context of my religious studies class in a yeshiva, a Modern Orthodox day school on Long Island. I have taught it to college upperclassmen, as well; there is no end to the dialogue it promotes. The themes the story raises and the essential questions it provokes make this narrative highly appropriate for any reader engaged in the subjects of defining one's identity and adherence to the values of family and community.

Four Goals

I set four distinct goals for my students in this four-period unit. First, I hope that by unpacking this simple piece of writing, rich in compression of details, actions, and emotions, my struggling writers will begin to note and appreciate (and imitate!) good writing and will reach for another story when they seek to know more about this era. The clarity of this literature with its photographic details helps us see the Radom Ghetto and its inhabitants vividly and memorably. I want them to experience the fact that literature is a great companion to history.

Next, I seek to offer them a taste of the complex world of the Jewish ghetto, the historical context in general and the Radom Ghetto in particular, because that is the setting of the story. By eighth grade, my students, and perhaps yours, have learned about the Holocaust as a collection of random facts and figures. However, without a human face, the task of ordering and making meaning from such statistics is gargantuan and, I believe, impossible. By introducing them to a teenaged Bernard Gotfryd, a profoundly believable adolescent with whom they can easily identify; and by offering just one episode as a paradigm for ghetto life, I seek to humanize and concretize the enormity of the ghetto experience. As one of my college students wrote, "Sometimes, even though we remember the Holocaust as a historical event, we forget the minute details that are so important. This story helps us remember the smaller parts, the day-to-day details of the lives of everyday people."

To help my students understand the specifics of Radom, I e-mail them a document called "Radom Ghetto" from the Web site *http://www.deathcamps.org/occupation/radom%20ghetto.html*. I ask them to download, read, and bring the article to class, where we will compare it to the story. (My kids seem to pay more attention to something they have to find and download than they do to what I give as an in-class handout.) To supplement the unit, I found *http://www.deathcamps.org/occupation/ghettolist.htm* fascinating. Called "Occupation of the East," the site provides the names of every ghetto in Eastern Europe, the number of Jews interned there, the camp to which they were usually deported, and the dates of the ghettos' existence. The United States Holocaust Memorial Museum Web site, *http://www.ushmm.org/education/foreducators*, is a vast, easy-to-negotiate resource, and, for a timeline of the Holocaust, *http://motlc.wiesenthal.com/site* is useful. For a projectable black and white map of the ghettos, go to *http://fcit.coedu.usf.edu/holocaust/MAPS/map006b.PDF*.

Third, because the story introduces the vitally important concept of spiritual resistance, I want my students to explore the nuances of such resistance, to understand and appreciate how even seemingly minor acts and trivial defiance served to embolden the spirit and feed hope. The concept of spiritual resistance is explored here through the family's commitment to keep religious law despite the hardships such adherence brings. Such otherwise small efforts carry larger significance precisely because they occur within the context of attempted domination and terror-control by the Nazis and their sympathizers. The young man in the story—and his mother by her ironic decision—display a kind of militant refusal to accede to the demands of the Nazis by their allegiance to an alternate value system, one that conflicts with the dictates of the dominant power. It is defiant and yet requires that no voice be heard, no placard waved, no weapon raised. Sometimes, the story tells us, we can do more to hamper the enemy's cause by unflinchingly serving the ends of our own ideology than we can by attacking him directly. To enrich the topic of spiritual resistance, see *www.ushmm.org/wlc/article* and *www.ushmm.org/education/foreducators/resource/resistance.pdf.*

In an English or history class, those goals would suffice; but because mine is a class in Jewish Law (in Hebrew, *halacha*), I have a fourth goal. I seek to synthesize what students have learned about *halacha* with what they learn about the ghetto and see if they can, by such synthesis, understand more clearly the ghetto conditions, the power of spiritual resistance, and the role that adherence to *halacha* played even in the most desperate times and extreme circumstances. Clearly, a rule of law must exist in any ordered society. What happens to that law when the pressures of morality and decency are stretched to their limits? Does the law fail? Does it bend? These essential questions form the heart of our exploration. For this, we use the text called *Responsa from the Holocaust* (2001) by Rabbi Ephraim Oshry. For an overview of Rabbi Oshry's life, try *http://www.nytimes.com/2003/10/05/nyregion/05OSHR.html.* While I am not accountable for New York State standards for teaching language arts, world history, or technology, this unit does meet performance standards for all three areas as delineated in this *Guide* (pp. 490–492).

In the Beginning

I begin this story at the *end* of a class in which we have analyzed various laws on the question of the necessity to eat meat on the Jewish Sabbath (*Shabbat* or *Shabbos*) and holidays. I distribute "A Chicken for the Holidays" and ask my students to read it for homework and come to class the next morning ready to discuss the story in detail. I do not assign directed reading prompts, but I do ask that they jot down in their journals, as they have been taught to do, questions and reflections as they occur. My students are highly grade-driven; a reminder that their participation in the next day's lesson will be tracked and graded is enough to ensure that they will read the story thoroughly.

I begin by posing simple comprehension questions on the plot, characters, setting, and outcome that can be answered in seconds or discussed at length, depending upon the teacher's purpose. I use them here to check for understanding; you may want to use them as an end-of-unit review before a summative essay or as guided or independent practice.

- Why does the narrator say he is "plotting" a trip to the Dombroski farm?
- How does the setting change as he nears the farm?
- What is his goal?
- What is his motivation?
- What do the Dombroskis give him?
- Why do they give him anything at all?
- What might the consequences of the boy's actions be?
- Why might his actions have those consequences?
- Why does he risk the consequences?
- What is so important to him? (Further discussion: Is the same thing important to us?)

- Why does the boy's mother respond the way she does?
- What are the two very different emotions that the mother shows? What does each show?

Clarifying the Background

To elicit my students' understanding of ghetto life, I ask them to find and read aloud only specific portions of the story that reference the rules, regulations, and penalties incurred for violation of instructions and prohibitions mandated by the Nazis who patrolled the ghetto. They offer, "My father gave up ... because of the danger of crossing city limits" (*Anthology*, p. 96); "It was a time of martial law: no hearings, no trials, no excuses"; "Open markets were banned"; and, most crucially, "To be caught without the armband was punishable by death" (p. 97). They are fully caught up in the text and frustrated by the life imposed on the Jews by the Germans.

"No matter what you did, it seems like you could be killed for no reason at all except the fact that you were Jewish," concludes Nataniel grimly.

"That's precisely the situation faced by our protagonist," I agree, "and by everyone else in the ghetto."

I ask them to sit with their partner (paired learning is called a *chavruta* in Jewish education), refer to their e-mailed information sheet on the Radom Ghetto, and take 10 minutes to read and respond to the following information, which I had written earlier on the board. I want to ensure that they read the fact sheet on the ghetto to help clarify the differences between a factual and a personal account and to stress the importance of using both in studying the Holocaust.

> We learn from our document on the Radom Ghetto that "on 7 April 1941, the ghettos were closed. No walls surrounded the ghettos, whose boundaries where indicated by surrounding housing. Although the Jews suffered from starvation, bad hygienic conditions, and persecution by the SS and Gestapo, compared to most other ghettos, overall living conditions were relatively bearable. Smuggling food into the ghetto, however, could have deadly consequences, and many paid with their lives for attempting to do so." *http://www.deathcamps.org/occupation/radom%20ghetto.html*

1. Do you get a stronger sense of the danger facing the narrator from the story or the document?
2. From which account do you get a stronger sense of the ghetto and its function? Explain, using specific details from the texts.

Formative Methods of Evaluation

The room buzzes with conversation, and I use this opportunity to find out what my students are thinking so I can assess and evaluate appropriately. When I listen to what my students say to one another in paired learning, I discover a great deal about their reading and thinking. When I see a frown, a yawn, or someone staring out of the window, I know there is a disconnect between this reader and the text, and I can attempt to address it on the spot, quietly. When I participate in a *chavruta*, even my most reticent students are willing to share their thoughts with me.

Confronting the Essential Quandary

Once I'm sure that the "stage" of the ghetto is set, and the narrator's situation is clear, I lead my class to explore the quandary he faced.

"What is the vision," I ask, "that drives his efforts to obtain a chicken for the family to eat on the upcoming holiday of *Rosh Hashana* (the Jewish New Year)?" The holiday meal that he dreams of, we decide, reflects several tiers of quest. The students turn to the text to find support.

First, and simplest among them, is the quest for a festive meal for his family who lives now in such deplorable conditions. This simple step is important, for it reflects the author's stated intent. Second is a child's quest to feel his parents' pride and joy at being able to offer such a feast. All children desire their parents' approval, and some undertake monumental risks to obtain it. I do not explore the young man's actions for their psychological implications; I wish simply to remind my students that the narrator is, at root, just a kid trying to make his parents happy and proud of him.

Compliant Defiance

Last, and perhaps so subtle that even our protagonist does not understand his own motive, is the quest for spiritual resistance, to preserve at least the trappings of his faith even while the madding world continues unabated. He seeks to obtain the bird, secured in defiance of his ghetto jailers, as a tangible symbol of his faith.

Another example of what might be called "compliant defiance," that is, seeming to go along with the rules but breaking them whenever one can without too much perceived risk, is hauntingly captured by the young man's mixed emotions as he replaces his arm band upon reentry to the ghetto and reflects on the implications of noncompliance vs. cooperation.

"To be caught without the arm band was punishable by death" (*Anthology*, p. 97), Gotfryd tells us matter-of-factly, as he removes it to begin his journey; but later, as he puts it on before returning to the ghetto, he realizes, "I was just as scared wearing the arm band as I was without it" (p. 100).

I ask, "How does this help us understand the Nazi treatment of the Jews?"

"It's what Nataniel said earlier," Chana volunteers. "The Nazis ruled as much by scaring you as with guns. You never knew what would get you killed, so you lived in constant fear. Maybe that was why people kept their faith. You felt you had no control over whether you lived or died—it was in God's hands."

We explore the son's efforts to save the spirit of the holiday and his other motivations as well.

"The adventure, the risk, and the pleasure he would bring to his mother all motivate the narrator," I summarize. "Which of the three seems to keep him going as the plot progresses?"

We turn to the mother and wonder: How and why is it possible that she is motivated by the *very same priority* that her son values but with such disparate conclusions? She pursues the same goal, to preserve the tenets of her faith, by rejecting the very offering that he made to satisfy those tenets. Mrs. Gotfryd explains that if she capitulates and compromises the dictates of her religion for the sake of a festive meal, she will have lost the war against those who seek to crush her. For the battle is won, she explains, not by having the holiday meal against all odds but by holding fast to the rules and beliefs of one's religion. "We're a people who must abide the laws, or else we'll cease to be a people" (p. 103), she explains, neatly encapsulating the story's major theme. Homework is four questions to be answered briefly in the students' journals:

1. The narrator may be trying to maintain his beliefs and resist the Nazis by celebrating the holiday in a particular way. Do you think he realizes that importance of his actions? Defend your position.
2. Why does the mother make the decision that she does? Does her decision make sense logically? Religiously? In the context of resistance? Explain.
3. The mother cries, and the boy cries, each for different reasons. What are they?
4. If the mother *had* used the nonkosher chicken for their holiday dinner, the story's theme would be different. What would it be?

In our second class, students share their responses. If time permits, you might have them share with a partner and then synthesize their findings for the class. Ariel begins. "From this story, we can understand the stress placed on the High Holidays in the ghetto. The family could not know if they would be alive at the next holiday, and maybe this was why the boy felt it was worth risking his life for a chicken."

"The boy went to great lengths to get the chicken," offered Nissim. "Even though he was scared, he was determined to go. I thought it was amazing that the mother said they couldn't eat it. By not eating it they are standing up to the Nazis, resisting the only way they can. So, yes, her decision did make sense in that context."

Tal agreed. "The Nazis try to dehumanize us, but we still are people of God and the Torah, and we will always do our best to follow its laws properly, even when it is hard. That's what the mother was teaching, so yes, her decision was logical religiously."

Lecture and Discussion

When the sharing concludes, I offer a brief lecture and discussion of *halacha* that dictates that when faced with the perceived necessity to violate an important, but not cardinal, law (i.e., everything but murder, prohibited sexual relationships, and idolatry), one can break the law without fear of the punishment of death, as required if one breaks a cardinal law. (Keep in mind that today this is purely theoretical, not what happens in fact if a Jew breaks one of those laws.) This humane sensitivity makes it possible to coexist with the demands of one's faith.

However, while this latitude usually operates, ironically, when the socio-political climate becomes hostile, as during the Holocaust, what was permitted by law beforehand may now rise to the standard of a cardinal offense, with the attendant instruction to sacrifice oneself rather than violate the rule. The rationale for this change of legal hierarchy is that the violation of the rule carries greater weight now that it has been attached to an external mandate. Because the enemy requires the action, defiance becomes all the more critical, even though the enemy may never know you are defying him.

I spent considerable time with the students exploring this curious phenomenon. "Why," I ask, "is this transformation of the law implemented? What values does it seem to reflect?" The students are able to understand the concept, though with some measure of difficulty. I think their hardship stems from the fact that they've been taught for years to learn something, categorize it, and keep it in its assigned place forever. Reassignment can be a considerable shock to young teens, who desire routine, regularity, and predictability, who still find comfort in the "blacks" and the "whites" of elementary school. It's very important to me to be sure that my students explore dichotomy and contradiction. It is only of late that they have begun to see a little more "gray"; I believe that it's up to us to widen that vision.

We examine the process of domination. Destruction of a person is accomplished, I suggest, by snuffing out not only life but also hope. When a person's soul is dead, you have won. If s/he still believes in something, however, you are defeated. The Holocaust, we discover together, is the battleground for this contest of wills.

Doing the Right Thing

To prepare students for the second night's assignment, I explain that even throughout the years of the Holocaust, there were men and women who remained committed to strictly following the laws that govern every aspect of daily Jewish life. Often, the conditions they confronted in the ghetto made it difficult or impossible to follow the laws as they understood them. So, they asked a rabbi what they should do if they were not sure. For example, it is a *mitzvah*, a religious commandment, to light candles just before *Shabbat* (also *Shabbos*), but no one had candles in the ghetto. What could they substitute? Some people may have said, "Who has time to worry about such luxuries?" Those who were committed to following Torah law did worry, and they sought out religious authorities to answer their questions.

Rabbi Oshry and the Kovno Ghetto

In general, when such questions were posed, rabbis in each community had to rely on their knowledge alone when making rulings, because they did not have their extensive libraries with them in the ghettos. A special situation existed in the Kovno Ghetto in Nazi-occupied Lithuania, though. (For general information on the Kovno Ghetto, go to *http://www.ushmm.org/kovno/*.) There the Nazis had decided to warehouse all of the books of Jewish law they had confiscated from the Jews. They wanted the collection for a museum they planned to build: "The Museum of the Extinct Jewish Race."[1] By chance, they appointed Rabbi Ephraim Oshry as the caretaker of the books in the warehouse from June 1941, when the Nazi occupation of Kovno began, until August 1944, when it was liberated. Thus, when people in his ghetto came with questions, he consulted the major books of rabbinic literature as he formulated interpretations of religious law, traditionally called *responsa*, to help his people.

Rabbi Oshry recorded—on paper torn from cement sacks—both the questions asked and the answers he provided, and he hid the papers in tin cans that he buried around the ghetto. When he was liberated in 1944, he retrieved his notes and published *Responsa from the Holocaust;* that text is integral to this lesson.

Although the situation of one ghetto may not apply to another, it is reasonable to assume that similar problems existed in every ghetto in Eastern Europe. Therefore, these questions presumably were asked by many Jews, not just those imprisoned in Kovno. As part of my final goal, I want my students to see and appreciate the commitment to their faith that these Jews, like the mother in our story, exhibited. I want them to explore how the quandary presented in each question adds to our growing knowledge and understanding of the historical context that gave rise to such questions. For homework, I ask students to write questions they might have about what we discussed in class, recognizing the subject's complexity.

The third day begins with a review of those questions; one provides a crucial segue to the day's lesson. (My response, too specific here, is in the Appendix.) Then Eyal wonders, "Maybe the family had an obligation to eat the chicken since it would have provided food to help them get through the hard times. The chicken could've saved their lives. What would Rabbi Oshry have said if they had asked him?"

"Fantastic question, Eyal!" I said. "My college students asked the same thing. However, I'm going to ask you to be patient because I don't want to answer it just yet. Instead, I want you all to explore some of the questions just like Eyal's that people really did ask the rabbi. Then, using what you've learned so far in our class on *halacha*, and keeping in mind the life-threatening conditions of ghetto life, sit

---

1 Historian Magda Veselska (2006), from the Prague Jewish Museum, says that there is no written German documentation to support this theory. "Moreover," she writes, "it does not seem probable that Nazis would have spoken about the exterminated race so openly in 1942 already." Other historians point out that such collections may have served the Nazi purpose of acquiring all Jewish property. (From the *Prague Daily Monitor*; reprinted in "Prague Jewish Museum paradoxically expanded during WWII" in *Martyrdom & Resistance*, March/April 2006, (16).

with your partner and figure out the response that you think the rabbi would give to the question posed. Be prepared to share it with us in 15 minutes."

Questions from Ghetto Residents

I chose three of the rules we had studied in previous classes[2] and gave to each pair of students one of the (abridged) questions posed by a ghetto resident:

Cooking on *Shabbos* in the Ghetto

"The accursed Germans," writes Rabbi Oshry, "took 1,000 men every day for slave labor in the airfield outside the city of Kovno. One … came to me with the following problem: He had the opportunity to work in the kitchen where they cooked the black soup that the Germans supplied the Jewish laborers. The problem was that he would be compelled to work there on *Shabbos* as well [Cooking, which is a category of "work" according to Jewish law, is forbidden on the Sabbath.]. One advantage to him, however, was that he would be spared the much more difficult slave labor at the airfield, which was psychologically as well as physically destructive. He would remain physically and mentally healthier and would perhaps be able to survive the general starvation of the ghetto. Another aspect of his question was whether he might be allowed to eat the soup he himself had been forced to cook on *Shabbos*." (p. 13)

Electric Lights as *Shabbos* Candles

"In 1942," Rabbi Oshry writes, "I was asked whether people could fulfill the *mitzvah* of lighting *Shabbos* candles by using electric lights, and whether they might recite the [same] blessing for lighting candles on those [electric] lights. People who had all their lives been careful to fulfill this *mitzvah* [each week] were unable to obtain candles because they were locked up in the ghetto. Electricity, however, was available." (p. 52)

Does a Ghetto Home Need a *Mezuzah*?

[Jews are required to place a small parchment scroll inscribed with Deuteronomy 6:4–9 and 11:13–21 inside a protective cover and affix it on the right-hand doorpost of all the entryways in their home or apartment.] "Since there was no way in or out of the ghetto without the Germans' permission," writes the rabbi, "and

---

2   These questions were chosen specifically for this guide, designed for use with a broad audience. Those readers well versed in halacha would choose responsa more closely aligned with the various laws on the question of the necessity to eat meat on the Jewish Sabbath and holidays. The focus of learning would be on the process of arriving at the answer rather than merely on the answer itself (Smith, 2007).

the ghetto was surrounded by an electrified barbed-wire fence, and machine-gun-armed guards made sure that no one even went near the fence, the dwellers of the ghetto were really no more than prisoners. Thus, does a prison dwelling need a *mezuzah* or not?" (p. 96)

Analyzing and Applying the Law

The period flew as the students, learning together, analyzed the law and tried to apply it to the restrictions faced by the ghetto Jews. I charted their responses; I like to make their thinking public because it makes them more responsible about what they say. I also did not want to lose the ideas they shared; they would be part of their evaluation. So, on a flip chart in the front of the room I wrote as students shared their conclusions.

Tova began by discussing the prohibition of cooking on the Sabbath: "We had to answer the question 'Can a Jew accept a job that results in his having to cook on the Sabbath?' The Torah states that the violation of Shabbat is permitted to save one's life, and this certainly was the case here. Life for the Jews couldn't get worse; with the lack of food, clothing, and shelter, they were really deprived."

Esther, her learning partner, continued. "When one Jew gets the chance to make life the slightest bit better or easier, it can save lives later on, because he will have more strength when the situation gets worse. Cooking in particular is important, because the person can sneak a few bites and because this job allows him to avoid the hard labor of the airfield. In the winter he has heat from a stove, and in the summer he can work inside. This man had a rare opportunity, and he shouldn't deny it to himself, especially because it's not violating any specific aspect of the Jewish law."

Shimon spoke next. "Both the story and this question show how people tried to keep their Judaism and the *halacha*. However, there is a big difference between saving your life and keeping the law. One question is if the man is allowed to eat the soup that he made on *Shabbat*. He didn't cook the soup on his own; the Germans made him work. That was what they wanted to do: to make the Jews violate Shabbat. Just like in the story, they wanted the Jews to eat nonkosher meat."

Simcha, his partner, continued: "We understand that you can violate *Shabbat* to save your life. I understood from the story and this question how things were difficult mentally, physically, and spiritually in those very hard times. So, in the story, eating the nonkosher chicken would not have saved their lives; they were not yet starving. But in this case, we think the man should take the job and eat the soup because that will save his life."

Leah raised her hand. "Tova and I don't think it's necessary for him to avoid the job. He has no choice. The Germans make him work where they want him to work. The enemy wants you to work on Shabbat, so it is important to show them that it doesn't matter to you."

"Do you think that the stakes are raised by the fact that the enemy *wants* you to break *Shabbos?*" I asked.

"Yes! Show them that you still believe in God and nothing will change that. By doing what they want, you show them that nothing matters. If you still have faith in the Lord, He will have faith in you," Tova said.

"That's exactly why you ought to defy them at that moment!" Yoni called out. "I have a question. Is the decision altered if the Germans gave the man a choice about which job to take? Should he avoid the kitchen job so that he can avoid the violation? I got the idea that he had no choice. It was take that job or maybe be shot, just like wearing the armband or taking it off—either one could cost you your life."

"I like your thinking on this," I said. "However, I want you to consider what you know about *halacha* and respond to the following thoughts tonight:

- Is it permissible for the man to eat the food that he has cooked on Shabbos? If not, should he take a job where he would be tempted to eat it?
- By taking this job, he is taking someone else's place and perhaps putting that person at greater risk for starvation or death from hard labor. If he had the choice, should he offer the job to someone who is older and weaker?"

When we moved to the question of the *Shabbat* candles, Shmuel said, "Yehuda and I agree that they shouldn't worry about that. It was very hard for them in the ghetto. They don't have candles, so they should use something else. If they have electricity, they should use it. At least they would have a glow of light to make Shabbat feel holy."

"We learned," Yehuda added, "that Jews in the ghetto tried their hardest to obey the commandments no matter what hardships they faced. So, this could be a way of obeying the commandment 'to kindle' the Sabbath lights."

"I'm aware," I answered, "that you feel strongly that they should not have had to worry about these questions in the ghetto, but they *did* worry. While perhaps they did not need not to be concerned with such things, it is this very concern that reveals their level of dedication to Jewish law. Can we say the same about ourselves? I think their situation teaches us to ask ourselves essential questions. What is our level of dedication to *halacha* in our current safe and comfortable lives? Think about it."

Effie spoke. "Michael and I had the question about the *mezuzah*. If you don't have a *mezuzah*, then there is nothing that you can do about it. If you step out of line trying to get it, that's taking a big risk, and we don't think life is worth risking for a *mezuzah*."

"Ordinarily, you'd be right," I said, "but the question that the story raises is whether the usual rules apply when someone is trying to crush your faith. What is normally not an issue worthy of risking your life may become a more important issue in times of trouble. The preservation of the law of *mezuzah* is no longer simply the symbol of a Jewish home. It has been transformed into the symbol of Jewish defiance and pride in the face of our enemies. Much as that boy risked his life for a chicken for the holiday, the people in the ghetto may have accepted unusual risks to show the Germans that they were not willing to obey and die without fighting back, even if only in a symbolic way."

Dana added, "Their so-called 'apartments' were barely livable! There was no room to live normally; everything was 'vacuum-packed.' The conditions were not like a house, so why should you put a *mezuzah* on the doorway of what you could barely call living space?"

"Also," Ilan spoke as he raised his hand, "I think that the Jews would be afraid that the Nazis would destroy the *mezuzah*, which is sacred. Maybe that's why they asked the question in the first place."

"Putting up a *mezuzah* would be an extra fulfillment of a commandment in the ghetto," reasoned Malka. "But if you have a *mezuzah* and the Germans see it, you might be punished. It's like the armband. You could be dead if you wear it and dead if you don't!"

Thinking along the Same Lines

To finish the class, I gave them a copy of a comment from one of my college students so they could see how closely their thinking matched:

"I sometimes wonder," Zev, a senior, had written, "how someone could go through that trauma and then live a normal life. After reading this story, I found one way to answer this question. The Jews of the ghetto suffered but were trying to live a normal life. Regardless of the difficulties, they tried to keep the tradition and religion. The Nazis gave them nonkosher food, but in order to live a religious life, they endangered themselves and tried to bring a kosher chicken into the ghetto. The Nazis forced them to work on the Sabbath, and the Jews agonized about doing the right thing. The struggle for normalcy then is probably one reason they were able to live a normal life afterwards."

For homework, I asked for responses to that comment and/or to the class in general. Now, in our fourth and final class on this topic, we would see if their rulings reflected what the rabbi had ruled in each of these situations. After reviewing the homework responses briefly, I distributed the text and directions:

- Use your Oshry text to look up his answer to your question.
- Reflect on his decision, and explain, by citing details from the question and the answer, what you have learned:
  - about religious resistance
  - about conditions in the ghetto
- Join another *chevruta* and exchange and discuss questions and answers.
- What are your thoughts regarding the responsa you read? What is the value of the responsa? What do they tell us about the life and times of those who posed the questions?

The students flew to find the answers. They high-fived one another as they realized their thinking reflected that of the esteemed rabbi.

Cooking on Shabbos in the Ghetto

"I ruled," writes the rabbi, "that he was allowed to cook on Shabbos, because the alternative of slave labor in the airfield on Shabbos was no less a desecration of Shabbos than the cooking. In neither case would he be desecrating Shabbos willfully, but solely out of compulsion. It was therefore preferable that he work in the kitchen where he would be given enough food to eat. I allowed him to eat the black soup that he himself would cook on *Shabbos* since it is not forbidden to eat the product of Shabbos labor where one eats it to preserve life." (p. 13)

Electric Lights as *Shabbos* Candles

"I ruled," writes the Rabbi, "that where it is impossible under any circumstances to obtain *Shabbos* candles, it is permissible to recite the blessing on electric lighting." (p. 52)

Does a Ghetto Home Need a *Mezuzah?*

"The ghetto rooms were unbearably overcrowded," the rabbi writes. "Beds were almost literally one on top of another. Such rooms could in no way be considered normal, permanent dwelling places, since if anyone was given the option he or she would leave as soon as possible. These dwellings were beyond any doubt temporary residences. A *mezuzah*, however, is required only in a permanent residence. ... I therefore ruled that those apartments and rooms did not need *mezuzahs*." (pp. 96–97)

The kids loved this period and shared their analyses gleefully until the bell. Our summary statements would be completed via e-mail.

E-Mail Summary Statements

As confirmation of the acquisition of ideas presented and discussed in class, e-mail correspondence between teacher and students is ideal. The students can reflect freely at home, contemplate conclusions they have drawn from the lesson, and write at their leisure. I can assess their thinking on my goals and evaluate from their written work the meaning they have constructed. I make sure that they receive my e-mail feedback, along with a grade for their participation, in a timely manner. The first message was waiting for me that afternoon. "The fact that the Jews asked the question shows a lot," wrote Mira. "They were in a horrible situation and still they were concerned about law."

"What I found most amazing from the *Responsa*," Andrew wrote, "was that the man was more concerned with following the *halacha* than he was with having an easier job and staying alive. Instead of taking a job that may save his life, he checks to make sure that it's halachically (legally according to Jewish law) permissible. It is good to know that there were Jews who kept their faith so strongly."

Raphi wrote, "I learned a lot about the hardships of the ghetto: the curfews, death sentence for removing the armband, poverty, and the sacrifices Jews wanted to make for Judaism, first by the kid to risk his life for the chicken, and then by the mother throwing it out, when it would have been so easy to eat it."

Riva told me, "I learned from the mother, as well as from the halachic questions, that even in incredibly hard times, these people didn't give up one ounce of *halacha*. Even where they could have done their best and it would be fine, they went out of their way to ask a rabbi whether it would be okay. I hope that in such a hard time, I would be willing to sacrifice so much for every inch of law."

"The rabbi is telling his people," wrote Esther, "that even in this darkest time, where it's extremely difficult to practice Judaism and live like the Torah tells us, we must do everything in our power to try. This is the message the mother teaches her son."

"This unit made me think about how much we take for granted," Daniel reflected. "We can follow the strictest laws, but instead, sometimes, we take advantage of this privilege and look for loopholes."

I write individual responses to everyone and send the following to the class: "I'm pleased that each one of you understood the most important point just as well as my college students did: that despite the horrendous conditions of the ghettos, still there were Jews who remained steadfast to the ways and teachings of their fathers. I think that's not because they knew that the Holocaust would turn out all right, because of course it did not, but because they knew that they could not abandon the truth that they had come to know, even in the face of intense adversity. When you are driven by that loyalty, sacrifices *al Kiddush Hashem* [in sanctification of God's Name], are, though excruciating, just simply part of the package that you buy into, for if you fail to remain true to these ideals, then, to borrow the mom's phrase, you cease to be a people."

I attached a response written by Dani in my college course. I wanted them to see their thinking reflected outside their classroom, and I wanted to end the unit on the very note he struck: "The resilience exhibited in "A Chicken for the Holidays" and by the Jews in the ghettos who asked halachic questions is remarkable. The Nazis waged a war on the Jews and their humanity. While they were successful in murdering millions and destroying the spirit of many, they were unable to extinguish the Jewish spirit that burned within these few. The boy had been stripped of his dignity and seemingly had no hope of survival, but he was on a continuous quest to maintain his Jewish identity—a holiday meal would do the trick. Food was scarce and eating nonkosher food was necessary to survive. While everyone understood that *halacha* dictated they could eat the food to survive, the mother felt that since the family was not yet starving, compromising the law would be giving in to the Nazis, and she was determined to resist. These people were threatened with extinction solely because they were Jewish, and still they were concerned with keeping the laws so they could remain true to their heritage. The Jewish spirit could not be beaten!"

APPENDIX

This question, which was raised in my class, is here for those who might find it interesting.

"According to Jewish Law, one must give his life up for three major sins. For all other sins, one is obligated to save oneself (except in various cases). In our story, perhaps the family had an obligation to eat the chicken, as it would have provided much-needed nourishment. Perhaps the chicken could've saved their lives. What do you, Rabbi, believe was the right halachic response to this case?"

"The halachic truth is that aside from the "Big Three" (murder, prohibited sexual unions, and serving other gods), all other Torah demands fall by the wayside. However, there is a notion in *halacha* of a *sha'at tzarah* (extenuating desperate times). During these times, a Jew may find himself faced with a violation of *halacha* that ordinarily would not rise to the level of challenging his elemental beliefs, but because of the circumstance he now faces, a greater offense to his religion will be committed. This is because the context has artificially erected a stage for a public statement on where he fundamentally stands. In such a situation, a Jew's behavior takes on a greater significance, and he ought to be mindful that others are watching—both for his defiance as much as compliance. In our 'chicken case,' any *rav* (rabbi) would say that one *can* eat the bird. However, the child was risking his life for *kavod Yom Tov* (the honor of the festival), hardly a worthwhile trade-off under normal conditions. Moreover, his mother's rejection of the chicken (again, not in accord with the notion of the *tzivuy* of *u'shmartem et nafshoteichem*—commandment of self-preservation) reflects a desire to preserve the minor tenets of faith, for it represents, to her, the preservation of all she holds dear."

References

Gotfryd, B. (2000). A chicken for the holidays. In K. Shawn & K. Goldfrad (Eds.), (2008). *The call of memory: Learning about the Holocaust through narrative: An anthology*, pp. 96–103). Teaneck, NJ: Ben Yehuda Press.

Martin, D. (October 5, 2003). Ephraim Oshry, 89, a scholar in secret during the Holocaust, dies. Source: *http://www.nytimes.com/2003/10/05/ nyregion/05OSHR.html. Retrieved April 26*, 2007.

Oshry, E. (1983, 2001). B. Goldman (Ed.). (translated by Y. Leiman.) *Responsa from the Holocaust*. Brooklyn: Judaica Press, Inc.

Smith, Y. (2007). Private conversation. New York: Yeshiva University.

Retrieved April 26, 2007, from *http://www.deathcamps.org/occupation/radom%20ghetto html*.

Retrieved April 26, 2007, from *http://www.deathcamps.org/occupation/ghettolist.htm*.

Retrieved April 26, 2007, from *http://www.ushmm.org/education/foreducators*.

Retrieved April 26, 2007, from *http://www.ushmm.org/kovno/*.

Retrieved April 26, 2007, from *http://motlc.wiesenthal.com/site*.

Retrieved April 26, 2007, from *http://fcit.coedu.usf.edu/holocaust/MAPS/map006b.PDF*.

Retrieved April 26, 2007, from *www.ushmm.org*.

Retrieved April 26, 2007, from *www.ushmm.org/education/foreducators/resource/resistance.pdf*.

Shattered Innocence, Shattered Lives: Jewish Children in the Netherlands

Diane M. Plotkin

Yad Vashem, the Holocaust Martyrs' and Heroes' Remembrance Authority in Jerusalem, includes a small, unique memorial. Hollowed out from an underground cavern, the space is a tribute to the approximately 1.5 million Jewish children who were murdered during the Holocaust. Inside, eternal, flickering flames of memorial candles, traditional Jewish symbols used to commemorate those who have died, are mirrored infinitely in the dark, cool, and somber place of remembrance and mourning. The effect, poignant and powerful in its simplicity, is of a black sky lit by millions of twinkling stars. Recorded voices intone, slowly and distinctly, the names, ages, and countries of origin of the murdered Jewish children, facts taken from documents of testimony housed in Yad Vashem's Hall of Names, creating an endless litany of anguish and loss.

How does one describe and memorialize the suffering of more than a million children? Perhaps the best way, perhaps the only way, is to start with one child at a time.

Clara Asscher-Pinkhof was a Jewish mother of six caught up in the Nazi net when Hitler's armies invaded and occupied the Netherlands. Like all other Jews, her life changed drastically after the German occupation of Holland in 1940. She moved to Amsterdam, where she worked as a teacher in the schools set up for Jewish children and as a volunteer assistant in the *Hollandse Schouwburg*, a Dutch theater that the Nazis used as a detention center, until her deportation in May 1943.

Already a writer of children's books and novels, she felt the need to describe the events she witnessed, the suffering of those she called the "Star Children." Her intent was to speak for those who could not, and she succeeded admirably, eventually producing 68 short narratives collected in a book called Star Children (1946, 1986) that details, episode by episode, the gradual process of the Nazis' attempts to identify, separate, humiliate, and dehumanize the Jews of Holland.

"I knew," she wrote, "that I had to be their voice—that I had to speak out and say what they had felt and suffered—what they were still feeling and suffering" (Asscher-Pinkhof, 1986, p. 18). She began to write, using her authenticity as an eyewitness to capture the puzzled and fearful perceptions and anguished responses of the children with the yellow star.

Through the voices and the eyes of the children, Asscher-Pinkhof helps readers begin to understand the conditions these innocents faced as the world they knew faded and became instead an inexplicable place of danger, anxiety, and loss. In the sensitive and deceptively simple stories "Grandson" (Shawn & Goldfrad, *Anthology*, 2008, pp. 104–106) and "White Lie" (pp. 107–109), she affords readers a glimpse of these children as they are confronted with a world of rejection and brutality.

"Grandson" is a seemingly simple story of an 11-year-old boy who, on his way to school one morning, witnesses his beloved, frail, elderly grandmother being forced into a deportation van along with others from the care facility in which she lives. He cannot respond outwardly to what he is seeing; he is immobilized by the horror of what is unfolding in front of him and could do nothing to help even if he were not. Marion Pritchard, a Dutch Christian rescuer, writes of a similar moment that she witnessed as a graduate student. One morning on her way to school she passed by a Jewish children's home:

> The Germans were loading the children, who ranged in age from babies to eight-year-olds, on trucks. They were upset and crying. When they did not move fast enough, the Nazis picked them up, by an arm, a leg, the hair, and threw them into the trucks. ... I could not believe my eyes. I found myself literally crying with rage. Two women coming down the street tried to interfere physically. The Germans heaved them into the truck, too. I just sat there on my bicycle. (Retrieved from *http://www.carlisle.mec.edu/curriculum/student_resources/facinghistory/Chapter%208.pdf*, p. 383)

Pritchard goes on to say, "That was the moment I decided that if there was anything I could do to thwart such atrocities, I would do it." For the Jewish child in "Grandson," however, no such option was possible. This is indeed a defining moment in the story, but it will bring him to actions and a future far different from that of Pritchard's. In the immediate present of the narrative, he stands and waits until the vans have sped away, and then he continues on to school. Numb, in shock, and despairing, he responds, when his teacher asks him why he was late, "I couldn't get by" (*Anthology*, p. 106).

This short story is more complex than it initially seems, as it provides opportunities for examination of the effects of the Nazis' brutality on child witnesses and, simultaneously, of the relationship between one's experiences of being cared for and one's ability to care, between strength and powerlessness. The grandmother appears to be the more delicate of the two and lacking in strength, as captured metaphorically in the opening sentence, "Grandma is made of porcelain" (p. 104). The image of her fragility and his contrasting strength is furthered by her grandson's thought that her thin white hands "would certainly fall into pieces" if grasped too tightly in his "strong boyish grip" (p. 104). She has been unable to move her legs for years, although they are described as "whole" (p. 104). Her grandson, on the other hand, is able to love her as much and as easily as he does only because her legs are unbroken. His weakness, the weakness of a child, is exemplified by the fact that things broken are "so dreary to him" (p. 104).

The grandmother's strength is emotional; she "cares very much. .... She looks at him with her sweet eyes" (p. 105), and she listens well, showing him that what he has to say is important, as she never nods until she has comprehended all that he has told her. In turn, the grandson loves her and tells her things that one does not ordinarily tell "porcelain" grandmothers. Thus, the strength of her affection, attention, and appreciation of him and all that he offers in turn elicits his strength, dependent in part on the security and constancy of her love.

The situation in Nazi-occupied Holland has become one in which "there is so much that is no longer allowed" (p. 105). Such things as public deportations have become commonplace, and there is nothing anyone can do about them. To go on afterwards, then, "you make a detour" (p. 105). Although the boy no longer finds such interruptions in his daily routine unusual, he is totally unprepared for the sight of "big vans parked in front of his grandmother's building" (p. 105). His "detour" will be emotional and long lasting.

Both he and his grandmother suffer a loss of strength when they are cruelly and suddenly separated. Neither is able to do anything about her being taken from him; they are both victims. As this shatters their relationship, it also shatters his sense of security in her love. While she is shoved into the van with the others, he is prevented from getting close to her "and he cannot stop it (p. 106)." As "something very terrible" (p. 105) happens to her physically, something equally dreadful happens to him psychologically. She will no longer be able to care for him; he, in turn, loses his capacity, and perhaps even his right, to care.

According to psychological studies, children who witness violence against a caregiver are indeed likely to develop strong negative reactions. Wondering what they could have done to prevent or stop it, they tend to internalize their feelings, becoming withdrawn and anxious (Osofsky, 1995, p. 4). This leads to anxiety, depression, and aggressive behavior in school-age children and results in a numbing of affect, profound personality changes, and indifference (Osofsky, 1999, p. 37; Osofsky & Scheringa, 1997, p. 170). As the grandson becomes aware of his loss and his helplessness in the face of it, "when his legs can move again and his head is no longer buzzing and whirring" (*Anthology*, p. 106), he drags himself to school. He becomes increasingly withdrawn, apathetic, and self-protective. This is exemplified by a quartet of repetitions we hear as Asscher-Pinkhof, the omniscient narrator, states his thoughts:

> He does not care about anything anymore. If a bomb falls, he does not care; if he comes home and father and mother have been taken away, he does not care; if the schoolmaster no longer wants him in the class, he does not care; if no one wants him anymore, he does not care—for grandma … has been bound up and shoved into a big van. (p. 106)

Nonetheless, as he enters class, life seems to be continuing both normally and silently, conditions representing, perhaps, those either unaware of, or unconcerned about, the danger engulfing the Jews. No one cares, the boy perceives; so he too no longer cares. In his response to his teacher's query, he answers, in the final sentence, "I couldn't get by" (p. 106), surrendering to his vulnerability in the face of such implacable adversity. Just as porcelain is easily shattered, so, too, are the lives of the grandmother and grandson and the ties that had bound them in a nurturing and primal relationship. He has become helpless in the face of violence, and as he becomes indifferent to his surroundings and his fate, love degenerates into apathy in a seemingly indifferent world.

While the first story raises questions about connectedness and trauma, the second, "White Lie," provides opportunities to explore issues of identity and, more provocatively, Jewish-Christian relations in the wake of the Holocaust. Jopie is an 8-year-old Jewish boy, small for his age and blond, two facts that allow his mother to consider sending him to a store without his mandated yellow star to buy apples for his father's birthday. Apples, like many other things, are forbidden to Jews; the store and the shopping hours are forbidden to them as well; but the family is hungry. They have run out of vegetables and have been eating nettles (a wild plant with serrated leaves covered with fine hairs that sting when touched) they have gathered from a place where there is no "Jews forbidden" sign. Nettles, they tell themselves, "tasted all right when mother had cooked them" (p. 107).

The mother, who, when considering his errand, "does not find it as easy as he does" (p. 108), recognizes the danger she is allowing her son to face; but in this tragic world, the providers of food were frequently the children, often the family's only possible link to the non-Jewish world they needed to access if they were to survive. Jopie's "Aryan" appearance and small stature will protect him, his mother hopes, but she worries because their last name sounds Jewish. In an effort to help him pass convincingly as a Christian boy, she instructs him not to tell anyone their real name, but to say instead to whoever asks that his name is *De Jong*, a surname that can be Jewish or Christian.

Starless, he ventures out feeling invulnerable. Now, even when he sees a Nazi, he is not afraid; he thinks, for these few minutes of heady freedom, "He can't do anything to me because he doesn't know that I'm Jewish" (p. 108). He walks into the store to buy the two kilograms of apples his mother has requested. When the friendly shopkeeper asks his name, he answers as he was told; but the woman smiles and says, "No, I mean your first name!" (p. 109) He freezes, fearing that *Jopie*, a Dutch diminutive for Joseph, might be recognized as Jewish. He does not know, and he senses danger, but the shopkeeper asks him again, and so he responds with the one name he believes will convince her that he is not a Jew.

"Jesus," he says (p. 109).

What are we to make of this? Is Asscher-Pinkhof simply describing a story she was told? Does she want her readers to wonder what this ironic "white lie" portends for Jopie? Might she also be urging us to recognize the fate that Jesus himself would suffer if he were in that city, or any place in Nazi-occupied Europe, at that time, and thus to confront and struggle with the cosmic question of how to resist the endless hatreds and killings that plague the world?

Etty Hillesum, a Dutch Jewish woman who was killed in Auschwitz in 1943, wrote in her diary, "True peace will come only when ... we have all vanquished and transformed our hatred for our fellow human beings—of whatever race—into love" (Hillesum, 1981, p. 151). Can Hillesum's words, and Jopie's truer-than-he-knows statement of identity, begin a classroom dialogue about Jewish-Christian relations in the wake of the Holocaust?

In his book *Jesus Through the Centuries*, Jaroslav Pelikan (quoted in Lederer, 1998) raises the issue of the theological focus that fueled the flames of Christian hatred of the Jews.

> Would there have been such antisemitism, would there have been so many pogroms, would there have been an Auschwitz, if every Christian church and every Christian home had focused its devotion on …. Jesus as Rabbi Jeshua bar-Joseph in the context of the history of a suffering Israel and a suffering humanity? (quoted in Charlesworth, 1992, p. 51)

Most provocative, Angelo Giuseppe Roncalli, the 262nd Pope of Rome, commonly known as Pope John XXIII, as part of his quiet work to save Jews during the Holocaust, advised a young Jewish boy who had been secretly baptized "to continue being a good Jew in [your] community, go to synagogue, support the Jewish school, because 'by being a Catholic, you do not become any less a Jew'" (Kaiser, 1963, p. 49).

Jopie, who thinks he has called himself by a Catholic name, has not become any less a Jew. He has instead inadvertently revealed his Jewish identity and has, at the same time, raised for all readers necessary questions that thoughtful consideration of the Holocaust must confront.

In these vignettes, Clara Asscher-Pinkhof accomplishes her stated aim: to be the voice for the millions of children who suffered during the Holocaust. At the end of her book she notes "a handful of star children chosen by chance" were able to go to "their own land and freedom," but she calls our final attention to "the crowds of star children who did not live long and happily, whose stars were torn off by God Himself and placed among the other stars in the heavens, as eternal evidence" (Asscher-Pinkhof, p. 255). These stories serve both as lasting testimony to those children and as a testament to the author's skill in engraving their experiences in our collective memory.

REFERENCES

Asscher-Pinkhof, C. (1986). Grandson. In K. Shawn & K. Goldfrad (Eds.). (2008). *The call of memory: Learning about the Holocaust through narrative: An anthology* (pp. 104–106). Teaneck, NJ: Ben Yehuda Press.

Asscher-Pinkhof, C. (1986). *Star children.* (Terese Edelstein & Inez Smidt, Trans.). Foreword: Harry James Cargas. Detroit: Wayne State University Press.

Asscher-Pinkhof, C. (1986). White lie. In K. Shawn & K. Goldfrad (Eds.). (2008). *The call of memory: Learning about the Holocaust through narrative: An anthology* (pp. 107–109). Teaneck, NJ: Ben Yehuda Press.

Charlesworth, J. H. (Ed.). (1992). *Overcoming fear between Jews and Christians.* New York: Crossroad. Quoted in Lederer, T. G. (1998). 2000 years: Relations between Catholics and Jews before and after Vatican II. New York: Seminary of the Immaculate Conception. Retrieved April 27, 2007, from *http://www.arthurstreet.com/2000YEARS.htm.*

Hillesum, E. (1981). *An interrupted life: The diaries of Etty Hillesum.* New York: Washington Square Press.

Kaiser, R. B. (1963). *Pope, council, and world: The story of Vatican II.* New York: Macmillan. Quoted in Lederer, T. G. (1998). 2000 years: Relations between Catholics and Jews before and after Vatican II. New York: Seminary of the Immaculate Conception. Retrieved April 27, 2007, from *http://www.arthurstreet.com/2000YEARS.htm.*

Lederer, T. G. (1998). 2000 years: Relations between Catholics and Jews before and after Vatican II. New York: Seminary of the Immaculate Conception. Retrieved April 27, 2007, from *http://www.arthurstreet.com/2000YEARS.htm.*

Osofsky, J. D. (1995). Children who witness domestic violence: The invisible victims. In *Social policy report: Society for research in child development.* Vol. IX, 3, 4.

Osofsky, J. D., & Scheringa, M. S. (1997). Community and domestic violence exposure: Effects on development and psychology. In D. Cicchetti & S. Torn, (Eds.), *Developmental perspectives on trauma: Theory, research and intervention.* Rochester, NY: University of Rochester Press.

Osofsky, J. D. (1999). The impact of violence on children. In *The future of children: Domestic violence and children.* Los Altos, CA: Packard Foundation.

Pritchard, M. Retrieved April 27, 2007, from *http://www.carlisel.mec.edu?curriculum/student resources/facinghistory/Chapter%208.pdf,* p. 383.

Clara Asscher-Pinkhof's "Grandson" and "White Lie": Stories of Separation

Krystyna Phillips

> *Did I enjoy childhood at all? Did another million children*
> *who suffered my fate have any childhood?*
> —Chava Kawinta

When I first began teaching eighth-grade language arts students about the Holocaust through literature, I was overwhelmed by the vast array of available novels, survivor testimony, poetry, short stories, memoirs, diaries, biographies, autobiographical fiction, and interviews. I didn't know which sources were best suited to or most "teachable" for my students. Furthermore, few age-appropriate materials were available in my school, a small, K-8 community Jewish day school in Iowa. Through numerous trials, errors, and successes over several years, I have found that short stories, often supplemented by film, poetry, and drama, are my medium of choice. Stories communicate so directly and concisely through details and imagery that understanding can happen in a moment; stories highlight essential truths of the human experience that history may not convey. Stories are teachable, to middle schoolers in particular, in ways that other literary sources are not.

For example, novels are time-consuming and may need to be read outside of class, leaving the teacher unsure that the book has been read. Poetry may intimidate students who think they can never understand it, and poetry about the Holocaust is often too abstract, oblique, or graphic for young adolescents. I prefer to use it on occasion to supplement, rather than facilitate, learning. Drama, including Readers' Theater, is an engaging method of reinforcing learning; adolescents live "in the moment" and prefer to participate rather than observe. However, students may be too caught up by the business of staging and performing to attend to learning content; drama works most effectively, I believe, after the essentials of the subject are taught.

The Benefits of Short Narratives

The genre of the story has none of the above drawbacks and many benefits. Stories involve and engage readers, allowing them to taste, smell, feel, hear, and see what is happening to one person at one moment in time. Because stories are typically short, they can often be read and discussed within one or two class periods. They have few characters, one main event, and involve us in only one situation, helping even the weakest readers to focus and comprehend. Because the genre is familiar to and comfortable for virtually all students, they are generally eager to read a story, approaching it with the confidence that they will understand it. Stories about children who were the age of the children in our classes are particularly effective; adolescents are always interested in what happens to other young people and in what they do and think. Stories, like drama, can always be read aloud or role-played, actively engaging students.

The stories I chose as an introduction to my students' learning about the plight of the Jews in Holland, as preparation for a later reading of *The Diary of Anne Frank*, are "Grandson" and "White Lie" (Shawn & Goldfrad, *Anthology*, 2008, pp. 104–106 and 107–109), two of a remarkable collection entitled *Star Children* (1986), begun by Clara Asscher-Pinkhof in 1943, as she herself, a Jewish teacher, was one of the persecuted.

"Grandson" and "White Lie," set in Holland under Nazi occupation, are told from a child's point of view, narrated in the third-person, plaintive voice of a child caught in a world beyond his understanding. Both the titles and the very brief texts appear simple at first glance, focusing on everyday life through the eyes of the child protagonists. They offer ordinary situations, at least as the stories begin, that allow readers to feel an immediate connection. Most middle-school students, for instance, have at least one living grandparent; some may live with, or be parented by, a grandparent; generally, being a grandchild is very important in the lives of children. Thus, the title "Grandson" has a built-in, concrete, subjective appeal. So too the title "White Lie" grabs readers' attention; students have all told white lies, allowing instant empathy with the character.

Simple Writing, Complex Content

The stories, however, are not simple. Each provides a multitude of layers in which one can feel, through a child's eyes, the bewildered fear and anxiety of being trapped in the Nazi net of identification, separation, isolation, ghettoization, and deportation. Yet, they are not violent or graphic, and this makes them appropriate for 7th and 8th graders in language arts or reading classes, where youngsters from the most gifted to the most challenged will be intrigued by the essential questions posed by the stories: "What was it like to be a child in a world where you were hated—hated for the crime of having been born?"(Asscher-Pinkhof, 1986, p. 11). How could children survive, let alone thrive, when adults in his community treat him as "the other," an enemy to be despised? What were the conditions of daily life for a Jewish child living under Nazi occupation? What is "childhood" to such children? What is the role of their parents? A million and a half Jewish children were murdered in the Holocaust; these stories give us a glimpse of the life they led before they were taken. Students with both a historical context and the imagination to reflect on the pain and terror of these children's experiences—only hinted at in these delicate readings—will be able to appreciate that the simplicity of the writing style belies the complexities of the time and place from which the characters speak.

"Grandson" and "White Lie" are short but powerful as they highlight the plight of Jews in the Netherlands and provide a window into the lives of children as the Nazis ravaged their cities. I find these readings extremely effective in teaching about the initial stages of the Holocaust: the identification, marking, restrictions, separation, and isolation forced on the Jews of Holland and every other occupied land. During this unit, students will be reading, discussing, and questioning; predicting; identifying cause and effect relationships; comparing and contrasting; identifying main ideas; and citing text to support theses. The questions, anticipatory reading guides that I raise for discussion, are designed to help students make sense of what they read, as many young learners require frequent pauses for clarification. As you listen to answers proffered, you'll be able to gauge students' understanding and correct any misunderstandings they may have about the setting, plot, characters, or context. The independent assignments I suggest focus on reflective writing, both before and after reading. My assessments are based on in-class journal writing, brief written assignments at home, class discussion, and the appropriate completion of the guided reading questions and discussion prompts.

I allow five class periods of approximately 40 minutes each to teach these stories and to incorporate the suggested activities, including assessment, assuming the students have prior knowledge of the events from 1933–1940. For additional background on the situation in Amsterdam, you may wish to begin with some of the earlier stories in *Star Children;* they provide a solid grounding, as well as a powerful follow-up, for the events of "White Lie." All of these stories are set in what the author calls "Star City," Amsterdam in the early stages of Nazi occupation.

Creating Connections

To begin, as well as to enrich, I use an activity designed to create connections between students and their past, helping to achieve one of my goals of making the time period of the stories accessible to young readers. I ask students to bring from home old family photos, particularly those of their grandmothers and great-grandmothers. If they don't have any photos, direct them to the United States Holocaust Memorial Museum Web site (*www.ushmm.org*) to select and print photos from the archival collection to bring to class. This activity allows students to enter the time period to be studied through something familiar, their own or a representative family, with their particular dress and surroundings; it also allows them to share connections to their grandmothers, laying the groundwork for an empathetic response to the boy in "Grandson," another goal in this lesson.

Ask students to share the photos and to identify similarities and differences among them. Some may have come from the "Old Country," while others will be from the United States. How can we tell the difference? Discuss clothing, hairstyles, poses, facial expressions, and background objects, eliciting strong and specific adjectives; this activity will resonate when students read "Grandson." After the readings, you may use these photos to have students create a collage of ancestors and today's families; see *www.ushmm.org* for more information on this extension or enrichment activity.

As this discussion slows, bring the class closer to one of the themes in "Grandson" by asking: "Who in these photos would be the people usually saved and protected first when there is an emergency? How would a grandmother or other old person be treated during an emergency today? Why?" You may connect this to a discussion about the movie *Titanic* if your students are familiar with it; lifeboats were filled with women and children first. The Nazis did the opposite, choosing instead to kill the past and future of the Jewish people by murdering old women and young children as well as everyone else.

Students may ask about the possible reasons for the Nazis' war against the Jews; this is a complex question that students will continue to raise, and teachers will attempt to explain, throughout middle school, high school, and college. Assuming a brief, prior overview of Holocaust history, students should be able to state that the Nazis believed, although it is not true, that Jews were a race and not just a religion. The Nazis believed that the "Jewish race" was both inferior and threatening to the German future. Europe has a long history of Christian antisemitism, and the Nazis, by making the antisemitism *racial*, were able to channel this long-standing hatred and make it murderous.

Focused Reading

On day 2, students read "Grandson" in class. To help them focus when they read, write the title on the board and discuss the following questions before distributing the story.

1. Keeping in mind yesterday's discussion, what might this story be about?
2. What does the term *imagery* mean? How do writers use it in a story? What imagery did we use yesterday to discuss our photos?
3. What were some descriptions we had of grandmothers? What does the word "porcelain" mean? (Fragile, expensive, old, precious china.) What would a "porcelain grandmother" look like?

After this discussion, introduce Clara Asscher-Pinkhof. You might offer the short biographical piece from the "About the Authors" section of the *Anthology* (Shawn & Goldfrad, pp. 267–268) and point out that the author wrote these stories at the very time she was experiencing these hardships herself. Distribute the text, the questions, below, and highlighters/markers. To begin, read aloud the first through fourth paragraphs. I read aloud to introduce stories because I find that students are less likely to race through the narrative once they are engaged by hearing it. Ask students to highlight the imagery in the paragraph as you read and then to answer the comprehension questions. Discuss their answers before proceeding with the rest of the reading. Possible answers follow.

- Write an example of imagery you highlighted. ("Grandma is made of porcelain; Grandma's hand would ... fall into pieces" (p. 104); everything about her is white and smooth and fine.)
- How old is Grandma? (She has white hair, so she is elderly.)
- What does it mean when it says "Grandma is made of porcelain?" (She is delicate; may break easily.)
- Why wouldn't the boy have loved his grandma as much if her legs were broken instead of whole? (Perhaps such a disability would frighten him, making her too vulnerable for him to feel safe.)
- Why are broken things "so dreary" (p. 104)? (Broken things don't work, they don't give pleasure, and they cause problems. For the more sophisticated reader, you might discuss this as a possible reference to the broken lives caused by the war, the occupation, and antisemitism.)
- Where does Grandma live? (A nursing home.)
- Why does the author use the word "white" so much? (Possibly to show the innocence or frailty of Grandma, or as a contrast to the "black and white" in which children view the world; the boy's hands are black.)
- At the end of paragraph 4, what are the things actually intended "for boys and not for white, porcelain grandmas" (p. 105)? (Possibly fights at school or the goings-on at the time, which may frighten her.)

Before reading paragraph 5, ask students why the author used an extra space before it begins. (To make the paragraph stand out; to show transition and change in tone.)

Students should now be well engaged; suggest that they read the next two paragraphs silently and answer the following questions in their journals:

- Why is the boy prevented from seeing his grandma? (The Nazis are taking her and the other old people out of the nursing home and putting them into trucks.)
- Where are Grandma and the other patients being taken? (We assume to a killing center.)
- What evidence in the paragraphs helps us know the boy is Jewish? (He wonders whether the schoolmaster will still want him in class, or whether anyone wants him anymore.)

Take a minute to share answers, and then have students return to the story and to the final questions.

- Why does the boy feel that he does not care that his grandma has been shoved into a van or if his parents are not home when he gets there? (He is frightened; he cares so much that he cannot admit it to himself; how could he ever cope if his parents met the same fate and left him alone? He is worried and uncertain about what has happened in front of him and what will happen next. Grandma was innocent; how can he understand why they took her away? How can porcelain, so breakable, be shoved into a van?)

- The author does not use the boy's name. Why? (He could have been any Jewish boy in Amsterdam; he is anonymous to his tormentors; also, it highlights the omniscient point of view.)
- Why was the story titled "Grandson" when it was equally about the grandma? Would "Grandma" be a better title? Why? (Answers will vary.)

Check for Understanding

You might use the student responses, either oral or written, for assessment and to check understanding. If you assign homework, you might ask students to write a one-page extended ending to the story predicting the outcome. What happens next? What does the teacher say? How does the boy get through his day at school? Students should maintain the story's tone and include enough detail from the story to provide realism and insight. They should be prepared to share the endings the following day.

On the third day, I ask the students to sit in groups of four to share their writing, and I circulate to ensure that each group remains on task, reading aloud within their group, listening, and commenting. If time permits, you may invite students to read their paragraphs to the class. For evaluative purposes I've designed a simple rubric to help students understand the criteria for grading; each question is worth 20 points:

1. Does the writing meet the page requirement and adhere to the class standards of spelling, punctuation, grammar, and usage?
2. Is the writing detailed and specific to the assignment?
3. Does the piece conclude in a realistic manner?
4. Is it written in the third person with the same tone as the story?
5. Is there evidence of insight/realism concerning the Holocaust?

After answering remaining questions, I ask students to recall the response that the boy gave to explain his tardiness. When they repeat, "I couldn't get by," I ask if they consider that to be a "white lie." To ensure that all students are engaged in this exploration and have a chance to express their thoughts, I require them to write in their journals, and I add additional questions: How do you define "white lie"? If you think the boy did tell one, do you understand why he did? What would have happened had he told the truth? Have you ever told a white lie? To whom? What would have happened had you told the truth? What were the consequences of your white lie? Was it harmful to you? To the hearer?

The discussion that emerges will be lively, but be sure to save a few minutes to introduce the story. Building on the momentum of this discussion will reinforce students' eager anticipation of the next day's reading.

Because our next story, "White Lie," is set in the same time and place as the earlier one, I ask, "Why might the main character be telling a white lie? Do you think that the word 'white' is significant? Would you expect a different story if it were called just 'The Lie'?"

The class will end, most likely, with a groan; students will be eager to hear more!

"White Lie"

On day 4, read aloud the first paragraph as students highlight every instance of color mentioned in the first paragraph, and ask for ideas about the theme of the paragraph. You'll elicit "hunger": for color, for food; you can almost see the boy salivating; he hungers for sustenance and simple childhood pleasures. Note the colors used: mustard, white, green, and beet. To check for understanding, ask students to write one question they have about the paragraph and exchange it with a neighbor. You might call on the students whose questions are the same, or ask students to classify their questions into types: are they about the meanings of words? About the plot? setting? characters? This simple exercise helps students become familiar with the language of literature and moves them from a typical, vague, "I don't get it!" to a specific "What are *nettles*?" A quick check for comprehension might include the following questions:

- Where does this story take place? (The city, first sentence.)
- What are *greengroceries*? (Grocers that sell only fruit or vegetables.)
- How do you know that the boy is Jewish? (Ask for textual references, such as the "Jews Forbidden" sign.)

I like to continue reading aloud, at least through the third paragraph. I read the long and detailed sentences slowly so students will hear and question the oppressive, senseless laws that keep the boy and the other Jews from living a normal life. To check for new learning, I might ask students to write two specific phrases or events from the reading that have provided them with new knowledge about daily life for the Jews under occupation. Answers may include:

- Jews are not free to shop in stores that are not owned by other Jews and cannot shop even in a Jewish store except between 3 and 5 p.m.
- In Holland, the SS wore green uniforms; the author refers to Nazis as "the men in green."
- It is dangerous to throw leftover, illegal food in the garbage can; the men in green search the trash to be sure Jews are not breaking their new laws.
- Jewish people had to wear a yellow Star of David on all of their outer garments so they could be easily identified as Jews.
- Jews 5 years old or younger were not required to wear a star.

Such responses might lead to a more wide-ranging discussion, including such questions as:

1. Why would non-Jewish neighbors turn the Jews in to the Nazi police if they saw them with forbidden food? Why would Jewish neighbors report other Jews for breaking the Nazi laws? (In any conversation about Jews turning in other Jews in order to protect themselves or receive extra rations or privileges, be sure to explain that we cannot judge the Jews' actions here. We cannot know the pressures brought to bear on the Jews at that time, and the Nazis forced the Jews to make choices that they did not want to make. This is part of the complexity of the Holocaust, and we learn a little more about it each time we study it!)

2. Why would the boy want to get the apples if it is dangerous? (The family was desperate for food, and it was Father's birthday.)

Journal Writing

Students will want to read the story through; ask them to respond to the following questions in their journals as they finish. If the period ends, assign the questions remaining for homework:

1. Why would the mother let her son do something so dangerous? (Parents are desperate for food. Again, these are choices that no one wants to make; the world of the Holocaust is an upside-down one. Everything that we know to be right was wrong; everything we know to be wrong was Nazi-enforced law. Some parents had to make the agonizing choice to allow their children to endanger their lives to help the family.)

2. What are the dangers the boy faces in his journey to buy apples? (The Nazi police, bombs, strangers on the street, shopkeepers.)

3. How did you feel when the boy realized that his Jewish identity might be discovered? (Answers may vary.)

4. Why would he use the name *Jesus*? (It's the only name he can think of that he believes for sure is Christian. Point out the irony of Jesus being Jewish; if he were standing there, would he be in the same position as the boy? What conclusions can you draw from this?)

5. Why is the word *green* used so frequently at the beginning of the story, but not on the last page? (It allows a transition from the story's setting to the story's central problem; what was hopeful and positive in the beginning is no longer.)

6. Do you consider the boy's response a "white lie" or a real lie? What are the consequences of his telling such a lie? What if he had told the truth?

7. Do you think the shopkeeper believes him? Why? If she does not, do you think she might go along with the "white lie" and let him go, or will she turn him in? What sentences from the text support your opinion?

Assessing and Extending Learning

On the fifth and final day of this unit, you'll want to answer students' remaining questions and assess their learning and understanding. One way to do this might be to share poems, such as Pavel Friedman's "The Butterfly," from *I Never Saw Another Butterfly: Children's Drawings and Poems from Terezín Concentration Camp 1942–1944* (1993), and ask students to compare them to the stories. Responses might include the ideas that all were written by or about young people who were marked, separated, isolated, and persecuted because of their Jewishness; all were written during the Holocaust; all have strong imagery; all use simple language to present a difficult reality; all help the reader understand the despair felt by Jewish children during that time.

After wrapping up what will surely be an engaging discussion, assign as homework the option to illustrate five specific aspects of Jewish life under occupation in Amsterdam and explain each to the class. Addressing the different learning styles and abilities of your students is key; these stories lend themselves to a variety of assessment opportunities.

From Teacher to Teacher

Clara Asscher-Pinkhof writes about these children, "I knew ... that I had to be their voice—that I had to speak out and say what they had felt and suffered" (in Plotkin, *Guide*, p. 184). From teacher to teacher: we bring this quietly eloquent voice into our classrooms as we introduce the third and fourth generations after the Holocaust to these tragic stories.

References

Asscher-Pinkhof, C. (1986). Grandson. In K. Shawn & K. Goldfrad (Eds.), (2008). *The call of memory: Learning about the Holocaust through narrative: An anthology*, pp. 104–106. Teaneck, NJ: Ben Yehuda Press.

Asscher-Pinkhof, C. (1986). *Star children*. Detroit, Michigan: Wayne State University Press.

Asscher-Pinkhof, C. (1986). White lie. In K. Shawn & K. Goldfrad (Eds.), (2008). *The call of memory: Learning about the Holocaust through narrative: An anthology*, pp. 107–109. Teaneck, NJ: Ben Yehuda Press.

Friedman, P. (1993). The butterfly. In H. Volavkova (Ed.), *I never saw another butterfly. Children's drawings and poems from Terezín concentration camp 1942–1944*. Revised and expanded by the *United States Holocaust Memorial Museum*. New York: Schocken Books, Inc.

Plotkin, D. M. (2008). Shattered innocence, shattered lives: Jewish children in the Netherlands. In K. Shawn & K. Goldfrad (Eds.), (2008). *The call of memory: Learning about the Holocaust through narrative: A teacher's guide*, pp. 184–189. Teaneck, NJ: Ben Yehuda Press.

United States Holocaust Memorial Museum. Retrieved on November 24, 2007, from *www.ushmm.org*.

Daily Life in the Ghetto

Listening to All the Human Stories
in "A Cupboard in the Ghetto"

Sharon Deykin Baris and Karen Shawn

This brief work, like others by Rachmil Bryks, takes place entirely within the confines of the Lodz Ghetto in Poland and seems in many ways as limited as its setting and as frail and unassuming as the cupboard in its title. Minimal in size and bare of adornments, "A Cupboard in the Ghetto" (Shawn & Goldfrad, *Anthology*, 2008, pp. 113–120) has little overt action to command the reader's immediate attention. Heightening the sense of this limitation is the fact that the central characters remain, with minor exceptions, indoors. Therein, very few lively feats or deeds can be seen or noted. What does occur, however, is another colorful form of action—or interaction—suggested in repeated comments, responses, riddles, and reassurances shared and exchanged by the characters in this tale. Enlarging upon the implications of their responses to one another's stories, whether spoken or implied, we, as readers, react in turn to such persistent interchange. We do so by recognizing the many human stories included in the "Cupboard," as we continue even now to tell, review, and re-imagine their implications.

As we discover at the outset of Bryks's narrative, Hershel Zeif and his wife, Henye, spend "most of the day" (p. 113) in their separate beds. We do not observe their efforts to lie down, how they rise, or even how they contend with their discomforts. All we see is the one dire and devastating shiver of their "writhing from hunger and cold, like all their neighbors" (p. 113). In those confines we can only imagine pale Hershel and thin Henye moving from bed to table to door as they sleep fitfully, prepare and eat the scant rations they have managed to gather, admit the tinsmith who arrives to repair their roof, and greet their occasional guest Mr. Bluestein, a helpful neighbor.

We are told that Hershel and Henye, once roused, spend a surprising amount of energy attending to their great array of clothing. Daily they manage to hang outside their window a variety of unused garments, their wedding wardrobe, which they brought with them into the ghetto and now air out to fight off the onslaught of mildew, although this attention brings only temporary results and little apparent benefit. Bryks presents the details of their clothing—the winter coats, the trousers with crease and cuffs, the boots, shoes, a half-dozen white shirts, hats, linens, and so on—but he does not describe, as he conveys this process, any gestures of the Zeifs, although we can envision their worried inspections of velvet collars or frightening near-misses in getting all that material onto some presumed clotheslines or outer hooks.

We are also told that Henye cooks, that Hershel formerly had run "to the Civil Administration every day looking for work" (p. 113) and that on one occasion he had taken a board and broken it "into small pieces for several days' fuel" (p. 116). What Zeif makes of this and other boards, needed as they are for the daily cooking, is reported by him with protracted attention: "I chopped up three boards, split two of them," and so on. Yet the only observable action is merely his "point[ing] to the bunches of wood which he had divided into four tiny strips each" (p. 116). The chopping and dividing go on unseen. Similarly, Henye's cooking is not described through her active preparations, with any flair of gestures, of bending, reaching, or even stirring. We are given, rather, a catalog of ingredients: unappealing cabbage roots and wild leaves that she uses to make nearly inedible concoctions of imitation appetizers, fish, soups, and tsimmes that she merely waits to "let" cook. The energetic feats that occur in the lives of this couple and their neighbors, we realize, take place beyond the margins of Bryks's text. Within, something else is being "cooked" (or cooked up!), instead.

Vitally astir in this household is a different and positive activity whose significance provides, metaphorically, the supportive structure for the frail cupboard at its center. A variety of lively forms of communication—including anecdotes, riddles, clues, and extensive guessing games—follow one upon the other throughout these pages as a vital dynamic that characters and readers alike can see and hear. To that end, the itemized clothing, particular roots, cabbages and other foods, and even the boards inside the cupboard—counted, recounted, and slowly dismantled—do serve a purpose. They become significant and necessary props for a focus upon the process of telling, listening, and responding to a wide range of deeply human stories told and heard within this ostensibly limited setting. It is this personal interaction in which the characters participate to their mutual benefit that lies at the heart of Bryks's compelling work.

These daily acts of acknowledgment become, far more than the drudgery of forestalling mildew or the daily task of preparing food, the mainstay of hope and sustenance for his characters as they heed one another's individual views. It is our own ability, in turn, to hear and respond to these actions that allows us not only to participate in the necessary process of writing and rewriting the Holocaust, as James E. Young (1988) has put it, but also, as a similar demand upon us, to rehearse (or re-"invent," to use an action Zeif himself deploys) and re-imagine their stories. Bryks's text thus presents itself as a call for attentive reader-responsive behavior, as it offers complex examples of personal interaction that defy simple distinctions, allowing—urging—each reader anew to accept its challenge.[1]

---

1 In another short story, written presumably at the same time as Bryks was completing "A Cupboard in the Ghetto," Bernard Malamud enacts a similar cry for reader response, or what can be called "reader responsibility," within the context of an American literary tradition. See Sharon Deykin Baris, "Intertextuality and Reader Responsibility: Living on in Malamud's 'The Mourners,'" *Studies in American Jewish Literature*, 11:1 (1992): 45–61.

Peppering the text, colorful iterations draw attention to the use of language itself. Terms relating to telling and responding to one another's stories provide a dynamic that is both remarkable—whether conveyed in the original Yiddish version or its subsequent translation—and essential to Bryks's design. What thus happens, seen in this textual and responsive light, might be listed as follows: The wedding clothes and the furniture that require so much daily attention from the couple and seem unnecessarily to crowd the spaces of this story and of the meager dwelling serve effectively, instead, as the external premise for another necessity, the internal drive to maintain the tales that need be told, of how "the war might end any minute" (*Anthology*, p. 114) and of how old patterns of decent living would somehow continue. While Bluestein and others urge Zeif to sell their goods for more material and useful means of sustenance, Zeif, with brave determination, refuses. He does so if only to demonstrate his wiser sense that another kind of survival—of the shared humanity they must bespeak and continue to uphold—is more crucially at stake. Thus the boards, so fully detailed and measured, should indeed be carefully counted. For they serve as a means not only of actual cooking but also of fueling up additional stories.

That too is what the barely standing but all-important cupboard, like the short narrative named for it, so centrally offers. From the first, references to stories heard and told progress in a litany of responsive interaction. There is reference to a significant interchange or "pact" between husband and wife about keeping their clothes ready for the day they will leave the ghetto and return home. Other repeated discussions between Henye and Hershel reflect their understanding and obvious mutual regard: "Yes, the war might end any minute. God can do anything, and we'll go home in our new clothes." To which his wife nods, "That's right" (p. 114), in simple, sure agreement.

Zeif and Bluestein interact through their own lively dialogue, as well. A mini-drama is staged between them in which a question posed by Zeif as a riddle requires Bluestein's scripted participation as he "wracked his brain. ... to guess the answer" (p. 115). To his confident but incorrect guess, Zeif gleefully shouts, "Ha-ha! A likely story!" (p. 115). Thereafter, however, a far greater challenge is demonstrated in a scene that requires more serious understandings between these figures, as a story within a story unfolds to become a test case of listening, attending, and rehearing. This scene is duly remembered and emphatically set off by an indicative notation: "This was what had happened" (p. 115).

What is the reality to which this colorfully reported scene is so clearly calling attention? It had "rained in," we are told, and "Zeif had to put pans on the beds" (p. 115). After much pleading by Zeif to the administrator of buildings in the ghetto, the tinsmith has at last come to repair the leaking roof. Instead, he steals some of its precious timber. Zeif, typically, takes little physical action during this trying event, even as he hears "boards being pried loose over his head" (p. 115). However, within the space of half a page in Bryks's text, a remarkable series of comments and shared understandings is exchanged among these people under stress. As they acknowledge one another's conflicting needs, they quietly but intensely perform what proves to be this story's most significant action.

The tinsmith, a Jew forced to labor at the behest of other Jews who themselves were forced to oversee the workings of the ghetto, is in a precarious position. Needing wood for his own cooking fires, he plunders timber from the Zeifs' roof, for the tinsmith has his own narrative to maintain, we can well presume. How is one to judge this moment? The reactions that follow are fraught with a careful testing and counter-testing of Bryks's characters and their differing yet distinctively personal perspectives.

Zeif first shouts, "You're a robber!" and then presses on with an ostensibly rhetorical question that encourages interaction and response. "Don't you have any feelings?" (p. 115). The tinsmith's calm reply, in his own defense, that his theft has presented no real danger, is, oddly enough, one that Zeif himself so often loves to say and hear: "Until it rains again the war might end. ... [B]y fall we'll all have forgotten that there was ever a war" (p. 115). Zeif interrupts, if only to modify this version of the often-told story: "God forbid the war should last until the fall" (p. 115), he asserts. The tinsmith reacts to this subtle sharing of views, however implicit, by thrusting one of the boards he had taken for himself under Zeif's willing arm, while agreeing, "Of course. Now take a board for yourself for fuel ... you'll see the end of the war" (p. 115). That brief interchange has been far more productive than any physical action each of them might have taken.

Bluestein is then expected to play his part, as they all turn to him, the one officially forced to see "that nobody steals any wood" (p. 116). Bluestein considers the fright of the tinsmith, endangered as he now is, even while he notes Zeif's position. As if to complete the verbal exchange underway, Bluestein offers the simple gesture of "look[ing] at him pityingly and *he* felt better [emphasis added]" (p. 116). The fact that the pronoun "he" in this passage could refer interchangeably to Bluestein or to the tinsmith (in the English translation and presumably similarly in the original Yiddish) serves to demonstrate how our thoughtful response to one another's views has proven to be our best, our greatest, form of action.

A heightened awareness of acts of personal understanding has readied us for the moment when all view the cupboard at the story's center. Zeif opens the cupboard "with the expression of an inventor demonstrating his work" (p. 116). The characters, and we, look in. As Bluestein silently wonders, "What is he trying to show me?" (p. 116), Zeif points to the neat paper shelving that presumably covers its original sturdy construction of whole boards. However, the carefully smoothed paper acts, we find, as a cover (or undercover) story, not only for a loss of boards but also for a seemingly analogous and yet opposite purpose. Zeif proudly lifts the paper that appears on "each level" of the cupboard, showing his guest that the glassware and linens are in fact supported only by strips of wood saved from its shelves cut up for use as fuel. Thus when Zeif asks, "Why do I need whole boards? ... The wooden strips are enough" (p. 116), we may understand that they are enough, in one sense, not for fuel but for maintaining the cupboard's centrally important physical presence. On another level, however, their greater promise exists in sustaining the stories that live at the heart of these individuals' persistent concerns.

As if to reinforce the need for re-rehearsing this central textual process, the story's interactive behavior continues, as Zeif two weeks later challenges his neighbor again to "be smart and guess" about some cooking underway. As the same game of questions and answers is reenacted, Zeif refers once more to the cupboard, now moving beyond shelves to consider its very backing. When he asks, rhetorically, "Why does a cupboard need a back wall? ... [N]ow I'll have fuel for a long time" (p. 117), an answer hangs in the air. Such fuel will, indeed, continue to supply their physical needs; but it will also allow for their "invention" of salted and "ersatz" scraps on their menu, which they enjoy to the tune of imaginative devices emphasized by Hershel's humming a hasidic tune and "drumming his fingers on the table in rhythm," his wife again nodding in harmony and "agreement as they ate with relish" (p. 117). While such artistic, sensual, and even musical responses from Zeif and Henye indicate their expressive capabilities, these moments provide a provocative counterpoint to the darker scenes that lie ahead.

Two weeks later still, the cupboard door is gone, but "the cupboard is still a cupboard!" (p. 117) Zeif insists, expanding the tale that posits their unspoken theme: Much can be taken from us, but as long as the essentials remain, we ourselves are still human. We, too, insist upon this by our humane ability to share personal narratives and acknowledge one another's perspectives. Bluestein, in the process of doing so, may have "ached," and Zeif himself bravely has "tried to smile, but a grimace distorted his face" (p. 118). Nevertheless, both have kept to the script of shared responses, and they will continue such important interaction when further troubles afflict them.

Zeif falls ill, and Bluestein comes to him, responding willingly to Mrs. Zeif's plea to "look what's happened to my husband" (p. 118). Bluestein now tries his best form of cure. It is a response at once ostensibly bland and yet powerful and deeply consoling. He repeats, nearly in Zeif's own words, the narrative that begs to be heard, slightly reshaped to fit the needful moment: "Don't worry, Mr. Zeif, the war will end any day now, and we'll go home together" (p. 118). He tries, briefly, to test some other possibilities for responding to the crisis, to far less helpful effect or consolation. So, at the door he turns back, as if to reassure the Zeifs of his ability to listen. He rehearses and reiterates the all-important message that evinces understanding, as he predicts, "Mr. Zeif, in the middle of the night I'll come running in to tell you that the war is over!" (p. 118). What Bluestein offers in this crisis, we understand, is the promise of telling tales of personal and communal humanity, ongoing day or night. "Be patient, Mr. Zeif," Bluestein assures him on another visit, "we'll go home together" (p. 119). This sharing of stories is the definitively human action fundamental to Bryks's powerful ghetto narrative.

As this work draws to its abrupt and puzzling end, such linguistic or textual markers continue to appear, underlining Bryks's insistence upon this deeper narrative current. We hear hopeful references to a "good sign," and also to mere "nonsense" in words "ranted," and even a flitting thought that Zeif has himself become a dire text, a kind of "obituary" about to happen—which he does not, as the story's conclusion affirms. Yet, finally, it is Bryks's last quotation pronounced by Hershel at the end of the narrative that indeed becomes most troubling. This quotation may, in one reading, foreshadow an ominous outcome for the brave tales of hope so persistently herein maintained.

While this story's last lines seem optimistic (a term one hesitates to use, preferring useful, provocative, or demanding intimations), a darker underlying threat rises to the surface as Henye and Hershel go on repeating their tales that "We'll survive the war" (p. 120). For even as this couple seem to thrive on their own and others' repeatedly hopeful words, they subsist on what has often been feed for cattle. This is what Hershel declares as he reports what "the ghetto Jews said," while eating unpeeled potatoes, "The peel is healthy. In the peel there is iron and under it there is sugar, and that's why cattle are so healthy and strong" (p. 120). Hershel's seemingly blithe observation can be interpreted as hauntingly predictive of terrible future journeys or darkly reminiscent, a fateful reminder—whether in resistance or denial—of another statement, harshly impersonal and grossly inhumane, which Bryks, earlier, has subtly included. It was the Nazi Hans Greizer ("may his name"—or his story—"be blotted out" [p. 119]) who had predicted, in a speech that ghetto residents had read about, that hunger would turn Jews into animals, "into mad dogs. ... They will devour themselves!" (p. 119). Such talk of "wild beasts" (p. 119), as Bluestein observes, is a statement that Jews most surely shall never acknowledge or abide. It is one against which this short story's responsive and personal dynamics have carefully and brilliantly forewarned.

Mr. Bluestein, Mr. and Mrs. Zeif, and even the tinsmith all have demonstrated, by the versions of their shared understandings, that this Nazi's cruel prediction will never prevail. If Bryks's "A Cupboard in the Ghetto" stops abruptly with talk of animals and of potatoes with their peels, his readers will nonetheless continue to follow the most profoundly human challenge imaginable, one that his story in its entirety has consistently offered. That is the ongoing challenge of hearing and re-imagining one another's personal narratives, to the very end.

A figurative second ending, one could argue, is written by Bella Bryks-Klein and Nathan Cohen in this volume (pp. 208–212) as Bryks-Klein tells how her father read this story aloud to her mother and herself as a child, creating a scene of its own retelling. Alvin Rosenfeld (1980), decrying a kind of fateful literary "double dying" endured when tales of the ghetto and Holocaust find themselves without any expected moorings in a familiar form or precedent (p. 22), turns toward Primo Levi's call, in the face of such lack, for other resources to be found even in the smallest act "or the simplest gestures of human kindness" (p. 57). Bryks's short work, as if in fulfillment of both observations, offers its readers the hope of a literary double living in a recognition of one another's stories as essential to human kindness. Suggesting ever-present forms of response, such action allows even us to continue the vital process of listening to Holocaust narratives, as we feel called upon to tell and retell them, including all those layered within an unassuming cupboard in the ghetto.

REFERENCES

Bryks, R. (1959). A cupboard in the ghetto. In Shawn, K. & Goldfrad, K. (Eds.). (2008). *The call of memory: Learning about the Holocaust through narrative: An anthology*, pp. 113–120. Teaneck, NJ: Ben Yehuda Press.

Bryks-Klein, B. & Cohen, N. (2008). The man behind the "Cupboard." In Shawn, K. & Goldfrad, K. (Eds.). (2008). *The call of memory: Learning about the Holocaust through narrative: A teacher's guide*, pp. 208–212. Teaneck, NJ: Ben Yehuda Press.

Rosenfeld, A. H. (1980). *A double dying: Reflections on Holocaust literature*. Bloomington: Indiana University Press.

Young, J. E. (1988). *Writing and rewriting the Holocaust: Narrative and the consequences of interpretation*. Bloomington: Indiana University Press.

The Man Behind the "Cupboard":
An Introduction to Rachmil Bryks

Bella Bryks-Klein with Dr. Nathan Cohen

I am the daughter of Rachmil Bryks and Hinda Wolf Bryks, two Holocaust survivors. Dr. Nathan Cohen is my professor of Yiddish literature at Hebrew University in Jerusalem. With his permission, I have used his scholarship to enhance and expand this brief personal introduction to my father and his work, particularly the story "A Cupboard in the Ghetto" (Shawn & Goldfrad, *Anthology*, 2008, pp. 113–120).

Rachmil Bryks, son of Tevye and Serl Bryks, was born in the village of Skarżysko Kamienna in central Poland in 1912. He was the third child in a family of eight siblings. As a young boy, he moved with his parents to Łódź. The son of a Hasidic Jew, he received a traditional Jewish education and some general education. At the age of 14 he began to work to help the family, first as a hat maker and then as a house painter. A young romantic, his literary talent found its first expression in print in a poem "Avenues" in the literary journal *Inzl* (Island), in March 1938. Shortly before the outbreak of the war, his first book of lyric poems, *Yung-grin-may* (Young-Green-May), was published in Łódź and critically acclaimed (Cohen, 2006, p. 1).

My father was confined to the Łódź Ghetto between May 1940 and August 1944. He lived at *Blech Gasse* no. 13, Flat no. 12. While coping with the day-to-day hardships of the hermetically sealed ghetto, he continued to write. Because the Nazis forbade such cultural activity in the ghetto, groups of writers used to meet in private homes, present their works to each other, and discuss subjects of mutual interest. The first literary circle was organized by the poetess Miryam Ulinover (1890–1944) in her private apartment, where he took part (p. 1). Here he continued to write poems as well as a ballad about the Jewish experience.

After the war, my father's writings were discovered buried underground at the site of the Łódź Ghetto. These original writings are now in the archives of the Jewish Historical Institute in Warsaw, Poland.

Some parents hid their ghetto and concentration camp experiences from their children, protecting them from hearing about the cruelties they endured, but my father insisted that we must know the truth even at a tender age. Discussion of the Holocaust was a major part of our daily family life and an integral part of my childhood. I have, therefore, always felt that the Holocaust is a part of *my* life and even my very existence. My father instilled in us from our earliest years that something terrible happened to the Jewish people, including to him and to my mother, and we must be aware of it; yet, at the same time, we must recognize as well our strength as a people.

Practically our entire family was wiped out: My father lost his father, Tevye; his mother, Serl; his sister Esther and her husband, Yehiel, and their two small children, Moishele and Ruchele; another sister, Tobtche, and her husband, Yidel, and their small child; and a third sister, Leah, and her husband and small child. All were taken from their village and murdered in Treblinka on the Jewish holiday of *Simchat Torah* in 1942. Another brother, Yitzhak, was murdered in Auschwitz in 1944. My mother, Hinda, lost her father, Zeev; her sister Chaya Sarah and her two small children; and a 16-year old sister, Miriam-Leah, in Bergen-Belsen in April 1944.

We were told of the brutality, of the cruelty of the Nazis, and yet, at the same time, my father instilled in us a sense of optimism, a sense of the resilience of the Jewish soul and the Jewish people. He repeated to us the fact that throughout Jewish history, an enemy has arisen determined to destroy the Jewish people, but we have always overcome.

I have always considered my father's books historical fiction; perhaps today they would be called testimonial literature. In his works, one can find a detailed description of ghetto life: What did Jews talk about? What did they feel and think? What did they dream about and how did the see the future? He describes their appearance, where they lived, what they ate, and how they cooked their "food." The events he describes are true, but he weaves them into a story.

One of the central questions that concerned the writers in his literary circle in the ghetto was if it is possible, or even allowed, to interpret/express through *belle lettres* the current horrific events. We don't know the position of each writer on this question, but, as Cohen notes, "By reading Bryks's works from after the war, we can assume that he may have approved of the approach that claimed that the events should be given a literary interpretation" (p. 2).

For example, my father knew the couple he described in "A Cupboard in the Ghetto," but in the story he renamed them: Hershel and Henye Zeif. My father himself is represented; he is the prototype for Mr. Bluestein, a kindhearted character. My father had been sent to work in forced labor at Ghetto Factory 76 where the Jewish workers were forced to process potato peels into alcohol. He was placed as a guard at the gate, and at the end of every day, he checked each worker to ensure no one smuggled out any peels or anything that could be used for food. At the risk of his own life, he overlooked what the Jewish workers managed to sneak out. In his own way, he felt he was righting an injustice and helping Jewish families to survive. We see even in this story that he lends half of his potato ration to Mr. Zeif when this proud and self-sufficient man becomes swollen and ill.

People in these ghetto stories are dominated by everlasting and tormenting hunger. In fact, ghetto residents used to grow various kinds of leaves, mainly beetroot, radish, and cabbage; and despite the fact that these leaves caused them physical harm rather than benefiting them in any way, they mixed them with food substitutes they possessed and, as in this story, "ate with relish. … From the roots and wild leaves Mrs. Zeif prepared appetizers, fish, meat, soups, tsimmes"

(*Anthology*, p. 117). People used to describe to their ... neighbors how delicious their "food" was and share the "recipes" with each other (Cohen, p. 6).

My father wrote this particular story, as I recall, in the summer of 1953. I remember that when he finished writing it, he gathered my mother, my sister, and me together and read it aloud to us. He did not have a title for it and asked us to help him think of an appropriate one. I suggested "The Cupboard that Cooks." Although he was amazed at my abstract thinking at the young age of five, he decided to use instead the straightforward, simple title it has today.

All the Jewish inhabitants of Lodz were concentrated in the ghetto: young couples, old people, and children of all ages. Cohen points out that in my father's works

> there is a clear division between bad people and good, and no one can misunderstand who is who. There are people who still believe in social or religious ideas and in universal values; there are some who are ready to help others and those who care only about themselves. (p. 7)

However, everyone believed that the war would end any day and the Zeifs, the newlywed couple who are the main characters in this story, are a symbol of optimism, methodically airing out their wedding clothes each day in their one sunny window so the garments would be ready to wear on the day the war ended.

Throughout the war, my father, like the Zeifs, remained optimistic. The belief that the Jewish nation cannot be destroyed and would overcome this new Haman kept him strong and enabled him to survive. During the last days of August 1944, together with the other Jews who, though weak and ill, still remained in the Łódź Ghetto, my father was deported to Auschwitz. From there he was sent to various labor camps in Germany, where he was released on May 2, 1945. After five years of grueling experiences, he was brought to Sweden for healing. There he engaged in cultural work among the survivors and resumed his literary activities. In 1945 he published several poems in the Israeli Yiddish periodical *Nayvelt* (New World) and in the collection *Zamlung fun katset un geto lider* (A Collection of Poems from Concentration Camps and Ghettos, Bergn Belzn, 1946). In November 1946, Bryks published his first work in prose, a short story called

"Berele in Geto," in the Yiddish children's magazine *Kinder zhurnal* in New York. The story, based on the reality of a most traumatic period in the ghetto history, the deportation of children and elderly people in the first two weeks of September 1942, evoked great interest and was reprinted in other Yiddish publications around the world (p. 2).

He continued lecturing before groups of survivors (*she'erit hapleita*), encouraging these refugees to go on with their lives in spite of being exiled from their *shtetl* (village) and their home and losing their entire families and possessions. At one such evening, my Polish father met a young Rumanian woman, Irene Hinda Wolf, who was born in Transylvania. They fell in love, married at the Great Synagogue of Stockholm, and my sister Myriam and I were born in Sweden. Because my father was a Yiddish writer, in Sweden he served as the representative of the New York City-based YIVO (*Yidisher visnshaftlekher institute,* Institute for Jewish Research). As such, he transferred documents and other materials concerning Jews in Scandinavia and Eastern Europe during the Holocaust to the Institute's archives in New York.

In March 1949, YIVO and the HIAS (Hebrew Immigrant Aid Society) sponsored the family, and we immigrated to the United States. We were raised on the Upper West Side in New York City. Of course, my father was a changed man and could no longer write about springtime, nature, and love. Believing it was his mission to do so, he devoted the remaining 25 years of his life to reminding the world what the Nazis did to the Jews, lest we forget, lest it happen again to other nations.

Although many years had passed since his liberation, in my father's mind, ghetto life remained very fresh. I remember once waiting at a bus stop in the Catskill Mountains north of New York City, and there were bushes at the side of the road. He brought some leaves to me and said, "You see, we used to eat these leaves in the ghetto."

In "My Credo: Essay" (1969), my father wrote,

> I felt that when one writes about millions of people, it weakens the tragedy. But if you tell the story of one individual, of one family, of one child, and you succeed in conveying their sufferings, their emotions, their state of mind, it [the tragedy] comes across. But it must be written in such a way that the individual or the family or the child should symbolize the whole mass, the millions who were slaughtered. (p. 490)

In "A Cupboard in the Ghetto," he focuses on the proud display of spiritual resistance of one Jewish couple and their response to their surroundings rather than on the Nazi actions; these individuals symbolize the millions of Jews who resisted by trying to stay alive. His narrative is an early documentation of what we know today to be fact. In his article "The Corpus of Yiddish and Hebrew Literature from Ghettos and Concentration Camps and Its Relevance for Holocaust Studies," Yechiel Szeintuch (1986) writes,

> We must extend the concept of "resistance" to apply not only to armed resistance, but also to the spiritual resistance that preceded armed resistance during the years of Jewish persistence in living a Jewish life in the ghettos and in the camps, a life of cultural activity, community organization, and self-help. (p. 188)

Part of this spiritual resistance was the cultural life in the ghettos and the residents' efforts to preserve human dignity; these efforts maintained them, as we see in the story of the Zeifs.

My father had been optimistic throughout the war years, but he told me more than once that a Holocaust could happen again, that it is possible even in the United States. Although we lived in an open, free society, my father still felt uneasy. Disappointed and disillusioned in the second half of the 20th century when he realized that the world remained unchanged despite the genocide of World War II, he concluded that nations had not learned anything. Antisemitism still existed.

I hope that "A Cupboard in the Ghetto" will help students understand how difficult it was to live in a ghetto imposed by the Nazis, and how strong one must have been to resist spiritually and to preserve one's humanity, as the characters in this story do. Hershel Zeif removed the wooden shelves, the back boards, and the doors of the cupboard in the ghetto, and yet it remained a cupboard. The Nazis confined the Jews, forcing them into small, meager dwellings, starving and weakening them, trying to remove from them every shred of individualism and dignity, and yet they remained human.

"As one who actually kept on living the ghetto … life," Cohen has written, "Bryks has created works that should be recognized as a unique literary expression of the period, or, as the historian Nakhmen Blumental defined them, as a museum" (p. 9).

We welcome you into this museum and urge you to touch the history you will discover here.

REFERENCES

Bialistotski, B. Y. (1952). *Der "keyser" un di "kats,"* preface to Rachmil Bryks, *Der "keyser" in geto.* New York: Buch Komitet.

Blumental, N. (1969). *Geshikhte in a kinstlerisher form,* preface to Rachmil Bryks, *Di papirene krvin.* (The "King" of the Ghetto.) New York and Tel Aviv: Buch Komitet with the assistance of the "Yidishe P.E.N." Club.

Bryks, R. (1959). A cupboard in the ghetto. In K. Shawn and K. Goldfrad (Eds.). (2008), *The call of memory: Learning about the Holocaust through narrative: An anthology,* pp. 113–120. Teaneck, NJ: Ben Yehuda Press.

Bryks, R. (1969). My credo: Essay. In J. Leftwich (Ed.), *The way we think: A collection of essays from the Yiddish,* pp. 490–491. New York, London: Thomas Yoseloff.

Cohen, N. (2006). Unpublished paper: An introduction to Rachmil Bryks and his work.

Glatshteyn, J. (1963). *Mit meyne fartogbikher.* Tel Aviv. Y. L. Perets Farlag, pp. 193–199.

Sadan, D. (1970). *Megey hahareiga.* preface to Rachmil Bryks, *Al kiddush Hashem.* New York: Rachmil Bryks.

Szeintuch, Y. (1986). The corpus of Yiddish and Hebrew literature from ghettos and concentration camps and its relevance for Holocaust studies. In *Studies in Yiddish Literature and Folklore.* Research Projects of the Institute of Jewish Studies, Monograph Series 7, pp. 186–287. Jerusalem: The Hebrew University.

Szeintuch, Y. (1995). *Yishayahu shpigel: Proza sipurit megeto lodge.* Jerusalem: Magnes.

Unger, M. (2005). *Lodge: Akhron hagetaot bepolin.* Jerusalem: Yad Vashem Press.

The View From a Crevice: Isaiah Spiegel's "Bread"

Phyllis Lassner

The story "Bread" (Shawn & Goldfrad, *Anthology*, 2008, pp. 121–130) is derived from two volumes of short fiction by Isaiah Spiegel and is based on his five-year incarceration in the Lodz Ghetto, from the 1939 Nazi takeover of Poland until the ghetto's liquidation in 1944, when he was taken to Auschwitz and then to a slave labor camp in Saxony.

While in the ghetto, Spiegel's daughter starved to death; his wife, his parents, and his three sisters perished in the camps. He was one of very few who survived both the ghetto and Auschwitz. After the war, he went back to Lodz and found his manuscripts, which he had buried in order to preserve them. He reworked them and composed other stories and poems based on his Holocaust experiences.

Collectively, Spiegel's stories represent one of the few eyewitness accounts of the Lodz Ghetto experience that survived the Holocaust. Rather than a diary, which narrates one person's experience, or a memoir, written after the fact, Spiegel wrote many of his stories at the time of the events he depicts. Rather than overlay the narrative with reflections gained with time, he offers a sense of immediacy through a panoramic but close-up view of ghetto life by condensing different horrors into sharply etched vignettes of individual and family lives. Written in a style he called "the laconic vision," Spiegel's stories resemble those of Ida Fink and Sara Nomberg-Przytyk (Furnish, 2003, p. 1190), whose work is also represented in this guide to the pedagogical use of Holocaust narrative. As Furnish notes, this is "an approach to fiction that is deceptive in its apparent simplicity as it exploits the symbolic and artistic dimensions of its narrative with keen economy" (p. 1190). Spiegel's symbolic and terse style conveys not only the material, external details that comprised the destitute lives of ghetto inhabitants, but also the felt sense of unending shocks that constitute the ghetto's "emotional landscape" (p. 1191).

Spiegel's story "Bread" depicts a family confined to the Lodz Ghetto and living in a disintegrating wooden hovel that overlooks a small street on the outside of the ghetto's wall. Mama Glikke (whose name, ironically for this story, means luck) is literally the breadwinner of the family: her husband, Shimmele; their 11-year-old son, Umele; and their younger daughter, Perele. It is the extreme scarcity of food that leads to the story's climax. The ritual of apportioning equal slices of the bread that serves as the family's primary nourishment is smashed when Shimmele yields to his ferocious hunger and gorges himself on the meager loaf meant for the whole family. Having retreated into prayer and emotional isolation before his breakdown, Shimmele recedes even further from his family in his shame. This emotional withdrawal then prefigures his actual disappearance when he is arrested by the Nazis, never to be seen again. Although deeply grieved by his disappearance, Mama Glikke and her children turn to his bread portion with the joy of anticipated nourishment.

Reflecting the ghetto's meager resources, the story's compressed method emphasizes the characters' emotional and social isolation. Paradoxically, they cannot express their anguish to each other because they are both deeply enmeshed and fearfully distanced in their shared needs. However, even if they had a listener, even if they could speak sympathetically to each other, language as an expressive vehicle would fail them.

As Charlotte Delbo (1995) and so many other Holocaust writers have emphasized, words that came close to representing the prisoners' prewar lives have little meaning when it comes to "[e]xplaining the inexplicable"—for example, the thirst that swells the tongue and freezes speech or the verb "to organize," which Auschwitz changed from its positive connotations to mean "improv[ing] your own situation, very often at someone else's expense" (p. 70). Applying Sara Horowitz's (1997) discussion of muteness in Jerzy Kosinski's *The Painted Bird,* but shifting it from the active to the passive voice to show a lack of agency, we can say that having been deprived of the "power of speech," Spiegel's characters have been deprived of the "ability to define" themselves or to tell their own story (p. 85). Theirs is not "a silence of agency, when victims use muteness to resist their own or other people's death" (p. 121). In "Bread," the characters' muteness bears not only symbolic meaning, but foretells their deaths (p. 91).

"Bread" fills but also questions the possibility of filling the void of Holocaust deprivation with its narration. In all its graphic detail, this short story represents what Michael Bernard-Donals and Richard Glejzer (2001) identify as "the junction of the compulsion to speak and failure of speech, where the witness manages to redeem the moment (to finally see what lies beyond or behind what can be told by history), to 'fall victim' to it, and leave a trace of it in language" (p. xi). Instead of compensating for the failure of speech and language with many descriptive or qualifying words, the story's language of witnessing functions like Delbo's use of "thirst."

Many more words, additional discursiveness, would only indicate the frustration and anxiety incumbent upon the search for an accurate or precise lexicon. By contrast, Spiegel's one word title assumes many meanings, including the opposite of its nominal meaning—nourishment—to convey the precise but "inexplicable" nature of the conditions and the physical and emotional pain that expresses the prisoners' responses. Instead of interior or exterior monologue or dialogue to convey the difficulties of communication in the ghetto family, the narrator plays the key role, speaking on the characters' behalf.

As Primo Levi (1989) reminds us in *The Drowned and the Saved,* "In short, the prisoner felt overwhelmed by a massive edifice of violence and menace but could not form for himself a representation of it ... their capacity for observation was paralyzed by suffering and incomprehension (p. 117). Although Levi speaks here of Auschwitz prisoners, the relationship he draws between those who could speak and the silenced ones parallels the expressive tensions among the characters in "Bread": "Weeks and months before being snuffed out, they had already lost the ability to observe, to remember, to compare and express themselves. We speak in their stead, by proxy" (p. 84).

Instead of serving as a proxy for the disoriented characters or as a guide for readers' responses, the narrator of "Bread" shares with readers what he is able to see and then impels us to see along with him, as though we are responding to Delbo's (1995) plea: "Try to look. Just try and see" (p. 84). For example, we read his effort in a response that reflects the pain of seeing. In a lamentation that prepares us for the tragedy that will inevitably befall Mama Glikke and her children, the narrator's voice becomes a wail of despairing, self-canceling hope: "Oh, God, if only it were possible to cut slice after slice from the loaf and not be terrified at knowing that with every slice the loaf gets smaller and smaller" (Shawn & Goldfrad, *Anthology*, p. 124).

As if the trajectory of the family's story were not hopeless enough, we must witness the constitutive powerlessness of the narrator's role. While his predominant presence and voice bring us as close as he can to the characters' lives, his presentation constantly reminds us that this may really be an impossible mission. The narrator also expresses this doubt as a tension in his temporal relationship to the story, where the continuous present tense prevails. While the continuous present is a familiar technique in Holocaust narratives, as in Tadeusz Borowski's (1967) stories, for example, offering a sense of immediacy and intimacy with the characters and their plight, as well as the valence of omnipresent, ongoing catastrophe, "Bread" counters this evocation.

Instead, Spiegel uses this technique to call attention to the impossibility of knowing. For example, despite his authoritatively graphic descriptions, the narrator offers no explanation to offset the characters' inability "to know how it came to pass" (*Anthology*, p. 125) that the father shames himself by losing control and devouring his family's bread. If such unknowingness is a logical extension of the characters' loss of interpretive capacity, it also leaves us wondering about the narrator and our trust in his intensely observed depictions. That the narrator may not be able to provide interpretations may simply be a function of the characters' unprecedented, otherwise inconceivable actions. Yet, as Bernard-Donals and Glejzer (2001) argue, even when it fails, testimony can allow us a momentary and deeply felt view of otherwise inconceivable events (pp. ix–x).

Even if we accept this definition of witnessing and testimony, the interpretive vulnerability of the story's narrator undermines the sense of control typically associated with an omniscient narrator who not only witnesses but organizes and sometimes even orchestrates the plot. In "Bread," it is as though despite his being there, despite hovering over the very events he witnesses, the narrator and his position cannot guarantee any knowing or understanding of what these events mean.

For Spiegel himself, whether he is writing from the ghetto or retrospectively, the problem of epistemological distance is all too similar. How can he represent the aspects of the Holocaust that he lives and witnesses firsthand when his own position is limited by the only power that would seem omniscient or omnipotent to the prisoners of the ghetto? This power is represented by the Nazis, whose motivations for brutality are always arbitrary or capricious and so remain beyond ascription or even scrutiny at the time. Indeed, the very idea of omniscient power becomes central to the story as we see in Shimmele's almost total immersion in prayer and in the narrator's lament quoted above. The narrator's appeal to God calls attention not only to his own subordinate and timorous position, but as so many Holocaust writers have grieved, he can expect no response. God may either have absented Himself from the Holocaust or, as a Jewish God, been exterminated along with His people. The position of the narrator in "Bread" is thus vexed, not unreliable, but compromised by the very intimacy and uncertainty he shares with the characters and their fates.

We read this compromised intimacy in the story's last line, when the narrator tells us, "That night they all sleep peacefully and soundly, and father, Shimmele, appears only to Umele in a dream. Umele sees him praying over a large, thick book" (*Anthology*, p. 130). While it appears that the narrator has access not only to the story's denouement, but to Umele's dreaming consciousness, the statement offers an ironic commentary on the dubious possibility of finding meaning even in what is assumed to be knowledge. On the one hand, the repose of the characters suggests that instead of being traumatic, the father's disappearance has healed the family's shock at his behavior. Of course, just as the father was arrested for no other reason than the exercise of Nazi caprice and power, so too the peaceful sleep of Mama Glikke and her children betrays the danger lying in wait for them. The haunting of Umele by an image of his father's emotional withdrawal would then not only prefigure the father's actual disappearance as an ongoing trauma, but serve as an ominous sign of how the "peaceful sleep" will be interrupted.

In forging a relationship with the reader, the narrator not only tells the story, but with all his complexity and the predominance of his voice, he becomes a featured character. He assumes qualities of a focalizing character whose point of view prevails, not to construct or understand his own sense of self, but as a mediating agent between himself and the characters, and between himself and the reader; he will show as much of the story's events as he can.

As though he understands the limitations of Holocaust representation, he emphasizes the paucity of descriptive language to convey the family's story, highlighting the circumstances that constrict, even erase the possibility of expressing that which would explain the characters' responses to themselves and to each other. Only when there is a dramatic, indeed, traumatic turning point, do the otherwise silenced characters find a voice, as when Mama Glikke discovers the devoured bread and when Umele sees the last bread taken from the bakery window. Although the narrator's use of exacting detail and his mediating role convey the urgency of bearing witness, these features only remind us how distanced in time and contexts we remain from the story.

It thus remains unclear how we will be able to understand the story and teach it as testimony. As Sara Horowitz (1997) reminds us, "The fragmentary nature of these traces of catastrophe complicates their import for us" (p. 224). Just as videotaped survivor testimony is mediated by the speaker's assumptions about listeners' frames of understanding, so too the construction of this fictional narrator is predicated on questioning the literary conventions that make a story accessible to readers.

Because our models for reading are called into question by the story, so is the viability of our role as witness. Within his mediating role, the narrator's representations only highlight the chasm between the characters' experiences and any possibility for interpretation applied from outside the text. Both the narrator and the extreme emotional, imaginative, and physical suffering he depicts dislodge any assumption by readers that we can follow the unfolding fates of characters who impel our involvement with the text. In turn, this disorientation dramatizes the questionable applicability of the hermeneutic models with which we learn to interpret non-Holocaust literary texts.

For example, the story's ending is ambiguous, not only in its omission of the terrible certainty of the father's arrest but in its affect and tone. We are not told what happens to Mama Glikke and her children after they "joyfully eat to their hearts' content" and "sleep peacefully and soundly" (*Anthology*, p. 130). But whatever pleasure we might take in this final scene does not mean that we can cling to the hopefulness that an open ending invites. We might then ask—if we feel we must ask—how can we orient ourselves in this unstable relationship with Holocaust stories? Speaking of Tadeusz Borowski's fiction, Inga Clendinnen (1999) notes that "the reader, struggling for a foothold, finding none, [becomes] the protagonist" (p. 169).

Self-conscious about these narrative complications, as we have seen with his narrator, Spiegel also dramatizes the relationship between readers and his stories through "Bread's" fable-like structure. The story's opening describes the family's hovel by endowing it with a voice, "like a person who laments: 'Oh—oh, what I have lived to see ... Oh my, such a fate'" (*Anthology*, p. 121). A speaking house coincides with elements of folktales or fables, which often anthropomorphize material objects and natural forces. Whether these objects and forces serve an oracular or guiding role or speak for characters who cannot, either because of youthful inexperience or some kind of oppressive condition, they also provide readers with a critical perspective or gloss on otherwise mystifying circumstances and events. In the case of "Bread," the speaking house and the story's sparse dialogue convey that silencing may not be the characters' ultimate deprivation, but that like their hut, it serves as an overdetermined metaphor of their starved lives.

If rescue plots are the stuff of oral traditions and folktales, the storyteller here must reverse their structure to portray the ever narrowing and more perilous spheres that entrap the characters. Instead of "Once upon a time," we read "Once there was a stroke of misfortune" (p. 124). Differences between the two designations are instructive. The first example suggests a timeless elsewhere and entices us with its evocation of universal meaning, as though the plot it introduces follows allegorical lines that are applicable to all our lives. Conventionally, the plot trajectory of folk or fairy tales includes adventure, danger, magical rescue, and resolution, a combination that expresses anxieties of separation but resolves them magically with reconciliation.

From the very start of "Bread," however, when the narrator points to "one narrow little window looking wistfully down at the small street" (p. 121), he is telling us that not only has he no magic to perform, but that like the family, our vision will be impaired. The window serves as the vantage point for the reader so that whatever contextual knowledge we bring to the family's story, our understanding of its plight derives from the "narrow" view afforded us. Moreover, like the meanings symbolized by the family's few material objects, anthropomorphizing the window gives expression to the despairing emotional state of the family and thus both represents and substitutes for the narrator's inability to provide psychological insight.

Instead, whether their scant possessions are religious objects such as Sabbath candelabras and a *tallis* (prayer shawl) or a lone pot, whether they are used or abandoned in a corner, they reflect the characters' exhausted emotional resources as well as the sparseness of ghetto living quarters. Despite their tarnished and often broken condition, they are reminders of the Jews' rich cultural lives before Nazi persecution while they also represent their owners' dislocated lives. Part of the poignancy of these displaced and abandoned objects derives from their connection to both the most ordinary domestic as well as sacred rituals. Reflecting the fracturing of a cohesive family structure, as well as the material and emotional states of parents and children, the objects lie "in a pile of junk, among empty pots and torn clothes" (p. 122).

The position and status of these objects suggest not only imprisonment by the Nazis but abandonment by everyone in the outside world. In addition to this reflection of external conditions, such objects resonate with the characters' feelings. With no outlets for expressing their anxieties and yearnings, both the "panic" of the first transports as well as the "ray of joy" (p. 130) of having something to eat are projected by the narrative onto the sight of a loaf of bread.

"Bread" dramatizes the attenuation of sensory expression and satisfaction through the power of sight. Deprived of any schooling or other distractions, the children relish the rare chance to steal into a tiny antechamber and peek through two crevices to see the world beyond the ghetto walls. The pleasure of this sight is also marked by danger, however, for seeing out means that the children could be seen and shot. Theirs is neither a game of hide and seek nor, as we shall see shortly, a treasure hunt. What entices Umele and Perele is that through the crevices, they can gaze at the windows of a bakery and a cheese shop where the sights are both tantalizing and taunting. Unlike the narrator who knows that his perspective is limited by the confines of the ghetto, the children's clandestine adventure is buoyed by fantasy: "the eye can escape into a free, uncaged world" (p. 128). We can almost hear their voices in reading the following entry from an anonymous Lodz Ghetto diary:

When we look at the fence separating us from the rest of the world, our souls, like birds in a cage, yearn to be free. ... How I envy the birds that fly to freedom. ... Will I live to eat bread and rye flour until I'm full? Meanwhile, hunger is terrible. (Langer, 1995, p. 42)

The children's escaping eye, however, does not point to a romantic characterization of children as visionaries. The very limits of the narrator's own perspective will disclaim both the children's fantasied yearning and the possibility that it will produce a sentimentally hopeful response from the reader. He thus intervenes by providing a critical edge to an image typically associated with freedom. Referring to the pigeons kept by the previous tenants, he reminds us that they are free to visit their old home and fly away, but the children's yearning for freedom will be dashed by the realities created by the Nazis. If imagination is a wellspring of childhood development in ordinary times, the necessity of betraying the children's imaginations represents the ghetto as designed to extinguish the possibility of childhood development.

Viewing the outside world and its food enflames but then frustrates the children's desires for knowledge, freedom, and nourishment. While this devolution from desire to frustration and then to an acute state of deprivation could very easily produce a response like their father's, it does not. Instead of modeling the children's reaction on his voracity, the story depicts the children as "feast[ing] their eyes" (*Anthology*, p. 124). If the father has turned inward, consuming both prayer and food, the children's sights turn outward, attempting to share in the world beyond them. However, the story also connects Shimmele's regression to the children's foiled imaginations to show how a story of the Lodz Ghetto must work against the plotting of a *bildungsroman*. "Bread" forecloses on both the children's vision and paternal protection and nurture which, in a *bildungsroman*, will chart a journey to self-determination despite a compromised and often disappointing conclusion. The progress of such a journey typically depends on a surrogate father figure or narrator situated beyond or outside the experience of young children so that he or she can guide or prod them through their journeys into adult disillusionment.

"Bread" dismisses such a tradition as inapplicable to a Lodz Ghetto story by yoking the limited knowledge of its narrator to the vulnerability of Perele and Umele. Expressing the interdiction of any journey from the ghetto, except to destruction, the story employs indirect free discourse to illustrate the anxiety shared by the narrator and the children that the death of imagination anticipates their own bitter end:

God forbid that Mama should find out about this. No, Mama must not know about this, because if she does, then the whole treasure is lost. It will no longer be possible to come into the little chamber and gorge oneself on rolls and loaves of white bread. (p. 128)

Despite the disconsolateness with which life in the ghetto hovel must be represented, we can also see the children's transgressive act as a rebellion against the forces that keep them incarcerated, ignorant, and in constant danger of deportation and murder. Where the logic of the Holocaust would decree a failed rebellion, the story offers perspectives that credit such risks like those the children take. And so the narrator focuses on their individual initiative and therefore endows Umele and Perele with the subjectivity denied to them by the Nazis.

"Bread" highlights the activated characters of Umele and Perele by depicting their father as paralyzed with fear and emotionally isolated. His immersion in prayer and religious books marks a deep and abiding commitment to religious faith, but his actions also isolate him from God, despite his envelopment in God's words. Even as we are guided by the narrator to view Shimmele's fears as logical to his conditions, we also find that extreme suffering is not redemptive here. In her discussion of Elie Wiesel's meditations on "traditional Jewish explanations of suffering against the challenge of the *Shoah*," Sara Horowitz (1997) offers an interpretive model for reading Shimmele's behavior:

> [A]t its most extreme, suffering isolates individuals from one another and from God. Despite the impulse to absorb traumatic events into the continuum of Jewish history, classical rabbinic Judaism sees extreme suffering as characterized by the impossibility of communication, of relationship, of narration, of explanation ... extreme suffering obliterates the means of its amelioration, along with the source of ethical values and comfort (Torah and prayer). ... In essence, then, the Talmudic text envisions the possibility of suffering so radical that it engenders a rupture with what comes before and what might come after, removing the sufferer from the continuum of Jewish history, community, texts, and values. (pp. 122–123)

The moment of Shimmele's most acute suffering not only "engenders a rupture" from his family and Jewish history, but also shows that the only "continuum" in which it participates begins with his isolating absorption in prayer and text. He has already created an irreparable fissure in encasing himself in his own needs and rescinding his bond with the suffering shared by those dependent upon him for comfort and guidance.

Ironically, his self-absorption erases the very spirituality prayer represents and paves the way toward the extreme physicality of his hunger. In turn, yielding to this hunger encourages a degraded spirituality that the story figures as both violating and fulfilling the paradoxically material but immaterial being the father has become: "That wasn't the father any more ... but some kind of enchanted shadow that had separated itself from him, that had issued from his hands and feet, some kind of accursed *dybbuk*" *Anthology*, p. 125)[1].Most recently, Yohanan Petrovsky-Shtern (2006) has broadened the meaning of dybbuk metaphorically to "indicate obsessions, double or false identities, corrupted *Doppelgangers* and insolent impostors ... in an inter-personal, social or even political context" (p. 4). Whereas in Ansky's version, the dybbuk is an ambiguous figure, driven by anguished love to invade his beloved, Spiegel interprets the spectral figure as a sign that Shimmele has alchemized into a voracious monster. Neither an imposter nor carrying a false identity, the father here has "corrupted" normative expectations of paternal feeling and behavior.

Readers can easily be torn between judging Shimmele as cruelly narcissistic or simply compelled involuntarily by desperate hunger. Following Delbo's depiction of such debilitation, we could see Shimmele as having improved his situation at his family's expense. However, regardless of the discomfort we might feel with his characterization or the ambivalent response to which we are led, these possibilities touch upon a central concern of writers and critics of Holocaust representation. As Levi (1989) urges us in his chapter "The Gray Zone" in *The Drowned and the Saved*, the Nazis designed the conditions of their prisoners to produce starvation, disease, and emotional and moral abjection, and the prisoners' responses defy our impulses to judge them. Although he writes specifically about Auschwitz, Levi's imperative applies to our responses to Shimmele:

> The prisoners of the Lagers, hundreds of thousands of persons of all social classes, from almost all the countries of Europe, represented an average, unselected sample of humanity. Even if one did not want to take into account the infernal environment into which they had been abruptly flung, it is illogical to demand—and rhetorical and false to maintain—that they all and always followed the behavior expected of saints and stoic philosophers. In reality, in the vast majority of cases, their behavior was rigidly preordained. In the space of a few weeks or months the deprivations to which they were subjected led them to a condition of pure survival, a daily struggle against hunger, cold, fatigue, and blows in which the room for choices (especially moral choices) was reduced to zero. Among these, very few survived the test. (pp. 49–50)

In "Bread," the starvation to which the characters are subjected produces psychological horror, not distinct from, but as only another component of the Nazis' physical brutality. The physical pain and suffering Shimmele experiences in his hunger leads to emotional deformity, and the combination forms a picture of the

---

1 Spiegel's use of the folktale specter who wanders in search of belonging and takes possession of another's mind and body recalls S-Ansky's play, written in 1920 and last performed before the Holocaust as a Polish movie produced in 1937 and directed by Michael Waszynski.

depraved Nazi plan to destroy human life in the ghetto even before deportation. In addition to starvation and disease, the ghetto conditions designed by the Nazis would include the dissolution of empathy and individuation. It is as though the Nazis' fantasy of the Jews as an undifferentiated and poisonous mass finds its logical consequence in policies and practices that transform fantasy into reality.

With all feeling collapsed into hunger, Shimmele represents another result of Nazi doctrine: that even though their suffering is shared, the Jews will become radically dissociated from each other as competitors for the same depleted nourishment. As Spiegel's narrative moves from Shimmele's alienation to his act of gorging on the family's bread it suggests that physical brutalization—abject hunger—incorporates a drive for satisfaction that obliterates his perception of another's presence. Prisoner of his own primal hunger, Shimmele loses sight of his family as human beings deserving their own integrity of being. By devouring his family's nourishment, he becomes complicit in their suffering. In effect, this implies a mortal blow to the others, as we hear in one of the few outbursts the narrative allows Mama Glikke: "When she read the truth in [Shimmele's] downcast eyes, she squawked like a slaughtered chicken: 'A father, eh? A fa—ther, is it? Murderer!'" (Anthology, p. 125). Of course, Shimmele has also murdered himself; when he devours the family's bread, he eats himself up.

Shimmele's unknown fate at the end, the fate that cannot be narrated, is already known to the reader, but as their behavior shows at the end, Mama Glikke and her children have intuited it as well. It is also as though they don't wish to know what happened to Shimmele, as he has already been dead to them like the father in Fink's (1995) story "The Key Game" (pp. 35–38). But whereas Fink's character of the father is rendered helpless and infantilized by the hysteria that paralyzes him. Shimmele is presented as helpless from the beginning, indeed almost inert, like the *musselmen* of Auschwitz, as though already dead. There is nothing in "Bread" that would indicate any active participation by Shimmele in a plan to survive. Yet, in judging Shimmele and our own responses, we cannot avoid the knowledge that Spiegel implies and that we bring to our reading decades later. Through his microcosmic view of the ghetto experience, Spiegel urges us to see, as his characters cannot, that their responses cannot represent the whole of Holocaust suffering but can offer a glimpse. In that sense, the metaphor of sight and vision central to the story helps us as well. In the line of vision from the children's imagination to ours, Spiegel and his narrator, like Delbo, ask us "to try to see" although we may never fully understand the nature or scope of the horrors of the Holocaust. Instead of condemning the victims for fulfilling the machinations of the perpetrator, "Bread" insists that we view the victims and their frailties as an essential Holocaust truth from which we cannot hide our eyes.

REFERENCES

Bernard-Donals, M. & Glejzer, R. (2001). *Between witness and testimony: The Holocaust and the limits of representation*. Albany: State University of New York Press.

Borowski, T. (1967). *This way for the gas, ladies and gentlemen*. New York: Penguin.

Clendinnen, I. (1999). *Reading the Holocaust*. Cambridge: Cambridge University Press.

Delbo, C. (1995). Voices. In Langer, L. L. (Ed.), *Art from the ashes*. 77–92.

Fink, I. (1995). The key game. *A scrap of time and other stories*. Evanston, IL: Northwestern University Press.

Furnish, B. (2003). Isaiah Spiegel. In Kremer. L. (Ed.), *Holocaust literature*. New York: Routledge: 1189-1192.

Horowitz, S. (1997). *Voicing the void*. Albany: State University of New York Press.

Kosinski, J. (1976). *The painted bird*. Boston: Houghton.

Langer, L. L. (1995). (Ed.). *Admitting the Holocaust*. New York: Oxford University Press.

Langer, L. L. (1995). (Ed.). *Art from the ashes*. New York: Oxford University Press.

Levi, P. (1989). *The drowned and the saved*. New York: Vintage Books.

Petrovsky-Shtern, Y. (2006). We are too late: Shloyme Ansky and the paradigm of no return. In Safran, G., & Zipperstein, S. (Eds.), *The worlds of Ansky: A Russian-Jewish intellectual at the turn of the century*, pp. 83-102. Stanford: Stanford University Press.

Spiegel, I. (1998). Bread. In K. Shawn & K. Goldfrad (Eds.). (2008), *The call of memory: Learning about the Holocaust through narrative: An anthology*, pp. 121–130. Teaneck, NJ: Ben Yehuda Press.

Dehumanization Through the Lens of the Lodz Ghetto: Rachmil Bryks's "A Cupboard in the Ghetto" and Isaiah Spiegel's "Bread"

Daniella Rotenberg

> *All history becomes subjective; in other words,*
> *there is properly no history, only biography.*
> —Ralph Waldo Emerson

At what moment does a cupboard cease to be a cupboard? At what moment does a human being cease to be human?

I am not an experienced teacher, nor am I a Holocaust scholar. Yet these questions reach out to me, an interested and curious student of the Holocaust, nonetheless. They challenge me to reconsider what it means to be human and to reflect on what it requires to fight to maintain one's humanity; they highlight for me the struggle between the Nazis' treatment of the Jews and the Jews' desperate and defiant resistance to that treatment.

Dates, names, and places are critical to a knowledge and understanding of history, as are visual images, documents, and artifacts. As a student in Holocaust courses and as a novice Holocaust educator for high school students, I depend on each of these historical tools. The voice of the victim as it projects from the pages of the short story, however, is an equally critical historical tool, and, in my roles as both learner and instructor, I welcome the use of literary works, both to introduce and to enhance historical knowledge of this subject.

In this unit of study, Rachmil Bryks's "A Cupboard in the Ghetto" and Isaiah Spiegel's "Bread" (Shawn & Goldfrad, *Anthology*, 2008, pp. 113–120 & 121–130) serve as the literary conduit through which students will encounter the Lodz Ghetto of the early 1940s and two of the families forced to endure life within its confines. Students will confront the protective veneer of optimism, faith, and wry humor in the former and the ravages of desperate hunger, shame, and despair in the latter. In both, they will come to understand the dehumanizing conditions of the ghetto and their effect on these two families.

Goals

My goals in teaching these stories include the following:

- ensuring that students understand the concept of dehumanization as it existed during the Holocaust in general and in these stories in particular;
- providing writing and discussion opportunities for students to empathize with those who struggled against and those who succumbed to the forces of dehumanization;
- helping students to contextualize the ghetto experience within the Holocaust;
- introducing students to an overview of conditions in the Lodz Ghetto; and
- encouraging students to humanize the ghetto experience by offering stories told by inhabitants themselves.

This unit of study, designed for high school and college students who have a basic knowledge of the Holocaust and an awareness of ghetto life, will require four 50-minute class periods and three homework assignments. Class sessions and assignments provide students with a framework of the concept of dehumanization and the Nazi rationale for its enforcement, contextualize the Jewish ghetto and its stories within the larger narrative of the Holocaust, and afford students opportunities to apply their understanding as they analyze and interpret these readings and share the meanings they make of each.

An Introduction to Dehumanization

Dehumanization, the process by which the Nazis attempted to destroy the will and very selfhood of the Jews, had many faces in the years between the Nazis' initial rise to power and the implementation of Hitler's Final Solution. "A Cupboard in the Ghetto" and "Bread" reflect the face that peered out from the Jewish ghetto. Efforts to dehumanize Jews were ever-present, yet my own encounter with these stories has taught me that for students to fully grasp and appreciate the specific manifestations of these attempts within the ghetto walls, they must first make sense of these attempts within the greater context of Holocaust history. To recognize the extraordinary will of those who remained able to resist dehumanization and to empathize with those who were forced to succumb, they must meet ghetto inhabitants through the unique medium of literature.

To enhance, then, students' understanding of the meaning and the essential questions raised both by these stories and by the history behind them, I suggest first exploring the concept of dehumanization.

- Write the word *dehumanization* on the board and ask: "What familiar word do you see within this word?" Once the students answer *human*, ask:
- "What makes something or someone human? How do you define the word *human*?" Next, ask:

- "Think about the term *human rights.* To what kind of rights do you think the term refers? Why are such rights granted to humans by other humans?" Finally, ask:
- "Now that we have an understanding of what it means to be human and to have certain rights, what might the word *dehumanization* mean? What can someone do to attempt to *dehumanize* someone else? How might one resist attempts at dehumanization?"

You might appoint a student to copy the proffered responses so you can refer to them as the unit progresses. Journals in which students write their reflections and reactions are invaluable; you might suggest here that students write their ideas before they make them public, for it is often only through writing that we come to know how we feel and what we think.

Jewish Passports

To highlight the methods by which the Nazis implemented the slow process of dehumanization, I suggest moving students from their exploration of the word itself to an examination of a sampling of the Nazis' subtle and overt tactics. To connect these tactics to the experience of the students, ask students to share the background of their own names. Conversation-starters include such questions as:

- Why did your parents choose your name? For whom, or for what event, were you named?
- How do you feel about your name? How do you feel when people mispronounce or misspell it?
- Have you had the experience of not being able to use your name as your e-mail address because someone else had already claimed it? How did the realization that others have the same name make you feel?
- Have you had the experience of having to change your name to conform to a new culture? If so, how did that forced change make you feel? Would you voluntarily change your first or middle name today? Why?

The goal is to elicit the strong sense of identity and pride, often ethnic, that one's name engenders. As I witnessed when I led students through this activity, creating this personal connection between the students and the historical material to come captures and holds their interest.

Next, explain that in August 1938, Nazi law forced all Jews to change their middle names on all official papers and passports. Jewish women had to assume the middle name "Sara" and Jewish men had to assume the middle name "Israel" regardless of their given middle names. In October 1938, all Jewish passports were stamped with the identifying letter "J." Have students examine Jewish passports on the following Internet sites: (*http://www.ushmm.org/lcmedia/viewer/wlc/document.php?RefId=1998SGBQ* and *http://www.exlibris.memphis.edu/Secher-Schab*). They will notice the stamped red "J"; guide them towards discovering the uniformity of the names "Sara" and "Israel." (On the first site, students can zoom in to see the name quite clearly. On the second, students can see that the middle name is inserted, which highlights the fact that the name was not originally on the passport.)

Ask the students how they think this affected Jews. Elicit the notions of stripped individuality and obliterated personal history. As an early, subtle method of dehumanization, the Nazis altered passports as a way to identify, separate, and humiliate Jews. Examining these passports will provide background for the more toxic forms of dehumanization imposed in the Lodz Ghetto, the setting of our stories.

The Jewish Star of David

A related activity centers on the *Magen David*, the Jewish Star of David, a symbol of both the Jews' freedom of expression and, later, the Nazi assault on Jews' dignity. It's important to explain, if your students do not know, that as the German army invaded and occupied countries throughout Europe, Jews were mandated to wear a cloth badge imprinted with or representing the Jewish star. Depending on the country, Jews were forced to wear these stars as arm bands or on the front and/or back of their outer garments. In some countries, the star was blue and white; in others, it was yellow. In 1939, this law was applied to all Polish Jews above the age of 10; in Lodz, the order for a Jewish badge was announced on November 16, 1939. Now, wearing the star was a matter of law, not choice. If a Jew was caught without a star, he or she could be arrested or killed on the spot. At *http://www.corkpsc.org/db.php?aid=15489*, students can read "Wear the Yellow Badge with Pride," an essay written in 1933 by Robert Weltsch. He urged the German Jewish community, reeling from the Nazi boycott of their shops and businesses on April 1 of that year, to embrace and wear as a sign of pride the very symbol the Nazis were using to mark and isolate Jewish stores and their owners. Elicit responses to the essay, reminding students that no one could have known, at that time, what the future would bring.

At *www1.yadvashem.org/Odot/prog/index_before_change_table.asp?GATE=Z& list_type=2-14&type_id=2&total=N*, students can scroll down to the third heading from the bottom, "The Berlin Bar Kochba Team in the Macabiya Jewish Olympics, Prewar," and click on the link to see a photograph of a Jewish Olympics ceremony in prewar Germany in which the Jewish participants are waving a flag emblazoned with the Star of David, illustrating the sense of pride that accompanied these events.

Ask students why they think there were "Jewish Olympics" in prewar Germany. Explain or elicit that after the 1935 Nuremberg Laws were passed, Jews were no longer allowed to participate in German sports leagues, so Jews created all-Jewish leagues. Players carried Star of David flags and sported uniforms that often had a large Jewish star sewn on the front. Ask students how they think the Jewish athletes felt as they competed in these uniforms and displayed this "badge." Elicit the idea that such exclusion forced them to take pride in their Jewish community and to reinforce their ties and commitment to it.

Next, focus on the later, *imposed* use of the Jewish star to give students a glimpse of the indignities that Nazi law forced on every aspect of the Jews' daily life. Use the following Web sites: *www.ushmm.org/wlc/en/* (click on the category "Ghettos"; scroll down to photo of star; click on "see more artifacts"); *www1.yadvashem. org/Odot/prog/image_into.asp?id=4406&lang=EN&type_id=7&addr=/IMAGE_ TYPE/4406.JPG,www1.yadvashem.org/Odot/prog/index_before_change_table. asp?GATE=Z&list _type =3-0&TYPE_ID=107* (see "Child wearing the Yellow Jewish Badge, Ghetto Lodz, Poland") and *www1.yadvashem.org/ Odot/prog/ index_before_ change_table.asp?GATE=Z&list_t*ype=1-4&type_id=2&total=N (see "Mogilev, Belorussia, Jews Wearing the Jewish Badge Clearing Rubble from the Street Immediately After Occupation"; the poignant "Lodz, Poland, Rumkowski Blessing a Bride and Groom"; and "Lodz, Poland, Jews Parting from Their Relatives Before Their Deportation"). While the star on the sports uniforms and flags had been displayed as a sign of pride, now the star on the clothing was a stigma, decreed by the enemy and worn only out of fear of reprisal.

For homework, I would ask students to choose and download two photos that speak to them most powerfully of dehumanization, paste them on card stock, and respond on the card, in a paragraph, poem, letter, drawing, or painting, to the indignity they see in the photo.

The Transition from Dehumanization to the Jewish Ghetto

In the second class, invite volunteers to share their homework and then ask all students to post their photos and accompanying text around the room for viewing before or after class.

I would then stress, in a brief lecture, that the ghettos they see in photographs were never intended to be the final stage of the Holocaust; they were instead a transitory phase and were often situated near railway lines so that the Jews could be efficiently transported to concentration and slave-labor camps and forced to work, albeit to their death, for the war effort. The ghetto was a temporary, preparatory stage predicated on the systematic dehumanization that began with the Nazis' rise to power and became increasingly intricate and harsh.

I would explain that from the very start of their rule, the Nazis used much of their energy to identify, separate, and isolate the half a million Jews who lived in Germany. The Nazis deprived these Jews of their livelihood and of their religious and cultural attachments in an attempt to force them to leave the country. From January 1933 through November 1938, some 150,000 Jews did leave. Those who remained, hoping that sanity would return to their beloved Germany, had no way of knowing that there would soon be no place in Europe for them to escape from Hitler and his henchmen. After *Kristallnacht*, under Gestapo pressure, another nearly 150,000 left (Dawidowicz, 1975, p. 191). When the Germans invaded Poland in September 1939, beginning WWII, the borders were sealed and emigration was an impossibility. The second stage of the Holocaust had begun. (For a general timeline of the Holocaust, go to *www.historyplace.com/worldwar2/holo-caust/timeline.html*. You might offer it before the lecture, as a visual break, or as a follow-up assignment.)

After stopping for questions, I would explain that in Poland and throughout most of the other countries that were soon conquered and occupied by German armies, Jews were forced from their homes and sent to live in ghettos. The Polish city of Lodz, for example, was a thriving center of Jewish culture before the Nazi invasion and occupation in 1939. In the months following the Nazi occupation, the Jewish inhabitants of the city were physically attacked and prohibited from such liberties as using public transportation and celebrating religious holidays. In February 1940, the Nazis established the Lodz Ghetto in the poorest quarter of the city and forced some 150,000 Jews to settle in the ghetto, which serves as backdrop to both "A Cupboard in the Ghetto" and "Bread." Conditions in the ghettos, including the required wearing of a Jewish "badge," random beatings and murders by Nazi guards, unbearable crowding, unsanitary conditions, and little or no food, were designed to strip the Jews of their essential qualities of being human and, sooner or later, to kill them. Students will more easily understand ghetto life as well as the events and the characters in our stories if the stories are framed within this context. To illustrate these points with statistics, maps, and photos, and to enliven the lecture format, you may wish to refer to the following Web sites:

http://www.deathcamps.org/occupation/lodz%20ghetto.html,
http://motlc.learningcenter.wiesenthal.org/pages/t045/t04597.html,
www.ushmm.org/lcmedia/animatedmap/wlc/flash/lodz.swf,

which you can project and discuss with your students or assign as an outside reference.

"A Cupboard in the Ghetto"

"A Cupboard in the Ghetto" is a story in which the characters retain their hope, faith, and humanity despite the deplorable conditions under which they suffer; "Bread" is a narrative of despair and longing, a tragic illustration of the effects of brutalization and starvation, two overt components of dehumanization. I believe that assigning "A Cupboard in the Ghetto" first will afford insight into the imaginative mechanisms employed by those who, somehow, were able to maintain their humanity; it will contrast starkly with the pitiable actions of the desperate father in "Bread."

Ask your students to read "A Cupboard in the Ghetto" for homework and give them the following chart to fill in as they read. They will complete half of it as they examine the plot, characters, and setting in "Cupboard" and half as they contemplate them in "Bread." Completing this chart will ensure close reading and will guide students to focus on elements of dehumanization and resistance to it found throughout the tales.

	Imagery of Dehumanization	Subtle Dehumanization	Overt Dehumanization	Succumbing to Dehumanization	Resisting Dehumanization
"A Cupboard in the Ghetto"					
"Bread"					

Responding personally to the stories is crucial in helping students articulate the meaning they make from their reading. Below are questions that will prompt readers to turn to the text to support their speculations and conclusions. I recommend distributing and reviewing the questions before the end of class and having students submit, or write in their journals, a one- to two-page written response to one question of their choice.

- Mr. Zeif insists that the cupboard in his dwelling remains a cupboard even after it loses its doors and its shelves. Do you agree? At what point, in your opinion, does an object cease to be what it once was? Is it possible for a human being to cease being human? Explain.

- Why might Rachmil Bryks have chosen to end his story with the line "And that's why cattle are so healthy and strong—because they eat the peel"? (*Anthology*, p. 120). Can you find a connection between the notion of dehumanization and the tone or the events of the story?
- How does the faith of the couple help them to maintain their humanity? Cite specific examples from the text. How might it hurt their chances of eventual survival?
- Do you consider "A Cupboard in the Ghetto" to be a romanticized or a realistic version of ghetto life? Explain, using specific examples from the text or from the Web sites we have examined to illustrate your point.

An Analysis of "A Cupboard in the Ghetto"

In the third class, ask students for their responses to the story; their reactions should spark insightful and lively discussion. The chart below may be used to elicit, focus, or summarize; you'll use it again for the second text. Prepare it in advance on the board, on an overhead projector, or on the computer and invite students to fill out the middle column, or give copies to individual or pairs of students to complete at their seats.

	"A Cupboard in the Ghetto"	"Bread"
Plot		
Setting		
Author's Tone and/or Attitude Towards the Husband		
The Role of the Wife		
Author's Effectiveness in Helping You Feel the Dire Circumstances		
Theme		
Point of View		
Author's Use of Compression: What You Inferred, or Teased Out, to Make the Story More Accessible to You		
What You Learned About the Daily Life of Jews Under Occupation		
Your Feelings Towards the Characters		
Most Powerful/ Profound Passage		

Next, assign students to groups of four or five and direct each group to discuss one of the homework questions that at least one student chose *not* to answer. This will encourage everyone to ponder questions whose answers may not come easily and will allow you to assess student thinking. After 10 minutes, ask members to share their ideas, including those written as homework, with the class.

As readers will discover, the Nazis employed overt as well as subtle methods of dehumanization. In "A Cupboard in the Ghetto," students will see that the methods now employed are ferocious and insidious as they force parallels between Jews and animals. Ask students to find such a parallel and read it aloud. ("The Jews are finished. Hunger will turn them into mad dogs. They will bite chunks of flesh from each other. They will devour themselves!" [p. 119]).

Distribute the following excerpt from the Nazi propaganda film *The Eternal Jew* (*www.holocaust-history.org/der-ewige-jude/stills.shtml*) and ask a volunteer to read it:

> Wherever rats appear they bring ruin, by destroying mankind's goods and foodstuffs. In this way, they (the rats) spread disease, plague, leprosy, typhoid fever, cholera, dysentery, and so on. They are cunning, cowardly, and cruel, and are found mostly in large packs. Among the animals, they represent the rudiment of an insidious and underground destruction, just like the Jews among human beings.

As students explore the connection between these words and the Nazis' actions cited earlier, they may well ask, "Why were the Nazis so intent on dehumanizing the Jews?" I have found this question is best explored through a combination of document-based lecture and discussion.

Some answers may be straightforward and simple: The Nazis separated and marked the Jews to identify and differentiate them from the non-Jewish population among whom they lived. The Nazis treated the Jews like animals because they actually believed that the Jews were subhuman.

Other answers are more complex. A considerable number of Nazis and their sympathizers were in contact and even closely acquainted with Jewish men and women before the Holocaust began. While we cannot know the inner workings of the Nazi mind as the atrocities of the Holocaust accumulated, we do know that some perverse mechanism must have allowed the wholesale murder of employees, colleagues, and neighbors, unarmed men, women, children, and babies. A large part of that mechanism was dehumanization, which allowed Nazis to accept the idea of, and then implement, the torment and murder of Jews. By stripping Jews of their individuality, history, and humanity, the Nazis could murder them without question or remorse. In short, the dehumanization of the Jews facilitated their eventual murder.

Interview with a Perpetrator

A concrete example of this fact is the following excerpt from an interview with one of the most infamous perpetrators. In 1970, journalist Gitta Sereny conducted interviews with Franz Stangl, an SS officer who served as commandant of the Treblinka extermination camp. The passage below, from *Into that Darkness* (1983), a compilation of Sereny's interviews with Stangl (also available at (*www. szasz.com/sereny.pdf*), provides vivid acknowledgment that Jews were perceived as animals and therefore it was possible to carry out their murders in vast numbers. The frankness of the imagery in this dialogue, while revolting, is an extremely relevant and powerful complement to this lesson. As students read this passage aloud, they will see that the stripping of the Jews' humanity profoundly affected not only the Jews but also the Nazi perception of them. To ensure a clear understanding of the text, you might assign one student to read Sereny's questions and another to read Stangl's responses.

> "Would it be true to say that you got used to the liquidations?" I [Gitta Sereny] asked. ...
> "To tell the truth," he [Franz Stangl] ... said slowly and thoughtfully, "one did become used to it."...
> "You became used to it in days? Weeks? Months?"
> "Months. It was months before I could look one of them in the eyes. ..."
> "Would it be true to say that you finally felt that they [the Jews on the transports] weren't really human beings?"
> "When I was on a trip once, years later in Brazil," he said. ... "my train stopped next to a slaughterhouse. The cattle in the pens, hearing the noise of the train, trotted up to the fence and stared. ... They were very close to my window, one crowding the other, looking at me through that fence. I thought then, 'Look at this, this reminds me of Poland; that's just how the people looked, trustingly. ...
> Those big eyes ... which looked at me ... not knowing that in no time at all they'd all be dead."
> "So you didn't feel they were human beings?"
> "Cargo," he said. ... "They were cargo."
> "There were so many children; did they ever make you think of your children, of how you would feel in the position of those parents?"
> "No, ... I can't say I ever thought that way. You see, ... I rarely saw them as individuals. It was always a huge mass. I sometimes ... saw them in the 'tube' [the path to the gas chambers]. ... How can I explain it? They were ... naked, packed together, running, being driven with whips, like ...."
> "Like cattle," he meant, but stopped short of saying it. (pp. 200–201)

It's a shocking and dreadful passage and will prompt responses that may range from silence to outrage, but it provides a culminating and graphic reflection on the results of the Nazis' attempts to dehumanize the Jews.

"Bread"

For homework, assign the reading of "Bread" and the completion of the chart. To prepare students for this distressing story, I ask them to keep in mind that unimaginable conditions, including desperate hunger, drove people at times to behave in ways that they would not have imagined behaving in another time and place. As Langer (1998) notes, "Starvation is an unholy partner in the quest for survival" (p. 132). He reminds us, as I remind students, that we must resist the impulse to condemn the actions of those weakened by starvation. We condemn instead those who created the conditions that provoked those actions.

You might wish to assign formal writing or journal entries of a page or two. As with "A Cupboard in the Ghetto," ask students to address one question that interests them.

1. In "Bread," horrific details of ghetto life are offered in the calmest manner. Give examples. How does this understated, laconic style underscore the tragic events?
2. What do you infer from the fact that "the two Sabbath candelabras are lying on the floor in a corner near the window, in a pile of junk, among empty pots and torn clothes" (*Anthology*, p. 122)? How does it clarify the process of dehumanization?
3. What was Mama Glikke's response to Shimmele? How did you respond as you were reading? What recognitions of your own did you add to make it meaningful/understandable to you?
4. Spiegel describes the children looking at and longing for the bread and cheese they see in the bakery window across from their room. What emotions did this description evoke in you as you read? How does the text help you to understand the meaning of ghetto hunger? How does it help you to understand the father's actions? Why is this kind of hunger dehumanizing?
5. At the end, why does Mama Glikke call the loaf "your father's bread"? The children and Mama Glikke "joyfully eat to their hearts' content" (p. 130). Did you find that description, given the circumstances of the father's deportation, odd, unsettling, offensive, justified? Does it work to defy or support the Nazis' intent to dehumanize the ghetto residents? Explain.

An Analysis of "Bread" and A Comparative Study

Begin the fourth class with a discussion of students' reactions to "Bread." Next, complete a sample chart (below) with responses to "A Cupboard in the Ghetto" to refresh the students' memories and to highlight the stories' differences.

	Imagery of Dehumanization	Subtle Dehumanization	Overt Dehumanization	Do the Characters Succumb to Dehumanization?	Do the Characters Resist Dehumanization?
"A Cupboard in the Ghetto"	There is much imagery that suggests that the characters are still quite vibrant; for example, the imagery of the wedding clothes and their belief that they will wear them again speaks of life and hope.	Their desperate hunger forces them to forage for cabbage roots. They are forced to destroy pieces of their home and belongings to burn them for heat.	Hans Greizer's quote: "Hunger will turn them into mad dogs!" (p. 119).	Not at all; Mr. and Mrs. Zeif treat each other with the sweet compassion of a married couple. Mr. Bluestein thinks, "[We] have not become wild beasts. .... He will not turn us into mad dogs!... [I]nside we have preserved the image of God" (p. 119).	They do resist; through their creativity, the Zeifs are able to make food for themselves; their unwavering optimism and faith allow them to stay hopeful.
"Bread"	Mama Glikke is described as a frightened bird; she "squawked like a slaughtered chicken" (p. 125). Shimmele salivates over the bread and stuffs it into his mouth, evoking the image of a wild beast that has not been fed for a long time, has been let out of its cage, and is now devouring anything it can get its paws on.	The family is trapped behind a wire fence, as animals would be treated.	The family is used as target practice by the German guard. They are forced to live without "a stick of furniture, no closet, no beds" (p. 122).	Shimmele, the father, can't control his hunger and thus eats his children's bread: "There is nothing lower ... except to cut a chunk out of the children and cook it" (p. 125) screams the mother. The father "has decided to give up his soul ... he is ... a dead man" (pp. 123–124). The father is deported, and on the same day, the mother and children eat his portion of the bread "joyfully," and "all sleep peacefully and soundly" (p. 130).	Shimmele and Avramele both turn to God and pray at different points in the story. Mama Glikke stands for hours each day to get a bit of food for the family.

Your students will now be able to compare both narratives. Through analysis and use of the chart, readers will have noted details of plot, characterization, setting, theme, and tone. These details, their differences and similarities, will be highlighted on one chart that can serve as a catalyst to return to the theme of dehumanization as you bring the lesson full circle.

Once the chart is summarized, assign students to groups of four or five and have each group discuss one homework question. This time, students may benefit from being placed with other students who answered the *same* question as they did, so that they can flesh out their ideas with others who are interested in the same aspect of the story. After 10 minutes, open the discussion to the whole class, as representatives share their thinking.

One difference between "A Cupboard in the Ghetto" and "Bread" is the absence of children in the former. Once students recognize this, you can expand the focus to include the manifestation of childhood in the ghetto if time and interest permit. In "Bread," for example, Spiegel writes, "The few ghetto months have completely transformed the children. They are no longer children, but ancients, on whose faces sit the ravages of heavy years" (p. 126). Each of the following quotes also draws upon the experiences of children engulfed by hunger and robbed of childhood. Utilize them as enrichment or individualized learning activities.

1. "I want everyone to know that there was no childhood; all were adults, everyone wanted to survive. Everyone knew what death was, and everyone knew that you had to eat, because without food you'd die" (Ernest, testimony).
2. "Indeed, how different we were here, between the walls! ... How much pain, and how much hunger! Hunger was now the lot of many people, even those who never lacked for anything" (Liberman, 2002, pp. 26–27).

Students can profit from reading and responding to the passages in a research or a writing assignment, in or out of class, as time allows. Encourage students to address such research issues as the impact of ghetto life on childhood, or, in an essay, to respond to a key question such as, "Do you think that the hopefulness and faith found in "A Cupboard in the Ghetto" would have been curbed or destroyed by the presence of hungry and desperate children?"

To elicit a final provocative and fruitful discussion, assign one question each to pairs or groups for 10 minutes of intimate, reflective dialogue; ask volunteers to share their conclusions.

- Locate and explain the role of faith and/or religion in each story. Do faith and/or religion seem to have the same effect in each? Be specific.
- Do you think that, with the passage of time, the couple in "A Cupboard in the Ghetto" would become similar to the couple in "Bread"? Why?
- Study the titles. How may each reflect the outlook of the characters in its tale?

- Identify the differences between at least two actions of the husbands in the narratives. Compare and explain your feelings for each man.
- "Bread" illustrates the inhuman demands of Nazi rule, which forced the nurturing instincts of parents to struggle with their need to survive. How does "A Cupboard in the Ghetto" capture the emotional conflict between one's need to survive and one's need to nurture?

Integration and Understanding

In concluding this unit, a goal for your students should be integrating and understanding the ideas that have thus far been illuminated. The following passage, used as a concluding homework assignment or summative essay prompt, may help you evaluate student thinking and learning.

> We who lived in concentration camps can remember the men who walked through the huts comforting others, giving away their last piece of bread. They may have been few in number, but they offer sufficient proof that everything can be taken from a man but one thing: the last of the human freedoms: to choose one's attitude in any given set of circumstances, to choose one's way. (Frankl, 1984, p. 75)

Do you agree that "to choose one's attitude" can never be taken from a person? Explain, using specific textual references from both stories to support your position.

Conclusion

By this time, your students will have experienced these narratives as literature and as manifestations of the dehumanization that was a defining characteristic of the Holocaust. Whether this lesson plan is part of a larger study of Holocaust literature or your students' sole encounter with such writing, be confident that your presentation will have provided students with ample grounding to continue their study of the nature and function of the Jewish ghettos and of the individual Jews who suffered within their walls while struggling to maintain a spark of humanity.

REFERENCES

Aktion Reinhard Camps. (2006, February 14). Lodz Ghetto. Retrieved April 8, 2006, from *http://www.deathcamps.org/occupation/lodz%20ghetto.html.*

Bryks, R. (1959). A cupboard in the ghetto. In K. Shawn & K. Goldfrad (2008). (Eds.), *The call of memory: Learning about the Holocaust through narrative: An anthology*, pp. 113–120. Teaneck, NJ: Ben Yehuda Press.

Dawidowicz, L. S. (1975). *The war against the Jews, 1933–1945.* New York: Bantam Books.

Emerson, R. W. (1841, reprinted 1847). History. *Essays, first series.* Boston: Munroe.

Ernest, I. *The testimony of Ernest Israel.* Yad Vashem Archives 0.3/10187.

Frankl, V. E. (1984). *Man's search for meaning: An introduction to logotherapy.* New York: Simon & Schuster.

History Place, The. (1997). Holocaust timeline. Retrieved April 8, 2006, from *http://www.historyplace.com/worldwar2/holocaust/timeline.html.*

Holocaust History Project, The. (1998, September 13). Still images from *Der ewige Jude (The eternal Jew).* Retrieved April 8, 2006, from *http://www.holocaust-history.org/der-ewige-jude/stills.shtml.*

Langer, L. L. (1998). The stage of memory: Parents and children in Holocaust texts and testimonies. In *Preempting the Holocaust*, pp. 131–145. New Haven: Yale University Press.

Liberman, C. (2002). *Celinqa: A child survives Auschwitz.* Jerusalem: Yad Vashem. *Shoah* Resource Center (2003). Retrieved April 8, 2006, from *http://www1.yadvashem.org/Odot/prog/index_before_change_table.asp?GATE=Z&list_type=1-4&type_id=2&total=N.*

Secher, H. P. (Ed. & Trans.) Secher letters collection of the University of Memphis Libraries, Special Collections. Retrieved June 23, 2006, from *http://exlibris.memphis.edu/Secher-Schab/reisepaj.gif.*

Sereny, G. (1983). *Into that darkness.* New York: Random House, Inc.

Sereny, G. (2004 October). *Into that darkness: 30 years on.* Presented at the Inner Circle Seminar, London, England. Retrieved June 23, 2006, from *http://www.szasz.com/sereny.pdf.*

Shoah Resource Center (2003).The Berlin Bar Kochba Team in the Macabiya Jewish Olympics, Prewar. Retrieved April 8, 2006, from *http://www1.yadvashem.org/Odot/prog/image_into.asp?id=7730&lang=EN&type_id=2&addr=/IMAGE_TYPE/7730.JPG.*

Shoah Resource Center (2003). Yellow Stars. Retrieved April 8, 2006, from *http://www1.yadvashem.org/Odot/prog/image_into.asp?id=4406&lang=EN&type_id=7&addr=/IMAGE_TYPE/4406.JPG.*

Spiegel, I. (1947). Bread. In K. Shawn & K. Goldfrad (2008). (Eds.), *The call of memory: Learning about the Holocaust through narrative: An anthology*, pp. 121–130. Teaneck, NJ: Ben Yehuda Press.

United States Holocaust Memorial Museum. German passport Issued to Erna "Sara" Schlesinger. Retrieved on April 8, 2006, from *http://www.ushmm.org/lcmedia/viewer/wlc/document.php?RefId=1998SGBQ*

Weltsch, R. Wear the Yellow Badge with Pride. Retrieved October 22, 2007, from *http://www.corkpsc.org/db.php?aid=15489*

Retrieved on June 7, 2007, from *http://motlc.learningcenter.wiesenthal.org/pages/t045/t04597.html.*

Retrieved on June 7, 2007, from *www.ushmm.org/lcmedia/animatedmap/wlc/flash/lodz.swf.*

Cause of Loss
Eli Ben-Joseph

As a survivor of the Nazi death machine, Bernard Gotfryd can rely on his experiences in writing about events that present the Holocaust reality. He survived six concentration camps, unsuccessfully tried to escape captivity, smuggled film of the murder of inmates to the Polish underground, and lost his family to the Nazis (Wenta, 2000). In the "The Last Morning" and "On Guilt" (Shawn & Goldfrad, *Anthology*, 2008, pp. 131–138 & pp. 139–148), both set in a closed Polish ghetto, Gotfryd generates meaning and arouses speculation about basic questions of human suffering, responsibility, and redemption. In these life episodes, he has written down, in the first person, final moments with his parents as the Nazi death plan devastated the ghetto where his family lived. Though these recollections are autobiographical nonfiction, Gotfryd exercises considerable authorial skill in presenting events, describing the people involved, and witnessing a terrible past.

These two episodes form a complementary sequence, or diptych, in which the author recalls the memory of his parents in their final days. In "The Last Morning," Gotfryd, the narrator, focuses on his mother, who must report to the ghetto center for deportation. Gotfryd recalls her crying in the garden, serving the family, and getting ready to leave. He observes his father cherishing their wedding picture, and his paternal grandmother, recovering from a stroke, preparing to report to the overcrowded and unequipped hospital, like all sick ghetto residents. The forced relocation of his grandmother foreshadows Mother's deportation in the first tale and gives a presentiment of Father's end in the second. At Mother's urging, the narrator and his older brother escape from the ghetto and hide in a stable, but the Polish stable hand discovers them and denounces them to the SS. The writer skillfully brings the tale to a crushing end with a triple climax recounting the terrible beating he and his brother receive from the SS, his confrontation with a "horse-drawn cart ... loaded with dead, naked bodies" on which he sees his grandmother, who, "seemed to be looking straight at" him (p. 137); and his allusion to the aftermath of the brutal deportation that has taken his mother, a scene that renders him wordless: "No dictionary in the world could supply the words for what I saw" (p. 137).

The story continues in "On Guilt," in which Father's fate is revealed. Gotfryd describes his father as bereft, forlorn, and preoccupied with his wedding picture. Where was he, Gotfryd wonders, when Mother was deported? Gotfryd's sister, Hanka, who gets no direct mention in the first tale, here becomes a central character. Caught up in the deportation but not taken, she later describes the mass confusion and terror of the selection. She explains that she tried to help her mother; she rejects her father's explanation that he had become disoriented and was thus unable to save his wife; she accuses her father of abandoning her mother. Eventually, Father, too, is deported. After the war the narrator learns that his brother saw their father shot on a wagon of exhausted inmates and interred in a mass grave as the Nazis were evacuating the camp near war's end.

The central setting is the Gotfryd home, whose garden is where the narrator recalls the bittersweet vision of his mother weeping "on a broken bench behind the lilac tree" (p. 131). The family has used the last of their fuel and prepares for deportation; Gotfryd hugs an old suitcase of his mother's as if to embrace her. Gotfryd deftly recreates for the reader the loving and respectful domestic scene that was his adolescence despite the poverty and impending doom.

The central focus of the diptych is on the parental archetypes, namely, Mother and Father. There is a difference between them as they go about their complementary tasks: Mother bears up while Father declines even within the range of what it is possible for him to do. Mother manages to gather and prepare food for the family despite the looming deportation, whereas Father, who cannot be fairly blamed for failing to accompany his wife to her death, does not even manage to provide his wife with a sandwich he has saved for the deportation. Mother is warm and comforting in spite of her tears. She urges her sons to go into hiding, save themselves, and tell the world of the Nazi evil. Father has naively miscalculated the reality before him, falls into depression, and relies on his son for life and hope. He becomes a lesser man whose only solace is the memory of his bride. Yet the narrator's loss of each parent is equally felt.

Hanka has a painful and ironic role as her father's accuser, maintaining that he shied away from accompanying his wife while she, Hanka, defended her. Yet even as Hanka narrates the events of night of the deportation, giving reasons for her ultimate failure to protect Mother—the confusion, the instinct for survival, the impossibility of actually accompanying Mother to her death—she inadvertently and unintentionally offers the narrator and the reader reasons that Father also could not have made any difference. Nevertheless, when she points the finger, she has already offered reasons that make it clear a sense of guilt may exist in spite of an inability to influence the outcome. At the same time, the reader has been made well aware of the Nazi regime as the only guilty party.

A sense of impending death pervades the diptych. The Gotfryd house is not the usual place of warmth and sustenance. The tension so stifles Gotfryd that he must get out; his walk takes him to the ghetto square, where he observes that the street lamps have been replaced with huge reflectors to be used on the night of the deportation. He reads the notice instructing the sick to report to the hospital and "tremble[s] at the thought of having to turn … [Grandmother] in" (p. 132). The hospital, he knows, is no longer a place of healing but of death. There is no relief within the ghetto; we feel its overwhelming oppression through a sensitive and relevant selection of images and reactions from Gotfryd's own recollections.

Among the persecuted, Gotfryd's grandmother is most noteworthy for her dignity and strength of character in walking unaided to the so-called hospital where it is assumed she can only, and actually does, meet her death. She would not endanger her family by failing to report. She asks, sarcastically, if one says "Be well" (p. 134) in such circumstances; perhaps this dark humor strengthens her in what she is about to face. Another strong character is Gotfryd's older brother, who accompanies him in his attempt to escape but is most important as a witness to their father's murder.

Adding to the picture crafted for the reader's understanding of the grim and frightening situation are the Zilber family and others stopping by "to confirm the rumors about the coming deportation and to say good-bye" (p. 133). Good-byes are still said in an apparent attempt to maintain a sense of normalcy, but these are farewells whose finality evokes much more than a temporary parting. A curious element is added by a passing ghetto resident who, despite the coming deportation, wants to know the time so he won't miss evening prayers. Is this an example of tenacity or absurdity?

Gotfryd offers well-chosen details to describe how he and his brother fled the ghetto, scaled the fence, and hid in a stable in a field, the setting for his eyewitness account of the deportation. Exhausted and terrified, he hears "cries and screams … rifle shots … [and] the cries of little children," and he recalls a comment of his friend Mr. Gutman who, some years earlier, "had claimed that God was in exile" (p. 136). His imagination adds to his terror as he pictures his aunt, young cousins, and his mother crying and helplessly awaiting deportation.

From a crack in the stable wall, he peers into the ghetto and sees the human roundup. He imagines that the prisoners become so numerous that the guards cannot control them, yet the reality, as recalled by the sister in the second narrative, contrasts sharply, for the people are all gone—shot mercilessly on the spot or sent to their death, leaving stench and litter as the only mementos of organized chaos. Gotfryd does not ask his readers to dwell on the horror; he shields them somewhat by shifting his focus to the unfolding fate of his family. Yet the crime against humanity gets told.

In the aftermath, Gotfryd assumes the responsibility of assuring his father that Mother is all right and will return, but the older man stands daily at the ghetto gate, nursing a sense of guilt and despair. Wherever Gotfryd takes us in this place, we see that the survivors cannot escape the morbidity and despair caused by the Nazi death machine.

Gotfryd has the maternally assigned role of survivor; he is to act as witness to what has happened to his community, and thus these Holocaust memoirs serve a didactic purpose. Yet they convey a vivid and engrossing reality as well because of the feelings and reactions Gotfryd details in place of a mere catalogue of accusations, though charges are included. In fact, his telling is more a recapturing of final moments with his parents than a cry of despair at his loss of them. He lives not only to report but also to retrace his own deprived adolescence. As a writer depicting his youth, he gains the sympathy of his readers. He reflects on his premature loss of innocence as he was forced to accompany his grandmother to her certain death, attempt escape, lose his mother, witness atrocities, hear and weigh his sister's accusation, and support his father emotionally and materially.

As a survivor, he offers his personal testimony of the premeditated attempt to execute his entire people.

The author uses three noteworthy stylistic elements that work to authenticate his testimony. First, he uses language that is standard and straightforward. This un-sensational mode of expression takes the reader from initial domestic scenes into the horrific events and circumstances of the ghetto world. The understated tone aids the reader in the absorption of shocking details.

Second, the episodes are interspersed with terse phrasing that fits the austere atmosphere of the ghetto. "The tension in the house nearly paralyzed me" (p. 132), he writes. "People "seemed like caged birds looking for an escape" (p. 134). "They were killing for sheer pleasure" (p. 140).

Third, dialogues offer confirmation of his recollection of events. They show their reliability in coming directly from the mouths of those who have lived through the events, as when Hanka vividly describes the night of the deportation. In short, the author's concise though emotionally expansive account facilitates the reader's comprehension of the perpetrators' extreme malevolence and the misery it created for victims and survivors alike.

As portraits of both of his parents under harrowing circumstances, the two tales are contrastive as well as complementary. "The Last Morning" is a nostalgic recollection of a mother's beauty, warmth, and care. It spotlights her nourishing resourcefulness and her parental caress. It is a longing regret for having missed her final moments at home. The first tale is, then, an exploration of the premature and profoundly unjust loss of a parent. "On Guilt," in comparison, is an excursion into the complex feelings of the surviving family members evoked by Mother's loss. The narrator regrets not having been present when Mother was deported; his sister agonizes over having been powerless at the final moment; and Father psychologically disintegrates over his inability to have played a husband's protective role toward his cherished wife, though her fate—and his—are sealed by the Nazis, who are the criminals.

The first tale differs from the second because it features positively Mother's ability to play her part, whereas the second tale highlights negatively Father's deficiency and survivor's guilt (compare Langer, 2001; compare Stark, 2001). Yet the tales are complementary in that the two consider the contextual horror that destroys both parents. Despite the author's uncertainty about understanding the terror ("I myself am not sure if I understand" [*Anthology*, p. 137]), meaning emerges from his retelling. Though different people bear ultimate pressures differently, it is tragic when survivors are passively contaminated by the morbid guilt the perpetrators have generated.

The diptych here considered is a representation that makes the Nazi-controlled ghetto accessible. In portraying the human condition in terms of filial longing, familial loyalty, and conscience under threat of slaughter, it universalizes by referring to family roles and leaving out or minimizing relatives' individual names. Thus, it is easier for the reader to enter the ghetto world and to learn how various characters coped with it. Persecutors are mentioned in terms of nationality only insofar as it identifies them. An officious SS officer sees Mother's papers as being in order for slave labor but is countermanded by an SS officer who rips up her papers and deports her to her death. While minor characters may play roles of comic relief in the most serious of tragedies, here they are joyless. They fit the necessary brevity of short-story depictions but play roles that add depth and poignancy to the descriptions of the efficient collaborators and the vulnerable and tragic victims of organized genocide. There is the sardonic sketch of the "free" Polish stable boy, for instance, who boasts that he can't be outsmarted as he leads the SS to Gotfryd's hiding place on the stable platform. Though mentioning the particular plight of Jews, the account does not dwell on Jewish particulars. Rather, it features antisemitism as an epitomic prejudice that must be exposed in its worst manifestations.

That the American armed forces were too late to save Gotfryd's parents and that non-Germans aided the Nazis in their persecution of Jews are matters that raise questions of the role that the rest of the world played in the Holocaust, whether failing to deflect it or lending a hand in carrying it out. One might want Gotfryd, who has the vantage of hindsight, to say something of the failure of the U.S. to disrupt the Nazi rail system that brought Jews to the death camps (compare Wyman, 1984) even as he reports "Allied air raids and attempted landings on the French coast" (*Anthology*, p. 143) to keep his father's spirits up; but would a storyteller do this? Perhaps such a shift in tone and time would divert the reader's attention from the stories' focus on loss.

Gotfryd's sensitivity to his readership surely owes much to his Americanization—he settled in the United States after the war, served in the U.S. Army during the Korean conflict, and became a prominent photojournalist in U.S. news media (Wenta, 2000). In line with American pluralism, his narrative hints at an inclusive answer to the question of Holocaust "ownership," that is, of special care for the suffering of a group the Nazis selected for extinction (compare Bernard-Donals, 2005). In Gotfryd's account, it is the protagonist's task to inform the world about what has taken place. Thus, he puts forth his own story as an instance in which the Holocaust against the Jews concerns all peoples, just as today genocide against any particular people may be internationally judged to be a crime against humanity.

Nevertheless, the victims—Jews or any people singled out for genocide—stay at the center of the horror. Despite postwar Judaism's resilience in pulling through the greatest threat ever posed to its religious and cultural cohesiveness (compare Flanzbaum, 2000), the harm done to the Jewish people is irreparable. Jewish ownership of the Holocaust remains a reflection of historical reality; and any attempt to rid the Holocaust of Jews by arguing that the target of the Holocaust was actually ubiquitous humanity may smack of insidious antisemitism, a not uncommon form of prejudice (Ben-Joseph, 1996). Gotfryd recalls that, as he lay in hiding in the stable watching the Polish stable boy come and go, he envied him and wondered, "Why was he free while I had to hide?" (*Anthology*, p. 135). Readers grounded in Holocaust history know very well that the answer is what Brustein (2003) has deemed the world's oldest irrational antipathy toward a single people: antisemitism.

REFERENCES

Ben-Joseph, E. (1996). *Aesthetic persuasion*. Langdon: University Press of America, 173.

Bernard-Donals, M. (2001). History and disaster: Witness, trauma, and the problem of writing the Holocaust. *Clio*, 30, 143.

Bernard-Donals, M. (2005). History in transit: Experience, identity, critical theory. *Clio*, 34, 505.

Bernard-Donals, M., & Glajzer, R. (2000). Between witness and testimony: Survivor narratives and the *Shoah. College literature*, 27, 1.

Brustein, W. I. (2003). *Roots of hate*. New York: Cambridge University Press, 337–355.

Flanzbaum, H. (2000). Sun turned to darkness: Memory and recovery in the Holocaust memoir. *Biography. 23*, 547.

Gotfryd, B. (2000). The last morning. In K. Shawn & K. Goldfrad (2008). (Eds.). *The call of memory: Learning about the Holocaust through narrative*: *An anthology*, pp. 131–138. Teaneck, NJ: Ben Yehuda Press.

Gotfryd, B. (2000). On guilt. In K. Shawn & K. Goldfrad (2008). (Eds.). *The call of memory: Learning about the Holocaust through narrative*: *An anthology*, pp. 139–148. Teaneck, NJ: Ben Yehuda Press.

Gotfryd, H. (1989). Foreword in B. Gotfryd (2000). *Anton the dove fancier and other tales of the Holocaust*. Baltimore: The Johns Hopkins University Press, x–xii.

Langer, L. L. (2001). Pursuit of death in Holocaust narrative. *Partisan Review*, 68, 379.

Stark, J. (2001). Suicide after Auschwitz. *The Yale Journal of Criticism*, 14, 93.

Wenta, A. (Spring 2000). Finding voice: How one Holocaust survivor gathered the courage to share his experiences with others. *Facing history and ourselves: New York update*, 5.

Wyman, D. S. (1984, 1998). *The abandonment of the Jews: America and the Holocaust, 1941–1945*. New York: The New Press, pp. 288–307.

Living With Loss:
Bernard Gotfryd's
"The Last Morning" and "On Guilt"

Diane E. Fingers

Step out of history
to enter life
just try that all of you
you'll get it then.
—Charlotte Delbo

Holocaust education, a "journey through the kingdom of fire and ashes," as it has been called by survivors, is a personal experience for both teacher and learner. Rarely will either make sense of their journey in just the same way, for each of us brings to the classroom diverse values, understandings, and ideas about, and responses to, trauma, loneliness, despair, perseverance, guilt, and memory. While some students, for example, may focus only on loss, others may look to the miracle of those who survived; while some may pledge to remember and share the stories they learn, others, overwhelmed by perpetrators' atrocities or survivors' pain, may choose to distance themselves, for the moment, from hearing more.

Before beginning any lesson, therefore, teachers might reinforce the importance of acknowledging and respecting divergent views, perceptions, and conclusions aired in an honest classroom community. Sometimes, this means that we will agree to disagree, as long as we share the desire to learn, communicate honestly, and grow. We who teach also face the task of knowing both the material and our students well enough to ensure that we have made the right match between them, that the history and the literature we offer on this subject are challenging enough to bring learners just to the edge of their comfort zone, but not so difficult or graphic that they cannot or will not participate in the journey.

This unit is a part of my sophomore course, "Diverse Voices: Literature and Composition," but it would work well with students in any high school or university literature or humanities class. Mine is a public, suburban high school where the majority of students are Caucasian and Christian. Literature from several countries is used to teach diversity and culture; this unit is designed to acquaint students with the Holocaust through survivor narratives. Numerous accounts allow us to hear and appreciate the survivor's voice, but two in particular, written by survivor Bernard Gotfryd and collected in Shawn & Goldfrad (*Anthology*, 2008), profoundly engage and move my students because of the author's spare and simple prose, clarity of tone, and forthright portrayal of moments of his life during his incarceration in the Radom Ghetto in Poland.

"The Last Morning" (pp. 131–138) is a story of loss, luck, survival, and memory. In less than one day, lives change forever. "On Guilt" (pp. 139–148) is an emotional roller coaster leading the reader to ponder the decisions and actions of a father even while feeling anguished empathy for him and his family and fury towards the perpetrators of the crime that engulfed the Jews of Europe. Bernard Gotfryd recounts his experiences so readers see the events through his details; his writings are photographs, vivid and clearly focused. He shares with us his family's experiences and thus provides a glimpse of the tragedies endured by all Jewish families torn apart. We begin, also, to understand, through his carefully told tales, the strength, spirit, and often just chance that allowed so many to continue living each day under unbearable circumstances.

Why I Teach Through Literature

I teach the Holocaust through literature for two reasons. First, I want to bring history into the realm of real life lived by real people, some just the age of my students. Tenth graders, who may soon forget dates and generalizations, connect to a straightforward narrative told by one man about himself and his family, describing a particular event that happened to him on one day during the thousands of days we call the Holocaust. Gotfryd has "stepped out of history to enter life" (Delbo, 1995, p. 278).

Second, I believe that learning from people who have experienced trauma, discovering how they felt, acted, coped, and put their lives together afterward, may help us in this world in which trauma threatens daily. My overarching goal is that my students will leave my classroom with an understanding of, and empathy for, the emotions, trials, behaviors, and fates of the people they encounter through literature, and that this understanding and empathy will remain with them and shape them as they mature and begin to examine their own humanity. Although this literary study of the Holocaust is not required, it is aligned with both my school curriculum and the Missouri State Communication Arts knowledge standards (Shawn & Goldfrad, *Guide*, 2008, pp. 490–492).

I teach Gotfryd's stories in the context of a larger unit of four to six weeks. Teaching these two stories, including prewriting, reading, and discussion, may take six 50-minute periods if all work is done in class, four if reading and writing are completed at home.

Laying the Foundation for Learning

While these stories stand on their own as literature, students who have a basic knowledge of Holocaust history will be far better prepared to make meaning from them. They need to have, at a minimum, knowledge of who was involved; an overview of the ordeal experienced by the Jews and other targeted people; and a general understanding of the aftermath from which the few who survived tried to begin again. Knowing the extent of your students' foundation will help you decide how much teaching is necessary before reading. One way to ascertain the level of prior knowledge is to use a K-W-L-H (Know/Want to know/Learned/How I learned) chart, either individually or in small groups. If most students have a fairly clear understanding of the basics, a round table review of key points might be all that is needed. If students have little or no prior knowledge, you may choose to partner with a history teacher, which will not only bring a fresh face to the classroom but will also give students a knowledgeable resource. Use reliable Internet sources: Visit *http://fcit.coedu.usf.edu/holocaust/default.htm*, useful for its timeline (click on left link), which leads to information on ghettos and a discussion of the aftermath; *www.ushmm.org*; or contact a local Holocaust museum for information and sound educational activities and resources. For specific information about the Radom Ghetto, the setting of our stories, visit *http://www.deathcamps.org/occupation/radom%20ghetto*.

Before Reading: Thinking About the Big Ideas

When the historical context is set, I ask my students to interpret concepts related to the reading they are about to undertake. For these stories, I write on the board the words "isolation" and "guilt' and ask students to take five minutes to write in their journals what each word means to them and to reflect on a time when they experienced at least one. (I assure students that I will not read them aloud or judge them for their experiences!) This activity connects the texts to the students' lives and provides an empathetic lens through which they will read.

Defining "isolation," Alicia personalized her feelings, writing, "Feeling alone, nobody cares, and I don't know what to do about it." Ann defined it as "Not just feeling alone, but it's when others purposely exclude someone." Jennifer was the philosopher: "I hate it when people make other people feel alone. It's hurtful and silly. Why should other people feel better for making someone feel worse?"

Kevin defined "guilt" as, "It's your gut telling you something is wrong." Katie explained, "Your heart lets you know you have something to feel sorry about." Joe took it a step further: "My mom makes me feel guilty when I do something that I know is wrong. Sometimes I think she just likes making me feel bad, but after it's over, I know I'm a better person for learning a lesson."

We will revisit these concepts throughout our discussions; now, I begin "The Last Morning," a sharply painful account of a day of disaster for the Gotfryd family, told from the point of view of the narrator, the teenage Bernard, who, at his mother's urging, escapes an impending deportation. I write the title on the board and ask students what they think it might mean. Nikki speculates that events would happen on "literally the last morning for something important. Any time it's the last time for something, it's a sad time. Even when we think it will be happy, there's usually something negative about it, like the last day of school. We can't wait for summer, but it also means the last time to see some friends."

Strategies for Reading

Most classes include readers of various abilities, so I utilize active reading strategies to accommodate different learning styles. Active reading demands participation from readers and assists them not only in remembering story elements but also in engaging them with the characters by providing a space where they can express thoughts and questions easily as they read (see Olson, pp. 102–116; Boettcher, pp. 294–308; and Humphrey, pp. 411–424 in this volume for additional ideas).

I give students class time to read so they can ask questions and receive immediate answers about the story and the reading strategy I've assigned. If time is a constraint, give the reading as homework with the reassurance that there will be ample time for discussion in the next class.

The first strategy requires a stack of Post-It notes for each student. As students read, they jot down thoughts and paste the note on the page where the thought was evoked. I tell my students to comment whenever they discover:

1. a character or a place that reminds them of another they have seen or known;
2. a question they would like to ask the character at that very moment;
3. a connection they see to another piece of literature, a film, or their life; or
4. anything else they wish to share.

Such writing can be difficult initially because many students want simply to read the piece without interruption. I assure them that once they become accustomed to reading actively by engaging with the text, they'll remember more about it and will participate more substantively.

Another method to use is the two-column response sheet, explained on p. 254 as the reading strategy for the next story. Try different strategies with each story or use the same one twice to provide guided practice. If you try both, encourage students to identify which one encourages a closer reading of the text. Students read silently and write on their Post-It notes for the rest of the class as I circulate and remain available for questions.

Student Commentary

In the second class, students gather in groups to comment on the notes made the day before. Examples follow:

Text	Post-It Note

"I found an old table top that father kept behind the house covered with sheets of tar paper. It was dry and burned well. I didn't tell my mother where the wood had come from; I was afraid she might not like the idea of putting a good table to the fire." (*Anthology*, p. 133)

> The table had been used to share family meals, to hold the family together. Now it has to be sacrificed to prepare the meal that barely feeds them, yet it still holds them together.

"An elderly man carrying a huge bundle on his shoulders stopped us and asked for the time. 'Why do you need to know the time? 'I inquired. He looked at me as if upset by my question and answered, 'Soon it will be time for evening prayers, don't you know?' And he went on his way, talking to himself and balancing the awkward bundle on his shoulders" (p. 134).

> Older people are used to living their lives by the clock. Younger people do what they want when they want. Older people are bound by tradition and routine. Maybe the younger ones are losing these things, abandoning their faith. Maybe the old man has lost his mind; he thinks he must go to pray, but public prayer was forbidden.

Referring to the sandwich found in his pocket, Bernard writes, "My mother must have put it there when my jacket was still hanging behind the kitchen door" (p. 135).

> This reminds me of my mother. She always made sure I had my lunch even when she was running out of time in the morning. Perhaps she had a sense of what was happening and was doing whatever she could to help her sons.

I find that in self-selected groups of three or four, students share more openly than they will with the entire class; alternatively, you may choose to group a very able student with those less able or eager to participate so he/she can serve as a guide. I monitor to ensure task-oriented behavior and participation of each student, briefly joining each conversation as an observer. Occasionally, I ask a student to elaborate on a note. Not only does this validate the student's work, but it also provides me with some understanding of how he/she is reading the text. I follow up on responses that lend themselves to research or extended learning.

After 15 minutes, I bring the class together to share thoughts. It never fails: Each group takes a different direction with ideas that enhance everyone's understanding. This is also the time to further examine the story, including its theme(s), symbols, and additional points the students or I would like to pursue. During our discussion, emergent themes were:

- "Although children and adults may understand events differently, children often know more than they're given credit for."
- "Parents protect and love their children through good times and bad."
- "Isolation, loneliness, and loss are integral to the Holocaust experience."

All themes provided a way in to the text as well as a connection to our lives, underscoring their universality.

Some symbols we discussed were:

- the suitcase: representing a lifetime of memories;
- the sandwich: representing love and support from the mother;
- the mouse: a small, frightened creature in hiding in a world where he, too, is at the mercy of predators.

As the discussion concluded, I assigned students in each group two questions to be answered in writing. Depending upon time constraints, this could be begun in class or completed for homework and shared the following day. My questions were arbitrarily assigned; you might choose questions for specific students. Individualizing and limiting required questions cuts down on copying and ensures more attention in class as each group shares something different.

Exploring and Responding to the Text

On the third day, students came fully prepared with their responses. Group 1 had been assigned the following:

1. How is Gotfryd's mother characterized?
2. In the first four paragraphs, what memories does the author share? What is his tone?

Travis surprised me by his nuanced assessment: "Gotfryd's mother is caring and vulnerable but not selfish. She is multidimensional, being both a softie and an incredibly tough woman." (Other answers might include: She is considerate, stoic, reflective, caring, and selfless. She cares deeply for her family, places their needs above hers, and is a quiet leader who, like all mothers, has dreams for her children.)

Kylie responded to the second question, "The memories were of his mother and his childhood. They give you a feeling for the character and what he has gone through. The tone is remorseful, like he is talking of his mother only for the reader, but he doesn't like to." (Additional answers include: His mother in the garden crying, his not knowing the exact date of his mother's birthday, his mother's caress, her last words to him, and the treat of margarine and jam. The tone is alternately peaceful, melancholy, sorrowful, helpless, and thoughtful.)

Students in Group 2 were asked:

1. What does the father mean when he says "I stopped thinking; it's better not to think" (p. 132)?
2. When Bernard finds the suitcase in the attic, he hugs it before he takes it downstairs. What do you imagine were his thoughts and feelings?

Naaseha observed that the father "stopped thinking about his life or what is going to happen to him. This is better for him because he isn't expecting something to happen; therefore, he won't be mad if it doesn't." (Other possible answers: Thinking about what might happen does not change events or outcomes. He feels as if he has lost control over his life and the lives of his family. Thinking is painful when one is powerless to affect change, as the Jews were in the Holocaust.)

Nikki understood that "there is something in that suitcase that he doesn't want to let go of, but he knows he will have to let it go." (Different answers include: He may be thinking of times when the suitcase was used for family trips that brought happy memories, while this trip would bring only sadness. He may be wishing he could go back in time to those happier moments. It is a moment of isolation for him, since he cannot share his pain with his family.)

Group 3 was assigned the following:

1. Why do you think this family spends the last hours together in silence?
2. Mother continues her routine this day just as any other. Why is this significant?

Hannah seemed to understand: "The family does not know what they want their last words to be, so silence is what they choose, to show that hopefully this was not a good-bye, just a see you later." (Other options: Each knows what is to happen, and words cannot express their feelings or thoughts. Sometimes what is not said is more powerful than what is. The pain of the situation and fear for the future may make each feel isolated even as they sit together.)

Kylie explained the second question: "This shows how bold she was. It was like telling the Germans that even though they were taking her life, while she was still free she wasn't going to let them get to her. She was still in control." (Additional responses: Mother is a creature of habit. As long as things seem normal, they feel normal. Keeping busy helps to keep her mind off the coming events. Mother is trying to keep things as calm and natural as possible; this is her role.)

Group 4 responded to the following:

1. Why is burning the table symbolic?
2. Why is the following image effective? "People. ... seemed like caged birds looking for an escape" (p. 133–134).

For the first answer, Kara wrote, "The table represents family and togetherness, and when burned, represents the destruction of the family." (Other answers: The table is the family refuge where the meals, day's events, and memories are shared. Just as the family is now being torn apart, so is a piece of furniture that represents so much of family life. Students may also connect the consuming fire to the consuming Holocaust.)

The second question elicited from Ali, "Gotfryd compares them to caged birds because they were caged in the ghetto until they met their fate." (Additional possible answers: Birds and people are meant to be free. Many seem to be walking around without direction as if seeking a way to escape.)

Group 5 dealt with issues of guilt and collaboration. I had asked the following:

1. While hiding in the hay, Gotfryd "started to recall the events of the entire day. I realized I had run out of the house without saying good-bye to my parents. Seized with guilt, I started sobbing" (p. 136). Is his guilt justified? Why?
2. Why does the Polish stable boy, who could have been in the same situation as Bernard, turn the boys in to the Nazis?

The group held different opinions on the first question. Kara wrote, "He did not need to feel guilt because his mom told him to leave right away. He was just doing what she said." Naaseha disagreed. "His guilt is justified because he knew that anything could happen these days. He should have remembered to say good-bye because he didn't know what could happen to him or if he would make it back." (Other possible answers: He should not feel guilty; he did not do it on purpose. It is not the Jews who should feel guilty, but the Nazis. He should feel sad; this may be the last time he sees his parents, but not guilty. It is another moment of isolation, loneliness, and profound loss.)

For the second, Natalie showed she understood the nature of collaborators: "The boy knew he could save himself by turning in Jews to get on the Nazis' good side." (Other answers: He may have been antisemitic and turned in the boys because they were Jews; he may have been afraid of being accused of helping Jews trying to escape, which could endanger his own life.)

I had asked Group 6 to respond to the following:

1. Bernard says that when he wants to remember his mother, "I close my eyes and think of the Sunday in August of 1942 when I saw her sitting in our ghetto

garden, crying behind the lilac tree" (p. 138). Why do you think this, and not another, is the memory that comes to him?

2. There is a distinct difference between the responses of the older people and the younger ones. What differences have you noticed? What might account for these differences?

Nikki thought that when Bernard "saw his mother behind the tree, he saw her completely being herself and not trying to put on a facade." Naaseha believed, "It is a memory different from all others because he didn't see her cry very often. When he did, he felt bad, and this memory evokes that emotion." (Additional answers: This is one of the last memories he has that also encompasses so many emotions. Despite the sadness of the day, she attempted to behave as normally as possible while caring for her family.)

Nikki answered the second question as well: "The older people seem calmer and just try to live their lives, while the younger people seem scared and panicked and don't know what to do. I think older people's maturity and experience in life help them cope." (Additional answers: Older people seem to let things happen to them rather than fighting them like the younger people do. Perhaps it is their faith; perhaps they, having lived longer, may be more prepared for death. Younger people seem to question more and fight ideas that are anathema to them.)

Students enthusiastically responded to one another's conclusions, debating or adding ideas to classmates' comments. They had connected to the author and his experience and were eager to begin "On Guilt" the next day, speculating that the author might continue his anguish over his mother's deportation.

"On Guilt"

For this story on the fourth day, I gave definitions for only two words:

1. Nazi *Gendarmes*: police officers within the ranks of the Nazi party
2. *Polizeiführer*: police leader

I wrote the title on the board and asked them to speculate about its meaning; Megan wrote, "It seems that during the Holocaust the wrong people were feeling guilty for things. Innocent people were made to feel guilty for things that were beyond their control, while the people who should feel guilty didn't."

Again students read silently. This time I asked them to use the two-column response sheet as they read. To use this strategy, have students fold a piece of paper in half lengthwise. As they read, they note in the left column any characters, events, questions, or any literary element that catches their interest. In the right column they react, questioning or explaining the entry on the left. Entries on the left may be chosen by the teacher at first until students become adept at developing their own entries; below are my suggestions and some student responses:

- Why do you think Father sells the chocolate-filled wafers? (Right column notes might include: He may feel guilty to have any pleasure in this desperate time. He may feel responsible for taking care of his family instead of enjoying the wafers himself. His guilt may be so overwhelming that he is unable to enjoy even a morsel. The consensus of my students was "Father needed to make money for his family.")

- Bernard has contradictory feelings about his father. How do we know this? (Right-column notes might include: "He started crying; … I muttered, 'Oh, I'm sure she's alive and we'll find her soon.' … It was extremely difficult for me to watch him suffer. At that moment I wished he had gone with Mother. At least then they would be together" [p. 143]. Bernard tries to console his father, hearing his nightly cries.)
- The daughter states, "If Father had gone with her, at least she wouldn't be alone, and that's what he should have done. She was his wife, and he owed it to her" (p. 145). Does the father owe anything to his children? (Possible comments: Yes, he owes them every opportunity at life, considering he did not take the opportunity to "escape." Because they are able-bodied, the children should do everything possible to take care of their father. Eric said, "They need him more than their mother did.")

Again, my students sit eagerly in their groups (you may choose to reorganize the groups), and I visit them as they use this reading strategy to take a position on each question. They are comfortable with the method, and their connection to the story and to the plight of the Gotfryd family is palpable.

One group leaps to the defense of the father even while recognizing his daughter's rejection of his actions. Holly observes, "The son and daughter have very different reactions to the father's story of what happened" and wonders why. The response is specific and substantive. Samantha reasons, "Bernard wasn't there, so he knows only what he has been told." Megan posits that the daughter believes the father abandoned his wife. "She was with Mother during the deportation," she reminds her group, "and she has firsthand memories of that night that don't coincide with Father's explanation." Holly thinks that "their memories may have changed over time, given what they have been through." Taking the daughter's point of view, Megan said, "The son believes his father and is sorry that he was helpless, but the daughter denies this. The reactions are different because the daughter was there and had to watch her mother being taken away, but the boy didn't have to witness that, so he feels remorse for his father." Samantha summarizes, "The daughter doesn't believe him; she thinks he left the mother on purpose. The son believes that he tried to find her, or, at the least, that he cannot be blamed for his actions that day." She urges the group to turn to the text for support. "Look, Gotfryd says to his sister on p. 145, 'Why the recriminations? Why torture one another? What it comes down to is that we all want to stay alive. No one is guilty for it.' That's what I think, too."

Eric's two-column note asked, "Why did Father choose this particular day to tell his son what happened? Why doesn't he tell his son and daughter at the same time?" During the group discussion, Samantha was astute in her answer: "Maybe the father doesn't expect to live much longer and thought his son should know, or maybe he has been silent for so long and really needs to talk. He chose to tell his son alone because his daughter thinks that he left their mother on purpose, so he needs his son to hear his side before the daughter puts doubts in his head."

Students agree that Father may be nearing his end mentally, physically, and emotionally. They acknowledge that he may have told each child separately because he knew that his daughter would remember details that might implicate him. He may also have wanted to feel more in control of the situation, Samantha posits; that's easier to do with one child at a time.

Such observant, fully articulated commentary made my assessment easy.

I call the class together for the final minutes of the period to congratulate them on their thoughtful analyses and we share last-minute thoughts.

Questions for Critical Thinking and Writing

For homework students may write any reactions they did not have time to express in class, and I assign the questions below to be discussed in our fifth class.

- The first four paragraphs of this story parallel the beginning of "The Last Morning." Comment on the parallels.

(Possible answers: Both describe a parent; the first is a warm, caring portrayal of a strong mother holding on to her hope and her family, while the second is a portrayal of a father broken by the despair of loss.) Megan felt that "The tone of the first paragraphs is loving and personal; in the second, the tone is objective, distanced, unsympathetic."

- "When dawn came, a strange calm prevailed" (p. 141). What does *dawn* typically symbolize? What does it represent here? Why is the calm strange?

(Possible answers: Dawn may symbolize a new day, freshness, beginning. Here it represents a new day with only sadness, fear, shock, pain, and longing. The calm is strange because only a few hours prior, this was a frantic, frenzied scene of a round-up of desperate and terrified Jewish men, women, and children; now, only scattered belongings and dead bodies remain. It is an eerie, morbid, dreadful scene.) Holly wrote, "*Dawn* typically means the beginning of something new when the bad is over. In this case, dawn represents the truth of what has just occurred. The calm is strange because after all the screams and shouts, it's over, and those left behind are silenced."

- Both Father and Bernard find a sandwich in their pockets. What might this symbolize?

(Possible answers: The sandwich could symbolize life, choice, freedom. Mother has attempted to care for her son while Father has attempted to care for his wife. While only one attempt might be considered successful, each ended in isolation, loss, and guilt.) Ali expressed it concisely: "The sandwich represents their possessions, love, and good-bye." Holly believed "the sandwich symbolizes their connection."

- What is significant about Mother having "nothing left, not even her pocket-book"?

(Possible answers: She tried to continue life as normally as possible while holding on to the few possessions that remained, and now she literally has nothing left, no connection to anything or anyone; she is utterly isolated from all that she knew and loved.) Jackie understood that, saying, "Her identity was taken away and she had nothing left."

- Father asks many questions of his son, to which he receives answers he doesn't seem to believe. Why does he continue to question?

(Possible answers: Inside remains a glimmer of hope that things are not as they seem. If one person can believe, then there is a chance that things could change. He may also be trying to make his son feel better by holding a conversation that involves hope.) Ali answers, "Though he knows the answers his son gives him are made up, they give him a sense of hope, and that is what keeps him going." Understanding false hope, Eric writes, "He continues to ask because he's waiting to get the answer he wants to hear." Megan, understanding the sense of loss, writes, "Father continues to ask his son questions because he needs hope; sometimes, believing is all we have."

- Why does Father continue to stand at the gate awaiting the mother's return despite his son's warnings?

(Possible answers: He may believe that as long as he stands there, she may return.) Holly notes, "He stands at the gate because his worries aren't about himself anymore and he misses his wife. He is a picture of isolation." Greg, with a surreal understanding, writes, "He stands there hoping to get shot and die so he can be with his wife, for he knows she's dead."

Discussion: Both Stories

Our analysis is complete; now, in our fifth and final class in this unit, we begin the synthesis as we compare these two narratives. We begin by sharing the homework. Students volunteer to read aloud their answers and their ideas are validated. When they have finished, they revisit the K-W-L-H chart and fill in the last columns, "Learned/How I learned it."

From there we turn to our summary discussion questions. To vary the procedure and to check for understanding, I ask students to sit in a circle next to a partner of their choice. I have questions, below, written on an overhead projector, and as I show one at a time, I ask students to spend two minutes discussing possible answers with their partner and share their conclusions if they are called on. Questions may also be used for written response or whole-class discussion.

- Why do you think the author remembers his parents' ages in each of these memoirs?

  Partners brainstorm: It is one element that he can hold onto despite the many memories that have been lost. Ages give his parents a place in his history to which other people, places, and events can be compared. Mary noticed, "He associates things that happened to his parents to a specific time in their lives, and knowing their ages helps him to relate to them as he gets older."

- What do these stories reveal about Gotfryd as a brother, son, and individual? Why are these two stories of significance?

  Partners agree: As a brother, Gotfryd is caring, respectful, and true to his siblings; as a son, he is, in addition, courteous, unassuming, and respectful to his parents and their memories. He stands out as an individual who is endearing, forthright, and sensitive. These stories are significant because they document the last time he saw each of his parents and several friends and other relatives. Jackie summarizes, "Each story tells of a specific event that shaped the person he became."

- Both stories are told in first person yet provide a different perspective on the same event. Discuss the perspectives and the effect each has on the reader.

  The partners concur: "'The Last Morning'" is still fairly early in Bernard's memories and is told in a hushed, fairly optimistic manner. 'On Guilt' is set several months later, when not only has the weather changed, but so too has the atmosphere surrounding what is left of the Jewish community. It seems as if Bernard has become, of necessity, hardened and cynical concerning his circumstances. Each story sets a mood for the reader. We see Bernard change from the boy he once was to the man he must become." Throughout both stories, there are times when someone either feels or is isolated from others. Partners identify feelings of isolation and guilt, overwhelming emotions that, left unchecked, can permanently change a person's outlook and demeanor. Self-imposed, emotional isolation may be harder to bear than physical isolation, and guilt from within, they state, produces a much stronger reaction than guilt placed on a person by another.

- What themes emerge from these two stories? The class as a whole responded with these universal themes:

  - "Family members can be emotionally isolated from one another even when they are physically together."

- "Sometimes families need to put aside negative feelings and stick together."
- "Survival can be as mental as it is physical."
- "Guilt is a very personal feeling, and it shouldn't come from other people."
- "Guilt is a pointless emotion unless it helps a person improve."
- "No one can tell you if your guilt is justified. You have to decide that for yourself, and you have to decide what you're going to do about it."

This theme, valid and specific for this particular discussion, emerged as well:

- "During the Holocaust, innocent people were made to feel guilty for things that were beyond their control, while the people who should feel guilty, didn't."

Again, this activity provided a simple method of assessing students' understanding, insight, interest, and ability to synthesize and draw conclusions from their reading while keeping them attentive and involved. Now I ask students to reflect on their initial notes on the story titles and on the words "isolation" and "guilt." I ask them how their initial ideas evolved to their current interpretation. Hearing this helps me to assess their understanding.

Closure and Summative Assessment Possibilities

For closure and summative assessment, I use a formal writing assignment; each option that follows meets curricular and individual student needs.

Cause/Effect Paper

Have students discuss causes and effects within the stories. They may focus on the cause/effect of a particular concept such as guilt, hate, or faith. They may use primary sources to explain the concept and show examples from related events, using the stories as support. This can be a difficult paper to write, but with guidance this assignment encourages students to examine issues and underlying causes.

Comparison Paper

Have students compare these narratives to what they learned about the same events from other survivors' stories or from their history text. They may compare Gotfryd's accounts of the deportation to accounts they have read in another text. A Venn diagram or other visual organizer can assist students, who will soon discover if they have enough information or if they need to continue reading to craft a thesis, flesh out their comparison, and draw a supportable conclusion.

Definition Paper

Students have defined the concepts of "isolation" and "guilt." Their definitions can be expanded into a formal paper that includes additional short stories, memoirs, or historical or current events. A definition paper goes beyond the dictionary definition of a term and examines it as a concept, not only in how it is shown through literature but also in its larger implications. Students may use these terms or others they have identified in their reading.

Finally, for those who need further challenge, I ask for a definition of "journey." As the Holocaust has been called a "journey through the kingdom of fire and ashes," students can define this journey and its impact either on a survivor or on themselves, the readers now attempting to understand and empathize 60 years after the event.

The Journey Ends—for Now

When I introduced the Gotfryd stories, my intent was to use just two. However, Gotfryd captivated the students, and they wanted to know more about him. So I added several more of his stories to my unit (see pp. 168–183, 294–308, and 411–424 in this volume for teaching suggestions on an additional four stories). For my sophomores, the knowledge that Gotfryd is not a fictional character connected them to his work and to the history of the stories he tells. They appreciated his gift for telling things as they happened, not glorified or enhanced for interest, just his memories of the real people and places that left an indelible mark on his life.

As Ben-Joseph (2008) notes in this volume, "Gotfryd generates meaning and arouses speculation about basic questions of human suffering, responsibility, and redemption" (p. 240). Through these stories, my students engaged in dialogue about family dynamics, decisions, consequences, loss, isolation, and guilt, concepts that allowed them to realize that the Holocaust is, first and foremost, about people just like them.

Not one of us can say that we understand the whole of the Holocaust, but we can begin this journey with our students, offering insight into a small but powerful piece of this dark time in history: the experiences of one man and his family in the Radom Ghetto and the residual memories ingrained forever in his mind.

References

Ben-Joseph, E. (2008). Cause of loss. In K. Shawn & K. Goldfrad (Eds.). *The call of memory: Learning about the Holocaust through narrative: A teacher's guide*, pp. 240–245. Teaneck, NJ: Ben Yehuda Press.

Boettcher, L. (2008). Two tales of protection: 'Kurt' and 'Helmut Reiner': Altruism or opportunism? In K. Shawn & K. Goldfrad (Eds.). *The call of memory: Learning about the Holocaust through narrative: A teacher's guide*, pp. 294–308. Teaneck, NJ: Ben Yehuda Press.

Delbo, C. (1995). *Auschwitz and after.* R. C. Lamont (Trans.). New Haven: Yale University Press, p. 278.

Gotfryd, B. (2000). The last morning. In K. Shawn & K. Goldfrad (2008). (Eds.). *The call of memory: Learning about the Holocaust through narrative: An anthology*, pp. 131–138. Teaneck, NJ: Ben Yehuda Press.

Gotfryd, B. (2000). On guilt. In K. Shawn & K. Goldfrad (2008). (Eds.). *The call of memory: Learning about the Holocaust through narrative: An anthology*, pp. 139–148. Teaneck, NJ: Ben Yehuda Press.

Humphrey, D. (2008). Living in the shadow: Bernard Gotfryd's "An encounter in Linz" and Elie Wiesel's "The watch." In K. Shawn & K. Goldfrad (Eds.). *The call of memory: Learning about the Holocaust through narrative: A teacher's guide*, pp. 411–424. Teaneck, NJ: Ben Yehuda Press.

Olson, C. (2008). Ordinary people, untold stories: Ida Fink's "The end" and "The threshold." In K. Shawn & K. Goldfrad (Eds.). *The call of memory: Learning about the Holocaust through narrative: A teacher's guide*, pp. 102–116. Teaneck, NJ: Ben Yehuda Press.

Choiceless Choices

"A Conversation," "Aryan Papers," and Ida Fink's Scraps of Time

Emily Miller Budick

"I want to talk about a certain time not measured in months and years," writes the narrator in "A Scrap of Time," the opening story of Ida Fink's (1995) award-winning short story collection of the same title.

> For so long I have wanted to talk about this time, and not in the way I will talk about it now, not just about this one scrap of time.
> … This time was measured not in months but in a word (p. 3) …

… a word, she goes on to tell us, that doesn't signify time at all. The measure of time, for Fink's narrator, and, I would venture, for Ida Fink herself (who survived the war in Poland, first in the ghetto and then in hiding) is the word *action*, or more precisely, the word in its German equivalent: *Aktion*.

Aktion is the technical word for the "rounding up" of the Jews for deportation and extermination, a word that also became a shorthand for the policy of extermination itself. "Action" is, the storyteller tells us, a word of "movement," as in "a novel or a play" (p. 4). It is also, we soon come to realize, a word signifying the inexorable fulfillment, in time, of the logic of a particular action—the *Aktion*—that for many Jews was the only action and synonymous with death itself.

"Action," then, as employed by Fink's book, closes down time. It signifies not a scrap of time but the scrapping of time. It is not movement but its end, as, we might say, also in a novel or play in which action also comes to an end, at the end of the story. Indeed, to pursue the literary metaphor further, there is no literal action of any sort in a written fiction. There are only, as in the set of stories before us in *A Scrap of Time* (first published both in Polish and in English in 1987) or in Fink's other published volumes (*The Journey* [1992] and *Traces* [1997]), the words on the page signifying action. What is "real" for the reader is, then, the activity of reading itself, the duration of time it takes the reader to read those words. If, therefore, "the scrap of time" is synonymous with the word "action"/*Aktion*, which isn't action but its opposite, that is, action halted or murder; if, in other words, the phrase "a scrap of time" signifies the end of time and action both, the scrapping and disposal (as of garbage or trash or the bits of cloth that are cut away from the fabric) of time and being, it is also, nonetheless, what remains, despite the devastation, at least for as long as it takes for us readers reading this text to keep these lives and events in mind. The English translation of the title is a fairly accurate rendering of the Polish original *Skrawek Czasu*. (A problem in reading Fink's fiction, which is a common one in the field of Holocaust literature, is that we of necessity read it in translation; much of what is written in native languages such as Polish is not familiar to most of the world's population; these languages also no longer function as a language of Jews). In Polish, the word for *scrap* (*skrawek*) is, as in the English, also not a temporal term (the word *czasu* means time). As in the English, it also refers to a remnant that is left over from something else and may not be worth saving. Fink's scrap of time is the leftover remnant, salvaged from the devastation, which has been knitted (to pick up on the major metaphor of the short story I now want to discuss) into a work of art: into, as it were, a quilt composed of scraps, not of fabric but of time, in which each scrap is nonetheless, as the title of the volume stresses, its own autonomous, independent moment, set apart from all others.

Like the other stories presented in Shawn & Goldfrad's (2008) *Anthology*, neither "A Conversation" (pp. 151–154) nor the other story I will be discussing, "Aryan Papers" (pp. 155–159), presents the ultimate, consummate atrocities and horrors of the death camps. Given the fate that befell the majority of Eastern European Jewry, 6 million of whom didn't even survive the war and countless others who endured the unimaginable torments and torture of the camps, one almost feels inclined to say back to the heroine Anna what Anna says concerning her and her husband's protector Emilia: "poor thing" (p. 152). Emilia, too, albeit a Pole and not a Jew, has suffered the consequences of a savage war: "since 1939, when her husband didn't return from the war, she has lived alone" (p. 152). How, natural, then, that she should turn to Anna's husband, Michal, for love and support: Michal, who now wears Emilia's husband's "mud-caked boots" and whose "sunburned face, which was also not his own" (p. 151) makes him that much more a Slav like her husband than a Jew like Anna. The war has changed Michal; it has changed Emilia as well. It has made a Gentile out of one of them, and a wanton woman out of the other. It has also transformed the once upper-class Jewish wife Anna, who, like her husband, knew nothing of farm life and the simple elemental rules of survival—such as splitting logs for firewood and knitting stockings for warmth—into the woman whose husband will now betray her with another woman.

Despite all the contextualizing, however, Anna is the primary victim in this story. As victim, her story can stand for that of the other people who suffered her fate. In a semi-autobiographical text like Fink's, it is even possible to imagine that this story, or the later story "Aryan Papers," reflects portions of Fink's own experience.

Anna's experience illuminates that of the other characters in the story as well. The story acknowledges, reluctantly and with pain (like the protagonist herself), that Anna's victimization is part of a much larger dynamic, which holds all three of the characters in its thrall. Anna is a prisoner of circumstance, in which her literal biological, physiological being, her "Jewish face," puts her in danger of being murdered—although, as "Aryan Papers" makes clear, passing as Aryan (as Anna's husband, Michal, can do) affords no real guarantee of protection, especially for women.

Anna is "grateful" to Emilia even now, when she comes to understand the price that Emilia will exact from them for their protection, for offering her and her husband refuge: Survival is the name of the game for the Jews, and if Anna's survival skills need to come to include not only her ability to knit "useful" stockings (p. 151) but also to accept the equally useful violation of her marriage vows, then (both Anna and the narrator concur) so be it: let no one judge Anna's actions, any more, perhaps, than Michal's, however unabatedly painful and offensive the reality of their situation is. As "Aryan Papers" will also suggest, what constitutes morality and ethics is, under the extreme conditions produced by the *Aktion* of these stories, no simple matter to determine. Indeed, this may not be the time for ethical conversation (concerning such matters as the sanctity of marriage, for example) at all.

Even though words of dialogue do pass between Anna and Michal, the story entitled "A Conversation" is not really a conversation. It is rather a pronouncement or decree, recognizing an inexorable fait accompli. Anna already knows what Michal is going to tell her before he begins to speak. Michal's body and its language—his sun-burned face and his slow, cautious pacing when he enters the room, the silent equivalent of the clicking of her knitting needles—have already told Anna everything she needs to know. While she permits him his denials and disclaimers, his professions of loyalty and love, and his offer of heroic self-sacrifice, she also knows what she has to do, for both their sakes. It is Anna who takes the initiative in this non-conversation: "with my face, without money … I won't survive, you know it" (p. 153), by which she means that he won't survive either. Once the awful logic of the Final Solution has been launched, there is no stopping the clock or its consequences, as the constant click, click, clicking of Anna's knitting needles, beating out time, reminds us. It is only a matter of time until the inevitable devastation of everything, from individual human lives and relationships to the sanctity of marriage itself, overtakes them. It is not that Emilia is, like the Nazis, taking a direct "action" against them, actively "driving [them] out." Yet, just as certainly and surely, Anna and Michal "have to leave" (p. 153).

Except that they don't leave. They stay. And who, the story dares us to say, will blame them?

It is the Holocaust itself (and not even Emilia) that has produced the bitter fruit of this thus far barren marriage, as Anna's knitting black stockings rather than pink or blue booties more than suggests. If, by the end of the story, Michal has become a Pole ("he has changed," Anna realizes; "he's not the same man" [p. 153]), Anna too has undergone a transformation. No longer is she the young Jewish bride. She isn't even any longer the Jewish prisoner, "condemned, isolated from the world and from people, imprisoned in this tiny room." In this story that is less about conversation than conversion, Anna is finally transformed into a Jewish "nun," "straightened up" and "stiffly" resigned, "stiff and straight," "counting" "stitches" (pp. 153, 154) that are as surely felt in her flesh (we realize) as they are set into motion by her fingers. Anna has learned to contain her pain, her "lips" moving "silently" (p. 154) as in prayer, to the "soft, monotonous clicking" (p. 152) of her knitting needles, her "white hands [dancing] rapidly and rhythmically to the beat of the metal sticks" (p. 153), which, in turn, we feel, beat to the rhythms of her wildly beating heart. Anna is the nun at her rosaries. Just as she "presses" her "panic-stricken, horrified" "scream" into the "horizontal, dark-blue line" (p. 153) of a voiceless grimace, so she converts her terror, horror, fear, anguish, humiliation, and pain into the "useful," not "unproductive," even sanctified art of knitting (p. 151), the clicking also recalling the typing of words on a page or the chanting of a prayer in church. She will not, contrary to her husband's request, "put down the needles," for, although he can't "stand that clicking," it is that very same "soft, monotonous clicking," that barely audible murmur of a prayer, which "keeps [her] calm" (p. 152) and thus enables her to save them. "You'd be surprised what I can do" to the clinking of these needles, Anna says to Michal (p. 152); and so he would. Anna is a miracle worker, a saint, the nun who has, of necessity rather than by choice, renounces the ways of the flesh to salvage what she can, for herself and for her husband, of the lives that have begun to unravel before their very eyes. In this way she would hold at bay the inexorable logic of the Nazi devastation.

"Aryan Papers" also begins with conversation and ends with counting. However, the "conversation" overheard at the opening of the story is only the threatening backdrop to the imminent sexual violation of the story's 16-year-old protagonist, while the counting that goes on at the end is of the money she has paid to her violator. This is a story about the insane economy of violation in a world gone mad. Like Anna in "A Conversation," "the girl" who is the nameless protagonist of "Aryan Papers" will suffer sexual humiliation, to which she will give her consent (in the name of survival) to someone who is *not* himself a Nazi but who becomes caught up in the inevitable, sinister logic of exploitation and abuse that the Nazi *Aktion* produces. Unlike Anna in "A Conversation," it is the young girl herself who will be the victim of the sexual liaison and who will be made to play the role of what her violator calls a "whore": "Who's the girl?" a friend of the girl's violator asks upon entering the room she is just vacating; "Oh, just a whore," the man responds. "I thought she was a virgin," the friend replies, to which the man rejoins: "Since when can't virgins be whores?" (p. 159). Reversing the grim logic of this, the story would ask "Since when can't whores be virgins?" The 40-year-old man who secures sexual favors from the 16-year-old protagonist may not be, as his friend suggests he is, a "philosopher" (p. 159). The author of this story is one, though, and so, soon, will be its reader.

Women's Holocaust stories, like the ones told in *A Scrap of Time*, were a long time in coming. This was due, in part, to the fact that the enormous, catastrophic dimensions of the Holocaust seemed to preclude the possibility that gender made any difference to the telling of the story of its horrors. Six million men, women, and children lost their lives and millions of others endured the hell of the ghettos, work camps, and concentration camps—starvation, exhaustion, the murder of loved ones, and so on. What difference could it possibly make if you were a man or a woman? It was also, however, the sexual nature of the abuses women often suffered that seemed to require protective silence. Indeed, this was a reason that women themselves did not speak of such events and often even denied the existence of rape in the camps and ghettos—a lie that easily seemed credible because of the race laws prohibiting sexual relations between Aryans and Jews. To have been raped or otherwise sexually compromised was to become in the eyes of the world, and, even worse, in the victim's own eyes as well, just what the man in this story calls his young victim: a "whore." It was to become garbage, trash, refuse, a scrap, to be tossed away and discarded.

Women might protect themselves, then, precisely by *not* telling their stories or, as in "A Conversation," by knitting or weaving their stories into other narratives that might conceal the actual nature of the events that had befallen them. Who will ever see in the black stockings Anna knits the true story they have painfully stitched together to conceal? Yet, how were women to escape their own sense of defilement, self-condemnation, and guilt if those stories could not be heard by the people who would place the blame squarely where it belonged: with the victimizer and not the victim? A rape victim is not a whore; and even a whore might remain a virgin, if only one knew how to consider the moral philosophy of these things.

It is to stress the problematical nature of guilt that the story doubles the motif of the young girl's selling sexual favors in order to secure her own and her family's survival. The protagonist has already repulsed the sexual advances of her co-worker, to which she will now yield. As a consequence, she has used up almost all the family's wealth obtaining papers that have failed to secure their safety. The family's future depends on her, she has failed them, and she feels enormous guilt. "I should have done this a week ago," she consoles herself; "We would already be in Warsaw. I was stupid" (p. 158). Having sex with her co-worker is not only what she should have done from the start, it is also a mode of self-punishment for not having found some other solution to her family's predicament.

She will now use up the last of the family's money, and she will sell her body as well to obtain new and presumably better documents, though there is no guarantee, the story makes perfectly clear, that these papers will prove any better than the earlier ones, despite, or rather because of her co-worker's protestations to the contrary. The Aryan papers are doubly paid for in cash, first to one greedy Pole and then another. That double payment is then redoubled by their being twice paid for again, with cash and her body, and still there is no guarantee that she will save either herself or her family. This is the extremity of impossible calculation that the "action"/*Aktion* of this story produces. In such an economy, what is the cost of freedom? Who is to say what is a fair price?

The Aryan papers, should they prove effective, will enable the young woman and her family to "pass" for Aryans. To pass for Aryan she has to play the whore. She has to, in other words, first pass for a whore; and this she does. Does this make her any more a whore than the Aryan papers make her an Aryan? If a Jew is a Jew even if she passes for an Aryan, isn't a virgin also always still a virgin, even if she passes for a whore? Her Aryan identity is only worth the paper it is written on, which is to say, it is of no worth whatsoever. The Aryan papers are no more than a scrap of paper, to be discarded when their usefulness is over, along with the identity they falsely declare.

The story itself represents a paper of a different kind. It is a scrap of time rather than of paper: It preserves the moment in time when a virgin resisted becoming a whore, and became, instead, like Esther of the Purim story, a hero of her people. As the story documents, it also grants license. It commemorates and memorializes as art what others would have discarded as not worthy of saying—both her physical body and the story of how that body was abused and survived nonetheless.

In this way, these short narratives are anything but passive acts of remembering the past. Rather they are performances "as in a novel or play." They are re-actions and counter-actions, resisting the *Aktions* of the Nazis and their allies. They are acts of recovery, fiercely salvaging those people, places, and events once deemed by the Nazis and their collaborators so much rubbish to be trashed and scrapped, and whose stories were later also refused by a population of readers who didn't want to hear these stories and the ethical, philosophical problems they raised. For this reason these stories do not simply take place in the time of those earlier "actions." Rather they construct in the disjunction between time and place (a *scrap* of *time*). They invent a wholly new psychological, aesthetic, human space, which is neither temporal nor geographical and yet both. In this space, time and place are simultaneously suspended, and yet both are very much present, very much capable of taking action and producing it. These slender stories are, in almost every sense, literal and figurative scraps, containing the discarded leftover remains of Jewish lives, which, in being rescued from the garbage heap, are reclaimed for the refashioning of Jewish mettle. These stories are the containers of such refuse, of the tragic remains of trashed lives, which we, the readers, can refuse only at the risk of repeating the original crimes these stories record. Insofar as the stories are also semi-autobiographical, they almost literally contain the remains of this witness—survivor herself: both what has died in her (her remains in this sense of the word) as well as what has remained startlingly and vitally alive, particularly in her memory and in her voice. What she has knit together let no wo/man rend asunder.

References

Fink, I. (1995). A conversation. In K. Shawn & K. Goldfrad (Eds.). (2008). *The call of memory: Learning about the Holocaust through narrative: An anthology*, pp. 151–154. Teaneck, NJ: Ben Yehuda Press.

Fink, I. (1995). *A scrap of time and other stories*. (M. Levine & F. Prose, Trans.). Evanston, IL: Northwestern University Press.

Fink, I. (1995). Aryan papers. In K. Shawn & K. Goldfrad (Eds.). (2008). *The call of memory: Learning about the Holocaust through narrative: An anthology*, pp. 155–159. Teaneck, NJ: Ben Yehuda Press.

Fink, I. (1992). *The journey*. (J. Weschler & F. Prose, Trans.). NY: Farrar Straus & Giroux.

Fink, I. (1997). *Traces*. NY: Henry Holt & Co.

Compromising One's Morality in Times of Crisis: Ida Fink's "A Conversation" and "Aryan Papers"

Loyal Darr and Barb Figg

One of my goals … is to evoke the moral dilemma of a human being in a situation of virtual powerlessness, since this is a concrete detail of the Holocaust that continues to elude our imaginative grasp.
—Lawrence L. Langer

"Stories like these represent moments in time for thousands of Jews throughout Poland in 1939 and the early '40s."

"She writes picture by picture, not talking about what happened before or after, only about what happened then, not historically, but as a moment in time."

These comments were among those made by 20 high school seniors in a modified Socratic seminar as they analyzed Ida Fink's purpose and style in "A Conversation" and "Aryan Papers" (Shawn & Goldfrad, *Anthology*, 2008, pp. 151–154 and 155–159). *A Scrap of Time and Other Stories* (1995), the title of Fink's book in which these stories originally appeared, suggests a fleeting glance at an incident—a snapshot, just as our students noted. These "moments in time" offered our students an enhanced understanding of the Holocaust experience that no history lesson alone could present.

For the past several years, Mullen High School, a co-ed, Christian Brother's college prep Catholic high school in Denver, Colorado, has offered a popular elective Holocaust course at the junior level to its ethnically and culturally diverse student body of some 1,000 students.

We had begun to look for literature, specifically short stories, to integrate into our course, because we had come to believe that the genre of the story, through its minimalist immediacy, helps students recognize and empathize with the very personal decisions—many involving issues of morality—that Jews faced during the Holocaust. Among the narratives we felt would most effectively do this are "A Conversation" and "Aryan Papers." We were so impressed by their potential that we wanted to field test immediately and not wait until our next scheduled Holocaust class. So we asked 20 seniors who had taken our course as juniors to volunteer to meet with us before school each day for a week so we could teach and gather feedback on the stories. We were elated that they all said yes, and thus the pilot began.

As both stories contained references to sexual behavior, we obtained approvals to teach the stories from the principal and the chairs of the English and social studies departments; parents signed permission forms, as well.

Our Teaching Goals

We were confident that these stories would prepare students to

- recognize, explain, and empathize with the very personal and agonizing decisions, including compromises, made by ordinary people to survive the Holocaust;
- analyze personal morality as it relates to life and death decisions made during the Holocaust;
- analyze the author's purpose in writing such stories about the Holocaust; and
- understand and explain the writing style used by the author to enhance readers' comprehension of the realities of the Holocaust.

Although it is not absolutely necessary, we feel that establishing a detailed context for the stories will allow students to obtain the fullest possible meaning from them. Thus, we highly recommend that teachers use the three background activities found in Appendix I. Based on the knowledge and abilities of the class, the teacher can adapt and present the essence of these activities in two 40-minute sessions.

We recommend, as well, that teachers discuss the brief biographical information about Ida Fink, which can be found in the Shawn & Goldfrad *Anthology* (pp. 268–269) that complements this *Teacher's Guide* or in a source of your choosing. We suggest you highlight the fact that Fink writes about the ways in which individuals survived, the strategies of resistance they chose, and the memories of their experiences.

Fink uses symbols, images, and metaphors not only to discuss the everyday events in the stories, but also to probe the subconscious mind of her characters and to look at moral and behavioral dilemmas confronted by those forced to make desperate decisions that they hoped would allow them to survive another day. Review her life in a ghetto in Nazi-occupied Poland, her survival, the style and topics of her stories, and the recognition she has received for her work.

In this way, students will feel an attachment to who she was, where she came from, and what obstacles she overcame to survive. We condensed these activities into our first day because we had taught these students before. The enthusiasm of our group was evident in their active participation in the background review and the discussion of Ida Fink.

We assigned both "A Conversation" and "Aryan Papers" to be read as homework. We reminded the students that the setting for both was Poland after the Nazi invasion on September 1, 1939, and we asked them to simply read the stories and think about the following:

- the setting (time, country, and immediate environment)
- the characters and their decisions and actions
- the plot
- the big ideas and questions raised by the story

The Big Ideas

We considered this last item, the big ideas and essential questions raised by the stories, to be the heart of our teaching. Although we did not pose specific discussion questions, we structured our planning, activities, and classwork around ones that we hoped students would raise and address:

- How does personal morality relate to life and death decisions?
- What motivates people to want to manipulate and/or control others in time of peril?
- How does an author's style enhance the understanding of a story?
- Why is the context of a story important to its understanding?
- Why does analyzing an author's purpose aid in understanding a story?
- What roles do economic gain and fulfillment of emotional needs play as those in power take advantage of the powerless in times of crisis?
- What does literature reveal about the capacity for good and evil in human beings?

Our methodology, we hoped, would (1) promote active participation, (2) structure learning activities so that students would progress in their analysis from the basic to the complex, and (3) conclude by eliciting a critical analysis of the ideas and questions raised by the decisions, the decision makers, the stories themselves, and the author's purpose and style. After reading the stories for homework, students were eager not only to discuss the plot and the themes but also to raise such varied questions as

1. "Are these stories really fiction?"
2. "Could these stories reflect the experiences of the author because she survived the Holocaust in Poland?"
3. "Did Michal and Anna decide to stay or leave?"
4. "Did the 16-year-old girl have any other choice?"
5. "Why did the characters have a given name in one story but not the other?"

These questions elicited the exact response we had hoped for in the classroom! The students plunged into interpreting the stories and found that they had divergent views of the plot, the characters, and the issues relating to survival. Many had a difficult time with "A Conversation" in particular; they weren't quite sure what was happening to Anna and Michal.

Getting Students Involved

We wanted to build on this initial burst of enthusiasm, to create an environment and a process that would capture and channel this zeal and allow students to articulate the meaning they made from these stories, so we rejected a traditional teacher-led discussion that allows only one student at a time to speak. Because we both believe that students learn best when they are actively involved, we would work for the next two classes in small groups using guided questions and the "jigsaw" technique to help students define the details needed to master the complexities of the context, plot, and themes and to empathize with the characters.

In the jigsaw technique, we break an entire reading assignment into discrete segments that students dissect and examine in small-group settings. Then, individual students from each group form new units to share their analyses of the details, making the story whole and coherent. This would prepare the class for their fourth session, where, in a modified Socratic seminar, students would progress to an analysis of the moral decisions made by these young Jews, as well as of the big ideas and essential questions raised by the stories.

We had five copies of each page of the stories and at least four questions, unique to each page, which ranged from simple recall of facts to scrutiny of the characters and the motivation for their actions and decisions. We invited students to add their own questions, the answers to which would help the entire class better understand the story.

"A Conversation"

We began with "A Conversation," randomly handing out numbered pages, 1–4, of this story, each with a different colored—red, blue, green, and yellow—dot in the bottom right corner. The students with the same numbered page (all the 1s, all the 2s, etc.) were assigned to meet in designated areas of the classroom, discuss their questions, come to a consensus, and then jigsaw the activity after approximately 15 minutes.

Each group focused on the following questions as well as those raised by the students themselves:

1. **p. 151:** Who are the main characters in the story? What is the situation of each? How did the hidden Jewish woman, Anna, feel about Emilia? Why? Why do you think Anna feels "imprisoned"? Describe your first impression of Michal. Why do you feel that he and his wife were so tense?
2. **p. 152:** In what manner did Anna question Michal about his relationship with Emilia? Why? What appears to be the year(s) of the story? What was happening in Poland at the time? What had happened to Emilia's husband? Why does Anna continue to knit during the conversation? Why does she "click" the knitting needles?
3. **p. 153:** How has Anna viewed the relationship between Michal and Emilia during the past month? What was Anna's reaction when Michal said they had to leave right away? Why? Why did Michal put off telling Anna about his encounter with Emilia? What are Anna's feelings about Emilia at this point?

Why? What did Anna mean when she said, "with my face, without money …
I won't survive"?

4. **p. 154:** At the end of the story, what decision was made between Michal
and Anna? What were the reasons for this decision? Why was Michal's face
flushed? What were Anna's fears? What enabled her to control them? What
analogy can best be used for her "counting her stitches"?

From the beginning, we were pleased with the seriousness of each group as
they questioned, compared suppositions, formulated theories, and identified the
significance of various details on their jigsaw piece. In moving from group to
group, we found that, in the beginning, students argued about whether Anna
and Michal had decided to leave Emilia or to stay. However, as they reread their
pages, constructed meanings, and cited text to support their conclusions, they
reached consensus on the basics.

As some students struggled with concepts, metaphors, and inferences, we
joined them and probed, asking, "Why is it significant that Emilia's husband has
been missing since the start of the war? What war? The author indicates the year
was 1939, so what was going on in Poland at this time? What was it like to be a
Jew in Poland at this time? Why? Why was Anna so torn between wanting to
leave and needing to stay?"

Getting the Big Picture

The students' focused work was rewarding to us. Once they had mastered their
part of the story, we had them jigsaw by forming a new group designated by the
colored dot on their page. Here a student representing each page of the story
shared his/her conclusions with the others. Each student soon evidenced appreciation for the "big picture" of the story and empathy for the characters. Typical
comments ranged from, "Now I understand what the story is really about!" to
"It must have been very difficult for Anna to stay, knowing that she was losing
her husband to Emilia." Some were angry with Michal because they felt he had
virtually abandoned his wife for his own needs, while others believed he was saving Anna's life by his actions. Regardless, most students agreed it must have been
almost unbearable for Anna to accept this burden in order to survive.

Each jigsaw unit was asked to conclude by revisiting, expanding, and sharing
their thoughts on (1) the setting, (2) characters, (3) plot, and (4) themes, ideas,
and questions raised by the story, and, through a spokesperson, share preliminary
conclusions with the class. Because this was a volunteer class, we assigned no
homework, although we did ask them to jot down further thoughts they might
have on both the story and the process.

"Aryan Papers"

The third class was essentially the same and the process went very smoothly.
This time we formed five groups since "Aryan Papers" was five pages. The focus
questions follow; a sampling of student questions is indicated by an (S).

- **p. 155:** What is the setting for the opening of the story? When and where do you think this took place? Why did the girl order tea and then haphazardly drink beer? Describe the girl's feeling about being in the bar. Was she relieved, fearful, or both about the meeting? Is there any evidence that the man and girl already knew one another? Why was she hoping that he wouldn't show? Describe the man's physical attributes. Why might he have dirty fingernails?

- **p. 156:** Why was the girl calling the man "sir"? What was his reaction to this? What is the significance of the line "the wolf is sated and the sheep is whole"? What is the man referring to when he says, "no cheating"? Why is the girl so nervous? (S)

- **p. 157:** Why did the man search out this particular young girl? How old is the girl? How did the man originally meet her? Why did he have her walk to his flat and not take the tram? Why was the mother of the girl being blackmailed? Why do you think the girl turned to the man for help? Do you think the girl trusted the man when he said, "I like to help people"? Why? (S) How was the girl able to work if Jews were kept out of so many positions? Why did the mother and girl need Aryan papers immediately? Where did they want to go? Do you think the man believed that she had no more money? Why?

- **p. 158:** Why did he ask for her address? What reason did this young girl give to justify being intimate with this man? What did the girl do to try and save herself and her mother? Were her actions in accord with her sense of morality? If not, why did she do it?

- **p. 159:** Who is the third character in the story, and what "business" do you think he might have had? What did the man count and why? Why did he say that "virgins can be whores"? (S) What role does the second man play in the story?

As we circulated, we noted that students' answers seemed to be more fluent than those from the first story. When we asked why, the students told us that they could identify more closely with this 16-year-old girl and her predicament, supporting the common wisdom that kids like to read about others their age, an important consideration in choosing Holocaust literature.

The groups completed their single-page assignment and moved smoothly to their new groups to jigsaw their conclusions. Each group concurred that the girl had little choice but to have relations with the man in order to get false documents, "Aryan papers," for herself and her mother, and thus survive.

To extend and vary the activity, we gave each jigsaw group an envelope with colored slips of paper indicating 15 major events of the story and asked them to sequence them, providing a visual time structure. Examples of the events included:

- She took his arm and hoped that they could take a tram.
- The man ordered double vodka and made her feel very uneasy.
- Shakily, she grabs the documents and puts them in her bag.
- He begins to take his clothes off, and she, humiliated, turns off the lights.

- The girl arrived and sat in the back of the room.

Students reported that they found the sequencing activity helpful in reiterating the complexities of the story and its flow from one scene to the next.

A Socratic Seminar

To bring closure to the discussions and to elicit essential questions, we planned for our fourth day a modified Socratic seminar. We felt this approach would allow the class to move from the stories to the philosophical questions they provoked. It would continue students' engagement, allow them "ownership" of the stories, and enable them to revisit and revise their preliminary conclusions in a nonthreatening environment. To prepare, we asked them to develop for homework three analytical, as opposed to content-based, questions about the issues raised by the stories; the author's intent, style, and/or motivation; and/or the meaning of the story to young Americans today.

Guidelines for a Socratic seminar are simple. Each student prepares questions; students sit in a peer-moderated circle; the moderator uses one random question to begin the seminar; and no one can speak a second time until everyone has spoken once. The moderator keeps track of who responds by putting a check beside his/her name. If a student is not prepared or opts out, he/she receives no credit, which rarely occurs. The teacher moves freely outside of the circle as an observer, listening to the students' views.

We were delighted at the quality of both the analytical questions raised and the intense discussion that followed. Virtually all comments lent themselves to enrichment or research opportunities, which we would pursue in a regular class. Here are examples of the students' thoughts; possibilities for extended activities are in parentheses:

Analytical Questions and Suggested Activities

1. Sarah was emphatic when talking about the protagonist: "What choices did the girl really have? What were the consequences of each? Which ones would most likely cause her to struggle with her sense of morality? Why?" (Research the concept of "choiceless choices" and apply the concept to these stories.)

2. Ryan seemed almost possessed with speculating about the author's purpose in writing. He challenged the class: "Do you believe these stories represent Fink's experiences? Her family's or friends'? Why?" (Research Ida Fink and her Holocaust experiences; analyze the differences among such genres as fictionalized autobiography, historical fiction, memoirs, diaries, and testimonies.)

3. Paul's conviction about the relationship between survival and morality was clear: "I believe survival trumped almost everything. The most important goal of any victim of the Holocaust was to survive!" (Research survivor testimony to affirm this belief. Sources might include the United States Holocaust Memorial Museum [*www.ushmm.org*]; Fortunoff Archives at Yale University [*www.library.yale.edu/vhi*]; USO *Shoah* Foundation Institute for Visual History and Education [*www.usc.edu/vhi*]; Illinois Institute of Technology *Voices of the Hol-*

ocaust, [*http://voices.lit.edu*]; and the British Library Living Words: *Voices of the Holocaust* [*http://www.bl.uk*].)

4. Becca, who had been intently listening but not contributing, said, "The reason that Ida Fink doesn't give us a lot of detail reflects how most Holocaust survivors did not want to share the details of what had happened to them." (Research survivors' experiences after the Holocaust, focusing on the issue of telling vs. "putting it behind them.")

5. Javon, an African-American, seemed reluctant to ask his question, but when he got it out, it sparked a class discussion on latent antisemitism. In essence, he asked the class to help him understand how and why the non-Jewish Polish citizens turned on the minority Jewish-Polish citizens, many of whom were long-standing influential contributors to Polish history and society. (Research the history of antisemitism in Poland.)

Closing Activities and Final Observations

As the seminar drew to a close, we praised the participants for their excellent analyses of the author and the stories. There would be time for final thoughts during our last class. Students took their seats in the seminar circle easily, agreeing they were sorry the meetings were coming to an end. The moderator took the last few comments, and we stayed together to read excerpts from "A Scrap of Time" (pp. 3–10) the introductory story in Ida Fink's book of the same name. It was the first time students had heard her first-person view of time when writing on the Holocaust, and it reconfirmed many of their perceptions. As we read, we reminded the class of its "moment in time" analysis, and we knew then, even before our formal poll, that these stories would become required reading for every Holocaust course at Mullen High School.

We administered a simple rubric we had developed as one measurement to help us determine whether the students learned what we thought we were teaching. This rubric, with the results, is found in Appendix II.

As we reflect on this teaching experience, we offer some general observations. Obviously, we would prefer to teach the narratives as an integral part of a regularly scheduled class. This semester we could not; next year we will. Our 20 volunteer students performed wonderfully well and indicated a high degree of learning and satisfaction with the class, but teaching the stories in a regular class will provide a pre- and post-story context and will allow time for extended and individualized activities.

Because so much in the texts is implied, we wondered whether they would be as effective with low-achieving students. It would probably depend on the teacher, but we do not know; it would be an interesting and rewarding case study. We do know that we would not use these stories with high school freshmen and sophomores because of the mature subject matter.

We have little doubt that teaching these stories is most effective in the context of a social studies, humanities, or English course. When teachers and students have some background and understanding of the Holocaust, the class will derive the most meaning from, and passion for, immersion in the texts. However, the stories are still of great value in a context in which teachers and students have little background as long as teachers use the material and data in our introductory lessons and the bibliographic resources to supplement them.

Further Reflection

After several weeks passed, we revisited the question of the value of using short stories to teach about aspects of the Holocaust. Based on our teaching and the students' evaluations, we feel our initial premise was confirmed—that these stories would effectively help students empathize with the very personal and difficult decisions that Jews had to make as they struggled to survive. These "moments in time" not only increased students' knowledge, but they also invited them to combine that knowledge with an intimacy—feelings, emotions, and compassion for the plight of the characters—rarely discussed in a traditional history classroom. Clearly, our American teenagers empathized with the painful and private moments young Jews faced, forced as they were to make choices that may have saved their lives but shattered their souls and spirit. The students clearly understood that daily moments of evil during the Holocaust caused individual tragedies perpetrated on the Jews not by Nazis only, but also by ordinary men and women who took advantage of those who were powerless. Because of the intimacy of such moments, students were able to see the victims as people much like themselves. As these stories become a part of our students, we believe they will want to learn more and, just maybe, as they draw their own conclusions about this watershed, they will commit themselves to speak out against events and decisions that have the potential to lead to future genocides.

APPENDIX I
Background Activity 1: Timeline

If students have little background, you will want to highlight key dates, events, and people. We placed a large timeline across the room with years 1933 through 1939 in bold numbers. We gave students a strip of paper noting a key event, below (taken from the United States Holocaust Memorial Museum's *Teaching About the Holocaust: A Resource Book for Educators*, pp. 29–43), by month and day, but not year (the year is listed below for your convenience) and asked each student to share the event and its significance and place it on the timeline. Class members—and then we—corrected or confirmed the placements.

Jan. 30, 1933	Hitler appointed chancellor
Apr. 1, 1933	Nazis boycott Jewish-owned businesses
Aug. 2, 1934	Hitler becomes Fuhrer
Sept. 15, 1935	Nuremburg "racial laws"
Jul. 6–15, 1938	Evian Conference
Nov. 9–10, 1938	Kristallnacht "Night of the Broken Glass"
May 13–Jun. 17, 1939	Voyage of the St. Louis
Sept. 1, 1939	Germany invades Poland; start of WWII
Nov. 23, 1939	Jews residing in the General Government required to wear white badges with a blue Star of David

We also included some key events from 1940–1945 from the above resource to complete the timeline on the war and the Holocaust:

May 20, 1940	Nazis establish Auschwitz concentration camp
Nov. 15, 1940	Warsaw Ghetto is sealed off
Jun. 22, 1941	German mobile killing squads—Einsatzgruppen
Nov. 26, 1941	Auschwitz-Birkenau established as a "killing center"
Dec. 7, 1941	Japanese bomb Pearl Harbor
Jan. 20, 1942	Wannsee Conference—Nazi plan for "Final Solution"
Jul. 22, 1942	300,000 Jews deported from Warsaw Ghetto to killing centers
Apr. 19–May 16, 1943	Warsaw Ghetto Uprising
May 15, 1944	Deportation of Hungarian Jews to Auschwitz
Jun. 6, 1944	Allied invasion of Normandy
Jan 17, 1945	Evacuation of Auschwitz; prisoners begin death march
Apr. 30, 1945	Hitler commits suicide
May 8, 1945	Germany surrenders
Sept. 2, 1945	Japan surrenders—WW II ends
Nov. 20, 1945	Nuremberg trials begin

Background Activity 2: The Participants

With classes with little background, you'll need to define and teach the categories of people in the Holocaust. We pair students and give each pair a strip of paper with a category: perpetrators, victims, bystanders, survivors, rescuers, resisters, liberators, witnesses, collaborators, revisionists, and deniers. In pairs, students confer briefly about their category; then, on the timeline, they highlight significant people, groups, countries, and their roles, including dates, in that category. (In our mini-class, we asked students to stress the people and their roles from 1933–1939, setting the stage for teaching our stories, which took place in Poland after 1939.)

Although the categories of liberators, revisionists, and deniers came into being only later, we include them to complete the key participants then and now. The students respond well to the active part of this learning; we find the retention rate greater than when the same facts are taught in a lecture.

Background Activity 3: Mini-Lecture on Polish Jewry in 1939

To further contextualize the stories, we offer some nonessential but meaningful Polish demographics, and an overview of the economic, political, social, and religious life of Polish Jewry in 1939 taken from *The Image of Polish Jewry between the Two Wars 1919–1939* (Kaye, 1995).

- Polish Jewry was unique in Europe at this time. Fifty percent of the Jews in Europe lived in Poland; almost 10 percent of the Polish population (3,350,000) were Jews, more than twice the number of the total of most countries. The Jews clustered in large and small urban centers. As Kaye points out, the smaller the town, the larger the share of Jews.
- This high concentration of Jews in urban areas helped shaped economic patterns and greatly influenced Polish political life. Seventy-eight percent of the Jews were employed in industry and trade; 4 percent were in farming. Urban Jews were at the forefront in creating schools, synagogues, and cultural and journalistic endeavors. Their influence was unmatched by other Jewish communities. As Kaye states, "Thus, on the eve of the Second World War, Polish Jewry lived under circumstances that were unparalleled in any other country" (p. 4).

We believe that with this background, students can more comfortably wrestle with these questions: What went wrong with Polish–Jewish relationships when Hitler invaded Poland in 1939? What happened to the apparent positive acceptance and influence of the Polish Jewish citizens?

The answer, in significant part, seems to be that although the roots of Polish Jewry were 700 years old, latent antisemitism was ever present, waiting for a spark to ignite it. Many non-Jewish Polish citizens had long resented their nation's forced signing by the Allies at the Paris Peace Conference of the Minorities Treaty of June 28, 1919. This treaty guaranteed the rights of national minorities in Poland and, in particular, prevented attacks against Jews. With the rise of Hitler in Germany and his signing a nonaggression pact with Poland in 1934, Poland no longer considered itself bound by the Minorities Treaty and disavowed it. The latent antisemitism in a country that seemed to be a place where Jews could live and thrive was about to be unleashed.

To conclude the presentation on Polish Jewry, we gave the students a concise general summary of antisemitism found in *Echoes and Reflections: A Multimedia Curriculum on the Holocaust* (2006) by the Anti-Defamation League. We also highlighted the major provisions of several relevant Nazi documents (pp. 173–192) from *Documents on the Holocaust: Selected Sources on the Destruction of the Jews of Germany and Austria, Poland, and the Soviet Union* (Arad, Gutman, & Margaliot, 1981).

APPENDIX II

Student Evaluation

You have completed our study of "A Conversation" and "Aryan Papers." Place an X across from each item indicating with what degree of confidence and quality you believe the class as a whole, and you as an individual, can:

	High Degree	Moderate Degree	Low Degree
✍ Place these stories in context			
✍ Recognize and explain agonizing decisions made to survive the Holocaust			
✍ Indicate empathy with such decisions			
✍ Discuss author's purpose and/or style			
✍ Relate personal morality to survival (life and death decisions)			
✍ Discuss why people want to manipulate/control others			
✍ Discuss roles of economic gain and fulfillment of emotional wants/need in the powerful taking advantage of the powerless in times of crisis			
✍ Discuss the ability of literature to reveal the capacity for good and evil in human beings			
✍ Refer to other ideas and questions raised by the stories			

Answer Yes or No to the following:

✍ Should we use stories such as these in the Holocaust course here at Mullen?

Yes   No

If yes, should the teachers use similar methods in teaching selected stories?

Yes   No

We were pleased that every one of our 20 students indicated "high degree" on every item and "yes" on the other two questions. These were serious and mature students who we believe indicated what they felt and not what they thought we wanted to hear.

A more detailed version could be completed by each student on him/herself and by the teacher on each student. The teacher and student would then meet, compare and analyze responses, and discuss the student learning and the teacher's goals. This is time consuming, but it can be done within a week by conferencing with students before/after school and during the lunch period.

REFERENCES

Anti-Defamation League. (2006). *Echoes and reflections: A multimedia curriculum on the Holocaust.* New York: Anti-Defamation League, Survivors of the *Shoah* Visual History Foundation, and Yad Vashem.

Arad, Y., Gutman, Y. & Margaliot, A. (1981). *Documents on the Holocaust: Selected sources on the destruction of the Jews in Germany and Austria, Poland, and the Soviet Union.* Jerusalem: Yad Vashem.

British Library Living Words: *Voices of the Holocaust http://www.bl.uk.*

Fink, I. (1995). A conversation. (M. Levine & F. Prose, Trans.). In K. Shawn & K. Goldfrad (Eds.) (2008), *The call of memory: Learning about the Holocaust through narrative: An anthology,* pp. 151–154. Teaneck, NJ: Ben Yehuda Press.

Fink, I. (1995). *A scrap of time and other stories.* Evanston, IL: Northwestern University Press.

Fink, I. (1995). Aryan papers. (M. Levine & F. Prose, Trans.). In K. Shawn & K. Goldfrad (Eds.) (2008). *The call of memory: Learning about the Holocaust through narrative: An anthology,* pp. 155–159. Teaneck, NJ: Ben Yehuda Press.

Fortunoff Archives at Yale University *www.library.yale.edu/testimonies.*

Illinois Institute of Technology *Voices of the Holocaust http://voices.lit.edu/index.html.*

Kaye, E. (1995). *The image of Polish Jewry between the two World Wars 1919–1939.* Jerusalem: Yad Vashem.

United States Holocaust Memorial Museum. (2001). *Teaching about the Holocaust: A resource book for educators.* Washington, DC: United States Holocaust Memorial Museum. See also *www. ushmm.org.*

USO *Shoah* Foundation Institute for Visual History and Education *www.usc.edu/vhi.*

The Gray Zone

Traces of Goodness:
"Kurt" and "Helmut Reiner"

Abigail Gillman

The resolve to savor the small traces of goodness within the most desolate of circumstances is a distinguishing feature of Bernard Gotfryd's stories—recollections of a Holocaust childhood first published 40 years after in the war in *Anton the Dove Fancier and Other Tales of the Holocaust* (1990). In her memoir *Still Alive: A Holocaust Girlhood Remembered* (2001), Ruth Kluger evokes Simone Weil's reflections on the good, and Hannah Arendt's notion of the banality of evil, to support her belief that the unexpected goodness that came her way as a prisoner was at least as fascinating as the massive evil with which so many are obsessed. To read Kluger's account of being spared during a selection thanks to one such inexplicable intervention is to understand that many of those who are "still alive," are so due to the acts of grace that came from the most unexpected of corners. Bernard Gotfryd takes the interventions of Gentiles not only as aids to physical survival but also as turning points in a psychological journey, even taking an interest in the mentality and motives of those who helped. A less tendentious narrator than Kluger, Gotfryd leads us gingerly through the dark landscape of his boyhood, taking as his stepping stones gestures of humanity that were offered under inhumane conditions, good fortune that occurred in the shadow of great misfortune, and acts of kindness by victims, perpetrators, and bystanders alike.

Two features render Gotfryd's stories especially accessible and edifying. First, he portrays each individual character with psychological acuity, creating character portraits reminiscent of the best-known Jewish writers from Central Europe, such as Arthur Schnitzler, Stefan Zweig, and Joseph Roth. Virtually all the figures in his stories, including many on the other side of the victim-perpetrator divide, are portrayed with humanity and empathy; Gotfryd's sensitivity leads him to suspend the dividing line between right and wrong action—to withhold judgment over the agonizing life and death choices so many were forced to make, even his own relatives.[1] A second priority—one that distinguishes him from

---

[1] The dubious actions of Bernard's father, for instance, lie at the center of a story titled "On Guilt" (Shawn & Goldfrad, *Anthology*, 2008, p. 139–148). Here the adult narrator intimates that the father has repressed the truth, yet he remains true to the child's charitable (and naïve) interpretation of events, motivated by the wish to spare his father any further pain. For further discussion, see, in this *Guide*, E. Ben-Joseph (pp. 240–245) and D. E. Fingers (pp. 246–261).

these imaginative writers, as well as from many other Holocaust survivors—is his commitment to providing a long-term perspective on his subjects, to filling in the "back story" in certain cases, and in others, to supplying an epilogue that follows his characters many years into the future. The commitment to continuity has the same humanizing effect as does his attention to psychological dynamics: It provides closure and at times even redemption from the scenes of extremis in which most found themselves.

Gotfryd is a photographer by profession, and this too affects his narrative voice.[2] Like the black and white studio photographs from early 20th-century Europe, his narrative compositions are artful, composed, yet not overly stylized. Each is a portrait drawn from a period of his life, from the experiences of family members going back to Radom in the 1930s, or from the lives of various people he encounters before, during, and after the war. What distinguishes Gotfryd's character portraits from those of many survivors is the fact that his have been fully processed, as it were, even framed. It is a measure of the temporal and psychological distance he has gained from the trauma that he is able to depict the Nazi soldier as a helper or friend. For Gotfryd, the story is a safe space of memory. As Rina Dudai (2002) has theorized:

> The poetic text is the space in which traumatic experience can be revived to a degree that permits its processing. It relocates the trauma in a protected arena, and permits expression of the worst-of-all, yet contains it without being engulfed and overwhelmed by it. In a poetic text the experience is assumed to retain some of the uncontrolled and terrible essence of the trauma, yet create an aesthetic, manageable distance from it. Similarly to rites and ceremonies, and to psychotherapy, literary work can expose the most terrifying events, yet observe them in relative safety. (*http://www. clas.ufl.edu/ipsa/journal/2002_dudai01.shtml*)

Gotfryd's work illustrates this; it must be emphasized that Gotfryd does not adopt the disjunctive idiom of many survivor-authors. In his "poetic texts," the descriptions are sober and yet compassionate. He evokes his traumatic memories without strain, without recourse to incomprehensibility, incommunicability, and other desperations. Episodes that had lain dormant for 40 years and longer have the character of vignettes that have aged naturally in the mind; they don't convey trauma as much as they create the requisite manageable distance and reveal the maturity and perspective that come naturally with the passage of time. Gotfryd manages this evenhanded style even when narrating from a young child's perspective. He recounts the events much as he experienced them in life, with relatively little commentary, without an ideological or philosophical agenda. Above

---

2 In the memoir itself, actual photographs are included, which serve to bring the dead along with the living into the present day.

all, the stories grant insight into a young man's struggle to make empirical sense of what he was experiencing.

Why would an SS man risk his life to give food and medicine to a Jewish family? How can we understand a German soldier who takes risks to protect one Jewish family, and on the same day, obeys the command to destroy another? These are the questions posed by "Kurt" and "Helmut Reiner" (Shawn & Goldfrad, *Anthology*, 2008, pp. 163–169 and 170–180), two stories that focus on interactions with Gentile "helpers." In varying degrees, the stories are also preoccupied with the motives of the helpers—at least one of whom is also a perpetrator—and with the physical and mental suffering they endured.

"Kurt" describes an encounter at a liminal moment in Gotfryd's wartime experience, detailing events in the years leading up to deportation and concluding with Gotfryd's thoughts from the freight car that is taking him away from Radom. The tale reveals that, beyond the material assistance, this intervention by a Gentile affected Gotfryd in a complex psychological way.

In "Helmut Reiner," the emotional impact of the intervention is examined from the opposite direction, namely, from the vantage point of a German soldier. While Gotfryd is absent as a protagonist in "Helmut Reiner," his presence as its narrator is unmistakable. He tells the story from within the psyche of a German soldier using techniques of quoted monologue and third-person narration. In marked contrast to the first story, however, the mental trajectory he describes is one of psychological disintegration, culminating in suicide.

Kurt comes one day to the photo shop where the young Gotfryd works as an apprentice and slips him a loaf of bread. On subsequent visits to the shop, Kurt, soon nicknamed by Gotfryd's extended family "the Jewish SS man" (p. 165) as the only way they can make sense of his good deeds, brings food and even medicine for the boy's grandmother, always refusing to accept any form of payment. The family not only comes to rely on him for aid, they begin to worry about him as well. "Kurt's disappearance became one more of our daily concerns" (p. 165). Kurt returns after a year's absence; he has lost his left arm. "Wars aren't much fun, but I still have my right arm" (p. 166), he remarks, adding that he refuses to get an artificial arm so he will not have to go back to the Russian front. The young narrator tries to make sense of Kurt. Is he "allowed" to feel pity for such a person? "I wanted to let him know how sorry I was about his arm, but I wasn't sure if I should. I felt awkward; being a Jew, I was hardly allowed such intimacy with a member of the *Herrenvolk*" (p. 166). The intimacy is unspoken but unmistakable. "I wasn't sure what he was implying. Could a man in an SS uniform possibly be against the war? I was confused. I couldn't figure him out" (p. 166). Already at this stage, Kurt and the alternative reality he represents loom large in the teen's imagination. Though too young to articulate it properly, the boy intuits the significance of the fact that "a man in an SS uniform" could oppose the war.

Kurt next appears after Gotfryd and his brother have moved into the smaller ghetto; he drops large packages of food over the wall at his own peril. Older now and familiar with this experience, Gotfryd feels secure enough to thank Kurt profusely and also to express his fears for Kurt's well-being. "*Danke sehr, vielen*

Dank'…'You shouldn't have done it. It's dangerous,' I told him, a teenage boy advising an SS man" (p. 168).

When Gotfryd sees Kurt for last time, on the day of his deportation, the connection acquires an altogether different significance. Already bereft of his parents and on the verge of being removed from his native town, Gotfryd looks to him for help. When it is not forthcoming ("I hoped he would notice me, but he wasn't looking in my direction. He was looking at the sky instead, as if trying to ignore what was happening around him" (p. 168), Kurt becomes the unwitting focal point for the young man's feelings of rage and impotence.

In this final encounter, Kurt lets Gotfryd down by avoiding his gaze. Yet, the episode is recounted in such a way that we are left wondering if in fact this two-armed soldier really is Kurt or just a fantasy inspired by wishful thinking on the boy's part. The more distanced the real Kurt is, however, the more vivid he becomes in Gotfryd's mind. In this traumatic moment, Bernard's attachment to Kurt reaches a new level of intensity. Through a crack in the train door, the boy's eyes fix on the soldier's form until it disappears from view "behind a thick screen of snowflakes," as the train travels farther and farther away.

> I was in a rage. I wanted to scream, just to let him know that this was probably the last time he would ever see me. … I can still remember the monotonous knocking of the wheels against the track seams, the arguments people were having over space in the overcrowded car, but mostly I remember my own fury over whether Kurt had seen me get on that train. (p. 168)

The fact that the boy's anger at Kurt, his intense desire to hold on to him, and the projection of reciprocity ("to let him know that this was probably the last time he would ever see me") surpass all other emotions at this moment is the kind of surprising yet believable detail one often finds in the narratives of child survivors.[3] In effect, Gotfryd uses Kurt to anchor his feelings of loss and betrayal. In this moment, the vanishing of the SS man from view becomes all important. Within the recollection, moreover, the scene functions somewhat like a Freudian screen memory (*Deckerinnerung*)—a disproportionately minor detail on which the mind fixes itself as a screen or "cover" for more charged memories or painful feelings: He claims to remember little of the horrific train journey, only his anger at Kurt for being helpless to stop the course of events, possibly even for choosing to look away. Kurt can no longer protect him, but Kurt's image (imago) empowers the boy to own his rage and thereby, one hopes, to safeguard even a small measure of his integrity.

In "Helmut Reiner," a Nazi's act of kindness towards a Jewish family is not enough to tip the balance in favor of exoneration. In this artful story, Gotfryd adopts the voice of an omniscient narrator who has access to both the inner lives

---

3 Kluger writes that her anger at her mother was in some ways more painful than what the Nazis were doing.

of a Jewish couple and those of a Gestapo officer and his wife over a number of years, and he relates the two perspectives in counterpoint. It is this narrative technique—highly unorthodox in Holocaust literature—that to some degree manages to "unify" these divergent perspectives and to emphasize that the two parallel plots are not only of equal interest but also equally devastating, if for different reasons.

The story begins as only an eyewitness would have told it [Gotfryd learned the story from the Orensteins, whom he knew well and with whom he remained in touch after the war.].

> On a very beautiful Sunday afternoon in August of 1942 a heavy-set man dressed in a Gestapo uniform, fully armed and wearing a steel helmet, left the Radom ghetto escorting a man and a woman and a sickly-looking little boy. (p. 170)

The officer, Helmut Reiner, is not singling out the Orenstein family for death; instead, he is taking them into hiding in advance of a deportation. Reiner was the Gestapo photographer, and Orenstein his expert negative retoucher. As long as Orenstein can continue to work for him, Reiner reasons, he may keep his job and avoid being sent to the Russian front. He escorts his charges to their former studio to hide, where he has provided food for a three-day stay.

In describing the tension enveloping the family and their escort, Gotfryd's filmic technique is clearly in evidence. We read of Reiner: "Heavy beads of perspiration rolled down his face onto his neck, dripping under the collar of his woolen tunic"; of Mr. Orenstein: "His pitch black hair was neatly combed and parted on the left side. ... The perspiration running down his forehead nearly blinded him, but he had no way of wiping it away"; and of Mrs. Orenstein: "There was fear in her eyes, but every now and then she would smile faintly at the boy to reassure him that all was well" (p. 171). The sick little boy similarly comes to life as he sits "in the crook of his father's arm, holding tightly to his neck. ... Only when he saw a woman with a dog come out of the building did his face light up; one never saw dogs in the ghetto" (p. 171).

The family is brought into the hiding place, and the fears and doubts they exchange as they hear "a deafening racket of rifle fire ... followed by loud roars of speeding vehicles" are again recounted in detail. Here Gotfryd employs a narrative technique called psycho-narration,[4] wherein the narrator has intimate knowledge of the characters' inner life. "Would they all be deported? Would anyone be left? Perhaps it would have been better to have gone with them?" (pp. 174–175).

Their rescuer, Reiner, is meanwhile called to participate in the evacuation of the ghetto. When he comes upon a woman and child who refuse to leave their

---

4 On the effect of this narrative mode, see Dorrit Cohn, *Transparent Minds: Narrative Modes for Presenting Consciousness in Fiction* (Princeton, NJ: Princeton University Press, 1978, pp. 21-57).

hiding place, he has no choice but to shoot them. "It made him sick, but he could not disobey the order. He fired" (p. 175).

Reiner and the Orensteins reunite when the officer returns to escort his charges to a new, smaller ghetto. Reiner is a visibly changed man; the Orensteins are "nearly blinded" by the sunlight that meets them as they emerge from the dark studio. They are, as they feared, the sole survivors of their family; their reprieve is short-lived, as all remaining Jews are deported the following year. They, but not their son, survive the camps and relocate to Sweden to begin a new life in the face of agonizing memories and guilt at having survived when many relatives perished. Reiner suffers from guilt of a different order; he cannot forgive himself for the murders he committed, despite his wife's efforts to convince him that "he might have done the woman and child a favor by killing them instantly and preventing humiliation, torture, and ultimately death by gassing" (p. 176).

Reiner and the Orensteins meet one final time, in 1945. When Reiner, standing in a breadline in Vienna after the war, is recognized as a former Gestapo member and arrested, his wife writes to the Orensteins asking them to come and testify on his behalf; they graciously agree. Reiner is acquitted by the military court, but at the celebration in his apartment that follows, it becomes inescapably clear that there can be no exoneration. He confesses, "Here I am celebrating … but my conscience will never be free. … Terrible things were happening in Poland, and it pains me that I was a part of it, that I didn't do enough to stop it" (p. 179). During the night, the Orensteins are preoccupied with similar thoughts as they struggle to comprehend Reiner's comments and grapple with their own feelings of guilt and grief.

The three lives have taken drastically different turns. Reiner had been excused from further military service due to illness, yet he remains a doomed man, haunted by the eyes of the child in the cellar. The Orensteins descended into the abyss of the concentration camps and emerged, somehow managing to begin new lives. The rescued ones have become the rescuers. Yet the essential trajectory of these three lives is the same in that none is free of the past.

The story concludes abruptly with a phone call informing the Orensteins of Reiner's "accidental" death. In a distinct departure from the omniscient narration utilized until now, the narrator is no longer privy to Reiner's last thoughts, nor does he opt to communicate Mr. and Mrs. Orensteins' reaction to the news. Leaving the reader hanging produces a striking effect; both silences resonate with humility and understanding.

The positive encounters between Germans and Jews, perpetrators and victims recounted in "Kurt" and "Helmut Reiner" become critical turning points in the lives of the characters as well as in the author's own life during and after the *Shoah*. These stories testify that the enemy could be a friend, that victims suffered from guilt, that Gentiles and Jews sometimes understood one another, and that closure on the past, however imperfect, was, for some, a reality. To read these tales is not to diminish the void separating Nazis and Jews; nonetheless, the narratives do serve to humanize the enemy to an extent not often possible in such memoirs. By avoiding the colorations of demonization and idealization, the stories communicate truths universal to the human condition. The accounts are, moreover, generous, unusual in their power to convey the fact that even against the overwhelming suffering of the Jews, the pain of some of the decent Gentiles was not trivial: Kurt loses an arm fighting on the dreaded Russian front; Herr Reiner commits suicide. That Gotfryd is able to bring these "back stories" sharply into view and make us care about these Germans, even as we sympathize with the Jews, is a tribute not only to his gift for understatement and the modesty of his writing but also, ultimately, to his character.

References

Dudai, R. (2002). Primo Levi: Speaking from the flames. *PsyArt: A hyperlink journal for the psychological study of the arts, article 020127.* Retrieved October 16, 2007, from *http://www. clas.ufl.edu/ipsa/.*

Gotfryd, B. (1990). *Anton the dove fancier and other tales of the Holocaust.* New York: Washington Square Press.

Gotfryd, B. (2000). Kurt. In K. Shawn & K. Goldfrad (Eds.). (2008). *The call of memory: Learning about the Holocaust through narrative: An anthology,* pp. 163–169. Teaneck, NJ: Ben Yehuda Press.

Gotfryd, B. (2000). Helmut Reiner. In K. Shawn & K. Goldfrad (Eds.). (2008). *The call of memory: Learning about the Holocaust through narrative: An anthology,* pp. 170–180. Teaneck, NJ: Ben Yehuda Press.

Kluger, R. (2001). *Still alive: A Holocaust girlhood remembered.* New York: City University Feminist Press.

Two Tales of Protection: "Kurt" and "Helmut Reiner": Altruism or Opportunism?

Lolle Boettcher

Let me be weighed in an even balance, that God may know me.
—Book of Job, 31:6

"Kurt" and "Helmut Reiner" (Shawn & Goldfrad, *Anthology*, 2008, pp. 163–169 and 170–180) tell stories of German soldiers who, each in different ways, come to the aid of Jewish families in Radom, Poland, during the Holocaust. I chose to teach these true stories specifically because my students frequently ask why more Christians didn't assume the responsibility to help Jews in danger.

In "Kurt," readers understand the acts of kindness from the first-person perspective of the Jewish narrator/author, Bernard Gotfryd. Bernard, a teenager during the Holocaust, served as an apprentice in a photography studio that serviced Nazi soldiers. Kurt, a *Waffen SS* soldier, is first a customer but soon becomes a benefactor to Bernard and his family.

In "Helmut Reiner," Reiner, a Nazi officer and Gestapo photographer, requires the skills of Mr. Orenstein, the Jewish negative retoucher in the studio, to ensure continuation of his successful work. Reiner hides Orenstein, his wife, and his young son, saving them from an impending deportation. Here the perspective is from the author as omniscient narrator, from whom we hear the thoughts of each character. Each story personalizes the dilemmas one might face when offering aid to—or accepting it from—an avowed enemy, during conditions life-threatening to both.

A Delicate Level of Trust

A delicate level of trust lies at the heart of these stories, which illustrate remarkably well the intricacies of the human soul and exemplify the truth that "among the many notions sabotaged by the Holocaust is the naïve opposition between good and evil or heroes and villains" (Langer, 1995, p. 10). We are neither all good, nor all bad. What conditions cause each of us to initiate or receive acts of courage are unpredictable; how we judge one another based on our actions or reactions to danger is just as enigmatic. These moral conundrums are a major appeal of these stories for adolescents ready to explore the shades of gray offered here.

Suggested Audience

I designed this unit for high school sophomores in a spring semester English class, but it is appropriate for students throughout high school, college, and graduate school and can easily be incorporated into humanities, psychology, history, or any classes involving morality, ethics, or social justice. I set aside six class periods of 50 minutes each, but the lessons can be condensed or expanded.

Thinking about Teaching

Before I began to teach, I resolved for myself the following questions:

1. What are my teaching goals? What do I want students to learn and to take away from this unit?
2. What strategies will I incorporate to achieve my goals? How can the lesson be taught so my students think critically about essential questions raised by this literature?
3. What historical background will I need to contextualize the stories? What must my students know in order to understand the plot, characters, setting, and theme?
4. What materials will I need to teach effectively?
5. How will the lessons be formatted and organized so that my goals are met?
6. How will I ensure student understanding and assess learning?

My hope was that students would take an emotional journey, putting themselves as much as possible in the shoes of the narrator after understanding the historical context. I wanted students to be able to describe the complexity of the dilemmas in each narrative; there are, after all, elements of trust, danger, and guilt involving each character. As a culminating activity and means of assessment, I wanted students to measure the acts of Kurt and Helmut Reiner by the standards set by the Department of the Righteous among the Nations at Yad Vashem, Israel's national Holocaust Memorial and Museum. Would Kurt or Helmut Reiner be a candidate for nomination as a hero, a "Righteous Gentile," an honor reserved for the special few who risked their lives to save a Jew? My students would analyze the documented requirements and make their case after the readings.

The Writing Journal

A staple of my class is the writing journal (see Appendix for journal rubric). It allows students to respond privately and thoughtfully to questions raised by the text; it gives each writer an opportunity to review his/her thought processes as the story unfolds; it allows me to see and comment on the process by which a student is developing thinking/learning; and it can support the students' final writing assessment as they turn to it to reevaluate and synthesize their conclusions.

The National Council of Teachers of English (NCTE) has a clear explanation of double-column journal writing at *www.ncte.org/collections/assessment*; see also the article titled "The Learning Response Log."

Providing the Historical Context

Because my 10th graders have had a general introduction to Holocaust history in their American and world history classes and have read Holocaust novels and memoirs in previous English classes, I begin with a brief lesson on the historical background and information on the Radom Ghetto. I use an overhead I made from the Web site *http://www.deathcamps.org/occupation/radom%20ghetto.html* to set the scene. Using an overhead or PowerPoint presentation to explain the formation of, daily life in, and ultimate destruction of, the ghetto allows you to present the information in stages that reflect the stories and helps students visualize the facts. Be sure to let the students know these characters are real; Gotfryd survived this ghetto and these experiences.

I begin with "Kurt" and give my students a brief synopsis to pique their curiosity, a character list that they must put in their journals to refer to as they read and make notes, definitions of words that I know they will find difficult, learning objectives, and several questions designed to focus their reading. You may prefer to have students do their own research and present it to the class, read the story without the overview, list the characters as they meet them, and define their own words; obviously, these decisions depend on your time constraints and the abilities of your students. You may choose to assign only one or two writing prompts and use the other questions as discussion starters and/or essay questions for a formative written assessment.

"Kurt": A Synopsis

In Radom, a ghetto in German-occupied Poland in 1941, Kurt, a young German soldier, gradually forms a relationship with a young Jewish photography apprentice (the author as a young man) that spans three years, a highly unlikely friendship. Kurt supplies food and medicine to the young man and his family, even as his actions place all of them in peril. Like many such encounters, this one raises more questions than it answers.

Characters

- Kurt: the *Waffen SS* soldier
- Bernard Gotfryd: the young Jewish apprentice to the shopkeeper who was the owner of the photography studio before the Nazis took over ("Aryanized") Jewish businesses.
- Gotfryd's parents and grandmother

Definitions

- *Waffen SS:* armed units of the *Schutzstaffel*, or *SS*, known for combat, but notorious for committing atrocities

- *Kommissarische Leitung:* commissary (government-owned) photography studio
- *Guten Morgen:* good morning
- *Herrenvolk:* ruling German Army; the exact translation is "ruling gentry"
- *Polizeifuhrer:* head of the occupying German police
- *Liquidated:* murdered
- *Danke sehr, vielen Dank:* thank you, thank you so much
- *Auf Wiedersehen, mein Freund:* good-bye, my friend.

I tell students that their goal in reading is to determine, through analysis, what motivated each rescuer and to identify the complicating situations that contributed to the outcome. I ask them to identify themes and to be prepared to discuss these essential questions:

- What motivates one to risk supporting or defending another targeted for persecution when the norm is to ignore, avoid, or persecute?
- Are there identifiable traits in one who receives mercy, who attracts the attention of another who can rescue?
- How do we understand someone who first opens and then hardens his heart to another in need?

We'll discuss a practical, researchable question as well: How would the committee at Yad Vashem's Department of the Righteous judge the person who saves two lives but takes two others?

Methodology and Questions for Discussion

My students and I share the reading aloud, at least for the first two pages, so I can check their understanding of the setting, characters, plot elements, and details. I model reading and note taking, pausing to make a journal notation on an overhead in response to a puzzling passage or to one of the questions assigned. Students read silently; I give homework questions in a handout. Suggested answers are in parentheses.

- What drew Kurt's attention to Bernard? Why is this important? (He was impressed with the young man's knowledge and mastery of the German language. Perhaps he assumed that Bernard took an interest in the society and culture of Germany before it threatened Poland. This recognition humanized an enemy, highlighting a common thread between them. Kurt also expresses an interest in photography.)
- "You speak much better than I expected," Kurt remarks. "Are you a Jew?" (*Anthology*, p. 164). When Bernard acknowledges his Jewish identity, Kurt reaches inside his vest and hands him a loaf of bread. Do you think that Kurt helped him *because* he was a Jew? If so, why? (Perhaps Kurt pitied him; answers will vary.)

- What was Bernard's parents' response to the gift of bread? (They thought the entire incident highly suspect and warned him not to ask the SS man for anything.)
- Kurt brings food for Bernard and his family, saying, "One day when this war is over, we'll have a long talk. Not now; it may be dangerous" (p. 164). What do you think he wanted to say to Bernard? (Perhaps he wanted to tell him that he was forced to be a soldier, but that he personally had nothing against the Jews; answers will vary.)
- When Bernard's grandmother needs medication, the boy asks Kurt "as a last resort" (p. 165) if he might obtain some. Kurt brings a long-lasting supply. Soon after, Kurt brings in a picture of his own grandmother and orders a copy. What do you make of this? (Perhaps Kurt is reminded of his affection for his grandmother; perhaps he now feels comfortable sharing the fact of that affection with Bernard.)
- When Bernard's parents see a copy of the picture of Kurt's grandmother, they comment, "She looks so Jewish" (p. 165). What is meant here by "looking Jewish"? (Generally, although by no means always, Polish Jews had dark hair and eyes; married women would have their hair covered.) What do you think the parents are implying? (They are looking for a reason that Kurt puts himself in harm's way. They suspect that he has Jewish relatives.)
- What is ironic about Mrs. Gotfryd's concern for Kurt when he is not seen for a few weeks? (The victims, those persecuted, are concerned about the safety of an assumed perpetrator.)

More Questions for Discussion

When the second class begins, the discussion is lively. Students have understood the text but puzzle over Kurt's motivation, and we discuss possibilities. I raise more questions, some merely to be sure that students did the reading, asking for a description, for example, of Kurt's appearance and demeanor when he returns after an absence of over a year. I confirm that he has lost his left arm.

Other questions encourage speculation and contextualization. I ask how Kurt's experiences might have changed him. Students posit that the battle experience, and losing an arm, might have made Kurt either more committed to helping Jews or less fearful of dying after having dodged death. Student note that Kurt has decided not to get an artificial arm because he believes this will keep him from returning to the Russian front. I take this opportunity to discuss the difference between fighting on the Russian front and being stationed in Poland to guard the ghetto. Russian winters are brutally cold, and the front is much more dangerous for soldiers, because there they fight other soldiers; in the ghetto, they face unarmed Jewish men, women, and children.

Still other questions are designed to lead students back to the text to cite support for their thinking. When I ask, "What confuses Bernard about Kurt's comments?" students find the response from the narrator: "I wasn't sure what he was implying. Could a man in an SS uniform possibly be against the war?" (p. 166). When I ask for examples of Kurt's generosity, students note that Kurt again produces a "voluminous" bag of food, and when Bernard begs him to accept some form of payment, Kurt says, "Take it. Your family must be hungry, and I have too much to eat" (p. 166).

Our discussion leads us to understand that even an offer of kindness posed a dilemma for Jews during the Holocaust. Bernard is afraid that Kurt is endangering all of them and stops accepting the much-needed food parcels.

As the deportations continue, the Gotfryds are forced to move into a smaller ghetto. Kurt throws bags of food over the ghetto wall to the boy. Bernard calls, *"Danke sehr, vielen Dank.* You shouldn't have done it. It's dangerous." Kurt answers, *"Auf Wiedersehen, mein Freund"* (p. 168). To check for all students' understanding, not just those whose hands are up, I ask each student to take two minutes to write a response to the question "Why do you think Kurt calls Bernard his friend?" As they write, I circulate and read answers: (Bernard and Kurt share a relationship based on caring, compassion, and trust; Kurt is lonely; Kurt feels sorry for Bernard and wants to make him feel that someone cares for him; Kurt wants Bernard to know that not all Nazis are bad.) If I see a misunderstanding ("I thought Bernard called Kurt his friend"), I can clarify on the spot.

The Use of Graphic Organizers

I introduce a "T-chart" that will be used for both stories. I like it because it can be made in a minute by students folding a sheet of notebook paper in half vertically. Across the top line, spanning both columns, they write the story title. Underneath, on the left side only, they write a smaller heading: "Kurt's Acts of Kindness"; on the right side, "Possible Motivations." Now they will list the kindnesses that Kurt offers and suggest motivations. The first kindness, for example, might be: "Kurt gives a loaf of bread to Bernard." On the left, the rationale: "Kurt hears Bernard speaking German and feels a connection with him."

Questions for Homework

For homework on the second night, I assign one question to each of my five rows of students; you can use any appropriate grouping device to individualize assignments. I ask for a thoughtful written response including text support and tell them that one representative from each row will share the group's insights in class tomorrow.

1. After the final exchange between Kurt and Bernard, Kurt turns to face Nazi officers. What is his response? (He raises his good arm and yells the Nazi salute. He may be using sarcasm in a subtle but disrespectful way that the German officers cannot detect. This is arguable; we are not in Kurt's head and can only surmise.)

2. As the ghetto is liquidated, Bernard and his family are marched to the train for deportation. Kurt is among the SS men standing guard. What does Bernard observe? What might this indicate? ("He had two arms; he must have gotten an artificial limb after all" (p. 168). Perhaps Kurt has responded to Nazi pressure to defend his country and, perhaps, Nazi ideology as well. It might

indicate that Kurt was given the arm by the Nazis and is now grateful to them. Perhaps he had to promise allegiance to them, a danger for Bernard and his family.)

3. Bernard files past Kurt fairly closely and hopes Kurt will notice and save him. What happens? How do you interpret this? (Kurt looks at the sky, as if trying to ignore what is happening around him. One can assume that Kurt has realized the dangers, both for himself and for the Gotfryds, or that Kurt's sympathies now lie with the Nazis, or that he simply did not see Bernard.)

4. What are Bernard's thoughts about Kurt's apparent rebuff? ("I was in a rage. I wanted to scream. ... I remember my ... fury over whether Kurt had seen me get on that train" (p. 168).

5. In retrospect, Bernard appreciates Kurt's generosity and regrets his inability to find and thank him. What is your reaction to Kurt's behavior, both his generosity and at the end, when he proves to be just another Nazi?. (Answers will vary and lay the groundwork for our discussion of the complexities of nominating someone for the title of Righteous among the Nations.)

Who Are the "Righteous Among the Nations"?

On the third day, students are eager to hear what their classmates have written. I give them 10 minutes to share their answers with those in their row and select a representative to report the group's conclusions, and then we go online. I introduce them to Yad Vashem via the Internet, *http://www1.yadvashem.org/righteous/index_ righteous.html*, and explain that this museum has a Department of the Righteous whose members utilize a complex process of study and verification of all nominations for the title "Righteous among the Nations." Together we study the criteria for recognition of the Righteous:

1. Aid was extended by non-Jews in situations where Jews were helpless and threatened with death or deportation to concentration camps. The aid must be described in its entirety.

2. The rescuer was aware that in extending such aid he was risking his life, safety and personal freedom. To what extent was there danger or risk?

3. No material reward or substantial compensation was exacted by the rescuer from the rescued as a condition for extending aid. At least two details must explain whether the aid was unconditional or conditional (was something exchanged with or promised to the rescuer, either materially or monetarily? Was it entirely altruistic, or was there something to be gained in any way by the rescuer?

4. Such rescue or aid is attested to by the rescued persons, or substantiated by firsthand eyewitness reports and, where possible, by *bona fide* archival documentation. What evidence from the rescued person supports the aid given by the rescuer? What documentation or witnesses support or dispute this person's selection?

5. Does evidence exist that questions the moral character of the rescuer outside of this act? If so, does it necessarily negate the actions of the rescuer? To what degree?

Would Kurt's actions fulfill the criteria? Will Reiner's? I ask my students to read the next story for homework with an eye to answering that question. First, we discuss how the progression of the war will make the situation six to nine months later even more perilous for the soldier and the Jews alike. Again, I suggest referring to the PowerPoint or notes on the Radom Ghetto. Here, too, I provide students with a story synopsis, a list of characters, and learning goals, and I ask them to define "altruism" and "opportunism," words key to our analysis of this story.

"Helmut Reiner": A Synopsis

In Radom, Poland, in August 1942, Helmut Reiner, a Gestapo photographer, hides a Jewish couple and their son during a deportation. On the same day, under orders by his superior officer, he commits murder. The internal struggle Reiner faces is the overriding theme of this tale. How are we to understand this rescuer/perpetrator? How does a murderer integrate the gratitude of another who sees him as a savior?

Characters

- Helmut Reiner, a Gestapo officer working as a photographer
- Trude: Helmut Reiner's supportive, sympathetic wife
- Mr. Orenstein: a master negative retoucher working for Reiner
- Mrs. Orenstein and their son, a sickly little boy

Questions for Comprehension and Critical Thinking

Homework includes six comprehension and critical thinking questions to be answered in journals:

1. The author's descriptions of setting and characters are detailed. What purpose does this serve? (The details add depth and paint a tense picture of the danger confronting Helmut and the Orensteins. All figures in this "walk away from death" clearly show the stress of the escape. Reiner has beads of perspiration rolling down his face, Orenstein has perspiration running down his forehead, Mrs. Orenstein "had ... fear in her eyes" (*Anthology*, p. 171). The author tells this tale through the senses so the reader can be there, right down to the echo made by Reiner's boots.)

2. The tensest moment, passing through the last checkpoint, is immediately followed by a scene in front of a church. Why does the author juxtapose these two extremes? (The church is supposedly a place of refuge; and yet there a young bride remarks, "'I wonder where he's taking them,' but no one answered" [p. 171]. Obviously the church did not offer refuge for the Jews of Radom.)

3. Two German soldiers notice the trio under escort and smile "knowingly" (p. 172). What may you assume they think they know? (that the Orenstein family is being taken to be executed)

4. Before leaving the Orensteins at their hiding place, what does Helmut tell them? Why is this important? (He tells them that the letter that allowed them to leave the ghetto was a fake, so they know that he, too, will be executed if his help is discovered; this helps establish trust on both sides. He says he will return in two days, that they must be absolutely quiet and not let anybody in.)

5. Reiner says he will be back when "everything will be over" (p. 172). To what is he referring? (to the liquidation of much of the ghetto)

6. How does the author detail the Orensteins' suffering? (They are exhausted from anxiety, concerned about their sick child, losing strength by the hour, and terrified by the noises outside. Mrs. Orenstein tries to take solace in their remaining together as a family; in contrast, Mr. Orenstein feels helpless and angry. They both worry about family and friends left in the ghetto.)

Thinking about Acts of Kindness

On the fourth day, we discuss the journal entries, and I respond to questions. Then, to change pace and to address individual abilities, I pair students to complete a T-chart on Reiner's acts of kindness and possible motivations. After five minutes, we discuss and compare them to the ones we did of Kurt. They consider the characters now through the lens of the "Righteous" criteria, and I see they answer more fully and thoughtfully as they begin to understand the complexity of these acts of kindness. Was Helmut opportunistic, saving the Orensteins only to save himself? The responses are conflicting; they'll need more time to support their conclusions.

Several students reflect on their assessment of Kurt, noting that, while his deeds were noble, he cannot be a nominee because of the requirement that aid "must be attested to by the rescued persons, or substantiated by firsthand eyewitness reports and, where possible, by *bona fide* archival documentation." There is no documentation or substantiation, and Mr. Gotfryd was never able to learn Kurt's last name.

Then I assign each dyad two questions (in a class of 24, the questions will repeat twice). Each student is to answer one, exchange it for the other and answer that; in a foursome (preassigned to avoid chaos!), exchange and answer the new questions; finally, discuss any differences of opinion. I circulate, listen, and comment.

1. Why has Reiner reasoned that the Orensteins deserved protection? What factors motivate Reiner? (Reiner "had known Orenstein …; he respected him. … Reiner knew he was taking a chance … but … it wasn't in his nature to turn his back on people in need of help, particularly on an esteemed friend" [p. 173].)

2. What is Reiner's ulterior motive? Do you consider him an opportunist? (He wants to remain in Poland. "If he could only have Orenstein, his photography

operation … might be assured, and he might not have to go to the east [Russia]" [p. 173]. He decides to rescue the Orensteins himself, "Just in case the tide turns. After all, this war won't go on forever" [p. 174]. Answers will vary.)

1. What were Reiner's internal struggles and external actions when he was told to kill a Jewish woman and her child? ("It made him sick, but he could not disobey the order. … After it was over … he still couldn't understand why the woman had refused to come out of the cellar. It was suicidal, he thought" [p. 175].)
2. How does his wife reassure him about the murders? ("His was not a premeditated murder. … He was under orders … he might have done the woman and child a favor by killing them instantly and preventing humiliation, torture, and ultimately death" [p. 176].)

1. What internal struggles do you think Reiner is confronting at this time? ("Being able to save the Orensteins … gave his bad conscience a sense of equilibrium. 'There was nothing I could have done about the woman and child. … They were going to die anyway'" [p. 176].) Do you think he knew what commands he would be required to obey? Did he have options to save the child and mother? Explain your thinking and include the dangers to Reiner. If Reiner were caught, what would happen to the Orensteins? Does Reiner's response to orders define his character? (Answers will vary.)
2. Reiner tells Trude about the death camps and gassings. She has difficulty believing such stories but tells him, "You must do what is right and just" (p. 176). What do you think she means? What irony or incongruity is evident here?

1. The Holocaust ends; Reiner suffers from nightmares, mostly of the woman and child he shot. What is his wife's response to his anxiety? How do you interpret it? ("Pull yourself together, Helmut. … Forget … the bad things. … start a new life. You did all you could, and there is no reason for you to feel the way you do. You were under orders" [p. 177].)
2. In 1945, Helmut is denounced by a neighbor and arrested. What does Trude Reiner do? (She checks the camp survivor registry, discovers the Orensteins living in Sweden, writes to them, and asks if they will come to Vienna to refute the charges. They agree, believing it is their chance to reciprocate the protection Helmut offered them.)

1. Why might neighbors turn in others when they themselves were bystanders or participants in the persecution of Jews? (Perhaps to turn in a perpetrator would relieve the guilt of those who were bystanders.)
2. Does it seem logical to you that the Orensteins would testify on Helmut's behalf? (Yes; he had saved their lives; no, they might not want to go to Vienna and have to relive the details by testifying.) If they had known that he also murdered two innocent Jews, do you think they still would have testified in his defense? (Answers will vary.)

1. When Helmut, freed, celebrates with his wife and friends, how does he show his gratitude to the Orensteins? (He introduces them to everyone, saying "I want you to meet my Jewish friends from Poland … my saviors" [p. 179].)
2. How do we know that Helmut is not celebrating with a clear conscience? (He says, "There is something that … disturbs my peace of mind. The eyes of a child follow me everywhere I go. … My conscience will never be free. … Terrible things were happening in Poland, and it pains me that I was a part of it, that I didn't do enough to stop it" [p. 179].) Why do you think the people at the celebration did not ask Helmut to say more? (They probably all had witnessed terrible things; perhaps they, too, felt guilty. The Orensteins likely assume that the "eyes of a child" of which Reiner speaks are their own son's, but they do not hold Reiner responsible.)

For their fourth journal homework assignment I ask students to comment on the day's discussion, summarizing the conclusions they have drawn about both men and their actions. I ask them to consider the dilemma of Helmut's potential for nomination: he saved two lives, but he took two as well. Is he a possible candidate for honor?

The Story's Ironic Conclusion

During our fifth class, we focus on the story's powerful ending. We talk about Trude's attempts to justify her husband's apparent breakdown, discussing whether Trude understands the despair her husband feels as he recalls his role in the deportations and killings, and we wonder if her response is a form of denial. Essential questions are raised: Could such thinking be, in fact, the earliest form of the Holocaust denial we know today?

Reiner's act of rescue is in stark contrast to the murder he committed. To Reiner himself, the truth could either be faced or buried, emblematic of the complexity of those who were complicit in committing atrocities in deed but not in thought. Such people either had to "face their demons" or use what might be termed "selective amnesia" to continue to function in a post-Holocaust world. Perhaps Reiner's ultimate action could be considered a form of personal justice.

We wonder if Trude's justification and support for her husband's actions will eventually lead her to believe that she contributed to his suicide. If, perhaps, she been a conscience instead of an enabler, he might have chosen a different path. Most students believe she does not understand his death to be a suicide at all, but rather the accident that she says it was.

The class focuses on the Orensteins' musings: "Why do you think Reiner risked his life to save us? I can't believe he could have done it for selfish reasons. One really has to be decent and courageous at heart, don't you think?" (p. 180). Mrs. Orenstein even comments that if the roles were reversed, she wonders if "they could equal him in his deed" (p. 180). We wonder: if the Orensteins had discovered Reiner's darker side, would their gratitude have been as great?

The ultimate irony is the guilt of the Orensteins, who continue to wonder about the fates of their deported relatives and friends, whom they felt they had betrayed, perhaps by surviving. Helmut committed suicide because of his deep remorse and guilt; perhaps the contrast between saving these two and murdering others is too much for him to face. We wonder: if the Orensteins hadn't survived, would the outcome for Reiner have been the same? I bring up the concept of "survivor guilt" and assign its exploration as an enrichment opportunity for several students. We conclude the discussion of Helmut's demons and Trude's denials with the realization that the only one who truly knows us is the person reflected in our mirror.

Thinking About Motives

For homework, I ask my students to prepare their support for, or rejection of, Helmut's nomination as a Righteous person. I provide the rubric I will use to evaluate their final responses, which we'll share in class.

Grading Rubric

(Grading power: 1 = poor, 2 = weak, 3 = average, 4 = detailed, 5 = in depth

A. Was the aid given fully and accurately described?

B. Were benefits to rescuer, if any, supported or disputed?

C. Was the issue of danger addressed?

D. Was motivation presented and supported by details?

E. Was evidence/lack of evidence for deeds addressed?

F. Was the moral character of the rescuer addressed, including its impact on the decision, and, if so, to what degree?

Total Score _____/30 points:
A=26–30, B=22–25, C=17–21, D=11–16, F= 10 or less

On the sixth and final day, the period flies as students sit in small groups to prepare their case. Each group appoints a spokesperson, who will have three minutes to convince the class to support its decision. The students are divided in their opinions about Helmut's potential to be nominated as a Righteous Gentile. A few defend his act of murder as "only following orders," insisting he had no choice. (What a perfect opportunity to discuss the Nuremberg Trials if students have learned about them previously or to connect the implications of these statements to current events!) They focus on debating the final criterion: "Does evidence exist that questions the moral character of the rescuer outside of this act? If so, does it necessarily negate the actions of the rescuer? To what degree?"

Was the murder committed by Reiner enough to question his moral character and negate his positive actions? The majority think it was. I explain that one could debate this in a classroom, but the Department of the Righteous is unambiguous; killing a Jew disqualifies a person from being honored as a hero. I suggest the following Web sites:

http://www1.yadvashem.org/righteous/index_righteous.html and

http://www1.yadvashem.org/education/entries/english/50.asp (scroll down the list of topics on the left hand side to find "Righteous Among the Nations), where interested students can read stories of the Righteous from a variety of countries to learn about those who have been awarded the title. (Additional research resources, including videos, are cited in the References below.)

This final assessment brings closure to the students, who become emotionally involved in supporting or rejecting the nominations for the honor of Righteous Gentile. I am proud of them. Close reading, research, and fact finding held sway over emotionality as students recognized the difficulties of offering and accepting aid during the Holocaust and of evaluating and rewarding that aid today.

Conclusion

My students' work and their comments afterwards make clear that they profit from reading, analyzing, and making meaning from these stories of life and death during the Holocaust. Gotfryd's writing style brings the student into the author's experiences, and with the critical thinking required by the evaluation of the actions of the titular characters, this lesson moves them a step closer to understanding the complexity of behavior during the Holocaust.

APPENDIX

Journal Rubric

This form is designed to help you evaluate student journals. Read each statement below and use the rating scale to assess students' work.

1–Weak, 2– Somewhat Weak, 3– Average, 4 – Strong, 5 – Very Strong

__ The topic of the entry reflects the assignment. All required notes are in place in the journal.

__ The student made a concerted effort to answer thoughtfully and completely.

__ The organization of the journal entries is clear.

__ Spelling, grammar, and punctuation reflect acceptable usage.

__ Entries are neatly typed or handwritten.

__ The journal is neat and organized; the cover is attractive.

__ The student has raised questions above and beyond those discussed in class.

__ The effort demonstrates the student's capabilities.

__ Additional relevant notes, photos, articles, or other material is included as appropriate.

Additional Comments:

Total Points: _____

REFERENCES

Dawidowicz, L. S. (1979). *The war against the Jews.* New York: Bantam Books.

Encyclopedia of the Holocaust. (1990). New York: Macmillan Publishing Company.

Gilbert, M. (1986). *The Holocaust: The Jewish tragedy.* London: William Collins Sons & Co., Limited.

Gotfryd, B. (2000). Helmut Reiner. In K. Shawn & K. Goldfrad (2008). (Eds.). *The call of memory: Learning about the Holocaust through narrative: An anthology*, pp. 170–180. Teaneck, NJ: Ben Yehuda Press.

Gotfryd, B. (2000). Kurt. In K. Shawn & K. Goldfrad (2008). (Eds.). *The call of memory: Learning about the Holocaust through narrative: An anthology*, pp. 163–169. Teaneck, NJ: Ben Yehuda Press.

Gutman, I., Bender, S., & Krakowski, S. (Ed.). (2005). *The encyclopedia of the righteous among the nations: Rescuers of Jews during the Holocaust in Poland.* Two vols. Jerusalem: Yad Vashem.

Langer, L. L. (1995). *Admitting the Holocaust: Collected essays.* New York: Oxford University Press.

Paldiel, M. (1993). *The path of the Righteous: Gentile rescuers of Jews during the Holocaust.* Jersey City, NJ: KTAV Publishing House, Inc.

WEB SITES

http://www1.yadvashem.org/righteous/index_righteous.html (Retrieved October 10, 2007)

http://www1.yadvashem.org/Odot/prog/index_before_change_table.asp?gate=1-10 (Retrieved October 10, 2007)

http://www.deathcamps.org/occupation/radom%20ghetto.html (Retrieved October 10, 2007)

http://www1.yadvashem.org/education/entries/english/50.asp (Retrieved October 10, 2007)

VIDEOS

Avenue of the just. (1983). New York: ADL.

The courage to care. (1986). New York: ADL.

They risked their lives: Rescuers of the Holocaust (1991). G. Block (Dir.). Teaneck, NJ: Ergo Media.

Weapons of the spirit. (1989, 1990). P. Sauvage (Writer, Prod., Dir.). New York: ADL.

The Narrating Camera:
Zofia Nalkowska's "By the Railway Track"

Orly Lubin

"The greatest writers are incapable of describing what the Holocaust means," states Elie Wiesel (2002) in *After the Darkness: Reflections on the Holocaust* (p. 5), and his comment is double-edged: How is one to convey the enormity and extent of the Holocaust? How can a reader relate to such unimaginable horror?

Nalkowska's "By the Railway Track," anthologized in Shawn & Goldfrad (*Anthology*, 2008, pp. 181–186), seems to be written in accordance with textbook advice: Do not try to tell the entire story; limit your tale to a single event and person. Do not try to explain; understanding will arise from the emotions the story evokes. Tell your story in the first person, or, if you were not a witness, tell it through a witness-narrator so readers can more easily believe and sympathize. Do not force judgment; show the complexity of evaluating morality—let readers feel, realize, how different their world is, so much so that none of our values or norms apply.

"By the Railway Track" is, indeed, shocking and may leave the reader overwhelmed, even numb. As horrible as it is, however, the reader does not doubt the story—after all, it is told by an eyewitness, the narrator, who himself admits to not understanding, thus helping the reader admit her own inability to comprehend and react. The individual suffering makes vivid the entire tragedy and allows the reader to feel strongly for the wounded woman and her death. Even the narrator requires sympathy, lost as he is in the memory he "can neither understand nor forget" (p. 182).

The Danger of an Emotional Reaction

While reading "By the Railway Track," however, a reader may experience an absence of emotion itself, of any knowledge of the thoughts and feelings of the protagonist and those surrounding her or of what effect the event—the "incident" (p. 181)—has on them. This absence overshadows other emotions the story evokes, thus undermining the above. The story is told as if viewed through a camera lens positioned at a distance, and only that which can be recorded is narrated: the scenery, one piece of land on which the focus of the camera is locked, its frame never changing, the lens never moving to another site or following those who can come and go. Verbal exchanges that can reach the far-removed camera are reported, but not the undecipherable whispers, too far to be heard. The actual killing of the young woman is blocked by the shooter bending over and cannot be described. The "camera" cannot penetrate the characters' hearts and minds and thus cannot know what the young man, "who ... continued to keep her company," (p. 184) feels; it can only show us what it sees—that learning from the woman herself that one of the dead was her husband "*seemed* to have caused him some unpleasantness" (emphasis added) (p. 184). The "camera" reports only that which is easily understood: common gestures: the policemen's hesitation, the villagers' turning away from the body; thoughts visible through actions: "the situation was clear" to the villagers, who refrained from saving the woman; the policemen "quickly sized up the situation and deliberated" (p. 184); or obvious observations: "They spoke as though she couldn't hear them" (p. 185).

This distancing from the minds and hearts of the characters results, inevitably, in lack of empathy. It is difficult for readers, through the usual literary conventions of empathy, to imagine themselves as either the wounded woman or the villagers. It becomes impossible to put oneself in their place, to adopt their thoughts and feelings and try to imagine how such an event would feel: for the woman, her wound, her loss, her impending and inevitable death; or for the villagers watching it unfold. As readers are pushed away, so to speak, from the domain of empathy, they lose the ability to feel sympathy. The loss of digested emotions, however, serves to expose the danger embedded in them. Without the protection, relief, and comforting self-esteem that come from empathy, they are left exposed to the demand posed by that other interpretative alternative: to evaluate the incident not as an emotional encounter but as one of responsibility.

The author distances the reader from the event both through the mediation of a narrator-character and by abstaining from revealing any thought, emotion, or even understanding. The narrator, the author informs us, saw the incident, but "couldn't understand it" (p. 186). By this distancing, the author demands a confrontation with the choices made by her narrator, the villagers, the policemen, the wounded woman, and the young man who shoots her. Through the moral issue specific to this single event, she gives rise to the troubling broader issues of how to tell the story of the Holocaust, how to judge the attempts to resist or to escape, and how to evaluate responsibility: that of the tortured prisoners for one another and that of the bystanders, witnesses who are not only the onlookers in the narrative but, through the use of the narrating "camera," are now the readers as well.

Toward the end of her argument on the effect of photographs of war and suffering, Susan Sontag (2003), in her last book-length essay, *Regarding the Pain of Others*, reminds us that

> images cannot be more than an invitation to pay attention, to reflect, to learn, to examine the rationalizations for mass suffering offered by established powers. Who caused what the picture shows? Who is responsible? Is it excusable? Was it inevitable? Is there some state of affairs which we have accepted up to now that ought to be changed? All this, with the understanding that moral indignation, like compassion, cannot dictate a course of action. (p. 117)

Nalkowska writes a story; by creating an effect of a "narrating camera" and by using gazing, looking, and seeing as markers of power relations and of catalysts of action, she achieves Sontag's awareness of the working of compassion as a different, interfering force, which diverts attention from the forceful demand addressed to the witness to acknowledge her responsibility and to take action.

Emotions Relieved from Responsibility

A comparison with a different translation from the Yiddish by Spiegel (in Glatstein, Knox, & Margoshes, 1973, pp. 361–363) reveals the effect of the literary devices that lead to lack of emotions in the story. In few minor changes and additions, Spiegel's slightly different version of the same story directs the reader's emotions and hence judgments. A man "reported the incident to the authorities" (p. 363); he thus sets an example by doing the right thing and is relieved of the moral accusation of not reacting actively and humanely. The same effect is achieved when the villagers justify their inaction, blaming the woman's exposed location. There she lies, elaborates Spiegel's translation, "visible from a distance" (p. 361) "in full view of the onlookers" (p. 362). "If it had happened in the woods, we could move her easily" Spiegel quotes the "old peasant woman" (p. 363). In Kuprel's translation, on the other hand, the old woman only states the general, impersonal, uncommitted remark: "From the forest she could easily have been taken somewhere" (Shawn & Goldfrad, *Anthology*, p. 185); somewhere, by someone, somehow.

Both translations explain that nightfall (in our translation), darkness (in the other) is necessary; but where Kuprel states merely, "Nothing of the kind [any form of help] would happen" (p. 185), Spiegel's translation explains: "The inhabitants were not prepared to cope with such an unforeseen tragedy" (p. 363). By replacing the formal, remote "incident" with the emotionally loaded "tragedy," Spiegel creates a fertile ground for empathy with the villagers, who were, simply, unprepared. Two men finally come for her "under cover of darkness" (Spiegel, p. 363) or Kuprel's straightforward "when it grew dark" (*Anthology*, p. 185). The foregrounding of the importance of darkness in both versions exempts the villagers from the obligation to help the wounded woman.

In Spiegel's translation the bystanders are also quite emotional. The young man does not feel "unpleasantness" (p. 184) but is, in fact, the one who tells the wounded woman that her husband is among the dead, and "his voice was husky with pity" (p. 362). The old woman "looked sadly," not "silently," "at the milk spilled on the grass" (p. 363); and upon hearing the shot, the villagers turned away "sadly" (p. 363), not "in disgust" (*Anthology*, p. 185). Finally, Spiegel's translation ends with an additional sentence, following the question from the man who reported the incident: "But why did he shoot her? ... Then from someone came the answer, 'There is such a thing as compassion'" (p. 363).

Action and moral responsibility are replaced by emotional reactions: pity, sadness, and compassion. The killing is now fully justified as a compassionate act, explained as such by the woman's own request to be killed, absent in our translation: she begs them to shoot her "instead of turning her over to the enemy" (p. 362).

The young man, by shooting her, relieves the policemen from the only choice presented—turning her over to the enemy and an even worse fate. He relieves himself and the villagers from the immoral choice to not help her and relieves the woman herself from an unforeseen but undoubtedly terrible fate. We do not feel anger or remorse at the action taken by the young man; we are coerced to support his action emotionally by the rhetoric of compassion, which returns in the final sentence to seal our doubts and judgment through numbing cliché reactions such as empathy, relief, compassion, and the stated fear of a painful death at the hands of the enemy.

In our translation, on the other hand, "she tried to negotiate with them, provided they keep the whole thing quiet" (*Anthology*, p. 184). The language of commerce and politics, together with the exchange offered—the killing in exchange for not reporting that people escaped and remain in the vicinity—are marks of community life, of an obligation to the collective. The policemen, same as the villagers, had an option: to kill her, not as an act of compassion but as a responsible response to the times and the situation, a response that will benefit both negotiating parties. They will not have to deal with the authorities, except for burial; they will be active and prove their superiority. She, meanwhile, will have saved those who managed to escape, and, especially important, will save herself from being the give-away, her live presence the mark of the possible presence of others to be hunted and murdered.

Now the shooting takes on a different meaning. It is part of a deal that the young man is the only one to fully understand and execute. When, in the dark a few hours later, the two men come to take her away, thinking her still alive, the reader is left with a dilemma: Was the shooting, after all, necessary? If the woman would have disappeared during the night, the villagers, even the policemen, would have been relieved of the duty to make moral decisions, and the woman would be still alive. "Why he shot her" (p. 186) is no longer clear to us. "Maybe he felt sorry for her" (p. 186) is offered as an explanation, a justification. However, this does not solve the moral issue; it is only a possibility. Other reasons for the shooting—the deal, her treatment at the hands of the enemy—still hover.

Now the reader needs to select the moral and immoral reasoning from among three different sets offered by the story or to organize all three hierarchically. The Kuprel translation does not state any one with certainty nor does it weave together "the greater cruelty of the enemy" with the actual shooting. Rather, the shooting is not only unexplainable, but it is also the source of the villagers' disgust as they turn away and are quoted as one collective, impersonal voice that says, "They could at least have called in someone. Not do it like that. Like she was a dog" (p. 185). The villagers try to disengage, to disassociate themselves from the incident; "they" could have called "someone," but to do what? Might they have called a priest? No, the dying woman was a Jew! Whom, then, might they have called and to what end? Obviously, the villagers would rather not be implicated, contaminated, by the murder.

The Spiegel translation, true to its attempt to justify morally the killing on grounds of compassion, has the villagers turn away not in disgust but in sadness. "It would have been better if we had called for help," someone says. "To shoot her like a dog ...'" (p. 363). It is an emotional comment referring to communal complicity in the shooting, which might have been mitigated by a higher authorization or permission to do the deed. The speaker would like to share the responsibility, but he is willing to take upon himself and his community some of it, knowing that the shooting is justified. She was, indeed, shot like a dog, but they all are, nevertheless, implicated by compassion.

Indecisive Men, One Active Woman

This indecisiveness is not only part of the unsolved moral dilemma but is also one of the story's rhetorical devices and the main characteristic of the villagers' actions. They would have acted, if it had only happened in the forest, says the old woman. She brings milk and places it in the wounded woman's hand, "left immediately," and observed "from a distance ... [to see] whether she would drink the milk" (*Anthology*, p. 184). She disappears "when she noticed two policemen approaching" (p. 184). The young man refuses the wounded woman's first request for Veronal, but "renders her [the] service" (p. 183) of buying vodka and cigarettes; the policemen "deliberated" and remained "undecided," "left, conferred, stopped, and walked on further" (p. 184); the villagers come and go, gather in groups and disperse and move about from one spot to another. The young man lights her cigarettes, stands, and starts to leave, only to turn back and remain, her only company, "the one who would no longer go away" (p. 185). Finally, the policemen again "still hesitated. ... debated, quarreled" (p. 185) and even the shooting is both determined, on the part of the young man, and questioned, by the villagers.

The only one who is resolute, certain, and active is the young wounded woman. In a role-reversal combining stereotypes of gender, race, health, and dichotomies of home and homelessness, winners and losers, the story lets the fleeing Jewish woman be active rather than passive, determined rather than hesitant, decisive rather than undecided. In opposition to all, it is the wounded woman who is decidedly taking control over her life, beginning with the escape.

She was not the first to jump from the boxcar; she was not the last, either. She was the third, and there were others after her. After she is shot, "It was she who asked if the ones in the forest were alive" when "no one uttered a word" (p. 183). She begs for Veronal and asks for vodka and cigarettes. She purposefully drinks the vodka and negotiates her death. She chooses to tell the young man about her dead husband, she tries to drink the milk, and she begs to be killed.

Her description as an unusually determined and brave woman begins after we know she is already dead. Her escape from the train calls for the kind of courage "even greater than that needed to go hopelessly, unresisting and meek, to a certain death" (p. 181). There is courage in going hopelessly to one's death, but certainty, even of death, does give comfort. It is uncertainty that calls for more courage. Thus, when the prisoners remaining on the train hear the shots and realize that those who tried to escape failed, they "could ride on calmly, ever closer to their own death" (p. 182), the certainty of their death ever so strong.

What Is Courage?

The wounded woman's choice is to take the risky action, and the author cannot hide her admiration. However, as the story continues, she also exposes her critique of romanticizing courageous acts. The woman's courage leads only to a death that is ugly and degrading, unnecessary and preventable. In fact, it is only in death, not by her attempt to escape nor her negotiations to be killed, that the young woman serves her community. Her presumed death serves as a calming factor for those who, afraid to try the uncertain, can "now regard the dark place left by the ripped-up boards as though it were the opening to a grave" (p. 182) and stop romanticizing bravery and resistance; and her killing prevents the authorities from looking for others who survived.

Although the challenges of escaping are minutely detailed, the technical language of this description enables a critical, coldhearted approach to the death that awaits them all. "She could only die, one way or another" (p. 185). All their deaths, finally, are ugly just the same; only her death, imagined by the prisoners on the train or real to the villagers, not her singular courage, can help the many. Her initial courage, to opt for the uncertainty of escape, is now replaced by another courageous choice: to opt for certain death. The hierarchy stated at the beginning—courage to escape being rated higher than courage to go without resisting—is now reversed.

The Politics of the Gaze: Responsibility

Nevertheless, the author does not interfere even when such a major transformation of values occurs. It is the protagonist who realizes the danger in which she put her fleeing mates and perhaps those left on the train, who might be punished once the escape is discovered. It is through yet another difference the woman has over the other characters that the author reveals the route to understanding responsibility, and this trait is also a reverse stereotype. Unlike the normative mode of representing women in Western culture, this author gives us a protagonist in control of her own gaze and with the power to look. Through her look and her refusal to look, she structures her world. She chooses when to look and when to shut or cover her eyes "so as not to see anymore" (p. 185). She does not gaze at the people surrounding her; maybe she does not dare, because her gaze does not represent any real physical or psychological power she might hold over them. Her gaze does, though, allow her to evaluate her situation. She "noticed new faces hovering around her," "but didn't count on anyone for help" (p. 183). She "noticed that the kind young man" (p. 184) followed the policemen as they departed. "She watched the policeman take out his revolver and hand it to the stranger" (p. 185).

Through her limited gaze she sees the entire world. After the train "disappeared into the darkness," "all that remained was the world" (p. 182). This world in its entirety that is separated from the train and its "cargo," the "non-world," is the subject of her gaze. When she shuts her eyes, it's "against the world" (p. 183). It is only after her acts of courage fail that the world shrinks to the size of her actual frame of vision and appears as it really is: "This emptiness was the whole of the world she saw" (p. 184). Now the very same gaze limits her world; it becomes the channel through which she takes in her surroundings and confronts her responsibilities to herself and to her community, her surviving friends in the forest.

The political role of the gaze in creating responsibility is highlighted by the villagers' refusal to gaze, to look, or to see. They "stood fearful, watching her from a distance." "They'd cast their eyes about nervously and quickly depart" (p. 183). The old woman, who refrains from looking when she brings milk and when she returns for the tin cup, recites her defensive speech to the others who, like herself, "spoke as though she [the wounded woman] … were no longer there" (p. 185), as though they cannot see her.

The wounded woman is either visible to all or concealed by her executioner from the "people standing further back" who "watched as he bent over her" (p. 185) and only heard the shot. That the woman is exposed but distant, avoided, and finally concealed from the onlookers defends them from the responsibility to help her. She is exposed so they can see her, but for the very same reason they cannot help her; she is distant, too far for them to help or see her clearly. It is only when she is entirely concealed that they can really *see* her and condemn the killing; otherwise, when seeing is possible, they avert their eyes or find refuge behind "the power that cut her off from all the others by forming a ring of fear [that] was unbeatable" (p. 184).

Between Looking and Seeing

The story does not formulate the relations among looking, seeing, and responsibility, nor does it spell out what this responsibility entails and whether it should manifest itself as action. The author mentions only one responsibility. When she details the escape, she notes that the prisoners "understood their obligation to help others" (p. 181). From where does this obligation come? Surely moral issues were not the primary concern of the "human mass" (p. 181) in the boxcar. They might be interested in helping some to escape so that they themselves will have some space; they might hope for the escapees' success, which will mean there can still be a future; or they might even become calmed by the escapees' deaths, they, who "back away fearfully" (p. 182) from the opening who will not have thus missed an opportunity to stay alive.

None are "obligations"; rather, they are self-serving reasons or lack of reasons to stand in the way. "The lesson of the camps is brotherhood in abjection" (p. 17) says Rousset (quoted in Levi, 1997, p. 216, and in Giorgio Agamben, 1999). The author herself does not pretend to substantiate the morality of the supposed obligation of solidarity, nor does she try to solve the moral issue of the villagers' obligation. If the woman who escaped is risking her life and the lives of others to no avail, why should the villagers be required to risk theirs, when it is clear to them they will achieve little or nothing at all?

In "One Day," one of the fragments in her book *Auschwitz and After* (1995, pp. 25–29), Delbo narrates her own witnessing of a woman trying to climb up from a ditch from among the ranks of several thousand women watched over by an SS officer. The woman can barely hang on; she is nothing but bones; but as she struggles, Delbo, the witness, imagines her thinking, "They look at me yet do not seem to see me. They cannot possibly see me, or they wouldn't stand there gaping. They'd help me climb up" (p. 26). Delbo differentiates between looking and seeing; to look does not necessarily mean to see; but to see, it seems, means responding to that which is seen by taking action. The narrator witness tries not to look so as to avoid seeing:

> I no longer look at her. I no longer wish to look. If only I could change my place in order not to see her. Not to see the dark holes of these eye sockets, these black holes. What does she want to do? Reach the electrified barbed-wire fence? Why does she stare at us? Isn't she pointing at me? Imploring me? I turn away to look elsewhere. Elsewhere. (p. 27)

The witness's attempts to avoid seeing fail; wherever she turns, she is looking at something or someone she can either not see, and thus eliminate, annihilate; or see, and then have to answer to the demand for action. There is no way she can help; if she moves, she'll be shot dead by the guard. Nevertheless, her gaze is not hers alone; it is resting, even if reluctantly, on a view that has moral value. The inability to help, or the futility of action, does not exempt the onlooker from actually seeing and taking some action. Hence eyes are diverted in the attempt to avoid looking so as not to see, and excuses are made, most of them blaming the victim's incompetence (the wounded woman should have made it to the woods, the villagers imply).

The ultimate manifestation of that from which one averts one's eyes is the camps' *Muselmann*. "[W]itnesses confirm this impossibility of gazing upon the *Muselmann*," says Agamben (1999) in his book *Remnants of Auschwitz: The Witness and the Archive*. Carpi (in Agamben, p. 41) defines the *Muselmann* as "living dead"; Agamben adds that it is "the extreme threshold between life and death, the human and the inhuman, that the *Muselmann* inhabits" (p. 47). The *Muselmänner* have lost not the will to live but the ability to will; it is this that makes them not only the unspeakable but the even more distancing *not-to-be-looked-at* following Laura Mulvey's famous definition of women's role on screen: "their to-be-looked-at-ness". The avoidance of looking, hence of seeing, may be explained by the effect of "a look into the future" that the *Muselmänner* leave with the spectator.

Delbo's woman, struggling up the slope of the ditch, is the image of the *Muselmann;* Nalkowska's protagonist is not. She is, indeed, "neither alive nor dead" (*Anthology*, p. 183) but does not become a *Muselmann*. They are entirely different in at least one major respect. Whereas the *Muselmann* cannot become, as Agamben defines him, a sacrificial offering that will, as Rene Girard (1977, 1978) shows, die in the service of the community, the wounded woman not only becomes a sacrificial victim for the good of the community but also makes it into her own, self-constituting decision—something (the act of deciding) that the *Muselmann*'s very definition obliterates.

Witnessing

"By the Railway Track," finally, is a discussion of the only moral action left when all moral judgment needs to be set aside: to bear witness. The story foregrounds not so much the necessity and obligation to testify or the heroism and sacrifice of the witness who testifies, but the conditions and the complexity of both. How does one tell about the Holocaust without reducing it to an easily understood emotional event and without relying on aesthetics? Is "true" testimony of the Holocaust possible at all?

> [W]e ... did not touch bottom. Those who did so, those who saw the Gorgon, have not returned to tell about it, but they are ... the submerged, the complete witnesses ... The destruction brought to an end, the job completed, was not told by anyone, just as no one ever returned to describe his own death. (Levi, 1989, pp. 83–84)

"It is not really possible to *tell the truth*, to testify, from the outside [of the camp, of the Holocaust]. Neither is it possible ... to testify from the inside," claims Felman in *Testimony: Crisis of Witnessing in Literature, Psychoanalysis, and History* (1992, p. 232,). Laub, her co-author, further explains that "what precisely made a Holocaust out of the event is the unique way in which, during its historical occurrence, *the event produced no witnesses*" (pp. 80–81). The combination of physical extermination together with the facts that "the inherently incomprehensible *and* deceptive psychological structure of the event precludes its own witnessing, even by its very victims"; and that "no observer could remain untainted, that is, maintain an integrity—a wholeness and a separateness—that could keep itself uncompromised, unharmed, by his or her very witnessing" leads Felman and Laub to conclude that no testimony is possible because there is no witnessing.

The protagonist of "By the Railway Track" is the living-dead who occupies the threshold, the very site of witnessing; she is the complete witness, as she, too, will soon see "the policeman take out his revolver" (*Anthology*, p. 185). It is a moment of not shutting the eyes, although her gaze is her own and she controls it; it is a moment of touching bottom. She herself, the witness, cannot testify; she can only stare at the gun. Her witnessing, not yet transformed into language, precedes language. It is up to the author to now "bear witness to a missing testimony" (Agamben, p. 34).

This round-about way of bearing witness, the only possible way, is fleshed out through yet another "detour" through the narrator. However, even this double mediation is not easily transformed into testimony. Hence, the absence of emotions; it is witnessing without the pretense of understanding that which is being witnessed. The narrator, being there and seeing it with his own eyes, is the optimal witness, the only one who can testify and the only one worth listening to, because he does not understand and thus cannot add, change, or aestheticize his testimony as is Montaigne's definition of a good witness. He bears witness to a missing testimony that the "complete witness," the wounded woman, did not, could not give.

The Spectacle

Neither the narrator nor the author has witnessed two events, one of which even those remaining on the train cannot witness because "there was no possibility of looking out through the sealed doors or high-set windows" (*Anthology*, p. 182): the escape itself. It is reported prior to the narrator's testimony, by the author, in a factual manner of an uninterested, uninvolved reporter. The other event is the shooting. This is, for the living-dead woman, the moment of seeing the Gorgon and not surviving this gaze. At this moment, she is transformed into a sacrifice, a memory, a corpse. Thus, the story shows the workings of three apparatuses: the first is the apparatus of sacrifice. It is an act performed for the good of the community but is always futile. It is always the demise of the individual and never the salvation of the many.

The second is the apparatus of committing an event to memory, thus transforming witnessing (an untainted gaze) into testimony (an untainted report) into narrative. However, this process also imprisons the commemorated: "One can make her [the young woman's] acquaintance only through the tale of a man. ... She lives only in his memory" (p. 181). The woman, the only active person throughout the incident, is confined, finally, to a place only in a man's memory, in a narrative organized by a mind "unable to understand."

To become a narrative, then, requires the third apparatus: the death of the bearer of the testimony, the carrier of the story. Narrated, non-embodied witnessing is a memory that is but a trace of a physical, corporeal existence. For that memory to keep alive, it needs to be repeated, like the annual, ceremonial repetitions of the survivors' personal stories, bearing witness to missing testimonies.

"Yet another person now belongs to the dead" (p. 181). The story opens when she is thus, a dead woman leaving traces in a man's mind, and we are already warned that this mind "is unable to understand." By the end of the story it is clear what is not understood: the process of the one complete witness becoming a missing testimony, the process of becoming a witness to that missing testimony, the process of sacrificing in the service of the community, and the process of turning the living dead, whom all try not to see, into a dead body that is the redemption of the killing community. Their deed of compassion exempts them from the responsibility to save and leaves them with the responsibility to witness and narrate a tale.

The gaze exposes the path from the heights of a courageous, resisting woman to the abyss of a sacrificial dead body committed to male memory and subject to compassion rather than responsibility. Her courage and sacrifice do not save her from becoming, like all other victims of the Holocaust, a missing testimony, now the responsibility of those who survived—and of those who read her story—to bear witness.

REFERENCES

Agamben, G. (1999). *Remnants of Auschwitz: The witness and the archive*. (D. Heller-Roazen, Trans.). New York: Zone Books.

Delbo, C. (1995). One day. *Auschwitz and after*. (R. C. Lamont, Trans.). New Haven: Yale University Press. pp. 25–29.

Felman, S. & Laub, D. (1992). *Testimony: Crisis of witnessing in literature, psychoanalysis, and history*. New York: Routledge.

Gerard, R. (1978). The plague in literature and myth. *To double business bound: Essays on literature, mimesis and anthropology*, pp. 136–154. Baltimore and London: Johns Hopkins University Press.

Gerard, R. (1977). *Violence and the sacred*. (P. Gregory, Trans.). Baltimore and London: Johns Hopkins University Press.

Levi, P. (1989). *The drowned and the saved*. (R. Rosenthal, Trans.). New York: Simon & Schuster, Inc.

Nalkowska, S. (1946). At the railroad tracks. (M. Spiegel, Trans.). In J. Glatstein, I. Knox, & S. Margoshes (Eds.). (1973). *Anthology of Holocaust literature*, pp. 361–363. New York: Atheneum.

Nalkowska, Z. (2000). By the railroad track. (D. Kuprel, Trans.). In K. Shawn & K. Goldfrad (Eds.). (2008). *The call of memory: Learning about the Holocaust through narrative: An anthology*, pp. 181–186. Teaneck, NJ: Ben Yehuda Press.

Rousset, D. (quoted in Primo Levi, 1997, p. 216). In Giorgio Agamben, 1999, p. 17.

Sontag, S. (2003). *Regarding the pain of others*. New York: Farrar, Straus and Giroux.

Wiesel, E. (2002). *After the darkness: Reflections on the Holocaust*. New York: Schocken Books.

Discarded Objects, Remnants of War:
Zofia Nalkowska's "By the Railway Track"

Christopher Gwin

> *There are guests who come no matter how tightly one's door is shut,*
> *as they are the thoughts surrounding our actions.*
> —S. Y. Agnon

I teach a full-semester social studies elective called "Holocaust and Geno-cide" at Haddonfield Memorial High School in New Jersey. The half-year course, which I designed in 1993, is open to all juniors and seniors. The offering grew out of a two-week pilot on the theme of the Holocaust and other genocides in the U.S. History II and German IV classes. My department supervisor, believ-ing in the power of Holocaust education to transform, generously supported this opportunity. More than 125 students showed initial interest after the pilot, and thus the elective was born.

Because it is an elective course, the credits do not count toward the New Jersey requirements for graduation, yet at least 25 students have filled my classes each semester for the last 15 years; more students enroll in it than in any other history elective offered in our school. I continue to be amazed at these numbers, consid-ering both the increased demands from the state in other areas of the school cur-riculum and the intensity of the study. The class has a reputation of being tough. Each session is 45 minutes and meets Monday through Friday, exposing the teens in the class to the history of the Holocaust every day for half a school year.

The curriculum is consonant with the National Council on the Social Studies (NCSS) standards; the teaching guidelines of the United States Holocaust Me-morial Museum (USHMM), available online at *http://www.ushmm.org*; and the New Jersey Core Content Curriculum Standards (NJCCCS), *http://www.state. nj.us/njded/cccs/ s6ss.htm*. It seems crucial to me to link the work in my course to state and national standards both to ensure its objective legitimacy and to prepare students for academic work beyond my classroom. What drives the classroom discussions and ultimately the curriculum, however, is the students' grappling with the "big questions" of humanity. In this inquiry-based learning approach, individual student responses shape and move the conversation; students' focus on essential issues makes the resulting exchange challenging and fascinating. Each group of students is unique, and their voices, even as they raise the traditional questions about the *Shoah*, make each semester's experience distinctive. The class repository of ideas, sparks, and insights, along with my continual reading, learning, discussions with colleagues, and rethinking materials and methodologies, keeps my teaching fresh.

Designing an Inquiry-Based Lesson

I believe that the synergy created by the atmosphere of open discussion is a significant way for students to deepen their capacity to interpret the world and their place in it. The discussion-based structure allows constant student input, creates an energetic classroom space, and allows students to feel that their life experience matters in the context of learning about history. The approach favors a constructivist model, and the chronological history is supported by constant connections to the world in which the students live today.

A good essential question is the principle component of designing inquiry-based lessons. Essential questions are those that probe for deeper meaning, establishing the structure for further questioning, and enhance the development of critical thinking skills and higher order capabilities, such as problem solving and understanding complex systems. I generally begin discussions with essential questions that demand that students apply what they are learning about history to how they are configuring their understandings of the world. These questions are derived from previous class discussions and my ongoing reflection on what emerged. I guide and facilitate class sessions by asking thought-provoking questions, but I try not to participate, explaining that the experience in the class will be more valuable to them if they are the active contributors, less valuable if they are merely passive listeners to lectures from me. This initial demand for their active participation sets up the structure in which the dynamism and immediacy of their life experiences can steer the discussions.

Even though I depend on this model as the predominant methodology, I know it demands great pedagogical consideration. I ask myself: Are my students mature enough to have developed opinions on the themes generated by reading about the Holocaust? Are they developmentally able at this stage in their lives to share experiences about themselves and use meta-cognitive skills to deepen their capacity to know what the Holocaust means to them? The answer varies from class to class and student to student and remains elusive, but I believe it is this quest to know that drives me to continue to structure the course in this way.

In the Beginning: An Overview

The semester starts with a methodology borrowed from Facing History and Ourselves (*http://www.facing.org*), in which students are confronted with opportunities to see how they fit into an "us vs. them" construction and to discover how they view humanity, social responsibility, and what is often called their "universe of obligation"; that is, for whom do they feel responsible? The material moves to the history of Judaism, the history of antisemitism, and the history leading up the National Socialist Party's rise to power. We attempt to explore every key historical piece from the late 19th century through 1945 and beyond. Early in the semester I present historical information in a lecture format. Within this less-popular methodology I incorporate charts, board work, and, every 10-15 minutes or so, as my listeners' attention begins to wander, I ask them to write for one minute on a point of particular interest as I circulate, allowing them to vary their learning modality and me to check for understanding. I find that such lectures, which involve visual and audio cues as well as active feedback from the students, are an efficient way to give over the solid foundation of historical facts and understanding, a critical base on which to build new learning.

The curriculum blends historical note taking and examination of original documents with film and literature. I think it is vitally important to present students with literature created by survivors as well as by current writers. The major piece we read in this course is *Night* by Elie Wiesel (1987). In addition, we participate in the International Book-Sharing Project sponsored by the American Friends of the Ghetto Fighters Museum (AFGFM). The project pairs us with an Israeli high school class in which students also read *Night*, and we discuss our reactions to it on *www.korczakschool.org*, a virtual school set up and monitored by the AFGFM. We also read several excerpts from *The Diary of Dawid Sierakowiak: Five Notebooks From the Lodz Ghetto* (1996), as well as various pieces from the ghetto diaries of Yitskhok Rudashevski of Vilna (pp. 190–225) and Ilya Gerber of Kovno (pp. 329–360) in Alexandra Zapruder's (2002) *Salvaged Pages*, a thoughtful collection of young people's diaries from the era.

The Importance of Keeping a Journal

One of the major curricular pieces I built into the course is journal writing. During the semester, my students write approximately 30 journal responses, which I use as part of my evaluation process. They write about five entries, which I collect and read every other week, depending on how the themes develop in the course. I think the International Book-Sharing Project, with its requirement of frequently exchanged e-mail with partners in Israel, expands the idea of journal writing, as it encourages participants to capture ideas and reactions in clear, concise, thoughtful writing and share them with an audience beyond their classmates and their teacher. I have come to know that this e-learning experience propels them to read young people's diaries and other literature with greater interest, and it also laid the foundation for a richer discussion of the imagery in Zofia Nalkowska's (1946, 1973, 2000) short story "By the Railway Track," anthologized in Shawn & Goldfrad (2008, *Anthology*, pp. 181–186) and the subject of this essay.

I like to layer and texture my teaching, presenting a short literary piece followed by an original historical document and then a film clip, for example, or whatever makes sense in the lesson at hand. My history students do not expect a focus on literary aspects of writing about the experience of those in Europe during the time of the *Shoah*, nor do they, in their English classes, become familiar with the works of writers from Eastern Europe. Thus, I welcomed the chance to introduce them to Nalkowska's short piece as soon as I discovered it.

"By the Railway Track"—Literally!

By chance, my first reading of Nalkowska was on a train ride one weekend. It immediately engaged me, evoking for me vistas and landscapes. The images in my mind came from the way the author described the first dreadful, haunting scene next to the railroad tracks.

> At the break of day, the woman with the crippled knee sat on the moist grass, beside the railroad track. Someone nearby managed to escape; another lay motionless at some distance, beyond the forest. A few more got away; two were mowed down. Only she lingered on, neither dead nor alive. (Nalkowska, 1946, in Glatstein et al., 1973, p. 361)

This stark opening gripped me with its power and bleakness, as did the entire brief story, and I began to think of the pieces with which I would connect it, anticipating the response it would evoke from my students if I were to use it. My trip and my arrival at the station were uneventful, the experience worlds apart, of course, from that of the woman with the crippled knee. The train ride connected me, however, to the story. I stood and stared at the railroad tracks for a while, noting how they impose themselves in the world, very straight and hard, against the backdrop of the softer, more random patterns of nature. The railway cuts through the landscape forcefully; nature is discarded, pushed to the sides of the tracks. I tried to see the tracks from the viewpoint of the wounded woman, and then from that of the narrator, the person writing about her, but my goal was elusive; the suffering of the *Shoah* is far away from our experience, all the more reason to bring this vivid account to my class. It was the perfect time in the curriculum for this addition; we had begun to examine the phenomenon of the camps and were deep into discussions about rescuers and resisters.

As I prepared material for the lesson based on the story I had read in Glatstein (1973), which had been translated from Yiddish by Moshe Spiegel and entitled "At the Railroad Tracks," I discovered that this version was an excerpt from Nalkowska's original full text, a slightly longer work. Published in *Medallions* (2000), translated from Polish by Diana Kuprel, and appearing in this *Guide's* complementary *Anthology*, the complete story opens with the very page that was omitted from the edition I read. Unlike the passage I had read, the original first paragraphs, below, contextualize the scene, leaving my readers much less to figure out:

> Yet another person now belongs to the dead: the young woman by the railway track whose escape attempt failed.
> One can make her acquaintance only through the tale of a man who had witnessed the incident but is unable to understand it. She lives on only in his memory. (Shawn & Goldfrad, *Anthology*, p. 181)

The translation of the complete text is less evocative and nuanced, more straightforward and dispassionate; the additional introductory page adds background, allowing the reader to understand the scene from which the woman fled. Had I read this complete text first, I do not know the direction my thoughts would have taken; they might have led me, perhaps, to begin the class with a discussion of choiceless choices, since the nameless woman was risking death to escape death; to a study of the transports, since the description of the "lead-sealed boxcar" from which she jumped is so vivid; or to an exploration of the bystander/ witness, who doesn't understand, but remembers. I might, with both versions in hand, have spent time analyzing the differences throughout the two translations. All of these paths would bear fruit, and I might well follow each of them as I continue to teach this story.

I was initially captured, though, by what I had thought was the opening paragraph, and that was what I wanted to present first to my students. In the complete version, that passage falls on the second and third page, translated less emotionally, presented more like a report than a story, but powerful nevertheless:

> When the new day broke, the woman was sitting on the dew-soaked grass by the side of the track. She was wounded in the knee. Some had succeeded in escaping. Further from the track, another lay motionless in the forest. A few had escaped. Two had died. She was the only one left like this, neither alive nor dead. (pp. 182–183)

I was convinced that a discussion built around the theme of vistas and landscapes, my original connection; of what we see discarded during the events of the *Shoah;* and of how we envision and personalize the countless human tragedies of the Holocaust would provide an excellent structure for my students to articulate and respond to essential questions derived from the text. I would have them dive into the Nalkowska piece the way I did, by reading the above passage from the second page as their introduction to the story.

Introducing the Story

I began my lesson by reading it aloud and asking the students to jot down what they envisioned and what they imagined was the setting. We don't often read aloud at the high school level; to do so adds a sense of weightiness to the material. The students were silent, writing. I wondered if they, too, would see vistas and landscapes. I wondered as well where they would place this text in the larger context of the Holocaust. What guesses would they make about where and when this was happening? I was very curious about what they would construct in comparison to what I experienced during my first quick read, moving forward on a train.

I began our discussion with these questions:

1. Who is she?

2. Where is she?
3. When is this happening?
4. Why is she there?

Various students called out responses and I mapped their ideas on the board, beginning to draw the scene as it emerged from their comments. One student thought it was in Poland; another said Western Europe. All agreed that it was during the war and that she was Jewish, and that she had been deported. Many realized that she had tried to escape, injured herself in the attempt, and was now unable to flee.

I read aloud the next paragraph, in which other people appear and scan the bleak scene, and asked my listeners to jot down their ideas about the impact of this new paragraph on their original suppositions. Students shared their thoughts, and I extended the map of ideas, and the emerging scene drawn on the board grew and took shape. We exchanged impressions of how the people dot the landscape, about the deposits, the remnants, of war. The conversation moved to the more general concept of things discarded, things left over; I elicited crumpled lyric sheets on a field after a concert, empty soda cans and chicken bones on the beach after a picnic. We talked about discarded objects left, damaged and alone, as a metaphor for victims of the *Shoah*.

I shared with them an excerpt from "On Guilt," by survivor Bernard Gotfryd in the *Anthology* (p. 139–148) in which he describes the morning after a deportation in the Radom Ghetto: "Littered with torn books, abandoned knapsacks, shoes, and clothing, the square looked like a battlefield. Here and there loaves of bread or half-eaten sandwiches could be seen in the gutters. Dead bodies were scattered all over the place" (p. 141).

Before I could mention the scene in *The Pianist* (2002) I had recalled and had ready to show, a student shared the exact same idea. Drew, a senior, said, "This reminds me of the suitcases discarded after Jews of Warsaw were forced into the trains in *The Pianist*," so we watched that scene on the DVD to reinforce Drew's comment. Having prepared it beforehand, I also showed the scene in *Schindler's List* (1993) where the character named Pfefferberg starts collecting suitcases and clearing the road in a last-minute attempt to save his life as the camp commandant Goeth and his men are rounding the corner; it had popped into my head when I read Nalkowska the first time, and it evokes a similar feeling. I also thought of similar scenes in the films *The Island on Bird Street* (1996) and *The Time of the Wolf* (2003), but time was limited, so I made a note to myself to include them next semester as good extension activities.

I read aloud the next paragraph, which speaks of the unease of the onlookers, and elicited what students were feeling now. Brittany, 17, said, "I cannot say what will happen to her. Is her life over, or are we to think that she can make it to the woods?" Hands sailed into the air as many were now eager to share their opinions, building on what had been offered initially. Suddenly, too soon, time was up. I concluded by explaining that I had read aloud from the second page, and that, in fact, the story begins earlier. I distributed the text and asked students to read the full piece for homework.

Questions for Discussion

On the second day, we started with a quick review of what they had in their notes from yesterday (especially important for those who were absent) and then I asked them to consider four key questions:

- Were you surprised by the ending?
- Did the young man do the right thing?
- Humaneness, self-sacrifice, choosing not to see, terror, antisemitism: each might be a theme pertinent to the experience of non-Jewish bystanders during the National Socialist era. Which of these themes do you see at work in this story?
- Does the last line reflect your definition of compassion?

The story's power was still palpable: there were so many hands in the air! The discussion was more intense than yesterday because two distinct camps formed: one that espoused that the action of the young man was cold-blooded murder; the other, that he was gently ending her misery, because her agonizingly painful death was inevitable. Derek, a senior, maintained, "He did the right thing. She asked him, and he obliged. We should not judge him." Joey disagreed. "It was murder," he said tersely.

I sat back and listened, occasionally interjecting a question to elicit clarification or to move the conversation in a new direction. Chris, a junior, agreed that the young man had done the right thing, "because obviously she is going to die soon anyway." I asked him, "But isn't there a possibility of rescue? What if the Nazis were on their way out of town, the Russians arrived, and the war ended for those villagers?"

Chris chastised me a bit, knowing I had no textual support. "Now we are just speculating, Mr. Gwin; we cannot say for sure."

"Why," I asked him, "do you feel that the police officer did not fulfill her request?" He responded, "The police officer was scared. The young man knew suffering better."

As the "murder vs. euthanasia" conversation continued, Gabby, 17, called our attention to the text that stated, "She pleaded with them to kill her, but without any expectation that they would do so" (*Anthology*, p. 185). "She begged to die," she reiterated, "so how can it be murder when he does what she begs him to do?" The conversation darted back and forth across the room. It was, as often happens, electrifying for a teacher: a room full of ticking brains, engaged, listening, pondering. I interjected, "What if there had been no police officer and no gun?" Several students responded, shared new ideas, and then we explored what her role in the escape attempt might have been as they weighed risk and retribution.

The question about the last line was particularly complex because I shared both translations, which were notably different in tone. In the full Kuprel translation, the last paragraph reads, "'Why he shot her isn't clear,' the narrator said. 'I couldn't understand it. Maybe he felt sorry for her …'" (p. 186). However, the same conclusion in the Spiegel (1973) translation, which feels bitterly ironic, reads, "'But why did he shoot her?'… Then from someone came the answer, 'There is such a thing as compassion'" (p. 363).

Spiegel, much more poignantly than Kuprel, forces the reader to confront the idea of the upside-down universe of the Holocaust, in which "compassion" was the cold-blooded murder of a wounded Jewish woman. Both versions, though, elicited strong responses from my class; the heated conversation stopped only in response to my reminder of reality: the dreaded bell to end the class would shortly ring.

Looking back, I wish I had developed these ideas more. This is one of the tricky parts of open-ended teaching. Students create intense discussion forums that we, as teachers, wish could continue, but the time simply runs out. It is eternally challenging to decide which themes or questions should be the initial focus and which to let fall by the wayside, discarding them, if you will. Even if I had deliberately created an open space in which to let these ideas float and dialogue to bounce, as it will, there can be no infinite open space. The class has only 45 minutes. The bell halts us abruptly like an unanticipated train stop.

To conclude the lesson, I asked the students to consider their responses to the situation of the woman, her now-lifeless body lying by the railroad tracks. I asked them to focus on what it conjured for them in comparison to other bodies they have seen discarded, lying lifeless in other vistas of Holocaust settings. I wanted them to concentrate their thinking on the idea of what remains after war:

- physically
- emotionally
- spiritually
- figuratively
- in the memories of the witnesses.

I asked them to think about other literary images in the text:

- "When the new day broke" (*Anthology*, p. 182): Does this foreshadow the end of war, a particular day, or perhaps liberation?
- "She was the only one left like this, neither alive nor dead" (p. 183): When is life not any longer life? Can we understand this state, this lack of an absolute?
- Clues to identity: How do we know who she is? Her eyes are described as "too-dark" (p. 183). What does this description mean in this context?
- The anonymous crowd, with their fearful, nervous whisperings: How do we make sense of their actions? What do they represent? How do they help us to understand the bystander, the witness?
- Escape: What does this mean in the context of this story? In the larger context of the Holocaust? Can we now escape, and do we want to escape, from the

images we've embedded in our brains, the indelible pieces of the *Shoah* our memories have captured?

Students' initial responses to the bulleted points led to a deeper examination of the idea of discarding and relinquishing. We discussed the idea of dehumanization, realizing that the use of the term "discarded" was evoked precisely because it reflected that process. We offered ideas as to where, when, and if she became a "discarded object," first to the Nazis, then to the townspeople, and finally to us. We spoke of what and how she herself chose to relinquish, and of what this means in the broader context of war; we looked at the concept of "choice" in her situation, understanding that what we really meant was a "choiceless choice." We looked at what we relinquish and when, how we discard parts of ourselves at various junctures in life and in certain situations.

Several students shared their realization that this story and its evocative and disturbing questions strengthened their understanding of what is precious in life. Even though they will never be able to understand the actions of the perpetrators and the bystanders in the Holocaust, they realized they can approach the particular actions they encounter on a personal level and make them make sense through these kinds of conversations. Nalkowska's imagery did that for this class.

As the discussion spiraled from the initial responses, I tried to facilitate a closer look at the blurred line between murder and euthanasia. I encouraged a more focused analysis of how this situation at the railroad track and the choice the young man made are linked to our understanding of the meaning and value of human life and choices we make. We examined as well the idea of the struggle of humanity in the context of the Holocaust, and the choices, perceived and real, that were available to people who had power. This drew the students back to their earlier framework about who in the Nazi Party had power and how they had achieved it.

Looking back, I think that framing the discussion around these key themes was a great way to allow students to peel away surface layers of the text to see what lay beneath. This particular class, representing a wide spectrum of student life at our school, including the top honors senior and a special needs junior who struggles to write, was completely captured by the images in the Nalkowska text in part because the diversity of thought and experience in the room enriched our interactions. Students heard ideas they had never considered in their isolated reading.

I asked them to consider these points for homework, and I assigned a close reading of the Bertolt Brecht (1995) poem "I, The Survivor" (p. 336) and Elie Wiesel's (1973) *Death Against Life* (p. 337); I wanted them to widen their focus on the issues by reading other related literary pieces to compare to their initial ideas.

Using Student-Created Art

In the next class, after discussing their notes on the prompts and responses to their assignment, we explored the idea of memory in response to the line, "She lives on only in his memory" (*Anthology*, p. 181). Over the years, my students have done visual arts projects for this course, and I have collected them all to have as a student-centered resource for teaching. I have found that using student-created work to teach connects to all students and yields profound results; accompanying the power of the essential-question framework, it motivates and provokes response. For this session, then, I had filled the classroom with student-created art about the Holocaust: pastels, drawings, sculptures, poems, and pieces of music; the classroom was transformed into an arts space, and we honored memory by examining each piece. We began with interpretation:

- Who created it and for whom?
- When you look at it, what do you think, feel, and know?
- What is the intended effect? The actual effect?

To deepen the discussion, we debated:

1. Can art teach?
2. What has been more powerfully lasting for you: the story, the excerpts and other assigned literature related to the story, the scenes in *The Pianist* and *Schindler's List*, or one of the pieces of art?
3. If you were to create a memorial for the dead woman in the Nalkowska piece, what would you create? Is this memorial a way to remember this one victim, a way to create a legacy for her life and suffering? Is a memorial for one specific victim appropriate for all those murdered in the Holocaust? Are there memorials that transcend art?

We spent more than a week talking about art as memory and examining art created by victims during the terror of war, including children's drawings from Terezin and 29 of survivor Nelly S. Toll's (1993) drawings from her book *Behind the Secret Window: A Memoir of a Hidden Childhood During World War Two*, and we compared these to mimetic approximation. Even though we really did not "have the time," this unit went on so long because students continued to wrestle with the issue of the possibility of creating memory by creating memorials.

This final week was richly engaging for me because the students wove the themes of Nalkowska's piece into those of the classroom art and the idea of memorials. This simple short story proved to be a vibrant catalyst for thinking, and I witnessed students' overall understanding expand as they compared each curriculum component to the other. I read other poems and short pieces with them throughout the semester, but this one had a particularly strong resonance for these young people at this time. I think it can be of great value in a class where the teacher has only a class or two to devote to it, and yet, as with my experience, it can extend and spiral to other curricular pieces over longer periods.

"Where's the Rigor?"

All of this good learning is challenged by the standardization of education. "Where's the rigor?" my old-school colleagues will trumpet. "Where are the standardized assessment outcomes? How do I know that they know?" These questions ring in my head. It is tough to measure student growth in quantitative terms, but anecdotal evidence written and gathered during and after the course proves its worth. I have 14 years of student journal samples, numerous visual arts projects, records of daily on-time attendance, titles of unassigned related books borrowed from our library, and many e-mails from appreciative students who stay in touch from college. They share what they learn about the Holocaust in college courses and explain what the foundations they laid in my course mean to them now. These notes, in particular, offer rewarding evidence that the deep understandings I believe my students develop in my classes remain as they seek to understand the world and their place in it.

Conclusion

I value my scribbly notes on what students shared; they push me harder to do what I have long considered doing: working with students to create a memorial to the Holocaust at our school. The discussion on what we discard and what remains applies to memory as well; the verve of student responses to the art and the energy of the conversations on the Nalkowska piece inspire me to use this concept as a framework to talk with a variety of community members about what the community discards from its collective memory and what is allowed to remain. This will help us, I believe, begin to consider a memorial site and its purpose.

The Nalkowska narrative also created tracks for me, carrying me in several new directions in thinking about teaching the Holocaust. It affirmed the idea that literature is key to building enduring understandings, and it substantiated the capacity of the short story to provoke meaningful discussion. I think that this is the power of "By the Railway Track": its spare, simple, straightforward language and moral ambiguity call students to search and discover, rethink and reevaluate the meanings they have made so far of the complex and distant universe of the Holocaust.

REFERENCES

Adelson, A. (Ed.). (1996). *The diary of Dawid Sierakowiak: Five notebooks from the Lodz Ghetto.* (K. Turowski, Trans.). London: Bloomsbury Publishing.

Brecht, B. (1995). I, the survivor. In *Holocaust poetry.* New York: St. Martins Press.

Gotfryd, B. (2000). On guilt. In K. Shawn & K. Goldfrad (Eds.), (2008). *The call of memory: Learning about the Holocaust through narrative: An anthology*, pp. 139–148. Teaneck, NJ: Ben Yehuda Press.

Haneke, M. (2003). Director, screenplay: *The time of the wolf.*

Kragh-Jacobsen, S. (1997). *Island on Bird Street.* Writers: Goldsmith, J., & Grisoni, T. (Screenplay).

Nalkowska, S. (1946). At the railroad tracks. (M. Spiegel, Trans. from Yiddish). In J. Glatstein, I. Knox, & S. Margoshes, (Eds.), (1973). *Anthology of Holocaust literature*, pp. 361–363. New York: Atheneum.

Nalkowska, Z. (1946). By the railway track. (D. Kuprel, Trans. from Polish). (2000). In K. Shawn & K. Goldfrad (Eds.), (2008). *The call of memory: Learning about the Holocaust through narrative: An anthology*, pp. 181–186. Teaneck, NJ: Ben Yehuda Press.

Polanski, R. (2002). Director & Producer *The pianist.* Focus Features (Distributors).

Spielberg, S. (1993). Director: *Schindler's list.* Universal Studios.

Toll, N. S. (1993). *Behind the secret window: A memoir of a hidden childhood during World War Two.* New York: Dial Books.

Wiesel, E. (1973). Death against life. In *Hunter and hunted.* New York: B'nai B'rith Commission on Adult Education.

Wiesel, E. (1987). *Night.* New York: Bantam Books.

Zapruder, A. (2002). *Salvaged pages, young writers' diaries of the Holocaust.* New Haven, CT: Yale University Press.

The Abyss

Elie Wiesel's "Yom Kippur: The Day Without Forgiveness": Manifestation of the Transcendental Paradox After the Holocaust

Sarah Fraiman-Morris

In one way or another, most of Elie Wiesel's novels and stories deal with his experiences during the Holocaust. Eliezer Wiesel was born on September 30, 1928, in Sighet (Romania). His memoir *Night* (1958) describes in detail how he survived the concentration camps of Birkenau, Auschwitz, and Buchenwald. His story "Yom Kippur: The Day Without Forgiveness" (Shawn & Goldfrad, *Anthology*, 2008, pp. 189–195), an additional testimony of his own concentration camp hardships, expresses a crisis of faith as a consequence of the Holocaust. Like so many Eastern European Jews, Wiesel grew up in an observant Jewish home. As Wiesel recollects in the story, he had learned in depth the classical Jewish sources: "Often, to outwit our hunger or to forget our reasons for despair, we would study a page of the Talmud from memory" (p. 190). Therefore, one might say that Wiesel represents all those who found their faith tested by the Nazi atrocities that brought immensurable suffering to the Jewish people. If God were just and good, how could He allow such horrible things to happen; how could He tolerate the torturing and murdering of millions of innocent people? Wasn't His letting such atrocities happen a proof that He did not exist? Many lost faith in God, as the narrator describes in *Night:*

> Never shall I forget that night, the first night in camp, which has turned my life into one long night, seven times cursed and seven times sealed. … Never shall I forget those flames which consumed my faith forever. … Never shall I forget those moments which murdered my God and my soul and turned my dreams to dust. Never shall I forget these things, even if I am condemned to live as long as God Himself. Never. (p. 32)

The decline of religious belief began more than a century before the Holocaust, "with the German 'poets and thinkers' who replaced Jewish-Christian monotheism with an aesthetic philosophy" (Maybaum, 1965, p. 13). The horrors of the Holocaust furthered agnostic thinking, and the questioning of God became a standard element in Holocaust literature. In Rolf Hochhuth's play *The Deputy*

(1963), for example, the entire last act deals with this question and is therefore entitled: "Auschwitz or Where Are You, God?" (*"Auschwitz oder die Frage nach Gott?"*) There, the satanic doctor (modeled after Mengele) claims that the creation *and* the creator are refuted through Auschwitz (p. 248), and that the only thing that can excuse God is that He does not exist (p. 247). In the same vein, Itzchak Katzenelson, who perished in Auschwitz in 1944, wrote in the ninth song of *The Song of the Murdered Jewish People* (*Dos lied vunem ojsgehargeten iidischen volk*, 1943) that, unlike what he used to believe, the skies do not contain God.

Yet, man's rebellion against God remains ambivalent. Wiesel's claim in *Night* that his faith is consumed forever and his God is murdered is followed by a statement affirming the eternal existence of God ("even if I am condemned to live as long as God Himself"). This religious paradox of belief *and* disbelief appears in many Holocaust texts, such as in Paul Celan's (1988) *Psalm*:

> *Niemand knetet uns wieder aus Erde und Lehm,*
> *Niemand bespricht unsern Staub.*
> *Niemand.*
> *Gelobt seist du, Niemand.*

> No-one kneads us again out of earth and loam,
> No-one bespeaks our dust.
> No-one.
> Praise onto Thee, No-one. (Steiner, pp. 166–169)

André Schwarz-Barth in his novel *Le Dernier des Justes* (1959) illustrates this paradox in chapter 8 with the known question whether God is so all-powerful that He could create a rock so heavy that He would not be able to lift it Himself. Schwarz-Barth's character, a Jew in a French concentration camp, admits to believe in both God *and* the rock.

The same kind of ambivalence permeates Wiesel's story "Yom Kippur: The Day Without Forgiveness" and manifests itself already in the very first paragraph, where Pinhas, the concentration camp inmate and former *rosh yeshiva*, "appeared to be arguing with someone within himself." As it turns out, he was debating whether to fast on *Yom Kippur* or not, and he "seemed close to admitting defeat" (*Anthology*, p. 189). As later he proclaims his intention not to fast, it appears that his defeat was in the domain of his adherence to the religious laws, meaning, in terms of his loyalty to God. This is how his friend, the narrator, interprets Pinhas's decision. The narrator immediately rationalizes it, saying to himself: "[T]he book of life and death was no longer in God's hands, but in the hands of the executioner" (p. 191). In other words, because God is not what He is supposed to be or what we thought He was, that is, all powerful, man is not obliged to keep his end of the deal, namely, to observe His commandments.

Pinhas seems to have come to the same conclusion:

Until now … I have told myself: "God knows what he is doing." I
have submitted to his will. Now I have had enough. I have reached
my limit. If he knows what he is doing, then it is serious; and it is
not any less serious if he does not. Therefore, I have decided to tell
him: "It is enough." (p. 191)

In Pinhas's mind, and, for that matter, for most people facing the conundrum
of the Holocaust, either God is unethical or powerless. The narrator admits that
he "was going through the same crisis," that every day he is "moving a little further away from the God of my childhood" (p. 191) who sometimes even seemed
to him to be his enemy. For Pinhas, "the break with God appeared complete" (p.
192), and also for the narrator.

Although the narrator participates in the prayers of the *Yom Kippur* service,
they ring false to him, and in his mind, he turns everything he utters into a farce.
Yet, his break with God is not complete, because at any moment he expects "the
Master of the universe to strike me dumb and to say: 'That is enough—you have
gone too far'" (p. 194). The narrator only rebels against the present manifestation
of God, and he hopes that if he were challenged, he would answer: "You also,
blessed be your name, you also [have gone too far]." The narrator has moved away
from the God of his childhood, from the naïve belief in a nurturing God who
takes care of the ones who believe in Him and punishes the ones who break His
commandments. His belief has adjusted to the new reality, but it has not yet been
lost. A sign of the narrator's deeply rooted faith is his belief that Pinhas will die
because he did not observe *Yom Kippur*, as is explicitly written in Leviticus 23:29
that anyone who does not observe this day shall be blotted out of His people.

In the end, Pinhas does fast, but, as he claims, "not out of obedience, but out
of defiance," "not for love of God, but against God" (p. 194). Pinhas did not break
with God, most likely because his faith, his relationship with God is so strong
(maybe out of habit) that it is inconceivable to him to terminate it. Therefore,
Pinhas keeps the relationship with God going, but in a paradoxical way: "Here
and now, the only way to accuse him is by praising him" (p. 195). By praising a
seemingly unjust God, man hopes to make God feel guilty.

Yet, such anthropomorphic thinking is quite inadequate when relating to a
transcendent force. In the biblical Book of Job, friends who come to visit Job
connect sin and punishment and therefore see Job's predicament as deserved.
Job opposes this simplistic view, but he does not have any explanation for what
is happening to him. Job, who became a symbol for Jewish suffering during the
Holocaust, finally realizes that he cannot measure God by human standards.

Anyone who has not gone through the horrendous experiences of the Holocaust cannot understand nor judge people who have. Therefore, I am hesitant to
continue a line of thought that is purely theoretical and based on the theoretical
analysis of others. Yet, many people who died in the death camps and many others who survived kept their faith. Thus, the narrator in Eli Wiesel's story, regarding the other Jews in the camp who were praying during the *Yom Kippur* service,
explains: "It was better to believe that our punishments had meaning, that we had

deserved them; to believe in a cruel but just God was better than not to believe at all" (p. 193). Yet, is this kind of belief—in a cruel God—real faith and not just a crutch?

Just like Job, who ultimately discerned that God's justice is not man's justice because God is beyond any human understanding, people with true faith submit to God. Realizing that human understanding is extremely limited, they do not attempt to grasp what is beyond their horizon. The religious philosopher Abraham Joshua Heschel developed this opinion in his book *Man is Not Alone* (Kaplan, 1996, pp.123–126). Kierkegaard already posited "the God of faith, who speaks to individual man and who imposes upon him a particular, at times even paradoxical, duty" (Glatzer, 1969, p. 253). The archetype of such faith is Abraham, ready to sacrifice his son Isaac. According to Kierkegaard,

> The man of faith ... "knows" nothing. Or rather, with Socrates, he knows only that there is "truth" as "the ultimate ground of all things," but he has no knowledge of what that truth is. ... This not knowing is the root of faith. (Glatzer, p. 253)

Wiesel, who deals with man's crisis of faith in most of his works, reveals man's lack of understanding due to his limitations in his novel *The Gates of the Forest* (1964). There, he has the prophet Elijah tell one of the characters, Gabriel:

> God's final victory, my son, lies in man's inability to reject Him. You think you're cursing Him, but your curse is praise; you think you are fighting Him, but all you do is open yourself up to Him; you think you are crying out all your hatred and rebellion, but all you are doing is telling Him how much you need His support and forgiveness. ... Later, you'll understand the importance of the mystery; you'll see the light and perhaps it will pervade you. (p. 33)

Although this is exactly the opposite phenomenon of the one in the "Yom Kippur" story, where Pinhas praises in order to accuse, in both cases man relates to God in a paradoxical way. As long as man does that, faith is still there, no matter how difficult it is to understand or explain the complexity of God's presence or absence.

In Jewish tradition, there is a concept that attempts to explain why God lets seemingly unjust human suffering happen. Based on Deuteronomy 31:17–18, and Isaiah 54:7–8:

> For but a brief moment have I forsaken you, and with abundant mercy will I gather you in. With a slight wrath have I concealed my countenance for a moment, but with eternal kindness shall I show you mercy, says your Redeemer, the Lord.

It is believed that at certain points in history, God hides His face, that He turns away temporarily. Martin Buber (in Glatzer, 1969) referred to it in his essay "A God Who Hides His Face." Maybe it just seems to us that God is absent, but in reality He has only turned away for a moment, for whatever reason, which we as humans cannot understand (p. 62).

It appears that Wiesel's faith is in tune with this attitude. In *The Gates of the Forest*, Gabriel declares: "It is in the silence after the storm that God reveals himself to man. God is silence" (p. 63). This could be understood as another paradoxical statement. Yet, it blends in with two Jewish concepts: for one, in the Book of Job, God reveals Himself to Job out of the whirlwind, the storm. After this revelation, in the silence that follows the storm, Job's faith has solidified. In addition, God's silence could in fact be understood as God hiding His face. Through this concealment, though, God reveals Himself, as the *Kabbalah* teaches. In fact, Wiesel was familiar with the concept of God concealing Himself (he refers to it in *The Gates of the Forest*, p. 154). He grew up with the traditions of Jewish Mysticism, as the fourth chapter ("Winter") in *The Gates of the Forest* indicates. In addition, *Kabbalah* sets forth the concept of the transmigration of souls, which might help explain what sometimes seems to be God's injustice: If people go through terrible experiences, it is possible that they atone for sins in a past life. Thus, man with his limited knowledge of only this life cannot judge God.

Wiesel's faith, and for that matter, the faith of his characters, might be more deeply rooted than one would expect at first sight. The prospect of breaking with God is too painful and even considered a defeat, as the first lines of the story indicate: "With a lifeless look, a painful smile on his face … Pinhas moved his lips in silence. He appeared to be arguing with someone within himself and, judging from his expression, seemed close to admitting defeat" (*Anthology*, p. 189).

In *The Gates of the Forest*, because of Auschwitz, the protagonist challenges the rabbi: "After what happened to us, how can you believe in God?"(p. 194) Although the rabbi's answers reflect Wiesel's own inner conflict (they are not representative of a truly religious person, even less of a *tzaddik*), Wiesel ends this book, which is an expression of his own struggle with God, by having his main character return to religion and submit to God. He embraces his Jewish name, Gabriel, and he says *Kaddish* (the prayer for the dead), "that solemn affirmation, filled with grandeur and serenity, by which man returns God his crown and his scepter" (p. 225). The *Kaddish* proclaims that God's ways "are righteous and impenetrable," and "that He has the right to hide himself, to change faces and sides, that He who gives life and light may also take them away" (p. 224). Very much like the biblical Job, Gabriel submits to God because man needs God.

The attitude reflected in "Yom Kippur: A Day Without Forgiveness" is less conciliatory in that the main characters do not submit to God. Yet, the only way Pinhas is able to rebel against God is within His law: Pinhas keeps the law by fasting on Yom Kippur, but he declares it as the expression of his rebellion. He also asks the narrator to say *Kaddish* for him after his death. Despite the facts of Auschwitz, Pinhas continues to believe in God, no matter whether He is just or unjust. Thus, he turns his death into an act of faith, as he had always hoped, although different from what he had envisioned, for it becomes, paradoxically, an act of faith.

REFERENCES

Glatzer, N. (1969). *The dimensions of Job. A study and selective readings*. New York: Schocken.

Hochhuth, R. (1964). *The deputy*. (Richard and Clara Winston, Trans.). New York: Grove.

Kaplan, E. (1996). *Holiness in words. Abraham Joshua Heschel's poetics of piety*. New York: State University of New York Press.

Katzenelson, I. (1943). *The song of the murdered Jewish people*. (N. Rosenbloom, Trans.). (1980) Israel: Hakibbutz Hameuchad Publishing House

Maybaum, I. (1965). *The face of God after Auschwitz*. Amsterdam: Polak and Van Gennep.

Schwarz-Bart, A. (1959). *Le Dernier des Justes. The Last of the Just* (S. Becker, Trans.) (2000) reissued) Woodstock, N.Y.: The Overlook Press

Steiner, G. (1988). The long life of metaphor. An approach to the *Shoah*. In B. Lang (Ed.). *Writing and the Holocaust*. New York, London: Holmes and Meier.

Wiesel, E. (1968). Yom Kippur: The day without forgiveness. In K. Shawn & K. Goldfrad (Eds.). (2008). *The call of memory: Learning about the Holocaust through narrative: An anthology*, pp. 189–195. Teaneck, NJ: Ben Yehuda Press.

Wiesel, E. (1966). *The gates of the forest*. (F. Frenaye, Trans. from French). New York: Holt, Rinehart and Winston.

Wiesel, E. (1960). *Night*. (S. Rodway, Trans. from French). Toronto: Bantam.

Crisis of Faith:
Elie Wiesel's "Day Without Forgiveness"

Lauren Kempton

> *Let us tell tales so as to remember how vulnerable man is*
> *when faced with overwhelming evil.*
> *Let us tell tales so as not to allow the executioner to have the last word.*
> *The last word belongs to the victim.*
> *It is up to the witness to capture it, shape it, transmit it.*
> —Elie Wiesel

Elie Wiesel's "Yom Kippur: The Day Without Forgiveness" (Shawn & Gold-frad, *Anthology*, 2008, pp. 189–195), a story about a crisis of faith, is difficult to comprehend and to teach. It is most appropriate for college students and high school seniors in literature or humanities classes. In schools where students have strong backgrounds in Jewish tradition, the story may be successful with sophomores and juniors as well. I teach it to sophomores for four sessions out of a 20-hour Holocaust literature and history course at MAKOM, a supplementary Hebrew high school in Woodbridge, Connecticut.

Just as in "An Evening Guest," another story in the Shawn & Goldfrad *Anthology* (pp. 67–73), here Wiesel is both author and narrator. Set in Auschwitz, the story introduces us, as Fraiman-Morris (2008) notes in this *Guide*,

> to a narrator who has moved away from the God of his childhood, from the naïve belief in a nurturing God who takes care of the ones who believe in Him and punishes the ones who break His commandments. His belief has transformed, it has adjusted to the new reality, but it has not been lost yet. (p. 337)

Wiesel's faith and religious adherence are integral to this story, so in teaching it, we must be comfortable speaking of the Jewish holiday of Yom Kippur and its traditions, faith and its questions, and, particularly, God, for in essence, He is the main character.

My students have been immersed in Holocaust history and literature, so I begin with a glossary of terms specific to this story:

1. **Yom Kippur:** Jewish Day of Atonement
2. **Days of Awe**: 10-day period between Rosh Hashana (Jewish New Year) and Yom Kippur, a time of introspection and repentance
3. **Talmud:** the Oral Law, which complements the Written Law or Torah; comprised of divinely revealed principles and rabbinically ordained legislation; includes the Hebrew Mishnah and the Aramaic Gemara
4. **Book of Life:** symbolic book in which God annually inscribes and seals the names of those who have been granted another year of life
5. *Kapo:* concentration camp inmate appointed by the SS to be in charge of a work detail
6. **Roll call:** the line-ups and prisoner checks at the camps
7. *Kol Nidre:* Aramaic opening prayer that is recited on the eve of Yom Kippur
8. *Kaddish:* more specifically, the Mourner's *Kaddish,* an Aramaic prayer that stresses the importance of sanctifying God's Name; recited for 11 months following the death of a close relative, and at other specified times
9. *Tisha b'Av:* Jewish fast day observed on the ninth day of the Hebrew month of *Av* to commemorate the destruction of the First and Second Temples in Jerusalem
10. *Vidui:* confessional prayer that is recited on Yom Kippur, in which all Jews atone collectively for the sins of the Jewish people
11. **Selection:** concentration camp practice of choosing some inmates for temporary work and others for immediate death

I give these words in a hand-out but ask students to reinforce the definitions by finding and highlighting, in their copy of the story, the line of text in which each word appears to appreciate it in context.

Because the setting is Auschwitz, the lesson must contain a brief description of the camp itself. An elaboration will be a group assignment. The date of this story is also crucial contextually. The eradication of European Jewry was a sophisticated and effective killing operation, and the Hungarian Jews were among the last Jews to be taken; Wiesel was deported in May 1944. Hitler was losing on all fronts, yet the deportations and extermination of the Jews were accelerating. My students have learned this and will design a contextual timeline as another group assignment.

Spiritual and Religious Resistance

The complex concepts of spiritual and religious resistance may be reviewed here: praying when prayer was forbidden; clandestinely retaining rituals and practices of faith when such activities were punishable by death. My students understood and took pride in the physical resistance young Jewish fighters exhibited when we discussed, earlier in the semester, the uprisings in Lachva, in the Warsaw Ghetto, and in various camps across Poland, but spiritual and religious resistance is less tangible, more nuanced. Until now, we have understood resistance to be anything one could do to stay alive another day. Understanding Pinhas' decision to fast, at least in the beginning of the story, rests upon understanding the concept of resistance as observing a sacred holiday under the most heinous conditions. However, fasting might hasten one's death; hence, we conclude that spiritual resistance is also remaining human in the face of the Nazis' wish to make us less than human, to destroy in us any spark of spirit or holiness.

Scaffolding the Learning

To connect the painful and difficult concepts explored in this story with the solemn holiday of Yom Kippur, the one part of the story familiar to them, we spend a few minutes discussing our experiences of Yom Kippur, the holiest day of the year for Jews, the day when we try to atone for our sins by fasting, praying, and eschewing all ordinary pleasures of life. I stress the difference between the hunger that we feel when we fast and the hunger that the camp inmates experienced; they are altogether incomparable. We begin the story and read together until the class ends; I clarify and respond to questions as necessary. I ask them to complete the story for homework and come prepared to discuss the theme and the characters. I'm saving discussion of plot and setting for group work. I offer journal prompts to help them continue to search for personal meaning in the story:

1. How does this story affirm the mandate to keep your religious traditions from generation to generation?
2. As grandchildren of survivors and/or refugees, do you have family stories of observance under persecution?

Harry begins the second class: "The theme of this short story is that the Book of Life is no longer in the hands of God, but in the hands of the executioners, the Nazis. For Elie and Pinhas, each day was Yom Kippur. Each day was a fast day because of the extremely meager rations doled out by the Nazis."

Anna jumps in: "It seems to me the theme is 'By any means necessary to keep their religion.' I mean, a service on toilet paper?"

"Yom Kippur must have had such a deeper meaning in the camps," Ian muses.

Alex concurs. "It shows us what believing in God meant to a 15-year-old Jew in late 1944."

I ask them to consider two aspects of conflict within the plot: man vs. man, that is, the Jews vs. the Nazis; and man vs. himself, that is, Pinhas struggling with the idea of fasting and struggling with his faith.

Matt's comment, "I am so surprised the guards let them have services," opens a discussion of the sentence "Officers and soldiers, machine guns in hand, had stood by, amused spectators, on the other side of the barbed wire" (*Anthology*, p. 192) as the Jews in the camp prayed. Heddy points out that the guards *played* with the Jews, motivated by what amused them: today, prayers did; tomorrow, perhaps, a beating or hanging would.

Harry offers, "Fasting at Auschwitz was the ultimate sacrifice. It is so noble! It was a sacrifice to defend his sense of truth."

"I agree," says Aubrey. "I think that fasting is praising God."

"In general, yes," I interrupt, "but here Pinhas says he fasted not to praise God but to defy Him, 'not for love of God, but against God (p. 194).' How do you understand that?"

"I'm not sure I do," she answers. "If I were to act against God, I just wouldn't fast. But Pinhas says that in the camps you have to make your indignation heard in a different way. I need to think about that."

"If you make yourself feel uncomfortable, you feel the power of what you've done," Ariella points out. "If you don't fast, you're not uncomfortable, you don't feel anything. But in the camps, of course, they were always starving, so I wonder how much more they felt their hunger on this day."

"I think we feel hungry and that is unusual for us, so we put the focus on ourselves, not on God," David adds. "But it seems that they really prayed and focused on God in spite of their hunger."

Rebecca responds to the personal connection their homework asked them to discover: "My grandfather always says he will fast on Yom Kippur, but his children say, 'You fasted enough in the camps.'"

We examine the characters through the lenses of physical characteristics, speech and actions, thoughts and feelings, and relations to other characters. I call on students to summarize in a way that allows them some activity and offers me the chance to check for understanding and assess responses. I ask students to volunteer to come to the board and write one sentence at a time when they know they can add to the sequence correctly and move the plot along.

They summarize:

> Elie, a Jewish boy of fifteen, is from an observant family from Sighet, Romania. He is very studious and well versed in Talmudic studies. Now he is in a work detail digging ditches at Auschwitz. He still believes in God and tries to follow Jewish law. Pinhas has become his close friend because they work together at Auschwitz. Prior to the war, Pinhas was the head of a rabbinical school. Pinhas is close to starving. He struggles, however, with a profound spiritual conflict: Should he fast on Yom Kippur although he is angry at God? He ultimately fasts, not "out of obedience" to God but "out of defiance." Pinhas know he will die soon, and he asks Elie to say *Kaddish* (the prayer for the dead) for him. Pinhas dies, a victim of the first selection.

However, the ending is not so simple. Matt points out that Pinhas' request that *Kaddish* be said does not mean he has forgiven God; instead, Pinhas explains to Elie, "The only way to accuse him is by praising him" (p. 195).

The class decides that God was a character, too. "I wonder if God heard their prayers that Yom Kippur," Maya says.

Harry believes He did. "I believe in God," he says. "We have survived for almost 6000 years. Don't blame Him for not being there."

I share with them a comment from Fraiman-Morris (2008), who writes in this *Guide* that Wiesel "represents all those who found their faith tested by Nazi atrocities, resulting in immeasurable suffering to the Jewish people" (p. 335). Does Elie believe that God is hiding, that He has turned His face from him and from Pinhas, Elie's beloved teacher and friend? *Hester panim*, the concept that there are times throughout Jewish history when God has hidden Himself from His People, is a fascinating one for more sophisticated students to explore if time permits.

Cooperative Learning

My students want another "silent conversation" (*Guide*, p. 127) because they found the one we did with "An Evening Guest" so rewarding; but I introduce a modified "jigsaw," a cooperative learning method that shifts responsibility for teaching to the students while the teacher becomes a facilitator. (See also Darr & Figg in this *Guide*, pp. 271–284, on this method). I tell my class they are to think of themselves as a "family" of four groups, each working to become expert on one aspect of the story. One person from each group will share his/her expertise with the family. As they work, they will assume typical cooperative learning roles: Reporter, Recorder, Researcher, Timekeeper, and Materials Scout. The assignments are as follows:

Group One will provide the historical context by finding or constructing and presenting an appropriate time line, including events from May 1944 to April 1945, which will help clarify the last year of the war and its effect on the assault on Jews and life in Auschwitz. The story is set late in the war. I want students to understand that the Final Solution was carried out with industrial efficiency. German soldiers were dying on all fronts, cold and hungry, without proper equipment and supplies; the postal system and food distribution were collapsing; and yet the gas chambers and crematoria were running at full speed. I ask them: What do you need to present to the class to help them understand this situation? I point them towards the school library and the Web sites of the United States Holocaust Memorial Museum at *http://www.ushmm.org/education/ foreducators* and Yad Vashem at *http://www.yadvashem.org*.

Group Two will present a "storyboard" overview of the plot to enhance understanding. I give them different graphic organizers, including one with blank text-box outlines, a storyboard that writers use in visually sketching a plot line of a show; they can add sketches to words if they choose. I encourage them to download their choice of graphic organizers from *http://www.eduplace. com/graphicorganizer/*, *http://www.teachervision.fen.com/graphic-organizers/ printable/6293.html*, or the very sophisticated *http://www.writedesignonline.com/ organizers/*, three excellent sites for every imaginable organizer and explanation of uses.

Group Three will present aspects of the barbed-wire, dehumanizing setting that will explain the extraordinary difficulties faced by those who tried to maintain some semblance of religious observance. Their task, I tell them, is to make vivid the time, place, and environment of the story, the barracks and work yard in Auschwitz in the spring of 1944. I suggest the Web sites *www.ushmm.org/wlc/ article.php?lang= en&ModuleId=10005189* and *http://www.auschwitz-muzeum. oswiecim.pl/html/eng/ start/index.php*; there are hundreds of others.

Group Four will produce one or more original pieces of music, poetry, or art that represent the story's theme. They may research and share existing works that capture what they wish to say in addition, or as an alternative, to creating original works. These students have the least structured assignment but have abundant resources to explore from our library and the Internet. I offer *www.ushmm. org/museum/exhibit/online/music* and *http://holocaustmusic.ort.org*, along with *art. holocaust-education.net*. Thousands more sites are devoted to poetry; I offer *www. auschwitz.dk/id6.htm* and *www.ushmm.org/museum/publicprograms/programs/ poetry*, which allows students to listen to poetry.

As experts, students will teach the "family" in the final class of this unit. For homework, they should begin to collect thoughts and resources; they are free to collaborate at home as well.

Gardner's Multiple Intelligences

This assignment reflects in part the work of Totten (2001), who puts forth a novel way to analyze a short narrative though the use of Gardner's (1983, 1993) "multiple intelligences." Totten notes, "As a rule, when I have my students read short stories about the Holocaust, it is to help illuminate some aspect of the history I am teaching" (p. 125). In this interdisciplinary course, I do the same. He explains that an exercise that makes use of the theory of multiple intelligences, that is, "the broad range of abilities that humans possess" (p. 126), "is a strategy that allows for open and creative responses by students to a piece of literature and reveals insights that might not be gleaned via a more traditional pedagogical approach" (pp. 125–126). He suggests defining the range of intelligences and letting students choose one to use to interpret the assigned story. However, time constraints led me to design the activity based only in part on multiple intelligence theory; I let students choose their preferred group rather than their preferred mode of expression.

To illustrate, the first group, the structured and defined timeline, might appeal to the intelligence defined as "logical-mathematical" (the capacity to reason well) and as "spatial" (perceiving the visual-spatial world accurately); the second, the storyboard, might be attractive to the intelligences defined as "spatial" and perhaps "interpersonal" (perceiving and distinguishing among "moods, intentions, motivations, and feelings"). The third group, expressing the dehumanizing setting, might reflect the "linguistic" (using oral and written words effectively) or Gardner's (1999) newest "'existentialist intelligence' … one that is concerned with issues of human existence and meaning" (p. 127); while the fourth group of artists, musicians, and poets might be consonant with intelligences identified as "spatial," "musical," "interpersonal," and "linguistic" (p. 126). The groups overlapped, because this was not a strict interpretation of Gardner, but the assignment did go beyond the typical essay that meets most effectively only the needs of those who shine with "linguistic" intelligence.

In the third class, students are eager to share what they have gathered at home and to make a cohesive presentation from disparate materials. I walk among the groups, listening, advising, probing, and ensuring that they move towards understanding and make progress on their products.

Anna, in the timeline group, comments that the story is "historical and autobiographical. It shows that the *Shoah* is real." Members have each brought their own timelines from a variety of Internet-researched sources and in-class texts; they reach consensus on dates and events they consider most crucial to the story line. They have brought foam board, black markers, rulers, and cardboard punchout numbers, and choose to illustrate their numerical timeline with photos, exhibiting their spatial intelligence.

Danielle, in the storyboard group, wonders: "How would you teach this to non-Jews?" and the talk veers off the topic; I urge them to remain true to the text. (Perhaps I should let them talk; yes, they are my students but also my teachers, and they, with their existential and interpersonal intelligences, raise a question with which I struggle. I have never taught this story to non-Jews, and I feel insecure about my ability to do so. I do not know if I could convey to them the depth of tradition and the profound importance of the Days of Awe and of Yom Kippur itself or the struggle against God so painfully and ironically expressed by Pinhas' decision.) The group has decided to list the events of the plot in an enlarged graphic organizer, highlighting the inmates' conflicts with God by typing and pasting statements on different colored paper. They show me the first four; I approve:

1. Elie wonders if in Auschwitz he can pray with the fervor he had when he was free.
2. Pinhas announces he will not fast on Yom Kippur.
3. Elie wonders if Pinhas believes he is dead in the eyes of God and man and therefore free to disobey the laws of God.
4. Elie reverses roles with Pinhas and becomes his teacher, advising him that he must eat to save his strength.

Here, I think, they exhibit both their logical and existential intelligences.

The third group, charged with presenting the setting, draws back from a toographic description of the workings of Auschwitz. Harry explains their sensitivity, saying, "I think you feel this story on a deeper level if you are Jewish." Harry shows yet another intelligence, defined as "self-knowledge and the ability to act adaptively on the basis of that knowledge" (p. 126). They struggle to represent their understanding that everyone in the barracks prepared for Yom Kippur. They have researched the setting and produce a PowerPoint presentation that incorporates illustrative text passages to accompany photos they found on the Internet.

The arts group is free-associating: "This story makes me think of dreams and flashbacks," Ariella says. They have each brought in scraps of random collage material, oil crayons, scissors, paper, and glue sticks to see how they can create a symbolic representation of faith, even a conflicted faith, as resistance during the Holocaust. Alex has highlighted the sentence, "To believe in a cruel but just God was better than not to believe at all" (*Anthology*, p. 193). Their desks are covered with Holocaust poetry downloaded from the Internet and photography books borrowed from the library; they seem to be comfortable expressing their linguistic and visual intelligences even as they avoid any musical exploration.

Giving Voice to Memory

The assessment is the presentation in our fourth class. Through shared inquiry and ownership, each student has become a teacher, responsible to us all. The groups have offered "varied, imaginative, and powerful interpretations" (Totten, p. 139) of the story, and I can assess their offerings in part by the content of their presentation, in part by the process that led to it, and in part by others' responses to it.

As I've done with earlier stories, I consider additional assessments in my final evaluation. As Totten (2001) affirms, "For a reader to get the most out of a work of literature, he or she must bring his or her own insights, knowledge base, and past experiences to bear on his or her reading" (p. 131). If a student can define and give examples of spiritual resistance in related literature, or draw and discuss Elie and the rebbe at Auschwitz, or research a poet of the *Shoah* and share the poetry, the assessment would be complete. If the students, in their journals or in our wrap-up discussion, comment on faith, spirituality, belief in or doubts about God's presence during the *Shoah*, as Michelle did, concluding a passionate journal entry by writing, "Many people lost their belief in God during the Holocaust, but I do not think many understand that the Holocaust was not God's fault," that, too, would be part of my assessment.

Through sharing what they learned through their group activity about Elie Wiesel's experience and the context in which it occurred, my students will remember, as Wiesel's epigraph that begins this chapter implores us to do, "how vulnerable man is when faced with overwhelming evil." My students will tell his story "so as not to allow the executioner to have the last word." By reading, discussing, and finding personal meaning in survivor narratives, they have become witnesses to the witnesses. With surprising seriousness they acknowledge their responsibility to "capture and shape" that last word, saving it from oblivion by making it a part of their lives; and to "transmit it" by recognizing and accepting their obligation to tell the tale.

REFERENCES

Darr, L. & Figg, B. (2008). Compromising one's morality in times of crisis: Ida Fink's "A conversation" and "Aryan papers." In K. Shawn & K. Goldfrad (Eds.). *The call of memory: Teaching about the Holocaust through narrative: A teacher's guide*, pp. 271–284. Teaneck, NJ: Ben Yehuda Press.

Fraiman-Morris, S. (2008). Eli Wiesel's "Yom Kippur: The day without forgiveness": Manifestation of the transcendental paradox after the Holocaust. In K. Shawn & K. Goldfrad (Eds.). *The call of memory: Teaching about the Holocaust through narrative: A teacher's guide*, pp. 335–340. Teaneck, NJ: Ben Yehuda Press.

Totten, S. (2001). Analyzing short stories about the Holocaust via a multiple intelligences and reader-response approach. In S. Totten (Ed.). *Teaching Holocaust literature*, pp. 125–142. Boston: Allyn & Bacon.

Wiesel, E. (1968). An evening guest. In K. Shawn & K. Goldfrad (Eds.) (2008), *The call of memory: Learning about the Holocaust through narrative: An anthology*, pp. 67–73. Teaneck, NJ: Ben Yehuda Press.

Wiesel, E. (1968). Yom Kippur: The day without forgiveness. In K. Shawn & K. Goldfrad (Eds.) (2008), *The call of memory: Learning about the Holocaust through narrative: An anthology*, pp. 189–195. Teaneck, NJ: Ben Yehuda Press.

WEB SITES

Retrieved October 22, 2007, from *art.holocaust-education.net*.

Retrieved December 17, 2007, from *http://holocaustmusic.ort.org*.

Retrieved October 22, 2007, from *http://www.ushmm.org/education/foreducators*.

Retrieved October 22, 2007, from *http://www.yadvashem.org*.

Retrieved October 22, 2007, from *http://www.eduplace.com/graphicorganizer/*.

Retrieved October 22, 2007, from *http://www.teachervision.fen.com/graphic-organizers/printable/6293.html*.

Retrieved October 22, 2007, from *http://www.writedesignonline.com/organizers/*.

Retrieved October 22, 2007, from *http://www.auschwitz-muzeum.oswiecim.pl/html/eng/start/index.php*.

Retrieved October 7, 2007, from *www.auschwitz.dk/id6.htm*.

Retrieved October 7, 2007, from *www.ushmm.org/museum*.

Retrieved September 9, 2007, from *www.ushmm.org/wlc/articlephp?lang=en&ModuleId=10005 189*.

Retrieved September 9, 2007, from *www.ushmm.org/museum/exhibit/online/music*.

The Ethics of Aesthetics:
Cynthia Ozick's "The Shawl"

Keren Goldfrad

> *Because Holocaust facts often seem so unimaginable, they assume the features of fiction;*
> *on the other hand, wary of promoting disbelief,*
> *Holocaust fiction clings to its moorings in the grim truths of the event.*
> —Lawrence L. Langer

Writing fiction about events that have, in fact, taken place poses unending moral problems for author and reader alike as they are asked to discern the reliability or to locate the borders between levels of truth. Such problems are especially keenly felt if the events portrayed were so inhumane as to be virtually indescribable in coldly factual terms. First, the literary or fictionally shaped reportage may seem so colorful, even powerfully so, as to entice the reader into believing that the imagined plot in all its detail actually took place. The writer, in this sense, could be called into account for deceiving the reader, almost playing, in effect, with the reader's highly wrought emotions. Second, by trying to reproduce the effect of past circumstances in presently readable terms, the writer could, in an oddly contradictory way, serve to reduce the impact of the event as it was known and felt by those who knew its reality. By portraying the past through some expected literary forms and genres, or by evoking well-defined literary structures and conventions that have developed through a long course of cultural expectations or logic, the writer might in that process decrease the reader's sense of the immediacy in transmitting a sense of the victims' suffering, as they experienced unprecedented events. In this manner, the writer is somehow taming those horrors while bringing them within recognizable terms.

Irving Howe (1988) in his article "Writing and the Holocaust" explains this seemingly unavoidable process when speaking of how the "representation of a horrible event, especially if in drawing upon literary skill achieves a certain graphic power." He notes how skill itself "could serve to domesticate it, rendering it familiar and in some sense even tolerable, and thereby shearing away part of the horror" (p. 180). That is why, I would suggest, some answer must be formulated to those who would argue that the fiction writer may be viewed as suspect, as if somehow legitimizing future denials of history itself—in the name of fiction.

In the past, the realms of fiction and autobiography were thought to be strictly separated; their differences were carefully defined in order to try, perhaps, to prevent the need to face such moral problems. Consequently, autobiographies were considered a realm apart from such questions of immediacy or authenticity. Yet, we need to be aware that even autobiographies, told in whatever vein of veracity, must inevitably contain a fictional quality, because imagination and perspective are never fully detached from one's experience. In a correlative and even heightened way, as we must further acknowledge, fiction, while not—or not only—based on factuality, can be equally complex in the truth telling it conveys. It can, in the very process of narration itself, invoke the reader's response as an acknowledgement of each and every person's perspective in shaping past and present readers' reality. Fiction, then, can be seen most reliably as an essential but provocative and challenging means for understanding historic events.

"The Shawl" (Shawn & Goldfrad, *Anthology*, 2008, pp. 196–201), a lyrical, meditative work written by Cynthia Ozick, an American author who had no firsthand Holocaust experiences to record, pushes such possibilities to their moral and artistic limits. This short story focuses on the experiences of three main characters during the time of the Holocaust: Rosa, her baby, Magda; and her niece Stella. Ozick manages to evoke the horror of the Holocaust through her compact depictions of the thoughts, emotions, and feelings that these three characters experience in the long march and during their internment in a concentration camp. Some people would argue that only survivors of the Holocaust can write about these experiences because they are the only ones who really know—and thus can truly record—what it was like. Indeed, the heightened fictionality that is made evident by Ozick through numerous artistic devices such as metaphors, similes, juxtapositions, or symbolic images might serve only to foreground such a fiction's greatest inadequacy. Hannah Arendt (1988), for example, argues that all such imaginative constructs must fail, because "our imagination cannot grasp" the horrors of the *Shoah* "for the very reason that it stands outside of life and death" (Kremer, 1988, p. 13). Does Arendt's claim, simply put, mean that whoever was not in the hands of the Nazis can never write about these events? "That innocence," writes Kremer, should not deny all writers "the privilege of writing about the Holocaust. Authority is not limited to those with personal suffering." All Jews "share the historic burden of Jewish history" (p. 15).

Such a sense of burden or historic responsibility, as Kremer shows, is established in ancient Jewish tradition. Kremer, for example, cites the example of the scene of Sinai itself: "Tradition commands all Jews to consider themselves figuratively present at Sinai to receive the Torah," and she continues the analogy forward through the Holocaust to the reader of another time. "Contemporary Jews increasingly feel that, geography aside, they were present at Auschwitz. American Jews carry the psychological burden of ... all the ... Nazi death factories where their relatives died brutal deaths" (p. 15). If Jewish writers feel the necessity to commemorate the death of the 6 million Jews who were murdered by the Nazis, those writers must also feel an obligation upon themselves to write such fictions that invoke our own critical and responsive actions. Reading and writing become means of warning future generations against allowing such a horrendous act to take place again. To that end, each individual writer feels compelled to devise a method of conveying a particular message, even while intimating prior forms of literary convention, to preserve an awareness of threatened human values, even if that entails the very possibility of blurring the edges of authenticity.

One particular message that Ozick thus so painfully conveys is that many Jews maintained fiction making in some form or another both before and during the Holocaust. It may prove all too true that the shattering of fictions for Rosa, a most painful aspect of suffering for her, has been an authentic factor, in and of itself, for the Jews in Germany at that time and thereafter. The assimilated Jews felt very much a part of the German society, so much so that many of them felt a stronger affiliation to Germany than to their Jewish identity. These perceptions prior to the war were shattered and crushed during the Holocaust. In addition, the Germans manipulated and confused the Jews' perceptions of reality throughout the war in order to increase fear and uncertainty among their victims and thus gain more power and control while avoiding any possibility for conflict and uprising. Deception was such a significant strategy in the hands of the Nazis that many witnesses were unable to perceive their own realities. As Dori Laub (1992) has wisely shown, "not only in effect did the Nazis try to exterminate the physical witnesses of their crime, but the inherently incomprehensible and deceptive psychological structure of the event precluded its own witnessing even by its very victims" (p. 80). Logically or psychologically speaking, if their minds could not grasp what had happened in the Holocaust, the victims themselves had to use their imagination in order to understand what they actually went through. Such imagining—somehow akin to the work of fiction—is not a negative aspect. On the contrary, it is essential.

The implicit message of Ozick's "The Shawl" and of theorists such as Kremer and Laub is the undeniable value of some imaginative or subjective shaping of facts in weighing testimonies. A fictional account of the Holocaust, seen from this vantage, can convey deeply appropriate sentiments that biographic recitation may cover. As Ozick's art would seem to say, even factual records require some framework, in the shape of fictional constructs or dreams, within which to make sense of ultimate horrors that have been endured.

It is important to note that even in her fictionalizing contexts Ozick does not flinch from creating a sense of harshest realities. There are on the one hand, in her pages, repeated evocations of the starvation, the endless walking, the piercing cold, hard labor, and the dehumanization elements that seize her readers' hearts. She strives to give an actual depiction of the physical settings—the concentration camp barracks, the morning roll calls, the electric fences, even the smoke-filled air.

At the very heart of this story is a crying need felt for vivifying history and enacting personal testimonies, which the act of writing itself seeks to fulfill. Such details, shaped in the telling of Ozick's prose, are certainly not to be rendered in the mode of the dry "data" or the "survivor syndrome" of false and despised researchers such as Ozick's character James W. Tree, Ph.D., who is mentioned in her sequel novel *Rosa* (1990), and who "scratch" at Rosa's life, as she puts it, "with lying theories" (Ozick, pp. 39–43). These careful, even colorful depictions, do add, instead, material that augments the mystery that Rosa herself so longs "to retrieve, to reprieve" (p. 45). Rosa's tellings are used, then, to a similar effect by the theorist Kremer in commenting on the method that writers of fiction employ to write about the Holocaust. Kremer, like the fictional Rosa, speaks of "retrieving" facts for "creative" reportage:

> Creative writers immersed themselves in the voluminous testimonials and diaries that were retrieved from hiding places, ghettos, camps and those that were written after the war in the histories and documents published by Holocaust researchers. Survivors have provided materials novelists have diligently studied—eyewitness accounts of the genocidal capacity of humankind, as well as its capacity to endure. (p. 29)

This method of retrieving factual data from other people's writings has a double dynamic, for it both "vivifies" or gives life to what seems dry record, and at the same time, these facts are revived by the desire to keep those truths alive. Such layered or embedded dynamic, in a sense, recalls Jacques Derrida's famous concept when he describes how our language, and even our thoughts, can and do "live-on" what has gone before. Derrida uses the term *survivre* to describe a dynamic in which words and texts always breed one upon the other "to go write-on-living" (Baris, 1992, p. 46).[1]

Yet, on the other hand, Ozick does repeatedly emphasize the fictionality of her work by forcing the reader to use the powers of imagination, as she allows herself to blend some symbolic elements within the historical truths. Ozick, for one, does not mention any dates or names of places. Moreover, there is no utterance of the word Holocaust throughout her work. Woven into her sensitive combination of facts and symbols are images that stimulate the reader's imagination. Andrew Gordon (1994), in his article "Cynthia Ozick's 'The Shawl' and the Transitional Object," emphasizes the delicate interrelation of fact and fiction Ozick achieves: "Ozick manages to avoid the common pitfalls of Holocaust fiction: on the one hand, she does not sentimentalize, but on the other, she does not numb the reader with a succession of horrifying events" (p. 1).

Even if, as Gordon correctly points out, Ozick does not mention the words "Jew" or "Nazi," that is not, as he goes on to suggest, for the sake of allowing "the historical and political context [to] disappear" in favor of a more narrow focus upon "the feelings of three characters as they struggle to survive moment by moment in extreme circumstances" (p. 1). Such feelings are the very essence, in her fiction as a report of reality, of the historical and political moment. There are times when words can make an event larger than it really is, but on other occasions feelings are stronger than words could ever be. Horowitz (1984) quotes

---

1 Baris further develops this idea, demonstrating that Derrida's theoretics show how all narratives indeed will thrive when "words breed one upon another to *sur-vivre*" (Baris, p. 53).

Delbo when arguing that language can be scarcely adequate when it comes to conveying the atrocious experiences that were felt by the victims:

> In *Mesure de Nos Jours*, Delbo echoes this frustration: *"Les mots n'ont pas le meme sense"* [Words don't have the same meaning]. She despairs of importing any idea of her dismal experience to any reader who has not shared it, since the words she needs to use— —words such as *"faim"* [hunger], *"peur"* [fear], *"froid"* [cold], *"soif"* [thirst], *"sommeil"* [sleep], *"mal"* [pain], even *"amitié"* [friendship, affection, kindness], exist for the uninitiated *"comme si ces mots- la n'avaient pas le moindre poids"* [as if these words don't have the slightest weight]. For her purpose, to render adequately her ac- count, *"Tous leurs mots sont légers. Tous leurs mots sont faux"* [All their words are light, thoughtless. All their words are false]. (p. 25)

Ozick's objective in "The Shawl" is hardly to obliterate the historical and po- litical context. On the contrary, one could argue that through her metaphors Ozick is compelling the reader to imagine the Holocaust. Her fiction works, one could say, to place each of us in the troubled position of those who are compelled to imagine, create, hence recreate, the truth of the Holocaust in its historical, political, and personal contexts.

Ozick's name symbolism is one way in which the writer conveys some of the pressure points traditionally felt in Western narratives. Magda, for example, the name of Rosa's baby girl, carries a complex connotation. Ozick may have derived that name from the Christian tradition of Mary Magdalene, who was a follower of Jesus, identified from early times as the "'woman which was a sinner'; it was she who anointed Jesus' feet in Simon's house." Thus, in a sense, Magdalene has been associated with sin; yet, too, she has risen from it and has repented. The doubleness in Magda's name—both as a Christian reference for a Jewish child, and within its own troubling connotations—could play its disconcerting part in Ozick's fictional framework, for Magda, in "The Shawl," may be the result of another mixture of physical sin and spiritual innocence. When Rosa looks into her daughter's face, she describes the tormenting personal and cultural *con-fusions* that the child represents. Her face is

> very round, a pocket mirror of a face: but it was not Rosa's bleak complexion, dark like cholera, it was another kind of face alto- gether, eyes blue as air, smooth feathers of hair nearly as yellow as the Star sewn into Rosa's coat. You could think she was one of *their* babies. (Shawn & Goldfrad, *Anthology*, p. 196)

The inference is that Magda's father was probably an Aryan. According to Nazi rule, it was a sin for an Aryan to have sexual intercourse with a Jew, even as Jews would likewise have thought of a relationship with a *Goy* (a Gentile).

Magda, therefore, as a product of sin, must pay for her very existence, and readers may even suspect her electrocution when thrown onto an electric fence by a German officer to be a kind of "crucifixion."

If one continues this line of thought in all its levels of complex significance, it could be argued that Rosa might be related mentally to Mary, who was often called "Mary the Rose" or Rosary (Oxford Dictionary of the Christian Church). Rosa usually signifies beauty, growth, livelihood, and colorful potential; yet the inverse here emerges, for in Ozick's story, this name is associated, through Rosa's experiences, with the atrocities of the Holocaust; her story turns the blooming Rose of faith or beauty—even in Christian terms—into a decaying figure defused of any motivation for life.

Similarly, one could argue that *Stella*, the name given to Rosa's niece, has both deceptive as well as Christian connotations. Stella can signify a *star*, a shining object. Rosa constantly stresses how Stella looks in terms of outer, distinctive, and lovely appearance, but inside, Rosa claims, she is "the angel of Death" (Ozick, in *Rosa*, p. 15). Rosa describes Stella as having "eyes like a doll's," her skin was "bright," "fine," and "pure," yet, as Rosa herself puts it, one "could not believe in what harmless containers the blood-sucker comes" (p. 15). Hence, the name Stella serves as a dubious label that plays—like Ozick's work itself—upon the frail distinctions between fact and fiction. In addition, the name Stella plays further upon a whole culture of such frail distinctions in that it can also be traced back to Christian theology; Stella Maris, the "Star of the Sea," has long been the preferred title by which seafarers have called on the Virgin Mary for the protection they seek.

A distressing question, then, arises as a consequence: Why would a Jewish writer such as Ozick, one who is so well acquainted with Judaism and so deeply concerned with Jewish identity, suggestively implement her case with Christian symbolism and its faithful connotations, especially when writing about the Holocaust? How could it be imaginably appropriate to give Christian connotation to the names of the Jewish victims in such a novel? Baris, who faced a similar question in her commentary on Malamud's "The Mourners," argues the following:

> The problem is not whether the literary reference or tradition invoked be the right one—either too American or not enough Jewish; the question, rather, is whether such recourse to literary reference (however elegantly evoked or appropriate the theme of Bartleby's [or Rosa's] or the cowboy's tales) in the mood of his time—and ours—be morally justified. (p. 54)

I argue that Ozick's device serves as a critique, fictionalizing action invoked by a mental process of assimilation of many Jews in seeking to abolish segregation from the local population. Ozick's naming in Christian terms could thus work to exemplify how easily and entirely engulfed some Jews—and some Jewish readers—might unconsciously wish to be. By blending Rosa's first name with the family name, Lublin, moreover, Ozick both points at the pre-Holocaust educated and cultured Jewish world of Poland and posits a question to be faced by readers of her texts today.[2] If in the Poland of that time Jews saw themselves as an integral part of their surrounding civilization, as when Rosa claims to Persky, "My Warsaw isn't your Warsaw" (Ozick, in *Rosa*, p. 19), then Ozick makes her important point even clearer for creators and readers of fictions thereafter. Persky's Warsaw, as Rosa imagines it, was Jewish, while "the Warsaw of her girlhood" was different. Hers was, as Ozick presents Rosa's view, "a great light ... the house of her girlhood laden with a thousand books" (p. 21).

While some Jews may have been disgusted by the traditional Jews: "these old Jew peasants worn out of their rituals and their superstitions, phylacteries on their foreheads sticking up so stupidly, like unicorn horns, every morning" (Ozick, p. 67), then in contrast, as Ozick's ironic mind-reading shows, other Jews might treasure their own fictions (a "thousand books") with far more satisfying results. Those Jews who adopted the Christian culture assume they would no longer be hated for harshly fictional or superstitious reasons.

Paradoxically enough, in historical terms, when the medieval Christian hatred towards Jews merged in Germany with the pseudoscientific notion that Jews were a "race," antisemitism became detached from religion and could be directed with equal intellectual validity at Jews who had assimilated into the German culture or converted to Christianity. It was the assimilated Jews who indeed became most particularly dangerous, in such perceptions, for their ability to carry Jewish corruption deeper into the core of German society. What Ozick's art conveys is the horrible shock felt by those Jews when their own imaginary distinctions have been shattered. Rosa's claim: "Imagine confining *us* with teeming Mockowiczes and Rabinowiczes and Perskys and Finkelsteins, with all their bad-smelling grandfathers and their hordes of feeble children!" (Ozick, p. 66) becomes all too painful. Rosa, like most Polish Jews who had come to demarcate their difference from other Jews, was not spared from "the final solution." Such failed fictions, indeed, became their most poignant reality when their dream-laden books required new contexts for reading.

Thoughts inscribed and memory invoked are insufficient tools to be used as the only true reflections of the past. It is the gaping space at the core of testimony that fiction, finally, must come to fill. The power of imagination can increase our intimacy with the horrors that cannot be articulated through facts. In Ozick's "The Shawl," fiction is not only a permissible tool in conveying testimony but also, as this paper has argued, a significant and essential mode of testimony. Its truth-telling powers should be fully esteemed.

---

2 Rosa's family name, Lublin, is not mentioned in the story "The Shawl," but it is filled in by Ozick in the sequel, "Rosa."

REFERENCES

Baris, S. D. (1992). Intertextuality and reader responsibility: Living on in Malamud's "The mourners." *Studies in American Jewish literature* 11:1 (1992): 45–61.

Felman, S. & Laub, D. (1992). *Testimony: Crises of witnessing in literature, psychoanalysis, and history.* New York: Routledge.

Gordon, A. (1994). Cynthia Ozick's "The shawl" and the transitional object. *Literature and psychology.* 40; 1–2: 1–9.

Horowitz, S. R. (1984). *Linguistic displacement in fictional responses to the Holocaust.* Ann Arbor, MI: University Microfilms International.

Howe, I. (1988). "Writing and the Holocaust," in B. Lang (Ed.). *Writing and the Holocaust*, pp. 175–199. New York: Holmes & Meier.

Kremer, L. S. (1989). *Witness through the imagination.* Detroit, MI: Wayne State University Press.

Ozick, C. (1990). Rosa. *The shawl.* New York: Vintage International.

Ozick, C. (1990). The shawl. In K. Shawn & K. Goldfrad (2008). (Eds.). *The call of memory: Learning about the Holocaust through narrative: An anthology*, pp. 196–201. Teaneck, NJ: Ben Yehuda Press.

An Examination of Loss in the Holocaust in Cynthia Ozick's "The Shawl"

William Younglove

> *From memory and its moral agent, metaphor,*
> *ensue the humane capacity to imagine another's pain*
> *and the moral obligation to honor the stranger.*
> —Elaine Kauvar

"The Shawl" (Shawn & Goldfrad, *Anthology*, 2008, pp. 196–201) is a fictional recounting of an incident in the lives of three victims enmeshed in the depths of Holocaust degradation-of forced marching, living in barracks, and assembling in the prisoners' roll-call arena in a concentration camp, enclosed by an electrified steel fence. We meet Rosa, the mother of infant Magda, and Rosa's niece, Stella, locked in a contest for survival. (Note: Only the later penned novella, *Rosa* (1988), clarifies this Rosa–Stella relationship.) Not a word is wasted in revealing a mother's effort to will her child to stay alive. Powerful figurative language paints a picture of escalating desperation.

This narrative will appeal to university students and those at the senior high level, chiefly in grades 11 and 12. While its use in an English class would permit maximum exploration of its depth, the story could be used in a history or social studies class to integrate skills and content and to personalize a Holocaust event. Even though it is a short story in both form and length, and could, therefore, be studied within a single period, I recommend that at least four class periods (50 minutes each) be allocated due to its sophisticated use of figurative language and symbols.

Theoretically, students have already been exposed in their grade 9 history/ social science course to the precursors of such a camp's existence: the rise of Nazi Germany and the origins of the Final Solution. In reality, "The Shawl" could stand on its own as an introduction to a Nazi camp death factory. Holocaust background must be broached, however, to contextualize the story. The teacher's main question to the students throughout "The Shawl" must be: *What is going on here?* If such an inductive approach is used, it is vital that ensuing lessons return to chief events and symbols in the story so that historical context is ultimately provided.

Rationale and Teaching Goals

My rationale for using "The Shawl," difficult though the story is, is that it focuses upon the desperate struggle for survival and ends in loss, an experience suffered by all too many of the nearly 6 million Jewish victims. Appelfeld writes (1988):

> Sometimes one hears this argument and warning: "Keep literature out of that fire zone. Let the numbers speak; let the documents and the well-established facts speak." I have no wish to belittle that claim, but I do wish to point out that the numbers and the facts were the murderers' own well-proven means. Man as a number is one of the horrors of dehumanization. ... Should we seek to tread that path and speak of man in the language of statistics? (p. 84)

Specific teaching goals include requiring students to delineate the characters, identify the elements of the setting, pinpoint the conflicts leading to the chief complication and climax of the story, evaluate the plot development and the way in which conflicts are (or are not) addressed and solved, reveal the significance of the author's tone, deduce plausible themes, including a central one; and state the denouement, the aftermath, of the story.

Today, many U.S. states set reading and language arts standards (pp. 490–492 in this volume) that require students to explore a work like Ozick's "The Shawl" in depth. Specifically, students must define specialized vocabulary words contextually and show ability to verify those meanings by definition, restatement, example, comparison, or contrast; identify significant literary devices (e.g., simile, metaphor, personification, etc.); analyze the chief symbols of the story, support written judgments and conclusions through text references, connect their own responses to the writer's narrative techniques that elicit those responses, and edit their own written manuscripts to ensure correct grammar, spelling, and mechanics.

Because "The Shawl" is presented as historical fiction, students should, to provide context, analyze the Nazi policy of pursuing racial purity, especially against European Jewry, which culminated in the Final Solution. The evolving plan of destruction of the Jews from 1939 to late 1941 resulted in their massive destruction between 1942 and 1945. Students *may* have previously achieved standards that discussed the human costs, civilian and military, including survivor returns to any postwar normalcy; and they may have learned to distinguish between primary and secondary sources.

Focus questions will permit an ongoing discussion about key story elements. I suggest a PowerPoint presentation of the following focus and essential questions to teach students how to read literary texts and how to talk about reading. That is, I want to teach habits of mind and of talk-strategies for collaborative literary engagement-that students might apply to multiple texts. Such questionings, derived from the standards and story content, might include the following:

- In "The Shawl," Rosa faced a dilemma, a problem with no satisfactory solution. The term "choiceless choices" is defined by Langer (1982) as "one form of abnormal response and another, imposed by a situation that is not of the victim's own choosing" (p. 72). It is not a choice between good and bad, or even between the lesser of two evils. It is forced choosing between the impossible and the unacceptable. What events limited Rosa's choices and in what sense may she have been left with a "choiceless choice?"
- Stella is alternately described as "cold," "jealous," and "ravenous" (*Anthology*, p. 196). How, then, are we to understand Stella's ultimate taking of the shawl for herself?
- Beyond the "margin of the arena" (p. 200), the place where the concentration camp prisoners assembled, was the electrified fence. What does Ozick's description of the areas on both sides of the fence reveal about the differences in the lives lived inside and outside of the camp?
- Magda's blue eyes and yellow hair likely gave rise to Stella's utterance of "Aryan" (p. 197). What significance might this have had at this time in history, for Magda, and indirectly for Stella and Rosa?
- The shawl is the only possession of the three characters in the story. How did the "magic" of the shawl likely contribute to the continued existence of the three camp inmates?

Beyond focus questions are those that loom large in light of the humanity that we, as teachers and students, share with the victims and survivors. These essential questions, while they have no definite answers, should evolve from discussion and examination of the text. I would include such essential questions as:

- Can one survive emotionally without the ability to feel pity?
- In what ways do our possessions sustain us-beyond their physical usefulness?
- How does one survive emotionally having made a "choice" to save her own life at the expense of another's?

As We Begin

I have found it useful to gather the following materials before I implement the lesson:

- an overhead projector
- Microsoft PowerPoint
- writing prompts (on transparencies)
- journals
- a K-W-L-H (Know/Want to know/Learned/How I learned) chart
- a professional audiotape of the story (optional)
- a class set of "The Shawl"
- TV/VCR (optional)
- two class sets of 3 × 5 cards

- a classroom dictionary and thesaurus (bilingual, if needed and available)
- an overhead transparency of the 20 key vocabulary words
- a brief list of Holocaust references (see list at chapter's end)
- Ozick biographical material from the Shawn & Goldfrad *Anthology* (2008, p. 271)
- a narrative writing rubric
- a date to use the writing lab, say a week hence, for a final computer draft

To help students connect their personal experiences with the lesson, I ask them to write a response to the following journal prompt:

> Most of us, growing up, had a favorite item to which we clung, sometimes long after it had worn out. It may have been a blanket, a toy, or some gift from a loved one. Think back to your early childhood. Identify one longtime keepsake, explaining how you obtained it, why you kept it as long as you did, what it meant to you, and how, ultimately, you came to set it aside.

I sometimes display and talk briefly about a fountain pen desk set, given to me by my grandmother, which allowed me as a preschool child to imitate the grown-ups around me who always seemed to be writing something. Provide a few minutes for students to write, and ask for sharing. Many students reference long-cherished items of every size, shape, and description, competing for "share and tell" time.

One poignant response came from Shashawna:

> I want to tell you about this seventh-grade picture of my little brother. I keep it in my purse billfold even though the photo is bent, cracked, and faded cuz [*sic*] his life was taken by a gang bang two years ago. I can't ever set it aside.

The importance that the often simple object held for each student will become clear as students respond. Be sure to collect the journals for later assessment.

Introduce the story by title, making sure that students understand what a shawl is. Ideally, exhibit one. Introduce the writer, Cynthia Ozick (b. 1928), an American author who has written extensively about Jewish life. "The Shawl" is a fictional attempt to depict the uncertainty of camp life during the Holocaust.

Pass out a K-W-L-H (Know/Want to know/Learned/How I learned) chart. Require the completion of the two left columns with at least four items revealing students' knowledge of and questions about the Holocaust. Collect charts in about 10 minutes to determine what students already know and what they wish to learn.

Read the story aloud together. With strong readers, I share the reading; with less proficient readers, I use a 15-minute-long tape read by Claire Bloom, available at *http://legacy.kcrw.com/jewish/jss.html*. I circulate to encourage students to follow the reading carefully.

Give students time to react in a double entry journal (Shawn & Goldfrad, *Guide*, p. 495). Students may select four or five passages they felt were crucial to the story. They may respond to key words, meaningful phrases, or writing style, or they might elicit questions about or challenges to the text, as the sample below illustrates.

Selected Text	Student Reflection
Roberto: "It was a magic shawl, it could nourish an infant for three days and three nights." (p. 197)	How can such a thing be possible—unless the shawl can absorb the dew or rain?
Munira: "Stella was waiting for Magda to die so she could put her teeth into the little thighs." (p. 197)	Was there actually cannibalism in the camp?
Clarence: Why did Magda's breath "smell of cinnamon and almonds"? (p. 197)	I thought food was nearly nonexistent. I don't get the combination of these two either …

(Compare this method with ones developed by Witty [pp. 78–94], Humphrey [pp. 411–424], and Olson [pp. 102–106] in this publication. I like their idea of dialectical journal highlighting or Post-it notes right on the original text.)

When students have responded, ask for entries they made regarding these previously-selected single words or phrases *only*, discussing each briefly. The words that follow are best approached in context before or after the story reading. The vocabulary and concept development objective is to have students identify and use the literal meanings of words and distinguish between the denotative and connotative meanings, interpreting the latter. A dictionary or thesaurus may be used as needed. These words, in order of appearance, whose meanings are crucial to understanding the story, include:

ravenous (starving)
windings (folds)
cholera (fatal disease)
elfin (dwarflike)
Aryan (so-called master race)
menstruate (have period)
annihilated (destroyed)
mute (speechless)
barracks (barn-like buildings)
arena (gathering place)

febrile (feverish)
larynx (voice box)
plundered (robbed)
carrion (dead flesh)
viscous (slimy)
phantoms (ghosts)
domino (black rectangular gaming piece)
goblet (rounded drinking glass)
loftiness (airiness)
saliva (spit)

Whatever your approach to vocabulary study, your goal will be to integrate the terms into students' usage. For example, class threesomes might work cooperatively with two words apiece, completing 3 × 5 cards via the following format, submitting the cards to use during discussion.

- target word _____
- story context (the entire phrase) _____
- what it is _____ what it is not _____ _____
- I would probably find this word in these contexts (places, events, people, situations) _____.
- I shall remember this word by connecting it to _____.

To accommodate second-language or underprepared students, you might offer, besides the taped reading, the bilingual dictionaries/thesauri, grouping those who share the same first language. Special needs students, too, can be grouped with stronger readers and provided with an aide, if available, to complete the writing prompt and the chart.

Questions for Discussion

When I begin, I address, via the overhead, identifiable events while drawing upon the words students listed in their journals as well as those I provided. Some questions I raise are:

- What is the relationship of the characters Stella, Rosa, and Magda? How do you know?
- What are the three settings referenced in the story? What is the overall setting?
- How does Rosa avoid conflict—until the very end?
- What is the climax of the story, Rosa's greatest conflict and her ultimate decision?
- How did the complication leading to her decision come about?
- Ozick tells the story in the third person. Only two voices, some six words, interrupt the narrative. How does such detachment reveal—or shape—the writer's tone (writer's attitude toward the material)?
- *Theme* is a central idea that underlies and unifies the elements of a story. What might be a chief theme of "The Shawl?"
- While the story ends rather abruptly, there can be little doubt about what happened. What is the significance, therefore, of the last five lines of the story, the denouement, that is, the final outcome of the complex sequence of events?

Language Shapes Thought

Ozick's use of figurative language in "The Shawl" is extensive. I think such layering of meaning is the real challenge in interpretation. The key to teaching about the figurative language is not simply to enable students to define the terms nor merely locate the figures of speech or even create them in their own writing. Rather, it is to help students understand that the writer wants to clarify a concept not immediately obvious. The author, therefore, links the lesser known, more abstract concept to one that most people can recognize. If the attempted connection works, readers should see a figure-an actual image-in their minds, which stands for the interrelated concept. The question regarding each figure of speech is the same: What image is the author trying to evoke at that moment, and why? I therefore suggest approaching the study of figures of speech in the following order:

1. Assign four students to a group. Provide them with definitions of each figure of speech.
2. Ask students to collectively choose and write the two most powerful similes, metaphors, and personifications in the story and explain their choices. In other words, the students will locate comparisons, those using "like" or "as" and those images directly compared, as well as things given human characteristics. I recommend integrating some of your own choices, from the list that follows, during group discussion. Scholar Keren Goldfrad (2008) suggests in this volume, "[T]hrough her metaphors Ozick is compelling the reader to imagine the Holocaust, that is to say, to identify with just those feelings aroused by historical and political contexts" (p. 354). Thus, this exercise provides a check on student understanding of the figures of speech and an opportunity for students to connect their chosen figures with both the story and with Holocaust-related events.

I have identified the following figures of speech:

Similes
Rosa ... [is] like ... a floating angel (p. 196).
Rosa's bleak complexion, dark like cholera (p. 196).
Magda's eyes blue as air; hair ... as yellow as ... the Star sewn into
    Rosa's coat (p. 196).
Stella's ... voice ... thin as a string (p. 197).
Stella ... [is] like a young cannibal (p. 197).
Magda's eyes ... watched like a tiger (p. 198).
Magda [was] ... as wild as one of the big rats (p. 199).
[The] ... shawl ... is like a flag (p. 200).
[Magda] looked like a butterfly (p. 200).
Below the helmet [is] a black body like a domino (p. 200).

Metaphors
Rosa [was] a walking cradle (p. 196).
Stella's knees were tumors on sticks; elbows [were] chicken bones (p. 196).
Magda [was] a squirrel in a nest (p. 196).
[Her] ... tooth [was] ... an elfin tombstone of white marble gleaming (p. 197).
Rosa's teats ... [were] duct-crevice extinct, a dead volcano, blind eye, chill hole
    (p. 197).
Magda [had] ... little pencil legs ... the little pencil legs faltered (p. 198).

Magda['s] ... cave of her larynx (p. 199).

they spoke of "flowers," of "rain": excrement, thick turd-braids, and the slow stinking maroon waterfall (p. 200).

light ... sparkled it into a goblet [shone off of a helmet] (p. 200).

pick up the sticks of Magda's body (p. 201).

Personification

Magda took the corner of the shawl and milked it (p. 197).

The shawl was Magda's own baby, her pet, her little sister (p. 198).

[Magda's] little pencil legs scribbling this way and that (p. 198).

ash-stippled wind made a clown ... of Magda's shawl (p. 199).

tiger lilies, lifting their orange bonnets (p. 200).

Rosa heard real sounds in the wire: grainy sad voices (p. 200).

electric voices began to chatter wildly (p. 200).

steel voices went mad in their growling (p. 201).

Rosa drank Magda's shawl until it dried (p. 201).

Allusion

A peculiar smell, of cinnamon and almonds, lifted out of [Magda's] mouth (p. 197).

[Rosa was] ... tasting the cinnamon and almond depth of Magda's saliva (p. 201). (These two substances may allude to (i.e., foreshadow) Magda's death since they were both used in embalming bodies in ancient Egypt.)

[Magda] looked like a butterfly touching a silver vine (pp. 200–201) (alludes to the contact Magda's hurled body had with the live current of the camp's electric fence).

Verbal Irony or Paradox

Stella, cold, cold, the coldness of hell (p. 196).

Symbolism provides yet another avenue for interpreting story events. Symbols, of course, represent something abstract by the use of something concrete, often revealing ideas or truths not directly expressed. Potential symbolic representations are interwoven within and throughout the figures of speech. I have found it interesting to probe with students, for example, the representations for: blue eyes/yellow hair, failure of Rosa and Stella to menstruate, dried up breasts, black wind that made eyes tear, the roll-call arena, ash-stippled wind, lice-head and body-butterflies in summer, innocent tiger lilies, bitter fatty floating smoke that greased Rosa's skin, and black domino body and black boots.

The linen shawl, of course, is the chief symbol of the story; these questions might aid analysis:

- What possible meaning does the shawl have for each of the three characters?
- How was the shawl used in ways other than as a wrap?
- What might the shawl symbolize at different points in the story?

As the discussion ends, I return the K-W-L-H charts to the students, requiring them to complete the "L" and "H" columns using at least four items in each. I explain that the "Learned" column must include statements that reveal the contextual meanings of the story's 20 vocabulary words. As students work, you might display on the overhead the vocabulary again for reference.

I model by displaying on the chalk or white board the K-W-L-H chart start:

K(now)	W(ant to know)	L(earned)	H(ow I learned)
Jewish people suffered humiliation, beatings, starvation, and murder in most camps.	Why did the Nazis single out the Jews?	Babies were destroyed so that no Jews were left to seek revenge and/or so that Jews would be denied a future.	from Ozick's story; class discussion; grade 9 history text

To check for understanding and to provide guided practice, I circulate and help. Students can use their notes, dictionary, and thesaurus as needed. For independent practice, I require students to complete the K-W-L-H chart at home and submit it the following day. A meaningful but simple closure is to hand students a 3 × 5 exit card and ask them to write the most important thing they learned and one further question that "The Shawl" raised for them about the Holocaust. I collect the cards at the bell to gain additional insights into student understandings, best discussed the next day.

Students Struggle to Make Meaning

After collecting the homework charts, I conduct a brief session regarding exit card questions not yet answered. Students have many questions, ranging from those the story and discussion generated (Alda: "Didn't people living near the camps know anything about them?") to those more tangential (Sonia: "Why did Hitler hate the Jews so much?"). You might open the floor for discussion here or direct students to the references included at the end of this lesson. Stadler (1994), Bresheeth, et al. (1994)[3], and Berenbaum (2003), particularly, do an excellent job of providing introductory overviews of the Holocaust. As you mention possible sources, you can also raise questions about student responses to the H(ow) col-

---

3 The Bresheeth et al. book is written in graphic arts form; it may, therefore be thought to be less scholarly than other sources. Brilliantly illustrated by Litza Jansz, however, the work evokes images by Art Spiegelman in *Maus I/II*. In addition to appealing to the students' visual intelligence, the book briefly raises the question of historical revisionism and Holocaust denial, something students may discover at any one of some 5,000 Internet sites.

umn of the chart. You might ask, for example, "What other primary and second-ary print resources are available? How can one determine which sources are most valid and reliable?"

I require one final writing task to discover how students connected with the story personally. The prompt, displayed on the overhead, requires them to adopt the point of view of one of the three characters. I also hand out the Holistic Rubric for Narratives (See Appendix A) to be used as a scoring guide after students revised and edited their rough draft. The final paper can be due within a week.

Background to Writing

As we have discussed, "The Shawl" is revealed almost entirely through the eyes of a third person narrator. The story, as told, may be closest to being Rosa's story, perhaps only because she is the dominant (chief) character.

Directions for Writing

Imagine that one of the three characters is telling us (the readers) the events directly. Choose one and retell the chief events of the story, in no fewer than 400 words, as though they were being seen, told (can be in the person's mind), and experienced directly by Stella, Magda, or Rosa (i.e., first person point of view).

Susanna drafted the following, excerpted, re-creation through Rosa's eyes:

> The wind bites at my flesh; the only warmth is between my breasts. I feel Magda move, searching for … food. "Suck, little one … suck shawl-giving life, all I have to give." It pains me to see you so rav-enous—and to see that Stella is so jealous. … She can't understand what I feel for you. Your struggle for life sustains me. Your spirit gives me strength. … As long as I am alive, I will not let Stella—or anyone else—take your food, your life, from me.

For a film that examines choiceless choices reflecting actual survivor testi-mony, consult the USHMM's Resource Book *Teaching About the Holocaust* or the Holocaust Resource Center and Archives at Queensborough Community Col-lege of the City University of New York's *Annotated Videography on the Holocaust and Related Subjects*.

Following the survivor testimony, I suggest returning to Rosa's climactic de-cision in "The Shawl," exploring this final question: "When the electric voices chattered, 'Maamaa …' in the camp roll-call arena, even though Rosa now pos-sessed the shawl, what choice did she really have?" I have never failed to have the question generate intense debate about the word "choice" and about what it meant to be a victim during the Holocaust.

Assessment Options

I suggest the following assessments as a way of rewarding students for those tasks that take the most time *and* yield the greatest range of thinking skills. Some teachers also like to offer oral response credit.

- A journal entry that addresses the first day's five key requests is worth five points. One point is deducted for each request not satisfactorily addressed.
- The K-W-L-H chart is awarded 16 points, four for each column completion with four entries minimum per column. If vocabulary is not defined correctly, I deduct up to four points from the total.
- The "changed viewpoint" essay will be graded by the attached (Appendix A) six-point rubric. If students revise, the narrative will be worth 18 points.
- Students who choose to read from Ozick's biographical works from various sources can be awarded extra credit.

Appelfeld saw Holocaust numbers only as deceptive, in accordance with Nazi "ledger keeping." He observed that fiction, although representational, often conveys experience best. Ozick's three fictional characters, bound together by a shawl in a concentration camp, have provided students with a glimpse of what it meant to be victims in the dehumanizing Third Reich. For my students, and hopefully for yours, "The Shawl" and other such narratives and their accompanying analyses and teaching guides in these volumes are the catalyst for further exploration of the Holocaust—and the students' own lives. Such stories have the power to raise questions for which the future lives of our students, only, may have the answers.

Appendix A

Holistic Rubric for Narratives[4]

6 DISTINGUISHED ACHIEVEMENT
intriguing, compelling, outstanding

Characterization: Writer uses more than one strategy to develop a single character. Character can be easily visualized, and actions are clearly understood.
Narrative: Story has a logical, organized plan and does not digress.
Setting: Setting is clear to reader and enhances narrative.
Unity: All parts of the story are balanced and cohesive. All elements contribute to the story.
Conventions: Reader rarely spots mechanics/usage/spelling errors. The writer seems in control of conventions of Standard Edited English

5 NOTEWORTHY ACHIEVEMENT
integrated, well-developed, effective

Characterization: One character is developed and understood. Not as easily visualized as in a 6. Most actions and motivations are understood.
Narrative: Story is logical and organized. Possible limited digression, or limited elaboration.
Setting: Same as 6—perhaps less vivid.
Unity: Most parts of the story are balanced—elements are generally balanced. Story is cohesive.
Conventions: Reader infrequently spots mechanics/usage/spelling errors. The writer may still be uncertain about some conventions or lack complete control of Standard Edited English.

4 SATISFACTORY ACHIEVEMENT
interesting, motivated, believable

Characterization: One character is adequately developed, but character's motivation may not be evident or consistent.
Narrative: Story follows a plan, but lacks complexity of a 5 or 6; story usually digresses or over-elaborates. Limited evidence of originality.
Setting: Setting is established and appropriate.
Unity: Paper is unbalanced. Some elements do not contribute to the story's purpose.
Conventions: Reader occasionally spots mechanics/usage/spelling errors. This writer clearly lacks complete control of conventions, but errors do not significantly interfere with understanding.

---

4 See usage considerations at rubric's end.

3 SOME INDICATION OF ACHIEVEMENT
general, ineffective, lacks believability

Characterization: Limited, sketchy development of central character. Some characters' actions may not make sense. Motivation must be inferred or is inconsistent.
Narrative: Story plan is illogical or confused.
Setting: Setting is either missing, inconsistent, or inappropriate.
Unity: Story is unbalanced and lacks cohesion. Narrative may dominate, or paper merely describes character.
Conventions: Reader is often aware of errors in mechanics/usage/spelling. The errors may cause some confusion or create ambiguity for the reader.

2 LIMITED INDICATION OF ACHIEVEMENT
unrealistic, inconsistent, unmotivated

Characterization: Minimal development of central character. No motivation is shown. Character's actions do not make sense, are illogical.
Narrative: No story plan. Hard to follow. May be brief or incomplete.
Setting: Not established or inappropriate.
Unity: May be pure narration. Difficult to follow and confusing.
Conventions: Reader is continually aware of errors in mechanics/usage/spelling. While the essay is still readable, the errors create confusion and ambiguity.

1 FEW INDICATIONS OF ACHIEVEMENT
undeveloped, rambling, confusing

Characterization: No central character. No development of any character. No connected actions or motivations.
Narrative: No plan. Incoherent.
Setting: None.
Unity: No apparent unity.
Conventions: Reader is bothered by numerous errors in every sentence or nearly every sentence. The error rate reveals a writer who seems to understand very little about the conventions of Standard Edited English.

0 INAPPROPRIATE RESPONSE
off topic
Conventions: Not applicable.

Usage Considerations

By *holistic*, I mean that the paper is judged as a whole, the scoring a general impression of the paper's merits. Such a rubric is not an aggregate of the paper's subpoints. If, for example, the paper achieves its distinguished rhetorical effect, but the conventions are weak, the overall score will be less than a "6" but would still be in the upper half of the 6-point scale. Specific placement would depend on the extent to which the lack of Standard Edited English *interfered* with the reading and understanding of the paper.

REFERENCES

Appelfeld, A. (1988). After the Holocaust. In B. Lang. (Ed.). *Writing and the Holocaust* (pp. 83–92). New York: Holmes & Meier.

Berenbaum, M. (2003). *A promise to remember: The Holocaust in the words and voices of its survivors*. Boston: Bulfinch Press.

Bloom, Claire. (1995). Jewish short stories from Eastern Europe and beyond. National Public Radio: National Yiddish Book Center. Retrieved June 24, 2007, from *http://legacy.kcrw.com/jewish/jss.html*.

Bresheeth, H., Hood, S., & Jansz, L. (1994). *Introducing the Holocaust*. New York: Totem Books.

Goldfrad, K. (2008). The ethics of aesthetics: Cynthia Ozick's "The shawl." In K. Shawn & K. Goldfrad (2008) *The call of memory: Learning about the Holocaust through narrative: A teacher's guide*, pp. 350–357. Teaneck, NJ: Ben Yehuda Press.

Holocaust Resource Center and Archives (2003). S. Roberts (Ed.). *Annotated videography on the Holocaust and related subjects*. Bayside: The City University of New York.

Langer, L. (1982). *Versions of survival: The Holocaust and the human spirit*. Albany: State University of New York.

Ozick, C. (1988). *Rosa*. New York: Vintage Books.

Ozick, C. (1980, 1983). The shawl. In K. Shawn & K. Goldfrad (2008) *The call of memory: Learning about the Holocaust through narrative: An anthology*, pp. 196–201. Teaneck, NJ: Ben Yehuda Press.

Shawn, K. & Goldfrad, K. (2008). *The call of memory: Learning about the Holocaust through narrative: A teacher's guide*. Teaneck, NJ: Ben Yehuda Press.

Stadler, B. (1994). *The Holocaust, a history of courage and resistance* (Rev. ed.). New York: Behrman.

United States Holocaust Memorial Museum. (2001*). Teaching about the Holocaust: A resource book for educators*. Washington, DC.

Sparks of Humanity

Encountering Ethics:
Sara Nomberg-Przytyk's "The Camp Blanket"

Joan Baker

"The Camp Blanket," reprinted most recently in Shawn & Goldfrad (*Anthology*, 2008, pp. 205–209), is taken from Nomberg-Przytyk's 1985 collection, *Auschwitz: True Tales from a Grotesque Land* (pp. 132–136). It is 35th in the sequence of 40 interlocking tales that chronicle the author's experiences from the time of her transport and arrival at Auschwitz in January 1944, to a forced march and transport to Ravensbrück a year later, followed by liberation on May 9, 1945, and the sobering journey back to Lublin, Poland. While chronicling events may fulfill a memoirist's historicist obligation, the linear trajectory of such events suggests that one's experiences, however traumatic, move one inexorably forward toward a kind of emancipatory telos. Survivors' testimonies and memoirs have refuted any such expectation.

"Coming out of the darkness," Primo Levi (1989) explains, "one suffered because of the reacquired consciousness of having been diminished" (p. 75). There was, he continues, a different "moral yardstick" in the camp, so that liberation was attended by the sobering "opportunity to measure our diminishment from the outside" (p. 75). For her part, Nomberg-Przytyk appears intent upon assessing the impact of the grotesque outer landscape upon the inner moral health of its prisoners. Thus, the *Tales*, each of which can be read independently, work not so much to move the reader through Auschwitz as to force the reader to pause in each vignette to consider how and to what extent the situation depicted in the tale determines the ethical response of the characters involved. In so doing, "she also reminds the readers to distrust their own automatic moral judgments in the face of such events" (Young, 1988, p. 44).

The series of vignettes itself works to preserve "the sense of broken time and lives that might have been artificially mended in one long story" (Young, pp. 43–44). She not only resists aesthetic "mending" but also eschews universalizing her experience. Instead, through a variety of narrative techniques, she provides a veritable chorus of female voices—from inmates of differing ages, ethnicities, religions, and political leanings to a hierarchy of camp functionaries—all of whom relate their stories or the stories of others to offer the reader an assemblage of remarkably diverse points of view of camp realities. The editors of the *Tales* note this distinctive handling of character in their Afterword:

It is through this subordinating of the horrors to the individual characters that Sara moves from documentarian to novelist, and it is as a novelist that she heightens the reader's awareness of the complexity of the moral and ethical problems posed by Auschwitz. (Pfefferkorn & Hirsch, 1985, p. 172)

If, then, situational ethics is the (dis)order of the day in the camps, we might also consider that by the time Nomberg-Przytyk sets to writing "The Camp Blanket," she feels compelled to frame the ethical dilemmas constantly faced by camp prisoners. To that end, she casts the anonymous benefactor's lifesaving gift in sharp relief to the lethal passivity of the other passengers; she then poses two questions in an attempt to evaluate the disparate responses. My concern in this essay is to illustrate how the Western tradition of virtue ethics proves utterly inadequate for evaluating Holocaust prisoners' responses. I also wish to suggest that the ethics of exteriority posited by Emmanuel Levinas offers a constructive approach both to reading the ethical encounter in "The Camp Blanket" and to achieving ethical relations in the post-Holocaust period. I will take up the major ideas of each element of moral philosophy in tandem with my discussion of the narrative.

Jean Améry (1977) states in *At the Mind's Limits: Contemplations by a Survivor on Auschwitz and its Realities:*

> It goes without saying, I believe, that in Auschwitz we did not become better, more human, more humane, and more mature ethically. You do not observe dehumanized man committing his deeds and misdeeds without having all of your notions of inherent human dignity placed in doubt. (p. 20)

Améry aptly reflects the narrator's state of mind in "The Camp Blanket" as she, the narrator, witnesses the brutal killing taking place around her in the freezing, crowded railway car when only a few paragraphs earlier news of freedom had seemed so close that it had "caused wings to grow on our shoulders" (Shawn & Goldfrad, *Anthology*, p. 205). Nomberg-Przytyk artistically sets the stage for the chilling silence that precipitates the first of the narrator's two ethical questions. It is January 1945. It has taken "the last remaining ounce of strength" (p. 205) for the contingent of Auschwitz women, who have been forced to march for days, to drag themselves forward. What faces them, however, finally immobilizes them not only physically, but emotionally and morally as well. In all the chaos and violence of packing the women into the railway cars, the narrator becomes separated from her friends, a significant event that deprives her of any solidarity. By her own admission, such solidarity would probably not have prompted any different response to her mute witnessing of the *kapos'* brutal murder of one of the young Polish girls, Zosiu or her friend, as they crawl towards their attempted escape. We don't know which girl is murdered because the narrator dared not "turn my head in their direction. I just listened carefully" (p. 206). As more women are murdered and tossed from the railcar, the grim thumping of their bodies appears to echo the hypnotic thumping of the train's wheels. Thus, all the conditions in the railway car threaten to dull the senses.

Nomberg-Przytyk presages the prisoners' deathly silence in repeated references to a nature turned violent: the wind that "almost tore our heads off" (p. 206) and "the wind and frost [that] were tearing my head off" (p. 208). Her imagination, as if seized by such grotesque images, conjures the possibility that the women packed together so tightly "would all become one stony mass with many heads" (p. 206).

Significantly, the narrator answers the first ethical question she poses.

> None of us said anything. No one could be found who reacted like a human being to this monstrous crime. Why did we keep quiet? After all, it was not fear that closed our mouths. They numbered about ten to fifteen, and we were more than a hundred. It was all part of the routine. In camp they were the ones who did the hitting, while we were the ones who got the beatings and who did not even have the right to defend ourselves or shield ourselves from the blows. That is what the camp had done to us. It had stripped us of the capacity to make a human gesture or to react normally when confronted by an enemy. (p. 207)

While the narrator exhibits no moral superiority during the event itself, she demonstrates an ethically conditioned understanding in the telling. By challenging the prisoners' silence in ethical terms, she does not relieve the prisoners of their responsibility to react *normally* but identifies the abuse that has deprived the prisoners of the powers of agency essential for the basic capacity to respond.

The bodies crammed into the railway car are depicted in stark contrast to Nomberg-Przytyk's imaginatively drawn characters, who, in her other stories, are remarkable for their individuality. Here, individuality is trampled on: "Where are you crawling, you louse?" (p. 207), the louse being Zosiu or her friend. The collective silence suggests that the inmates have come close to perceiving each other in the same way that they are perceived by their captors. We recognize, then, the need for the author's intervention at this point: Where there is shouting as opposed to dialogue and silence when protest is called for, the narrator must assert herself didactically in order to explicate the ethical situation. By rhetorically posing the question in order to frame the answer, she invites us to consider which, if any, aspects of classical (Aristotelian) ethics of virtue can encompass the moral choices available to one trying to stay alive in a death camp.

In his text *Moral Responsibility in the Holocaust: A Study in the Ethics of Character*, Jones (1999) enumerates the powers essential for the basic capacity of *responsibility* or what is also understood as *agency:*

1. Sufficient *cognitive powers* to understand the difference between right and wrong and the likely consequences of one's actions (p. 28).

2. Sufficient *powers of deliberation* "to make informed choices and decisions in the light of one's aims and goals" and "available evidence about which of the alternative means of reaching these goals is likely to achieve them" (p. 29).
3. Sufficient *powers of volition* "to enable one to carry out decisions and choices in action" (p. 29).

To assess the efficacy of virtue ethics for reading "The Camp Blanket," the pattern of cognitive and deliberative activity prior to the prisoners' moral collapse should first be traced. Although their physical and emotional reserves have been depleted by the freezing, starvation, exhaustion, and pain they have endured on the march, the women stagger on, prodded by the prospect of freedom. Now, also emotionally agitated, they appear in a constant state of anxiety. As we recall, one rumor fuels hope; the next, despair. Note that the narrator logically refutes the rumor that machine guns have been set up in the forest to slaughter the marchers: "Don't babble nonsense," I said sharply. "There are too many of us. They wouldn't have time to cover their tracks. The escorts are afraid of the Russian army. They won't do it" (*Anthology*, p. 206).

Once she is packed into the railway car, the narrator appears acutely alert—as do the two young Polish girls anxious to escape—cautiously gauging whether or not the *kapos* or Hungarian soldiers pose an imminent threat. The Hungarians, she concludes, are distracted by their own problems. It would, she deliberates, be possible to escape from the open car; one of the young Polish girls clearly thinks so and quickly acts on her own volition. Just as quickly she is martyred as "evidence" of the consequences of any attempted escape. Despite the fact that the prisoners outnumber the functionaries by perhaps 10 to 1, no individual capable of summoning the energy for so much as a gesture of protest could reasonably count on the volition let alone the support of the others.

Elsewhere in the *Tales*, the women of Auschwitz have exercised their human agency, albeit diminished, in collectively deciding—often after considerable debate—sometimes to remain silent to protect a sister inmate from knowledge, sometimes choosing, instead, to convey knowledge. What we now witness in this narrative is the near destruction of what the author has, to this point, depicted as the women's struggle to sustain a semblance of humanity, even community. Thus, on the one hand, the criteria of traditional virtue ethics do appear to support the narrator's explanation of the women's silence: The women have indeed been stripped of powers *sufficient* for human agency, for response (ability). However, examined closely, with reference to Jones's summary above, such terms as "informed choice," "choice of action," "consequences," "goals," and "alternative means of reaching goals" appear utterly incongruous with the reality of Auschwitz. Survivors speak instead of the choice that is no choice.

"At the first blow," Améry (1977) tells us, "trust in the world breaks down" (p. 28). He concludes: "Whoever has succumbed to torture can no longer feel at home in the world. The shame of destruction cannot be erased. Trust in the world, which already collapsed in part at the first blow ... will not be regained" (p. 40). In his analysis of survivors' "tainted memory," Langer (1991) offers another reason for the breakdown of human agency: "Because the moral systems that we are familiar with are built on the premise of individual choice and responsibility for the consequences of choice," courageous acts therefore appear "based on the conviction that the agent is in control of the results of his action" (p. 125). The tragic outcome for Zosiu or her friend, however, would shatter any remnant of such conviction for their sister passengers.

This failure of traditional moral systems to which Langer refers can be attributed in part to those assumptions of virtue ethics that place the ethical subject rather than actions at the heart of ethics. For Aristotle (upon whom much of Western ethical tradition is based), "human excellence is fixed independently of the specificity of the subject who realizes it. Any particular human being will realize human excellence only by fulfilling in his own life an already determinate universal ideal" (Cordner, 2002, p. 117). A person's character, then, is measured in terms of virtues and vices according to an ideal standard; or, as Cordner, drawing from Taylor, explains, virtue ethics is concerned with "what it is good to *be*" [emphasis mine] alongside concern with "what it is right to *do*" (p. 104). This is not to say that in his *Nicomachean Ethics* Aristotle (1947) disregards the notion of voluntary versus involuntary behavior (Bk. III: Ch. 1, pp. 347–352), only that he attaches little importance to idiosyncrasies and variety among people because such differences for him lie outside their human and moral essence (Cordner, pp. 117–118). Nor does this mean, Berel Lang (2000) asserts, "that there are no general or universal moral issues or principles, but that when such issues are viewed only or initially at that level, they remain abstractions and are therefore misleading," and nowhere more so than in the death camps (p. 43).

It would be fair to ask at this point why I have discussed virtue ethics in this reading, knowing that it cannot encompass the Holocaust. It is because virtue ethics, albeit centered on self-mastery for the elite and assuming an ordered world, is, nevertheless, the standard by which the Holocaust's victims and survivors will be measured by others. This realization may lead to a situation where the responses expected by others Holocaust survivors will expect of themselves, and therefore they will judge themselves accordingly. Nomberg-Przytyk knows that this is the pending shame that stalks freedom, the shame that Primo Levi (1989) describes that accounts for suicides *after* surviving victims return to the normal world where their camp behavior is measured against traditional moral standards (pp. 75–76). Therefore, Nomberg-Przytyk, who usually leaves the ethical questions she poses for the reader to answer, here feels compelled to answer the first question she raises in "The Camp Blanket" in order to leave no doubt as to the cause of the women's apathy and silence.

Up to this point, I have been speaking of *responsibility*, a notion critical to any discussion of ethics. In *The Writing of the Disaster*, Blanchot (1995) asks in frustration, "Will we sustain the enigma of what is announced in the term 'responsibility,' the term the language of ordinary morality uses in the most facile way possible by putting it into the service of order?" (p. 26). In post-Holocaust thought, "order" has acquired a threatening, if not lethal, aspect. Rather than view "responsibility," which Blanchot considers "a banal word, a notion moralistically assigned to us as a (political) duty," we should, he urges, "try to understand the word as it has been opened up and renewed by Levinas" (p. 25).

Blanchot here refers to philosopher Emmanuel Levinas (1906–1995) who has profoundly influenced the post Holocaust discourse of ethics. A Lithuanian Jew, Levinas fled Kovno as a refugee during World War I, and later, as a philosopher (and French citizen) teaching in Paris, was drafted into the army, captured, and forced to do hard labor as a prisoner of war for most of World War II (Critchley, 2002). Most of his family members were murdered in Nazi pogroms, including his mother, father, two brothers, and mother-in-law. In his writings, Levinas has stated that "his life had been dominated by the memory of the Nazi horror" (Critchley, p. 1). We recognize, then, why Blanchot asks that we entrust Levinas with a post-Holocaust definition of responsibility.

For Levinas, ethics is based on a relation of responsibility to another person. His ethics of *exteriority* is directed toward others. "For Levinas, an *ethical* relation is one where I *face* the other person. It is this ethical relation to the other person that was lost in both the fact of National Socialist antisemitism and in its philosophical apologias" (Critchley, p. 26).

It is, for example, difficult to sustain a stereotype or prejudice when one's face-to-face experiences with the other contradict the stereotype. An ethical relation with another also ideally allows that individual to remain absolutely "Other" to oneself. Although I will not specifically apply the notion of the absolute Other in the discussion that follows, it is important to mention it here in order to appreciate why alterity is synonymous with Levinasian ethics. In ethical relations the other remains absolutely Other. Simply put, this means letting the other person be herself without trying to alter her to be more like oneself—one's alter-ego, so to speak—or the "Same." Alterity is privileged; alteration, or our efforts to change others, eschewed. Levinas (1969) critiques philosophy for having suppressed alterity, a consequence, he argues, of philosophy's almost exclusive focus on ontology—the issues of being—at the expense of addressing real and perceived differences among human beings. The danger of ontological thinking is that the individual becomes subsumed into a category.

It is exactly this mode of thinking that breeds such negative consequences as stereotyping or *totalizing*, the suppression of difference that we see manifest in its extreme form in the Holocaust. Thus, according to Levinas, only an exteriorizing mode of thinking that is oriented toward other individuals and engages others in ethical, face-to-face human relations holds the possibility of deterring disaster (see Levinas, 1969).

Shifting now to the railway car, let us consider the ethical encounter, the gift of the camp blanket, in light of Levinas's notion of exteriority. We find that the narrator, not unlike the young Polish girls before her, is "seized with a desire" (*Anthology*, p. 208) and feels a powerful burst of agency once she spots the booth where she can sit on a bench. The "nagging idea" (p. 208) that she could literally put the murderous scene behind her momentarily kills her fear of being killed.

She assesses her situation: She is a safe distance from the *kapos* and protected by a barrier of women crowded together. Any exhilaration she feels once she reaches the booth is tempered by the fear of being discovered; any pride in her newfound comfort is as quickly dispelled by her realization that, in contrast to the women pressed against each other, she is now alone and freezing. Has she succeeded only in trading one misery for another? "The Camp Blanket" depicts the perilous nature of any "choice" in Auschwitz, choices that can mean the difference between life and death: the near impossibility, for example, of gauging the consequences of one's decisions from moment to moment or of imagining a genuinely altruistic gesture from a stranger. By first rendering the women's deadened humanity in the starkest possible terms, Nomberg-Przytyk heightens the incongruity of the ethical encounter so that both narrator and reader can rejoice in its very possibility, however remote.

The distinctive features of the ethical encounter itself forcefully draw the reader's attention. First of all, the encounter—albeit dialogue *sans* face-to-face—does occur one-on-one. Logistically, of course, rescue is more possible under more isolated conditions. I wish to stress that it is only because the narrator has secured a separate, isolated space in between the cars that the one-to-one ethical encounter can take place.

Logistics aside, the whispered exchange from within and without the booth appears supremely moral in contrast to the earlier scene. The benefactor has visually evaluated the narrator's condition and responds with exceptional sensitivity to [an]other. As we see, or rather hear, in their brief encounter, her language speaks to her ability to "read" the narrator's reluctance to accept the blanket. The benefactor first warns the narrator somewhat gently not to fall asleep, advice that proves impossible to follow. She then recognizes that she must switch to the imperative. Whereas her first courteous "Please, ma'am" seems an incongruous address considering the setting, the second "Please, ma'am" (p. 208) conveys urgency, imploring the narrator to stretch out her hand to take the blanket.

We need to pause to consider why the urging voice from the other world insists *"Please don't think about it"* (p. 208). Words offering warmth do indeed appear to issue from a world other than Auschwitz if only because one's sister inmates are the least able to extend help. Thus, the gift elicits disbelief from our narrator: "[S]omeone from the car *really* [emphasis mine] handed me a gray blanket from the camp" (pp. 208–209). Only someone who shares the narrator's grotesque world would know that she (the narrator) would have to "think about it," would have to second-guess the gesture: Is it a trick? What is expected in return? Will I have to reveal myself? Implicitly, the benefactor's voice is saying "Trust me."

It is not only the narrator who must "think about it." It is unlikely that the benefactor has acted spontaneously. We recall that the benefactor and her daughter possess two blankets and have been able to keep warm with just one. The benefactor has enough to share without increasing their suffering. Nonetheless, the extra blanket could be sold, bartered, or used as a bribe; certainly the entrepreneurial inmate skilled at "organizing" would definitely think about it before parting with a blanket. Any such reflection on the benefactor's part merely reflects the reality of the camp and in no way diminishes her compassionate act. In his study of altruism, Cordner (2002) notes that self-concern of this nature is "not only compatible with an ethical orientation, but even ... required by it" (p. 46). He also qualifies or modifies a Levinasian ethics [discussed previously] that privileges alterity so as to appear to preclude any sense of common humanity such as that which moves persons to come to the aid of others in times of tragedy. Citing the rescuers of Jews, he emphasizes that they were "not oblivious to differences among them. ... The point is rather that these differences ceased to be salient" (Cordner, p. 79).

The same could perhaps be said for the narrator and her benefactor except for the fact that they remain anonymous to one another. That the narrator asks if her savior needs the blanket returned, however, exemplifies the reciprocity engendered in ethical relations. The benefactor seals the fragile bond that has been forged between them with her offering of the crust of bread. This gesture, coupled with the narrator's liturgical chanting of "Your name, your name, your name" (*Anthology*, p. 209) and the benefactor's mysterious silence appears to confer a sense of the transcendent or to sacralize their encounter. This reading is not inconsistent with Levinasian thought, but in *The Female Face of God in Auschwitz*, Melissa Raphael (2003) offers an intriguing alternative in which this story

> evokes an elusive but providential divine female presence. ... The moments when God might just have caught the whisper of the first ... of her names were among women who offered care even when they had nothing left to give but the self they would soon cease to be. (p. 113)

In Goldenberg's (1996) estimation, "where giving comfort was criminal and caring was an act of courage," our nameless giver of blanket and bread, of temporary warmth and sustenance, exemplifies "gentle heroism" (p. 92).

"The Camp Blanket" is but one of several tales that depict the women of Auschwitz, who, in spite of being stripped of any sense of individual *self*, reach out toward others to create close friendships, surrogate families, and social groups in the blocks. These extraordinary attempts at human solidarity undertaken in the context of the death camp testify to the moral potential inherent in the individual, face-to-face encounter espoused by Levinas. For this reason, as I hope this essay has made clear, the moral apathy displayed in the railway car is all the more devastating an indictment—not against the women, but against the totalitarian regime that has tortured them. It is as if Nomberg-Przytyk resists perpetrating the same violence in her writing; she resists any move toward universalizing (totalizing) or abstracting what various inmates variously experience. As we have seen, she is equally intent upon portraying the conflicting demands of making moral choices and staying alive and on forcing her readers to examine their basis for judging those choices.

References

Améry, J. (1977). *At the mind's limit: Contemplations by a survivor on Auschwitz and its realities.* (S. Rosenfeld & S. Rosenfeld, Trans.). Bloomington: Indiana University Press.

Aristotle. (1947). *Nicomachean ethics.* In R. McKeon (Ed.). *An introduction to Aristotle*, pp. 347–352. New York: Random House.

Blanchot, M. (1995). *The writing of the disaster.* (A. Smock, Trans.). Lincoln: University of Nebraska Press.

Cordner, C. (2002). *Ethical encounter: The depth of moral meaning.* New York: Palgrave.

Critchley, S. (2002). Introduction. In S. Critchley & R. Bernasconi (Eds.). *The Cambridge companion to Levinas*, pp. 1–32. Cambridge: Cambridge University Press.

Goldenberg, M. (1996). Lessons learned from gentle heroism: Women's Holocaust narratives. *The Annals of the American Academy of Political and Social Sciences*, 548, 78–94.

Jones, D. (1999). *Moral responsibility in the Holocaust: A study in the ethics of character.* Lanham, MD: Rowman & Littlefield.

Lang, B. (2000). *Holocaust representation: Art within the limits of history and ethics.* Baltimore: Johns Hopkins University Press.

Langer, L. L. (1991). *Holocaust testimonies: The ruins of memory.* New Haven: Yale University Press.

Leder, S. (2003). Sara Nomberg-Przytyk. In S. Kremer (Ed.). *Holocaust literature: An encyclopedia of writers and their work*, pp. 884–888. New York: Routledge.

Levi, P. (1989). *The drowned and the saved.* New York: Random House.

Levinas, E. (1969). *Totality and infinity: An essay on exteriority.* (A. Lingis, Trans.). Pittsburgh: Duquesne University Press.

Nomberg-Przytyk, S. (1985). The camp blanket. *Auschwitz: True tales from a grotesque land*, pp. 132–136. (R. Hirsch, Trans.). E. Pfefferkorn & D. Hirsch (Eds.). Chapel Hill: University of North Carolina Press.

Nomberg-Przytyk, S. (1985). The camp blanket. In K. Shawn & K. Goldfrad (Eds.). (2008). *The call of memory: Learning about the Holocaust through narrative: An anthology*, pp. 205–209. Teaneck, NJ: Ben Yehuda Press.

Pfefferkorn, E. & Hirsch, D. (1985). Editor's Afterword. In *Auschwitz: True tales from a grotesque land* by S. Nomberg-Przytyk. (R. Hirsch, Trans.), pp. 163–181. Chapel Hill: University of North Carolina Press.

Raphael, M. (2003). *The female face of God in Auschwitz: A Jewish feminist theology of the Holocaust.* New York: Routledge.

Young, J. (1988). *Writing and rewriting the Holocaust: Narrative and the consequences of interpretation.* Bloomington: Indiana University Press.

Survival and Hope in Sara Nomberg-Przytyk's "The Camp Blanket"

Patrick Connelly

> *"If we do not learn how it is possible to act well even under the most trying circumstances, we will increasingly doubt our ability to act well even under less trying ones."*
> —Pierre Sauvage

Sara Nomberg-Przytyk's *Auschwitz: True Tales from a Grotesque Land* (1985) offers readers a grim yet compelling record of her experiences as a prisoner, both in the infamous death camp and during its evacuation. "But while she records unimaginable atrocities, she also richly describes the human compassion that stubbornly survived despite the backdrop of camp depersonalization and imminent extermination" (*http://uncpress.unc.edu/books/T-965.html*). Each story offers a snapshot in which hope and despair, belief and disbelief, the taking and the saving of life, and survival and surrender are juxtaposed. One such tale is "The Camp Blanket," a short narrative I have taught to my classes of Catholic sophomore and senior high school students studying the *Shoah*. Newly republished in Shawn & Goldfrad (*Anthology*, 2008, pp. 205–209), it is a perfect addition to any undergraduate or graduate school literature, humanities, or religion class as well.

Goals and Learning Objectives

One of my goals in teaching Holocaust narrative is to encourage students to read critically, reflectively, and empathetically. To examine students' shared experience of interacting with the text, I provide ample opportunity for them to convey their ideas and feelings through written expression and discussion. My class discussions require active listening with tolerance and respect for different opinions and with awareness of the variety of responses and experiences brought to and taken from the text.

"The Camp Blanket" helps me achieve other learning objectives as well. It humanizes the history by offering a first-person, eyewitness narrative by a young Jewish woman. It reminds students of the importance of being sensitive to the pain of others. It fosters an understanding of the consequences of indifference. It increases students' awareness of the compassion and humanity of the victims in the face of the brutality of their oppressors. It underscores the one fact that all students of the Holocaust should learn: Even in the midst of atrocity, selfless acts of lifesaving kindness, though few in number, did occur.

Child survivor and filmmaker Pierre Sauvage notes, "If we remember solely the horror of the Holocaust, we will pass on no perspective from which meaningfully to confront and learn from that very horror" (as cited in Roth, 1989, p. 250). My primary goal in teaching this story is to help students recognize and affirm the possibility of courage and the necessity of kindness even in the midst of desperation and despair. This goal dovetails with the mission of the school where I have taught for 22 years. As a Catholic school, we seek to foster the learning and implementation of Gospel values in our students. Curricula in all studies include some emphasis on the moral responsibility we as human beings have to help others who are in need.

This, of course, is not unique to Catholic schooling. The directive of Leviticus 19:18 to love one's neighbor as oneself is shared by Judaism and Christianity. Muslims are taught in the Qur'an, *surah* 2:83, to treat with kindness those in need; this is not so different from the "Golden Rule," to do unto others as you would have them do unto you. In Judaism, the Babylonian Talmud, Tractate Shabbos 31a, relates: "That which you dislike don't do to your fellow."

The Qur'an, *surah* 5:32, also states, "If anyone saved a life, it is as if he saved the life of a whole people." The same concept is expressed in the Babylonian Talmud, Tractate Sanhedrin 37a: "He who destroys a life is as if he destroyed an entire world; and he who saves a life is as if he saved an entire world." Teaching this story, then, can be effective in any setting that values and promotes caring responsible citizens and a democratic society.

I, like most teachers, lament the fact that there is never enough time to do justice to the topic of the Holocaust. Yad Vashem's e-newsletter for Holocaust educators reports that since the hours allotted to the subject usually are insufficient for comprehensive coverage, teachers often give precedence to facts and figures. However, "by using literature in the classroom, Holocaust studies can be translated from a massive historical process to a series of events that directly affected the life of an individual" (*http://www1.yadvashem.org/education/newsletter/english/fourth/main_article.htm*).

Short stories in particular help teachers, within their time constraints, to translate statistics into people, a must for Holocaust educators. Narratives written by survivors offer testimony and personal reflection, an enhancement to any history lesson. The rationale for teaching "The Camp Blanket," then, is well supported.

Supporting Materials

I have taught "The Camp Blanket" to my seniors and sophomores only after each group had a basic familiarity with a timeline of Holocaust events, and only after much study and discussion of perpetrators, collaborators, bystanders, and victims. My sophomores study the Holocaust as a unit in their global studies, English, and theology courses. My seniors have elected to enroll in my 10-week-long course entitled "Confronting Hate: Lessons from the *Shoah* for Today." My senior group benefits from their prior knowledge and from the luxury of an entire half-semester, so we can delve into wide-ranging aspects of this subject. Before reading this story, we focus, for example, on exploring the question Christopher

Browning raised in his book *Ordinary Men: Reserve Battalion 101 and the Final Solution in Poland* (1993): How did ordinary people become accomplices to genocide? We wrestle with Elie Wiesel's *Night;* we analyze an excerpt from a speech entitled "The Perils of Indifference: Lessons Learned from a Violent Century" that Wiesel delivered as part of President Clinton's Millennial Evenings at the White House program in 1999 (*http://www.americanrhetoric.com/speeches/ ewieselperilsofindifference.html*); and we confront issues of evil raised in the PBS. *Frontline* video *Faith and Doubt at Ground Zero* (*http://www.pbs.org/wgbh/pages/ frontline/shows/faith/etc/script.html*).

Following the story, I traditionally screen the PBS video *Daring to Resist* (*http:// www.pbs.org/daringtoresist/tgtranscript.html*), the story of three women who, each in her own way, fight the Nazis' genocidal efforts. The video recounts the intertwined stories of those who chose to act, illustrating the point that simple acts of courage and kindness can make a difference. We also read Simon Wiesenthal's (1997) *The Sunflower.*

The Right Story at the Right Time

I introduce "The Camp Blanket" at the point in the course when we shift from perpetrators and victims to resisters and rescuers, and it has proven to be the right story at the right time.

Though not *the* story of the Holocaust, acts of resistance in their varied forms and acts of altruism, great and small, are integral to the study. To understand what contributes to resistance and altruism, we investigate examples of spiritual, religious, and physical resistance throughout the ghettos and camps of Europe. We read testimony and history written by and about those Righteous Gentiles who saved Jews and by those Jews who were saved, sometimes by simple acts of kindness offered by total strangers. However, to understand what *inhibits* resistance and altruism, students must examine the concept of indifference. According to Holocaust scholar John Roth, "The truth about the Holocaust cannot be taught unless indifference is examined, and it is important to remember that from time to time, courageous resistance did save lives and did prevent the Nazis from doing their worst" (1989, p. 240).

This is certainly the case in the life of Sara Nomberg-Przytyk. The anonymous woman on the transport who gives Sara both a blanket and a morsel of food is clearly not indifferent to the suffering of another human being. Her act of generosity, selflessly sharing what she has with Sara, can be seen as an act of spiritual resistance, altruism, or both. It saved Sara's life, becoming then, as well, an act of rescue. Yet, until its climactic ending, indifference permeates the story. Its stark descriptions of apathy towards the sufferings of the Jewish women prisoners on the transport from Auschwitz to Ravensbrück are punctuated only by the cruelty and sadism of the Hungarians and Germans who guard them.

Getting Started

To begin the first lesson of this four-period unit, I distribute the story and ask students to read silently. Allowing valuable class time for silent reading in my short 41-minute period may be controversial, but I do it because I know that not all of my students will read at home. If class discussion is to be inclusive and meaningful, all students must participate and be informed. So, I make time for them to read in class. When they finish, I distribute a worksheet with focus questions, below, to be answered in their literature journals. I do not distribute the questions along with the reading because some students will simply skim the text looking only for answers to the questions.

- Document, by page number and paragraph, an example of:
  a. hope
  b. despair
  c. belief
  d. disbelief
  e. taking life
  f. saving life
  g. survival
  h. surrender
- How do the perpetrators treat the women prisoners in the story? What is the reason for this treatment?
- What is Sara's explanation for her and the other women's silence and passivity when sister prisoners are mistreated?
- Is extending a helping hand to those in need an act of resistance? Of altruism? Explain your thinking.
- What factors might have prompted Sara's rescuer to act?
- What can we learn from the fact that Sara's rescuer remains anonymous despite Sara's insistent attempts to learn her name?
- Where is God in all of this?

As the faster readers finish the story, they begin to consider the questions. Once all students have completed their reading, I ask everyone to listen and follow along as we reread the story, this time aloud, together. They would probably not read it a second time on their own, but two readings will ensure that students will be prepared to respond thoughtfully to the questions and will be more likely to use textual support during discussions. Hearing the story also helps aural learners, which is important to keep in mind as we seek to address each student's learning style. I identify which student will begin and ask that the reading shift to the next person in the row at each natural break in the text so the flow will not be interrupted by my calling on readers. They read, willingly and fluently.

Little time remains; I ask students to complete the questions for homework and be prepared to discuss their answers in class the next day. The seniors need no more direction than that, and what follows for the next two periods is impressive as they not only share all that they were able to take from the text but also connect it with much previous learning, always a great satisfaction to a teacher!

Maturity Counts

The lesson was more successful with seniors than with sophomores in my first attempt, perhaps because the seniors had much more background information and preparation for the story than did the sophomores. Their age, maturity, and experience, as well as an advantage of being part of an intimate, elective course where they all know and trust one another, provided a comfort level that was lacking in the sophomore class. I asked my seniors for their advice on using the story with sophomores, and I am grateful for their input regarding the discussion points and activities used in this chapter and with subsequent groups of sophomores. My latest experiences with sophomores have been far more rewarding than my first with this age group, and I am convinced that the story can be used very effectively in grades 10–12, even without months devoted to historical background, if the groundwork is carefully laid, the reading is focused, the questions are specific, and the class has been nurtured to become a caring community of learners.

Examining the Text

We begin the second class by examining the responses to the homework and documenting the passages easiest to identify, the taking of life and the saving of life. The Polish girl trampled as she moves to jump off the train, the woman who could stand no longer and so sits and is pounced on and thrown off the car, and the other women who were thrown off the car so the *kapos* would be more comfortable are the obvious examples of the taking of lives. Conversely, the anonymous woman who acted with kindness in sharing her blanket and food with Sara is the clear and only example in the story of the saving of life.

We move to discuss the examples students cite about hope and despair. Hopeful passages include the news that the Bolsheviks are getting closer, news that "caused wings to grow on our shoulders" (Shawn & Goldfrad, *Anthology*, p. 205). Zenia's whisper of a special company of soldiers sent to liberate the transport and listening for the echo of shots while waiting for freedom are also examples of hope. At the same time, the description of the terrible walk, no longer being able to tell the difference between night and day, and the thought "if we had to travel this way for any distance, no one would survive" (p. 206) reveal Sara's inner desperation.

Some students cite as an example of despair the plan that two young girls have to jump off the train. Others interpret the same passage as survival, while still others included it under belief, citing Sara's comment that it would have been possible to escape. Students soon conclude, in animated discussion, that hope and despair, belief and disbelief, survival or surrender are not polar opposites but rather interrelated possibilities along a continuum. Through shared responses, students examine setting, plot, characterization, and thematic elements of the story, rethink perspectives, and reinforce their growing understanding that there is more gray than black and white in the world of the Holocaust.

My seniors expand our discussion and connect the scene described in "The Camp Blanket" with their previous reading of *Night*, where belief/disbelief, truth/rumor, hope/despair all play a role. The atrocious conditions described—flatcars covered in ice, people squeezing in together, and the chaos of shrieks, beatings, and shootings—prompt a conversation about how one survives in such a state. My seniors make a further connection with *Night* as they turn to that text and discuss a scene (pp. 22–25) in which a character loses her sanity and is dealt with severely by others in the car. You might excerpt this scene or read it aloud to students to promote additional discussion in your class.

As we analyze the treatment of the women prisoners, we review significant descriptive elements of the story that lead to an enhanced understanding of the concept of dehumanization. (For an in-depth focus on this concept, see Rotenberg's [2008] essay in this *Guide*, pp. 224–239.) The description of the flatcars, "the kind that you ship lumber in" (*Anthology*, p. 205), of the crowding "so tightly that we could not even move an arm or leg" (p. 206) and of the exposure of the women to the harsh winter elements in an open, speeding train reinforces the fact that the Nazis treated the transports as cargo, not human beings. Sara observes that the escorts "did not even look at us" (p. 206); the soldiers refer to the Polish girl moving in the car as "louse" (p. 207) before beating her with a stick, leaving her to be trampled to death and tossed off the train. With no respect for life, women are killed and their bodies are thrown off the train by *kapos* to make more room "so they would have more comfortable accommodations" (p. 207).

Dehumanization often leads to the inability to respond as a human being. Sara explains:

> It was all part of the routine. In the camp, they were the ones that did the hitting, while we were the ones who got the beatings and who did not even have the right to defend ourselves or shield ourselves from the blows. That is what camp had done to us. It had stripped us of the capacity to make a human gesture. (p. 207)

To a person, my seniors express their revulsion and pain at the treatment of the women in the flatcar. Sandra put it succinctly when she said she had read about atrocities from many sources, yet she was still shocked, angered, saddened, disgusted, and scared that people were treated in the barbaric way described. After ample opportunity for others to share similar reactions, we review previous lessons that explored factors that influenced choices made by perpetrators to treat the victims so inhumanely.

Connecting the Text with the World

Earlier, I had shown the PBS *Frontline* video *Faith and Doubt at Ground Zero*. The documentary had affected them profoundly, and now they connect it to our story. We revisit the comments of Rabbi Brad Hirshfield about the perpetrators of September 11th:

> Evil. ... Is it inside of us? ... [O]utside? ... [I]f "outside of us" means that there's a devil out there who's ... orchestrating this stuff, no, I don't believe that. If ... "inside of us" means, can it ever be that big through the hand of one person alone? I don't believe that either. So I don't know if it's inside or outside or some combination. But I know it's ... the overwhelming destruction and disregard for the value of life. (*http://www.pbs.org/wgbh/pages/frontline/shows/faith/interviews/ hirschfield.html*).

On the same tape is National Public Radio (NPR) correspondent Margot Adler. She discusses an interview with Vladimir Putin who, in talking about Osama bin Laden and the terrorists, said, "We are as dust to them." She concludes,

> So maybe ... evil is ... when you ... believe in something so utterly that you lose your sense that a human being is a human being, when you feel that you can ... kill 3,000 people, and it doesn't matter because you are so focused on what you think is perfection and good. ... It's a kind of estrangement ... from your connection that these other human beings, the ones that are jumping out the window to the bottom, are just like you. (*http://www.pbs.org/wgbh/pages/ frontline/shows/faith/etc/script.html*)

The period ends as I ask them to respond to the following sentence in their journals: "We are as dust to them." We are all chilled, knowing the tragic results of dehumanization yet again, 60 years after Auschwitz.

Plunging into a Moral Turmoil

"The Camp Blanket" at first lends itself to a simplistic identification of good and evil. There is no disagreement in categorizing those mistreating the women or the woman who saves Sara. I caution my students, however, about oversimplifying matters related to Holocaust. As Lawrence L. Langer (1989) warned, "One is plunged into a moral turmoil that may silence judgment" (pp. 225–226). How does one categorize the reactions of those on the transport? We are told in the story that the German *kapos* murder the women and direct the Hungarian soldiers, the escorts, to throw the bodies from the train. The soldiers do this several times, simply ignoring both the barbarity of the murders and the intense suffering of the remaining women, and resume their conversation. How do the soldiers compare to the *kapos*? What are we to make of the silence of the Jewish women prisoners, including Sara?

In this, our third class period, Mike was the first to make the connection with a scene from *Night* in which, on the very first day in the camp, Elie witnesses his father being struck and remains silent. Wiesel (1960) writes that the guard

> dealt my father such a clout that he fell to the ground, crawling back to his place on all fours. I did not move. What had happened to me? My father had just been struck, before my very eyes, and I had not flickered an eyelid. I had looked on and said nothing. Yesterday, I should have sunk my nails into the criminal's flesh. Had I changed so much since then? So quickly? (p. 37)

Langer coined the phrase *choiceless choices* to apply to situations such as those the Jewish women and Wiesel encountered. Students learn to suspend quick judgment in such cases. We revisit Wiesel's "The Perils of Indifference." In this speech, Wiesel asks,

> What is indifference? Etymologically, the word means "no difference," a strange and unnatural state in which the lines blur between light and darkness, dusk and dawn, crime and punishment, cruelty and compassion, good and evil. ... Indifference is always the friend of the enemy, for it benefits the aggressor, never his victim, whose pain is magnified when he or she feels forgotten. ... And in denying [the] humanity [of the victim], we betray our own. (*http://www.historyplace.com/speeches/wiesel.htm*)

The students are quick to observe that the Wiesel excerpts from *Night* and from his speech relate directly to the question about Sara's explanation of the prisoners' response when others are mistreated. When the Polish girl's body is thrown from the train, Sara comments, "None of us said anything. No one could be found who reacted like a human being to this monstrous crime." She goes on to say, "Why did we keep quiet? After all, it was not fear that closed our mouths ... It was all part of the routine" (*Anthology*, p. 207). The class now understood well the reason for the dehumanizing treatment of the Nazis towards the Jews throughout their incarceration in ghettos and camps.

Resistance and Altruism

With our fourth question, about resistance and altruism, we return to the climactic scene where a woman makes the choice to act—to not sit idly by, to not remain silent or indifferent. She pleads with the dozing Sara, "Please, ma'am, don't sleep. It's dangerous! You will freeze" (p. 208). A second time, the woman knocks on the wall to awaken Sara, concerned for her well-being. This time she asks Sara to stretch out her hand, and she gives her a gray blanket she had managed to carry from the camp, leaving only one blanket for protection from the bitter cold for her daughter and herself. She also gives Sara a dry crust of bread, a morsel she had saved.

To help clarify the concept of spiritual resistance, sometimes a difficult one to understand, I distribute copies of "Faces of the Uprising," from Haim Guri and Monia Avrahami (*http://gfh.org.il/Eng/Index.asp?ArticleID=73&CategoryID =61&Page=1*). The poem is a collection of definitions of resistance; I focus on one: "To extend a helping hand to those in need—was to resist." We consider the definition of such an action as resistance.

"The woman on the transport, then, in extending a helping hand, resists," says Mike. Her choice to help, in contrast to the "choices" made by the other women to remain indifferent, by the *kapos* to murder viciously at will, and by the escorts to collude in the murders, provides much fodder for discussion about judgment and moral decision making.

Our discussion flows logically to the fifth question, the factors prompting Sara's benefactor to act. Without knowing what is in the mind of the woman on the transport, we can speculate that she may have been motivated to help as an act of resistance, the only one she could offer. We can conclude as well, as my students always insist, that "People in the darkest hour will help others!" I tell them that one of the teaching guidelines from the United States Holocaust Memorial Museum is to stress that just because something happened does not mean it was inevitable. I ask, "Was it inevitable that someone would have the courage to resist, to help, to save?"

Lisa comments that she is haunted by the scene at the end, asking herself, "Would I have done the same thing, would I have offered the blanket and food to the woman in need?" To me, her questions provide evidence of her involvement, empathy, and sensitivity. She has undertaken an honest assessment of whether she could have done this, fearing that she, like so many others, would not have. Her questions also underscore the judgment she has made about what *should* be done in the situation. Realizing that the "what would I do?" question is unanswerable, given the fact that we are so far removed from the situation of the women on the transport, we say instead, "This is what *should* be done." We also realize, however, that we don't always act as we should. Allowing students to explore these issues is of great value, as is stressing the fact that the only certainty is that there are no easy answers and no simple solutions.

This story can be a perfect introduction to *The Sunflower*. On the one hand we read Wiesenthal's question: "You who have just read this sad and tragic episode in my life can mentally change places with me and ask yourself the crucial question, 'What would I have done?'" (1997, p. 98). On the other hand, we have a provocative and fascinating response by Langer (1998) to the posing of that question. In "Wiesenthal's *Sunflower* Dilemma: A Response" (a necessary companion essay, I believe, to *The Sunflower*), Langer writes,

> I have no idea what I might have done in Simon Wiesenthal's place, nor do I believe that the question is a legitimate one. Role playing about Holocaust reality trivializes the serious issues of judgment and forgiveness that *The Sunflower* raises. (p. 181)

Langer offers alternative questions about choices relevant to our discussion:

> The vital question[s] to ask about this text … [are] why the SS man, as a young boy, … joined enthusiastically the activities of the Hitler Youth; … why he *volunteered* for the SS (as free a choice as a man could make at that time); why he then pursued a career in that murderous league of killers without protest; … and why he had to wait until he was dying to feel the time had come for repentance and forgiveness. (p. 185)

I found that encouraging deliberation of the construct of choice and the would/could/should issue during our analysis of "The Camp Blanket" helped reduce platitudes and facile responses in later discussions about *The Sunflower*. Even with my sophomores, who are not assigned *The Sunflower*, consideration of these central questions has challenged them to higher levels of thinking.

Examining Acts of Kindness

In our discussion about the acts of kindness in Sara's story, seniors Brianne, Sandra, and Justine highlight the importance of giving the dry crust of bread. Each claims that this act dispels any notion a reader might have that the helper was simply giving her excess, that is, she gave the blanket because she had a second one. Most others in the class disagree with their premise, arguing that no reader would belittle her gift even without the second generous act of giving bread, citing the harsh conditions and the absence of anything that could be categorized as excess. For them, and many of my sophomores, the gift of the blanket was enough.

All agree that the woman's generous sharing of the little that she and her daughter had lessened their chances of survival, of withstanding continued frigid cold and hunger. Furthermore, had they been noticed performing this act of resistance, they would surely have been murdered by the Nazis. While all appreciate the courageous, heroic behavior of women who themselves were imprisoned, starved, and abused, they raise questions about their motivation. Was the fact that they shared in Sara's pain, being in the same camp, on the same transport, a factor? What motivates a person to help another in need? In my senior course, we discuss "hidden children" and their rescuers. With this topic, too, there are no easy answers, no simple formulas about what would make one person help and another remain indifferent. Was it simply because it was the right thing to do? Does religious training or belief play a role in why one becomes a benefactor and another doesn't? Why were there not more rescuers? We note that in *The Sunflower*, in talking about perpetrators and victims, Simon asks, "Are we truly all made from the same stuff?" (Wiesenthal, p. 7). And what does it mean that, in the Judeo-Christian tradition, we have the belief of being made "in the image and likeness of God?" Is it all about free will, then, and the choices we make? I ask students to respond to these last three questions in their journals for homework.

Mary asks, "Why, in the midst of these extreme conditions, would someone help another, someone she didn't even know?" Two other students speak up, declaring that it was "stupid" of the woman to not give her name and take credit for her good deed. The sophomores, too, are amazed by the fact that the helper remains silent at the request for her name. Perhaps today's students are products of a culture intent on giving credit where it is due, reveling in recognition, where self-esteem and popularity go hand in hand; these may be reasons so many students are quick to dismiss the woman's silence as "stupid." What results is a wonderful opportunity to discuss what prompts "right behavior." Is it the fact that it is simply the right thing to do or is it the credit and attention that one gains from an act? Does the unselfish act then become a selfish one, given what has prompted that behavior? This could lead to study of rescuers' stories, like the flawed Schindler, or Christian families who sheltered Jewish children in exchange for money. Does the motivation behind the act make a difference?

Among some of the seniors who are puzzled by the woman's choice to remain anonymous, a much less dismissive attitude prevailed. It is clear that she chooses to remain anonymous given the silence after multiple requests for her name. Without being able to answer the question of why she chooses silence, they wonder what we can learn from this. Remaining anonymous may be perceived by us, the readers, as a challenge to do the same. It was not just that individual, not just "her"; rather, this personification of altruism may be seen as an allegorical representation of a model for behavior, of what should be expected of all of us as we act to help others in need. The anonymous helper is a contrapositive to the behavior of others on the train. My students extrapolate the lesson that being kind to someone a person doesn't even know can make an enormous difference. In this case, of course, a life was saved. This is a point agreed upon by all, even those who had earlier categorized the altruistic act as foolish.

Constructing Personal Meaning

It was this part of the discussion that prompted Lisha to share her journal writing. Lisha said she liked the story very much because it gives the reader hope. She insisted that throughout our discussions, we have all missed the point, that this story is about how God works through people to save. For her, the story is all about God. As a class of Catholics, we have dealt with this question of God in the midst of suffering throughout the course, so it was not surprising that Lisha would raise it here. Several students concur with Lisha, referring to Wiesel's memoirs and to his "Perils of Indifference" speech mentioned earlier, particularly the following segment:

> Rooted in our tradition, some of us felt that to be abandoned by humanity then was not the ultimate. We felt that to be abandoned by God was worse than to be punished by Him. Better an unjust God than an indifferent one. For us to be ignored by God was a harsher punishment than to be a victim of His anger. Man can live far from God, not outside God. God is wherever we are. Even in

suffering? Even in suffering. (*http://www.historyplace.com/speeches/ wiesel.htm*)

Yet how, why? Herein lies more unanswerable questions. At their request, I replay Rabbi Hirshfield from the *Frontline* video *Faith and Doubt at Ground Zero.* That students were able to compare situations from two sources spoke to me of successful learning experiences and supported my goal for the development of their critical thinking skills.

> Since September 11, people keep asking me, "Where was God?" And they think because I'm a rabbi, I have answers. ... I actually think that my job as a rabbi is to help them live with those questions. If God's ways are mysterious, then don't tell me about the plan. Live with the mystery. It's upsetting, it's scary, it's painful, it's deep, it's rich, and it's interesting, but no plan. ... [I]f you're going to tell me about how the plan saved you, you'd better also be able to explain how the plan killed them. And the test of that. ... [is] saying it to the person who just buried someone ..., "God's plan was to blow your loved one apart." If you can say that, well, at least you're honest. I don't worship the same God. But that at least has integrity. ... It's too easy. That's my problem with the answer. ... It's easy because it gets God off the hook, and it's easy because it gets their religious beliefs off the hook, and right now everything is on the hook. (*www.pbs.org/wgbh/pages/frontline/shows/ faith/interviews/hirschfield.html*)

Mystery: How else are we to deal with the question of God's presence in all of this, in Sara's situation in the flatcar? If, indeed, God were working through Sara's rescuer in the story, then why just Sara? Where is God in the face of the treatment of the others? Where was God for the girls who were beaten, killed, and thrown off the train? Haunting questions: mystery.

Assessment and Evaluation

Because school and its grading periods are a reality, I do assign a final essay on the story for the fifth and final class. The topic is purposefully broad to allow wide-ranging thoughts students may not have had the chance to express in class, and open-ended enough for me to evaluate how well I have achieved what I set out to do. I begin by commenting on the author's writing: "'Though Nomberg-Przytyk writes with remarkable detachment about her experiences ... she remains fascinated by the human personality, which was never before exposed to conditions so barbarously cruel. There is much to learn here about ... the range of human behavior' (Wisse, 1985, book jacket). Write a five-paragraph essay," I instruct, "describing what you learned about the range of human behavior or about anything else from our careful reading and discussion of 'The Camp Blanket.'"

I use rubrics to minimize some of the subjectivity in assigning grades for student writing. For the journal writing, I use a simple, 1–4 scale rubric; for the final evaluative in-class essay, I adapt one from the Northwest Regional Educational Laboratory's 6+1 Traits of Analytic Writing Assessment Scoring Guide (*http://www.nwrel.org/assessment/pdfRubrics/6plus1traits.PDF*).

I think it is impossible to evaluate objectively whether a lesson about helping those in need is learned, taken to heart, and practiced. Is the desired outcome for the student to factor moral responsibilities into their decision making? If so, how can this be measured? Is a desired outcome that students will perform authentic and spontaneous acts of kindness, be less selfish, and know that it is not enough to just be compassionate, that one must also act? If so, how can this be documented, assessed, and evaluated objectively within the parameters of a grading period?

The success of this unit can be evaluated, however, in tangible ways. How does one document success in one's teaching and in student achievement? I see responsiveness and ease in the flow of discussion, a measurable increase in the numbers of students who share their thoughts, insights, and reflections freely, and who are comfortable responding authentically to their peers. Sometimes they affirm, sometimes they politely disagree, sometimes they probe; their interactions with one another are respectful and tolerant. They are engaged and involved with the text and its essential questions of action and indifference, good and evil, God and humanity. They are speculating, reflecting, responding, learning.

I don't grade participation in discussion with a daily grade; I feel that such a grade may inhibit a student from asking authentic questions, exploring, and taking risks. Many will play the "school game" and perform for a grade at the expense of sincere engagement with the material, their peers, and me. Thus, I assess their performance instead by their daily attendance, eagerness to come to class, attentiveness, requests for additional readings, and the ongoing search for personal meaning they try to draw from our study of the Holocaust, measurable by their questions, observations, interpretations, and conclusions.

Success here, to me, is also about meeting my objectives for using the story. Students speak and write perceptively, sensitively, and significantly, explaining what they learned about inhumanity and indifference and their consequences, both during the Holocaust and today. They struggle to find textual support for their suppositions about resistance, altruism, and rescue, and they reference especially the values of selflessness and compassion.

The greater lessons, of course, are those that have an impact on the decisions my students will make throughout the journey of their lives, and it is only along the course of life's journey that these lessons may manifest themselves by engendering more caring, responsible citizens of the human family. "The Camp Blanket," I believe, offers an unforgettable story of a woman who chooses to come to the aid of someone in need, a paradigm of the way to live in this world. It is my hope and prayer that my students and I would exhibit that same kind of courage and selflessness when faced with a challenge, refusing the ease of indifference and choosing instead to act.

REFERENCES

Adler, M. The question of evil. In *Frontline: Faith and doubt at ground zero.* Retrieved October 18, 2005, from *http://www.pbs.org/wgbh/pages/frontline/shows/faith/etc/script.html* and *http://www.shoppbs.org/sm-pbs-frontline-faith-and-doubt-at-ground-zero--pi-1403901.html.*

Browning, C. (1993). *Ordinary men: Reserve battalion 101 and the final solution in Poland.* New York: HarperCollins Inc.

Guri, H. & Avrahami, M. *Faces of the uprising.* Retrieved October 18, 2007, from *http://gfh.org.il/Eng/Index.asp?ArticleID=73&CategoryID=61&Page=1.*

Hirshfield, B. The question of evil. In *Frontline: Faith and doubt at ground zero.* Retrieved October 18, 2005, from *http://www.pbs.org/wgbh/pages/frontline/shows/faith/interviews/hirschfield.html.*

Langer, L. L. (1989). The dilemma of choice in the death camps. In J. K. Roth & M. Berenbaum (Eds.). *Holocaust: Religious & philosophical implications* (pp. 222–226). St. Paul: Paragon House.

Langer, L. L. (1998). "Wiesenthal's *Sunflower* dilemma: A response." In L. L. Langer (Ed.), *Preempting the Holocaust* (166-186). New Haven: Yale University Press.

Nomberg-Przytyk, S. (1985). The camp blanket. In K. Shawn & K. Goldfrad (2008). (Eds.), *The call of memory: Learning about the Holocaust through narrative: An anthology,* pp. 205–209. Teaneck, NJ: Ben Yehuda Press.

Northwestern Regional Educational Laboratory. *6+1 Traits of analytical writing assessment scoring.* Retrieved October 16, 2007, from *http://www.nwrel.org/assessment/pdfRubrics/6plus1traits.PDF.*

Pfefferkorn, E. & Hirsch, D. H. (Eds.). (1985). *Auschwitz: true tales from a grotesque land by Sara Nomberg Przytyk.* Chapel Hill: The University of North Carolina Press. Retrieved October 18, 2006, from *http://uncpress.unc.edu/books/T-965.html.*

Rodbell, B. *Daring to resist. Women Make Movies. http://www.wmm.com/girlsproject/c483.htm.* Clips retrieved on October 5, 2007, from *http://www.pbs.org/daringtoresist/tgtranscript.html.*

Rotenberg, D. (2008). Dehumanization through the lens of the Lodz Ghetto: Rachmil Bryks's "A cupboard in the Ghetto" and Isaiah Spiegel's "Bread." In K. Shawn & K. Goldfrad (2008). (Eds.), *The call of memory: Learning about the Holocaust through narrative: A teacher's guide,* pp. 224–239. Teaneck, NJ: Ben Yehuda Press.

Roth, J. K. (1989). *On losing trust in the world.* In J. K. Roth & M. Berenbaum (Eds.), *Holocaust: Religious & philosophical implications.* (pp. 240, 250). St. Paul: Paragon House.

The United States Holocaust Memorial Museum. *Guidelines for teaching the Holocaust.* Retrieved October 16, 2007, from *http://academic.kellogg.edu/mandel/bartel.htm.*

Wiesel, E. (1960). *Night.* New York: Bantam Books.

Wiesel, E. (1999). *The perils of indifference: Lessons learned from a violent century.* Sunburst Creative Group, Inc. Washington, DC: White House Millennium Council. Retrieved September 18, 2005, from *http://www.americanrhetoric.com/speeches/ewieselperilsofindifference.html.*

Wiesenthal, S. (1997). *The sunflower.* New York: Schocken Books.

Wisse, R. R. (1985) in Eli Pfefferkorn and David H. Hirsch (Eds.). *Auschwitz: True tales from a grotesque land by Sara Nomberg-Przytyk.* Chapel Hill: The University of North Carolina Press, back cover.

Yad Vashem. (September 2005. *Teaching the Holocaust through literature.* Retrieved on October 18, 2007, from *http://www1.yadvashem.org/education/.*

Trying To Start Anew

Transformative Encounters:
Portraits of a Holocaust Journey

Abigail Gillman and Karen Shawn

Bernard Gotfryd's "An Encounter in Linz" (Shawn & Goldfrad, *Anthology*, 2008, pp. 213–219) is a first-person account of a young survivor's first few hours of his journey back into life from the hell of the Holocaust. Literature describing one's descent into hell, one's experiences there, and one's return, permanently but indescribably altered, may be perceived, according to Rina Dudai (2002), "as a rite of passage in which multiple processes take place in the forming and molding" (*http://www.clas.ufl.edu/ ipsa/journal/2002_dudai01.shtml*) of the identity of the protagonist. While only Gotfryd's *return* is the focus of "An Encounter in Linz," and of this essay, it is fascinating to trace briefly this clearly identifiable rite of passage in several other Gotfryd narratives in the Shawn & Goldfrad collection.

Dudai discusses three phases of these processes identified by anthropologist Arnold van Gennep (1960/1977). The first is "separation from childhood and transformation into adulthood" (Dudai, 2002, para. 12). In Gotfryd's "A Chicken for the Holidays" (*Anthology*, pp. 96–103), the narrator, though a teenager, is still a child. He knows that "to be caught without the arm band was punishable by death" (pp. 97), yet he has not internalized the concept of death; he removes his arm band and leaves the closed ghetto in search of a chicken for his family's holiday meal despite his friend's warning that what he is doing "is an insane idea" (p. 97). As he nears the Jewish cemetery, he sees "a military truck surrounded by people in uniform" and "realizes how insane" he was to be there but writes, "I wasn't about to turn back" (p. 97). He hears "a salvo of rifle shots" coming from the cemetery but cannot process what that must mean; when he "started hearing children's voices. ... a whole chorus," he "stopped and turned to look, but nobody was there." He adds, "I didn't think I was hallucinating" but can make no further sense of this disturbing scene except to underscore his child's view of his world: "It was eerie" (p. 98). He has not yet lost enough of his innocence to comprehend what the images show "through sound, context, and hindsight. ... it is obvious that the truck contained Jews who were herded out by SS soldiers and shot, perhaps even after having dug their own mass grave" (Levene-Nachshon, *Guide*, 2008, p. 164).

In "The Last Morning" (*Anthology*, pp. 131–138), however, such finality has become an actuality to him; his earlier childish daring has been transformed into an apprehensive acceptance of adult reality as he describes his neighbors' preparations for the looming deportation. "I couldn't bring myself to say good-bye to anybody; I feared that I would never see them again" (p. 133). He still "needed to cry" but was now "ashamed to do so" (p. 134) in the presence of his older brother. In hiding, he again hears "rifle shots"; now, though, "the cries of little children made me shudder" (p. 136). He imagines the screams of his desperate family; he is "frightened and burdened" with misgivings; again he is committed "to go on, not to give in" (p. 136) but with an adult's resolve rather than a child's bravado.

The second stage of this process of the descent into hell is entering "the liminal region, marked in space by means of a forest, a desert or hell. These sites stand for non-normative, unknown spaces, from which 'otherness' is perceived (like Odysseus in Hell)" (Dudai, para. 12). Gotfryd's forced glimpse of the deportation puts him at a point of conscious awareness for which he has no words and beyond which he cannot venture: "No dictionary in the world could supply the words for what I saw next. … All these years I've been talking and telling, and I'm not sure if anybody listens or understands me. I myself am not sure if I understand" (*Anthology*, p. 137). In the companion narrative "On Guilt" (pp. 139–148), Gotfryd's sister shares and confirms Gotfryd's perceptions of the deportation: "It is difficult to describe what went on that night," she recounts. "If there is a Hell, I thought, this is probably what it looks like" (p. 141). In "Kurt" (pp. 163–169), Gotfryd has already witnessed two consecutive deportations; his mother has been taken and his grandmother has been shot. As the story ends, he himself is "marched to the train. … Exhausted and hungry, I slipped to the floor of the moving car" (p. 168).

"The third stage," Dudai continues, "is the return from Hell into civilization. This reunification phase is marked by a new insight into reality. This process is occasionally perceived as rebirth, as an acquisition of a new identity" (para. 12). Thus in "An Encounter in Linz," we find Gotfryd on the brink of an utterly new existence. At the opening of this story, 24 hours after he was liberated from a concentration camp, he wanders the streets of Linz, Austria, thinking:

> As I had walked out of that hell I had promised myself to forget everything I remembered. … I wanted a new identity and a new lease on life; I felt … totally detached from everything I had once known. (p. 213)

Once again, as in "Kurt," a chance meeting with the "other"—in this case, an elderly Austrian couple—provides something of a foil for the complexity of his new life, his after-life, so to speak. Feelings of hope and anticipation prompt him to stop and chat with an elderly couple sitting on their porch—an impulsive act that itself is the prerogative of a free man! The couple invites him to tea and then to dinner, giving him his first cookies in over a year and feeding him his first meal as a liberated person. Initially, the site of the encounter is an oasis of hospitality, where Gotfryd's most basic needs for enough food and safe, clean shelter are met for the first time in years.

As one might expect, of course, there is a marked difference in the narrator's degree of self-consciousness as he moves from the telling of the earlier stories to that of "An Encounter in Linz," but in each case, encounters trigger an emotional transformation that is also a stepping-stone to greater ethical awareness; it is as if these were key episodes in the narrator's *Bildung,* his moral and spiritual formation in the early stories and his *re*-formation in the later one. As dramatic as is the contrast among the portraits of the naïve boy in "A Chicken for the Holidays," the fearful and grim youth in "The Last Morning" and "On Guilt," the raging teen in "Kurt" heading into hell in that cattle car, and the young adult survivor walking away from the hell of the camps in "An Encounter in Linz," so too are the psychological dynamics in the latter story radically different, though no less complex.

As part of this stage of "rebirth," Gotfryd speaks freely of his imprisonment. He finds the Gartners "understanding and very apologetic" though ignorant, apparently, of the journey to hell and back that Jews such as Gotfryd experienced; Herr Gartner claims to be "very fond of Jews" (p. 214), and the couple describes their own difficult wartime experiences, the rationing and long lines, and worst of all, the loss of two sons and a nephew who had served in the *Wehrmacht.* The couple invites their guest to spend the night in their son Horst's bedroom, and he doesn't hesitate to accept the invitation; he "immediately got to like the Gartners" (p. 215).

However, all too quickly, the space of nurturing is transformed into a danger zone, provoking intense anxiety but also, interestingly, a moral dilemma that the now mature young man is able to articulate and act upon. The transformation occurs when he is left alone in Horst's room. Two very different images hang on the wall—his own face as seen in a mirror, and a framed certificate welcoming Horst into the *Waffen SS*—and trigger a kind of emotional breakdown.

The use of the mirror in literature to teach, to caution, or to indicate the stages of one's life journey is not unfamiliar. In the formative myth of Perseus, for example, no one could survive a direct stare at the Gorgon Medusa but could observe it once removed, by gazing at its mirrored reflection. The metaphor suggests, perhaps, the relationship between the Holocaust itself and survivors' distancing narratives that only *reflect* its terror.

The mirror's purpose in Holocaust literature may be both literal and metaphorical, revealing a message and marking, as it often does, a transition. For instance, in Aranka Siegal's *Upon the Head of the Goat* (1981), a look in a mirror marks a young girl's transformation from child to adult as she is forced to accept the privations of a ghetto life that do not allow her the luxury of keeping her long hair clean. Here she confronts her newly shorn image:

> I bit my lips and listened to the ... sound of the shears as they clipped away my ... hair. ... Mother ... pulled a small hand mirror from her apron pocket and gave it to me. "Take a look. I think this length suits your face. It makes you look more grown-up, don't you think?" ... I relaxed my teeth and tasted blood. ... "I like it," I said to Mother. (Siegal, p. 153)

In Elie Wiesel's *Night* (1960, 2006), a mirror reveals the return of the survivor from hell into civilization:

> One day [weeks after his liberation from Buchenwald] when I was able to get up, I decided to look at myself in the mirror ... I had not seen myself since the ghetto. From the depths of the mirror, a corpse was contemplating me. The look in his eyes as he gazed at me has never left me. (p. 115)

Gotfryd, too, newly emerging from hell, peers into a wall mirror: "I had not seen myself since before the camps. Reflected was the face of a perfect stranger— gaunt, gray, wholly unfamiliar. I was shocked" (p. 215); seeing his own reflection provokes a profound sense of differentiation and identity. His own "unfamiliar" visage reminds him of *who he no longer is,* and at the same time, *of who he still is.* In the warmth and safety of this bedroom, his physical needs met, Gotfryd makes contact with his pure self, and he begins to mimic the expressions of his loved ones.

> I tried to smile and do imitations ... I made myself into my uncle from Warsaw. ... I stood in front of the mirror making faces until I ran out of characters to imitate and finally gave up. This was how I remembered my relatives. They became real; the mirror brought them back. (p. 216)

This poignant attempt to use a mirror to find and hold those lost to us recalls others; Urtecho (1967), for instance, writes: "When looking at myself/ in the mirror/ I see in my face the face of my father" (p. 15); and an anonymous Korean poet (translated by Pai, 1975) wrote, "When my father died,/ I saw him in my brother's face./ When my brother died/ ... I went down to the valley/ and sat by a pool./ There I saw my father's face,/ and then my brother's too" (p. 102). Like the poets, Gotfryd's mirror image reminds him that the prewar past, his childhood self, and the relatives he has lost are with him, body and soul.

On the heels of this discovery and others—that he has survived without becoming engulfed and overwhelmed, that he is able to maintain a life-preserving distance from the terrifying events that befell him— further details in the room intrude and have the effect of reactivating his defenses. Framed certificates from the Hitler Youth and from the *Waffen SS,* a photograph of a young man in a uniform decorated with the skull-and-crossbones insignia, and, stored in the night-table drawer, a packet of letters that Gotfryd feels compelled to read make clear that Horst Gartner served with the *Einsatzkommando* and not as a mere conscript in the German army. The safe space of the bedroom becomes a chamber of terror.

Gotfryd begins to fantasize that Horst is hiding and "might come at any moment to his parents' house. ...I was a nervous wreck. The slightest sound made me jump. I imagined all kinds of things; *I couldn't forgive myself for having been so truthful*" (p. 217; my emphasis); he quickly resumes the persona of a prisoner in fear for his life. He escapes early in the morning while the Gartners are out at the breadline, but he takes time to pen an excuse for leaving abruptly and offers his thanks for their hospitality. His commentary, "I was sorry to leave so rudely, but I had no alternative; to me they were part of a conspiracy, parents of a murderer" (p. 217), reveals an uncommon ethical sensibility—must one be so considerate to the parents of a *Waffen SS* soldier?—and calls to mind Simon Wiesenthal in *The Sunflower* (1997), who, like Gotfryd, meets the mother of a young Nazi murderer, now dead. Unaware of the boy's monstrous crimes, she describes her son as "such a good boy" (p. 95). Wiesenthal muses, "Perhaps it was a mistake not to have told her the truth," but he writes, "I took my leave without diminishing in any way the poor woman's last surviving consolation" (p. 94), just as Gotfryd leaves from the Gartners' home.

On his way out, Gotfryd spies silver candlesticks and a Passover goblet, leaving him mystified and angered about the mix of hospitality and apparent complicity with Nazi crimes that the Gartners represent. It is a perfect metaphor for the onset of the post-war period and the ethical dilemmas that arose around stolen property (or that given for "safekeeping" and never returned), many items of which are still being negotiated 60 years later.

The dilemma is ultimately resolved in Gotfryd's mind, however, as illustrated by the coda of "An Encounter in Linz." Two years after he immigrates to America, Gotfryd, having "still remembered their address" (p. 219), contacts the Gartners. We aren't told what prompts him to do so, but Wiesenthal asks the questions that Gotfryd's action provokes:

> What link was there between me, who might have been among her son's victims, and her, a lonely woman grieving for the ruin of her family amid the ruins of her people? I saw her grief and I knew my own grief. Was sorrow our common link? Was it possible for grief to be an affinity? (p. 92)

Herr Gartner writes back to Gotfryd at once, providing perhaps a kind of closure on the encounter, even a taste of redemption. Mrs. Gartner had apparently "suffered a heart attack when she had found out that their son Horst was tried by a Polish court and subsequently executed." He states that he is suffering from diabetes and "would be very grateful" if Gotfryd "could mail some insulin to him, as there was a shortage of it in Austria" (p. 219). Whether out of a desire to return their hospitality, out of sheer mercy, or out of "an affinity of grief," Gotfryd sends him insulin regularly. The survivor has reentered life and matured to the point where he can offer help to the father of his erstwhile enemy.

His gesture is reciprocated in turn. In the same way that Kurt came into his own as the "Jewish SS man" (p. 165), Herr Gartner, upon his death, bequeaths to Gotfryd the "silver wine cup and two silver candlesticks" (p. 219) in his possession. The fate of these objects—perhaps pillaged from a Jewish home, but ultimately restored to a Jewish home—represents the emotional and moral trajectory that leads to a reconciliation of sorts between Gotfryd and the Gartners. In this encounter, the rare humanistic impulse, the uncommon ability of each person to see the other, may mark one small and quiet step away from the sins of the past.

REFERENCES

Dudai, R. (2002). Primo Levi: Speaking from the flames. *PsyArt: A hyperlink journal for the psychological study of the arts, article 020127.* Retrieved October 16, 2007, from *http://www. clas.ufl.edu/ ipsa/journal/2002_dudai01.shtml.*

Gotfryd, B. (2000). A chicken for the holidays. In K. Shawn & K. Goldfrad (Eds.). (2008). *The call of memory: Learning about the Holocaust through narrative: An anthology,* (pp. 96–103). Teaneck, NJ: Ben Yehuda Press.

Gotfryd, B. (2000). An encounter in Linz. In K. Shawn & K. Goldfrad (Eds.). (2008). *The call of memory: Learning about the Holocaust through narrative: An anthology,* (pp. 213–219). Teaneck, NJ: Ben Yehuda Press.

Gotfryd, B. (2000). Kurt. In K. Shawn & K. Goldfrad (Eds.). (2008). *The call of memory: Learning about the Holocaust through narrative: An anthology,* (pp. 163–169). Teaneck, NJ: Ben Yehuda Press.

Gotfryd, B. (2000). On guilt. In K. Shawn & K. Goldfrad (Eds.). (2008). *The call of memory: Learning about the Holocaust through narrative: An anthology,* (pp. 139–148). Teaneck, NJ: Ben Yehuda Press.

Gotfryd, B. (2000). The last morning. In K. Shawn & K. Goldfrad (Eds.). (2008). *The call of memory: Learning about the Holocaust through narrative: An anthology,* (pp. 131–138). Teaneck, NJ: Ben Yehuda Press.

Levene-Nachshon, C. (2008). From the Gotfryd family album: "A chicken for the holidays." In K. Shawn & K. Goldfrad (Eds.), (2008). *The call of memory: Learning about the Holocaust through narrative: A teacher's guide,* (pp. 161–167). Teaneck, NJ: Ben Yehuda Press.

Pai, I. K. (1975). (Trans.). Together in me. Author unknown. In *Flight plan.* B. D. Stanford & G. Stanford (Eds.). p. 102. New York: Harcourt Brace Jovanovich.

Siegal, A. (1981). *Upon the head of the goat: A childhood in Hungary 1939–1944.* New York: Penguin Books.

Urtecho, J. C. (1967). Self-portrait. (Janet Brof, Trans.). In *Flight plan.* B. D. Stanford & G. Stanford (Eds.). p. 15. New York: Harcourt Brace Jovanovich.

Van Gennep, A. (1960, 1977). *The rites of passage.* Trans. Vizedom and Caffee. London: Routledge and Kegan Paul. Cited in Dudai, R. (2002). Primo Levi: Speaking from the flames. *PsyArt: A hyperlink journal for the psychological study of the arts, article 020127.* Retrieved October 16, 2007, from *http://www.clas.ufl.edu/ipsa/journal/2002_dudai01.shtml.*

Wiesel, E. (1960, 2006) (Stella Rodway, 1960; Marion Wiesel, 2006, Trans.). *Night.* New York: Hill and Wang.

Wiesenthal, S. (1997). *The sunflower.* New York: Schocken Books.

Elie Wiesel's Watch:
Transmission of a Legacy in Time and Spirit

Efraim Sicher

Elie Wiesel, who was deported with his family from his native Sighet to Auschwitz in 1944, is constantly returning in time and space to his hometown, and in "The Watch" (Shawn & Goldfrad, *Anthology*, 2008, pp. 220–224) he goes back there in his imagination. In *La Ville de la Chance* [1962] (published in English as *The Town Beyond the Wall* [1964]) or *L'Oublié* [1989] (published in English as *The Forgotten* [1992]), his characters also make fictional trips back to Romania. Why does Wiesel feel compelled to return to a childhood home that revives traumatic loss and to a town where few Jews live? Is he moved by some morbid curiosity to see if that vanished world of thriving Torah Judaism, that vibrant self-sustaining Jewish community, miraculously still lives on?

The return to the past, to a world that no longer exists, is common to a number of Holocaust writers who take us back with them to their childhood, which is remembered partially, and at best selectively. Aharon Appelfeld, for example, reinvents various fictional childhoods for his child survivors in his stories and novels. Writing brings a memory of what preceded the concentration camps and the harrowing journey through death, a journey which was generally innocent of prescience, since the Nazis kept the destination secret, though in hindsight any hope was delusory. We need to go back in time and space to prove that the survivor was there, that there was a historical reality in which everything—literally everything—was taken away and destroyed, leaving only memory that haunts the survivor's mind. If there is only one's own memory, one might well wonder if one was insane. This is especially true when Holocaust deniers claim it never happened and the world, which was silent and did nothing to save the Jews, is indifferent, or has forgotten. Moreover, if the traditions and heritage of an East European Jewish family have vanished forever, what meaning remains, Wiesel seems to be asking, in the survival of the Jewish people?

The watch, we should note, is both an actual artifact and a symbol of that treasure, the heritage of the Jewish people, conferred upon the boy when he became a bar mitzvah. He was then considered to be a Jewish man, obligated to observe the commandments and to be responsible for his actions. It is a coming of age, however, that is overtaken by history. Instead of being able to celebrate the festivals and study the Torah alongside other adult Jews, the boy in the story, like Wiesel himself, is initiated into a very different experience: Auschwitz. That experience of coming of age is described in *La Nuit* (1958; *Night*, 1960). It is a *rite de passage* into a mad hell where babies are burned alive and a Jew must struggle to hold on to his faith, to his love for his father, to the last dregs of his humanity.

"The Watch" does not expose us to those horrors. Instead, the watch serves as a keepsake, albeit a virtual one for the narrator, of what was lost and yet must be somehow retained. A watch is a timepiece. It measures our daily lives in terms of our duty as adults to fulfill the requirements of Jewish ritual that are associated with various times of the day. In this way, the watch indicates at every moment the responsibility of Judaism's moral precepts, as well as its requirement of diligence in study—from our rising in the morning to our lying down at night, as the *Shema* (the daily credo) states it. It is thus a suitable gift for a 13-year-old boy who must rise in the morning for prayers and know when to perform religious duties.

The watch measures another scale of time, too: the "timeless" laws of the Torah and the timeless existence of the Jewish nation, which spans centuries and continents. The watch will continue to mark that larger, eternal scale that measures the covenantal relationship between God and the Jewish people. However, when, under the Vienna Accords, the Hungarians take over the town, Jewish time is threatened. After confining them to ghettos, the Nazis order the deportation of the Jews. The watch has to be buried, along with the family's other valuables. As in Wiesel's *Night,* the family, like other Jews of the town, naively expects to come back home and reclaim their possessions. They do not know, indeed they cannot imagine, what awaits them. The boy cannot know that immediately following the deportation of the Jews, a mob will leave no trace of the valuables the Jews have so carefully hidden. We might reasonably assume the watch is, in fact, stolen, lost forever. Yet, it is not lost within the writer's mind. In his imagination, he has the power to do what he cannot do in reality: to regain time, to go back across closed borders and impassable historical time zones in order to search for this gift that has so much significance in personal and collective memory.

Twenty years have passed, but the watch is no longer there to tell the narrator what time it is. On a brief visit to his hometown, Wiesel is seized by an obsessive compulsion to retrace his steps to the garden of his family's house and to dig for his treasure. He is almost defying time, trying to exhume "time itself, the soul and memory of that time" (*Anthology*, p. 222). It is as if real time stopped at the moment of destruction, and what followed was a surreal nightmare. If we look at it in the cabbalistic terms that are familiar in Wiesel's work, we can say that in order to achieve *tikkun*, cosmic repair, time must be both regained and repaired.

A similar notion of the violent disruption of time and its recovery through the imagination, though seen from a very different theological and philosophical perspective, can be found in the figure of Menachem, the watch repairer in Primo Levi's *Se non ora, quando?* (1982; *If Not Now, When?* 1986). As Yaffa Eliach has observed, it is as if time were out of joint because of the cataclysmic rupture that the Holocaust has caused. Storytelling is the only way Levi can resume mastery over time and retell the story that was taken over by the Nazis. Here too, telling the story is a form of resistance to the Nazi conquest of Jewish time and their abolition of its festive calendar and traditional cycle (Eliach, 2001, pp. 24–26; see Sicher, 2005, p. 65).

We might expect the adult narrator to dig for his watch in his backyard and to be disappointed when he finds nothing, when he discovers that he has been transposing then and now, the "over there" of pre-Holocaust Europe and present-day America; or perhaps he is dreaming the entire episode. However, when he digs into the earth, his fingers do touch a solid object, the box that hides his watch. Perhaps we need to know that the treasure of the past is real and that it has a continuity in our present lives, that there is a secret knowledge hidden away. This treasure was spared, even if the burning bush of the rebbe's faith in Wiesel's story has burned itself out in the fire of the crematoria (to paraphrase Wiesel's parallel), contrary to the biblical account of Moses' vision in the Book of Exodus. There the burning bush signifies the eternal flame of the Torah and the eternal presence of the *Shechinah* (the Divine Presence) that accompanies the Jewish people, even in exile. And certainly Wiesel's own faith has not burned out but has risen phoenix-like from the flames of Auschwitz.

However, the watch has not itself withstood the test of time and has rusted, as one would expect if time has nevertheless proceeded along its natural course. The narrator is gripped by disappointment. He has been engaged in what psychologists call a *reenacting* of a traumatic memory in order to acquire knowledge of the past. He initially feels panic that the box may be empty and his search for knowledge might be in vain. Then, he realizes that the rusty, dirty watch is also a kind of survivor, a mute witness to its own story of destruction. He might yet get a jeweler to polish it and recover its "memory of the past" (*Anthology*, p. 223).

This is where the story takes an inexplicable turn, that irrational twist in Wiesel's stories when the survivor can give no logical or plausible explanation for his actions. He suddenly thinks of himself as a thief who has stolen something from the tenants' yard. He retraces his steps and replaces the watch. Perhaps, he reasons, he wished to leave something of himself, to wreak delayed vengeance when some child would later discover his watch. The child would discover together with the watch the story of the former owners of the house, a murdered Jewish family whose home had been usurped, as well as the story of the narrator's own childhood that had been stolen.

Yet there is a deeper, somewhat more elusive explanation. This narrative appears in Wiesel's volume of reminiscences, stories, and essays, *Entre deux soleils* (1970) (translated as *One Generation After* [1970]), a book that marks a quarter of a century since the liberation of the camps. The book, like the watch, marks the passage of time, a generation dividing the horror of history and the ambivalent memory:

> Children condemned never to grow old, old men doomed never to die. A solitude engulfing entire peoples, a guilt tormenting all humanity. A despair that found a face but not a name. A memory cursed, yet refusing to pass on its curse and hate. An attempt to understand, perhaps even forgive. That is a generation. Ours. (Wiesel, 1972, p. 8)

In other words, there is an almost unbearable conspiracy between time and history that defeats memory. If the instrument of time can be found, perhaps the memory might be preserved intact and oblivion arrested. With the first man on the moon, Wiesel believes a new era is dawning in which the systematic murder of the Jews ought to be inconceivable, but it is nevertheless the writer's task to be himself that instrument of time and to be a witness to the dark face of our planet. In a radical revision of the tale in the Talmud (Sukkah 28a) about Yonatan ben Uziel whose fiery zeal for learning the Torah scorched birds that flew too close, Wiesel says that this was a kind of burning bush and that the writer too may be burned by the flames if he gets too close to Auschwitz, the antipode of revelation at Sinai (Wiesel 1972, p. 16). Auschwitz may be a creative force for literary inspiration, but it can also be destructive. *One Generation After* asks how one can commemorate the death of an entire community and preserve its remembrance as something living and meaningful while remaining sane.

Wiesel concludes the story with the narrator's ritual reburial of the watch that has acquired for him such importance. The reburial completes the work of mourning for his family and for a whole community that was wiped out, with no tombstones to mark the loss. Having accomplished this task, small in itself but heavy with responsibility to future generations, he can come to terms with the past. In his mind's eye he can hear the children studying Talmud and the Hasidim praying at the time he was given the watch. The watch will continue ticking in its tomb, telling time beyond death. In telling the story of the watch, Wiesel has now passed on to us, across a generation, the transmission of memory. The town of his birth has become for Wiesel the face of time itself, the face of a watch.

REFERENCES

Eliach, Y. (2001). Primo Levi and his concept of time: Time of the gun, time of the spirit. In R. S. Kremer (Ed.). *Memory and mastery: Primo Levi as writer and witness*, pp. 21–34. Albany: State University of New York Press.

Levi, P. (1986). *If not now, when?* (William Weaver, Trans.). New York: Simon & Schuster, 1985; London: Michael Joseph.

Sicher, E. (2005). *The Holocaust novel*. New York: Routledge.

Wiesel, E. (1960). *Night*. (Stella Rodway, Trans.). New York: Hill & Wang.

Wiesel, E. (1964). *The town beyond the wall*. (Stephen Becker, Trans.). New York: Holt, Rinehard & Winston.

Wiesel, E. (1965, 1967, 1970). The watch. (Lily Edelman & Elie Wiesel, Trans.). In K. Shawn & K. Goldfrad, Eds. (2008). *The call of memory: Learning about the Holocaust through narrative: An anthology*, pp. 220–224. Teaneck, NJ: Ben Yehuda Press.

Wiesel, E. (1972). *One generation after*. (Lily Edelman & Elie Wiesel, Trans.). New York: Avon.

Wiesel, E. (1992). *The forgotten*. (Stephen Becker, Trans.). New York: Summit Books.

Living in the Shadow:
Bernard Gotfryd's "An Encounter in Linz"
and Elie Wiesel's "The Watch"

Dana Humphrey

No one recovers because nothing is recovered,
only uncovered and then re-covered,
buried again beneath the fruitless struggle to expose "the way it was."
—Lawrence Langer

The war is over. The camps are liberated. The prisoners are free.

For most students, the end of the war marks the end of their study of the Holocaust and their connection to its victims. Knowledgeable about the conditions Jews were forced to endure during the Holocaust, students often have no concept of the anguish confronting these tragic souls, many of them lone survivors of their entire extended families, once they were free. Students may believe they joined in the frenzied flag-waving of those whose countries were now liberated from the yoke of Nazi occupation and, along with other refugees, made their way back to their homes, friends, and communities, shoving memories of their horrific past into a dark corner and picking up their lives as best they could.

However, it wasn't that simple. Jewish survivors had no homes or communities to which to return; all were plundered, stolen, destroyed. They had no families or friends; virtually all were murdered. Too many times we forget this part of the suffering; we end our units of study in 1945, and we do not teach about the slow and painful piecing together of shattered lives that was the Jewish experience in the aftermath of the Holocaust.

Why I Teach These Stories

My goal is to help my students understand the difficulties faced by survivors in the years following the Holocaust. I want them to realize that the Holocaust didn't end with the liberation of the camps, that, in fact, survival afterwards was sometimes even more difficult than living through the war. I seek to make them conscious of the shadow from which survivors are never really able to emerge, a past that time cannot erase. Hearing stories of survivors told in their own voices allows my students to accomplish this goal; it is the most authentic and immediate way to understand the survivors' struggle.

Bernard Gotfryd's "An Encounter in Linz" and Elie Wiesel's "The Watch," in Shawn & Goldfrad (*Anthology*, 2008, pp. 213–219 and 220–224), tell of two survivors' attempts to come to terms with loss. Taught together, these stories, unique in voice and symbolism, give a name and face to individuals beginning life after the Holocaust and provide evocative parallels for rich and fruitful discussion.

I use "An Encounter in Linz" and "The Watch" in my eighth grade English class near the end of an eight week unit on the Holocaust, but the stories will engage high school and college readers as well. Through age-appropriate primary sources, memoirs, survivor testimony, and nonfiction text, students have gained a solid background in prewar Jewish life, Hitler's rise to power, and life in hiding, ghettos, and camps. They keep a reflective response log that I regularly read and evaluate. Logs not only give students a safe place to process and ponder new information and ideas, but they also allow me to monitor individual reactions and initiate conversations to guide their understanding. Eight weeks is a long time to teach this subject to young teens, and I take care that my material, age-appropriate though it is, does not overwhelm them.

I am passionate about, and dedicated to, teaching my eighth graders to look for lessons they can draw from the Holocaust. I want them to learn not only *about* the Holocaust but also *from* it, making meaning where they can. I want them to recognize that prejudice, stereotyping, racism, bullying, apathy, and fear of speaking out for what is right, elements present in our world today, helped to lay the groundwork for this genocide. I want them to understand that the Holocaust was not inevitable; its seeds were able to take root in Germany because people stood by and allowed it. English class provides the perfect setting for such a topic. Compelling and worthy of study in and of itself, the Holocaust as a unit also meets state knowledge and performance standards in communication arts (Shawn & Goldfrad, 2008, *Guide*, pp. 490–492).

Our unit's culminating focus, life after the Holocaust, takes approximately six 55-minute class periods. I use short literature rather than historical documents for this segment because the survivor–authors and their vivid first-person accounts invite students to become personally involved, providing bridges to understanding that history alone may not be able to do.

I begin first to focus their thinking by asking my students to respond briefly in writing to two essential questions evoked by the stories' themes, providing a framework to connect the text to students' lives:

- Can we ever forget our past?
- How does our past affect who we are?

Students write with thought and insight. Chrissie, for example, answered, "No, we can never really forget our past. It is as much a part of us as our arms and legs. Even if bad things have happened to us, we have learned through our trials and they have made us stronger. To forget our past would be like losing a part of ourselves."

Lauren agreed. "Knowing our past is what makes us who we are today. It's how we prevent our mistakes from recurring."

April noted, "Our personality depends on the things we've gone through."

Kameo concurred, explaining, "Our past teaches us things about life, and sometimes it defines who we are."

Using their words as a springboard, I ask students to reflect on their personal history and identify an experience that helped shape who they are today. In a think-pair-share dyad (Kagan, 1997), they briefly discuss the experience they consider formative. Then they write, describing the occurrence and how it has defined them. Volunteers share their sometimes moving, always perceptive log entries. I lead them to the story by noting that if their relatively normal and benign life experiences shape them, how much more so would a life be shaped by the experience of the Holocaust!

"An Encounter in Linz"

Before we read "An Encounter in Linz," I "front-load" the story by providing general background knowledge of the narrator and the setting to aid comprehension (Wilhelm, 2005). We note the date, May 6, 1945, recognizing that Hitler is dead and both the war and the Holocaust in Europe are over. Our story takes place after the Nazi regime was crushed by the Allies and the Jews were liberated, free to come out from the hiding places and camps they had been forced to endure. I tell them that the author–narrator was a Polish Jew active in the Jewish underground until he was captured and deported from the Radom Ghetto where he had been confined with his family. Imprisoned in six different camps, including Maidanek, he was liberated from Gusen, a forced-labor camp in Austria, when U.S. troops came upon it in 1945.

I show them a map (Gilbert, 1992) of Nazi-occupied Austria and the location of the camp. I think students should have some idea of Gusen (*www.gusen.org*) in addition to what they already know of the ghetto and camp experience; this camp's reputation of harsh conditions and high prisoner mortality may help them understand more clearly the narrator's thoughts and actions in this tale set just 24 hours after his liberation.

Most of the vocabulary is familiar, but be sure students know the definitions of *Wehrmacht* (Nazi Germany's army), Hitler Youth (Nazi youth organization), *Waffen SS* (military branch of the SS), and *Einsatzkommando* (mobile killing squads), as all are important to understanding the actions of the narrator. High school and college students may be assigned these terms to research.

I distribute the story, asking students to read actively by writing on Post-It notes questions, comments, and key phrases that strike them (see Olson [pp. 102–116], Fingers [pp. 246–261], and Boettcher [pp. 294–308] in this *Teacher's Guide*.) Such notes, which they will place next to the passages, are vital to their understanding (Harvey and Goudivis, 2000) and will serve as a basis for the next day's activity. Students work silently until the class ends.

Students Process Their Learning

In class the second day, I place students in predetermined groups of four and ask them to participate in a "write-around" (Daniels, 2005). In this process, students initial the left margin of their paper and, for a full three minutes, write a reaction to the story, using as a guide the notes they made as they read. I give them a 30-second notice to wrap up; they then pass their paper, without talking, to the next person, who will read and respond to it. The process ends when all members have responded and each paper is back in the hands of the original writer.

The write-around is thoroughly engaging, as students discuss the story in written dialogue. It provides a safe space for reflection and response to another's thoughts and encourages respectful attention to peers' differing perspectives, as evidenced by these examples:

"I liked this story. Trying to find a new way of life after the war seemed hard. [It was] certainly better than the camps, though. It was surprising how the Gartners acted even though their son served for the Nazis. They did seem like good people—they gave the narrator the wine glass and candlesticks in the end. B. J."

B. J. passed the paper to A. S., who added, "I agree, they were nice, but I don't understand how they could approve of what their son was doing and then act like they were against the Nazis. I couldn't believe a nice family like that could have such a bad son."

He handed the page on, and B. T. wrote, "Giving material possessions doesn't mean you are a good person, but I see where you are coming from. I also don't see how the Gartners could approve of what their son did and then act like everything was okay with the narrator."

K. M. had the last word; she wrote, "I agree with all three of you. They are good people who had a son who did bad things. Maybe they had no control over him. They were still kind to the narrator and, in the end, the narrator understood that."

Group work concludes with discussions of the write-arounds, and the class comes together. Now that they have processed other perspectives, I ask them to reread the piece for homework for greater understanding, again marking the text with Post-It notes, this time answering questions they posed during the first reading or noting new perceptions, and to write in their logs, focusing on insights and discoveries. The response log compels students to participate in the story again and prepares them for our next discussion (Kooy and Wells, 1996).

A Second Look

In the third class, again in groups, everyone takes a turn reading and commenting on response log entries. Thus, each student participates actively as reader, listener, and responder, gaining the multiple perspectives that collaboration offers (Wilhelm, 2005). April's response illustrates the efficacy of the second reading:

"After rereading, I have different questions. I wonder if the old couple read the letters from their son, and if the same nephew in the war was the one who sent the narrator the cup and candleholders. Now I feel sad for the couple and the narrator. I did not find the answer to my question of why the couple had Jewish items if they weren't Jewish."

As groups finish, I assign questions, differentiating learning by giving group-appropriate material. Whether they measure comprehension or analysis, all questions require the use of details and text support.

Group A

1. Why do you think the narrator stopped at the Gartners' fence? What drew him there?
2. Why do you think Frau Gartner invited him for tea? What prompted the invitation?
3. What is the significance of Herr Gartner telling the narrator that he "had become friendly with a number of Jewish families. He was very fond of Jews" (Shawn & Goldfrad, *Anthology*, p. 214)?
4. How do you feel about Herr Gartner comparing the loss of his family to the narrator's experience?

Group B

1. When the narrator looked into the mirror, he did not recognize himself. What is significant about this?
2. How does the mirror help him remember his family?
3. What might the mirror symbolize? Why is it important to the story?

Group C

1. Why was there a cold sweat running down the narrator's back as he looked at the photograph of the Gartners' son?
2. What is the difference between Horst Gartner's actions as a member of the *Waffen SS* and what his father believed his son did as a soldier in the *Wehrmacht*?
3. What do we learn about the Gartners' son from his return address: "*Scharenfuhrer* Horst Gartner of the *Einsatzkommando* of *Feld Post* at the *Ostfront*" (p. 216)?
4. The narrator is shocked that Herr Gartner appears not to know what his son was doing in the war. Do you think the father believed his son was merely a soldier? Explain.

Group D

1. Why do you think the narrator thought that Horst might be hiding and might soon come home?
2. The narrator felt the Gartners "were part of a conspiracy, parents of a murderer" (p. 217). Is he justified in this feeling? How do you feel about the Gartners?
3. The narrator imagines Horst following him and describes Horst's eyes in his photograph. "I knew those eyes ... that sized up the victim while they waited

for the kill" (p. 219). What does this tell us about the narrator and his experiences?

Group E

1. Why did the narrator feel he could not face the Gartners after what he discovered about their son?
2. Why didn't the narrator tell his hosts the truth about his leaving? Why didn't he discuss their son with them?
3. What is the significance of the clock striking? What might the clock symbolize?
4. What is the significance of the silver candlesticks and the Passover wine cup? Why do you think the Gartners had them? How might they have gotten them?

Group F

1. Why did the narrator memorize the Gartners' address before he left?
2. Why did he write to the Gartners two years later?
3. Why do you think he regularly sent Herr Gartner insulin?
4. Why do you think Herr Gartner left the silver wine cup and the two silver candlesticks to the narrator in his will?

Beyond the Basics

After 15 minutes or so, I project each group's questions on the overhead as representatives summarize their conclusions. Additional comments and reactions follow. These questions guide the class in an introspective exploration of the text, moving students beyond basic comprehension and facilitating analysis and evaluation. Students begin to empathize with the narrator and become aware of the difficult process survivors faced as they tried to move forward with their lives.

As an informal assessment and homework assignment, I ask students to respond in writing to the following, which circles back to the essential questions: "At the beginning of the story, the narrator states, 'I had promised myself to forget everything I remembered' (p. 213). Is this possible? Can he forget what has happened to him? Please use specifics from the story to illustrate your answer."

"No," Lauren wrote, "I don't think it is possible for him to forget what happened—the brain is designed to remember, not forget. He memorized the Gartners' address and, after he was in America, wrote to them. If he wanted to forget, he would not have done this. His past makes him who he is. I can understand him wanting to forget, but I don't think it is possible, especially if he now owns the wine cup and candlesticks, physical reminders."

Lauren's response indicates a connection; she empathizes with the narrator's actions and emotions. She realizes that forgetting the past and resuming normal life are not easy; she is beginning to understand the complex sentiments survivors battle as they struggle to move beyond their past.

"The Watch"

"An Encounter in Linz" describes Gotfryd's responses during his first days of liberation. Wiesel's "The Watch" is a dramatic illustration of how, even 20 years later, the author is still trying to cope with his experiences. A powerful story that shows that time does not heal all wounds, that memories can't be buried, it is a graphic description of the wrenching sorrow memories evoke for survivors.

Introducing the Narrator

On the fourth day, I begin with a brief lecture on Wiesel, using pictures, excerpts from his writing and speeches, and biographical information (*www.achievement.org*). I show a photo of Elie with his mother and sister, a portrait of him at age 15, just before he was deported, that famous picture of him in the bunks of Buchenwald, and of him today speaking, teaching, signing books—surviving.

I show on a map his home town of Sighet, Hungary, and explain how his childhood home became part of the ghetto in Sighet. I share with them his belief in being a silent witness, how silence in itself is a way of communicating, and I tell them of his discovery of the "kingdom of night" and how night has become a prevalent symbol in his writing. I do this to personalize the story, to give a face to the narrator, and because I believe students need this information to understand Wiesel's distinctive voice and the impact of the very private event in the story.

I read this story aloud. I find Wiesel's sentence structure and word choice to be difficult for my less fluent readers, and I do not want this to interfere with their comprehension. Reading aloud allows me to clarify passages they would not understand on their own, such as "the very day my native town became the pride of the Hungarian nation" and "the sorrow and reward of long years of toil" (*Anthology*, p. 220). I identify and discuss literary elements and devices in the story, such as rising action, mood, and personification. In addition, I can define what for my students is unfamiliar vocabulary, especially the religious terms, which I distribute on a prereading handout:

bar mitzvah: a religious milestone marking the attainment of a boy's religious maturity and responsibility at the age of 13; comparable to confirmation in Christianity

Torah: all the teachings of Judaism, including a legal and ethical system and a narrative account that begins with Creation; comparable to the Bible in Christianity

kaftan: long robe or coat worn by some Orthodox Jews

Shabbat: the Sabbath, from sundown on Friday until an hour after sundown on Saturday

rebbe: spiritual leader or rabbi; comparable to a priest or minister in Christianity

phylacteries: small leather cases containing scriptures traditionally worn strapped to the forehead and arm of Jewish men when they pray each weekday morning

prayer shawl: fringed shawl worn by Jews during morning prayers

Yom Kippur: Day of Atonement, the most solemn religious holiday for Jews; marked by intense prayer, introspection, repentance, and fasting

Talmud: compilation of rabbinic commentary on and interpretation of the Torah and Jewish law

Hasidim: a sect of Orthodox Jews who strictly follow religious law

incantations: a ritual, recitation of words

I read and ask students to mark the text as they follow, just as they did with the first story, looking specifically for vivid images, such as, "The ghetto was changed into a cemetery and its residents into gravediggers" (p. 220) or "I take the box from its tomb" (p. 222). When the story ends, the class is silent; I see they are both sad and puzzled, and I ask them to write their thoughts in their logs. Their initial responses reflect their inability to understand why Wiesel does not keep the watch he has found despite all odds.

Exploring Motivation

"I have lots of questions!" wrote Cole. "Why didn't he keep the watch? Why does he consider himself a thief? Why didn't he look for the things his family buried? Why did he go through all the trouble to accomplish nothing?"

"I don't understand why he wouldn't keep the watch," Chrissie wrote. "He needed it to cope with his past."

Ginny commented, "I liked this story and how he found his watch, but why would he put it back? Was it to forget his past?"

It struck Alan "as a story meant to bring understanding to the Holocaust—not the war or the camps but how the people felt and that they were truly leaving behind themselves, not just objects. It was shocking that the narrator's motives for taking the watch brought him back to leaving it." These initial responses indicate that students are moving beyond the literal text and seeking to understand the complexity of survival. To facilitate discussion, I ask students to answer two of the following questions in preparation for a "fishbowl" in our next class: (see Darr & Figg, pp. 271–284 in this *Guide*.)

- Elie Wiesel returns to his home in Sighet 20 years after he buried his bar mitzvah watch. Why?
- Wiesel writes, "All that matters in this town is my gold watch and the sound of its ticking" (*Anthology*, p. 221). What might the ticking symbolize?
- Explain Elie's comment, "I was laboring to exhume not an object but time itself, the soul and memory of that time" (p. 222).
- Explain Elie's observation that the watch was "the last relic, the only remaining symbol of everything I had loved, of everything I had been" (p. 222).
- What might the watch symbolize to Elie as he is digging for it? After digging it up?
- Elie's first thought is to have the watch repaired by the best jeweler in the world. What does this suggest? His original plan was to retrieve the watch and take it. What was he really trying to get back?

- Why is it ironic that he describes himself as a thief?
- In the end, Wiesel returns the watch to its original burial spot. Why do you think he does this?
- At the end, Elie Wiesel says he could hear "the tick-tock of the watch I had first buried" (p. 224). What might this sound symbolize?
- What do you think Elie means when he says, "Since that day, the town of my childhood has ceased being just another town. It has become the face of a watch" (p. 224)?

I print three to four copies of each question on individual sheets, making sure I have enough for each student to have two different questions. Students randomly draw questions and formulate responses as homework.

The Fishbowl

On the fifth day, the seats are arranged in two circles, the inner with three to five seats and the outer with those remaining. I give each student a copy of all 10 questions with space between each for written reactions. In the inner circle, I seat those who responded to question one. Students follow simple guidelines:

1. each student must respond;
2. no one may interrupt; and
3. no one may speak a second time until everyone has had a chance to speak once.

I read the question aloud; students have three minutes to address it. Those in the outer circle listen, take notes, and add reactions; after the three minutes, they may enter the inner circle and join the discussion for an additional minute. After four minutes, the inner circle disbands, and students who answered question two refill the seats. The process repeats until all questions have been addressed.

I collect students' notes and hold them accountable for participation. The fishbowl technique affords class collaboration as students construct meaning and make connections with others in a lively, nonthreatening atmosphere.

Reinforcing the Learning

Next, I show a segment from the PBS video *First Person Singular: Elie Wiesel*, in which Wiesel narrates this story. Hearing it from him touches students and deepens their appreciation of the literature they have just read. Now they see and hear the pain of one who—like the watch—survived, but who must live with the fact that his childhood, family, and the life he had known did not. As the segment ends, I ask students to reflect on their original written response after first hearing the story and to comment on their understanding now enhanced by the tape and the fishbowl activity.

Ronan says, "I understand why he buried the watch again, because every time he would look at it he would remember his family and the fact that they weren't with him. That's why he didn't keep it. He knew it would hurt too much."

Kara draws a parallel: "The watch and Wiesel made it through hard times, both of them, by themselves. As the watch became dirty and rusty, Elie had to endure the mental and physical pain the Nazis brought on him. The watch kept going, just as Elie did."

Students are eager to share their thoughts. It is an opportunity for them to express not only their reaction to the story but also their often emotional and empathetic responses to a man who cannot forget the images of the past.

"How is Wiesel similar to the watch?" I ask. This is an easy question now; the comparisons it elicits show a measurable depth of sensitivity and understanding:

- Both survived the Holocaust—Elie in a camp, the watch in the ground.
- Both appearances changed; both became worn.
- The watch physically tells time; Elie's memory records his time.
- Time has changed them; neither is as "shiny" as before; both need repair.
- Time did not conquer them, but stopped for them; both suffered.

We talk about the watch as symbol; students quickly recognize the metaphor of time and how it, like Elie's losses, can never be recovered. They point out that the watch could be repaired, but Elie could not. They discover a parallel between the watch ticking and Elie's heart beating. Time and living are clearly defined and separated for them.

Next, to further connect the readings, I ask students to return to "An Encounter in Linz" and compare Gotfryd to Wiesel. Groups are assigned one of the following elements: setting, symbols and symbolism, conflict, theme, and mood. Using a T-chart (see Glossary in this volume, p. 496), students compare the literary element, using details from the texts to support their findings. As groups present their parallels, the charts reveal comparisons that move beyond literal interpretation. They vividly show similarities the two survivors faced, the constant reminders of a past they are unable to forget.

For example, students immediately recognize that Wiesel experienced the same emotions of panic, paranoia, and distress 20 years after his liberation that Gotfryd experienced only hours afterwards. They understand the significance of the watch, candlesticks, and wine cup for the characters, seeing that the objects were part of each man's identity. They recognize the similar internal conflicts each survivor confronts, the daily struggles faced with varying degrees of anguish. They easily see that time does not change the effects of the past; time does not fade the memories for survivors.

Writing to Learn

For a summative essay, I ask students to consider the stories' parallels as they refer to our initial essential questions. I ask for a thesis statement, four parallels supported by text, and a conclusion about survival in the aftermath of the Holocaust. These essays allow me to see my students' understanding of the text as well as their emotional connection to the authors.

Our final activity is a different kind of writing. I ask students to create a "found poem" using Wiesel's evocative language or, if they prefer, Gotfryd's more concrete words. A found poem is created by locating vivid and powerful language from prose, extracting it, and arranging it into lines and stanzas of poetry. The language itself is "found," but the poem is created.

The results are powerful and compelling.

Skye shares what she "found" in Wiesel's writing:

Time

Tick-tock of the watch
The magnificent, gold watch
The first gift
The last gift
Curiosity
Obsession
In a dark, deep hole
Determined to keep its secrets
It too is a survivor
The only remaining symbol of
Everything I had loved
My past
My pride
I heard it
Distinctly
The tick-tock of the watch
The magnificent, gold watch.

Nick arranged words in a poem he called "The Tomb":

The Tomb

The ghetto
Changed into a cemetery
Its residents into gravediggers
Digging feverishly
Consigning to the earth
The reward of long years of toil
The earth would give it back
A first gift
A last gift
A magnificent gold watch
In a dark, deep hole
The earth would give it back
A magnificent gold watch
Defying all laws of probability
Survived
By accident
It is unrecognizable
The last relic
The only remaining symbol
of everything I had loved
Everything I had been
It contains nothing
Emptiness
Obsolete memories
An epilogue to my childhood
The earth would give it back.

From Gotfryd's piece, Avery found "I Remembered":

I Remembered

I promised myself:
Forget everything
I wanted a new identity
A new lease on life
I remembered
I felt at a loss
Totally detached
Faint images
Strange faces
I felt as if I were in a dream
I remembered
A perfect stranger
Gaunt
Gray
Wholly unfamiliar
I remembered
I was shaking with rage
It was unforgivable
I remembered.

After the writers present their poems, we display them on a bulletin board to honor not only Gotfryd and Wiesel but all survivors. They are a reminder of precious time that has been lost and can never be recaptured, a reminder that life, for survivors, did not pick up where it left off when the Holocaust swept them up in its fury, a reminder that lives are not like watches that can be polished, rewound, and continue as if nothing ever happened.

Students see the painful, parallel experiences of the narrators and have moved toward understanding the difficulties survivors face each day. They realize, as Fern Schumer Chapman (2000) observes in *Motherland*, that a survivor is "like an amputee who still feels her toes" (p. xi). They recognize the powerful aftermath of the Holocaust and the burden of memory from which survivors are never free. These stories have touched my students, who, I know, will seek to learn more about survivors and the event that has so profoundly shaped them and, still today, shadows their lives.

REFERENCES

Boettcher, L. (2008). Two tales of protection: "Kurt" and "Helmut Reiner": Altruism or opportunism? In K. Shawn & K. Goldfrad. (Eds.). *The call of memory: Learning about the Holocaust through narrative: A teacher's guide*, pp. 294–308. Teaneck, NJ: Ben Yehuda Press.

Chapman, F. S. (2000). *Motherland*. New York: Penguin Books.

Daniels, H. (2005). NCTE Convention Program. Pittsburgh, November 20.

Darr, L. & Figg, B. (2008). Compromising one's morality in times of crisis: Ida Fink's "A conversation" and "Aryan papers." In K. Shawn & K. Goldfrad (Eds.). *The call of memory: Learning about the Holocaust through narrative: A teacher's guide*, pp. 271–284. Teaneck, NJ: Ben Yehuda Press.

Fingers, D. E. (2008). Living with loss: Bernard Gotfryd's "The last morning" and "On guilt." In K. Shawn & K. Goldfrad (Eds.). *The call of memory: Learning about the Holocaust through narrative: A teacher's guide*, pp. 246–261. Teaneck, NJ: Ben Yehuda Press.

Gilbert, M. (1992). *Atlas of the Holocaust*. New York: William Morrow and Company.

Gotfryd, B. (2000). An encounter in Linz. In K. Shawn & K. Goldfrad (2008). (Eds.). *The call of memory: Learning about the Holocaust through narrative: An anthology*, pp. 213–219. Teaneck, NJ: Ben Yehuda Press.

Harvey, S. & Goudivis, A. (2000). *Strategies that work*. Portland, ME: Stenhouse Publishers.

Kagen, S. (1997). *Cooperative learning*. San Clemente, CA: Resources for Teachers

Kooy, M. & Wells, J. (1996). *Reading response logs*. Portsmouth, NH: Heinemann.

Langer, L. L. (1995). *Admitting the Holocaust: Collected essays*. New York: Oxford University Press. 15.

Olson, C. (2008). Ordinary people, untold stories: Ida Fink's "The end" and "The threshold." In K. Shawn & K. Goldfrad (Eds.). *The call of memory: Learning about the Holocaust through narrative: A teacher's guide*, pp. 102–116. Teaneck, NJ: Ben Yehuda Press.

Public Broadcasting Service. (2002). *First person singular: Elie Wiesel*.

Shawn, K. & Younglove, W. (2008). State standards and student learning objectives. In K. Shawn & K. Goldfrad (Eds.), *The call of memory: Learning about the Holocaust through narrative: A teacher's guide*, pp. 490–492. Teaneck, NJ: Ben Yehuda Press.

Wiesel, E. (1965). The watch. In K. Shawn & K. Goldfrad (2008). (Eds.). *The call of memory: Learning about the Holocaust through narrative: An anthology*, pp. 220–224. Teaneck, NJ: Ben Yehuda Press.

Wilhelm, J. (2005). *Inquiring minds learn to read*. New York: Scholastic.

Retrieved August 13, 2007, from *www.achievement.org*.

Retrieved August 13, 2007, from *www.gusen.org*.

Memory as Accomplice to History: Trauma and Narrative in Elie Wiesel's "An Old Acquaintance"

Victoria Aarons

Can one die in Auschwitz, after Auschwitz?
—Elie Wiesel

Elie Wiesel's short story "An Old Acquaintance" (Shawn & Goldfrad, 2008, *Anthology*, pp. 225–237) opens with a seemingly ordinary set of circumstances: a man riding on a bus through the streets of Tel Aviv shortly after the liberation of the camps on an otherwise unremarkable summer evening.

This opening scene, however, is anything but ordinary. For the story's narrator, an anonymous passenger traveling by bus to an undisclosed destination, the seemingly mundane and benign movement of the bus as it navigates the crowded streets of Tel Aviv becomes unbearable. The characteristic heat of the sultry summer day produces not the usual sedative, hypnotic effect one might expect. Instead, the heat claws; the atmosphere is stifling, oppressive, so much so that the very air is suffocating, requiring, as the narrator complains, "immense effort" (p. 225) just to breathe.

As the bus moves through the busy thoroughfare, the narrator's anxiety increases, and ordinary sensations are heightened, elongated, and strangely distorted. The heat closes in on him, "weighs on every gesture and breath, blurs every image" (p. 225). The narrator's reiterative focus on the heat, on the piercing bodily and psychic sensations that it generates, is, by contrast, painfully compressed into the sharp, slicing language of the narrative. His words are abrupt, halting and punctuated; such terse expression seems to arrest the very movement of the bus: "slower and slower and soon it will come to a standstill" (p. 225). The landscape itself, both inside and outside the bus, is aggressive, and the heat "insinuates itself into every pore" (p. 225). As the bus drags itself through the sweltering streets, the narrator can barely contain the apprehension, anxiety, and dread that he so acutely feels.

In an attempt to distract himself from the constricting heat and from his escalating discomfort, the narrator plays a game in which he randomly chooses another passenger on the bus with whom he establishes a "mute exchange" (p. 225). He silently studies him, arranging his life, imagining his occupation, his disposition, and his character. It is, admittedly, the narrator's favorite game, one he's played many times before. However, here, it's a game that proves dangerous, for, in the oppressive heat of the bus, a heat that distorts his vision, this pastime is suddenly no longer a mere diversion.

The game finally will be the source of the narrator's undoing, because it takes on the illusion of reality. As he studies the other passenger, with a sudden clarity born of increasing apprehension, the narrator believes himself to know the man whose being he conjures. With chilling and utter conviction, he believes himself to recognize this anonymous and otherwise inconspicuous passenger. He sees in this man his tormentor, a Jewish barracks-chief in Monovitz-Buna, one of the forced labor sub-camps in Auschwitz, the concentration camp where, in another time and place, the narrator had been imprisoned. At this singular moment of recognition, the bus is hideously transformed, and the narrator's destination, previously undisclosed, is now in fantasy revealed. As the stifling, claustrophobic heat closes in on him, cutting off his attempt to breathe, the bus becomes a cattle car delivering the narrator back in time to a reenactment of the trauma that he is compelled endlessly to repeat.

The bus, a graveyard site of memory reawakened, transports the narrator back to a place of the dead, and it's a memory upon which he cannot entirely depend. As the narrator finds himself losing control, the forward movement of the bus seems to reverse itself, thrusting him into a past from which he believes himself to have escaped. Liberated from the camps, the narrator, in exile in a fledgling country, remains anonymous, isolated by his sense of foreboding from the other faceless passengers, who "read the newspaper, chat, scan the advertisements for wines, shaving creams, cigarettes" (p. 225).

For the narrator, however, this ordinary bus, no more than a means of public transit and so commonplace as to render itself invisible, becomes a hostile and menacing space. The narrator is assaulted by a memory so palpable as to transport him back to a place from which there is no escape, the instant made all the more disturbing because of the ordinariness of the conditions that take him there. The haze and claustrophobia on the bus establish an atmosphere of unreality, dragging the narrator under, plunging him, as he fears, "into the void" (p. 225). Ferried by a pragmatic and single-minded Israeli Charon, the bus carries him back to hell, and the narrator can't resist passage, can't control the uncontainable panic that paralytically keeps him on the bus. We are meant to understand that for the narrator, a survivor of the Holocaust, there can never again be anything "normal." To be sure, outside the bus lies the city, "so close," and yet "so unreal" (p. 230), but the world taking place outside the windows of the bus is not the world in which he psychically resides.

Wiesel encases his narrator in a moment frozen in time and contained in a private, individualized space, the occasion of this survivor's traumatic experience. Both conditions—freezing time and creating an isolated stage upon which the trauma is played out—are characteristic conceits in Wiesel's writing. Typically in his Holocaust narratives, time is arrested; no longer linearly unfolding, time stops at those moments of discovery, moments of reawakened traumatic memory.

In such moments, past and present coalesce, and the reality of the external world gives way. In such moments, time is transformed; so too, quite radically, is place.

As the narrator of "An Old Acquaintance" reveals at the instant of his supposed recognition of the man from the camps, "the time changes pace, country" (p. 226). Memory takes him back in time and in place, and he and the man on the bus seem to share this space alone. As the bus becomes a cattle car, carrying the narrator again to the place of his undoing, he finds himself psychically transported to the concentration camp where he was subjected to the cruelty of the barracks-chief. However, as Wiesel makes clear, memory is slippery, deceptive, distorted by ambiguities arising from the trauma, altered both by the defenses of forgetting and by the impossibility of doing so.

The narrator's conviction that he knows the man on the bus to be the perpetrator of his suffering is curiously framed. Wiesel makes his recognition of the man too sudden, too overly determined, as if the narrator is relieved that he has found a specific target upon which to displace his anger and thus focus his debilitating anxiety, and it is not at all clear that the barracks-chief on the bus exists anywhere outside of the narrator's ruined imagination. There is, as we find here and elsewhere in Wiesel's Holocaust narratives, no stable shape to memory. Instead, memory exists in shards, fragments, the sharp pieces of an abused past, recalled by chance encounters, random occasions and events when one least expects them. Unprotected ultimately by repression, the narrator is ambushed by memory and held captive by past trauma. It's a quietly insinuating ambush of memory that shows itself symptomatically in the narrator's uncontrollable disorientation and uncontainable and irrational dread.

This, then, is why the narrator of "An Old Acquaintance" must create a narrative of the man on the bus. His initial effort to control his immoderate and phobic response by displacing his anxiety onto the bus driver fails. The driver symbolizes the control that the narrator lacks; it is, after all, the one at the wheel who is in charge of navigating the bus. He alone will determine its destination. In the rising tide of the narrator's fear of entrapment, the bus seems to stop its progress. He wants to get off the bus, to flee from his fear, but he can't bring himself to move, and so blames the driver for his own paralysis. Because it is, after all, the driver who sets the terms of the passage, and "the doors do not open until the bus comes to a complete stop" (p. 225), the narrator suspiciously fixates on the driver, believing that the driver is the sole obstacle to his exit. In doing so, the narrator projects his unease onto the driver in order to free himself from it: "Useless to argue: the driver's nerves are up to anything. Not mine" (p. 225). His unnecessary protests—"Not mine"—reveal his futile attempts to will his own agency, undermined by his conscious efforts to do so. However, such displacement fails to alleviate his discomfort and anger at his own helplessness because he cannot control the driver. In other words, his transference fails. Because the driver is aloof and in control, the narrator cannot know anything about the driver's motivations and intentions and thus cannot displace or transfer his fantasies onto him. As a result of the failed transference, the narrator responds with aggressive resentment toward the driver, but such a response only increases his vulnerability and reminds him all the more that he cannot control his situation.

In an effort to curb his rising panic and gain some control over his escalating anxiety, the narrator turns his attention from the bus driver to himself, as he now begins to manufacture a set of circumstances that he believes himself capable of controlling. After all, the game he has been playing with the unsuspecting passenger on the bus is *his* game, a scenario in which he alone invents, assesses, and passes judgment on the character of this other man. The narrator's assessment smugly exposes the other traveler's failings, his weakness, and, indeed, his utter banality: "Easy to classify ... anonymous ... avoiding extremes, responsibilities ... takes orders only to transmit them ... not at the top of the ladder nor ... at the bottom" (pp. 225–226). In writing the script of this other man's life, the narrator sets the terms of the relationship, a condition he was unable to achieve earlier in relation to the bus driver. Here, rather, the narrator can strip this banal man of his anonymity; but in doing so, he finds that he knows this fellow all too well or at least knows his "type." His memory is a liability, so vivid as to replace the present with the past.

Significantly, as the narrator fixates on this one fellow passenger, all others on the bus blur; they move aside, readying the stage for the contest that will ensue. In focusing exclusively on this sole passenger, the object of his scrutiny, the narrator blocks out everything else around him. His attention, focused microscopically on this one man, is excessive. It is as if they are in a kind of hiatus alone together, a space inhabited only by the two of them, not only the physical space of the bus, but the psychic space as well. Their proximity is appropriate, for as the narrator projects the other man's life and character, his growing identification with this man becomes increasingly obvious. Indeed, it's clear that the narrator has selected this particular man because, unconsciously, he reminds him all too acutely of himself.

This is no chance encounter, at least not psychologically, though it is, of course, by the "rules" of ordinary life. As the language of identification grows, it is no longer clear whether the narrator is describing himself or the other man. The narrator's phobia surfaces as a split self, a condition in which he becomes the other, the object of his seemingly detached reflection. Although initially defended by his sense that, if he controls the narrative, he will maintain the necessary separation between them, he comes to recognize himself in the other and the other in himself. His aggressive, menacing posture toward the other man becomes his own self-hatred and disgust manically revealed. In his obsessive fixation on the other man, the narrator not only identifies with him, but becomes him; that is, he freely assumes his character:

> I put myself in his place. ... I am the one his wife will greet with love or rancor; the one who will drown my resentment in sleep or in solitary drinking; the one my friends betray and my subordinates detest; the one who has wasted my life and now it is too late to begin again. (p. 226)

Indeed, he does not resist the temptation to step into the other man's life. The narrator all too willingly assumes the posture of the unwitting target of his attentions: "I think and dream like him" (p. 226), the unconscious identification with the object of his desire. Were he to become the other man, then their roles would be indelibly reversed, victim becoming victimizer, revealing the narrator's desire to revise the narrative and thereby rewrite his history. In such a transfer of identities, the man on the bus becomes the narrator's resistant double, the man a projected image of the narrator himself. The narrator's identification with the object of his fixation exposes a complex web of motives that are entirely unclear to him.

Significantly, it is the point at which the narrator assumes the identity of the other man, or rather, sees himself in the other man, that the moment of recognition takes place. His increasingly narrowed scrutiny of the other is finally reduced to a pinpoint of despair, for, in the instant at which the narrator remembers the man on the bus, "the present is in the grip of all the years black and buried" (p. 226). The narrator cannot dismiss the other man, for to do so would be to exonerate himself from his own guilt at not having fought back, or, conversely, to succumb to the depths of his terror and self-loathing. It is only in the relationship between the two men that both lose their anonymity, and that their personal destination and assignation, previously hidden, are now clear. Despite the narrator's many defenses, he is transformed by his treacherous memories of the camps, and while the narrator ascribes the fear of such memories to the other man, it is clear that it is the narrator himself who is deeply apprehensive of "thinking … memories … words" (p. 226). Indeed, what emerges throughout the unfolding of the narrative is undisguised terror, his anxiety now out of control, so much so that he is transported back in time to the place of his despair and overwhelming fear.

Up until this point, what transpires between them has been, as the narrator puts it, an entirely "mute exchange" (p. 225). Ironically, however, the silence has only been external, for the narrator's growing anxiety has created a kind of cacophonous, internal noise, which is a reflection of the phobic reaction that he has tried to contain through the creation of an imaginary narrative. However, as the language of the narrative reveals, it is, in large part, his own character that he has been describing. We are alerted to this early on when Wiesel makes the narrative "I" emphatic. In doing so, Wiesel has constructed an unreliable narrator, one whose perceptions we cannot entirely trust, and this unreliability causes our initial confusion. We want to believe that the man on the bus is the barracks-chief, because if he is, then a scene is constructed in which justice might be meted out, crimes addressed; but there has been a nagging sense from the very beginning that the man the narrator sees and selects for his attention is not the barracks-chief. Wiesel's careful construction of the opening scene, the narrator's claustrophobic obsession with the heat and his desperate attempts to control his ever-increasing anxiety, places him at a remove and thus makes the narrator the object of our attention. It is important that the story is told in first-person narration, for we see the events as they unfold entirely from the narrator's limited perspective, and his perceptions have been skewed from the very start by the heat, which inflames him and blurs his vision.

Typically with an unreliable narrator, the more he talks, the more his unreliability is evident. The narrator has designed a one-way interlocution, but his obsessive words give him away. Wiesel intentionally makes ambiguous the circumstances of the confrontation. Does the narrator speak to the man on the bus so that the man and other passengers can hear him, or is this an internalized monologue only? The ambiguity is amplified because the narrator "speaks" uninterruptedly, whether silently or aloud. The reader overhears his speech, but isn't told who else hears it. Indeed, the narrator tells us that the other man "does not hear. He is playing deaf, blind, dead" (p. 227). The narrator's monologue provides only a false semblance of control, inasmuch as there is no one outside himself with whom he must contend, no one who challenges the progression of his narrative. As soon as he steps out of his silent maneuvers, however, and confronts the other man directly, he gives himself over to the very dissociative behavior that he has been trying to avoid.

Eventually the man on the bus responds tersely, but only to deny the narrator's accusations. Stripped of his anonymity by the narrator's aggressive pursuit, the man on the bus is revealed to be a Jew, who, like the narrator, was imprisoned in Monovitz-Buna. However, unlike the narrator, he was purportedly an inmate with special privileges, a *Kapo,* one of the barracks-chiefs, who "knew neither hunger nor weariness nor sickness," a "collaborator," who "had jurisdiction over the life and death of hundreds of human beings ... the ally of evil, of hunger, of cruelty" (pp. 229, 231). The narrator seems to remember him all too well, because he was one of the prisoners in this man's barracks and thus the victim of his callous brutality and self-serving malice. For the narrator, the man on the bus is not an abstraction; he is, rather, the worst kind of Jew, whose crimes are now, after the liberation of the camps, "punishable by law" (p. 231). Indeed, in a reversal of roles, the narrator will try the former *Kapo,* the bus now a court of law in which victimizer becomes victim, predator becomes prey, guard becomes prisoner, and executioner the condemned.

Significantly, this story takes place shortly after the liberation of the camps, when Israel is, as the narrator puts it, a "country ... bursting with former deportees who refuse to reason" (p. 230). These are survivors of the Holocaust, who have come to Israel in search of a country over which they have autonomous control, a land that they can call their own. However, these are also people who arrive stunned, in the wake of immense loss. As the narrator makes very clear, these survivors want a public reckoning and retribution for the crimes committed against them. The narrator has witnessed several of the trials that have taken place of those accused of complicity: a former *Kapo,* a member of the *Judenrat,* a ghetto policeman. He will now reenact a trial in the courtroom of the bus; he will put the *Kapo* of barracks 57, the man he believes responsible for his own terrible suffering, on trial for having "rejected your people, betrayed your brothers, given aid to the enemy" (p. 231).

Previously imprisoned in the camps and rendered silent by fear, the narrator will now speak. He will play the role of prosecutor to the former *Kapo's* defense. Of course, in this first-person story of extreme psychic distress, the narrator will play all the parts; he will appoint himself witness, judge, prosecutor, defense attorney, while the prisoner will play only a single role: that of the accused. The narrator, once again in an attempt to gain control and demand autonomous agency—no longer the subject but the object of fear—will pronounce judgment and suitable punishment: "Full powers will be conferred upon me, my sentence will be without appeal. Facing the accused, I will be God" (p. 232). The central question that guides the inquest, that of the collaborator's guilt, has already been determined by the narrator. So the real question that emerges in the growing confusion and uncertainty of the court of law finally reveals itself: How can one judge those who chose self-preservation over sacrifice? What the narrator discovers is exactly what he has feared all along: that the act of judging itself aligns him in uneasy ways with those he condemns.

The competing voices of the prosecution and the defense bring into sharp focus the problem of how we judge those Jews who collaborated with the Nazis, those who aided the enemy in the "organized insanity" of the camps (p. 233). Unlike the appointed head of the Jewish council in the Ghetto of Krilov, who, when ordered to submit a list of 30 people to be sent to hard labor, returned to the Germans his own name written 30 times, there were those who "sold [their] soul" (p. 231) to save their own lives, those who agreed to the terms of their survival by sacrificing others. Yet, the verdict, as the narrator discovers, is not as unambiguous as he would have it, for, as the defense puts it, "to judge without understanding is a power, not a virtue" (p. 232). The prosecutorial arguments center on actions, while the defense is interested, primarily, in motives. The prosecutor unequivocally argues that those who collaborated by accepting the special privileges sadistically bestowed upon them were cowards, complying with the perpetrators and thus facilitating their actions. The defense, no less certain in its position, contests that no one had a choice, that all involved were victims, all dying a slow death whether one bargains for one's life or succumbs to the hardened will of others. To think otherwise, to believe to have located the truth of the camps, is dangerously to delude oneself.

The closing arguments made, the narrator, depleted and pained, is forced to concede that in such trials "the prosecutor told the truth, so did the defense" (p. 232). Yet he is haunted by the near certainty that "no one had told the truth, that the truth lay somewhere else—with the dead. And who knows if the truth did not die with them" (p. 232). The narrator, trapped, falsely believes that, if he can level a verdict against the man he wants to hold accountable for crimes committed, he can free himself. What becomes very clear is that, in exposing his "victim," the narrator exposes himself. In questioning the other man, the narrator loses touch with reality, with the performance that he has staged, as if he were speaking to "someone else," someone "dead a long time" (p. 229). The narrator's perception of the other man is skewed by his hesitation, confusion, and disorientation. Indeed, it is not clear whether it is he or the other man whose "efforts not to betray himself are becoming visible now" (p. 229). The intentional ambiguity that Wiesel establishes is crucial here, as it has been all along, for it sets the stage for the final confrontation between the two, which becomes the narrator's own encounter with himself, so long avoided. It is not vindication alone that he desires, but rather, expiation for his own paralyzing guilt at having survived at the expense of others.

As the bus approaches the "end of the line" (p. 232), the narrator's phobic dissociation, his split from reality, takes him back to the originating place of trauma. In a flashback, the narrator finds himself uncontrollably witnessing once again the scene of the crime, the accused handing out meager rations of soup all the while beating the emaciated prisoners. The narrator, standing by the barracks with his father, is approached by the barracks-chief, who forces him to take from his father the little soup that he has left. The narrator's guilt in succumbing to the *Kapo's* threats, in taking the food from his father, is magnified by the pleasure he takes in eating it; his shame is intensified by the "immense well-being" (p. 233) that the paltry bowl of soup brings him, in the face of the knowledge that his increased chances of survival come at the expense of his father's. The narrator fears that, in submitting to the *Kapo's* orders, he showed himself to be both "slave and … accomplice" (p. 234) aligned with his tormentor. As such, the narrator believes himself to have capitulated to the immutable law of the camps: "Every man for himself, every man the enemy of the next man, for each lived at the other's expense" (p. 234). For this betrayal, he cannot forgive himself; and so when, at the close of the trial, he asks *Well then? Guilty or not guilty? … What are you now compared to what you were then?"* (p. 235), the accusation is directed at himself as much as at the other man, who all along has been his unbearable double.

When the bus comes to its final stop, the two passengers, at the driver's insistence, disembark together, the "two speechless … phantoms" (p. 235) descending the bus at the same point. As they stand on the sidewalk alone, the narrator is deflated, once again unsure of his rights, no longer certain that his fellow passenger is, indeed, the barracks-chief. The narrator's memory deceives him, and even the sound of the other man's voice is no longer recognizable. Once "gruff, cutting," it is now "clear, humane" (p. 236). Momentarily, the narrator is stunned, hesitant, and vaguely embarrassed, as if he has awakened from a nightmare. Previously impervious to reason, his capacity to appraise the external world and its generally accepted meanings is conditionally restored, and his impulses are once again repressed, his emotional outburst exhausted. His seeming return to a stable, reasonable place, however, is only a temporary stay against his disorientation and difficulty in adjusting to the world outside the camps. His unconscious, aggressive attempts to assuage his fear by confronting it in the other man fail, for, abruptly, the other man is transformed back to the source of the narrator's deep fear and unresolved rage.

Just at the moment of hoped-for resolution, when the narrator eagerly anticipates that the other man will disclose "this mystery to which we remain chained forever" (p. 236) and so free him to experience some relief from his incapacitating anxiety, the passenger is once again the barracks-chief. The narrator looks to the other man for the answer to the mystery of their mutual bondage because he can't find it in himself. Once again the narrator must replay the trauma. Once again, in the narrator's psyche, the two men have returned to their place of origin, "no longer in Israel but somewhere in the universe of hate" (pp. 236–237). Once again, the barracks-chief makes threats, asserts his dominance; but this time he shouts insults in German, not in Hebrew. He is grotesquely, pathologically transformed into the barracks-chief, a Jew with terrible authority over the other prisoners in the camps, but also a Nazi with ultimate power over the narrator. The very confusion in the language, the rapid undergrowth of building hysteria, the abrupt shifts from first- to third-person narration, the jumble of tenses, past and present colliding, all speak to the narrator's disintegrating hold on reality. The narrator depends upon the other man; he holds onto the barracks-chief, or the fantasy of the barracks-chief, because to let him go would be to exonerate himself. Finally, he must separate himself from the man he fears himself to be.

The narrator's awareness, at the story's close, of the entwined nature of their mutual bondage, ironically sets both men free. They are, if not historically at least psychically, in the imagined space of the "universe of hate," old acquaintances, bound together in the knowledge of evil. However, understanding the motives that drive human beings to unspeakable acts eludes him still. The narrator's Joban acknowledgment of and resignation to the limits of his own knowledge and understanding of an unjust world would seem to be the catalyst for an acceptance of his fate, yet unlike Job, there is no room on the bus for God. The capacity for evil and the perilous confusions between courage and cowardice are solely and sorely all too human. The recognition of the limits of self-knowledge, the knowledge of one's own obscure motives, impulses, and constraints, will let the narrator free himself from his captor. The story's ending, however, is ambiguous, for the narrator's liberty depends upon freedom granted by the other, by the ever-watchful memory of trauma unresolved. At the story's end, the narrator is seen running from the man he imagines is following him still. Ultimately, Elie Wiesel suggests, memory, for the survivor, is endlessly destabilizing. His freedom is conditional, the future limited by the past. Wiesel thus speaks to the limits of bearing witness and to the lamentable but inevitable inadequacy of language as a form of representation. The trauma of history is the survivor's personal trauma, where past, present, and future are indelibly shaped and delimited by the master narrative of the Holocaust.

REFERENCES

Wiesel, E. (1968). An old acquaintance. In K. Shawn & K. Goldfrad (Eds.). (2008). *The call of memory: Learning about the Holocaust through narrative: An anthology*, pp. 225–237. Teaneck, NJ: Ben Yehuda Press.

Confronting the Memory of Evil
in Elie Wiesel's "An Old Acquaintance"

William Younglove

> *I died in Auschwitz, but no one knows it.*
> —Charlotte Delbo

Elie Wiesel's "An Old Acquaintance" (Shawn & Goldfrad, 2008, *Anthology*, pp. 225–237) is a short story that will appeal most to college and university students but will also intrigue high school students in grades 11 and 12. Its use in an English class will permit in-depth analysis of its levels of introspection and its varied diction. Its length and straightforward narrative style can be studied within one or two class periods, but I allocate three or more class periods of 50 minutes each for an in-depth exploration.

The story is a fictional recounting of an incident in the life of a man who survived the camps during the Holocaust. The narrator tells of traveling on a slow-moving bus down a street in Tel Aviv, Israel, on an exceedingly hot, oppressive summer evening. Slowly, he realizes that the man seated across from him is the former head of his barracks at Auschwitz III (Monovitz-Buna). He confronts the Jewish collaborator while trying to decide upon the type of vengeance—or justice—he, a former victim, should pursue, up to and including summoning Israeli authorities to arrest him.

Ideally, students will have already been exposed to the precursors of concentration and death camp existence: the rise of Nazi Germany and the origins of the Final Solution, that is, the evolving destruction of the Jews. In fact, I find the story an excellent window through which to help students understand the system that produced victims, collaborators, perpetrators, and bystanders—and allowed, most often by sheer chance, survivors. (Such categories, of course, fail to take into account Jewish victims who were forced to collaborate, such as the titular character in this narrative.) I believe the chief question the story raises is: What does it mean to be a survivor, to have survived a Holocaust death camp? I prefer to use an inductive teaching approach to study "An Old Acquaintance," going from text to focus questions to essential questions, but it is very important that any lessons include an investigation of the chief events and various roles described in the story to provide historical context for the students.

Rationale and Teaching Goals

"An Old Acquaintance" uniquely captures the affective concerns and actions of one who physically survived the horrors of the camps. I tell students that few other survivor writers have chronicled what it means to endure as a survivor as has Wiesel. Reflecting upon what such endurance means, a student, Esperanza, wrote: "I don't think there are words to describe how many people survived [the Holocaust] but are killed emotionally in their hearts and who will never be mended for as long as they live."

My specific teaching goals include enabling students to

- determine the believability of the characters;
- evaluate the setting, analyze plot conflict and story climax in light of the historical period that shaped it;
- analyze the ways in which irony, tone, and mood achieve specific rhetorical purposes; and
- relate the work and the author to major themes and issues of the era, and state the denouement, the aftermath, of the story.

Many states require goal fulfillment via student achievement of reading and language arts standards (Shawn & Goldfrad, 2008, *Guide*, pp. 490–492). To meet these standards, I want my students to

- detail the way in which meaning is affected by the repetition of main ideas, syntax, and word choice in the text;
- analyze the author's implicit and explicit philosophical assumptions and beliefs about a subject;
- evaluate the political influences of the historical period that shaped the characters, plot, and setting;
- analyze the philosophical arguments presented in the literary work to determine how the author's position contributed to the credibility of the characters; and
- edit their own manuscripts to ensure correct grammar, spelling, and mechanics.

Focus questions raised by the story content, broached for discussion after the reading, might include the following:

1. What does it mean to "survive" the Holocaust?
2. How is it possible to go forward in its wake, to find meaning and live productively?
3. Once people are reduced to the status of objects, how can they relate to other human beings?
4. How does a Holocaust victim turn from becoming a prisoner of the past to being able to connect not only with his past, but with the present, and, more importantly, with hope for the future?

5. How are Jewish survivors, especially, to judge those Jews in the camps who collaborated, even limitedly, with the Nazi hierarchy?
6. What measure and means of vengeance, or justice, can/should the liberated Holocaust victim expect/demand?

The essential, debatable question, evolving from the final focus question, is tripartite:

a. What does it mean to confront evil?
b. How does one confront evil in a meaningful way?
c. What is the desired outcome from such a confrontation?

Preparing to Teach

I find the following materials useful when I implement the full lesson:

1. class sets of the anthology including Wiesel's "An Old Acquaintance";
2. an Anticipation/Reaction Sheet handout to evaluate students' changing thoughts and feelings (two class sets for pre- and post-measurements);
3. an overhead transparency or handout of 25 key vocabulary words;
4. the "Elie Wiesel: Witness to the Holocaust" Nobel Prize Series video of his Nobel Acceptance Speech (1990) [the speech is available at *www.eliewiesel-foundation.org/ElieWiesel/NobelSpeech.htm* (1986).]
5. if available, an audiotape (professional or teacher-created) of "An Old Acquaintance";
6. a Holistic Rubric for Story Completion (at the end of this lesson plan); and
7. student access to computers.

I explain to the students that they are going to read and study Wiesel's narrative "An Old Acquaintance," originally part of a collection of short philosophical essays and other narratives called *Legends of Our Time*, published in English in 1968 (translated from the 1964 French *Les chants des morts*).

To help students connect their personal beliefs to the story, I hand out a copy of the "An Old Acquaintance" Anticipation/Reaction Sheet and review the directions briefly. We discuss the five underlined terms by citing examples of such roles from Holocaust memoirs, before the students mark the 10 items as agree, disagree, or unsure. (See Appendix A.) I collect and file the sheets for use toward the lesson's end.

Introducing Elie Wiesel

I provide a capsule summary: Wiesel, born in Sighet, Hungary (alternately Romania), in 1928, survived the Auschwitz death camps and Buchenwald concentration camp from May 1944 to April 1945. Family members, including his parents and little sister, were murdered in the camps.

After a decade of vowed silence, Wiesel wrote what became *Night* (in English, in 1960). In reality, *Night* is the sole book in which Wiesel provides us with ongoing reporting of what actually occurred in the death camps. I ask who has read or studied *Night* and note names for later use. Ten more books followed in the next decade, including *Legends of Our Time*. These are Wiesel's last works dealing directly with the Holocaust. In almost all of his later texts, Wiesel refers to the Holocaust indirectly via innuendoes, fleeting references, or through the enduring effects residing in the souls of survivors.

I help students define "acquaintance" (Webster's derived meaning is "to know perfectly"). One of the most famous uses of "old acquaintance" is from Robert (Bobby) Burn's lyrics "Auld Lang Syne." The title refrain refers to "an old kindness." Burns and his predecessors, however, posed a deeper, more telling question: "Should auld acquaintance be forgot, though they return with scars?" (Dick, 2007) *With scars* (emphasis added), I tell students, has much to do with Wiesel's story.

Essential Vocabulary Study

Next, I write on the board 25 vocabulary words essential to understanding Wiesel's story:

1.	sultriness	14.	flagrant
2.	insinuates	15.	dossier
3.	void	16.	protégés
4.	rancor	17.	servile rag
5.	subordinate	18.	incandescent
6.	tenaciously	19.	immutable
7.	jurisdiction	20.	writhing
8.	*groosh*	21.	contemptuous
9.	emaciated	22.	expiation
10.	Kapo	23.	inertia
11.	*Judenrat*	24.	default
12.	obliterates	25.	certitude
13.	indulgence		

I ask the students to copy the words, including the first two examples provided by me (see chart, Appendix B), on the left-hand side of their notebook paper, using only every other line. During the reading (the tape, if used, can be paused briefly after any paragraph in which the words appear), they'll write their contextual guesses on the right side; later, they'll write the actual meanings as well as an appropriate sentence, and I'll collect the sheets *following* the story work. To help the students note context, you can request that they use only words in their contextual guess that can actually be *substituted for* the vocabulary word. The following actual meanings can also replace the form and meaning of the vocabulary word in context. (See Appendix B for full [Actual Meaning] definitions.)

Reflection, Reaction, and Response

Ask students to use Post-It notes to mark passages to which they would like to respond. We begin the story together. With strong readers, I share the reading;

with more limited readers, a well-read tape is better. The use of the tape allows me to circulate to make sure that all students are following as the story is read. For the remainder of the period, students react in their journals. They choose four or five passages that they felt were important to the story and respond, noting interesting phrases and style, challenging the text, and raising questions. Reactions such as those in the chart, below, will be credited.

To accommodate second-language or underprepared students, I recommend, besides the taped reading, student access to bilingual dictionaries/thesauri, the *USHMM.org* Web site to access the *Holocaust Encyclopedia*, and the grouping of students who vary in language strengths. Special needs students can be grouped with stronger readers and provided with classroom help, if available. You can offer accelerated students additional readings about Wiesel from his referenced memoirs, the *USHMM.org* site, or the school library.

Selected Text	Student Reflection
Cardiss: "He [the passenger] has just lost his anonymity, returned to his prison, but he does not know it yet." (*Anthology*, p. 226)	What prison is the narrator talking about?
Felix: "Is your memory still alive? Or did it bury us all a second time?" (p. 230)	I don't think a memory can bury. Can it?
Khala: "With other Jews. You are Jewish, aren't you?" (p. 229)	How could the barracks-chief be Jewish, too?

I return the vocabulary worksheets, requiring students to complete the *My Sentence* column, as the examples in Appendix B illustrate; then I collect them.

Questions for Discussion

My initial discussion of the story addresses identifiable events in light of short story elements. The questions I include are:

1. Seemingly, there are four characters in the story: the nameless narrator, the barracks-chief, the PROSECUTION, and the DEFENSE. The narrator said that he was playing a game. What has happened to the narrator's "game"?
2. The setting might be said to be intermittent and in the background, except perhaps at the beginning. Scholar Victoria Aarons (2008) has noted in this *Guide* that Wiesel "encases his narrator in a moment frozen in time and contained in a private, individualized space, the occasion of this survivor's traumatic experience" (p. 426). How does the milieu of the ambling bus permit events to become selective? How is this setting crucial to the narrator's thoughts, words, and actions? To the barrack-chief's words and actions?

3. Describe the initial plot conflict, telling where the story takes place. At what points is the conflict heightened? Why? What is the climax of the story (the point at which we know the outcome for the chief character)?

The narrator invents characters, the PROSECUTION and the DEFENSE, which reveal a subplot within the narrator's own mind, interspersing itself with Wiesel's story. (In a fascinating analysis, Aarons posits that the whole encounter is within the narrator's mind only: "It is not at all clear," she writes, "that the barracks-chief on the bus exists anywhere outside of the narrator's ruined imagination" (p. 439).) Here is a good place to draw upon those who read *Night* and teacher expertise to establish the following text-based historical occurrences:

Providing the Context
- Twenty years before this story was first written (in French) was 1944.
- Evening soup distributed in tin plates to a pack of starved corpses raises images of concentration camp victims.
- Germany was the site of a number of concentration camps, including Buchenwald and Bergen-Belsen.
- In occupied Poland, death camps included Maidenek, Treblinka, and Auschwitz (plus its subcamps). In occupied Lithuania, near Vilna, was Ponar, the site of Nazi-initiated and Lithuanian-assisted massacres of Jews.
- Numbered blocks at Monovitz-Buna included barrack 57.
- Collaboration with the Nazis by some Jewish prisoners did occur.
- Kapos, Jewish and Gentile, did act as block or barrack leaders in concentration camps in return for more rations and better living conditions until 1944, when Heinrich Himmler issued an order prohibiting Jewish Kapos.
- Elders of the Jewish Councils, called the *Judenrat,* did help administer many Nazi-occupied cities in Eastern Europe; their degree of collaboration varied.
- Jewish ghetto policemen were induced by Nazis to enforce Reich laws, for the same reasons that the *Judenrat* was utilized.
- There were confusing and painful trials, including the Klaus Barbie trial, in Lyon, France, in 1987.
- Many accused Nazis did not recognize the legitimacy of the courts in Nuremberg and post-Nuremberg Trials.
- There were those in the camps who sometimes refused or shared soup with a loved one, claiming themselves "not hungry."
- Those in camps were advised by barracks-chiefs, at times, about the philosophy of the concentration camp: Every man for himself.
- Prisoners gave up clothes (shirts, shoes) to collaborators/perpetrators as demanded.
- There was an "Angel of Death" in the person of Dr. Josef Mengele, the SS physician and selection head at Auschwitz-Birkenau.

All fifteen of the foregoing events of the World War II and the post-war period, told by the narrator of "An Old Acquaintance," were experienced by Wiesel himself. Here, I raise the questions: To what extent, then, is Wiesel's writing autobiographical? To what extent does he use autobiographical data to create the tone (i.e., the writer's attitude toward a subject) and story mood, or atmosphere (i.e., establishing an appropriate state of mind for events to come)?

Fostering Student Responses

I handle the following discussion items on the chalk or white board or on the overhead to foster student interaction and dialogue. You may, again, wish to have students enter related notes in their journals, awarding points in the process. We turn to some rhetorical devices the writer uses. For example, when the bus crawls down Allenby Street in Tel Aviv one sultry night through numerous bottlenecks, the narrator exclaims, "And to think we are in the land of prophets!" (*Anthology*, p. 225). I ask: How does the story context reveal this statement to be an example of verbal irony (a contrast between what is said and what is meant)? At what other points in the story does Wiesel use irony?

- Matthew cited p. 228 when the narrator says, "How odd, so is mine" (bus stop is further on) as an example of situational irony, a contrast between expectation and occurrence.
- Cheri identified p. 232, "Luckily, I am witness and not judge: I would condemn myself," as more verbal irony.
- Domingo and Bianca pointed out (p. 233), "Hurry up and die. ... Give your bread to the young, at least do[ing] one good deed before you croak!" as still more verbal irony.
- Junior Kahlil viewed (p. 233), "My father murmured, 'He's [the barracks-chief's] a good man, charitable,'" as ironic.
- Antonio asked if the barracks-chief, making God visible (p. 235) with "I am God," was not also ironic.
- Senior Nika said that the bus driver's shouting (p. 235) "You must be deaf! Don't you understand Hebrew?" is ironic.
- I ask if Wiesel is being ironic in his final lines (p. 237): "He [the barracks-chief] let me go. He granted me freedom." At this point many students want to debate the narrator's seeming overall reversion to prisoner status, asking: Is that not the greatest irony in the story? Tupasi and Sharna, for example, strongly disagreed over the steps, literally, that the narrator took.

However students analyze the language of Wiesel, I let them know that he has not forsaken humor, be it ironic or even sardonic. As Kolbert (2001) noted, Wiesel adopted the formula of the French writer Camus: In a universe of misfortune, one must create happiness. Wiesel indicates there remain for humans but two choices: to be an optimist who cries or a pessimist who laughs. Irony, Wiesel insists, is a way of not talking about the unspeakable. It can be used to deflect or even to deny what is difficult, painful, or dangerous (p. 185).

Wiesel's Use of Language

Before turning from Wiesel's use of language, I point out elements of style, specifically, sentence length and the repetition of words and phrases. The near absence of transitional words adds to the effect, helping to focus the story. Brevity and repeating subject/verb order help to create a rhythm:

1. the short staccato sentences in the opening three paragraphs (*Anthology*, p. 225),
2. the uses of repetition: "frighten him" (p. 226), "no ... no ... no" (p. 228), "you are"; "not you" (p. 229), "We didn't ... we thought ... we hoped" (p. 231), "You were ... you lived ... you were" (p. 234), "I do not ... I let ... I am ... I will ... I behaved ... I will" (p. 237).

Since the bus setting is itself limited space, a good question for student exploration, I find, is: What is the total time passage in the story?

Next, I return briefly to the titles of both the story and of the collection: *The Call of Memory*. The previously referenced "Auld Lang Syne" song lyrics referred to the scars that can accompany memory. I thus ask, "In what way might the phrases 'an old acquaintance' and 'the call of memory' be referencing the scars that the narrator bears from his imprisonment in the camps?"

The story's final question, "Is he following me?" (p. 237) creates a mystery. Either answer, yes or no, has to be puzzling, because either raises the question of, now, just who is the pursuer and who is the pursued? Nguyen and Shamela, in debating the question, argue that Wiesel answered that question in his final sentence: "He granted me freedom" (p. 237). The problem with Wiesel's cryptic answer is this: Is Wiesel's narrator free now of someone who still had some potential to hurt him, do him evil? Would he have felt that he himself was somehow standing by had he not openly confronted the barracks-chief? Or is he somehow, as a result of the encounter, freed from the compulsion to confront his demons in the future? (Remember, just a portion of an hour ago he was on a slow bus ride, headed toward an appointment, content to play his "watching game," when he felt compelled to challenge this "old acquaintance.")

Cynthia, Josie, and Adriana pointed out that, three paragraphs before the story's end, "the man who measures himself against the reality of evil always emerges beaten and humiliated" (p. 237). I asked: Is this because the choices narrow themselves down to being either a judge or a victim? I argued that, if so, I believe the narrator wants never to allow himself to be victimized again. Yet, I admit that the narrator himself muddied the judicial waters when, earlier, he intoned, "I often left the courtroom depressed, disheartened, wavering between pity and shame. The prosecutor told the truth, so did the defense. Whether for the prosecution or for the defense, all witnesses were right" (p. 232).

"All witnesses were right," however, is an outcome that, I would argue, cannot be—in a normal, rational, and legalistic world. In "The Gray Zone" (Levi, 1988) of the *Lager* (camp), however, power tolerated and encouraged privilege. Collaboration itself bought privilege—for a while. In the most extreme example, the

Sonderkommandos, special squads of Jews, processed corpses from the crematoria at Birkenau, in exchange for privileges such as food, alcohol, and sleep, during perhaps four extended months of life. The rightness of the squads' actions needs to be examined in light of the following facts: the members were shot if they refused and they were doomed to be killed afterward. Dead, really, before dying, they were robbed of their souls—to the extent that many killed themselves (pp. 36–69).

Essential Questions

I inform students that in this story, Wiesel seems to be raising the very question that Arendt raised in 1963 with her publication of *Eichmann in Jerusalem,* asking serious questions about the "complicity" of *Judenräte* (Jewish Council members) at certain times and places. Arendt was attacked for her characterization of the "banality of Nazi evil," a term she used to imply that the evil was commonplace, made up of thoughtless acts, rather than ideologically driven. Is it possible that the *Judenräte,* set up and dominated by the Nazis, simply went along with the Nazis' evil schemes?

The Jewish barracks-chief in this story perhaps represents that banality. I share with the students that I thought the narrator might have the wrong man, but given that he was the right man, there was now a more difficult problem: How to judge the degree of evil in this man. Given an opportunity to turn him over to authorities, the narrator chose instead to "let him go free" (*Anthology,* p. 237). I remind students that four paragraphs before the end of the story (p. 237), the narrator asks: "Can one die in Auschwitz, after Auschwitz?" That tormenting question, one that so many survivors raise about the past and present merging and shaping their post-Holocaust years, suggests, I believe, the following question: Can one become free of the scars caused by evil and go on to live a normal life? I explore with students the role that memory plays in revealing these scars. I tell them that Wiesel says remembering is a moral duty. It prevents the victims' life stories from becoming banal—and events from appearing necessary. What one does with the memories of the victims' lives is paramount. When we share memories of their agony and suffering, we inform those about us in order to inform those who come after us. How will those of us who will bear witness for the witnesses of atrocity rescue the memories of the victims? Students might respond to these questions in light of the following statement from the first volume of Wiesel's (1995) memoirs:

> To remember is to live in more than one world, prevent the past from fading, call upon the future to illuminate it, revive fragments of existence, rescue lost beings, cast harsh light on faces and events, drive back the sands that cover the surface of things, combat oblivion, and reject death." (p. 150)

I ask the students: Which of his ways of remembering, just noted, does "An Old Acquaintance" seem to address? Wiesel (2005) also said at a special session of the United Nations, commemorating the 60th anniversary of the Allied liberation of the Nazi death camps, "His [the victim's] memory is a part of yours. … And what is memory if not a noble and necessary response to and against indifference?" (paras. 2; 10). I share the following from Wiesel's (1999) second volume of his memoirs, "Some scholars contend that I was the first to give the term 'Holocaust' a modern usage by introducing it into our contemporary vocabulary. Why did I choose that word over another?" (p. 18). He explains that "Holocaust" is a translation of "annihilation by fire," but he also proffers *Shoah* (natural catastrophe) and *Churban* (destruction of First and Second Temples). I point out to students that many writers have since written what has been called Literature of the Holocaust, revealing via memories, ways in which survivors, damaged, traumatized, and numb, yet functioning, have tried to come to grips with their pasts.

Wiesel was key in organizing the Gathering of Holocaust Survivors in Washington, DC, in the early 1980s. I ask students: Why did it take close to 40 years for such a reunion? Student answers vary. Aleisha and Jonathan suggested that silence and the passage of time may have been necessary for survivor memory to "catch up."

If the video *Elie Wiesel: Witness to the Holocaust* (1990) [22 minutes] is available, play the excerpt of Wiesel's Nobel Prize acceptance speech. For a hard copy, go to *http://www.pbs.org/eliewiesel/nobel/index.html*. Therein, Wiesel avowed, "I have tried to keep memory alive. … I have tried to fight those who would forget … if we forget … we are accomplices." I ask: In what way(s) is the narrator in "An Old Acquaintance" fulfilling the promise referenced by Wiesel in his 1986 speech?

By now, many students have remarked upon the similarity in the narrator's actions and Wiesel's pronouncements. I then revisit the ending of our story, challenging students to address the following prompt:

Background to Writing

Geoffrey Hartman (1994), scholar of literature and the Holocaust, writes, "The entanglement of memory and revenge does not cease" (p. 14). As noted in the last two paragraphs of Wiesel's short story, the barracks-chief is threatening the narrator. The reverse, however, is not true. Then comes that hard-to-interpret last line: "He [the barracks-chief] granted me freedom" (*Anthology*, p. 237). The question is: freedom to or freedom from? In other words, what has happened to the vengeance, or justice, the narrator was seeking?

Directions for Writing

You will be teaming with a partner to create a new story ending, starting two paragraphs before the present story ending, one which examines what means and measures vengeance, or justice, might take. One of you will write from the narrator's perspective; the other, the barracks-chief's, passing your dialogue paper back and forth after each entry. Your story outcome will be very different from the Wiesel version, but you must remain true to the story background information. You will have one opportunity to revise and edit your ending tomorrow, adding any narrative to the dialogue you wish. See the outline model that follows, plus the rubric (Appendix C). [Place the model on the overhead or board.]

Barracks-chief:
Narrator:
Barracks-chief:
Narrator:
Barracks-chief
Narrator:
(Through at least the eighth exchange)

I recommend forming the same partnerships that were used during the previous lesson. I distribute the "Holistic Rubric for Story Completion" (Appendix C) and instruct them to use their dictionaries/thesauri to complete the assignment. To check for understanding and for guided practice, I share with students how narration and dialogue can enhance and illuminate each other. I recommend a ratio of two parts narration to one part dialogue, meaning that most papers will be at least two to three pages in length. I circulate to help partners as they revise yesterday's start and begin to edit the copy. As a model, best displayed on the overhead, I have students look at an excerpt from "An Old Acquaintance" to see how Wiesel combines narration and dialogue, as well as paragraphing:

"How odd, we're getting off at the same place."

He steps back quickly to let me pass. "I made a mistake, my stop is further on."

I too pretend to step down and immediately turn back. "How odd, so is mine."

We remain standing near the door. Two women have already taken our places. (p. 228)

After examining the above passage and other excerpts, Latisha and Shala wrote the following conclusion:

"You don't really know me. You only think you do," said the barracks-chief, brushing by me in the darkness.

"I know you well enough," I shouted, grabbing at his arm. We struggled a bit. As he tried to move away from me more rapidly, I started yelling loudly.

The barracks-chief stopped, seemingly startled.

From the shadows appeared a man in uniform, a Tel Aviv policeman, who began to question us both ...

"This man," I said, suddenly short of breath. "This man ... from the camps ... Poland ... caused death ..."

Then I saw it—the tattoo on the policeman's arm.

"Say no more," the policeman replied quietly as he cuffed the barracks-chief.

"An old acquaintance from my life in death," I managed to whisper.

Finally, I share with students a Wiesel response to post-Holocaust Nazi encounter questions asked by interviewer Bob Costas in 1993:

B. C.: Did you ever, subsequent to Auschwitz, come face to face with Gestapo officers?
E. W.: No.
B. C.: Former Nazis? Not once?
E. W.: No. I came face to face, and I wrote about it in one of my books, in Israel, during the Eichmann trial. I saw Eichmann at the trial, but he was in a glass cage. But later, I saw, in a bus, going from Tel Aviv to Jerusalem, a man that I—I recognized his neck. He was a kind of blockhouse, or barracks, head in Auschwitz. My barracks head. And I passed him, and all of a sudden I said, 'Tell me, where were you during the war?' And he said, 'Why?' And I said, 'Aren't you a German Jew? Weren't you in Poland?' He said, 'Yes.' 'Weren't you in Auschwitz?' 'Yes.' 'In the barracks?' 'Yes.' I gave him a number, at which point he paled because had I said, 'You were a head of a barracks,' they would have beaten him up during the Eichmann trial, and for a few seconds, I became his judge. Literally, I had his fate in my hands. And, then, I decided, I am not a judge; I am a witness. I let him go. (p. 97)

I then ask students how this anecdote is reflected in "An Old Acquaintance": In what ways does the artistic narrative differ from the anecdote? How are they similar? Most importantly: Do the final lines of the anecdote help us to understand the narrative better? Do you believe that the message of the anecdote is the same, or different, from the underlying message of the narrative? Now, what do you understand the message to be?

Finding Closure

For closure, I give out a fresh Anticipation/Reaction sheet (Appendix A) of 10 items and require that students mark, once again, agree (A), disagree (D), or unsure (U). I collect the papers, promising to share the pre/post results tomorrow.

Assessments

I recommend the following overall assessments to reward ongoing student involvement with the story exploration. In addition, you may wish to provide an individual oral response grade.

1. Credit any student who completed the pre/post Anticipation/Reaction Sheet, all 10 items and oral follow-up, with 20 points. Pre- or post- only is worth 10 points. Reduce points for no responses. Note that each student's pre/post sheets need to be placed side by side so that any item marked differently on the two can be so noted. Look for the total number of items changed (e.g., agree to disagree or the reverse) and which items, if any, are changed by the most students. Class aides can help with the tabulations. I share with my classes any shifts regarding student thoughts and feelings about the roles of perpetrators, collaborators, victims, and bystanders during the study.

2. Reward the vocabulary worksheets (Appendix B), all four columns completed and all 25 words addressed, with 25 points. For each original sentence whose vocabulary word is used contextually incorrectly, reduce the total by one point.

3. The story completion, judged by the four-point holistic rubric (Appendix C), will earn a maximum of 20 points.

4. Journal reactions and notes on discussions can earn a maximum of 15 points. My basis for evaluation is the depth and range of reactions and notes. You may wish to award extra credit to any students who researched and presented, orally or in writing, information about Wiesel's life and writings.

One such student researcher, Jerard, discovered that Wiesel was one of 400 or so young boys taken from Barrack 66 of Buchenwald to a group home in France after the war. There, the wild boys, rage often simmering just below their surface actions, began their slow recovery (Krell, 2000). Jerard thus asked if the narrator's encounter in "An Old Acquaintance" had not caused "a fresh wound in place of the camps' scar."

Wiesel (2001) himself has spoken more than once of the youthful survivor's "hidden childhood ... a place that ... is so wounded and so protected [that it] remain[s] fresh always" (p. 57). "An Old Acquaintance" is perhaps the embodiment of that wounded memory, impervious to true healing—ever.

Appendix A

"An Old Acquaintance" Anticipation/Reaction Sheet

Definitions needed to complete this sheet:

crimes: may include robbery, rape, neglect of all human needs, torture, (mass) murder
perpetrators: people who initiated and carried out crimes
collaborators: people who helped the perpetrators
victims: people suffering under or murdered by the perpetrators and collaborators
bystanders: uninvolved people, neither against perpetrators/collaborators or for victims

Directions: To the left of each statement put the letter of your opinion about each statement:

Key: A = Agree   D = Disagree   U = Unsure

——**1.** A victim needs a future or a beloved, or that person will lose the will to live.
——**2.** A collaborator who is only following orders is not morally responsible for acts, even inhuman ones, s/he carries out.
——**3.** Justice requires that everyone guilty of a crime, perpetrator or collaborator, must be punished.
——**4.** Forgiving and forgetting are essentially the same thing.
——**5.** Collaborators always have a choice. There is no such thing as "no choice."
——**6.** The further a crime is in the past, particularly if the collaborator has led a decent life since, the less severe a punishment is deserved.
——**7.** Being forced to take part in a crime is different from voluntarily taking part in a crime.
——**8.** Everyone who perpetrates or collaborates in a crime should have a right to a fair and impartial trial.
——**9.** A victim of a crime at the hands of a collaborator has a right, if not a duty, to carry out a sentence personally to set things right.
——**10.** Victims who do not confront and help bring to justice collaborators may be said to be bystanders themselves.

Appendix B
Vocabulary Worksheet

Page Number	Word	Contextual Guess	Actual Meaning	My Sentence
225	sultriness	heaviness	heat, humidity	Santa Ana winds produce sultriness.
225	insinuates	infiltrates	indirectly introduces	Coach insinuates that I am lazy.
	void		empty space	
	rancor		bitterness	
	subordinate		lower-ranked persons	
	tenaciously		persistently	
	jurisdiction		control	
	groosh		old Israeli coin/"penny"	
	emaciated		very thin, starving	
	Kapo		head person of a barracks in a concentration camp	
	Judenrat		Jewish Council in a ghetto	
	obliterates		destroys	
	indulgence		lenient treatment	
	flagrant		deliberate	
	dossier		papers in a report	
	protégés		trainees	
	servile rag		useless slave	
	incandescent		glowing with intense heat	
	immutable		unchangeable	
	writhing		twisting	
	contemptuous		disdainful	
	expiation		act of atonement	
	inertia		slowness to move	
	default		fail	
	certitude		assuredness	

Appendix C
Holistic Rubric for Story Completion

(See usage considerations at rubric's end.)

4	Excellent Achievement

Has a minimum of eight complete exchanges between characters.

Dialogue is realistic, reflecting characterization revealed in story.

Dialogue reflects events referenced earlier in the story.

Narrative enhances the dialogue-driven events.

Provides a clear-cut climax, in which the reader knows the degree to which or in which the narrator or barracks-chief prevails during their encounter.

Conventions: Reader rarely spots mechanics/usage/spelling errors.

3	Above Average Achievement

May have only five to six exchanges between characters.

Dialogue represents characterization to a degree.

Dialogue references story events.

Narrative clarifies the dialogue-driven events.

The climax at least infers the outcome for the prevailing character.

Conventions: Reader occasionally spots mechanics/usage/spelling errors.

The few errors slow the reader down a bit.

2	Adequate Achievement

Exchanges may be only four or very brief ones.

Dialogue appears a bit stilted or artificial coming from the two characters.

Dialogue reflects the story events only intermittently.

Narrative adds minimally to the dialogue.

Climax outcomes are unclear for at least one character.

Conventions: Reader is often aware of errors in mechanics/usage/spelling. Re-readings are necessary.

1	Inadequate Achievement

Exchanges may not be clear-cut, may be very brief, or nonexistent.

Dialogue sounds totally unrealistic.

Dialogue barely reflects story events.

Narrative is lacking or is disconnected from the dialogue.

No real climax outcomes.

Conventions: Serious errors occur in nearly every sentence.

Nearly unreadable as a result.

Usage Considerations: By holistic, I mean that the paper is to be judged as a whole, the scoring being a general impression of the paper's merits. Such a rubric is not an aggregate of the paper's subpoints. If, for example, the paper is excellent rhetorically, but its conventions are weak, the overall score would be less than a "4," but it would not fall to the lowest rubric numbers unless the lack of Standard Edited English made the reading and understanding of the paper very difficult.

REFERENCES

Aarons, V. (2008). Memory as accomplice to history: Trauma and narrative in Elie Wiesel's An old acquaintance. In K. Shawn & K. Goldfrad (Eds.). *The call of memory: Learning about the Holocaust through narrative: A teacher's guide*, pp. 425–433. Teaneck, NJ: Ben Yehuda Press.

Arendt, H. (1963). *Eichmann in Jerusalem: A report on the banality of evil.* New York: Viking.

Costas, B. (1993). A wound that will never be healed: An interview with Elie Wiesel. In *Night and related readings* (pp. 81–106). New York: Glencoe McGraw-Hill. (Reprinted from *Telling the tale: A tribute to Elie Wiesel on the occasion of his 65th birthday*, by James Cargas, Ed., 1993, St. Louis, MO: Time Being Press, Inc.)

Dick, J. Auld lang syne—Its origins, poetry, and music. Retrieved on June 18, 2007, from *http://www.electricscotland.com/history/articles/langsyne.htm.* Para. 7.

Elie Wiesel Foundation. (1986). Nobel Acceptance Speech Page. Retrieved January 10, 2005, from *http://www.pbs.org/eliewiesel/nobel/index.html.*

Hartman, G. (1994). *Holocaust remembrance: the shapes of memory.* Oxford: Blackwell.

IMG Educators. (Producer). (1990). *Elie Wiesel: Witness to the Holocaust*: Nobel Prize Series. [Motion picture]. New York: International Merchandising Corporation (Interview).

Kolbert, J. (2001). *The worlds of Elie Wiesel.* London: Associated University Press.

Koppel, G. & Kaufman, H. (1974). *Elie Wiesel: A small measure of victory.* Tucson: University of Arizona.

Krell, R. (2000, October). *Child survivors of the Holocaust: The children of Buchenwald.* Oral presentation at the "1939" Club Lecture Series at Chapman University, Orange, CA.

Levi, P. (1988). *The drowned and the saved.* New York: Random House, Inc.

United States Holocaust Memorial Museum. *http://www.ushmm.org/* See *Holocaust encyclopedia* (en Espanol); also Inside Education: For Teachers: Elie Wiesel.

Wiesel, E. (1960). *Night.* New York: Hill & Wang.

Wiesel, E. (1968). An old acquaintance. In K. Shawn & K. Goldfrad (Eds.). (2008). *The call of memory: Learning about the Holocaust through narrative: An anthology*, pp. 225–237. Teaneck, NJ: Ben Yehuda Press.

Wiesel, E. (1995). *All rivers run to the sea.* New York: Alfred A. Knopf.

Wiesel, E. (1999). *And the sea is never full.* New York: Alfred A. Knopf.

Wiesel, E. (2001). Hidden memories. In Robert Krell (Ed.). *Messages and memories: Reflections on child survivors of the Holocaust* (2nd ed.). (p. 57). Vancouver, BC: Memory Press.

Wiesel, E. (January 24, 2005). *Bearing witness, 60 years on.* United Nations address. Retrieved on January 10, 2005, from *http://www.beliefnet.com/story/160/story_16004_1.html.*

The Second Generation and Beyond

"Because One Did Survive the Wreck": Kurt Vonnegut's "Adam"

Kinnereth Meyer

> *Star, you were once my dear friend,*
> *Come, stand for the words that have come to an end.*
> —Abraham Sutzkever

Many writers have expressed similar thoughts about the insufficiency of language, or what George Steiner (1967) called the "diminution of linguistic possibility" after the Holocaust (p. 49). Kurt Vonnegut's narrative "Adam," in Shawn & Goldfrad (*Anthology*, 2008, pp. 241–249), provides an interesting variation on the motif of the "incommunicability of suffering" (Trilling, 1953, p. 256). Heinz Knechtmann, a Holocaust survivor and the main character in this brief tale, lacks not language, but listeners. Overwhelmed with an irrepressible need to *tell the story* of his son's birth in America, he has the words but fails to find even one person who will truly "listen." Like Iona Potapov, the sledge driver in Chekhov's beautiful short story "Misery" (1886), Knechtmann "thirsts for speech" just as a man thirsts for water. Knechtmann's thirst is slaked only when he finally speaks to his wife, Avchen; only his partner in suffering can become his partner in joy and his partner in speech.

Like Chekhov, Vonnegut questions whether the emotions surrounding life and death can be communicated and shared. In the Chekhov tale, the cabman Iona cannot find a partner with whom to share his grief following the death of his son. At the end of the story, he is reduced to sharing his sorrow with his little mare. Conversely, Heinz cannot find a partner with whom to share his joy and can only "speak," ironically, when he *hears* his wife's words:

> "They couldn't kill us, could they, Heinz?"
> "No."
> "And here we are, as alive as we can be."
> "Yes."
> "The baby, Heinz—" She opened her dark eyes wide. "It's the most wonderful thing that ever happened, isn't it?"
> "Yes," said Heinz. (*Anthology*, p. 249)

Heinz's double "yes" concludes the story with an existential affirmation. Yet, in spite of their differences, "Misery" and "Adam" complement, rather than contrast each other. Vonnegut takes Chekhov's insight into the insularity of human suffering one step further. Heinz's joy is inseparable from his grief; the marvel of his son's birth is an assertion of life after the world has been blotted out by the Holocaust. He and his wife are "still members of the human race"; their joy is the joy of continuation after the cancellation of body and spirit.

Wisely, Vonnegut did not try to write a "Holocaust story." Despite his experiences as an American POW in Dresden during the Allied bombings in 1945, he was, in all common senses of the word, an "outsider," a fourth-generation non-Jewish American of German extraction. Yet, as George Steiner has written, while Jews everywhere were "maimed by the European catastrophe ... the massacre has left all who survived (even if they were nowhere near the actual scene) off balance" (p. 168). Steiner wrote "all who survived" in the context of a discussion of non-European Jews, but the phrase can be also read as a deliberately inclusive category, applicable to both Jews and non-Jews. It suggests that when it comes to the Holocaust, there are no outsiders; all are affected by the European catastrophe. Thus, it may be that Vonnegut chose a name for his main character—Heinz Knechtmann, and for his infant son, Peter—that are not obviously Jewish, in order to underline how the Holocaust affected "all who survived." Vonnegut's attempt to universalize (and, to some degree, sentimentalize) what is primarily a Jewish experience may be problematic for some readers; it is to Vonnegut's great credit, however, that the story reflects not only his knowledge of the horror, but also his awareness that knowledge is another kind of witnessing, one that must be recorded and remembered. "Adam" is one American writer's attempt to deal with the unbalanced state of a post-Holocaust world.

"Adam" is a miniature: a nine-page, economically constructed narrative. Beneath its placid surface, however, courses what Ozick (1989) calls a "torrent of truth" (p. 39). On one level a tale about ordinary, good-hearted Americans, the story also evokes the personal suffering and historical devastation of an entire culture.

"Adam" begins in the waiting room of a Chicago lying-in hospital. Two expectant fathers, Mr. Sousa and Mr. Knechtmann, await news from the delivery room. Mr. Sousa, a "sullen gorilla" (*Anthology*, p. 241) of a man, receives the news of the birth of his seventh daughter, an event that he interprets as a severe blow to his masculinity.

"Seven girls I got now," he complains to Knechtmann. "A houseful of women. I can beat the stuffings out of ten men my own size. But, what do I get? Girls" (p. 241).

Heinz Knechtmann is the almost comic counterpart to Sousa. A small man with a bad spine, he is hunched over "as though forever weary." Only 22, he "seemed and felt much older." The weight of his past suffering seems to literally press down upon his bent spine: "He had died a little as each member of his family had been led away and killed by the Nazis, until only in him, at the age of ten, had life and the name of Knechtmann shared a soul." Heinz and his wife,

Avchen, had "grown up behind barbed wire" (p. 241). This will be their second child; the first, Karl, died in a Displaced Persons camp in Germany.

Vonnegut's description of Heinz's illustrious and creative family functions both as an individual family history and as a synecdoche for the enormous loss of physical and spiritual life in the Holocaust. As he awaits the birth of his child, Knechtmann's mind was "a medley of proud family names, gone, all gone, that could be brought to life again in this new being—if it lived" (p. 242). The placement of this medley of names, of family history, precisely before the news of his son's birth underlines the proud yet painfully tenuous expectations that are being placed upon this child: "Peter Knechtmann, the surgeon, Kroll Knechtmann, the botanist, Friederich Knechtmann, the playwright." Knechtmann's mother, Helga, had played the harp, not surprising in the context of his thought that "the Knechtmann women were all lovely as angels" (p. 242). After the glassily grinning nurse announces the good news of the birth of his son, Knechtmann responds by repeating his name, thus countering the bland American rendering "Netman" and reasserting his identity. In "an exaggerated Old World pronunciation" he bows (to the wall) and states, "The name is Knechtmann. … *Khhhhhhhh hhhhhhNECHT!mannnnnnnnnnnn*" (p. 242). The German *knecht* suggests someone who is servile, or menial. For Knechtmann, however, the birth of his son is a truly noble arrival, granting a lost dignity to his family, and, it is suggested, to the entire human race as well.

While Sousa's wife, thoroughly integrated into American consumer culture, turns out babies like a "regular pop-up toaster" (p. 243), Knechtmann's wife, by contrast, suffers from pelvis trouble, the result of childhood malnutrition. The doctor with the comic-strip name who has just delivered his baby is revered by Heinz as an omnipotent figure:

> "Dr. Powers!" cried Heinz, clasping the man's right hand between both of his. "Thank God, thank God, thank God, and thank you."
> "Um," said Dr. Powers, and he managed to smile wanly. (p. 243)

The minimized vocabulary in the doctor's response to Knechtmann's effusive gratitude ("'Uh huh. 'S O.K. … 'Night. Luck" [p. 243].) presages the responses of everyone else that Knechtmann approaches in his effort to find someone who will share his joy and his wonder at the appearance of this "little spark of Knechtmann" (p. 244).

Baby Peter Knechtmann may not be like the all-American baby ("Got hair like Buffalo Bill" described by another new father whom Heinz meets at the telephone booths, but he is a "treasure house" all the same. "Everything is saved in you" (p. 244), Heinz whispers to Peter on the other side of the nursery glass; but who wants to hear about treasure houses and nobility? The "fat and placid" nurse "missed an urgent invitation to share for a moment his ecstasy" (p. 244). The phone booths in the hospital corridor remain empty; for Knechtmann, "there was no one to call, no one waiting for the news" (p. 245). Sousa and the bartender in the neighborhood bar, both of whom have huge families, are deaf to Heinz's philosophical "Boy, girl, … it's all the same, just as long as it lives. … A miracle over and over again—the world made new" (p. 245). Their response to Heinz's toast to his son–"Here's long life and great skill and much happiness to—to Peter Karl Knechtmann"—is to raise a "cursory salute" to the at least nominally Americanized "Pete K. Netman" (p. 246). Yet, before Heinz can move on to the next step and propose a toast to the entire human race, "of which the Knechtmanns were still a part," the bartender counters with a roaring toast of his own: "Here's to the White Sox!" True to his namesake, John Philip Sousa, "The March King" and composer of "Stars and Stripes Forever," Sousa rousingly adds, "Minoso, Fox, Mele." Although Heinz is standing in the bar with Sousa and the bartender, he suddenly finds himself "all alone again, with twenty feet of bar between him and the other two men" (p. 246). Deep in the analysis of baseball strategy, Sousa and the bartender ignore the miraculous in favor of the mundane.

Even a co-worker and his giggling girlfriend (another incipient tale of procreation and plenty?) whom Heinz meets at the railroad station can only respond to Heinz's great news with the colorless and conventional, "I think that's swell, Heinz, perfectly swell" (p. 247). Heinz's co-worker, Sousa, the bartender, and the other characters in the story are all part of the American mainstream, busy, working, taking the paradise of their freedom for granted. Their horizons do not stretch beyond the White Sox winning the pennant or going out for an evening's entertainment. Their strength is in their ordinariness.

Still, Knechtmann knows that he is in the midst of an extraordinary event. On this level, the story is more than a tale of birth and continuation after the suffering and devastation of the Holocaust. It is also more than a commentary on the cultural isolationism or philistinism of the average American. Who is the "Adam" of the story? Is it Heinz—the beginner of the human race, as is every Holocaust survivor? Little Peter Knechtmann, a "miracle" born into the paradise of the New World? Or is it the writer—who writes out of a need to constantly engender his artistic heritage? The answer, of course, is that it is all three.

"Adam" evokes Theodor Adorno's (1981) qualification of his earlier dictum (1955) that "to write poetry after Auschwitz is barbaric" (p. 34). Explains Adorno:

> Perennial suffering has as much right to expression as a tortured man has to scream; hence it may have been wrong to say that after Auschwitz you could no longer write poems. But it is not wrong to raise the less cultural question whether after Auschwitz you can go on living—especially whether one who escaped by accident, one who by rights should have been killed may go on living. (1973, p. 362)

Heinz is Adam because he goes on living; the "yes" that he utters on the occasion of his son's birth constitutes the only possible answer to Adorno's existential question.

Baby Peter Karl Knechtmann is also Adam, not only because he is an American Adam, heir to the freedom and riches of the New World, but also because through his illustrious name, he renews the cultural heritage that was almost obliterated by the forces of darkness. After the devastation of the Holocaust, asks Adorno in *Negative Dialectics* (1973), how can we affirm or posit transcendence? If the Holocaust was a "denial of the creative instinct" (Kremer, 1989, p. 28), then Peter's role as a "treasure house" of the spirit counters this denial with the promise of cultural continuation.

Steiner wrote that "All great writing springs from *le dur désir de durer*, the harsh contrivance of spirit against death, the hope to overreach time by force of creation" (p. 21). Thus, in grappling with a question of major cultural import for the writer, Vonnegut, too, is Adam. Like his creation, Heinz, Vonnegut is a listener-speaker who communicates the tangled connection between suffering and joy, death and birth, devastation and art. Having listened to Knechtmann's suffering, Vonnegut subsequently seeks a listener-reader himself, one who will bear this tale of regeneration and figuratively start the human race anew.

"Adam" comes from the Hebrew word for "earth": *adamah*. "In the sweat of thy face shalt thou eat bread, 'til thou return unto the ground (*adamah*); for out of it [the earth] wast thou taken," says God to Adam in Genesis 3, "for dust thou art, and unto dust shalt thou return." Those who did not survive the Holocaust were literally turned to dust. Similarly, the long-held idea that "culture is a humanizing force" (Steiner, p. 15) was also turned to dust. Composed out of the dust and earth of the European catastrophe, "Adam" is Vonnegut's *dur désir de durer*—his minimalist but vital contribution to the survival of the human race.

REFERENCES

Adorno, T. W. (1981). *Prisms*. (Samuel & Shierry Weber, Trans.). Cambridge: Harvard University Press. Originally (1955) published as *Prismen, Kulturkritik und Gesellschaft*.

Adorno, T. W. (1973). *Negative dialectics*. (E. B. Ashton, Trans.). New York: Continuum Press.

Chekhov, A. (1886). Misery. (C. Garnett, Trans.). New York: W. W. Norton.

Kremer, L. (1989). *Witness through the imagination: Jewish American Holocaust literature*. Detroit, MI: Wayne State University Press.

Ozick, C. (1989). I required a dawning. Interview with Kim Heron. *New York Times Book Review*. September 10, 1939.

Steiner, G. (1967). *Language and silence*. London: Faber and Faber.

Trilling, L. (1953). *The liberal imagination*. New York: Doubleday.

Vonnegut, Jr., K. (1954). Adam. In K. Shawn & K. Goldfrad (Eds.). (2008). *The call of memory: Learning about the Holocaust through narrative: An anthology*, pp. 241–249. Teaneck, NJ: Ben Yehuda Press.

"Everything Is Saved in You":
Exploring the Legacy of the Second Generation
Through Kurt Vonnegut's "Adam"

Keith Breiman

> *Everything new must have its roots in what was before.*
> —Sigmund Freud

I envision ten intense, middle-aged, Jewish men and women sitting around a conference table with me. Most people looking at the group will use the designation "Baby Boomer" as the common group identity, as those in it were born in the first decade after World War II. However, their more important affiliation, and the reason that they will be part of the eight-week reading and discussion group I plan to facilitate, are the commonalities they share as members of the "Second Generation," now frequently called "2Gs," children born to Jews who survived the Holocaust. These adult children of survivors will come together to explore the Holocaust legacy bequeathed to them by their parents.

The term "Second Generation" was coined in the mid 1970s, when the psychological community began to form a consensus about a set of common circumstances, characteristics, and themes shared by children born in the postwar years to the few European Jews who had survived the Holocaust. Initial research on the Second Generation focused on early and ongoing parent-child interactions, the nature of which had its roots in events that took place before the birth of these children. There was general agreement that these survivors, who were mostly adolescents and young adults when caught up in the deadly brutality imposed on them during the Holocaust, responded to the blessed occasion of the birth of their children with psychodynamic dilemmas that were, generally, different from the non-survivor peers.

I plan to advertise the group in local Jewish newspapers, and conduct phone interviews with prospective members. During the initial interviewing and registration process, I will explain that, while I am not a 2G myself, I do have postgraduate certification and previous experience in working with survivors and their children. I will also explain that these two-hour weekly sessions will not be conducted as a therapy group addressing maladaptive thoughts or behaviors, but rather as a literature-based discussion group. There is now a considerable body of literature written by and about the Second Generation, facilitating an exploration of common themes and experiences group participants may have shared. To this end, there will be a reading component—a short story, a testimony, a poem—for each session, and members will be encouraged to keep personal journals that connect their responses to the readings with issues and events in their own lives.

My goal, taken in part from the writings of Hoffman (2004), is to help participants, as they try "to understand the past retrospectively" (p. 187), to search for the "intimate history" (p. 188) of their parents, to reconstruct their parents' fragmented stories and construct their own identity, and to "decode" (p. 187) their place within their family narratives. This chapter describes the content of the first meeting only.

Recognizing that the legacy of the Second Generation was transmitted first and most strongly through the survivor parents, "with its beginnings in enormous loss and mourning" (p. 190), and often through what Hoffman calls "condensed feelings" (p. 187), I chose the short story "Adam" by Kurt Vonnegut, Jr., (Shawn & Goldfrad, 2008, *Anthology*, pp. 241–249), which begins as the main character, Heinz, a survivor, awaits the birth of his child. Although brief, it underscores, in a compressed but vivid telling, interpersonal and psychological dilemmas survivors faced in their new lives within the postwar American society. It is fiction, but it is an authentic portrayal of the notion that, for children of survivors, the most important event of their lives happened before they were born.

Because the group is literature-based, I believe my suggestions for this first session can be adapted easily to an educator's classroom audience and goals. The story, with its accessible plot, familiar vocabulary, and straightforward narrative structure, is suitable for students in 9th grade through graduate school. While I will use "Adam" to spark a discussion of the complex emotions our 2Gs' parents may have experienced at the time of their birth, high school teachers and college professors may wish to use it as they conclude their teaching of the Holocaust. Their goal might be to introduce their students to the difficulties survivors faced years after the Holocaust ended, even as they married and began families.

The World Begins Anew

Vonnegut sets "Adam" in the early postwar years in Chicago, Illinois. The protagonist, Heinz Knechtmann, is introduced to us in the waiting room of a hospital. He's diminutive and hunched-over, only 22 but old before his time. His name, we learn, is always mispronounced, its European "K" reduced to an American "N," much to his frustration. Currently employed as a presser for a dry cleaner, he is a Holocaust survivor, who, by age 10, was the last surviving member of a large, extended Jewish family whittled down, murdered, one by one, by the Nazis. We intuit that he spent his formative adolescent years behind barbed wire in concentration camps witnessing further brutality and death. The story takes place in the few hours before and after his wife, Avchen, who also grew up "behind barbed wire" (p. 241), gives birth to a child.

In this opening meeting, my goal is to immerse participants in the complicated cognitive and emotional network of Heinz Knechtmann as he approaches the birth of his son to help them reflect on the wounds, scars, vulnerability, or depression that may have haunted their parents and shaped their early, preverbal experiences. Professors might have as a goal that their students will understand that the Holocaust did not end with liberation; rather, it profoundly and irrevocably affected the generation born after its conclusion. As psychologist and child of survivors Haas (1996) explains, "The agony of our parents did not end ... at the close of WWII. Their legacy of pain and changed personalities dramatically affected a generation that never saw an SS storm trooper." Children born to survivors, he continues, have been "involuntarily grafted onto this ignominious period of human destruction" (p. 6).

Hoffman (2004), herself a child of survivors, concurs, suggesting that one of the commonalities among the members of the Second Generation is that their defining moments live in their "prehistory" (p. 28). Consistent with this idea, one of my aims is to help participants recall and share personal and collective memories of their formative years by looking at them through the prism of Heinz's and Avchen's earliest responses to parenthood.

To help accomplish this aim, each participant will have a copy of the anthology containing "Adam" before our first session, along with questions about the story that they are to answer in journals as preparation for our meeting:

1. What scenes resonated most for you? Why?
2. What character images were strongest for you?
3. What changes and/or contradictions did you see in the characters? What might have caused those changes/contradictions?
4. Can you ask your parent(s) and/or other family members about the circumstances of your birth? For example, who was present? Who was missing? What were your parents' reactions? Were there any related anecdotes that became part of family history?
5. For whom are you named? How familiar are you with the life and personality of this person? What do you understand your legacy from this person to be?

These questions are appropriate in a classroom as well; the last two, in fact, might serve as an excellent pre-reading assignment. In class, as students share these family anecdotes and then read the story, the comparisons between their parents' experiences and Heinz's, a survivor, will become clear.

Meeting the Group

In the group, we'll begin with brief introductions. Knowing that some people will be more comfortable and/or eager to share details than others, and wanting everyone to participate equally, I'll limit responses to four minutes or so. I'll clarify that the purpose of this exercise, which should take less than an hour, is not to tell the breadth of their or their parents' stories, but is merely to provide a starting point to discuss "Adam." As part of their introduction, I'll ask them to share from their journal assignment a summary of what they learned of their parents' circumstances and reactions at the time of their birth; we'll discuss these accounts more fully in the following hour as we analyze the story. I'll suggest that they talk about their ordinal place within the family structure, their earliest knowledge of the person for whom they were named, and their perceived legacy from, and responsibility to, that person as well as their parents. I'll request that there be no interruptions or verbal interactions as members give these synopses; instead, I'll suggest that listeners write in their journals questions or comments about the speakers, about themselves, or about the 2G experience as a whole after hearing each narrative. As the introductions conclude, I'll invite people to share key questions or concerns.

While group interaction often leads members to refine their initial agendas, I think it will be valuable to focus the group on the story for the next hour. In the classroom, I would set aside two 40- or 50-minute periods for reading and discussion.

In the group, just as in the classroom, we'll begin with a consideration of the contrast drawn between two expectant fathers as the story opens in the hospital waiting room. One, Mr. Sousa, is described as "a sullen gorilla," sitting through "a tiresome and familiar routine" (*Anthology*, p. 241), almost resentful of the birth of his seventh child, the seventh daughter. The other, Heinz Knechtmann, is portrayed as solemnly and introspectively awaiting the birth of his second child. Vonnegut shows Sousa stomping impatiently out of the waiting room while Heinz sits, his thoughts wandering somberly. He recalls not only his murdered relatives, but also his first child, who died at birth in a Displaced Persons' camp in Germany. This son was to have been named Karl, after Heinz's father, "one of the finest cellists ever to have lived" (p. 242).

I will ask the group to consider the disparity between Vonnegut's depiction of Mr. Sousa, the quintessential blue-collar, assimilated American father; and of Heinz, the representative of some 300,000 Holocaust survivors who emigrated from Europe to the United States following WWII. Here we'll explore research that supports the characters' differing responses, such as that which suggests that while parenthood is a wondrous experience to most new parents, "the fact that parents and children are alive is taken for granted" (Bergman, 1982, p. 295). However, to Holocaust survivors, the birth of a child is looked at with a double incredulousness: first, that they survived; and second, that they were able to perpetuate the memories of those lost by creating new life. At the same time, the birth of a child exacerbated the pain of the survivors' loss of family. A teacher's goal might also be to help students see the contrast between the characters as Vonnegut's way of defining the survivor's "differentness" within the context of American society in the late '40s and early '50s.

My goal in discussing Heinz's thoughts and feelings is to encourage the participants to consider the mixed emotions their parents, particularly their fathers, may have experienced at the time of their children's births. Students might consider this as well, but from an objective point of view.

I would find it valuable at this point to introduce a research finding by Yael Danieli (1981), an Israeli psychiatrist who suggested that male survivors entered postwar parenthood with even greater burdens than females. Her premise was that men felt that this was a second chance to prove that they could ensure the safety of family members, something that they couldn't do during the Holocaust. This finding may help participants identify with their fathers as well as Heinz as he sits waiting, his thoughts shuttling between past memories and future hopes. My intent will not be to make gender-based comparisons as to whether men or women had the harder time but to sensitize the group to Heinz's thoughts and actions in the story. Of course, women too faced extremely painful psychological dilemmas as they approached motherhood after the war, and I'll assure the group that later sessions will focus on female/maternal issues. In this short story, however, it is clear that Heinz, as the expectant father, is the author's focus, and thus ours in this session.

I will not be surprised if one or more participants had siblings who died before, during, or soon after the war, and this might be a topic for later discussion. This in turn might lead to a discussion about how the deaths of siblings or relatives were either shared or kept hidden within the family, and the emotional atmosphere that surrounded such information might also be examined. However, this meeting, as in a class, will focus only on responses to the story.

As the group members refer to the questions mailed to them, I'll encourage them to expand on their earlier summaries of the stories they were told about their births and the knowledge they have of their parents' emotional state at that time. My aim, similar to a teacher's, will be to help participants articulate and compare how the portentous, almost overdetermined meaning the upcoming birth had for Heinz mirrored or contrasted with their understanding of the meaning their births had in their parents' lives.

I might ask the group to consider Vonnegut's curious use of seemingly contradictory language, as he describes Heinz as "so overcast with good-humored humility as to be beautiful" (*Anthology*, p. 241). By directing their attention to the pairing of "overcast" and "good-humored humility," my intent will be to have the group discuss the ambivalent strands in Heinz' cognitive and emotional approach to fatherhood. In the classroom, teachers will also appreciate Vonnegut's language. His skillful use of descriptors affords students the opportunity to identify the few but crucial words that make his characters vivid: the nurse, with the "prim smile and officious, squeaking footsteps" (p. 242); the "very young" doctor, "with a pink face and close-cropped red hair," who had "circles under his eyes" and "spoke through a yawn" (pp. 242–243); and Knechtmann himself, "a small man with thin wrists and a bad spine that kept him slightly hunched, as though forever weary" (p. 241).

I expect that most of my group members will be highly educated professionals, as so many 2Gs are, and will thus be aware that the psychological aftermath of Jewish survivors and the losses they experienced during the Holocaust have been the subject of multiple research studies by mental health professionals. Niederland (1968) suggested that repeated psychic trauma had both short- and long-term effects on the postwar psyches of Holocaust survivors, predisposing them to emotional isolation, with difficulties in forming and sustaining social relationships. Eitinger (1968), a survivor as well as a psychiatrist who treated many survivors in his practice, suggested that persecution left survivors with a propensity to states of chronic anxiety and depression. Haas (2001) speaks about the intergenerational transmission of trauma internalized by children. To explore the possible origins of these constructs, I'll ask group members, as you might ask your students, to focus on Heinz's experiences as he attempts to connect and communicate the breadth and depth of his feelings about his impending fatherhood to the non-survivors he encounters.

As the discussion progresses, we'll note that the initial description of Heinz as he waits for the birth of his child does not fit the research profile. (Examining the literature on survivors after the Holocaust would make a rich extension assignment for an interested student.) Heinz is initially *not* portrayed as emotionally isolated, depressed, unable to laugh or feel, and without desire to establish interpersonal contacts with others. To the contrary, he actively seeks connection with and understanding from others during this significant episode. However, by the end of the brief time we spend with Heinz, less than 12 hours, we watch as he is transformed before our eyes from someone eager to share his pride and delight with others into a gray, detached everyman, "seemingly incapable of surprise or wonder, joy or anger" (*Anthology*, p. 248).

Active Reading

To ensure active participation from all, to check for understanding, and to make the written words come alive, I'll suggest, just as you might in a classroom, that participants take turns reading aloud the series of empathic disappointments for Heinz, beginning with his conversation with Mr. Sousa. The next is with the delivery room nurse who responds to his queries about his wife's well-being cursorily, telling him that there is still no word on his wife's birthing process. Next, we meet his wife's doctor, who, after initially mistaking him for Mr. Sousa, announces the delivery of his son. Heinz, who had waited for 12 hours for this news, responds with a burst of emotional appreciation. The tired doctor, in turn, smiles "wanly" at him while walking away. Heinz, desperate for an emotional connection, pursues the doctor: "It's the most wonderful thing that ever happened," he says, following him to the elevator that "slithered shut" before the doctor "could show a glimmer of response" (p. 243) to Heinz's profound gratitude to him.

The group will stay with the story line, reading aloud and commenting on the scene of Heinz walking alone down a deserted hospital corridor as he makes his first visit to see his son in the nursery. There, an unemotional nurse fails to notice the wide smile on his expectant face, thus missing "an urgent invitation to share for a moment his ecstasy" (p. 244).

We'll continue to read aloud and share observations as Heinz listens as a soldier, with whom he spent time in the waiting room, talks to his mother on the phone, describing his newborn child. Heinz looks at the bank of empty phone booths, aching also to share the momentous event:

> There were five other booths, all empty, all open for calls to any-
> where on earth. Heinz longed to hurry into one of them breath-

lessly, and tell the marvelous news. But there was no one to call,
no one waiting for the news. (p. 245)

Here might be a perfect time to ask participants, and students as well, to take a moment to respond to this passage in their journals, exploring the personal meaning this survivor's sorrowful reality has for them.

Research shows us that the absence of extended family further complicated the emotional life of survivors, with feelings of isolation exacerbated by lack of empathy from the non-survivor communities, precisely what we see in the experience of Heinz as he tries unsuccessfully to connect with the people around him.

We follow Heinz to a bar as he searches for camaraderie after seeing his son for the first time. However, in response to his offer to buy drinks in honor of his naming his son Peter Karl Knechtmann, the bartender responds, "Here's to the White Sox!" (p. 246) while the still-bitter Mr. Sousa downplays fatherhood. Neither man understands, and hence both ignore, the significance of the boy being named after Heinz's murdered uncle, a famous surgeon; and his murdered father, the cellist.

We watch as Heinz's affective interpersonal world is further constricted when his efforts to share his joy and delight with a work colleague and his girlfriend at an unexpected late-night meeting on a train platform are met with barely hidden discomfort and derision. Heinz retreats, embarrassed and alone.

Participants will recognize, as they focus on Heinz's experiences, that both the wartime trauma and the postwar disconnection from society contributed to their parents' affective responses to parenthood. Highlighting the polarities of Heinz's experience should help our 2Gs to comprehend their fathers' state of mind on the occasion of their birth. On the one hand, we experience Heinz's growing sense of forlorn isolation based on repeated interpersonal disappointments. On the other, we see his profound investment in his newborn son as he looks at him for the first time with awe and wonder. Students need this understanding as well if they are to learn how the trauma of the Holocaust shaped the generation that followed it.

Haas (2001) suggests that the first child born to Holocaust survivors absorbs the largest quota of compensatory parental expectations, particularly relevant to those firstborns in our group as well as to Heinz's new son. This mantle of uniqueness is both a gift and a burden to the child, for with it comes a sense of vast, almost immeasurable expectations to fulfill, the conviction that these children born from the ashes "must justify [their] existence by great deeds" (Kestenberg, 1982, pp. 97–98).

We see this dynamic in Heinz's rapidly shifting responses to fatherhood. He cannot look at his baby without remembering, by name, the myriad family members murdered in the Holocaust; yet, almost immediately, he shifts to the affective and symbolic meaning of his son's birth, crooning, "Little spark of Knechtmann, you little treasure house. Everything is saved in you" (*Anthology*, p. 244).

This might be an appropriate time to raise questions, in class as well as in my group, about Vonnegut's choice of "Adam" as the title for his story, because, as we learn from the reading, there is no Adam in the story—or is there? My hope is that the discussion will elicit the idea that the title suggests a parallel between the newborn child and the biblical Adam, with Heinz seeing his son as the first human being to emerge from the ashes of the Holocaust, and with the implicit expectation that from him, all future life will derive. Furthermore, like Adam, Heinz's son was born with a reservoir of purity and innocence unblemished by hatred, sin, and human tragedy, the first child in a new world.

Meyer (2008), in this volume, suggests additional interpretations: "Heinz is Adam because he goes on living"; the new baby is Adam: "He renews the cultural heritage that was almost obliterated by the forces of darkness"; "in grappling with a question of major cultural import for the writer, Vonnegut, too, is Adam"; and Adam may be even a "listener-reader himself, one who will bear this tale of regeneration and figuratively start the human race anew" (p. 457).

We'll conclude the discussion as we analyze the final scene. Here the stage is set for the Knechtmann family to form a self-sustaining emotional triad, as Heinz's painful and disappointing experiences with outsiders contrast with his feelings towards his wife, for whom he feels "love and aching awe and gratitude" (*Anthology*, p. 248). The final image is that of Heinz and his wife forming a separate, insular, almost self-contained universe predicated on their joy and gratitude in being alive.

"They couldn't kill us, could they, Heinz?" Avchen asks, and adds, "And here we are, alive as we can be" (p. 249).

The story concludes with the reaffirmation of their mutual and shared belief that their son's birth was "the most wonderful thing that ever happened" (p. 249).

The likelihood is that my group (and your now-sensitized students) will be steeped in emotions as they process the final interchange between Heinz and his wife and the implication that their future world will be self-contained, yet emotionally volatile, consisting of the two of them, their child, and their memories and expectations. Heinz's experience of the hours surrounding his son's birth is quite different from Avchen's; his isolation, his slow recognition and bitter acceptance of the essential meaninglessness of this birth to the rest of the world can never be shared with his wife, the first, perhaps, of the "encapsulated sagas" and "family secrets" (Hoffman, pp. 187–188) that bring many adult children of survivors to groups such as mine.

This hidden divergence of the couple's experience as they begin parenthood may resonate with group members as they reflect on their parents' earliest reactions to them and their siblings. Group members and students, as well, will need time to articulate and respond to questions raised by this story, setting the agenda for the second group session or class.

Setting the Agenda for Our Second Meeting

As we end, I'll distribute the following questions for participants to consider as they write in their journals:

- Why is there no mention of the persecutions Heinz or his wife suffered? How would such mention enhance or detract from the story?
- How is Heinz's experience with others on the night of the birth of the child different from his wife's? How might these differences be manifested in each parent's response to the child?
- Why do you think Vonnegut focuses on Heinz and not his wife?
- What do you make of the responses of the other characters to Heinz? Were the responses realistic given the post-wartime setting of the story?
- What do you make of Heinz's solitary conclusions expressed to himself in German as the summer night ends?
- What response from the non-survivors in the story did you experience as the most painful? Why?
- How do you understand Heinz's monosyllabic responses to his wife at the story's end?

Again, these questions are also appropriate for a homework assignment for students, providing a focused starting point for the next day's discussion. A teacher might have students sit in small groups and discuss their responses to one question only and then have group representatives summarize their conversations for the entire class; this will ensure the active engagement of all students and provide a simple way to check for understanding.

Perhaps the most obvious methods of determining the success of such a meeting are to see who returns the following week and to ask the participants if the session met their expectations. In a classroom, of course, your measures and methods must be different. You may wish to assess understanding by assigning an essay about these readings to be completed at home. A sample writing prompt follows:

> The aftermath of the Holocaust brings its own despair, helping us to understand that there is no 'happy ending' to the story of the Holocaust. Choose two stories from among the works we've read and discussed in class. In a two- or three-page analytical essay, illustrate the ongoing trauma of the Holocaust on survivors, their children, and their grandchildren, citing two specific references from each story.

This first-session plan is not meant to be definitive, as too rigid a structure and process would defeat the purpose of an open-ended discussion group such as the one I propose here. Thus, the classroom teacher can easily adapt this design as she concludes her unit on the Holocaust with this brief study of its aftermath and the shadow it casts on survivor families.

As the facilitator of a group of adult children of survivors, I want to be flexible enough to let group agendas emerge as necessary, but I believe that beginning with a thorough discussion of the story "Adam," supported by research on the survivor family and children of survivors, should provide a thought-provoking framework, rich in imagery and metaphor, as the group begins the difficult task of defining, embracing, and sharing their legacy and their unique role in the history of the Holocaust.

REFERENCES

Bergman, M. V. (1982). Thoughts of superego pathology of survivors and their children. In M. V. Bergman & M. E. Jucovy (Eds.). *Generations of the Holocaust* (pp. 287–311). New York: Basic Books.

Danieli, Y. (1981). Differing adaptational styles in families of survivors of the Nazi Holocaust. *Children today*, 10(5), 6–10, 34–35.

Eitinger, L. (1968). *Concentration camp survivors in Norway and Israel.* London: Allen and Unwin.

Epstein, H. (1979). *Children of the Holocaust.* New York: Penguin Books.

Haas, A. (1996). *In the shadow of the Holocaust.* Cambridge, England: Cambridge University Press.

Hoffman, E. (2004). *After such knowledge: Memory, history, and the legacy of the Holocaust.* New York: Public Affairs.

Kestenberg, J. S. (1982). Survivor-parents and their children. In M. S. Bergmann & M. E. Jucovy (Eds.). *Generations of the Holocaust* (pp. 83–102). New York: Basic Books, Inc.

Meyer, K. (2008). Because one did survive the wreck: Kurt Vonnegut's "Adam." In K. Shawn & K. Goldfrad (Eds.), *The call of memory: Learning about the Holocaust through narrative: A teacher's guide*, pp. 453–457. Teaneck, NJ: Ben Yehuda Press.

Niederland, W. C. (1968). Clinical observations on the "survivor syndrome." *International journal of psychoanalysis*, 49, 313–315.

Vonnegut, K. (1954). Adam. In K. Shawn & K. Goldfrad (Eds.), (2008). *The call of memory: Learning about the Holocaust through narrative: An anthology*, pp. 241–249. Teaneck, NJ: Ben Yehuda Press.

The Problem of Holocaust Remembrance in Israel of the 1950s: Aharon Megged's "The Name"

Dvir Abramovich

> *The Holocaust is a central event in many people's lives,*
> *but it also has become a metaphor for our century.*
> *There cannot be an end to speaking and writing about it.*
> *Besides, in Israel, everyone carries a biography deep inside him.*
> —Aharon Appelfeld

"The Name," published in 1955 by Israeli author Aharon Megged and now in Shawn & Goldfrad (2008, *Anthology*, pp. 250–265), is a searching, visceral, and observant parable that tackles several themes. First, it is a story about a bitter and heartbreaking familial conflict. Second, it dramatizes the clash of values and lack of understanding and communication among three generations in Israel of the 1950s, particularly the relationships between Israelis and the Jews who came to Israel from the Diaspora of Eastern Europe. [We define the Diaspora as all places where Jews reside outside of Israel.] Third, it details the troubling internal contradictions and strain that struck at the very core of the Jewish state in its first years regarding Holocaust memorialization. Fourth, it depicts two groups, two equivocal poles, living side by side, who are at a standoff and cannot find a common bond. Above all, the subtext of this cautionary tale is that a nation that does not embrace its past, that fails to take into account the magnificent foundations of its heritage, will not have a future.

There is little action or movement in "The Name." It is economical and tightly structured. Formally, the story consists of episodes, meetings, and extended conversations, leavened with complex ideas and ideological inflections. In a sense, it is a compendium of the cardinal threads and fissures that permeated the canvass of the post-*Shoah* generation in Israel regarding memory and memorialization, as well as the negation of the values of the Old World. It contains a series of interlocking segments of confrontation, leading up to the climactic finale. Admirably, it does not resolve everything in the end, does not find any big solutions to the predicament that studs the lives of the characters. Besides weaving disparate strands to braid a realistic portraiture of Israeli society, the story carries universal echoes because it foregrounds themes about the generation gap and fissures within families that resonate everywhere.

Set in Israel in the 1950s, the narrative introduces us to Grandfather Zisskind, a Ukrainian Jew who left his country before the systematic extermination of Jews began. He lost his son Ossip and grandson, Mendele, to the Nazi genocide and wants his granddaughter, Raya, and her husband, Yehuda, to name their soon-to-be-born son after the murdered boy to sanctify his memory. In Ashkenazic Judaism, naming a baby after a deceased relative is a long-standing custom. The idea of this sacred obligation and practice is to invest that family member with new life through the cherished child who will serve as a reminder of the departed one. The young couple, however, adamantly resists. For them, the Yiddish-oriented name "Mendele" evokes unpleasant images from Jewish life in Europe, and in particular the Holocaust. These are images that they would rather efface from the collective, national narrative. In addition, the name Mendele, and the Hebrew alternative, Menachem, are for them names that are not uniquely Israeli, which is the identity and cultural cluster to which they feel the most affinity.

The Hebrew title of "The Name" is "Yad Vashem." In 1953, the Israeli Parliament established Yad Vashem, The Holocaust Martyrs' and Heroes' Remembrance Authority. The name is taken from Isaiah 56:5: "And to them will I give in my house and within my walls a memorial and a name (*yad vashem*) ... that shall not be cut off." In Hebrew, *yad vashem* can be interpreted to mean a memorial and a name. Megged borrows the two words *yad* and *shem* and employs them according to their original import—bestowing a name on a person. Like the founders of the national memorial, Grandfather Zisskind, too, wants to ensure that the memory of his beloved grandson, who has no grave, is never erased.

The third generation, as signified by Raya and Yehuda, are entrusted with the enormous responsibility of preserving the legacy of the Holocaust. It is up to them to create a *yad vashem* for the victims of the Holocaust. However, the moral imperative to *never forget* does not hold sway with them, and in "The Name," such essential memorialization fails to occur. There is a disturbing gulf, although the ending of the story implies, if delicately, that this divide may be bridged.

Yad Vashem, the Martyrs' and Heroes' Remembrance Authority, commemorated, in the main, the bravery of Jews in Europe. It put the accent on valor—an emphasis that colored Israeli attitudes for a lengthy period. To a large extent, this action stifled real identification and understanding of the world of European Jewry, for whom survival in the camps was as much an act of heroism as armed resistance (Porat, 1991, pp. 157–174). Regrettably, most Jews who either perished in occupied Europe or survived were viewed by native Israelis (known as *sabras*) as passive weaklings who were led to their death like "sheep to the slaughter" and never offered resistance to their Nazi interlocutors.

It is pivotal to understand that the nascent Israeli state was little concerned about young Israelis' indifference and apathy towards the horrible events of the Holocaust as the nation sought to "emphasize the regenerative force of the Jewish people as demonstrated in the valiant founding and the heroic defense of the Jewish State" (Brenner, 2002, p. 1). Instead of affording the survivors the respite they so craved, as well as the opportunity for some psychological relief, the state and its native-born dealt the survivors a crushing blow, crippling any opportunity they sought to foster positive self-images away from the damaged self-esteem of the past.

During the 1950s, Hebrew fiction had a substantive impact on the formation of Israeli national identity and values. Modern Hebrew literature did not skirt the edge of controversy and was uncomfortable with the fact that the glorification of Israel "superseded the grief and mourning of the Holocaust destruction" (p. 1). As a result, authors such as Megged attempted to show, through works such as "The Name," the problems with this ideological position. In doing so, they demonstrated that it was not realistic to assume that Holocaust survivors effortlessly and painlessly integrated into their new home. All told, during the formative years of Israeli statehood, writers had a profound involvement in the evolution and construction of the 'New Jew.' It has been observed that

> It is hard to think of another field of modern cultural activity that provides, as does Hebrew literature, such a luminous mirror both of the creative élan and of the deep perplexities of Jews trying to define some relationship to an age-old heritage in a radically unfamiliar new world. (Alter, 1975, p. xi)

Megged, who immigrated to Palestine from Poland when he was six, was one of the first Israeli artists to examine the subject of post-Holocaust dynamics and Israel's attitude to the Holocaust. Certainly, "The Name" was a breakthrough, one of the first literary pieces in the Hebrew canon to explore the issue, to note but one, of forgetting versus memorialization of the *Shoah*. Hence, it came to manifestly define a watershed, a template for a work of fiction that delved deeply into socio-cultural currents that still pulsate within the Israeli psyche and are still debated today. Also, it was hailed as an original variation because it featured an elderly hero from another land at a time when the mainstream narrative focus was on young soldiers busy with the War of Independence and the pioneering effort.

In "The Name," the author attempts to demonstrate the difficulties inherent in remembering and the condemnatory sentiments of the young Israeli generation. On the one hand, Raya, to some extent, understands Grandfather Zisskind's wish. On the other, she, and more acutely her husband, Yehuda, seek to find for their first child a suitable name that will link him to the Land of Israel. Essentially, the young couple is caught between competing memories. In the end they choose the one with which they are most comfortable. In the process, they embrace and celebrate the heroic *sabra* ideal, as well as lionizing and enshrining the doctrine of the "New Jew"—fierce, strong, courageous, self-reliant, carefree—who broke away from the 2,000 years of Jewish suffering in exile.

Significantly, native-born Israelis saw themselves anchored to the land rather than to the painful and somewhat uncomfortable memory of the *Shoah*. For them, the lengthy Jewish history with which they were asked to associate was pervasive with oppression, vilification, persecution, and martyrdom—the antithesis of Zionism, a national movement suffused with triumph and independence. Among other things, Zionism argued that the moribund Diaspora would simply wither away and could not survive. The solution to this "Jewish problem" was a Jewish state. Seeking to confect a new entity, divorced from its historical antecedents and liberated from the shackles of Jewish history, a new group was created in Israel. Convinced that the Holocaust proved once and for all that European Jews were cowardly, depleted, and vulnerable, the young generation deserted any shades of that history. This type of thinking became known as "Negation of the *Galut*" or the Canaanite movement. In compression, "Canaanism" promoted an outright severing of the ties with the Diaspora. It rebelled against the historical belonging to the Diaspora, wanting to form a nation based on the Hebraic, Semitic-Canaanite civilization, independent, different, and free from the Jewish nation of their ancestors.

In an informative interview, Megged discussed his motives for penning "The Name." He revealed that as a teenager he knew very little about the East European Jewish communities. Yet, in contrast to his peers, who viewed Diaspora Jews with contempt and revulsion, he felt a deeply veined kinship to his European brethren. Furthermore, Megged believed that his contemporaries' attitude was very superficial, that a secular Israeli culture, severed from the traditional roots of Jewish culture, including literature, folklore, and art, would lead to a shallow and ignorant society. Megged disclosed that it was while working in Haifa Port that he met Holocaust refugees who spoke Yiddish and described the horrors they encountered. Engaging with those people, of whom he grew fond immediately, helped Megged understand the injustice and pain Israel society was inflicting on those who had suffered enough (Lavi, accessed 2006).

After the publication of "The Name," Megged wrote a scathing disquisition in which he criticized Israel's estrangement from the annals of European Jewry and explicitly from the Holocaust (Megged, 1955, p. 16). In the main, he called for a rethinking of the disparaging attitude rendered against the eviscerated European Jewish culture. In a separate essay published more than 30 years later, Megged confessed a burning need to come to grips with and understand the *Shoah*, an urge fuelled by a compulsive engagement with memoirs and diaries written by survivors (Megged, 1989, p. 158).

At heart, "The Name" is a story with an educational message. Its nucleus narrative intelligently maps out the crosscurrent of divergent values and beliefs that seemingly cannot be reconciled. Megged seeks to demonstrate the unfavorable stereotypes that operated within Israeli society by employing the figures of Raya and Yehuda. All in all, it was Megged's desire that the gulf between the Israeli-born generation and European Jews be bridged. Similarly, he wanted to bring the *sabras* closer to their Jewish roots, encouraging the study of literary texts that encased within their midst a more positive image of the Diaspora Jew and jettisoned the standard ghetto Jew protagonist.

Hence, in "The Name," we encounter, through the memory of Zisskind, his son Ossip, a successful, warmhearted, and intelligent engineer; and his grandson, Mendele. Both are painted in glowing hues. Mendele was a prodigy, a boy who was versed in Hebrew, who, at the age of 11, could declaim by heart poems by Bialik and independently read Hebrew's foremost novelists. There is little question that Megged yearned to influence positively Israeli thought and opinion towards the Diaspora and towards those who had gone through the hell of the Holocaust.

"Zisskind" in Yiddish means "sweet child." Indeed, through flashbacks, he is portrayed as good-hearted and gracious, "his tranquil face from which a kind of holy radiance emanated, and his quiet, soft voice that seemed to have been made only for uttering words of sublime wisdom" (Shawn & Goldfrad, *Anthology*, p. 251). He had always taken an active interest in his granddaughter, helping her with schoolwork, and he had infused his daughter's house, where they all lived, with his warmth and humor. When the loss of Ossip and Mendele is confirmed, however, his life is arrested. Crushed by the news, he begins to regress and drift away, enveloped by a sense of irreparable mourning and loss.

> For many weeks afterward it was as if he had imposed silence on himself. ... Now he seemed to cut himself from the world and entrench himself in his thoughts and his memories, which none of the household could penetrate." (p. 254)

Aloof and remote, Grandfather Zisskind becomes rigid and inflexible. His sense of reality is impaired. At one point, Raya and Rachel return home to find him dressed in his best suit: it is Mendele's birthday. He forgets incidents that took place two days earlier, but he meticulously recalls events of 30 years before that occurred in his town. In contrast to the younger Israeli generation, his attachment to the Holocaust is sturdy and firm. Ossip and Mendele's spirit is forever etched in his soul. It is plausible to aver that the natural mourning period endured beyond an appropriate suffering cycle and evolved into a prolonged fixation that alienated those close to him. The story is punctuated with scenes that stress the increasingly tense relationship between Zisskind and his daughter. Eventually, he relocates to a little house some distance away from Rachel and Raya. Wholly absorbed in the past, the present irrelevant, he resists the historical fate forced upon him.

Consider the flat to which he moves. Its furnishings attest to the aging character's petrified interior state. There are books with thick leather bindings, an ancient walnut cupboard, antique furniture, and in the corner, sooty kerosene burners, a kettle, and saucepans. The tone of the apartment's setting and objects reinforces an image of a lonely man shipwrecked on an island of distant memories. We read that even though it was hot, he would wear long-sleeved winter clothing, more appropriate for and emblematic of the Ukrainian weather than the blazing Israeli climate.

The broken clock that Grandfather Zisskind took with him when he left Rachel's home to live by himself occupies a symbolic place in the narrative. Inside the clock, the old man keeps a "cloth bag with a black cord tied around it" (p. 252). The cloth enrobes an eight-page essay that recounts the history of Zisskind's hometown and the subsequent liquidation of its residents. What is the role of the clock and what does it embody? In literature, a clock normally represents multiple levels of the concept of time. The clock personifies Grandfather Zisskind's emotional condition; like the clock, he is frozen in time. He does not care to repair the clock that had stopped working a long time ago. He does not need to know the actual time; his rhythm of life stopped with the death of Mendele and Ossip. The clock contains all of Grandfather's shattered past, including the narrative of his demolished Jewish community. Metaphorically, it functions as a shrine for those who perished, epitomizing a time that has stood still; so it is small wonder that he vehemently safeguards it; his life story and precious memories are enshrouded inside. When Raya mentions to Yehuda during every visit that they should buy her grandfather a new clock, she is obliquely underwriting her desire to replace the archaic with the contemporary. One has to wonder how Grandfather Zisskind would react to such a gift. One could also assert that the clock motif represents the young generation, moving according to its own pace and the winds of modernity and unwilling to pause and reflect on Grandfather's era.

During every visit from his grandchildren, Grandfather Zisskind extracts the cloth bundle from the clock, reads the essay, and recounts the story of Mendele, showing pictures of him and sharing the letters he wrote. He repeats his eulogy for Mendele, proud that the child had won a scholarship and was an outstanding violinist. His genuinely dedicated exaltation would culminate with a sorrowful, "Not a trace" (p. 253). By habitually extracting and reciting this narrative, Grandfather Zisskind is performing a ritual for the dead. Additionally, he seeks to overlay the new society and identity in Israel with the cache of the glory of Jewish life in Europe. More than anything else, the horrors of Auschwitz and the communities it devoured constitute not only an historical record, but for Zisskind they also typify crucial values, vital for the future path of the Jewish people in Israel. The old man deeply yearns for his granddaughter to honor her forebears from the Old Country.

The young couple recoil from such an attempt. His repository of memories is alien and discomfiting to them. They do not want to be reminded of the perennial Jewish destiny of defeat and death. They are symbolic agents of the *sabra* ethos, longing to mold their individual identity in the "here and now," in the language and the land that is not marked by an allegiance and deference to the East European forefathers. Notice the effect this agonizing lament solicits from the married couple: "A strained silence of commiseration would descend on Raya and Yehuda, who had already heard the same things many times over and no longer felt anything when they were repeated" (p. 253). The old man tries to draw them both into his own world, into his whirlpool of aching memories, into his time-haunted domain, but the memories do not elicit pity, responsiveness, or rapport, but embarrassment. The couple, especially Yehuda, repudiates his effort to unload a freight of guilt about the ghosts and traumas of the past.

The dislike for the *Galut* is epitomized most acutely in the character of Yehuda. He personifies the Israeli who is absent any roots to his Jewish legacy, and in a way personifies, more broadly, the Canaanite thinking. From the first pages, Yehuda's aversion to Grandfather Zisskind and what he exemplifies is showcased. On visits, the young husband is revolted by the jar of preserves, fruit, and biscuits laid out on the table by the old man. After Raya's gentle pleas, he tastes a little of the "nauseating stuff" (p. 252). To alleviate Yehuda's boredom, Raya attempts to keep the conversations affable, and it does bear noting that Yehuda and Raya deal with the old man, notwithstanding his oft-repeated anecdotes and idiosyncrasies, with respect. For example, although adumbrated as irritated and impatient during the visits, which, for Yehuda, were "unavoidable torment" (p. 252), he would time and again accede to Grandfather's request to listen to the elongated essay without fail.

Rachel, Zisskind's daughter and Raya's mother, is sensitive to the tension, and often admonishes her father for forcing the young couple to listen to his talk about Mendele and his native town in the Ukraine. If she happens to visit while Raya and Yehuda are there, she reprimands her father, "Stop bothering them with your masterpiece ... if you want them to keep on visiting you, don't talk to them about the dead. Talk about the living. They're young people and they have no mind for such things" (p. 256).

The moment he hears of Raya's pregnancy, Grandfather Zisskind, in an act completely out of character, ventures out from his apartment—a metaphor for the past— to call on Raya and Yehuda for the first time, exemplifying the present and future. The possibility that their newborn might sustain Mendele's slowly disappearing image activates a change in the old man's deportment and disposition. Dressed in his holiday clothes, eyes sparkling, he walks through the apartment, full of vigor and generous with his praise. He does not reference Mendele in the conversation, which is peppered with jokes and witty remarks. Finally, for the old man, a possibility has materialized that the unspeakable darkness will be redeemed and restored by the light of a great-grandson, in a way, a memorial candle to Mendele.

Grasping the background and prevailing attitudes of the period greatly assists us in coming to terms with the purpose of "The Name" and the response of the couple to Grandfather's profound wish. Rivkah Maoz (1989) offers a sensitive insight into the context and period in which this narrative was written. She points out that in 1955 the name *Mendele* was closely associated with the Jewish East European writer Mendele Mocher Sefarim because his tales were part of the teaching syllabus in Israeli schools. Maoz observes that the stories were taught with the unequivocal aim of "instilling Zionist ideology—the negation of the *Galut* and of the passive, submissive, wretched ghetto Jew" (pp. 71–72). Moreover, Mendele Mocher Sefarim was (incorrectly) presented to the students as the "official" chronicler of Diaspora life, even though his stories depicted distinct Jewish communities and were satirical in nature. Therefore, for a majority of Israeli teenagers, Mendele functioned as the primary authority regarding the lives of Jews in Eastern Europe.

The conversation between Raya and her mother about the possibility of electing Mendele as a suitable name dramatically evinces the view of European Jewry. Raya objects strongly, calling Mendele a Ghetto name, ugly, horrible! I wouldn't even be capable of letting it cross my lips. Do you want me to hate my child? ... I should hate him. It's as if you'd told me that my child would be born with a hump ... You know, Mother, that I am ready to do anything for Grandfather. ... I love him, but I am not ready to sacrifice my child's happiness on account of some superstition of his. (*Anthology*, p. 258)

Simultaneously, high school students were also taught the poem "In the City of Slaughter." Written by Hayyim Nahman Bialik (1873–1934), considered to be the greatest and most influential Hebrew poet of all time, Bialik penned "In the City of Slaughter" after he was sent to interview survivors of the Kishinev pogroms and prepare a report. Aside from foregrounding the chilling bloodbath by the merciless perpetrators, which resulted in the death of more than 100 Jews, Bialik scolds and lashes out at the victims. Russian Jews are painted as cowards and weaklings. It is not surprising, then, that young Israelis in general, and Raya and Yehuda here, faced a difficult task. As a result of such dissonant portraits, they and the rest of their generation were unable to sympathize with the suffering of the victims and truly understand the Holocaust.

Rachel, "midway between the two generations" (p. 257), is drawn as a person who oscillates awkwardly between the polar universes of her daughter, Raya; her son-in-law, Yehuda; and her father, Zisskind. She is torn between her loyalty and affection for her daughter and for her father. During the friction around the naming of the baby, she is pulled in opposite directions. She comprehends the respective position of both sides and proposes an alternate name that she feels will satisfy both parties. She suggests the Hebrew name *Menachem*, which means "comfort," to accommodate the warring parties. Interestingly, the usually intransigent old man is open to negotiation, while the young couple, expected to exhibit a spirit of flexibility, are acutely obstinate and immediately say no.

"Menachem is a name that reeks of old age," Raya insists, "a name that for me is connected with sad memories and people I don't like. Menachem you could call a boy who is short, weak, and not good looking" (p. 259). In one sentence, she encapsulates and summarizes the undertow of her generation's avoidance of the stifling Diaspora. Mixed into the emotional brew are ingredients of embarrassment and shame. Mendele and Menachem are both names typically associated with the Jewish Diaspora. As such, the couple ferociously reject their appropriateness. They want a name for their newborn that is purely aligned with Israeli society and culture and stripped of European vestiges, a name that would be more acceptable within the Israeli public sphere. For Raya and Yehuda, choosing Mendele or Menachem would mean choosing an old-fashioned, antiquated name that denotes *shtetl* life. It would mean welcoming and picking up the attendant box of memories allied to that name. Mendele/ Menachem would distressingly call attention to the narrative of horrors they would rather shunt to the margins.

The exchange between mother and daughter soon expands into a discourse about the gravity of eternalizing the murdered. "Perhaps all the same we are bound to retain the name of the dead," Rachel asserts, "in order to leave a remembrance of them" (p. 259).

Raya elucidates her opposition. "But I don't always want to remember all those dreadful things, Mother. It's impossible that this memory should always hang about this house and that the poor child should bear it" (p. 259).

Gradually, as she struggles to discover a road of accommodation, Rachel objects to and challenges her daughter's reasoning and deportment, viewing her logic as flawed and superficial, symptomatic of the malaise affecting young Israelis. Indeed, Rachel tells Raya, "At times it seems to me that it's not grandfather who's suffering from loss of memory, but ourselves. All of us" (pp. 259–260). Nevertheless, she is impotent to resolve the impasse, unable to find a middle path.

The couple wants to call their son Ehud, a very popular name overflowing with self-definition and vitality, denuded of the weight of history and symbolizing modernity and freshness over archaic tradition. According to Maoz (1989), the name Ehud can be traced to the biblical judge Ehud Ben Gera, a heroic and capable leader. The eagerness by Israelis to fashion a reality separate from the traditional Jewish way of life in Europe was evinced in the names they chose for their children. Yiddish, the dominant tongue of the *shtetl*, was belittled and maligned, so any names with Yiddish echoes and sounds were discredited. Thus, many Israeli citizens changed their European-sounding names to Hebrew names. The story makes abundantly clear Raya and her husband's ideological agenda: to exclude the historical bond with the Jews of Eastern Europe.

Even though Raya loves and respects her grandfather, this affection has limits. She is unwilling to "sacrifice" (p. 258) her child's happiness to fulfill her grandfather's desires. Her rejection of his wish may also imply that there are multiple ways of remembering the annihilation of 6 million Jews. Naming a child after a deceased relative is only one way to commemorate the tragic past, not necessarily the only way. The reader must determine if the couple's refusal to give their son a name that would carry the burden of the Holocaust and the death of the 12-year-old Mendele is unreasonable.

For Grandfather Zisskind, of course, it is. Dismayed by Raya and Yehuda's disquieting insistence on forgetting the family's past, as if what happened in Europe is unworthy of perpetuation in Israel, the aged survivor still clutches the credo that the collective past matters. When he realizes that Yehuda especially is disgusted by the taint of the Diaspora affiliated with the name of his lost grandchild, he issues a startling warning,

> O children, children, you don't know what you're doing. ... You're finishing off the work which the enemies of Israel began. They took the bodies away from the world, and you—the name and the memory. ... No continuation, no evidence, no memorial and no name. Not a trace. (p. 262)

Here another of the story's buried themes, the veneration of the *Galut*, surfaces, powerfully conveyed in this scene in which Grandfather Zisskind castigates Yehuda, telling him that Mendele and Ossip were among the finest in Ukrainian society, treating with contempt his simplistic and ignorant biases. When Yehuda explains that Menachem is a name from the *Golah*, the old man launches into one of the text's most gripping jeremiads. The juxtaposition between the Israeli and the Diaspora Jew is neatly reinforced when we recall that Ossip named his son after his dead brother, even though he was acutely aware that such a name would not fit easily in a society populated by non-Jewish Russians. However, as Grandfather Zisskind highlights, Ossip, while not a Zionist, was first and foremost a Jew. The story invites the reader to conclude that Ossip's shimmering superiority to Yehuda the *sabra*, in all its manifestations, is undeniable. Moreover, this scene hints that "The Name" is also fearfully concerned with Israel as a modern, secular state eschewing and dimming the towering achievements of Judaic tradition, failing to tap the rich the fount of wisdom of Yiddish and Judaism.

It is significant that Yehuda distinguishes between being Israeli and being Jewish. In effect, he regards the two identities as incongruous and not as rings on the same historical golden chain. In his mind, a new breed has been born in Israel. The adversarial dialogue between Yehuda and Zisskind is highly illuminating. Grandfather Zisskind explains that all Israelis came from the *Galut*, to which Yehuda replies that they—he and Raya—were born in Israel, which for him is different and separate. The wounded old man, seething with anger and shaking with rage (the story says that he "looked as if he could wring Yehuda's neck" [p. 261]), accuses the heartless young man of ignorance, of being a fool for expressing such opinions. Rightly, he emphasizes and elucidates that ties are remembrance, that a person is guyed to his people, to his nation, because he never forgets his ancestors. Still fuming, Grandfather Zisskind lashes out at Yehuda and accurately zeroes in on his and Raya's sin of omission:

> You're ashamed to give your son the name Mendele lest it remind you that there were Jews who were called by that name. You believe that his name should be wiped off the face of the earth. That not a trace of it should remain. (p. 262)

Even in the face of such agony, Yehuda remains obdurate and unsympathetic. Lamentably, Yehuda and Raya cannot see through the old man's eccentric and often infuriating conduct, cannot help support the immense love he shoulders for Mendele and Ossip.

As the story nears the end, Grandfather Zisskind holds back from acknowledging his new great-grandson when the couple brings him for a visit. It is not illogical to assume that in his mind he feels that the moment he accepts Ehud, the living boy, the unmemorialized Mendele will undergo a second death. On one level, endorsing Ehud's presence and name will demolish the world of yesteryear to which he so impassionedly clings. "You haven't seen our baby yet" (p. 263), Raya tells him ruefully. Yet, Grandfather Zisskind ignores her supplication.

Instead, as he has done numerous times earlier, he pulls up the chair and climbs up to the clock to retrieve the documents. Raya, no longer patient, cannot bear to once again absorb the horrific details of Grandfather's history. Emotionally devastated, she tells Yehuda that they should leave. Outside, with tears streaming down her cheeks, she bends to kiss her son's chest.

It is too late, but in this painful and symbolic passage, Raya, at that instant, recognizes the absolute chasm between her son and her grandfather: "At the moment it seemed to her that [her son] was in need of pity and of great love, as though he were alone, an orphan in the world" (p. 265). Yes, she closes the door. Yes, she is no longer willing to tolerate her grandfather's unremitting, singular preoccupation with the Holocaust. Yes, she and Yehuda prevailed over the forlorn refugee. Yet, in that small scene, her heart opens slightly, and she moves toward her grandfather, perchance propelled by a fear that her son will grow up without any attachment to his history. Suddenly, Raya understands that the complicated matter of the name has far more meaning than she at first believed. Could it be that she undergoes a conceptual and cultural shift, appreciating that Grandfather's appeals and convictions were not just the ramblings of a man with a weak mind?

Herein lies the paradox. Israel was a nation that was born in the shadow of genocide and the promise of "Never Again." Yet, afterwards, it acted ambivalently towards the Holocaust, denying several aspects of that memory so it could renew and re-construct itself. Clearly, Megged endeavors to demonstrate that Raya and Yehuda, by rejecting a memorial and a name, were erasing the dead grandson's presence. In effect, the young couple, and by extension, young Israelis, were expunging the rich tapestry of life that existed before the State of Israel was founded. As Megged frames the unfolding of this sequence, he undermines Raya and Yehuda's deep-seated rejection of the *Galut* and hammers home the criticism that this disconnection, this lack of solidarity, this Israeli condition was shortsighted, malicious, immoral, and unfair. We understand Megged's underlying message, epitomized by the isolated, pitiable "orphaned" infant: Jews must continue to uphold and secure within the collective record the disaster that befell their brothers and sisters in Europe. Without a past, there can be no future.

REFERENCES

Alter, R. (Ed.). (1975). *Modern Hebrew literature*. New York: Behrman House.

Brenner, R. F. (Spring 2002). Discourses of mourning and rebirth in post-Holocaust Israeli literature: Leah Goldberg's "Lady of the castle" and Shulamith Hareven's "The witness." *Women in Judaism*, 1–12. Retrieved August 12, 2007, from *http://www.utoronto.ca/wjudaism/ journal/spring2002/ documents/brenner.pdf.*

Lavi, I. (Interviewer). *A conversation with Aharon Megged about Yad Vashem*. Reshet Bet, Israel. Retrieved October 10, 2006, from *http://msradio.huji.ac.il/wwwroot/ulpanpatuach.htm.*

Maoz, R. (1989). Ideational and ideological principles in constructing teaching syllabus criteria for selecting literary works and their teaching as reflecting and shaping opinion. 65-82. In Janet Aviad (Ed.). (1989) *Studies in Jewish education*. Volume IV, Jerusalem: The Manes Press, The Hebrew University.

Megged, A. (1955) The name. In K. Shawn & K. Goldfrad (Eds.). (2008). *The call of memory: Learning about the Holocaust through narrative: An anthology*, pp. 250–265. Teaneck, NJ: Ben Yehuda Press.

Megged, A. (September 16, 1955). Our old and new culture. *Massa*.

Megged, A. (1989). I was not there. In *The Writing Table*. Tel Aviv: Am Oved.

Megged, A. (1992) Israeli literature over time. *Jewish Studies* 32, 35-43.

Porat, D. (1991). Attitudes of the young state of Israel toward the Holocaust and its survivors: A debate over identity and values. 157–174. In L. J. Silberstein (Ed.). *New perspectives on Israeli history: The early years of the state*. New York and London: New York University Press.

Ramras-Rauch, G. & Michman-Melkman, J. (Eds.). (1985). *Facing the Holocaust: Selected Israeli fiction*. Philadelphia: Jewish Publication Society.

Generational Divide:
Tradition in Transition
in Aharon Megged's "The Name"

Evelyn Ripp and Norbert Ripp

Those who experience the war or its half-life know that it lives on;
the war's clock has no numbers, no spring, no plug to pull.
—Fern Schumer Chapman

Aharon Megged was born in 1920 in Poland, and his family immigrated to Palestine when he was six years old. He began publishing in 1938 and is a recipient of many literary awards. In his writings, Megged creates overviews of society at large by focusing on the relationships between individuals. He is particularly concerned with the "new" Israelis, the *sabras* (those who were born in Israel), and their attempts to discard the cultural heritage of the Diaspora. When we were asked by the editors of this text to choose a story that we would like to teach young people today if we were given the opportunity to do so, we selected Megged's narrative "The Name" (Shawn & Goldfrad, 2008, *Anthology*, pp. 250–265) to present to students because it deals very sensitively with the life of a man in the grip of his memories after the Holocaust. As survivors, we, too, believe in remembering. To us, it is a moral imperative.

Teaching Goals, Audience, and Time Frame

We are retired educators as well as survivors, so we understand well the complexity and the importance of teaching this subject carefully. We know we cannot teach the entirety of the Holocaust; we have chosen a story set after it ended with the understanding that students will be grounded in Holocaust history and have a rich context in which to place this story and its dilemmas. Because we believe that "the history of the Holocaust cannot be transmitted without taking into account the history of its aftermath, the history of survival" (Stark, 2000, p. 4), our goal here is to help students to understand that the Holocaust did not end with the liberation of the camps; the aftermath was long and lingers still today. We want to make students aware that children and grandchildren of survivors still live in the shadow of the Holocaust. We want students to empathize with each of the characters and thus with each survivor family they meet. We want them to maintain their awareness of each character as an individual with his or her own background, viewpoint, concerns, needs, and expectations. We also have a goal specific to literature, namely, that students will recognize and explain the inferences used by Megged to reveal an intimate look at life.

As Dvir Abramovich (2008) writes in this *Guide*, "At heart, 'The Name' is a story with an educational message. Its nucleus narrative intelligently maps out the crosscurrent of divergent values and beliefs that seemingly cannot be reconciled" (p. 471). Although this story is set in Israel and presents a conflict within a Jewish family, it can well be of interest to young adults of all backgrounds because of its underlying universal theme, the yearning to be understood and accepted on the basis of one's own life experiences. Our teaching guide is designed for high school juniors and seniors and college and university students in a literature class. We suggest scheduling four or five 40-minute sessions to cover this complex story adequately.

An Overview of the Story

We offer this brief plot summary for our readers' edification. You may wish to present it as an introductory overview or assign a student to prepare and present it, or you may require that students write their own summary in their notes after they read the story.

Studies show that, despite their scars, many survivors were able to resume their lives, work, establish families, and function successfully as parents and active members of their communities. Yet the psyches of most survivors harbor deep wounds that have never fully healed. There are those who are so psychologically scarred that, like Grandfather Zisskind in "The Name," they are powerless to let go of their tragic history, unable to adjust to the world as it is in the present, and unwilling to face a future that fails to acknowledge and learn from the past.

Raya and Yehuda, a young married couple, often visit Raya's maternal Grandfather Zisskind, a Holocaust survivor, on the Sabbath. The ritual does not vary: He offers refreshments, makes small talk, removes from the wall clock that "had long since stopped" (*Anthology*, p. 251) sheets of paper on which he had recorded the story of the destruction of his *shtetl* and the slaughter of its Jews, and reads it to Yehuda, oblivious to Yehuda's dread of this ritual. Zisskind deeply mourns the loss of his grandson, Mendele, killed by the Nazis at age 12. When Zisskind finds out that Raya is pregnant, his depression lessens. Rachel, Raya's mother and Zisskind's daughter, explains that his transformation results from his expectation that they will name their baby after his grandson. This is the dramatic tension in the story.

Preparing the Students

To prepare students for the reading, which they will do, for the most part, at home, we suggest introducing the vocabulary first, as the terms embody concepts that go beyond simple definitions. These words demand attention because they help provide the background information necessary for understanding this nuanced story. List the words on the board, elicit definitions where possible and fill in as necessary, as the backgrounds of our students dictate, and then ask students to share any connotations these words evoke for them as a way of scaffolding the information, beginning the connection between the literature and the reader.

1. **Holocaust**: The term comes from classical Greek and means "consumed by fire: a burnt offering." The word denotes the murder of 6 million Jews by the Nazis. In Hebrew, the Holocaust is called *Shoah*, which means "catastrophe."
2. *Golah* (Heb.): **Diaspora** (Eng.): The term originally refers to the uprooting and dispersion of the Jews from their homeland, but today commonly refers to anywhere outside of Israel where Jews live.
3. **Ghetto**: A section of town, separated from the general community, serving as a compulsory, enclosed residential quarter for Jews.
4. *Shtetl* (Yiddish): A small Eastern European town with a proportionately significant Jewish population.
5. **Torah:** The term refers to all the teachings of Judaism.
6. **Zion:** The term refers to the Jewish homeland and is symbolic of Judaism or of Jewish national aspiration.
7. **Zionism**: An international movement originally for the establishment of a Jewish national or religious community in Palestine and later for the support of modern Israel
8. **Zionist**: A member of the Zionist movement founded during the 19th century to secure the return of Jews to Palestine (Israel).

In addition to the vocabulary as necessary background information, we will acquaint students, in a brief lecture, with the fact that when the State of Israel was created, ardent young Zionists wanted to expunge all vestiges of the Diaspora from their restored homeland. This also included rejection of the cultural heritage of the *shtetl,* down to its very language, Yiddish. This was in reaction to the persecution, the discrimination, and the sense of helplessness that had been the lot of so many Jews throughout the ages.

Without any personal experience of the Holocaust, this new breed of young Israelis could not understand their fellow Jews, who, they believed, let themselves be led helplessly to their deaths "like sheep to slaughter." This was, of course, a misconception, because there was much Jewish spiritual, religious, and even physical resistance. As a result of this myth, young Israelis considered themselves superior to the survivors, who felt misunderstood and isolated.

It was only during the 1990 Persian Gulf War, when they were bombarded with Scud missiles and confined to their air raid shelters, that some of the young Israelis began to understand what it is like to be rendered helpless in the face of terror. As an alternative or in conjunction with this lecture, you might assign or read aloud from the superb and detailed discussion of Israeli society in the 1950s offered by Abramovich in this volume (pp. 468–479) to fully contextualize the narrative.

The introduction and overview of the story, the vocabulary discussion, and the contextualizing lecture will take close to the full period. Distribute the reading in class and assign its completion as homework for the next session. To check for understanding, ask the students to select five sentences they consider most crucial to their comprehension of thematic elements, essential questions, and philosophical issues raised by the story and write them in their notebooks or journals.

Monitoring Progress

In the second lesson, monitor progress in comprehension by asking students to cite and discuss their sentence selections. Because these are young adults, they can help facilitate the discussion, providing a change of pace from the traditional lecture modality. Ask five volunteers to write one of their sentences on the board and explain their reasons for their choice. Then, group students in small clusters around the room and have them conduct a 15-minute exchange of ideas with the twin goals of

1. determining the importance of each of their chosen sentences to the story's essence; and
2. analyzing the structural components of the sentence—its words, tone, symbols, inferences, compression—to reach consensus on what makes the sentence crucial.

A volunteer then reports the group's analysis to the whole class. Our goal here is to provide students with the opportunity to hear their peers' interpretations and insights into the implications and subtleties that they might not have recognized during their silent reading. The homework assignment that follows can be informal; we suggest that students list in their journals any questions the story or the small-group discussion may have raised for them.

Continuing the Analysis: Characters and Inferences

To assess students' comprehension, you might design individualized group work for the third class. For example, in a class of 20 students, ask them to form five groups of four. In the first four groups, randomly assign one of the four characters in the story for study and analysis; we want students to be sensitive to each character's individuality and needs. We also want students to recognize and explain the inferences used by Megged, so the fifth group will explore the larger meanings implicit in his writing. Assign these students to reread the story closely to identify and examine Megged's use of inference.

Each student in each group has an independent task which s/he must complete and share with the others to fulfill the assignment. A group representative shares the conclusions with the class. With each person taking one aspect of the assignment, the groups assigned to a character will describe/illustrate with text citations:

- the character and his/her role or position in the story;
- his/her described or implied desires/needs/expectations/demands;
- his/her past, described or implied; and
- its effect on his/her current and future thoughts and/or actions/behaviors.

The fifth group identifies, citing page and paragraph number, and states directly what Megged has only implied for at least eight inferences in the story; each group member contributes two. To ensure that students remain on task, we suggest that you limit the time they work together, allowing 20-25 minutes for this activity.

These are the characters in the story and our responses to the assignment for your convenience; your students' responses will, of course, vary:

Grandfather Zisskind (the name literally means "sweet child" in Yiddish) lives in the State of Israel. He has no place in the new society. He is deemed irrelevant—powerless and voiceless. Zisskind has been seriously affected by his painful past. The Holocaust is a part of his history and remains a dominant part of his life. He lives with those memories and carries his loved ones deep in his heart. What he wants is for his legacy to live on through his soon-to-born great-grandchild. "He has one wish—that if it is a son, he should be named. ... Mendele" (*Anthology*, p. 257). Naming a newborn after a deceased relative had been a long-held, important, and all but religiously ordained tradition that has been discarded by the new, secular generation of Israelis. Now, his granddaughter and her husband are expecting their first child, and he hopes that they will name him after his grandson, Mendele, who was killed during the Holocaust. He maintains this hope and is grief-stricken when he learns that it will not be fulfilled. The name Mendele is a window to the past for Zisskind, a metaphor for the spiritual sustenance that he needs. When it is not forthcoming, his physical and emotional health quickly begin to fail.

Raya is Zisskind's granddaughter and has a close and loving relationship with him. However, she does not understand him and is unable to assimilate his needs with her own, which include giving her baby a modern Israeli name. She has her own dreams of such names for the baby she expects and intends to choose one of them. Her past has led her to feel that "Mendele" and other Yiddish names are "Ghetto names" (p. 258). She doesn't realize how much pain her words will trigger in him when she refuses to name the baby after Mendele, should it be a boy.

Yehuda is Raya's husband. He is particularly unempathic and unwilling to fulfill Zisskind's needs. He doesn't grasp Zisskind's dilemma, and in fact becomes annoyed and numbed by Zisskind's insistence on repeating stories of the past whenever they visit: "He had heard these same things many times over and no longer felt anything when they were repeated" (p. 253). It is clear that he tolerates the old man only out of respect for his wife. He, too, derisively rejects Mendele as a possibility for his son's name. Ultimately, he is considered by Zisskind to be "a wretched boor, an empty vessel," a "good for nothing" (p. 261) for so casually discarding the bonds that tie him to the past.

Both Raya and Yehuda are young and unable to see Zisskind in the context of his life. They cannot relate to his suffering on a personal level and cannot help him overcome it. After all, he knew the *Golah*, and they will never suffer exile. They're of a different breed and have grown up in a different culture. They belong here. Their reaction to Zisskind's request also contains an element of the new generation distancing itself from events of the past, the pain and destruction that is, after all, beyond their comprehension.

Rachel is Raya's mother and Zisskind's daughter, the mother of a *sabra* but the daughter of a survivor, caught between them both. She sympathizes with both views, and tries, unsuccessfully, to find a compromise. When her daughter rejects it out of hand, she despairs of finding common ground between her past and her future.

Below are inferences we have expanded upon; our suggested responses are included. Students' conclusions will vary.

- What is the significance implied by the white tablecloth and the remnants of the Sabbath meal? (Covering the table with a white cloth is traditional among observant Jews, and that, together with the leftovers from the Sabbath meal, indicates that Zisskind is religiously observant.)
- Can we infer anything about the religious observance of Raya and Yehuda? (Depending on the reader's knowledge of Jewish ritual, the following things may be noted: On the one hand, Raya and Yehuda come to visit almost every Sabbath afternoon and knock on the door, perhaps in observance of the prohibition not to ring a door bell on the Sabbath. On the other hand, they do not greet him with any customary Sabbath greeting and seem reluctant at best to share any part of the Sabbath meal with him, so perhaps they are not observant. Later, their adamant refusal to even consider naming their soon-to-born child Mendele seems disrespectful of Jewish tradition.)
- What can we infer about the religious differences between Raya and her husband and Grandfather Zisskind? (Religious differences may contribute to the tension between them. Zisskind may feel that they have no regard or respect for any aspect of the past that he cherishes. They may feel that he lives in the past and is unable, then, to function in what they see as the modern world.)
- What can we infer from the symbolism of the broken clock on the wall and the fact that it is now used as a storage place for Zisskind's Holocaust testimony? (The clock, which has not been running for a long time, could imply that Zisskind's own life has come to a stop. In his granddaughter's estimation, he is, like the clock, stuck in the past, albeit a painful one that she cannot understand or appreciate. Alternatively, we might infer that nothing can go forward after the Holocaust for those who survived but still suffer so profoundly. Like Zisskind, the clock is the receptacle of the story of Holocaust losses; that is its only current use. It can no longer be what it was meant to be.)
- What can we infer from the reluctance of Raya and Yehuda to accept the refreshments offered them by Grandfather Zisskind? (Their reluctance to eat might imply a rejection of Zisskind himself, or of what they consider old or unappetizing food, or of tradition, since he always serves the same refreshments, or simply that Yehuda is so irritated by Zisskind and his habits that he does not want to do anything to prolong the visit or get comfortable while he is there.)
- What is the implication of the dread Yehuda experiences upon hearing Zisskind read his story? (We may infer that Yehuda had become desensitized to

the constant repetition since Grandfather insists on reading it aloud to Yehuda during each of his visits, or that the whole subject is one that, in Yehuda's opinion, is in the past and should be forgotten. Alternatively, we may infer that Yehuda is afraid that the repetition will make it impossible for him to ever forget, which may be Zisskind's motivation in telling him each week, but the burden of memory is not something that Yehuda wants to accept.)

- What is the inference in the following sentence?: "Although it was very hot, he [Grandfather Zisskind] always wore a yellow … vest" (p. 250). (At the risk of reading something into the text that may not have been intended at all, to us the color yellow recalls the yellow Star of David that Jews were required to wear as an identifying mark. It is as if the yellow vest reaffirms his identification with the tragedy of the Holocaust and connects him to his lost family. He has not moved forward since that time.)

- What are we to infer from the fact that Grandfather Zisskind is the only one in the story who doesn't have a given name, while each of the other characters has a first name only? (We might infer that Grandfather symbolizes a generation of survivors; he speaks for all of the "sweet children" whose childhoods were destroyed by the Nazis. Raya and Yehuda, on the other hand, represent the new generation that has broken with tradition; they have forgotten the centrality of Jewish continuity, of transmitting one's heritage *midor l'dor*, from generation to generation. They are leaves without roots, with modern first names but without a family name that binds them to their past.)

For the final 15 minutes of the class, students will share their character analyses and their explication of Megged's inferences.

For homework that night, assign the following interpretive questions to continue to assess comprehension and to offer students an opportunity to express themselves. You may choose to individualize the assignment by giving one question to each of your five groups.

- Grandpa Zisskind is sad, and he knows the source of his sadness. Explain, citing text to support the premise.
- What literal significance does the name "Mendele" have for Grandfather Zisskind? What symbolic significance does it have?
- Both a *deep* connection and a *disconnection* exist between Raya and Yehuda and Grandfather Zisskind. Defend or reject this statement, citing specific examples from the text as well as your own inferences.
- Rachel, "midway between the generations, was of two minds" (p. 257). Discuss the difficulties she faced. Does her position represent that of all mothers *vis-á-vis* their parents and their children, or is her position singularly reflective of an adult child of survivors? Explain, using text support where possible.
- Each of the characters has different needs, but each has a support system. Agree or disagree with this statement as you comment on the relationships between:
  a. Grandfather Zisskind and Raya

b. Grandfather Zisskind and Yehuda
c. Grandfather Zisskind and Rachel
d. Rachel and Raya
e. Raya and Yehuda

Evaluation and Closure

In the fourth and final session, have students offer their responses to the homework questions, and evaluate them in terms of the logic of their conclusions and the use of text-based support. In addition, to provide closure and to encourage students to expand their personal connections to the narrative, ask them to take a position on the following timeless, essential questions appropriate for every ethnic group in every generation:

- Should we want and expect our children to be familiar with their parents' and grandparents' past? Is an awareness of family history central to one's own identity?
- How do you feel about giving a newborn child an ethnic versus an assimilated name? How did your parents select your name? What are your feelings about the process and the choice they made? What is the impact one's name may have on one's development as a person?

These provocative questions lend themselves well to discussion in dyads and small groups as well as to a written response. You might ask students to write informally in their journals first to articulate their thoughts, then share with a partner, and then summarize their conclusions with the class.

We like to complete units of study with a writing assignment given as homework; you may wish to use an additional period for students to write in class. For a summative assessment, assign a two- or three-page reflective narrative essay that requires students to explore the divide between and among the generations in "The Name." If the essay and the group work assessment are each given a value of 40 points, and class participation earns 20 points, you have offered students the opportunity to earn a perfect score for this unit. A writing prompt follows:

> Read and explain the following quotation by the American writer John Dos Passos: "Our only hope will lie in the frail web of understanding of one person for the pain of the other." (10 pts.) Then, applying this quotation to the characters in "The Name," address the following in an integrated, first-person, reflective essay, using the text wherever possible to support your opinion.

1. What is "our only hope" for this family? (10 pts.)
2. Do you think there is a "frail web of understanding"
   a. of Raya for the pain of her grandfather? (5 pts.)
   b. of Yehuda for the pain of Grandfather Zisskind? (5 pts.)
   c. of Rachel for the pain of her father? (5 pts.)

3. Does the story lead you toecific family to the world in general, can we today live up to the ideal expressed in the words of Dos Passos? (10 pts.)

The brief unit of study on this story is traditional, using literature and vocabulary study, lecture, class and small-group discussion, and writing as learning modalities. However, the co-editor of this guide, Keren Goldfrad, shared with us the unusually creative dramatic presentation her daughter was offered when she completed this story in her ninth-grade class in her school in Israel, an option you might try.

As an extended learning opportunity, the classroom teacher assigned several students to summarize the story to the entire grade assembled in the school auditorium. A student then announced that the conflict had so distressed Grandfather Zisskind that he had petitioned the Family Court in closed session to have the baby's name changed to Mendele over the parents' objections. The judge who heard the arguments, the student continued, felt that the issue was potentially so divisive to the entire community that a public trial was in order, and the case was to be heard immediately.

Volunteers from the audience became the jury on stage, and students from the class took the roles of the characters, defense and prosecution lawyers, the judge, bailiff, and other courtroom personnel. Each character took center stage to tell his/her story, and appealed to the jury to rule in his/her favor, using, of course, arguments based only on the text and what the readers could infer from it. The jury was given 15 minutes to deliberate the case offstage, while teachers met with the "spectators," the students in the audience, in small groups in and around the auditorium to discuss the case as well.

The judge called the audience to order. The jury returned a verdict, which the judge announced, and ordered the family to go for counseling to help each member learn to hear and respect one another. The jury, along with the audience, was dismissed with thanks from the judge.

We thought this idea was a wonderful way to bring closure to the reading, particularly for younger students, an authentic, real-world, fully-engaging, independent practice of facts and concepts taught and meaning made. The students who experienced and participated in this drama went back to their classes never to forget Megged's powerful story, always to remember one aspect of the painful legacy of the Holocaust borne by survivors and their descendants.

REFERENCES

Abramovich, D. (2008). The problem of Holocaust remembrance in Israel of the 1950s: Aharon Megged's "The name." In K. Shawn & K. Goldfrad (Eds.). *The call of memory: Learning about the Holocaust through narrative: A teacher's guide*, pp. 468–479. Teaneck, NJ: Ben Yehuda Press.

Megged, A. (1955). The name. In K. Shawn & K. Goldfrad (2008). (Eds.). *The call of memory: Learning about the Holocaust through narrative: An anthology*, pp. 250–265. Teaneck, NJ: Ben Yehuda Press.

Stark, J. (2000). Retrieved July 23, 2007, from *http://www.library.yale.edu/testimonies/publications/Newsletter_2000.pdf, p. 4.*

State Standards and Student Learning Objectives

Karen Shawn and William Younglove

Standards in learning are not new, and yet standards-based learning has come about largely only since 1989. From state to state and nation to nation, standards differ; even when the same terms are used, meanings differ; hence our glossary (*Guide*, pp. 493–496).

Most American states have developed subject matter content standards. English language arts, for example, encompass the communication skills of listening, speaking, reading, and writing; research and technology are often listed as adjunct content standards. In 1996, the National Council of Teachers of English and the International Reading Association jointly issued a dozen standards encompassing such literacy growth skills. At the same time, National Standards for History were published, delineating specific content that learners need to know en route to becoming informed, responsible, and contributing citizens.

This teacher's guide addresses and meets or exceeds the following general state and district standards and student objectives in reading, writing, speaking, listening, and viewing that require that students

1. read, understand, interpret, and evaluate a variety of materials and works including fiction, poetry, drama, and nonfiction;
2. write and speak formally and informally for a variety of purposes and audiences;
3. read to locate, select, and make use of relevant information from a variety of media, reference, and technological sources;
4. identify and evaluate relationships between language and culture;
5. read and recognize literature as a record of human experience;
6. participate in discussions of issues and ideas;
7. conduct, refine, and present research and investigations in a variety of forms;
8. analyze the duties and responsibilities of individuals in society.

The lessons and suggestions presented here

- offer opportunities for independent and shared silent and oral reading;
- challenge students to use comprehension, interpretation, evaluation, and appreciation strategies with a variety of texts to increase empathy for and understanding of the dimensions of human experience;
- encourage students to read complex literary works, using one to deepen knowledge in another;

- provide opportunities for students to recognize themes and theses, supporting details, cause and effect, and authors' purposes;
- elicit students' predictions, opinions, questions, comparisons, conclusions, extrapolations; and paraphrases or retellings;
- enhance students' participation as thoughtful, reflective, and responsive members of a literacy community;
- incorporate journal writing and formal writing as an integral part of assessment.

Specifically, in history, social studies, and geography, students

1. listen and read to acquire information and understanding;
2. draw on prior experience and interactions with other readers and writers and examine the ways that personal identity and human behaviors are shaped by one's culture;
3. think and analyze systematically personal, national, and global decisions, interactions, and consequences;
4. analyze historic events by examining accounts written from different perspectives;
5. analyze the roles, duties, responsibilities, and contributions of individuals and groups to social, political, economic, cultural, and religious practices and activities;
6. interpret and analyze documents related to significant developments and events in world history;
7. understand the chronological organization of history and know how to organize events and people into major eras to identify and explain historical relationships;
8. understand how to use the processes and resources of historical inquiry;
9. understand that societies are diverse and change over time;
10. understand specific political institutions and theories that have developed and changed over time;
11. understand how economic, political, cultural, and social processes interact to shape patterns of populations, interdependence, cooperation, and conflict;
12. apply knowledge of people, places, and environments to understand the past and present and to plan for the future.

In addition, the lessons provide connections among the disciplines of literature, geography, history, culture, current events, and technology, offering students opportunities to

1. examine interactions among places, regions, events, and people in the historical events under discussion;
2. judge the reliability of sources, including those on the Internet;
3. read and respond, through discussion and writing, to a variety of texts, including primary sources, literature, and historical narrative;

4. form and express text-based opinions and judgments;
5. become thoughtful, tolerant participants in our multicultural, democratic society;
6. collect data, facts, and ideas;
7. discover relationships, concepts, and generalizations;
8. obtain, use, and communicate accurate and relevant information from a range of electronic sources;
9. routinely and efficiently use and evaluate online information resources to collaborate, research, and communicate in ways that suit their purpose and audience.

We believe the lessons written by our teacher/authors will help their colleagues

- encourage the individual child and capitalize on his/her capabilities and strengths;
- respect and demonstrate caring and concern for each child's interests, needs, and background;
- provide opportunities for students to work cooperatively in dyads, triads, and groups;
- check for understanding, assessing students' comprehension with multiple assessment opportunities, including traditional and alternative modes that accommodate diverse learners;
- connect new learning to previous knowledge and interests;
- provide organizational strategies for learning the required material;
- promote independent learning and research, encouraging students to use technological and informational resources to gather, analyze, and synthesize information;
- teach to students' learning styles, using a variety of strategies, approaches, and modes;
- present engaging direct instruction, practice, and authentic tasks.

Glossary of Educational Terms

Because terms used in standards-based learning are not uniformly defined, the following definitions, culled largely from American states that have adopted world-class standards (e.g., California) will be referenced. Please note that not all elements appear in each teacher's guide, and applications of definitions may be fluid within lessons.

Anticipatory Set: The "hook" at the start of the lesson to connect the experiences of the students to the objectives of the lesson.

Assessment: Students' independent application of the skills or content objectives to reveal the extent to which they achieved them.

Chavruta (Alt., *chavrusa*): Related to the Hebrew word for "friend"; a minimum of two study partners who learn a biblical or Talmudic passage and accompanying commentaries; here used to refer to study partners of any text under discussion. *Chavruta* learning is characterized by reading and discussing the meaning of the text, raising detailed questions, and offering potential answers and explanations. In an effort to deepen the level of the textual study and understanding, study partners or *chavrutas* challenge one another's answers and explanations, thereby sharpening one another's learning.

Check for Understanding: Teacher seeks feedback from students, before practice, to see if they will be able to perform the objective.

Closure: Teacher checks students' perceptions of how well they learned the lesson; can include teacher questions about or student summary of the content standard's concepts or skills.

Content Standards: Specify what the students should know and be able to do.

Curriculum Objectives: Describe the instructional means to achieving the content standards, i.e., the goals of classroom instruction, including cognitive, affective, and psychomotor objectives.

Double-Voice (or Dialogue) Poem: The use of two voices to write a poetic response to a narrative. A student may take two points of view in such a poem, or two students may take turns responding, writing a poetic dialogue.

Enrichment Opportunities: Offerings going beyond the lesson objectives of content and skill mastery to deepen and/or broaden a specific concentration of study.

Essential Questions: Open-ended questions that suggest investigation and inquiry and act as concept organizers.

Evaluation: Collection of student data to determine achievement of objective.

Extended Learning: Lesson-related learnings that go beyond the classroom and the school schedule.

Found Poetry: Students use specific words or sentences found in a narrative and highlight its theme or essence by writing them in poem form.

Front-load: Describes building and activating prior knowledge before reading a selection, for example, giving information about a particular location to help students understand the setting.

Gallery Walk: Students stroll, singly or in small groups, past teacher-displayed artifacts, often primary source documents, preceding the study of a literary work, writing questions or comments upon hung white paper en route—or to view such final products.

Goals, Teaching and Learning: Broad aims or outcomes.

Group Work:

> **Cooperative**: Group work with positive interdependence and shared responsibility, yet individual accountability.
>
> **Collaborative**: Participants work in small groups toward a class goal, addressing group dynamics through an agreed-upon process.
>
> **Jigsaw**: Resource interdependence created in class by dividing materials/information among groups; holding each group responsible for teaching part of the material to the class.
>
> **Small-Group Discussion**: Class divisions to help students process content and skills and increase individual responses.

Guided Practice: Opportunity for each student to demonstrate grasp of new learning while applying specific teacher input.

Habits of Mind: Sixteen types of intelligent behavior:

1. persisting
2. managing impulsivity
3. listening with understanding and empathy
4. thinking flexibly
5. thinking about thinking
6. striving for accuracy
7. questioning and posing problems
8. applying past knowledge to new situations
9. thinking and communicating with clarity and precision
10. gathering data through the senses
11. creating, imagining, and innovating
12. responding with wonderment and awe
13. taking responsible risks
14. finding humor
15. thinking independently
16. remaining open to continuous learning

Independent Practice: Students apply newly taught skills or concepts in familiar formats or tasks, reinforcing their acquisition during dependent practice with the teacher.

Individualized Assignments: Differentiated tasks provided for students that include special scaffolding to help those students achieve the objective.

Journal, Dialectical (Double Entry); Literary; Writing: Student-written short responses to literature, media, and/or personal experience. Bisected page diacritical journal, often called double entry, allows text passage selections on the left side and critical analyses and questions on the right.

K-W-L-H Chart (Know/Want to Know/Learned/How I Learned): Four columns provide an opportunity to "pretest" students on any material (K-W), while allowing for "post-test" gains and an examination of the value of utilized source material (L-H).

Lecture: A formal discourse by a teacher to instruct the class to help fulfill course objectives.

Literacy: Ability to read, write, and understand texts in varied academic discourses and from different academic disciplines.

Modeling: Teacher- or student-provided representations, often demonstrated, so that students can see the shape, component parts, or arrangement of what they are producing.

Multigenre: A collection of texts that rely upon a variety of reading/writing types.

Multimodal Literacy: Metacognitive strategies for developing literacy practices that can be carried across multiple sites/texts/media, rather than a set of practices tied to specific sites.

Objectives: What students will know and be able to do by the end of the lesson.

PhotoPoem: A multi-modal presentation using photographs to illustrate and enhance a poem or using lines of poetry to illustrate and enhance related photographs; ideally, the poetry and the photographs are the students' original work. See *http://www.usd.edu/dwp/activities/photopoem.html* for suggestions for a classroom lesson.

PowerWords PowerPoint: A brief PowerPoint presentation using particular parts of speech (adjectives, verbs) from a poem or story illustrated and enhanced by related art, photographs, voice-overs, and/or music.

Procedure/Method/Input: Teacher-sequenced scaffolded activities that students will need to do during the lesson, including accommodations for special needs students.

Quick-write, parallel quick-write: An assignment of two or three minutes in which students write a response summarizing points every ten minutes into a lecture; or articulating their response to literature or an aspect of it. A parallel quick-write is used for team or group work, usually on different but related stories or on two or more aspects of the same story. Quick-writes may be for the students' own use as a study guide; for the teacher's use as a way of assessing understanding, and as a classroom activity in which they are exhibited and analyzed publicly.

Readers' Theater: Short literary material, often adapted into script form, to be enacted by a class, with minimal props or rehearsal.

Rubric: An assessment tool to measure students' achievement, consisting usually of a scaled scoring guide (e.g., 1–6) with stated criteria at each numerical level.

Share and Compare: Student pairs or small groups share and compare their individual findings on an assigned topic, coming to a consensus, or not; explaining their reasons for either to the class.

Silent Conversation: Similar to a Gallery Walk, students move around the room while writing, with markers, responses and questions about posted studied text and, possibly, about each other's comments. Without discussion, teacher synthesizes responses into common themes and essential questions for future class discussion.

State Standards: Designate what students will learn at specific grade levels.

Storyboarding: A tiered-learning activity in which more visually oriented students express the ideas of the narrative fully by drawing simple figures and writing minimal text in sequenced boxed scenes.

T-Chart: So called because the perpendicular center line on the paper from the top center downward allows text entry on the left and student commentary about the text selected on the right, serving as a graphic organizer.

Tiered Learning: Scaffolded lesson segments that approach reading, writing, speaking, and listening with audiences of varied size and background.

Venn Diagram: Traditionally, two overlapping circles (can be three) whose largest left-right parts contain direct opposite statements about the studied material, while the center overlap contains similarities, serving as a graphic organizer.

Whole-Class Discussion: Traditionally teacher initiated and directed class give-and-take conversation to utilize higher-order thinking skills in achieving objectives; can use randomly mixed student name cards to ensure inclusion of all students.

Write-Around: A written reaction to a reading selection before any discussion occurs. Participants write for two to three minutes, and then pass the response to the next person in the group. The first response is read, and then responded to. Additional comments may be introduced. The process continues until all group members have responded in writing to the reading selection.

Writing Prompt/Journal Prompt: Teacher-provided short invitation for the student to write on the given topic, consisting of very brief background and a set of directions.

About the Contributors

Victoria Aarons, Ph.D., Professor and Chair of the English Department at Trinity University, Texas, received her Ph.D. at the University of California, Berkeley. She is the author of *A Measure of Memory: Storytelling and Identity in American Jewish Fiction* and *What Happened to Abraham? Reinventing the Covenant in American Jewish Fiction*, both of which received a Choice Award for Outstanding Academic Book. Aarons has published essays and book chapters in a variety of volumes and reference works and is a contributor to *Holocaust Literature: An Encyclopedia of Writers and Their Work*. She teaches courses on American Jewish and Holocaust literatures.

Dvir Abramovich, Ph.D., the Jan Randa Senior Lecturer in Hebrew & Jewish Studies, is Director of the Centre for Jewish History and Culture at the University of Melbourne. He is editor of the *Australian Journal of Jewish Studies*, the country's only peer-reviewed journal dedicated to the field of Jewish Studies, and president of the Australian Association for Jewish Studies. Dr Abramovich has written and lectured extensively on Israeli and Jewish literature and is currently co-editing a reference work on Hebrew authors and a publication on testimonies of Jewish Holocaust survivors.

Barbara G. Appelbaum served for 22 years as Director of the Center for Holocaust Awareness and Information (CHAI) at the Jewish Community Federation of Greater Rochester (JCFGR), NY, where she created an oral history archive, trained teachers, and hosted annual interschool conferences. She has taught at Nazareth College and interviewed survivors for the Shoah Visual Documentation Project. She co-edited, with Barbara Lovenheim, *Perilous Journeys: Personal Stories of German and Austrian Jews Who Escaped the Nazis* (1990, JCFGR) and co-authored, with Peter Marchant, *Angie's Story* (2006, JCFGR), developing study guides and DVDs for both. Barbara studied at the Yad Vashem Summer Institute.

Joan Baker, Ph.D., is Associate Professor of Medieval Studies in the Department of English at Florida International University in Miami, Florida. Her research has included editing a Middle English romance, *Robert of Sicily*, derived from the legends of Solomon. Her publications include essays on editing medieval texts, Middle English romance, Chaucer and Langland, and poverty in William Langland's poem "Piers Plowman." Recent papers focus on a study of Jews in this poem. Dr. Baker served as an interviewer for the Shoah Visual History Foundation.

Sharon Deykin Baris, Ph.D., Senior Lecturer in English and American Literature in the Department of English at Israel's Bar-Ilan University, chairs the Kaplan Program for American Literature. She has published on Hawthorne, Melville, James, Eliot, Stevens, and Welty, among others, in such journals as *MLS*, *The Henry James Review*, *Prospects*, *Southern Literary Journal*, *Hebrew University Studies in Literature*, and *Common Knowledge*. Her work has also focused on Jewish writers including Sachs, Malamud, and Kellerman, published in *Studies* *in American Jewish Literature* and *Jewish American Women Writers*. She is completing a book on Eudora Welty on the political and cultural contexts of her times and another on the influence of the biblical Book of Daniel on the American imagination.

Aden Bar-Tura is the Managing Editor of Bar-Ilan University's interdisciplinary journal *Common Knowledge*. Her research interests include anthropological approaches to 19th- and 20th-century American literature and Holocaust texts. She is currently writing on the construct of taboo in American literature.

Eli Ben-Joseph, Ph.D., is Head of English Studies at the Western Galilee College in Israel. His dissertation was interdisciplinary: historical biography, literary analysis, and the social psychology of antisemitism. This work was later published by the University Press of America as *Aesthetic Persuasion: Henry James, the Jews, and Race* (1996). During his doctoral studies, Dr. Ben-Joseph researched Holocaust bystander history. He has given talks at the Ghetto Fighters' Museum on the literature of Holocaust victims and on literary antisemitism and has given presentations at Pennsylvania State University, Mount Union College, Ohio, and the University of Trier, Germany. More recently, he has authored a paper entitled "Cultural Studies in English" for the anthology *How Globalization Affects the Study of English* (Mellen Press, 2006).

Lolle W. Boettcher retired from the Missouri Public School system after teaching middle school English for 25 years. She studied the Holocaust at Yad Vashem and at the Ghetto Fighters' Museum. Ms. Boettcher serves on the Missouri Holocaust Education and Awareness Commission. In her association with the St. Louis Holocaust Museum and Learning Center, she serves on their Governing Board and their Education Council, facilitates the "Teaching Trunks" program, and conducts Law Enforcement and Society workshops for the St. Louis Metropolitan Police Force and Academy. She is a USHMM Teacher Fellow as well as a member of its Regional Education Corps. She is the recipient of the Janusz Korczak Teaching Award.

Keith Breiman, Ph.D., is a supervisor of Child Study Teams in the New Jersey public school system. A clinical social worker, he completed an advanced certificate program in Counseling Holocaust Survivors and the Second Generation at New York's Training Institute for Mental Health and served as interviewer and clinical coder for the Jerome Riker Foundation for the Study of Organized Persecution of Children under the direction of Dr. Judith Kestenberg.

Bella Bryks-Klein is the daughter of Holocaust survivor and writer Rachmil Bryks. Born in Stockholm after the war, she immigrated with her family to New York as a baby. She attended Stern College (Yeshiva University) and is presently a graduate student in Yiddish Literature at the Hebrew University of Jerusalem. Active in the Yiddish world in Israel, she lectures and translates, belongs to the Association of Yiddish Writers and Journalists in Israel, administers the Arbeiterring Tel Aviv, and is a member of Dorot Hemshech, the Second Generation to the Shoah, an organization sponsored by Yad Vashem. She interviewed survivors for the Shoah Visual History Foundation.

Emily Miller Budick, Ph.D., holds the Ann and Joseph Edelman Chair in American literature and is Chair of the American Studies department at Israel's Hebrew University. She has published widely; her books include *Emily Dickinson and the Life of Language* (Louisiana State University Press, 1986), *Fiction and Historical Consciousness* (Yale University Press, 1989), *Nineteenth-Century American Romance* (Twayne Publishers, 1996), *Engendering Romance* (Yale University Press, 1994), *Blacks and Jews in Literary Conversation* (Cambridge University Press, 1998), and *Aharon Appelfeld's Fiction: Acknowledging the Holocaust* (Indiana University Press, 2005). She has written numerous essays primarily on American literature and is now writing on American and Hebrew Holocaust fiction. Professor Budick is the editor of *Ideology and Jewish Identity.*

Nathan Cohen, Ph.D., is a senior lecturer at the Center for Yiddish Studies at Bar-Ilan University. He is the author of *Books, Writers and Newspapers: The Jewish Cultural Center in Warsaw, 1918–1942* (Hebrew, Jerusalem 2003) and is an associate editor of *Yad Vashem Studies.* The central themes of Dr. Cohen's research and of teaching are the historical aspects of the cultural life of Polish and East European Jewry in the late 19th and first half of the 20th centuries.

Patrick Connelly has taught theology at The Aquinas Institute of Rochester, NY, for 22 years. He studied at Yad Vashem and received a National Endowment for the Humanities (NEH) Summer Seminar grant to study "Cultural Responses to the Holocaust in America" at the Jewish Theological Seminary in New York. Patrick is a Museum Teacher Fellow of the USHMM. He is the recipient of the Janusz Korczak Teaching Award and the Louis Yavner Award.

Loyal Darr now works with the Teacher Education Program at the University of Denver in Colorado following early retirement from the Denver Public Schools where he served as a teacher and supervisor of K–12 Social Studies. He studied at Yad Vashem and has taught the Holocaust at the middle school, high school, and college levels. He has been honored with the State of Colorado Martin L. King, Jr., and Beth Joseph Congregation Humanitarian Awards.

Barb Figg teaches about the Holocaust, Advanced Placement United States Government and Politics, and Recent U.S. History to seniors at Mullen High School, a college prep Catholic school in Denver, CO. Barb twice participated in the National Bearing Witness Program in Israel and in the March of the Living Catholic Teachers in Poland. She received the University of Denver's Judaic Studies Department Vinnick Scholarship to study at Yad Vashem's Summer Institute, and she works closely with Colorado's governor to plan the Holocaust Awareness activities for the state.

Diane Fingers, NBCT (National Board Certified Teacher), is a Language Arts teacher at Francis Howell North High School in St. Peters, MO. She teaches the Sophomore Diverse Voices Communication Arts Honors courses as well as the Senior European Voices program.

Josey G. Fisher is Director of the Holocaust Oral History Archive of Gratz College in Pennsylvania and Holocaust education consultant to the Auerbach Central Agency for Jewish Education and the Jewish Community Relations Council. An instructor in Holocaust education at Gratz College and adjunct faculty in history at Moore College of Art and Design, she sits on the Pennsylvania Holocaust Education Council. Honors include the Mordechai Anielewicz Award for Teaching the Holocaust and the Korczak Teaching Award (together with colleague Christopher Gwin). Her publications include *The Persistence of Youth: Oral Testimonies of the Holocaust*, contributions to *The Holocaust: A Grolier Student Library*, and a foreword to this volume.

Sarah Fraiman-Morris, Ph.D., is Assistant Professor of Comparative Literature at Bar-Ilan University, Israel. Her field of expertise is German literature. She is the author of *Judaism in the Works of Richard Beer-Hofmann and Lion Feuchtwanger* (1998) and has also published various articles on German-Jewish writers such as Stefan Zweig, Franz Werfel, Joseph Roth, Heinrich Heine, and others. In addition, she has written on the Faust-motif in German literature as well as in connection with the Holocaust.

Mark H. Gelber, Ph.D., is Professor of Comparative Literature and German-Jewish Studies at Ben-Gurion University in Israel and permanent member of the board of the Rabb Center for Holocaust and Redemption Studies at BGU. He has been a visiting professor at the University of Pennsylvania, the University of Graz (Austria), and Yale University. He is an expert on the literary and cultural legacy of Central European Jewry, including Cultural Zionism, and the author of numerous studies on the literature of exile, which focuses on authors of Central European provenance including Nelly Sachs, Jakov Lind, Stefan Zweig, Joseph Roth, Georg Hermann, Max Brod, Else Lasker-Schueler, Elias Canetti, and others.

Abigail Gillman, Ph.D., is Assistant Professor of German and Hebrew at Boston University in Massachusetts. Her research focuses on German Jewish literature and culture, and she has published essays on Kafka, Hofmannsthal, Schnitzler, and Freud. Another article studies the architecture of memory in the Jewish Museum of Vienna and Rachel Whiteread's Holocaust monument on the Vienna *Judenplatz*, and her essay on Yehuda Amichai's novel *Not of This Time, Not of This Place*, appeared in the Encyclopedia of the Holocaust. Her first book, *Viennese Jewish Modernism: Genres of Memory*, is forthcoming from Penn State University Press. Her current research is on the history of the German Jewish Bible, 1780-1937.

Keren Goldfrad, Ph.D., studied English literature, French, and comparative literature at Bar- Ilan University, Israel. Her Ph.D. dissertation, completed with highest distinction, focused on literary styles in Holocaust literature. Keren twice received the Rector's Award for Excellence in Teaching from Bar Ilan University, where she was also recognized for research excellence; she is also the recipient of the Nahum, Sarah and Baruch Eisenstein Foundation Prize from Yad Vashem. She teaches English in the English as a Foreign Language Department at Bar-Ilan, where she is the e-learning coordinator. She also teaches Holocaust literature at Orot College in Elkana and is a member of the Mofet Institute's Holocaust Consortium in Tel Aviv.

Brana Gurewitsch is an archivist and curator at the Museum of Jewish Heritage in New York City. A Holocaust educator and oral historian for 40 years, she has curated special exhibitions at the Museum, including "Ours to Fight For: American Jews in the Second World War," and "Daring to Resist: Jewish Defiance in the Holocaust." Ms. Gurewitsch has advised scholarly and educational projects, including the Survivors of the Shoah Visual History Foundation. Her publications include *The Liberators: Eyewitness Accounts of the Liberation of Concentration Camps* (1981), the *Oral History Manual* (1991), *Mothers, Sisters, Resisters: Oral Histories of Women Who Survived the Holocaust* (1998), and *Daring to Resist: Jewish Defiance in the Holocaust* (2007).

Christopher Gwin teaches at Haddonfield Memorial High School in New Jersey. His semester elective on Holocaust and genocide laid the groundwork for the statewide, student-facilitated Spring Student Summit on essential Holocaust and genocide themes. Mr. Gwin is Vice Chair of the Pennsylvania Holocaust Education Council. He is a USHMM Mandel Fellow, recipient of the Janusz Korczak Teaching Award, and recipient of the Sarna Family Foundation Summer Study Exploration in Israel award, which allowed him and four of his seniors to spend two weeks in Israel analyzing Israel's theory, design, and practice of memorialization.

Jakob Hessing, Ph.D., was born in Poland in 1944; grew up in West Berlin, and immigrated to Israel in 1964. Hessing studied history, English literature, and comparative literature at the Hebrew University in Jerusalem, where he is now Associate Professor for German Literature and head of the German Department. Among his books are *Else Lasker-Schüler, Deutsch-Jüdische Dichterin* (1985), *Der Fluch des Propheten. Drei Abhandlungen zu Sigmund Freud* (1989), and *Der Traum und der Tod. Heinrich Heines Poetik des Scheiterns* (2005).

Dana Humphrey is the Communication Arts Curriculum Coordinator, Department Chair, and 8th grade Communication Arts teacher in the Fort Zumwalt School District in O'Fallon, MO. A USHMM Teacher Fellow, she serves on the Education Committee of the St. Louis Holocaust Museum and Learning Center and developed their "Teaching Trunks" program and guide. Dana is the recipient of a State Department grant for Holocaust education and was appointed by the governor to Missouri's Holocaust Education and Awareness Commission.

Lauren Kempton, Ed.D., is an adjunct Assistant Professor of Education at Sacred Heart University in Fairfield, CT, and Director of the Holocaust Education and Prejudice Reduction Program of the Jewish Federation of New Haven. She is an alumna of the American Gathering of Jewish Holocaust Survivors Summer Study Fellowship on Holocaust and Jewish Resistance, interviewed for Shoah Visual History Project, and co-authored *Man's Inhumanity to Man*, the Connecticut Department of Education teaching manual on the Holocaust. She is currently conducting research for a book on Petr Ginz and Terezín.

Phyllis Lassner, Ph.D., teaches Holocaust Studies, Gender Studies, and writing at Northwestern University in Illinois. She is the author of two books on the Anglo-Irish writer, Elizabeth Bowen, many articles about interwar and World War II women writers, *British Women Writers of World War II* (Macmillan/Palgrave 1998), and most recently, *Colonial Strangers: Women Writing the End of the*

British Empire (Rutgers UP, 2004). She also serves as co-president of The Society for the Space Between: Literature and Culture 1914–1945.

Chana Levene-Nachshon is a senior faculty member of the English as a Foreign Language unit at Bar-Ilan University, Israel. Her degrees are in English literature, but her love and focus of recent studies is Yiddish. She is a certified translator-interpreter and co-translated Yad Vashem publications such as *Rescue Attempts During the Holocaust* and *Patterns of Jewish Leadership in Nazi Europe 1933–45*. She has recently been appointed Director of Public Relations of the Salzburg Seminar Israel Alumni Association.

Avidov Lipsker, Ph.D., teaches in the Department of Jewish Studies at Bar-Ilan University, Israel. His principal research areas are Modern Hebrew Literature from the turn of the century to the present—his books on modern Hebrew poetry include *The Poetry of S. Shalom* (1990) and *The Poetry of A. Broides* (2000)—and Thematology of the Literature of the Jewish People. In this sphere, he and Professor Yoav Elstein created a multisystem model dealing with versions of the Jewish story, and published the *Thematological Encyclopedia of the Jewish Story: Sippur Okev Sippur* (Bar-Ilan University Press 2005). His study proposes a new theoretical approach, Cultural Ecosystem, which provides an explanation for replacement of poetic models in the ecological literary habitat.

Orly Lubin, Ph.D., is the former chair of the Department of Poetics and Comparative Literature and of the National Council of Jewish Women's (NCJW) Women and Gender Studies Program, both at Tel-Aviv University. She teaches feminist theories, visual culture, literature, and cinema, and co-developed "Holocaust Memory in Israel and the US: Identity, Gender, and Generations," a course taught long-distance simultaneously and collaboratively at Dartmouth College and Tel-Aviv University.

Rabbi Daniel Mayer holds a Master's Degree in Law from the Benjamin Cardozo School of Law at Yeshiva University, New York City, and is a doctoral student at Yeshiva University's Azrieli Graduate School of Education. He teaches Judaic Studies at the Yeshiva of Flatbush High School in Brooklyn, NY.

Kinereth Meyer, Ph.D., Senior Lecturer in English at Bar-Ilan University, Israel, has written for *Modern Language Studies*, *Genre*, *Religion and Literature*, *Comparative Drama*, *American Poetry*, *American Literature*, *Nineteenth-Century Literature*, *Prooftexts*, and *Christianity and Literature*. Her essays, devoted primarily to modern poetry and drama, have also appeared in a number of books. She has been a guest lecturer at many conferences, including those sponsored by the American Studies Association, American Literature Association, Christianity and Literature, and the T. S. Eliot Society. Dr. Meyer has recently completed (with Rachel Salmon Deshen) a book entitled *Reading the Underthought: Jewish Hermeneutics and Christian Poetry*.

Carrie A. Olson teaches at Kepner Middle School in Denver, CO, offering an elective for students who want to travel to Washington, DC, and to Europe, where the students study the Holocaust. She is founder and Executive Director of Kepner Educational Excellence Program, a nonprofit organization that assists in funding students for these journeys. A graduate of the Yad Vashem Summer

Institute, she volunteers at the Holocaust Awareness Institute at the University of Denver, where she is a doctoral candidate in Curriculum and Instruction and Judaic Studies. Ms. Olson was awarded the "Excellence in Education" award from the Institute.

Krystyna Smeltzer Phillips, a 2004 Covenant Fellow, has been a Holocaust educator in the Des Moines, IA, Jewish Federation Community School, a guest lecturer in the public elementary schools, and a writing instructor at the Des Moines Area Community College. Previously the Director of the Iowa Jewish Historical Society, she has resumed a career as an English and reading teacher at Herbert Hoover High School in Des Moines, IA.

Diane M. Plotkin, Ph.D., a registered nurse, returned to school to complete a Master's degree in nursing but instead graduated with an M.A. and a Ph.D. in Humanities, concentrating on interviews of survivors and liberators. She teaches world literature and history and Holocaust literature at Brookhaven College, a junior college in Texas, and Yiddish literature and "The Holocaust in Film" at the University of North Texas, Denton. She has presented internationally on women in the Holocaust, Holocaust revisionism, America's response to the Holocaust, methodologies of teaching, shtetl life in Yiddish literature, and, most recently, on the roots of Fundamentalist Islam. Diane co-authored, with R. A. Ritvo, *Sisters in Sorrow: Voices of Care in the Holocaust* (Texas A & M University Press, 1998).

Evelyn Ripp, née Romanowsky, was born in 1930, in Lachva, Poland. She is a Holocaust survivor, and her experiences under Nazi occupation during World War II are described in her memoir *The Abandoned: A Life Apart from Life* (2004, Margate, NJ: ComteQ Publishing). After the war, she settled in the United States, where she received an M.A. in Russian from New York University and an M.A. in English from Fairleigh Dickinson University in New Jersey. She has taught both Russian and English.

Norbert Ripp, D.D.S., was born in Bochum, Germany. He left his home and family at the age of 11 in 1939, and, by himself, entered Holland illegally. When the German invasion came, he was part of the only group of refugees to be evacuated to England on the *Kindertransport.* He, his two older brothers, and his parents survived the Holocaust, and he was reunited with them in America after a separation of five and a half years. Dr. Ripp, now retired, was Assistant Clinical Professor of Dentistry at the Columbia University School of Dental and Oral Surgery.

Daniella Rotenberg studied history and psychology at Columbia University in New York City, and is pursuing a Juris Doctorate at Harvard Law School. As a Lipper Intern at The Museum of Jewish Heritage: A Living Memorial to the Holocaust in New York City, Ms. Rotenberg taught public school students about the Holocaust through multimedia presentations and guided students on tours of the Museum. She served as an ICHEIC (International Commission for Holocaust Era Insurance Claims) Service Fellow. Her recent research includes the role of children's literature within the Nazi regime, described in a paper entitled "The Poisonous Teachings: Children's Literature as Nazi Propaganda."

Karen Shawn, Ph.D., is an adjunct Associate Professor of Holocaust Education at Yeshiva University's Azrieli Graduate School of Jewish Education and Administration. A recipient of the Israel Summer Study Fellowship on the Holocaust and Jewish Resistance, the Mt. Scopus Fellowship, and the Covenant Award, she served for 10 years on the staff of Yad Vashem's Summer Institute for Educators from Abroad and as the educational consultant for the American Friends of the Ghetto Fighters' Museum. She has written extensively on Holocaust education, including *The End of Innocence: Anne Frank and the Holocaust* (1992, New York: ADL).

Susan Prinz Shear is a child of Holocaust survivors and a former teacher. A graduate of Yad Vashem's International School for Holocaust Studies, she interviewed survivors for the Shoah Visual History Foundation and served as Education Director for the Holocaust Awareness Institute at the University of Denver. Her workshop and a curriculum entitled "No Way Out: Letters and Lessons of the Holocaust" and a Readers' Theatre play, *No Way Out Readers' Theatre*, have been published and performed at Holocaust centers, theaters, universities, and the United States Holocaust Memorial Museum. Ms. Shear is currently working on producing *No Way Out* as a full-length play.

Efraim Sicher, Ph.D., is professor of English and comparative literature at Ben-Gurion University of the Negev , Beer-Sheva , Israel . He completed his doctoral studies at Oxford University and has published widely on 19th-century realism (particularly Dickens and Eliot), dystopia, and modern Jewish culture. He is the editor of a collection of essays on the writing of the generation after the Holocaust, *Breaking Crystal: Writing and Memory after Auschwitz* (Illinois University Press, 1998), as well as a student guide to Holocaust fiction, *The Holocaust Novel* (Routledge, 2005).

Miriam Sivan, Ph.D., who is originally from New York, now lives in northern Israel and teaches literature and writing at the University of Haifa. She has published scholarly articles on the American writers Cynthia Ozick and James Baldwin and is currently writing a book on contemporary American literature that deals with the Holocaust. She has also published numerous short stories, some of which are about the intersection of love, marriage, and war. Her novella, *City of Refuge*, was dramatized and staged in London. She is currently at work on a novel, *Make it Concrete*.

Tova Weiss, Director of the Holocaust Education Resource Center of the Jewish Federation of Northeastern Pennsylvania, has created and implemented Holocaust programming for 13 years. A member of the Pennsylvania Holocaust Education Council, she has coordinated and conducted teaching workshops, and her collaborative efforts with local institutions and agencies reach the arts, legal, social work, and education communities. Tova, who has taught the Holocaust in Connecticut and Pennsylvania, participated in Yad Vashem's Summer Institute and studied in a year-long course for teachers at Yad Vashem as a Fellow in the Melton Senior Educators Program at Hebrew University.

Emily Amie Witty, Director of the Educational Resource Center of the Board of Jewish Education of Greater New York (BJENY), worked at Yad Vashem's

International School for Holocaust Studies and has taught in public and parochial schools in the metropolitan New York area. She authored *It Is My Business: Selected History from 1933–1945* (2005, BJENY), co-authored the Educator's Guide for Volume I of *The Years Wherein We Have Seen Evil: Selected Aspects in the History of Religious Jewry During the Holocaust* (2003, Jerusalem: Yad Vashem), and served as the language editor of Volumes I and II of the same publication. She serves on the Educational Advisory Committee of New York's Museum of Jewish Heritage, where she is a docent.

William Younglove, Ed.D., is an instructor/teacher supervisor at California State University Long Beach, after serving for 38 years as a high school teacher and community college instructor. His Holocaust studies include a USHMM Mandel Fellowship; Yad Vashem Summer Institutes, including the Graduates' Seminar in Eastern Europe; and the Holocaust and Jewish Resistance Teachers' Program. Recent publications include "Children's Holocaust Literature" in the *Encyclopedia Judaica* (2007) and "A Case for Teaching the Literature of Atrocity" in *California English* (April 2007). Dr. Younglove is recipient of the California Association of Teachers of English and the National Council of Teachers of English High School Excellence Awards. A member of the UCLA Alumni Bruin Caucus, he lobbies on educational matters.

Peer review board members:

Beryl Bresgi is a librarian at the Solomon Schechter Day School of Bergen County, NJ. She serves on the Children's Book Committee at Bank Street College of Education, which publishes an annual list of the best children's books.

Denise A. Coleman is a USHMM Teacher Fellow, has led Holocaust education workshops at Rutgers University, and has written curricula for the Marlboro, NJ, Board of Education, where she has taught for the past 15 years.

Shannon Kederis is an Advanced Placement high school social studies teacher at DuPont Manual High School in Louisville, KY. Shannon was a participant in the Pluralism and Democracy seminar in Israel and the recipient of the Korczak Teaching Award and a USHMM Teacher Fellowship.

Brooks Parmelee is a forensic social worker employed by the Connecticut Judicial Branch in the New Haven criminal courts.

Pamela Vissing teaches Holocaust literature at McAuley High School, a Catholic school in Cincinnati, OH. She helped develop *Mapping Our Tears*, an interactive theater/museum experience of Holocaust and World War II testimonies at the Hebrew Union College Center for Holocaust and Humanity Education.

Beit Lohamei Haghetaot, The Ghetto Fighters' Museum, is located in the western Galilee, just north of Haifa, Israel, on the grounds of Kibbutz Lohamei Haghetaot, the Ghetto Fighters' Kibbutz. It was founded in 1949 by survivors of the Jewish resistance as the world's first Holocaust Museum.

Today, the Ghetto Fighters' Museum includes extensive historical exhibits, an historical archive, a large collection of film and photography from the period of the Holocaust, a large art gallery and collection of Holocaust art, a Center for Humanistic Education, and a teachers' seminar center, where many of the contributors to this book studied.

About The Cover
"Transports"

81 hours
1985
25" × 22"

Inspired by the monument in Westerbork, the track symbolizes the beginning of a journey to the frightening unknown—bent back in grief and sorrow, the journey to nowhere.

Although I had done needlepoint for many years, it was not until 1984 that I started my first piece with the Holocaust as a focus. This came when I heard Elie Wiesel urging survivors to bear witness to the evils perpetrated by the Nazis. Mine is the last generation who, by telling our stories, can help people to be more aware of the consequences of evil gone unchecked.

My memories are expressed in a language of line, tone, and texture. The unexpected pairing of thread and art was inspired by my family. In my recollections of my mother, she was always engrossed in some form of needlework, while my father was an avid collector of paintings and drawings that decorated our home. My work reveals the blending of both of their interests, combining cultural and familial influences.

I call my collected works "Every Stitch a Memory." The number of hours I spent completing this piece is listed under the title, emphasizing the endless number of stitches eliciting memories.

Scattered throughout the mostly somber tones of black, gray, and brown are bits of color, symbolizing the wish to hold on to life and hope. While the memories are there, my work helps me to move beyond.

Netty Vanderpol
Boston, MA

RECEIVED

MAAN 11 28 20112

JAN 1 8 2012

		DATE DUE	

**JAMAICA HIGH SCHOOL
167-01 GOTHIC DRIVE
JAMAICA, N.Y. 11432**

Printed in the United States
101984LV00004B/5-8/P